THE LAW AND PRACTICE OF MARINE INSURANCE IN CANADA

THE LAW AND PRACTICE
OF MARINE INSURANCE
IN CANADA

George R. Strathy, B.A., M.A., LL.B.
George C. Moore, B.Comm., F.I.I.C.

The Law and Practice of Marine Insurance in Canada

Members of the LexisNexis Group worldwide

Canada	LexisNexis Canada Inc, 75 Clegg Road, MARKHAM, Ontario
Argentina	Abeledo Perrot, Jurisprudencia Argentina and Depalma, BUENOS AIRES
Australia	Butterworths, a Division of Reed International Books Australia Pty Ltd, CHATSWOOD, New South Wales
Austria	ARD Betriebsdienst and Verlag Orac, VIENNA
Chile	Publitecsa and Conosur Ltda, SANTIAGO DE CHILE
Czech Republic	Orac sro, PRAGUE
France	Éditions du Juris-Classeur SA, PARIS
Hong Kong	Butterworths Asia (Hong Kong), HONG KONG
Hungary	Hvg Orac, BUDAPEST
India	Butterworths India, NEW DELHI
Ireland	Butterworths (Ireland) Ltd, DUBLIN
Italy	Giuffré, MILAN
Malaysia	Malayan Law Journal Sdn Bhd, KUALA LUMPUR
New Zealand	Butterworths of New Zealand, WELLINGTON
Poland	Wydawnictwa Prawnicze PWN, WARSAW
Singapore	Butterworths Asia, SINGAPORE
South Africa	Butterworth Publishers (Pty) Ltd, DURBAN
Switzerland	Stämpfli Verlag AG, BERNE
United Kingdom	Butterworths Tolley, a Division of Reed Elsevier (UK), LONDON, WC2A
USA	LexisNexis, DAYTON, Ohio

National Library of Canada Cataloguing in Publication Data

Strathy, George R., 1948-
    The law and practice of marine insurance in Canada / George R. Strathy, George C. Moore.

Includes index.
ISBN 0-433-44007-4

    1. Insurance, Marine — Canada. I. Moore, George C. (George Cameron) II. Title.
KE1135.S87 2003   346.71'08622   C2003-901440-1
KF1135.S87 2003

Printed and bound in Canada.

This book is dedicated to our families:

Elyse, Arundel, Sarah, Anna, Maeve and Alexandra Strathy

and

Maria, Robert and Shirley Moore

About the Authors

GEORGE R. STRATHY

George R. Strathy is the founder of the Toronto law firm of Strathy & Associates, having practiced law for over 25 years, primarily in the field of maritime law. His clients include most of the leading Canadian and international marine insurers as well as shipping and transportation companies and related businesses. He has taught Maritime Law at the Faculty of Law, University or Toronto, and also established and taught a course entitled "Maritime Law for Marine Insurers", sponsored by the Canadian Board of Marine Underwriters. He has served as Chairman of the Canadian Association of Average Adjusters and as Vice-President (Ontario) of the Association of Maritime Arbitrators of Canada. He has also held executive positions in the Canadian Maritime Law Association and the Canadian Bar Association.

GEORGE C. MOORE

The late George C. Moore was a senior Canadian marine insurance broker who was employed for many years by Reed Stenhouse (now Aon), attaining the position of Vice-President. Following his retirement, he served as a Marine Insurance Consultant and expert witness on marine insurance matters. He also taught a community college course on marine insurance to freight forwarding students and was well-known for his commitment to the education and training of marine insurance professionals.

Preface

Writing a book on a subject like marine insurance is a lesson in humility. I recommend it to anyone who thinks he or she knows something about their profession. I have practiced maritime law, with a particular emphasis on issues affecting marine insurers, for over twenty-five years, and began this project more than ten years ago. At the beginning, I thought I knew something about marine insurance. At the end, I realize how much there is to learn. I hope, however, that this book will serve as a useful tool to the practitioner, whether lawyer or marine insurance professional, and that any shortcomings in the work will be brought to my attention, gently, for future correction.

Marine insurance is a fascinating subject, not only for its ancient origins and orderly principles, but also because it involves a body of law that has evolved over hundreds of years, to deal with the practical needs of the international maritime community. I have been fortunate in my legal career to have worked with many members of the Canadian maritime community, including outstanding marine lawyers, insurance brokers, underwriters, claims people, adjusters and surveyors. I am particularly grateful to my former partners, Arthur Stone (now of the Federal Court of Appeal) who introduced me to maritime law, and to Kristine Connidis, John Morin and Paul Richardson who have given me their friendship and encouragement in this part of my legal practice. I have been fortunate to have had many clients and friends who have given me an understanding and appreciation of the practical side of the marine insurance business. In the course of researching this book I was introduced to George Moore, who agreed to assist in the task, adding his enormous experience and insights to the text. I am sorry that he did not live to see its publication, but hope that it serves as a memorial to him and to his commitment to sharing his knowledge through education.

I owe a particular debt to the Canadian Board of Marine Underwriters, which, in the finest tradition of marine insurance, agreed to "underwrite" this book. Particular thanks go to Mike Wills, President, and Margaret Struhanyk, Chair of the Education Committee, for their support and encouragement. I thank as well my "task force" of insurance professionals who have read and commented upon most chapters, in draft form: Susan Kowan and Allan Murray of Vancouver and Jim Spicer of Toronto. Chris Giaschi of Vancouver, Ron Eldridge, Linda Erwin, Alan Jervis and Mel Fernandes of Toronto and Peter Wyld of Montreal have also commented on various chapters and I thank them for their contributions. I thank as well Jerry Rysanek and Jason Mutch of the Canadian Department of Transport. Others, who prefer to remain anonymous, have provided suggestions, commentary and assistance. Research and editorial commentary has been provided by Mona Anis and Krista Saunders and by my colleagues at Strathy & Associates, Anne Walker and Amy Pressman. I also wish to acknowledge the very professional support and editorial assistance I have received from Gian-luca DiRocco and Michelle Ecker of LexisNexis Canada Inc. Like all authors, I accept full responsibility for any omissions or inaccuracies in this text.

I wish to thank the Standard Steamship Owners' Protection and Indemnity Association (Bermuda) Limited, the International Underwriting Association, Witherby & Co. Ltd., the Comité Maritime Internationale (the official custodian of the *York-Antwerp Rules)*, the Canadian Board of Marine Underwriters, and the Marine Insurance Association of British Columbia, (formerly the Association of Marine Underwriters of British Columbia) for permission to publish extracts from their copyrighted material in this book.

It would have been impossible to complete this project without the encouragement and support of my family — my wife Elyse and my daughters, Arundel, Sarah, Anna, Maeve and Alexandra. I dedicate this book to them, with my profound gratitude.

Table of Contents

Table of Cases

PART I

THE PRINCIPLES OF MARINE INSURANCE

Chapter 1

Overview of Marine Insurance

1.1 INTRODUCTION

Marine insurance provides security for those engaged in maritime commerce: buyers and sellers of goods and owners and operators of ships, as well as their respective financiers. It allows them to diminish the risk of ruinous losses by sharing that risk with their insurers — referred to as "underwriters". It covers the risk that the ship will be lost or damaged, the risk that its cargo will be wholly or partially destroyed, the risk that the voyage will be interrupted and the shipowner's profits reduced, and the risk that third parties will be injured as a result of the operation of a ship. For centuries, marine insurance has fulfilled this role — it "underwrote" the great voyages of exploration, trade and colonization of the seventeenth, eighteenth and nineteenth centuries, and in the twentieth and twenty-first centuries, it has continued to be a vital underpinning of maritime trade.

The distinguishing feature of marine insurance is its subject-matter. It insures against losses incidental to a "marine adventure"[1] — a circumstance in which a ship, goods or other movable property is exposed to perils incidental to navigation.[2] The expression "marine adventure" comes from the days when the ocean voyage was a joint venture between the owner of the ship and the owner of the

---

[1] Canadian *Marine Insurance Act*, S.C. 1993, c. 22, subs. 6(1):

> 6(1) A contract of marine insurance is a contract whereby the insurer undertakes to indemnify the insured, in the manner and to the extent agreed upon in the contract, against
>
> > (a) losses that are incidental to a marine adventure or to an adventure analogous to a marine adventure, including losses arising from a land or air peril incidental to such an adventure if they are provided for in the contract or by usage of the trade; or
> >
> > (b) losses that are incidental to the building, repair or launch of a ship.
>
> For convenience, the Canadian *Marine Insurance Act* is referred to in this book as the "*C.M.I.A.*" The English *Marine Insurance Act* of 1906 is referred to as the "*M.I.A. 1906*".

[2] See *C.M.I.A.*, subs. 2(1); see also *Regal Films Corp. (1941) Ltd. v. Glens Falls Insurance Co.*, [1946] 3 D.L.R. 402 (Ont. H.C.J.), aff'd. [1946] O.R. 341 (C.A.), in which it was held that the policy in question, although titled "Inland Marine Policy", was in substance a policy of insurance against fire and lightning and not a marine policy, and therefore the statutory conditions in the Ontario *Insurance Act*, R.S.O. 1990, c. I.8 were applicable to the policy. The substance of the policy, and not its name, determined its real nature. See also *Staples v. Great American Insurance Co. of New York*, [1941] S.C.R. 213, 2 D.L.R. 1.

cargo. In those times, it was common for the owner of the cargo to be a part-owner of the ship or to travel with the ship with a view to selling the cargo at the port of destination. As joint venturers, the ship owner and the cargo owner had a common interest in the successful completion of the voyage.

There are four basic types of marine insurance, classed according to subject-matter. *Hull and machinery insurance*, as its name suggests, insures the owner's interest in the hull and machinery of the ship. Shipowners could not afford to risk millions of dollars in capital to purchase ships (nor would their bankers or investors provide them with that capital) without the security of marine insurance to protect them in the event of loss of or damage to the ship. Hull and machinery insurance provides them with the means to repair the ship if it is damaged or to replace it if it sinks or is otherwise totally lost.

Cargo insurance insures goods sent abroad by sea, air or post, or which are water-borne at any stage of their transportation. A contract of marine insurance may insure against mixed marine, air and land risks where goods shipped internationally travel by several conveyances, including a ship, from seller to buyer.[3] Policies of "inland marine insurance" cover loss of or damage to property while in transit by air or land or during delay incidental to such transit.[4] Buyers and sellers of cargo rely on marine insurance to protect their investment during the transportation of the cargo. Without marine insurance, financial institutions would be unwilling to lend money to finance the purchase of goods.

Freight insurance insures the earnings of an owner or charterer of a ship who may lose revenue if the ship or the cargo it carries is lost or damaged.[5] It provides the shipowner or the ship operator with protection against the loss of earnings suffered as a result of a maritime accident affecting the ship or its cargo.

Liability insurance provides shipowners and others engaged in marine operations with insurance against their liabilities to third parties.[6] The most important liabilities arising out of the ownership, operation or use of ships are covered by collision liability insurance and protection and indemnity insurance (sometimes called "P. & I. Insurance"). The liabilities associated with the ownership and operation of ships, particularly liabilities arising from environmental damage,

---

[3] *C.M.I.A.*, s. 6.

[4] See, for example, the Ontario *Insurance Act*, where "inland transportation insurance" is defined in s. 1 as "insurance (other than marine insurance) against loss of or damage to property *(a)* while in transit or during delay incidental to transit, or *(b)* where, in the opinion of the Superintendent, the risk is substantially a transit risk".

[5] See *Jordan v. Great Western Insurance Co.* (1885), 24 N.B.R. 421 (C.A.), rev'd. (1886) 14 S.C.R. 734; *Troop v. Merchants Marine Insurance Co.* (1886), 13 S.C.R. 506; *Driscoll v. Millville Marine Insurance Co.* (1883), 23 N.B.R. 160 (C.A.). In marine insurance language, "freight insurance" refers to insurance on the price paid for the carriage of goods and "cargo insurance" refers to insurance on the goods themselves.

[6] For example, charterers of ships, ship repairers, stevedores and terminal operators and freight forwarders — these subjects are discussed in Chapter 21, *Insurance of Particular Risks*.

are so substantial that shipowners could not afford to run the risk of operation without such insurance.[7]

Part I of this book examines the principles of marine insurance, initially developed by the common law and now embodied in statute. Part II examines some of the principal forms of marine insurance, cargo, hull and machinery, P. & I. and various common insurance forms. Part III gives an overview of the subject of General Average. Finally, Part IV examines some issues relating to the practice of marine insurance as well as the roles played by insurance brokers and marine surveyors.

1.2 HISTORY OF MARINE INSURANCE

To truly understand marine insurance, one must appreciate its origins.[8] Suffice to say that marine insurance has ancient roots, going back thousands of years and is unquestionably the predecessor of all other forms of insurance. Rudimentary examples of marine insurance can be found in the practices of the ancient maritime trading nations such as China, Greece, and Phoenicia. Marine insurance codes were developed by the Babylonians and the Rhodians.[9] Many writers have suggested that "bottomry" — a form of loan on the security of the vessel, was an early kind of marine insurance.[10] Others have pointed to the ancient practice of general average as a form of risk-spreading similar to insurance.

Modern marine insurance, however, had its genesis in seventeenth century England and derives its traditions and principles from the practices of merchants, "brokers" and "underwriters" in the London insurance markets, the most notable of which was, and still is, Lloyd's. Edward Lloyd's coffee house in London became a gathering place for owners of ships and cargos and for those prepared to finance or insure maritime trade. It was here that the process of having marine risks insured by obtaining the signature of various insurers underneath a description of the voyage on a "slip" (hence "underwriters") was

---

[7] For examples of protection and indemnity insurance, see *Western Assurance Co. v. Desgagnés*, [1976] 1 S.C.R. 286; *Catherwood Towing Ltd. v. Commercial Union Assurance Co.* (1996), 26 B.C.L.R. (3d) 57, 35 C.C.L.I. (2d) 124 (C.A.), aff'g. (1995), 30 C.C.L.I. (2d) 135, [1995] I.L.R. ¶1-3245 (B.C.S.C.).

[8] For a partial review, see the decision of the Supreme Court of Canada in *Zavarovalna Skupnost Triglav (Insurance Community Triglav Ltd.) v. Terrasses Jewellers Inc.*, [1983] 1 S.C.R. 283, [1983] I.L.R. ¶1-1627.

[9] It is said that the practice of marine insurance was introduced in England by the Lombards in the early thirteenth century. The word "policy" is said to derive from the Italian "polizza", meaning "promise" or "undertaking". W.R. Vance, *Handbook of the Law of Insurance*, 3rd ed. (St. Paul, Minn.: West Publishing Co., 1951), at p. ll, notes that "polizza" in turn was apparently derived from the Latin "politicum", based on a Greek word for "folded writing".

[10] The Supreme Court of Canada accepted this historical link in *Zavarovalna Skupnost Triglav (Insurance Community Triglav Ltd.) v. Terrasses Jewellers Inc.*, [1983] 1 S.C.R. 283, [1983] I.L.R. ¶1-1627. The loan was secured by a "bottomry bond" which was not repayable if the ship was lost.

initiated — a process still used in the industry today.[11] In 1769, a society of Lloyd's underwriters was formed and in 1779 Lloyd's subscribers agreed on a standard form of marine insurance policy.[12] London also served as a centre for the establishment of insurance companies, apart from Lloyd's, who were prepared to insure marine risks.

The first English statute dealing with marine insurance was introduced by Sir Francis Bacon in 1601 and was entitled *An Act concerning Matters of Assurance among Merchants* (sometimes referred to as the *Arbitration Act*).[13] Its Preamble acknowledged the long history of insurance:

> And, whereas it hathe bene, tyme out of mynde, an usage among the merchants, both of this realme and of forraine naycons, when they make any great adventure (especiallie in remote parts) to give some Consideracion of money to other persons (which commonlie are in no small number), to have from them assurance...

Early marine insurance legislation in England was designed to prevent the practice of using insurance as a form of gambling. While marine insurance protected the owners of ships and cargos, some unscrupulous merchants would put insurance on adventures in which they had no interest, hoping that if the ship was lost, they would recover under the insurance. Recognizing the mischief of such practices, Parliament passed statutes making it an offence to engage in "wagering" contracts of insurance — contracts in which the "insured" had no interest in the subject-matter of the insurance.[14]

In the latter part of the nineteenth century, attempts were made to reduce the uncertainty produced by two hundred years of litigation of marine insurance disputes by legislative codification of the law.[15] In 1906, largely as a result of the

---

[11] While a definite usage governing marine insurance was developed at Lloyd's, the industry "continued to be largely informal, governed by no fixed rules or regulations, either as to the membership in the company of attending brokers, or as to the terms and incidents of the contracts made" for approximately 100 years following the establishment of Lloyd's Coffee House: W.R. Vance, *Handbook of the Law of Insurance*, 3rd ed. (St. Paul, Minn.: West Publishing. Co., 1951), at p. 18. V. Dover, *Handbook to Marine Insurance*, 5th ed. (London: H. F. & G. Witherby, 1962), at p. 45 states:

> It is a curious fact that marine insurance was practised for many years before any attempt was made to reduce it to precise legal form. In the early legislation on the subject, no effort was made to elaborate a legal system to govern contracts of insurance, the statutory provisions being confined normally to the prescription of particular practices and usually directed to the elimination of speculation, the reduction of fraudulent activities and the retention of business in particular centers by means of discriminatory regulation. What is clear is that merchants and shipowners, as well as their insurers, were for long content to accept 'what was wont to be done'.

[12] This was made the standard form by Parliament in 1795 (35 Geo. 3, ch. 63) and is appended to the *M.I.A. 1906* as a Schedule.

[13] 43 Eliz. Cap 12 (1601).

[14] The *Marine Insurance Act*, 1745 (19 Geo. II, ch. 37). The Act was repealed by the *M.I.A. 1906*, s. 4 which contains a prohibition of "no interest" policies.

[15] In 1884 a Bill was presented in the House of Commons by Joseph Chamberlain, President of the Board of Trade. The bill was reportedly not well received and a Royal Commission was appointed to study the matter. Ten years later, in 1894, a "Marine Insurance Codification Bill" was

work of Sir Mackenzie Chalmers, the great English codifier, *The Marine Insurance Act, 1906*[16] (referred to in this book as the "*M.I.A. 1906*") was passed by Parliament. The purpose of this act was to state all the important principles of marine insurance as they had been expressed by the courts or understood by the insurance community at the time. The *M.I.A. 1906* continues in force in the U.K. in its original form today, subject to a minor amendment in 1959. It has served as the model for marine insurance legislation in Canada and elsewhere in the British Commonwealth and, indeed, around the world.

The basic principles of modern marine insurance, codified by Chalmers in 1906, were the product of the preceding 300 years of the practices of marine insurers and decisions of the courts. These developed in the age when underwriters wrote with quill pens and international trade and communication took place by sailing ship. They also developed in a time when maritime commerce carried with it extraordinary risks and rewards and when the strength of the merchant fleet was central to a nation's power and prestige. The milieu in which marine insurance developed helps to explain some of its most important principles.

1.3 DEVELOPMENTS IN CANADA[17]

Canada is usually thought of in terms of its land border with its southern neighbour and major trading partner, the United States. In fact, however, Canada has one of the longest maritime coastlines in the world, bordering the Atlantic Ocean to the east, the Pacific to the west and the Arctic Ocean to the north. As well, Canada's great inland seaway, the St. Lawrence River, serves as an entrance to the Great Lakes and to the North American industrial heartland.

There is little doubt that the explorers, fishermen and merchants who came to Canada in the two centuries before Confederation in 1867 brought with them the principles and practices of marine insurance as they had been developed in England and the continent. The pre-Confederation law books make it clear that in the early nineteenth century, and probably long before, the principles of marine insurance were being applied in Canada. The earliest reported Canadian marine insurance case is *Attwood, Hunt and Wilson v. Trustees of Samuel Kough & Co.*,[18] in which it was held, without citing any authority, that the party who had procured insurance on a vessel on behalf of its owner was liable to the

---

introduced by Lord Herschell in the House of Lords. The bill had been drafted by Sir Mackenzie Chalmers, a judge and Sir Douglas Owen, an underwriter. The bill was referred to a committee under Lord Herschell, consisting of insurers, adjusters, lawyers and shipowners, who received comment and suggestions from other interested parties. Having been reintroduced in the House of Lords in 1895, 1896 and 1899, it was ultimately enacted on December 21, 1906 and came into force on January 1, 1907.

[16] 6 Edw. VII, c. 41. In 1909, the *Marine Insurance (Gambling Policies) Act* was enacted to strengthen the anti-gambling provision in the 1906 Act by adding criminal sanctions.

[17] For analysis of the law of marine insurance in Canada, see: R.M. Fernandes, *Marine Insurance Law of Canada* (Toronto: Butterworths, 1987); C. Brown, *Insurance Law in Canada* (Toronto: Carswell, 2002), chapter 19, *Marine Insurance*; F. Laverty, *The Insurance Law of Canada*, 2nd ed. (Toronto: Carswell, 1936).

[18] (1818), Nfld.

underwriter for payment of the premium. There were relatively few reported cases in the early nineteenth century, possibly because Canadians followed the English practice of resolving marine insurance disputes outside the courts. As Chief Justice Robinson of Upper Canada stated in a case in 1851, *Crawford v. St. Lawrence Insurance Co.*:

> We are not yet very familiar with actions on marine policies, and the courts in England do not furnish many cases: the losses, when they occur, being usually amicably adjusted by reference to merchants, or to counsel, when questions arise.[19]

A sampling of the nineteenth century Canadian marine insurance cases reveals that the courts examined authorities from England — and often the United States and other jurisdictions — as a matter of course in reaching their decisions, particularly where no Canadian precedent was available. For example, in *Canada Fire and Marine Insurance Co. v. Western Insurance Co.*,[20] the Ontario Court of Appeal cited a text largely based on American case law and adopted it "as a statement of our own law", adding that this was something "we may fairly do". In *Meagher v. Aetna Insurance Co.*,[21] Chief Justice Robinson of Upper Canada, in rejecting a test for abandonment proposed by one of the parties, stated: "But it is enough to say that there is no authority for applying such a test according to the law of this province — in other words, the law of England, for we have no peculiar law or custom on the subject."[22]

In *Danson v. Cawley*, the effect of a surveyor's certificate was at issue, and Chief Justice Tucker stated:

> And here I can derive no positive direction from the law of England, which can furnish no rule relative to surveys which are unknown to it. In the practice of other countries, and in general principles, I must seek then to discover that light by which my determination upon this point ought to be guided.[23]

He thereupon went on to consider the law of France on the subject.

The decision of the Nova Scotia Court of Appeal in *Creighton v. Union Marine Insurance Co.* contains an interesting statement of judicial awareness of the need to adapt English rules to Canadian conditions. Chief Justice Haliburton stated:[24]

> The common law is elastic, it is remarkable for its plasticity and adaptation to all varieties of circumstances. In a new country like this - changing in its aspects, condition, requirements with every turning year; where new interests, new combinations, and new difficulties are perpetually arising, it is impossible to apply stringent rules with the same unvarying fixity that marks their applicability to the circumstances of older and more stable countries. How can the same commercial

---

[19] (1851), 8 U.C.Q.B. 135 (C.A.).
[20] (1880), 5 O.A.R. 244.
[21] (1861), 20 U.C.Q.B. 607, 20 Gr. 345.
[22] *Meagher v. Aetna Insurance Co.* (1861), 20 U.C.Q.B. 607 at 620.
[23] (1823), 1 Nfld. Rep. 377 at 380.
[24] (1854), 2 N.S.R. 195 at 213.

rules be applied to a sparsely populated country - designated only by its latitude and longitude and a few log huts - as apply to Gibraltar or Malta? Our trade is different in many respects, and, among others, we know that the traders along our coast are often obliged to collect their cargos in different harbours, because many of them are so small that a whole cargo cannot be obtained at a single port. This course of trade is notorious, and must have been well known to these underwriters.

In the colonial period preceding the Confederation of Canada in 1867, the applicability of English law to a colony depended on whether it was acquired by Britain by settlement or by conquest and cession; in the former case, "the settlers from Britain were considered to have brought with them to the new territory so much of the total existing body of English common law and statute law as was suitable to conditions in the new place"; while in the latter case, pre-conquest private law of the colony "remained in effect and continued in force, unless and until altered by the appropriate British authorities in London".[25] The date of reception of English law in a settled colony is generally accepted as being the date of the institution of its local legislature.[26] Thus, in *Blazer & Co. v. Horwood Lumber Co.*, Justice Kent stated:

> It is...clear that, long before the establishment of a legislature in this country, the rule which has originated as a custom had received the sanction of legal decision and so had been engrafted upon and become part of the Common Law of England. It is therefore presumed to have been part of the law of this country at the time our legislature was established. It has been held and frequently acted upon by this Court that the law of England so far as it was applicable to this Colony was, up to and at the time our local legislature was established, the law of this country. The rule that a broker might sue for premiums was as applicable to marine insurance brokers here as it was in England. In my opinion the rule is part of our law and the plaintiffs are entitled to recover these premiums from the defendant.[27]

French civil law in all but criminal matters was established in Quebec by the *Quebec Act* of 1774.[28]

The *British North America Act, 1867* (now the *Constitution Act, 1867*)[29] created the Dominion of Canada, composed of the provinces of Upper and Lower Canada (later divided into Ontario and Quebec), Nova Scotia and New Brunswick, and envisaged the admission of other provinces and territories in the future, as in fact occurred. The *British North America Act* allocated legislative jurisdiction between the federal and provincial governments. Among the powers

---

[25] W.R. Lederman, "The Extension of Governmental Institutions and Legal Systems to British North America in the Colonial Period", in *Continuing Canadian Constitutional Dilemmas: Essays on the Constitutional History*, Public Law and Federal System of Canada (Toronto: Butterworths, 1981), at pp. 64-65.

[26] *Ibid.*, at p. 67; for specific dates, see G. Gall, *The Canadian Legal System*, 2nd ed. (Calgary: Carswell, 1983), at pp. 43-44.

[27] (1924), 11 Nfld. Rep. 319 at 322.

[28] G. Gall, *The Canadian Legal System*, 2nd ed. (Calgary: Carswell, 1983), at p. 135.

[29] Originally the *British North America Act*, 30 & 31 Vict. c. 3; subsequently the *Constitution Act, 1982*, enacted as Schedule B to the *Canada Act 1982* (U.K.) 1982, c. 11.

allocated to the federal government were the power to make laws with respect to "the regulation of trade and commerce",[30] and "navigation and shipping".[31] The *Act* conferred on the provincial legislatures jurisdiction in relation to "property and civil rights"[32] as well as "all matters of a merely local or private nature" within the province.[33] The Act did not confer specific jurisdiction with respect to the subject-matter of "marine insurance", but as we shall see in the next section, after the enactment of the *M.I.A. 1906*, a number of Canadian provinces enacted marine insurance legislation modeled on this statute.

1.4   MARINE INSURANCE LEGISLATION IN CANADA

Prior to the passage of the Canadian *Marine Insurance Act* (referred to in this book as the *C.M.I.A.*) in 1993,[34] five Canadian provinces had enacted statutes modeled on the *M.I.A. 1906*, it being assumed, without question, that they had the power to do so as part of their legislative jurisdiction over "property and civil rights" within the province.[35] British Columbia was the first of these in 1925,[36] followed by Nova Scotia in 1941,[37] New Brunswick in 1943,[38] Manitoba in 1945[39] and Ontario in 1946.[40] The Quebec *Civil Code* (first enacted in 1866 as the Civil Code of Lower Canada and substantially revised in 1994) deals with marine insurance in articles 2505 – 2628.[41] It is in most respects the same as the *M.I.A. 1906*. In Saskatchewan, Prince Edward Island and Alberta, marine insurance is dealt with by the provisions in the insurance statutes dealing with

---

30   *Ibid.*, s. 91.2.
31   *Ibid.*, s. 91.10.
32   *Ibid.*, s. 92.13
33   *Ibid.*, s. 92.16.
34   *Marine Insurance Act*, S.C. 1993, c. 22.
35   See for example the Ontario *Marine Insurance Act*, R.S.O. 1990, c. M.2; British Columbia *Insurance (Marine) Act*, R.S.B.C. 1996, c. 230; Manitoba *Marine Insurance Act*, R.S.M. 1987, c. M40; New Brunswick *Marine Insurance Act*, R.S.N.B. 1973, c. M-1; Nova Scotia *Insurance Act*, R.S.N.S. 1989, c. 231, Part IX; Quebec *Civil Code*, S.Q. 1991, c. (4), arts. 2505-2628.
36   *Marine Insurance Act* (S.B.C. 1925, c. 21; presently R.S.B.C. 1996, c. 230). An earlier *Marine Insurance Act*, S.B.C. 1911, c. 116 (R.S.B.C. 1924, c. 118), prohibiting wagering policies, was repealed by the 1925 Act.
37   *Marine Insurance Act* (S.N.S. 1941, c. 7; R.S.N.S. 1954, c. 166). This Act was repealed by the *Insurance Act*, S.N.S. 1962, s. 274), and the *M.I.A. 1906* was incorporated as Part IX of the *Insurance Act* (presently Nova Scotia *Insurance Act*, R.S.N.S. 1989, c. 231).
38   *Marine Insurance Act*, S.N.B. 1943, c. 40 (presently R.S.N.B. 1973, c. M-1).
39   S.M. 1945, c. 29, presently Manitoba *Marine Insurance Act*, R.S.M. 1987, c. M40.
40   S.O. 1946, c. 51, presently R.S.O. 1990, c. M.2.
41   See F. Laverty, *The Insurance Law of Canada*, 2nd ed. (Toronto: Carswell, 1936), at p. 1 for a discussion of the Insurance Title of the Code; Laverty's extensive chapter on marine insurance is replete with comparisons between the Civil Code provisions and those of the *M.I.A. 1906*. The Quebec Civil Code Revision Office issued a Report on Marine Insurance in 1976, in which draft legislation based largely on the *M.I.A. 1906* in a modern and revised format was proposed, and this was subsequently enacted in 1991. For a discussion of some of the provisions of the Civil Code in relation to marine insurance, see: *Fairway Life & Marine Insurance Ltd. v. "Susan Darlene" (The)*, [1987] 2 F.C. 547 (Prothonotary); *Marine Insurance: The Silent Export*, 2nd ed. (Canadian Board of Marine Underwriters, 1994).

insurance contracts generally.[42] Newfoundland,[43] the Northwest Territories[44] and Yukon[45] exclude marine insurance from the general insurance legislation, in spite of the fact that they have no specific marine insurance legislation of their own. In the provinces which have enacted marine insurance laws, the general insurance legislation typically excludes marine insurance from its ambit. In the case of Newfoundland, which did not enact marine insurance legislation, it has been held that the *M.I.A. 1906* codified the common law and could be looked to as an accurate statement of the law in that province.[46]

The enactment of the *Federal Court Act*[47] in 1971, constituting the Federal Court of Canada as the successor to the Exchequer Court as a court with Canada-wide jurisdiction in, among other things, maritime matters, resulted in a series of cases clarifying the scope of the court's jurisdiction and, incidentally, Parliament's jurisdiction in relation to navigation and shipping.[48] The decision of the Supreme Court of Canada in *Zavarovalna Skupnost Triglav (Insurance Community Triglav Ltd.) v. Terrasses Jewellers Inc.*[49] was an important turning point in the development of Canadian marine insurance law.

In *Terrasses Jewellers*, the appellant challenged the constitutionality of section 22(2)(r) of the *Federal Court Act*, giving concurrent jurisdiction to the Trial Division of the Federal Court of Canada over claims arising out of or in connection with a contract of marine insurance. The action concerned a policy of marine insurance issued by the appellant, a Yugoslav company, to another Yugoslav company, covering transportation of certain goods from Yugoslavia to Montreal. When the shipment arrived in Montreal, a case of jewellery containing gold, silver and platinum was missing and a claim was made under the insurance policy. The appellant argued that marine insurance was a matter of "property and civil rights", falling within the exclusive jurisdiction of the provincial legislatures and argued that there was no federal marine insurance law to be applied by the Federal Court of Canada. The appellant pointed out that a number of provincial legislatures had enacted marine insurance legislation and argued that because there was no federal legislation there was no "federal law" of marine insurance for the Federal Court of Canada to administer.[50]

---

[42] Saskatchewan *Insurance Act*, R.S.S. 1978, c. S-26; Prince Edward Island, *Insurance Act*, R.S.P.E.I. 1988, c. I-4; Alberta *Insurance Act*, R.S.A. 2000, c. I-3.

[43] Newfoundland *Insurance Contracts Act*, R.S.N.L. 1990, c. I-12.

[44] *Insurance Act*, R.S.N.W.T. 1988, c. I-4.

[45] *Insurance Act*, R.S.Y. 1986, c. 91.

[46] *Amo Containers Ltd. v. Drake Insurance Co. Ltd.* (1984), 8 C.C.L.I. 97, 51 Nfld. & P.E.I.R. 55 (Nfld. S.C.); see also *Biggin v. British Marine Mutual Insurance Association* (1992), 101 Nfld. & P.E.I.R. 156, 14 C.C.L.I. (2d) 66 (Nfld. S.C. T.D.).

[47] R.S.C. 1985, c. F-7, as amended.

[48] For a discussion of the history and development of admiralty jurisdiction in Canada, see *Inter-municipal Realty Corp. v. Gore Mutual Insurance Co.*, [1981] 1 F.C. 151, 112 D.L.R. (3d) 432 (T.D.).

[49] [1983] 1 S.C.R. 283, [1983] I.L.R. ¶1-1627.

[50] Referring to earlier decisions of the Supreme Court of Canada in *McNamara Construction Western Ltd. v. The Queen*, [1977] 2 S.C.R. 654 and *Quebec North Shore Paper Co. v. Canadian Pacific Ltd.*, [1977] 2 S.C.R. 1054.

The question, as the court neatly put it, was whether marine insurance was a part of maritime law, since it was clear that the Parliament of Canada had jurisdiction to establish the Federal Court to administer maritime law, as it fell within federal jurisdiction over "navigation and shipping".[51] Justice Chouinard began by reviewing the nature of marine insurance. He stated:

> Marine insurance, which preceded other forms of insurance by several centuries, originated as an integral part of maritime law.

> It had its origin in bottomry and respondentia, which are defined as follows in art. 2693 of the *Civil Code*:

>> 2693. Bottomry is a contract whereby the owner of a ship or his agent, in consideration of a sum of money loaned for the use of the ship, undertakes conditionally to repay the same with interest, and hypothecates the ship for the performance of his contract. The essential condition of the loan is that if the ship be lost by a fortuitous event or irresistible force, the lender shall lose his money; otherwise it is to be repaid with a certain profit for interest and risk.[52]

He noted that the Hindus, Greeks and Romans had recognized "bottomry", whereby a loan on the hull or "bottom" of a ship might be forgiven if the ship was lost. He also referred to a statement in one of the leading English texts on marine insurance: "Of the origin of marine insurance, all that can be said with certainty is that it is 'veiled in antiquity and lost in obscurity'. The concept of protection against loss by maritime perils has been traced back to B.C. 215."[53]

The judge then referred to Bonnecasse, *Traite du Droit Commercial Maritime*, No. 29, in which it is stated:

> Marine insurance is an institution without which maritime trade and navigation would be almost inconceivable; we would go so far as to that that in the absence of insurance it would be meaningless to speak of the ownership of vessels and their operation. In view of the large sums committed by participants in an ocean voyage and the frequency and seriousness of maritime risks, the merchant shipping industry would be at an end, and with it sea transportation, if persons engaging in them felt that they were threatened without compensation with loss of the ship and of the cargo. That in brief accounts for the close and indissoluble link between chartering and insurance; and for the dependence of a prosperous maritime trade on an effective insurance system. [translation][54]

After reviewing these authorities, Justice Chouinard summed up as follows:

> It is wrong in my opinion to treat marine insurance in the same way as the other forms of insurance which are derived from it, and from which it would be distin-

---

[51]   See *Tropwood A.G. v. Sivaco Wire & Nail Co.*, [1979] 2 S.C.R. 157.
[52]   [1983] 1 S.C.R. 283 at 293, [1983] I.L.R. ¶1-1627.
[53]   V. Dover, *A Handbook to Marine Insurance*, 5th ed. (London: H.F. & G. Witherby, 1957), at pp. 1-2.
[54]   [1983] 1 S.C.R. 283 at 297-98.

guishable only by its object, a maritime venture. It is also incorrect to say that marine insurance does not form part of the activities of navigation and shipping, and that, although applied to activities of this nature, it remains a part of insurance.

Marine insurance is first and foremost a contract of maritime law. It is not an application of insurance to the maritime area. Rather, it is the other forms of insurance which are applications to other areas of principles borrowed from marine insurance.

I am of the opinion that marine insurance is part of maritime law over which s. 22 of the *Federal Court Act* confers concurrent jurisdiction on that Court. It is not necessary to determine what other courts may have jurisdiction concurrent with the Federal Court, nor to determine the scope of their jurisdiction. I am further of the opinion that marine insurance is contained within the power of Parliament over navigation and shipping, and that accordingly a negative answer must be given to the constitutional question.[55]

Referring to other decisions of the Court but without specifically identifying the body of "federal" marine insurance law, he concluded that the Federal Court had jurisdiction over the case.

The *Terrasses Jewellers* case confirmed that the Federal Court of Canada has jurisdiction over a marine insurance dispute, but it also raised questions about the validity and application of provincial marine insurance legislation. A demand for reform, led by legal and marine insurance organizations including the Canadian Maritime Law Association and the Canadian Board of Marine Underwriters, resulted in the enactment by Parliament of the *C.M.I.A.* in 1993. This statute is, except for some minor modernization of the language, almost identical to the *M.I.A. 1906*.

Before the *C.M.I.A.*, it was probable that the body of common law dealing with marine insurance could be regarded as "federal maritime law" which would nourish the jurisdiction of the Federal Court of Canada under section 22(2)(*r*) of the *Federal Court Act*. With the enactment of the *C.M.I.A.*, there can be no doubt of the existence of such a body of law or of the jurisdiction of the Federal Court of Canada to administer that law, concurrent with the superior courts of the provinces.

Case law since *Terrasses Jewellers* has confirmed the broad and exclusive nature of federal legislative jurisdiction under the "navigation and shipping" power and the limited scope for the application of provincial laws to maritime matters.[56] In *Whitbread v. Walley*,[57] the issue was whether the provisions of the

---

[55] *Ibid.*

[56] *Ordon Estate v. Grail*, [1998] 3 S.C.R. 437, 166 D.L.R. (4th) 193, aff'g. (1996), 30 O.R. (3d) 643, 140 D.L.R. (4th) 52 (C.A.); *Monk Corp. v. Island Fertilizers Ltd.*, [1991] 1 S.C.R. 779, 80 D.L.R. (4th) 58, rev'g. (1989), 97 N.R. 384 (F.C.A.), 19 F.T.R. 220 (T.D.); *Whitbread v. Walley*, [1990] 3 S.C.R. 1273, 77 D.L.R. (4th) 25, aff'g. (1988), 51 D.L.R. (4th) 509, [1988] 5 W.W.R. 313 (B.C.C.A.), rev'g. (1987), 45 D.L.R. (4th) 729, 19 B.C.L.R. (2d) 120 (S.C.); *Bow Valley Husky (Bermuda) Ltd. v. St. John Shipbuilding Ltd.*, [1997] 3 S.C.R. 1210.

[57] [1990] 3 S.C.R. 1273, 77 D.L.R. (4th) 25, aff'g. (1988), 51 D.L.R. (4th) 509, [1988] 5 W.W.R. 313 (B.C.C.A.), rev'g. (1987), 45 D.L.R. (4th) 729, 19 B.C.L.R. (2d) 120 (S.C.).

Canada Shipping Act,[58] permitting a ship owner and operator to limit his or her liability for damages in a marine accident, were constitutionally applicable to a pleasure craft operating in British Columbia's coastal waters. The vessel struck a rock, causing serious injuries to one of the passengers and rendering him quadriplegic. He sued the owner and operator. The issue was whether the statutory limitation of liability under the *Canada Shipping Act* was applicable to a pleasure craft, the argument being that the limitation was designed to benefit commercial shipping and that its application to pleasure craft was both unnecessary and unfair, as it would have substantially reduced the plaintiff's damages. The Supreme Court of Canada, agreeing with the British Columbia Court of Appeal, held that the legislation was constitutionally valid. In the course of its reasons, the Supreme Court confirmed that Parliament's jurisdiction over navigation and shipping permits it to enact maritime legislation that is uniform throughout the country and that this does not depend on whether the waters in question are tidal or non-tidal, coastal or inland. The liability for the accident, and the rights of the affected parties, would be the same regardless of where in Canada the accident occurred.

In *Ordon Estate v. Grail*, the Supreme Court dealt again with the ambit of Canadian maritime law and with the interaction between federal and provincial legislation in the context of two boating accidents in Ontario waters. At issue, among other things, was the application of the Ontario *Family Law Act*,[59] granting rights of action to relatives of people killed in accidents and of the provincial *Negligence Act*,[60] providing for apportionment of responsibility and contributory negligence. The Supreme Court confirmed, as it had in *Whitbread v. Walley*, that Canadian maritime law is a uniform and comprehensive body of law dealing with maritime and admiralty matters. The court noted that much of maritime law is the result of international conventions and said that the nature of shipping is such that, in a country like Canada, uniformity of law is essential. The court set out a four-part test for the determination of whether a provincial statute would be applicable in the context of a maritime negligence action. First, said the court, it must be determined whether the subject-matter of the provincial law falls within the exclusive federal jurisdiction in relation to navigation and shipping. If so, one must ask whether there is a counterpart to the provincial legislation within existing Canadian maritime law. If not, the court must ask whether it is appropriate to "reform" the non-statutory federal maritime law in such a way as to give effect to the principle expressed in the provincial law. It is only if this stage is reached, and the court determines that it would not be appropriate for it to reform the law, should the court decide whether the provincial statutory provision should be applicable. Applying this test, the Supreme Court held that it would be inappropriate to apply provincial law to maritime accidents of this kind, since they were the subject of a comprehensive federal legal regime within the exclusive jurisdiction of Parliament.

---

[58]   R.S.C. 1985, c. S-9.
[59]   R.S.O. 1990, c. F.3.
[60]   R.S.O. 1990, c. N.1.

In light of *Terrasses Jewellers*, the enactment of the *C.M.I.A.* and the Supreme Court's decisions in the *Whitbread v. Walley* and *Ordon Estate v. Grail* line of cases, it is difficult to see that there could be any scope for the application of provincial legislation in the field of marine insurance. While the provincial and territorial marine insurance acts remain on the statute books and will be valid until declared unconstitutional by the courts, it is doubtful that those statutes could have any application in the face of a comprehensive federal statute dealing with the same subject-matter. In view of the case law concerning the interplay of federal and provincial legislation in maritime matters, it would appear that the provincial legislation on the subject has no constitutional basis and is, at best, inoperative and at worst unconstitutional.[61] While there has been some suggestion that the provincial legislation might continue to be applicable to marine insurance risks on inland waters, the more likely conclusion is that Canadian maritime law (of which marine insurance is a part) is national in scope and uniform in nature, even where the geographic location of the risk is inland waters wholly within the province.[62] In the marine accident field, the Supreme Court has said that federal law applies, whether the accident occurs on inland waters or not and whether the vessel is a pleasure craft or a commercial ship. The same principle should apply to marine insurance.

A troublesome issue remains with respect to the application of provincial law to issues not addressed by the *C.M.I.A.* That statute deals almost exclusively with the substantive law of marine insurance. It does not deal with procedural matters, such as the manner in which a claim must be presented, the time limits applicable to claims or actions, and the rights and responsibilities of the parties when a claim is filed. The provincial general insurance statutes deal with matters of this kind and the question has arisen in the past as to whether they are to be applied in the marine insurance context. While some decisions have answered this question in the affirmative,[63] their validity is in doubt in light of *Terrasses Jewellers*, *Ordon Estate v. Grail* and subsequent case law. Considering the national and international nature of marine insurance, the importation of

---

[61] In *C.C.R. Fishing Ltd. v. British Reserve Insurance Co.*, [1990] 1 S.C.R. 814, 43 C.C.L.I. 1, the Supreme Court of Canada considered the provisions of the *Insurance (Marine) Act* of British Columbia without commenting on its constitutionality.

[62] The provisions of most provincial marine insurance legislation reflect s. 2(1) of the *M.I.A. 1906* which provides that a marine insurance policy may by its express terms or usage, extend to inland waters. For example, the British Columbia *Insurance (Marine) Act*, R.S.B.C. 1996, c. 230, s. 3(1) provides:

> 3(1) A contract of marine insurance may, by its express terms or by usage of trade, be extended so as to protect the assured against losses on inland waters, or on any land risk that may be incidental to any sea voyage.

See also the Ontario *Marine Insurance Act*, s. 3(1). Oddly enough, this provision was not included in the *C.M.I.A.* The case law, including *Whitbread v. Walley*, [1990] 3 S.C.R. 1273; and *Ordon Estate v. Grail*, [1998] 3 S.C.R. 437, 166 D.L.R. (4th) 193, aff'g. (1996), 30 O.R. (3d) 643, 140 D.L.R. (4th) 52 (C.A.), would suggest that the federal law of marine insurance applies, regardless of the location of the risk.

[63] *Porto Seguro Companhia de Seguros Gerais v. Belcan S.A.*, [1997] 3 S.C.R. 1278, 153 D.L.R. (4th) 577, rev'g. [1996] 2 F.C. 751, 195 N.R. 241 (C.A.), aff'g. (1994), 82 F.T.R. 127 (T.D.).

provincial laws, with their varied requirements, many of which are not consistent with the practice of marine insurance, could be a source of conflict and confusion.

Prior to 1993, the Canadian federal Parliament made only limited, and very specific use of its ability to pass legislation in relation to marine insurance. The *Marine War Risks Act*,[64] provides for marine insurance coverage by the federal government through the Ministry of Transport in the event that Canada becomes engaged in a war. This legislation is necessary because commercial marine war risks insurance policies provide for automatic termination in the event Canada enters a war. The availability of a merchant fleet during wartime is considered so necessary to national security that the government makes war risks insurance available.

The federal government also administered a marine insurance program pursuant to the *Fishing Vessel Insurance Regulations*,[65] whereby a fishing vessel with a Canadian home port could be insured against marine perils. Claims under this program, which has been discontinued, generated considerable litigation.

1.5 BASIC PRINCIPLES OF MARINE INSURANCE

This book will examine the basic principles of marine insurance, as they have been developed and applied in Canadian law and practice. The following summary is provided in order to give the reader an overview of the content of this book.

Marine insurance is a contract of indemnity. This statement makes two points — first, marine insurance, like all insurance, is a *contract*. It must be contained in one or more documents which make up the *policy*. Second, it is a contract which provides an *indemnity* — an undertaking by one party to make up for the losses of another. The contracting parties are known as the *insured* (in traditional marine insurance language, the "assured") and the *insurer* (sometimes called the "underwriter"). Typically, the marine insurance is effected through an intermediary, known as a *broker* who is engaged by the insured and who has important obligations to both the insured and to the insurer. The insured pays a *premium* in order to buy the insurance. In order to purchase insurance, the insured must have an *insurable interest* in the subject-matter of the insurance, if not at the time the insurance is placed then at the time of the loss. When the contract is made, *good faith* must be observed by both parties and the contract may be rendered void if it was not. The contract evidencing the insurance will be contained in a *policy* which will describe the *subject-matter insured*, the *sum insured* and the *perils* insured as well as the *insured value* and the *measure of indemnity* payable in the event of loss. Different types of *losses and charges* may be *recoverable* depending upon the damages suffered and the coverage provided by the policy. Losses which are, under maritime law, considered to fall on all parties to the marine adventure are described as *general average* losses and are usually insured under marine policies. In order for the insured to recover

---

[64] R.S.C. 1970 c. W-3.

[65] C.R.C. 1978, c. 325, as amended.

under the contract of insurance, an insured peril must be the *proximate cause* of the loss. If the property is not fully insured, there may be *underinsurance*, which requires the insured to bear some of the loss him or herself. There may be contractual terms or *warranties* which oblige the insured to engage in or refrain from certain conduct. After suffering an insured peril, the insured is required to *sue and labour* — to make efforts to minimize or avoid the loss. On payment of a valid claim pursuant to the policy, the insurer becomes entitled to rights of *subrogation* against third parties responsible for the loss. There may be *reinsurance* in place which allows the insurer to spread some of the risk it has incurred; or, there may be *double insurance*, which permits the insurer to recover some of its outlay from another insurer. There may have been an *assignment* of the policy, whereby the insured has transferred the right of indemnity to another party.

1.6 MODERN MARINE INSURANCE IN CANADA

Canada has a sophisticated and mature marine insurance market, with a number of domestic insurers and managing general agents offering marine insurance coverage. Specialist marine insurance brokers have the ability to place insurance in the domestic and international marine insurance markets. Marine insurance professionals including marine surveyors, average adjusters and maritime lawyers provide support and assistance to these insurers, brokers and insureds.[66]

The Canadian Board of Marine Underwriters ("C.B.M.U.") was founded in 1917 and provides a focus for the discussion of marine insurance issues and the promotion of the interests of those involved in marine insurance. It works at both the domestic and international levels and is a member of the International Union of Marine Insurers ("I.U.M.I."). It also works with the Canadian federal government. Its committees, which deal with insurance clauses, loss prevention, legislation and education, among other things, promote matters of interest to the marine insurance community. The C.B.M.U. has published hull and machinery insurance clauses for vessels trading on the Great Lakes.[67]

The Marine Insurance Association of British Columbia is a provincial organization designed to deal with matters of particular interest to marine insurers on Canada's west coast. Formerly known as the Association of Marine Underwriters of British Columbia, it has published insuring clauses which are particularly applicable to west coast risks.

The Association of Average Adjusters of Canada was founded in 1967. Its objects are the promotion of the correct principles in the adjustment of averages, the promotion of the uniformity of practice amongst adjusters and the promotion of other matters of interest to the average adjusting profession. The association provides accreditation to average adjusters in Canada — candidates must pursue

---

[66] For a description of aspects of the Canadian marine insurance market, see *Marine Insurance: The Silent Export*, 2nd ed. (Canadian Board of Marine Underwriters, 1994).

[67] Known as the C.B.M.U. Great Lakes Hull Clauses (Sept. 1, 1971). See Appendix G and Chapter 19, *Hull and Machinery Insurance*.

a course of study and successfully sit exams. The association maintains ties with its counterparts in the United States, England and on the Continent.

The Canadian Maritime Law Association was founded in 1951 and has as its mandate the advancement of the development of effective, modern commercial maritime law within Canada and the international community. It is composed of lawyers, insurers, brokers, shipowners, cargo interests, government officials and others involved in the maritime industry and interested in maritime law. The C.M.L.A. is Canada's representative on the "Comité Maritime Internationale" ("C.M.I.") which is the international maritime law body, founded in 1897 to promote uniformity in and reform of international maritime law. In conjunction with the United Nations Committee on Trade and Development ("U.N.C.T.A.D."), I.U.M.I. has been responsible for the drafting of a number of international conventions dealing with maritime matters.

The Association of Maritime Arbitrators of Canada was incorporated in 1986 to provide services for the arbitration of maritime disputes in Canada. It has published marine arbitration rules and a roster of arbitrators. It also undertakes educational programs designed to promote awareness of maritime arbitration. The membership of this organization includes maritime lawyers, insurers, brokers, surveyors and others connected with the marine industry.

The importance of marine insurance in modern Canadian commerce is reflected by the substantial number of marine insurance decisions which have emanated from the highest courts in the federal and provincial legal systems, many of them dealing with important principles which have an international reach. These decisions, the principles expressed in the *C.M.I.A.* and the practice of marine insurance in Canada, are the focus of this book.

Chapter 2

The Marine Insurance Contract

2.1 INTRODUCTION

A marine insurance policy is a contract — a bargain between two parties, insured and insurer. The Canadian *Marine Insurance Act*[1] ("*C.M.I.A*") provides a set of principles applicable to marine insurance contracts, but, like the English *Marine Insurance Act* ("*M.I.A 1906*"),[2] it preserves freedom of contract. The parties are free in most respects to write their own contract and, in practice, they invariably do so. The interplay of the needs of insureds, the ingenuity of brokers and the willingness of insurers to accept new risks (on certain terms and at a certain price) has driven the evolution of marine insurance. This chapter considers the basic requirements of a marine insurance contract as well as the main types of marine insurance contracts.

A contract of marine insurance must be in writing to be admissible in evidence[3] and must be signed "by or on behalf of the insurer",[4] The other requisites of a marine policy under the *C.M.I.A.* are:[5]

  (*a*) the name of the insured or of a person who effects the insurance on behalf of the insured;

  (*b*) the subject-matter insured;

  (*c*) the perils insured against;

---

[1] S.C. 1993, c. 22.

[2] 6 Edw. VII, c. 41.

[3] *C.M.I.A.*, subs. 25(1). See also s. 23 of the Ontario *Marine Insurance Act*, R.S.O. 1990, c. M.2: "A contract of marine insurance is inadmissible in evidence unless it is embodied in a marine policy in accordance with this Act…". In *Green Forest Lumber Ltd. v. General Security Insurance Co. of Canada*, [1977] 2 F.C. 351, [1977] I.L.R. ¶1-849 (T.D.), aff'd. [1978] 2 F.C. 773, 34 N.R. 306 (C.A.), aff'd. [1980] 1 S.C.R. 176, 34 N.R. 303, the trial judge noted that under English authority, an action for specific performance could be brought to enforce an agreement to issue a policy. In that case, it was held that the certificate of insurance contained all the necessary ingredients of a marine policy, but the court rejected a claim for coverage under clauses not embodied in a marine policy. See also *General Marine Assurance Co. v. Ocean Marine Insurance Co.* (1899), 16 Que. S.C. 170 in which it was held that an interim memorandum issued by the underwriter could be a valid contract and that the insured was allowed a reasonable time to provide particulars of the cargo to be insured.

[4] *C.M.I.A.*, subs. 27(1).

[5] *Ibid.*, s. 26.

(*d*)   the voyage or period, or both, covered by the insurance;

(*e*)   the sum insured; and

(*f*)   the name of the insurer.

The subject-matter of the insurance must be specified with reasonable certainty, but it is not necessary that the insured's interest, or the extent thereof, be specified.[6] An "interim covering memorandum", insuring cargo to be shipped on a particular vessel, with a policy to be issued on receipt of particulars, has been held to be an enforceable marine insurance contract, even though the particulars had not been provided at the time of the loss.[7]

2.2   THE FORMATION OF THE CONTRACT

A contract of marine insurance is "deemed to be concluded when the proposal of the insured is accepted by the insurer", whether the insurance policy is issued at that time or not.[8] Marine insurance is usually effected by a marine insurance broker, acting as the agent of the insured, thus the "proposal" is usually the broker's submission to the insurer.

In traditional marine insurance practice the broker prepared a piece of paper known as a "slip", identifying the insured, the risk to be insured, and the insuring terms required. The broker then called on underwriters, attempting to gain their acceptance of the terms and their participation in a percentage of the risk. Usually, the broker found an underwriter to take the "lead" or a substantial part of the risk and to fix the premium. Other underwriters would "follow" and accept percentages of the risk, and of the premium. The underwriters subscribed to the risk by signing the slip. The lead underwriter might amend the terms being proposed by the broker, qualifying or limiting the risk accepted, or imposing warranties. These qualifications would initially take the form of amendments to the slip. Once the risk was fully subscribed, the broker prepared the policy, based on the terms accepted by underwriters. The policy was then forwarded to all the underwriters for signature. This might occur some considerable time after the risk had attached and the insurance had become effective.[9]

In Canada today, market practices vary. Most cargo insurance is placed through open policies issued to freight forwarders or large exporters, and takes the form, from the insured's point of view, of a marine insurance certificate containing a reference to the insuring terms. The insurance of commercial hulls is invariably placed with underwriters by specialist brokers, and hull and machinery policies are typically prepared on the broker's manuscript wording, containing tailor-made clauses and generally incorporating standard Canadian or

---

6   *Ibid.*, s. 28(1).

7   *General Marine Assurance Co. v. Ocean Marine Insurance Co.* (1899), 16 Que. S.C. 170.

8   *C.M.I.A.*, s. 23.

9   See *O'Keefe & Lynch of Canada Ltd. v. Toronto Insurance and Vessel Agency Ltd.* (1926), 59 O.L.R. 235, [1926] 4 D.L.R. 477 (H.C.) for a discussion of the making of insurance contracts in that particular era.

United States hull insurance wordings. Pleasure craft and yacht insurance is usually provided on standard form wordings issued by the leading marine insurance companies. Protection and indemnity insurance may be written on standard market forms or may be placed with a P. & I. Club which issues a Certificate of Entry, incorporating the Club's Rules Book.

2.3 TYPES OF MARINE POLICIES

Apart from classification according to subject-matter (cargo, hull and machinery, freight or liabilities), marine policies can be classified in other ways — whether the policy is valued or unvalued,[10] whether it is written on a time or voyage basis, whether or not it is a floating or open policy[11] and whether it is a subscription policy.

2.3.1 Valued and Unvalued Policies

The *C.M.I.A.* distinguishes between "valued" and "unvalued" policies. Most marine insurance policies are valued policies. A valued policy specifies the agreed value of the subject-matter.[12] In contrast, an unvalued policy leaves the insured value of the property to be determined by a set of rules contained in the *C.M.I.A.*[13] In the absence of fraud, the valuation in a valued policy is binding on both the insured and the insurer.[14] The subject of valuation is discussed in Chapter 6.

2.3.2 Time Policies and Voyage Policies

The *C.M.I.A.* also distinguishes between time policies and voyage policies.[15] A time policy insures the subject-matter for a definite period, typically one year. A voyage policy insures the subject-matter for a specified voyage. A cargo voyage policy is generally referred to as a "single shipment policy" and the "voyage" is normally extended from the seller's warehouse to the buyer's warehouse and on all intermediate conveyances.

Voyage policies were of much greater significance in the days of sailing ships than they are today. In the past, it was common to insure a ship for a single voyage or to issue a "voyage" policy of cargo insurance. Today, most of the world's tonnage is insured under time policies and most cargo insurance is placed under open policies with terms of a year or more. "One-off" shipments of cargo are generally insured by declarations under open policies of freight forwarders.

---

[10] See Chapter 6, *Insurable Value*.
[11] Referred to in s. 31 of the *C.M.I.A.* as a "floating" policy. See Chapter 18, *Cargo Insurance*.
[12] *C.M.I.A.*, subs. 30(2).
[13] *Ibid.*, subs. 30(3); see also s. 19.
[14] *Ibid..*, subs. 30(4).
[15] *Ibid.*, s. 29. For an example of a time policy, see *Dimock v. New Brunswick Marine Assurance Co.* (1848), 5 N.B.R. 654 (C.A.).

2.3.3 Open and Floating Policies

The *C.M.I.A.* makes provision for "floating" policies, or what are sometimes referred to as "open policies". A floating policy is one that "describes the insurance in general terms and leaves the name of the ship and other particulars to be defined by subsequent declarations, either by endorsement on the policy or in any other customary manner".[16] Strictly speaking, the modern "open policy" is not the same as a "floating policy", which was the type of policy in use in England when the *M.I.A. 1906* was drafted. A floating policy specified a maximum amount of insurance, which was drawn down upon through declarations until the limits of the policy were exhausted. Open policies, which came into common use in the United States and Canada in the 1940s, do not have a maximum amount of insurance (although there is usually a limit for individual shipments) and generally remain in force until cancelled.

Open policies are commonly issued by marine insurers to importers and exporters who find it convenient to have one policy covering all their requirements. The insured reports all shipments by means of declarations under the policy and pays a monthly, quarterly or annual premium based on the insured value of all shipments falling within the policy. Open policies are frequently issued to freight forwarders as a simple and efficient means of providing insurance to their customers.[17]

In the case of open policies covering exports sold on a C.I.F. basis, it is the general practice for the exporter to furnish evidence of insurance to the buyer in the form of an insurance certificate. These forms (which are provided by the insurer) are completed by the exporter/seller and, when delivered to the buyer, function as proof of insurance. They enable the foreign buyer of the goods to present a claim to the local "settling agent" or survey firm nominated by the insurer. One copy of the certificate, forwarded to the insurer, serves as a declaration under the open policy.

In *Standard Marine Insurance Co. v. Whalen Pulp & Paper Co.*,[18] the British Columbia Court of Appeal, described the operation of an open policy, adopting the words of Lord Blackburn in *Ionides v. Pacific Fire & Marine Insurance Co.*:

> The contract of an underwriter who subscribes a policy on goods by ship or ships to be declared is, that he will insure any goods of the description specified which may be shipped on any vessel answering the description, if any there be, in the policy, on the voyage stipulated in the policy to which the assured elects to apply the policy. The object of the declaration is to earmark and identify the particular adventure to which the assured elects to apply the policy. The assent of the assurer

---

[16]   *Ibid.*, subs. 31(1).
[17]   See Chapter 21, *Insurance of Particular Risks.*
[18]   [1922] 1 W.W.R. 679 (B.C.C.A.), aff'd. (1922), 64 S.C.R. 90, 68 D.L.R. 269. This case is also discussed under the subject of open policies in Chapter 4, *Good Faith: Misrepresentation and Non-Disclosure.*

is not required to this, for he has no option to reject any vessel the assured may select.[19]

In most open cargo policies it is common to incorporate a classification clause (such as the Institute Classification Clause 13/4/92) specifying limitations to the class, age and tonnage of vessels that may be used to transport cargo insured under the policy. Provided a vessel falls within the parameters of the classification clause, the marine insurance rates contained in the policy's rate schedule will apply. If a vessel is used that is not within the requirements of the classification clause, it is usually accommodated by a "held covered" provision permitting the insurer to surcharge the normal rates.

Often the party issued with a certificate of insurance under the open policy is not the actual holder of the open policy and may not be privy to its terms. For example, in the case of an open policy held by a freight forwarder, the forwarder's customer will simply receive a certificate of insurance, attesting to the fact that insurance on the goods has been effected under the open policy and identifying the insuring conditions. It has been stated that the holder of a certificate is entitled to obtain the full policy.[20] Similarly, the holder of a certificate is not bound by unusual clauses in the underlying insurance policy that are not referred to in the certificate and that limit his or her rights.[21]

2.3.4 Subscription Policies

A marine policy is often a "subscription policy" — the policy is underwritten or subscribed to by a number of insurers, each taking a percentage of the risk. In that case, unless the policy otherwise provides, each insurer is severally liable for its percentage of the risk and the policy is a distinct contract with each subscribing insurer.[22]

2.4 ALTERATION OF THE CONTRACT

No party to a contract may alter it without the agreement of the other party. A broker cannot unilaterally alter the contract, except to the extent permitted by the policy, without the insurer's agreement, and any such alteration renders the policy void.[23] Similarly, the insurer cannot amend the contract without the consent of the insured. An amendment to the contract must be made in writing in order to be effective.

---

[19] *Ibid.*, at 680 (W.W.R.), citing (1871), L.R. 6 Q.B. 674 at 682.

[20] See *Browning v. Provincial Insurance Co.* (1873), L.R. 5 P.C. 263, although this case did not involve an open policy.

[21] See *Ronald A. Chisholm Ltd. v. Agro & Diverses Souscriptions Internationales — A.D.S.I.-S.A.* (1991), 2 C.P.C. (3d) 120 (Ont. Master), aff'd. 4 O.R. (3d) 539 (S.C.).

[22] *C.M.I.A.*, subs. 27(3).

[23] *Atlantic & Lake Superior Railway Co. v. Empress Assurance Corp.* (1899), 15 Que. S.C. 469, aff'd. (1900), 11 Que. K.B. 200.

2.5 ATTACHMENT OF THE RISK

There is often a difference between the date of the marine insurance contract and the date when the contract becomes effective or "attaches" to the property at risk. This is because the policy is usually prepared in advance of the voyage or time period for which the property is to be insured. The policy is said to "attach" to the property at the time the insured risk commences. The policy itself will describe the voyage or period during which the risk is insured.

In the case of hull and machinery time policies, the insurance attaches at the inception time and date stated in the policy. In voyage policies, the risk attaches when the voyage begins.[24] It is, however, common practice in time policies to insure short periods of time in port prior to the commencement of the voyage and/or following the vessel's arrival at destination.

Open cargo policies usually contain an "attachment clause" stating that the policy attaches to all shipments made on or after a specified date. In effect, the open policy is a facility covering specified shipments from their origin ware-house, during their ordinary course of transit, and until they are delivered to the final warehouse at destination. An open policy is really a convenient means of covering a series of single shipments. If no shipments are made under a single shipment policy or an open policy, neither policy will attach as there is no subject-matter to insure. A single shipment policy will normally state that the insurance attaches from the time the goods leave the warehouse at the place named in the policy.

2.6 TERMINATION OF THE CONTRACT

The policy itself generally describes its duration. A voyage policy comes to an end automatically on the conclusion of the voyage named in the policy. A time policy comes to an end at the expiry of the period named in the policy. The policy may come to an earlier end in a variety of circumstances:

(a) where one party exercises its right to "avoid" (treat as void) the policy as a result of the misrepresentation or non-disclosure by the other party;

(b) where there has been a breach of warranty which discharges the insurer from liability from the time of the breach;

(c) where the policy gives one party a right of cancellation.

The subjects of misrepresentation and non-disclosure are dealt with in Chapter 4. Warranties are the subject of Chapter 8.

---

[24] See *Great Northern Transit Co. v. Alliance Insurance Co.* (1898), 25 O.A.R. 393 (C.A.), where a vessel was insured "whilst running on inland lakes...etc." The vessel was in fact at dock at the inception of the policy and remained there for two years until destroyed by fire. It was never navigated during that time. It was argued on behalf of the insurer that the risk never attached since the vessel was insured during the navigation season only when running. It was held that the risk had attached and that the quoted clause was used merely to limit the geographic risk.

2.7 RENEWALS

Marine insurance contracts are frequently renewed at the time of their expiry. It has been held that a renewal is a separate contract.[25] An insured or its broker seeking to renew the contract must therefore make full disclosure of any new and material circumstances since the policy was originally effected which might affect the judgment of the insurer as to whether or not to accept the risk and what terms or premium to require.

A time policy on a vessel will often be renewed for another year. Although some insurers make a practice of issuing open cargo policies on an annual basis, with an expiry date one year from inception, most such policies remain in force until cancelled by either the insurer or the insured in accordance with the policy cancellation clause. Insurers maintaining open cargo policies usually have a system for periodic reviews of the underwriting results; thus, if an individual open policy has been sustaining adverse claims experience, the insurer has the option of sending a cancellation notice to the insured.

2.8 CANCELLATION OF THE CONTRACT

A party may wish to cancel the policy before its term ends. The insured may dispose of the property covered by the insurance and may have no further need for the policy. The insurer may decide that the insured's loss record makes the policy unprofitable and may wish to end its exposure. The *C.M.I.A.* does not deal with the cancellation of the policy, but policies frequently contain cancellation provisions. Where the policy permits the underwriter to cancel it on giving due notice, the provisions of the policy must be strictly observed and notice must be given in the manner specified in the policy. In *Atkinson v. State Farm Fire & Casualty Co.*,[26] it was held that the sending of notice by registered mail canceling a policy on a cabin cruiser was effective since it was done in accordance with the policy, even though the insured claimed that he had never received the notice of cancellation.

In *Nuvo Electronics Inc. v. London Assurance*,[27] the insurer contended that an open cargo policy of insurance had been cancelled at 12:01 a.m. on August 10, 1996 and did not attach to a shipment by air departing at 20:23 hours on August 10, 1996. The policy attached to all shipments "made on and after August 1, 1994". It had no fixed term but remained in force until cancelled by one of the parties. The policy contained a cancellation clause stating that it could be cancelled by the insurer giving 30 days written or telegraphic notice. Another clause provided that notice *mailed* to the broker would be deemed to be notice to the insured. On July 10, 1996 the insurer prepared a letter to the broker purport-

---

[25] See *Neepawa Yacht Ltd. v. Laurentian Property & Casualty Insurance Co.* (1994), D.R.S. 95-04330 (B.C.S.C.), holding that each renewal is a separate contract, citing *Stokell v. Heywood* [1896] 1 Ch. 459 and *Benson v. Ibbott-Seed Insurance Agencies Ltd.* (1966), 60 D.L.R. (2d) 166 (B.C.C.A.).

[26] [1982] I.L.R. ¶1-1525 (Ont. S.C.J.).

[27] (2000), 49 O.R. (3d) 374, 19 C.C.L.I. (3d) 195 (S.C.J.), additional reasons at (2000), 23 C.C.L.I. (3d) 231 (S.C.J.), appeal withdrawn, Jan. 28, 2002, Ontario Court of Appeal.

ing to cancel the policy by giving 30 days notice of cancellation effective August 10, 1996. The letter was sent by facsimile to the broker on July 10, 1996 and a copy was also sent by courier the following day. It was not "mailed" to the broker.

Expert evidence was led as to the various times used in marine insurance policies for the attachment or termination of the insurance[28] and as to the manner of calculation of notice periods. An insurance broker testified as an expert witness that although the policy wording required notice to be mailed, "convention" would permit facsimile communication. Justice MacFarland concluded that the policy had not been effectively cancelled at the time of the shipment. She stated:

> Where marine custom traditionally recognizes three times used in policy wordings and where the notice of cancellation is vague and imprecise in its language and merely states that cancellation '...is to be effective August 10, 1996' without more, it is insufficient to bring home to the insured or his agent that the coverage expires one minute into August 10, 1996.

> In my view, the insurer bears the primary responsibility, when it wishes to cancel its policy, to be specific in terms of the time when the cancellation is to be effective and here the insurer did not do so. Its notice could be interpreted to mean that coverage would be in force for the entire day of August 10, 1996 but not beyond. It is no answer for the insurer to say that if there was confusion about the time of cancellation the broker ought to have clarified it, in circumstances where the insurer created the confusion.

> In my view, this alone is enough to find that the policy continued to attach throughout August 10, 1996 and hence provided coverage for the subject loss but there is more.[29]

The judge then noted that the insurer had not complied with the cancellation terms of its own policy because the notice was sent by facsimile rather than by mail. As well, the policy provided not only cargo coverage but also coverage for buildings, equipment and stock and, said court, it was therefore subject to the Statutory Conditions contained in the Ontario *Insurance Act*.[30] Those statutory conditions required that notice of cancellation be given directly to the insured, either by registered mail or by personal delivery. There was, therefore, a conflict in the form of notice required by the policy. Justice MacFarland concluded that

---

[28] The expert witness testified that three times are traditionally used in marine policy wordings: 12:01 a.m., 12 noon and midnight or 11:59 p.m. He stated that it is up to the parties to choose whatever time they wish for the commencement and termination of the policy and that, typically, the time is noted in the policy. He testified that in this case, because the policy attached "on and after August 1, 1994", "marine tradition" would dictate that the policy would attach at 12:01 a.m.

[29] (2000) 49 O.R. (3d) 374 at 383-84 (S.C.J.).

[30] R.S.O. 1990, c. 18.

"Minimally, the language of the policy is ambiguous and the insurer has failed to give proper notice of cancellation."[31]

The *Nuvo Electronics* case illustrates just how strictly the courts will interpret cancellation provisions and how important it is for the insurer, when canceling the policy, to comply literally with the requirements of the policy. In the event of conflicting provisions with respect to cancellation, the court will require exact compliance with the most generous provisions.

Notice of cancellation must be given before a loss occurs. Thus, in *Osborne v. R.*,[32] it was held that the notice of cancellation given by the Fishing Vessel Insurance Plan for non-payment of premium was ineffective because it was not received by the insured before the loss.

Care should be exercised in the cancellation of the policy, as the act of cancellation itself may be treated by the court as confirmation that there has been a valid policy in effect up to the time of cancellation. Where the underwriter has advised the insured (or the broker on behalf of the insured) that the policy is "void *ab initio*" as a result of fraud, or when there has been a misrepresentation or non-disclosure entitling the underwriter to avoid the policy, it is arguably unnecessary to cancel the policy, since the policy ceases to apply by operation of law in these instances. The act of cancellation may in fact be regarded as an affirmation of the contract in circumstances where it would otherwise have ceased to be operative. Even in the case of breach of warranty, which has the effect of discharging the insurer from liability from the date of the breach, care should be taken in cancellation to avoid the inference that the insurer regards the policy as being operative up until the cancellation date.[33]

2.9 RATIFICATION OF THE CONTRACT

Section 24 of the *C.M.I.A.* provides:

> 24. A contract effected in good faith by a person on behalf of another person may be ratified by that other person even after that other person becomes aware of a loss.

This simply means that an agent for a party may contract on behalf of that party and the knowledge of a loss at the time the party ratifies or "adopts" the contract does not affect its validity.[34]

---

[31] (2000) 49 O.R. (3d) 374 at 385 (S.C.J.).

[32] (1983), 3 C.C.L.I. 154, [1984] I.L.R. ¶1-1724 (F.C.T.D.); See also *Brown v. British American Assurance Co.* (1875), 25 U.C.C.P. 514 to the effect that the policy must be cancelled before the loss in order for the cancellation to be effective.

[33] See Chapter 8, *Warranties*.

[34] See *Seaman v. West* (1885), Cout. S.C. 723, Cass. S.C. 388, aff'g. 17 N.S.R. 207 (C.A.), where it was held that the person for whose benefit a contract of insurance was made could ratify it expressly or by implication.

2.10   MARINE INSURANCE FORMS

The starting point for the analysis of most marine insurance problems is the identification of the contract of insurance. This is not always an easy task, as the contract may be made up of several documents or may make reference to policy forms that may or may not be attached to it.[35] It is common for marine insurance contracts to incorporate standard forms by reference to the name of the form, without actually attaching the form to the policy. In the past, a policy might not be issued unless specifically requested by the insured or in the event of a claim under the policy. Good practice requires that all relevant forms be attached to the policy, properly completed where necessary and deleting redundant, unnecessary or inconsistent clauses.

There are a number of "standard form" contracts in use for all types of marine insurance. The most commonly-used forms, whether Canadian, U.S. or British, are referred to at various points throughout this book, and some of the details of the most important forms are discussed. In Canadian marine insurance practice, it is common to insure cargo using English forms prepared by the Institute of London Underwriters and known as the "Institute Cargo Clauses" 1/1/82.[36] In hull and machinery insurance, there is a choice of Canadian clauses unique to the Pacific Coast and to the Great Lakes, American hull clauses and English market forms.

The *M.I.A. 1906* incorporated a standard form of insurance policy, known as the "S.G. Form".[37] This form, which had been used in the marine insurance markets for many years, was appended to the statutes of most Canadian provinces. The form has fallen into disuse and was not incorporated into the *C.M.I.A.* In 1982 many of the English marine insurance clauses, notably the Institute Cargo Clauses, were revised with more modern language and in this connection a new policy form, known as the "MAR" form, was produced. The form provides spaces for the insertion of certain essential information, including the insured, the vessel, the voyage or time period insured, the subject-matter and the proportion underwritten by each insurer. The applicable clauses are then attached to the form.

In Canada, it is common for the larger insurance brokers to have their own standard policies for various types of insurance which typically incorporate the standard Canadian, English or U.S. "market" policy forms but also containing additional clauses specially prepared by the broker using its own "manuscript" wordings.

---

[35]   See Chapter 3, *Construction of the Marine Policy.*
[36]   See Appendices B, C, and D.
[37]   Generally considered to stand for "Ship and Goods".

Chapter 3

Construction of the Marine Policy

3.1 INTRODUCTION

As noted in Chapter 2, the Canadian *Marine Insurance Act* ("*C.M.I.A.*")[1] allows the parties the freedom to write their own contract. Section 90 of the *C.M.I.A.* provides:

> Any right, duty or liability that arises under a contract by implication of law, or that is established by this Act and may be lawfully modified by the parties to a contract, may be modified or varied by express agreement or by usage of the trade if the usage binds both parties to the contract.

While the Act provides a framework for the solution of marine insurance problems, it is invariably necessary to have reference to the insurance contract itself, since it is the expression of the parties' particular bargain. The starting point is a careful reading of the policy, but in most cases, the solution also requires an understanding of marine insurance law and practice followed by the interpretation of the policy using the principles of construction laid down by the courts.[2] This chapter deals with those principles.

The *C.M.I.A.* has little to say about how a contract of marine insurance is to be interpreted, although like the English *Marine Insurance Act* ("*M.I.A 1906*"),[3] it contains a Schedule defining the meaning of certain terms used in a marine policy.[4]

---

[1] S.C. 1993, c. 22.

[2] For discussions of the principles to be applied in the interpretation of marine insurance policies, see A. Parks, *The Law and Practice of Marine Insurance and Average* (London: Stevens & Sons, 1988), chapter 4; Arnould's *Law of Marine Insurance and Average*, 16th ed., Vol. I (London: Butterworths, 1981), chapter 3; E.R. Ivamy, *Marine Insurance*, 4th ed. (London: Butterworths, 1985), chapter 23.

[3] 6 Edw. VII, c. 41.

[4] Section 3 of the *C.M.I.A.*: "Subject to this Act, and unless a contrary intention appears, the words and terms set out in the schedule have, when used in a marine policy, the meaning assigned by the schedule." The defined terms in the Schedule include "barratry", "goods", "pirates", "thieves", "all other perils", "arrests, &c., of kings, princes and people", "lost or not lost", "at and from", "perils of the seas", "safely landed", "from the loading thereof", "stranded", and "at any port or place whatsoever". These terms have been the subject of consideration in English case law. The term 'perils of the seas' refers only to fortuitous accidents or casualties of the seas. It does not include the ordinary action of the winds and waves: *Century Insurance Co. of Canada*

3.2 IDENTIFYING THE CONTRACT

The right of the insured to indemnity is governed by the contract terms.[5] The process of interpretation begins with the identification of the documents containing those terms. In some cases, the insurance contract will be one document covering a single interest against specified perils. In other cases, there may be several documents created at different times. The policy may not have been issued at the time of the loss. It may be a *pastiche* of several documents, some standard forms and some prepared by the broker specifically for the particular insured. The insurance may have been arranged under an open cover incorporating a variety of forms, and declarations may have been filed or insurance certificates issued. Subsequent endorsements may have been issued to vary, extend or renew the insurance. Where the insurance has been placed through a broker, as is often the case, the broker may have retained the contract or the "slip" and the insured may have received nothing more than a cover note or other confirmation of coverage.[6]

Regardless of the manner in which the insurance contract is made, one must distinguish between documents which are merely antecedents to the contract and those which are truly part of the contract itself. If there is no ambiguity in the contract, only the policy should be referred to — antecedent documents, such as the slip or application should be ignored. Where there is ambiguity in the policy, courts have referred to the slip to determine the true contract to which underwriters subscribed.[7]

---

     v. Case Existological Laboratories Ltd., [1983] 2 S.C.R. 47, 150 D.L.R. (3d) 9, aff'g. (1982), 133 D.L.R. (3d) 727, 35 B.C.L.R. 364 (C.A.), rev'g. (1980) 116 D.L.R. (3d) 199 (S.C.). This subject is discussed in Chapter 7, *Perils Insured*. "Barratry" is defined in the Schedule as including "every wrongful act willfully committed by the master or crew of the insured ship to the prejudice of the owner or charterer of the ship" but it does not refer to negligent acts: see *O'Connor v. Merchants Marine Insurance Co.* (1889), 16 S.C.R. 331; *Spinney v. Ocean Mutual Marine Insurance Co.* (1890), 17 S.C.R. 326.

[5]   Section 6 of the *C.M.I.A.*:

     6. (1) A contract of marine insurance is a contract whereby the insurer undertakes to indemnify the insured, *in the manner and to the extent agreed in the contract*, against

         (a)   losses that are incidental to a marine adventure or an adventure analogous to a marine adventure...

[6]   For examples of the interpretative difficulties that can arise from the use of policy forms, see: *MacMillan Bloedel Ltd. v. Youell* (1991), 2 C.C.L.I. (2d) 241, 79 B.C.L.R. (2d) 326 (S.C.), var'd (1993), 95 B.C.L.R. (2d) 130 (C.A.), leave to appeal refused (1994), 23 C.C.L.I. (2d), 18*n*. (S.C.C.); *Burrard Towing Co. v. Reed Stenhouse Ltd.* (1996), 19 B.C.L.R. (3d) 391, 35 C.C.L.I. (2d) 145 (C.A.), rev'g. (1994), 100 B.C.L.R. (2d) 92, 29 C.C.L.I. (2d) 29 (S.C.); *Catherwood Towing Ltd. v. Commercial Union Assurance Co.* (1996), 26 B.C.L.R. (3d) 57, 35 C.C.L.I. (2d) 124 (C.A.), aff'g. (1995), 30 C.C.L.I. (2d) 135, [1995] I.L.R. ¶1-3245 (S.C.).

[7]   See, for example, *Robertson v. Lovett* (1874), 9 N.S.R. 424 (S.C.), where the court held that the insured could not circumvent a time limitation in a policy of insurance by bringing suit on the slip. The slip was not the contract. On the other hand, in *McKenzie v. Corbett* (1883), Cass. S.C. 385 (S.C.C.), rev'g. (1882), 16 N.S.R. 50 (C.A.), it was held that it was permissible to read the slip, the application and the policy together.

Once the contract has been identified, it is necessary to examine and to read all its components in order to interpret it. In *Mowat v. Boston Marine Insurance Co.*, Chief Justice Strong of the Supreme Court of Canada stated:

> The policy, certificate and memorandum together constitute the contract between the parties, and we must read them together as if they had been embodied in the same instrument, and doing this, we are bound to construe them, so far as we reasonably can, in such a way as to avoid any repugnancy between the provisions of the several instruments in which the parties have thus formulated their entire contract.[8]

The documents forming the contract, and the contract itself, should be construed, if possible, so as to find harmony and logic. Even when the policy is a single document, the whole document must be examined in order to fully understand the coverage it provides and to ensure that the interpretation of the part is consistent with the meaning of the whole.[9]

3.3   THE PRINCIPLES OF CONSTRUCTION

3.3.1   The Intention of the Parties

The object of the interpretation of a contract of insurance is the same as in the case of any other contract — to find the intention of the parties as manifested in the words they have used to express that intention.[10] In *Pense v. Northern Life Assurance Co.*, it was stated:

---

[8] *Mowat v. Boston Marine Insurance Co.* (1896), 26 S.C.R. 47 at 53, rev'g. (1895), 33 N.B.R. 109 (C.A.): the policy, certificate and memorandum should be read together as if they were embodied in the same document and should be construed, if possible, so as to avoid repugnancy; see also *Creighton v. Union Marine Insurance Co.* (1854), 2 N.S.R. 195 (C.A.); *British America Assurance Co. v. William Law & Co.* (1892), 21 S.C.R. 325, aff'g. (1892), 23 N.S.R. 537 (C.A.); and *Wilson v. Merchants' Marine Insurance Co.* (1872), 9 N.S.R. 81 (T.D.). In *Catherwood Towing Ltd. v. Commercial Union Insurance Co.* (1996), 26 B.C.L.R. (3d) 57, 35 C.C.L.I. (2d) 124 (C.A.), aff'g. (1995), 30 C.C.L.I. (2d) 135 (B.C.S.C.), the British Columbia Court of Appeal said at C.C.L.I. 128 that the interpretation of the contract was to be determined by "the terms of the policy, the schedule, the terms and conditions appended and the endorsements" and not the history of the preceding policy or the binder in respect of this policy.

[9] For an example of this approach, see *Nanaimo Shipyards (1985) Ltd. v. Underwriters, Lloyd's London* (1992), 66 B.C.L.R. (2d) 162, 7 C.C.L.I. (2d) 1 (C.A.), rev'g. (1991), 56 B.C.L.R. (2d) 149, 3 C.C.L.I. (2d) 1, leave to appeal refused (1992), 143 N.R. 286*n*, 70 B.C.L.R. (2d) xxxiii, where the Court considered all the language in the policy to determine that it was an occurrence policy rather than a claims made policy.

[10] *Robertson v. French* (1803), 7 R.R. 535 at 540, 4 East 130, *per* Lord Ellenborough at 135: "the same rule of construction which applies to all other instruments applies equally to...a policy of insurance". In the non-marine context, see C. Brown and J. Menezes, *Insurance Law of Canada*, 2nd ed. (Toronto: Carswell, 1991) at p. 138, referring to *Poole & Thompson Ltd. v. London & Lancashire Guar. & Accident Co.*, [1938] 4 D.L.R. 6 (S.C.C.), aff'g. [1938] 1 D.L.R. 334 (P.E.I.S.C., App. Div.), aff'g. [1937] 1 D.L.R. 588 (P.E.I.S.C.); *Seagate Hotel Ltd. v. Simcoe & Erie General Insurance Co.*, [1980] I.L.R. ¶1-168 (B.C.S.C.).

There is no just reason for applying any different rule of construction to a contract of insurance from that of a contract of any other kind; and there can be no sort of excuse for casting a doubt upon the meaning of such a contract with a view to solving it against the insurer, however much the claim against him may play upon the chords of sympathy, or touch a natural bias. In such a contract, just as in all other contracts, effect must be given to the intention of the parties, to be gathered from the words they have used. A plaintiff must make out from the terms of the contract a right to recover, a defendant must likewise make out any defence based upon the agreement. The onus of proof, if I may use such a term in reference to the interpretation of a writing, is, upon each party respectively, precisely the same. We are all, doubtless, insured, and none insurers, and so, doubtless, all more or less affected by the natural bias arising from such a position; and so ought to beware lest that bias not be counteracted by a full apprehension of its existence.[11]

In one of the earliest English marine insurance cases, *Robertson v. French*, which has been referred to repeatedly in England and Canada, Lord Ellenborough stated with reference to an insurance contract:

In such a contract, just as in all other contracts, effect must be given to the intention of the parties to be gathered from the words they have used.[12]

The parties' subjective intention may not, in fact, be properly expressed in the words they have used, but the law of contract is based on the objective manifestation of their intent and not on their unexpressed wishes or expectations.

While some nineteenth century cases suggested that the words used in the contract were less important than the meaning that was to be given to them based on the practices of merchants, shipowners and insurers,[13] the primary

---

[11]   (1907), 15 D.L.R. 131 at 137, 15 O.L.R. 131 (C.A.), rev'g. (1907) 14 O.L.R. 613. This passage was adopted by the Supreme Court of Canada on appeal (1908), 42 S.C.R. 246. It was also approved by the Supreme Court in *Consolidated Bathurst Export Ltd. v. Mutual Boiler & Machinery Co.*, [1980] 1 S.C.R. 888, 112 D.L.R. (3d) 49.

[12]   (1803), 7 R.R. 535 at 540, 4 East 130. The logical inconsistency in this approach is exposed by the following statement by the Judicial Committee of the Privy Council in *Beacon Fire & Life Insurance Co. v. Gibb* (1862), 1 Moo. P.C. N.S. 73 (P.C.), 15 E.R. 630 (C.A.), quoting from Lord Denman in *Rickman v. Carstairs*, 5 B. & Ad. 663: "The question in this and other cases of construction of written instruments is, not what was the intention of the parties, but what is the meaning of the words they have used?" For a somewhat different approach, see Justice Southin in the British Columbia Court of Appeal in *Burrard Towing Co. v. Reed Stenhouse Ltd.* (1996), 19 B.C.L.R. (3d) 391 at 397, 35 C.C.L.I. (2d) 145 (C.A.), rev'g. (1994), 100 B.C.L.R. (2d) 92, 29 C.C.L.I. (2d) 29 (B.C.S.C.), quoting from Lord Sumner in *Becker v. London Assurance Corp.*, [1918] A.C. 101 (H.L.):

      One need only ask, has the event on which I put my premium actually occurred? This
      is a matter of the meaning of the contract, and not, as seems sometimes to be sup-
      posed, of doing the liberal and reasonable thing by a reasonable assured.

[13]   According to this approach, language used in marine insurance contracts had taken on its own meaning, with which all involved in the business were familiar and the contract should be interpreted in order to give effect to this meaning. As early as 1849 in *Gillespie v. British American Fire & Life Insurance Co.* (1849), 7 U.C.Q.B. 108 (C.A.), an Upper Canada court adopted the statement in Park's *Treatise on Insurance* that: "a policy of insurance being a contract of indemnity and being

modern rule of construction is to focus on the words used by the parties to discern their "intent". In *Ocean Fisheries Ltd. v. Pacific Coast Fishermen's Mutual Marine Insurance Co.*,[14] the Federal Court of Appeal stated that a marine insurance contract should be interpreted in the same manner as any other insurance contract and the objective should be to give effect to the intention of the parties:

> While we are here concerned with the construction of a contract of marine insurance, such a contract is to be construed in the same way as any other contract of insurance: *Robertson v. French*…The primary objective is to discover and give effect to the intention of the parties as disclosed by the words used by them, the context in which those words appear and the purpose sought by the words employed at the time the contract was entered into.[15]

The Court of Appeal referred to two prior decisions of the Supreme Court of Canada, to the effect that the "cardinal rule [in the interpretation of insurance policies] is that the intention of the parties must prevail" and that "particular consideration must be given to the terms used by the parties, the context in which they are used and finally the purpose sought by the parties in using these terms".[16]

---

only considered as a simple contract, must always be construed as nearly as possible according to the intention of the parties, and not according to the strict and literal meaning of the words; and that as the benefit of the insured and the advancement of trade are the great objects of insurance, policies are largely to be construed in order to attain these ends." See Lord Esher M.R. in *Stewart v. Merchants Marine Insurance Co.* (1887), 16 Q.B.D. 617 at 627 (C.A.):

> But ought we in the case of an instrument like an English policy of insurance or a charterparty to apply the rules of construction which are applicable to other instruments? Anything more informal, inartistic, or ungrammatical than those policies or charterparties cannot be found … I protest against the attempt to construe these policies by the rules of construction applicable to other instruments, and where they are construed without the assistance of the jury I think the proper way is to consider them with the aid of our knowledge of business, and to take it for granted that merchants and insurers have acted in a businesslike way.

See also Lord Mansfield C.J. in *Stevenson v. Snow* (1761), 3 Burr. 1237 at 1240: "These contracts are to be taken with great latitude; the strict letter of the contract is not to be so much regarded as the object and intention of it."

14 [1998] 1 F.C. 586, 220 N.R. 68 (C.A.), aff'g. (1997), 128 F.T.R. 232 (T.D.).

15 [1998] 1 F.C. 586, *per* Stone J.A. at 597.

16 *Frenette v. Metropolitan Life Insurance Co.*, [1992] 1 S.C.R. 647, (1992), 89 D.L.R. (4th) 653, *per* L'Heureux-Dubé J., at S.C.R. 667-68; *Brissette Estate v. Westbury Life Insurance Co.*, [1992] 3 S.C.R. 87, 96 D.L.R. (4th) 609, aff'g. (1990), 74 O.R. (2d) 1, 72 D.L.R. (4th) 138 (C.A.), rev'g. (1989), 69 O.R. (2d) 215, 60 D.L.R. (4th) 78 (H.C.J.), *per* Sopinka J. at S.C.R. 92-93; see also: *Consolidated-Bathurst Export Ltd. v. Mutual Boiler and Machinery Insurance Co.*, [1980] 1 S.C.R. 888 at 900-901, 112 D.L.R. (3d) 49.

The words of the policy should be understood in their plain and ordinary sense,[17] unless they have taken on a special meaning through the custom of the trade or practice.[18]

---

[17] *Campbell v. Canada Insurance Union* (1877), 12 N.S.R. 21 (C.A.). The Nova Scotia Court of Appeal adopted a statement by Lord Ellenborough C.J. in *Robertson v. French* (1803), 7 R.R. 535, 4 East 130 at 135:

> ...it is to be construed according to the sense and meaning, as collected in the first place from the terms used in it, which terms are to be understood in their plain, ordinary and popular sense, unless they have generally, in respect to the subject matter, as by the known usage of trade or the like, acquired a particular sense, distinct from the popular sense of the same words, or unless the context evidently points out that they must in the particular instance, and in order to effectuate the immediate intention of the parties, be understood in some other special and peculiar sense.

This observation was adopted by the Nova Scotia Court of Appeal in *William Law & Co. v. British American Insurance Co.* (1892), 23 N.S.R. 537 (C.A.), aff'd. (1892), 21 S.C.R. 325. Words are to be understood in their ordinary grammatical meaning: *London Assurance Corp. v. Great Northern Transit Co.* (1899), 29 S.C.R. 577. In *Gorgichuk v. American Home Assurance Co.* (1985), 5 C.P.C. (2d) 166 (Ont. H.C.J.), the court refused to permit a party to introduce expert evidence concerning the rules of English grammar to assist in the interpretation of an insurance policy. In *Gerow v. ProvidenceWashington Insurance Co.* (1890), 17 S.C.R. 387, aff'g. (1889), 28 N.B.R. 435 (C.A.), it was held that the terms of the policy should be taken to have been used in their "popular commercial sense", as understood by the business people who relied on the contract. The court referred to Lord Herschell's remarks in *Hunter v. Northern Marine Insurance Co.*, 13 App. Cas. 726:

> I agree with the view which has been more than once expressed by learned judges that in construing such a contract as that with which we are dealing the [words] must be taken to have been used in [their] popular or commercial sense that is to say, as [they] would be understood by shippers, shipowners and underwriters. Where there is a common understanding among such persons as to the [application of the terms used] the matter is free from difficulty.

See also *St. Paul Fire & Marine Insurance Co. v. Troop* (1896), 26 S.C.R. 5, aff'g. (1895), 33 N.B.R. 105 (C.A.) to the effect that the words should be construed according to their popular and commercial sense as they would be understood by shipowners, shippers and underwriters.

[18] The policy is to be construed in the context of a commercial transaction and it is permissible to look at the surrounding circumstances: *British America Assurance Co. v. William Law & Co.*, (1892) 21 S.C.R. 325, aff'g. 23 N.S.R. 537 (C.A.). In *Merchants' Marine Insurance Co. v. Rumsey* (1884), 9 S.C.R. 577, aff'g. (1883), 16 N.S.R. 220 (C.A.), the court construed the term in a policy "merchandise under deck on trading voyage from Halifax to Labrador, and back to Halifax on trading voyage" to cover not simply the cargo originally shipped at Halifax but also cargo taken on board at other places during the voyage for the return trip. The court said that the purpose of the voyage was to sell the original cargo and to bring back a return cargo. The reason for this principle was set out in *Spooner v. Western Assurance Co.* (1876), 38 U.C.Q.B. 62 (Ont. C.A.), quoting from *Noble v. Kennoway*, 2 Doug 510, 512:

> Every underwriter is presumed to be acquainted with the practice of the trade he insures, and that whether it is established or not. If he does not know it, he ought to inform himself. It is no matter if the usage has only been for a year.

In order for a usage or practice to be considered binding on the parties, it must be established that the practice was "notorious" — that is, well-established and well-known: *Hennessy v. New York Mutual Marine Insurance Co.* (1863), 5 N.S.R. 259 (C.A.); *Young v. Dale & Co.*, [1968] I.L.R. ¶1-200 (B.C.S.C.), where it was held that there was no evidence that the term had a particular technical meaning. The interpretation of the contract should be governed by the rule that the

3.3.2 Contra Proferentem

There is a rule of interpretation applicable to all contracts, expressed in the Latin maxim, *verba cartarum fortius accipiuntur contra proferentem* — where there is ambiguity in a contract, that cannot be resolved through the application of other rules of construction, the ambiguous provision is to be construed against the party who prepared the contract. Where there are two or more possible interpretations of the document, it will be read in the light most favourable to the party who is the "proferens" — in the case of insurance, this is usually the insured.[19]

The *contra proferentem* rule has been applied in Canada from the earliest times. In an 1866 Ontario case, *Berry v. Columbian Insurance Co.*,[20] Vice-Chancellor Mowat stated: "In interpreting this provision, it is to be remembered that the policy was prepared by the company in an accustomed printed form, and every ambiguity in the instrument is therefore to be construed against the company."[21]

The rule has been applied in the non-marine insurance area partly due to the prevalence of standard policy forms. Thus, in *Wigle v. Allstate Insurance Co. of Canada*, where it was stated that "[t]here can be no doubt that the Court must treat insurers with the same fairness and impartiality that all litigants should receive",[22] Justice Cory, then on the Ontario Court of Appeal, stated:

---

words should make sense to those most likely to read and rely on them: *Burrard Towing Co. v. Reed Stenhouse Ltd.* (1996), 19 B.C.L.R. (3d) 391, 35 C.C.L.I. (2d) 145 (C.A.), rev'g. (1994), 100 B.C.L.R. (2d) 92, 29 C.C.L.I. (2d) 29 (S.C.) — whether a barge chartered by demise to the insured was included within the words "the property of the assured". The conduct of the insured, which must have been known to the underwriters, was consistent with the belief that they thought they were covered. See also *Provincial Insurance Co. of Canada v. Connolly* (1879), 5 S.C.R. 258.

[19]   *Re Arbitration between Terra Nova Mutual Marine Insurance Co. Ltd. and Blackwood*, [1952] I.L.R. ¶1-074 (Nfld. S.C.) at 304:

> It is hardly necessary to cite cases to show that the words of a marine policy or like document are, in the absence of special circumstances, to be construed *contra proferentem*, in other words, against the insurer and in favour of the insured. Perhaps *pro forma* we may cite *Metal Stampings Ltd. v. Standard Life Assce Co.*, [1952] I.L.R. 1-038, [1952] 1 D.L.R. 105, but the books list long strings of cases in support of that doctrine. Ambiguous words are to be construed against the insurer who dictates the terms of insurance.

A branch of this rule is that where a clause is capable of two different constructions, one broad and the other narrow, the broader one should be preferred. See *Chartered Bank of India v. Pacific Marine Insurance Co.* (1924), 33 B.C.R. 91 (C.A.).

[20]   (1866), 12 Gr. Ch. R. 418.

[21]   (1866), 12 Gr. Ch. R. 418 at 424. See also *Mowat v. Boston Marine Insurance Co.* (1896), 26 S.C.R. 47, rev'g. (1895), 33 N.B.R. 109 (C.A.): Chief Justice Strong stated at S.C.R. 54: "Further, on well established principles, the whole contract of insurance to be gathered from the policy, certificate, and memorandum must, so far as there is any ambiguity, be construed as against the underwriters in whose language it is expressed...for all these three instruments emanated from them."

[22]   (1984), 49 O.R. (2d) 101 at 115, 14 D.L.R. (4th) 404 (C.A.), aff'g. 44 O.R. (2d) 677, 5 D.L.R. (4th) 327 (H.C.J.), leave to appeal refused [1985] 1 S.C.R. v. To a similar effect, see *White v. Dominion of Canada General Insurance Co.* (1985), 11 C.C.L.I. 121 (Ont. H.C.J.) at 132-33:

It is difficult to conceive of an individual bargaining with a general insurer, either as to the terms of a standard policy of automobile insurance or with regard to the standard form of an endorsement added to the policy. Can it really be said that the average individual is capable of understanding the provisions of such a contract himself or is likely to engage his solicitor to review the terms, advise him of the dangers and complexities of the contract, what is included and what excluded from the coverage, and to then submit an amended contract to the insurer? The very concept of a standard form of insurance policy argues against this vision of equality of bargaining. The individual can do no more than accept or reject the policy. A standard form contract may have benefits for the insured by reducing the amount of his premium and for the insurer by setting out the contractual terms without the necessity of bargaining with each individual applicant.

Given these characteristics of the standard form contract, I think that it is reasonable and equitable to conclude that if the standard form is ambiguous, any ambiguity should be construed against the insurer. Surely it is the insurer who has more control of the writing of the contract. It is the insurers who will make submissions to the Superintendent of Insurance and who will accept the final standard form or determine that they will not offer that standard form of endorsement to their clientele. It would not be reasonable for the insurer to say that it did not draw up the contract, that it was really the Superintendent of Insurance who is responsible for its wording. That, I think would be an unrealistic and unwarranted approach to the situation. Without knowing what is included and what is excluded from the coverage when the terms are ambiguous, the ordinary member of the public cannot make an informed decision as to whether he should accept or reject the standard form presented to him.[23]

In *Consolidated Bathurst Export Ltd. v. Mutual Boiler and Machinery Insurance Co.*,[24] the Supreme Court of Canada interpreted a policy of insurance covering a paper plant in Quebec. Justice Estey, who gave the judgment of the majority of the Court, stated:

Insurance contracts and the interpretative difficulties arising therein have been before courts for at least two centuries, and it is trite to say that where an ambiguity is found to exist in the terminology employed in the contract such terminology shall be construed against the insurance carrier as being the author, or at least the party in control of the contents of the contract. This is, of course, not entirely true

---

...in principle, the identity of the draftsman is immaterial...the harm is done when the policy is marketed. An insurer knows, or has ready means of knowing, that a policy form is uncertain or ambiguous...If the insurer elects to market insurance in a form which he knows or has the means of knowing is unclear or ambiguous, he cannot wait until a claim arises and then elect the interpretation most favourable to him in the circumstances of the case...[T]he insured has no way of negotiating or amending the coverage, even if he is aware of the problem. His choice is merely to take it or leave it.

[23] (1984), 49 O.R. (2d) 101 at 116.
[24] [1980] 1 S.C.R. 888, 112 D.L.R. (3d) 49.

because of statutory modifications to the contract, but we are not here concerned with any such mandated provisions.[25]

Justice Estey referred to the words of Justice Meredith in *Pense v. Northern Life Assurance Co.*, that "effect must be given to the intention of the parties, to be gathered from the words they have used".[26] He described this as "step one in the interpretative process".[27] He went on to say that "Step two is the application, when ambiguity is found, of the *contra proferentem* doctrine."[28] He continued:

> Even apart from the doctrine of *contra proferentem* as it may be applied in the construction of contracts, the normal rules of construction lead a court to search for an interpretation which, from the whole of the contract, would appear to promote or advance the true intent of the parties at the time of entry into the contract. Consequently, literal meaning should not be applied where to do so would bring about an unrealistic result or a result which would not be contemplated in the commercial atmosphere in which the insurance was contracted. Where words may bear two constructions, the more reasonable one, that which produces a fair result, must certainly be taken as the interpretation which would promote the intention of the parties. Similarly, an interpretation which defeats the intention of the parties and their objective in entering into the commercial transaction in the first place should be discarded in favour of an interpretation of the policy which promotes a sensible commercial result. It is trite to observe that an interpretation of an ambiguous contractual provision which would render the endeavour on the part of the insured to obtain insurance protection nugatory should be avoided. Said another way, the courts should be loath to support a construction which would either enable the insurer to pocket the premium without risk or the insured to achieve a recovery which could neither be sensibly sought nor anticipated at the time of the contract.[29]

It has been repeatedly stated that the *contra proferentem* rule is one of "last resort" and that it may not be invoked unless there is a real doubt as to the meaning of the particular clause.[30] In the *Consolidated Bathurst* case, the Supreme Court of Canada referred to the judgment of Justice Cartwright in *Stevenson v. Reliance Petroleum*, in which it was stated that "The rule expressed in the maxim [*contra proferentem*] was pressed upon us in argument, but resort is to be had to this rule only when all other rules of construction fail to enable the court of construction to ascertain the meaning of a document."[31] Unfortunately, all

---

[25] *Ibid.*, at 899.
[26] *Ibid.*, citing (1907) 15 O.L.R. 131.
[27] *Ibid.*, at 900.
[28] *Ibid.*
[29] *Ibid.*, at 901-902.
[30] See, for example, *Cornish v. Accident Insurance Co.* (1889), 23 Q.B.D. 453 (C.A.).
[31] [1980] 1 S.C.R. 888 at 901, citing [1956] S.C.R. 936, 5 D.L.R. (2d) 673, aff'g. [1954] O.R. 846, 4 D.L.R. 730 (C.A.), aff'g. [1953] O.R. 807, 4 D.L.R. 755 (H.C.J.). See also *Derksen v. Guardian Insurance Co. of Canada* [1976] I.L.R. ¶1-773 at 225 (Alta Dist. Ct.), referring to *Kruger v. Mutual Benefit*, [1944] O.R. 157 at 161:
> The contract of insurance should be given a reasonable interpretation. The Court should endeavour to see that the insured obtains all the benefits fairly and reasonably

too often the courts appear to treat the rule as one of first resort and apply it without really attempting to determine whether the contract can be given a reasonable and plain interpretation.[32]

The *contra proferentem* rule has been expressed by the Supreme Court of Canada in a number of cases, including *Consolidated Bathurst Export Ltd. v. Mutual Boiler and Machinery Insurance Co.,*[33] *Simcoe & Erie General Insurance Co. v. Reid Crowther Partners Ltd.,*[34] *Frenette v. Metropolitan Life Insurance Co.*[35] and *Brissette Estate v. Westbury Life Insurance Co.*[36] These cases confirm that the goal of interpretation is to find the intention of the parties as expressed in their words, to avoid, if possible, unreasonable, unrealistic or unfair results, and that, if ambiguity is found in the policy, it should be interpreted against the insurer.

In *1013799 Ontario Ltd. v. Kent Line International Ltd.,*[37] the court declined to apply the *contra proferentem* rule to resolve an ambiguity in the policy where

---

>   in contemplation of the parties at the time the policy was issued. In a case of doubt or uncertainty, the Court should not readily be persuaded to negative or minimize the obligation of the insurer. But the application of the principle mentioned requires that there should be an obscurity, uncertainty or ambiguity in the policy. The doubt or difficulty in construction must not be fanciful, it must be real.
>
>   See *J.P. Porter & Son Ltd. v. Western Assurance Co.,* [1938] 1 D.L.R. 619, 12 M.P.R. 469 (N.S.C.A.), aff'g. [1938] 1 D.L.R. 619 (N.S.S.C.), where it was held that the words "in tow of two approved tugs" were ambiguous and should be construed against the insurer so as to permit separate towing (*i.e.,* not that two tugs would tow the ships but that each could be towed by a separate tug).

[32]   See: *Strangemore's Electrical Ltd. v. Insurance Corp. of Newfoundland Ltd.* (1997), 151 Nfld. & P.E.I.R. 317, 43 C.C.L.I. (2d) 322 (Nfld. S.C.); *Federal Business Development Bank v. Commonwealth Insurance Co.* (1983), 2 C.C.L.I. 200 (B.C.S.C.) where the doctrine was applied in favour of the insured; *Burrard Towing Co. v. Reed Stenhouse Ltd.* (1996), 19 B.C.L.R. (3d) 391, 35 C.C.L.I. (2d) 145 (C.A.), rev'g. (1994), 100 B.C.L.R. (2d) 92, 29 C.C.L.I. (2d) 29 (S.C.).

[33]   [1980] 1 S.C.R. 888, 112 D.L.R. (3d) 49.

[34]   [1993] 1 S.C.R. 252, 99 D.L.R. (4th) 741, aff'g. (1991), 77 D.L.R. (4th) 243, 70 Man. R. (2d) 36, supp. reasons (1991), 73 Man. R. (2d) 128 (C.A.), rev'g. (1990), 66 Man. R. (2d) 142 (Q.B.).

[35]   [1992] 1 S.C.R. 647, 89 D.L.R. (4th) 653; see also *Ocean Fisheries Ltd. v. Pacific Coast Fishermen's Mutual Marine Insurance Co.,* [1998] 1 F.C. 586, 220 N.R. 68 (C.A.), aff'g. (1997), 125 F.T.R. 20 which refers to the *Frenette, Brissette Estate* and *Consolidated Bathurst* cases.

[36]   [1992] 3 S.C.R. 87 at 92-93. In *Simcoe & Erie General Insurance Co. v. Reid Crowther Partners Ltd.,* [1993] 1 S.C.R. 252, 99 D.L.R. (4th) 741, aff'g. (1991), 77 D.L.R. (4th) 243, 70 Man. R. (2d) 36, supp. reasons (1991), 73 Man. R. (2d) 128 (C.A.), rev'g. (1990), 66 Man. R. (2d) 142 (Q.B.), the Supreme Court of Canada referred to (1) the *contra proferentem* principle; (2) the principle that coverage provisions should be given a broad construction and exclusions should be given a narrow construction; and (3) the desirability, at least where the policy is ambiguous, of giving effect to the reasonable expectations of the parties. See also *Panzera v. Simcoe & Erie Insurance Co.,* [1990] 2 S.C.R. 1029, 74 D.L.R. (4th) 197, rev'g. [1988] 20 Q.A.C. 226 (Que. C.A.), rev'g. [1985] C.S. 1263 (Que. S.C.) at S.C.R. 1043:

>   Additionally, I am of the view that to adopt the interpretation of the Court of Appeal would be to ignore the well-recognized principle that it is necessary to interpret insurance contracts as they would be understood by the average person applying for insurance and not as they might be perceived by persons versed in the niceties of insurance law.

[37]   (2000), 21 C.C.L.I. (3d) 312, [2000] O.T.C. 635 (Ont. Sup. Ct.).

it found that the insured had not read the policy and had not been misled by the ambiguous language.

In Canada, policies are frequently prepared by the broker and not by the underwriter. This is particularly so in the case of comprehensive "Open Cover" marine cargo policies and complex hull and machinery policies covering larger fleets. The policy itself is likely to be a "broker's manuscript" wording, tailor-made by the broker to reflect its particular preferences and the needs of its client. Sometimes there will be negotiations between the broker and the underwriter with respect to particular clauses, but in other cases, particularly involving a substantial broker with a major piece of business to market, the policy may be presented as part of the package. In such cases, the language used in the policy is as much the language of the insured, through the broker, as it is the insurers. While it is reasonable to say that the insurer is bound by the language to which it subscribes, is it reasonable to interpret the policy against the insurer in such cases? One could still make the case that in the event of true ambiguity, that is, two equally *reasonable* meanings of a given clause, there is no reason to adopt the most restrictive meaning. The touchstone, however, should be "reasonableness".

3.3.3 Reasonable Expectations

The Supreme Court of Canada has said that effect should be given to the "reasonable expectations of the parties" in the construction of insurance contracts. In *Reid Crowther & Partners Ltd. v. Simcoe & Erie General Insurance Co.*,[38] the court referred to three principles for the interpretation of insurance policies: (1) the *contra proferentem* rule, (2) the broad construction of coverage provisions and the narrow construction of exclusion clauses and (3) the desirability, at least where the policy is ambiguous, of giving effect to the reasonable expectations of the parties.[39]

> I turn to the third relevant principle of construction, the reasonable expectation of the parties. Without pronouncing on the reach of this doctrine, it is settled that where the policy is ambiguous, the courts should consider the reasonable expecta-tions of the parties: *Wigle v. Allstate Insurance Co. of Canada*...The insured's rea-sonable expectation is, at a minimum, that the insurance plan will provide coverage for legitimate claims on an ongoing basis. The presumption must be that the intention of the parties is to provide and obtain coverage for all legitimate claims on an ongoing basis, whether through renewal with the same insurer or through securing new insurance with a different insurer. This presumption is con-sistent with the discovery principle discussed earlier in these reasons, in that the insurer is able to secure a means of certainty in calculating the risk without un-

---

[38] [1993] 1 S.C.R. 252.

[39] *Ibid.*, at 253.

fairly creating gaps in coverage. Yet the construction of the policy which the insurer urges upon us may well not achieve that goal.[40]

The obvious difficulty with the "reasonable expectations" test is that it requires the court to go beyond the expressed intent of the parties to presume an "expectation" which the parties had in their minds but did not express in their written contract. While courts occasionally "imply" terms into contracts[41] to make them commercially effective, the reasonable expectations test goes considerably farther than this and has the potential of rewriting a contract which expresses the expectations of the court and not of the parties.

3.4 OTHER AIDS TO CONSTRUCTION

There are a number of secondary rules the courts use to interpret insurance contracts.

3.4.1 Reasonable Result

The courts interpret contracts, whenever possible, to produce a reasonable result. In *British America Assurance Co. v. William Law & Co.*, Justice Strong stated:

> The well established rule of construction applicable to all deeds and instruments, and especially to policies of marine insurance which are mercantile deeds not prepared by lawyers, is that they should be so interpreted, if possible, as to be valid and effectual and not in such a way as to be void.[42]

The contract should be interpreted, if possible, to avoid inconsistencies[43] and to find harmony between its various parts.[44] It has been said that terms in the contract should be interpreted to give a reasonable and not an absurd result.[45]

---

[40] [1993] 1 S.C.R. 252 at 269, referring to C. Brown and J. Menezes, *Insurance Law of Canada*, 2nd ed. (Scarborough: Carswell, 1991) at pp. 123-24, and *Brissette Estate v. Westbury Life Insurance Co.*, [1992] 3 S.C.R. 87, 96 D.L.R. (4th) 609, aff'g. (1990), 74 O.R. (2d) 1, 72 D.L.R. (4th) 138 (C.A.), rev'g. (1989), 69 O.R. (2d) 215, 60 D.L.R. (4th) 78 (H.C.J.). For a discussion of the "reasonable expectations" doctrine in the United States, and a comparison with the "Canadian Approach", see the dissenting judgment of Justice Cory in the Supreme Court of Canada in *Brissette Estate v. Westbury Life Insurance Co.*, [1992] 3 S.C.R. 87, 96 D.L.R. (4th) 609, aff'g. (1990), 74 O.R. (2d) 1, 72 D.L.R. (4th) 138 (C.A.), rev'g. (1989), 69 O.R. (2d) 215, 60 D.L.R. (4th) 78 (H.C.J.). See also J. W. Stempel, "Reading between the Lines: Insurance Contract Interpretation" (September 1995) Trial, 31n.q., at p. 74 for a discussion of the "reasonable expectations" doctrine in the United States. The author notes that the acceptance of the doctrine is not by any means universal.

[41] See "The Implication of Terms", Section 3.5.1 below.

[42] (1892), 21 S.C.R. 325 at 327-28, aff'g. (1892), 23 N.S.R. 537 (C.A.).

[43] *Mowat v. Boston Marine Insurance Co.* (1896), 26 S.C.R. 47, rev'g. (1895), 33 N.B.R. 109 (C.A.).

[44] *Catherwood Towing Ltd. v. Commercial Union Insurance Co.* (1996), 26 B.C.L.R. (3d) 57, 35 C.C.L.I. (2d) 124 (C.A.), aff'g. (1995), 30 C.C.L.I. (2d) 135 (B.C.S.C.).

[45] See, for example, *London Assurance Corp. v. Great Northern Transit Co.* (1899), 29 S.C.R. 577.

3.4.2 Specially Written Clauses Should Be Given More Weight than a Pre-printed Form

It is presumed that, in the case of ambiguity, the clauses which the parties have taken the trouble to write out reflect their true intention more than the printed form itself.[46] In *Morrison Mill Co. v. Queen Insurance Co. of America*,[47] the British Columbia Court of Appeal stated:

> It was strongly contended, and I think rightly, that the written matter in the printed forms used should be given the controlling weight when there is any doubt or ambiguity, and it is clear that applying that as a rule, the insurance of the raft was insurance as a separate entity, such as a ship or boat in tow.[48]

3.4.3 Deletions Should Not Be Regarded in the Interpretation of the Remainder of the Document

It is common for clauses in pre-printed forms to be crossed out. The proper rule of construction is to ignore these clauses as if they were never part of the printed form.[49]

3.4.4 Respect Should Be Accorded Settled Meanings

It can be assumed that the parties are aware of previous judicial interpretations of the terms they have used and that they would expect the court to apply those interpretations in the construction of their contract. For this reason, the courts should apply the settled interpretation of a particular clause.[50]

3.4.5 Exceptions To Be Construed Against the Insurer

In *Reid Crowther & Partners Ltd. v. Simcoe & Erie General Insurance Co.*, the Supreme Court of Canada confirmed that exceptions from coverage should be construed strictly and against the insurer.[51]

---

[46] *Meagher v. Home Insurance Co.* (1861), 11 U.C.C.P. 328 (C.A.); *Meagher v. Aetna Insurance Co.* (1861), 20 U.C.Q.B. 607, to the effect that a clause written over the face of a policy will prevail over printed provisions of the policy which are inconsistent with it.

[47] [1925] 1 D.L.R. 1159, 1 W.W.R. 691 (B.C.C.A.).

[48] *Ibid.* at 1165.

[49] See *Wakeham & Sons Ltd. v. St. Lawrence Cement Inc.* (1995), 26 O.R. (3d) 321, 86 O.A.C. 182 (C.A.), rev'g. (1992), 8 O.R. (3d) 340, 9 C.C.L.I. (2d) 211, leave to appeal refused [1995] S.C.C.A. No. 553.

[50] See *Catherwood Towing Ltd. v. Commercial Union Insurance Co.* (1996), 26 B.C.L.R. (3d) 57, 35 C.C.L.I. (2d) 124 (C.A.), aff'g. (1995), 30 C.C.L.I. (2d) 135 (B.C.S.C.) *per* Goldie J.A. at 61, citing *Shell International Petroleum Co. Ltd. v. Gibbs (The "Salem")*, [1983] 1 All E.R. 745 (H.L.) to the effect that "Settled meaning, given to [the standard policy's] description of the perils insured against is not to be interfered with lightly, if at all."

[51] [1993] 1 S.C.R. 252. See also *Trenton Cold Storage Ltd. v. St. Paul Fire & Marine Insurance Co.* (1999), 11 C.C.L.I. (3d) 127 (Ont. S.C.J.), rev'd. (2001), 199 D.L.R. (4th) 654, 146 O.A.C.

3.5   WHERE THE INTENTION IS NOT EVIDENT FROM THE DOCUMENT

3.5.1   The Implication of Terms

A court may "imply" a term in a contract — a term not found in the express words of the contract is "read into the contract" as if it were part of the contract. An implied term may not displace an express term. Where the parties have dealt expressly with a subject it is not appropriate to imply a term that is inconsistent with their express terms.

The court will imply a term of the contract where it is necessary to give business efficacy or sense to the contract.[52] Sometimes this is expressed by asking the question: "If the parties had been asked, at the time they made their contract, whether the term to be implied was a part of their agreement, would they have answered emphatically 'Of course!'?" If the answer is "yes", the court may imply a term into the contract if it is necessary to do so in order to make the contract commercially effective.

As provided in section 90 of the *C.M.I.A.*, quoted at the outset of this chapter, terms may be implied in an insurance contract by custom or practice, provided that the custom is not contrary to the express terms of the contract.[53] In *Hennessy v. New York Mutual Marine Insurance Co.*,[54] the Nova Scotia Court of Appeal stated that a policy can be interpreted in accordance with a clear and notorious usage in a particular trade because the parties must have been intended to contract with reference to that usage. The fact that one of the parties may have been ignorant of the usage will not negate its application, provided that it is shown that insureds and insurers are generally familiar with it. The usage must be proved by evidence of actual instances, rather than by the opinion of witnesses as to its existence and it must be proven to be so clear, certain and accepted that it can be said that the parties contracted with reference to it.

3.5.2 Parol Evidence Rule

Where the parties have recorded their agreement in an unambiguous written contract, extrinsic evidence is not permissible to establish that their "true intention" was something different from the plain meaning of their words. The contract itself is regarded as the expression of their intention and neither party is allowed to give evidence as to what was really intended. This is known as the "parol evidence rule". There are exceptions to this rule, one being that in the case of ambiguity it may be permissible to introduce evidence of intention, such as evidence of the parties' negotiations or conduct; but the evidence must not be

---

348 (C.A.): exclusion clauses should be construed narrowly and must use language that clearly expresses the intent and scope. In the Court of Appeal, it was concluded that the policy was one of excess insurance and there was no double insurance.

[52]   *The Moorcock* (1889), L.R. 14 P.D. 64.

[53]   Section 90 of the *C.M.I.A.* contemplates that any term implied by law may be varied by the express terms of the contract or by usage of the trade.

[54]   (1863), 5 N.S.R. 259 (C.A.).

used for the purpose of *creating* an ambiguity which does not exist on the face of the document.

In *Shearwater Marine Ltd. v. Guardian Insurance Co. of Canada*,[55] a policy on a vessel contained a warranty: "Warranted...Vessel inspected daily basis and pumped as necessary." The defendant insurer wanted to introduce the evidence of an underwriting agent to explain the reasons for including the warranty and his "expectations" regarding the daily inspections. The Court refused to permit this evidence, referring to the expression of the parole evidence rule by the House of Lords in *Shore v. Wilson*:[56]

> ...where the words of any written instrument are free from ambiguity in them-selves...such instrument is always to be construed according to the strict, plain, common meaning of the words themselves; and...in such case evidence [outside] the instrument, for the purpose of explaining it according to the...alleged intention of the parties...is utterly inadmissible.

The judge continued:

> While modern authorities are replete with exceptions (or refinements) to that general rule, my conclusion is that the interpretation of [the warranty] requires no out-side or parole evidence.[57]

He held that the warranty did not require that someone actually go on board the vessel to inspect it and that daily observation was sufficient. He also held that the warranty should be construed *contra proferentem*.[58]

3.6 RECTIFICATION OF THE POLICY

The court has the power to "rectify" a contract which does not incorporate the true intention of the parties,[59] but will generally not do so when the contract has

---

[55] *Shearwater Marine Ltd. v. Guardian Insurance Co. of Canada* (1998), 60 B.C.L.R. (3d) 37 (C.A.), aff'g. (1997), 29 B.C.L.R. (3d) 13 (S.C.).

[56] (1842), 8 E.R. 450 (H.L.), referred to in *London Drugs Ltd. v. Truscan Realty* (1989), 3 R.P.R. (2d) 60 at 68 (B.C.S.C.).

[57] *Shearwater Marine Ltd. v. Guardian Insurance Co. of Canada* (1997), 29 B.C.L.R. (3d) 13 at 18 (B.C.S.C.).

[58] The subject of warranties, and their interpretation, is discussed in Chapter 8. Due to the drastic consequences of a breach of warranty — the discharge of the insurer from further responsibility under the policy — the courts interpret warranties strictly and, in case of ambiguity, against the insurer. See, for example: *Federal Business Development Bank v. Commonwealth Insurance Co.* (1983), 2 C.C.L.I. 200 (S.C.) at C.C.L.I. 204: "If there be any doubt as to what the parties intended when they included the warranty in the form set out in the second endorsement, the court should invoke the *contra proferentem* rule and interpret the words against the insurer."; *Staples v. Great American Insurance Co.*, [1941] S.C.R. 213, [1941] 2 D.L.R. 1; *Provincial Insurance Co. v. Morgan*, [1933] A.C. 240 at 254: a warranty or condition, "though it must be strictly complied with, must be strictly though reasonably construed"; *Tulloch v. Canada (Department of Fisheries & Oceans)* (1988), 21 F.T.R. 72, 32 C.C.L.I. 36 (T.D.), aff'd. (1988), 96 N.R. 51, 37 C.C.L.I. 229 (F.C.A.).

[59] See *Wylde v. Union Marine Insurance Co.* (1875), 10 N.S.R. 205 (C.A.); *Cusack v. Mutual Insurance Co.* (1862), 6 L.C. Jur. 97.

been acted on by one of the parties.[60] In *Toron Construction Ltd. v. Continental Insurance Co.*, it was stated:

> There is a presumption that the policy contains the real terms between the parties and unless it is clearly proved that the policy is incorrect rectification will be refused and the parties remain bound by the policy as issued.[61]

3.7 A SUGGESTED GUIDE TO CONSTRUCTION

Marine insurance is an international business which uses policy forms which have been developed by the maritime community, insurers, brokers, shipowners and cargo interests, for the facilitation of maritime commerce. There has been a simplification and modernization of many of the standard insuring clauses, such as the Institute Cargo clauses 1/1/82 (A), (B) and (C)[62] and the Institute time and voyage clauses for hulls issued in 1983 and 1995. Insurers of yachts and pleasure craft have developed "plain language" policies. Many of the clauses have been interpreted by the courts or have been given a meaning through application and practice. It has been noted elsewhere in this book that marine insurance is vital to international maritime commerce, be it the international sale of goods or the insurance of ships and their liabilities. It is impossible to properly interpret a commercial policy of marine insurance without appreciating the setting in which the document was prepared and the legal and business purposes it was intended to serve. The policy will only make sense if it is understood as a maritime contract and as a commercial contract. Many of its terms — "constructive total loss", "general average", "free of particular average", "sue and labour" and so on — are terms of art which can only be understood with a full appreciation of how they fit into the scheme of maritime law and marine insurance law. Marine insurance policies have been crafted over the centuries – particularly many of the standard form policies — by brokers on the one hand and underwriters on the other hand, with a view to including certain losses and excluding others. While the intention of the parties must be found in the words that they have used, and imprecise expressions of that intention should not be to the detriment of the insured, these policies were not developed overnight nor were they crafted with one transaction in mind. The interpretive process should include a genuine appreciation of the setting in which the policy evolved and with a desire to find meaning and consistency, rather than ambiguity, in the contract. If there is true ambiguity, no one could

---

[60] *Robertson v. Lovett* (1874), 9 N.S.R. 424.

[61] (1982), 34 Alta. R. 456 (Q.B.). See *Marine Underwriter, Lloyd's London v. Protection Mutual Insurance Co.* (1991), 58 B.C.L.R. (2d) 290, 4 C.C.L.I. (2d) 219 (C.A.), aff'g. (1989), 40 C.C.L.I. 303 (S.C.), where rectification was ordered because the court was satisfied that the insurance policy did not fully express the terms agreed upon; *Wylde v. Union Marine Insurance Co.* (1875) R.E.D. 203 (N.S.S.C.), aff'd. (1875), 10 N.S.R. 205 (C.A.), where rectification was ordered because the policy did not contain terms stated in the application.

[62] See Appendices B, C and D.

argue with the application of the *contra proferentem* principle but it is in danger of becoming a rule of construction, rather than a rule of last resort.

The starting point to interpretation should be the identification of the contract in all its component parts, in order to examine the documents that are contractual and to exclude those that are not. In the case of cargo insurance, this may consist of the open policy, the certificate and the insuring clauses, such as the Institute Cargo Clauses (A), 1/1/82. There may be endorsements to be taken into account. A similar approach will have to be taken in the case of hull and machinery and P. & I. insurance. Once the contract is identified, it should be read carefully, to understand its overall scope and purpose and how its pieces or sections fit together. A focus on one or two clauses in isolation may lead to an inconsistent or unduly narrow construction of the policy or a failure to appreciate its full scope and intent.

Once the policy has been read, the question is whether, on its face, the loss is covered by the policy. Does the loss fall within the insuring terms of the contract? This approach was noted by the British Columbia Court of Appeal in the case of *Burrard Towing Co. v. Reed Stenhouse Ltd.*[63] The plaintiff, a towing company, was hired by a client to transport cargo. The plaintiff in turn hired a barge in order to fulfill its contract with its customer. While being towed with the customer's cargo on board, the barge capsized and the cargo was lost. The customer made a claim against the towing company which sued its insurers claiming that they were required to indemnify it against the customer's claim. The trial judge held that the policy provided coverage. The British Columbia Court of Appeal reversed and held that there was no coverage. Justice Southin, giving the decision of the majority, stated:

> In approaching any question of this kind, one must start with the principle expressed by Lord Sumner in *Becker v. London Assurance Corp.*, [1918] A.C. 101 (H.L.) adopted by this Court in *Collier v. Insurance Corp. of British Columbia*, (1995), 100 B.C.L.R. (2d) 201 at 223 (C.A.):
>
> > One need only ask, has the event, on which I put my premium, actually occurred? This is a matter of the meaning of the contract and not, as seems sometimes to be supposed, of doing the liberal and reasonable thing by a reasonable assured...
>
> He was there speaking of the causa proxima rule but the principle is the same whether one is discussing the causa proxima rule or any other aspect of marine insurance law. (For an interesting application of this rule, although it is not mentioned by name, as well as the importance of maintaining the orthodox meaning of words used in contracts of marine insurance, see *Shell International Petroleum v. Gibbs*, [1983] 1 All E.R. 745 (H.L.)

---

[63] (1996), 19 B.C.L.R. (3d) 391, 35 C.C.L.I. (2d) 145 (C.A.), rev'g. (1994), 100 B.C.L.R. (2d) 92, 29 C.C.L.I. (2d) 29 (S.C.).

So, in this case, the question is: Did these insurers undertake the risk of indemnifying this insured for legal liability to the owner of a cargo for loss or damage to that cargo carried upon a dumb barge which this insured supplied for the purpose.[64]

For the purpose of this exercise, the exclusions from coverage should generally be ignored, since they can only apply to losses which are otherwise covered. If the insuring terms do not, on their face, cover the loss, then that should usually be the end of the exercise. If the insuring terms appear to cover the loss, then reference must be made to any exclusions which might take the loss outside the policy. The exclusions must be read carefully, to determine whether they apply to all parts of the policy or only to some of the coverages.

Overall, the object of the exercise should be to give a sensible commercial meaning to the contract of marine insurance. This involves a recognition that, in many cases, the terms embodied in (or excluded from) the contract are a reflection of the price the insured is willing to pay and the risks the underwriter is prepared to accept.

If there is ambiguity in the policy, then recourse may be had to various aids to interpretation, including, in particular, the *contra proferentem* rule.

In view of the fact that the *C.M.I.A.* is based on the *M.I.A. 1906* and that the same or similar insuring forms are in use in the two countries, as well as our common heritage in marine insurance law, it makes sense that Canadian courts should follow English precedent unless there is some compelling reason not to do so. The international nature of marine insurance makes it highly desirable that the interpretation of similar statutory provisions, and similar clauses in marine policies, should follow the same course.[65]

---

[64] (1996), 19 B.C.L.R. (3d) 391 at 397.

[65] See *H.B. Nickerson & Sons Ltd. v. Insurance Co. of North America*, [1984] 1 F.C. 575, 49 N.R. 321 (C.A.), leave to appeal refused (1984), 54 N.R. 80n, where the trial judge had stated at [1984] 1 F.C. 575 at 584:

> The parties have agreed that the insurance policy…is to be construed in accordance with the laws of England relating to marine insurance generally and hull and machinery insurance in particular. The onus is on the plaintiff to establish…that the [vessel] sank because of a peril insured against. Only after that, must the defendant show that she sank for a cause not covered.

Chapter 4

Good Faith: Misrepresentation and Non-Disclosure[1]

4.1 INTRODUCTION

The principle of the "utmost good faith" is a cornerstone of marine insurance and is enshrined in section 20 of the Canadian *Marine Insurance Act* (*"C.M.I.A"*):[2]

> 20. A contract [of marine insurance] is based on the utmost good faith and, if the utmost good faith is not observed by either party, the contract may be avoided by the other party.

The principle finds its most famous expression in the leading case of *Carter v. Boehm*,[3] which involved a policy of insurance taken out by the governor of Fort Malborough, on the island of Sumatra, against the taking of the fort by foreign enemy. The fort was taken by the French within the year. In a suit on the policy it was contended by the underwriter that the insurance could be avoided because there had been concealment of the weakness of the fort's defences and of the probability of it being taken by the French. In rejecting this contention, Lord Mansfield made his famous remarks on good faith:

> Insurance is a contract of speculation. The special facts, upon which the contingent chance is to be computed, lie most commonly in the knowledge of the *insured* only; the underwriter trusts to his representation and proceeds upon confidence that he does not keep back any circumstance in his knowledge to mislead the underwriter into a belief that the circumstance does not exist, and to induce him to estimate the risque, as if it did not exist.

> The keeping back such circumstance is a *fraud*, and therefore the policy is *void*. Although the suppression should happen through *mistake*, without any fraudulent intention, yet still the underwriter is *deceived*, and the policy is *void*; because the

---

[1] This chapter, since revised, was initially prepared as a paper entitled "Good Faith in the Canadian Law of Marine Insurance", presented at a seminar of the Canadian Maritime Law Association and the Federal Court of Canada.

[2] S.C. 1993, c. 22

[3] (1706), 3 Burr. 1905.

risque really run is really different from the risque understood and intended to be run at the time of the agreement.

The policy would equally be void, against the *underwriter*, *if* he concealed; as, if he insured a ship on her voyage which he privately knew to be arrived: and an action would lie to recover the premium...

Good faith forbids either party by concealing what he privately knows to draw the other into a bargain, from his ignorance of that fact, and his believing the contrary.[4]

While *Carter v. Boehm* was a non-marine case, it is apparent why the principle of utmost good faith had particular significance in marine insurance. In most cases, the interest to be insured, a vessel or a cargo, was located far away, perhaps on the other side of the world. The voyage might be in progress when the insurance was placed. The underwriter usually had no means to inspect, assess or verify the risk. Communication was rudimentary, slow and unreliable. The underwriter was at the mercy of the insured for information concerning the risk and accordingly there was a real opportunity for fraud. The law stepped in to provide balance to the "informational disadvantage" between underwriter and insured. The good faith rule required full disclosure to ensure that the underwriter was in a position to fairly assess the risk and to set appropriate premium and policy conditions. Harsh consequences — complete avoidance of the contract — served as a deterrent to concealment and misrepresentation.

From the middle of the nineteenth century, Canadian courts followed the English lead by demanding the utmost good faith in marine insurance contracts. In one of the first reported Canadian marine insurance cases, *McFaul v. Montreal Inland Insurance Co.*,[5] a decision of the Appeal Division of the Court of Queen's Bench in Upper Canada in 1845, the plaintiff had insured a shipment of wheat on board the schooner "Wellington", on a voyage from Presqu'Isle on Lake Ontario to Gananoque. The plaintiff failed to inform the underwriter that the vessel had been forced into Presqu'Isle by a storm and that other vessels, which had sailed from Presqu'Isle after it, had reached Gananoque in safety, but that there was no word of the "Wellington", which had last been seen in a heavy squall. On the date that the insurance was placed, the same date that the other vessels had arrived safely, the "Wellington" was overdue. The Appeal Division held that the plaintiff had not established that he had filed the proper notice, on oath. The court further held that it would have dismissed the claim on the basis of non-disclosure. Chief Justice Robinson stated:

If we had not found it necessary to direct a nonsuit on this ground, we would not have refused a new trial, on the evidence, for nothing can be clearer than that the law exacts the utmost good faith in these transactions, and there is strong evidence that the plaintiff did not obtain his insurance fairly, but that on the contrary, he

---

[4]   *Ibid.*, at 1909.
[5]   (1845), 2 U.C.Q.B. 59 (App. Div.).

concealed important facts that were known to himself, and which would most probably have led the defendants to decline the risk or at least to exact a different rate of premium...In such transactions, almost more than in any others, the utmost good faith should prevail. Any suppression of a fact, on which it may be important to the insurer that he should be allowed to exercise his judgment, either as to taking or refusing the risk, or in fixing the rate of premium, invalidates the policy.[6]

In the *McFaul* case, the insured possessed information, or suspected facts, that the underwriter had no way of knowing. The insured attempted to use his special knowledge to obtain insurance when he had reason to believe that a loss might have occurred. There is a strong suspicion that he was attempting to deceive the underwriters. The court emphasized the fundamental fairness of ensuring that the degree of risk was equally known by both parties to the contract of insurance.

Other early cases in Canada suggest that candour and good faith were not always shown by insureds in applying for insurance and that the courts were sensitive to protect underwriters from the insured's unfair non-disclosure of pertinent information.[7] The principle of good faith remains alive in the modern world and was confirmed by the Supreme Court of Canada in an aviation insurance case, *Coronation Insurance Co. v. Taku Air Transport Ltd.*[8] In that case, Mr. Justice Cory stated:

The uberrima fides doctrine is a long-standing tenet of insurance law which holds parties to an insurance contract to a standard of utmost good faith in their dealing. It places a heavy burden on those seeking insurance coverage to make full and complete disclosure of all relevant information when applying for a policy.[9]

The good faith principle finds specific expression in two ways: by requiring *full disclosure* by the insured and by requiring *truth in representation* before the contract is concluded.

4.2 DISCLOSURE

The duty of disclosure is set out in section 21 of the *C.M.I.A.*, which provides in part:

21.(1) Subject to this section, an insured must disclose to the insurer, before the contract is concluded, every material circumstance that is known to the insured.

---

[6]   *Ibid.*, at 61.
[7]   For early examples of the avoidance of a marine insurance contract due to non-disclosure, see: *Mahoney v. Provincial Insurance Co.* (1869), 12 N.B.R. 633; *Smith v. Royal Canadian Insurance Co.* (1884), Cout. S.C. 723, Cass. S.C. 386 (S.C.C.), rev'g. (1884), 17 N.S.R. 322 (C.A.), in which the insured had placed insurance without advising the underwriter that the ship had been in a serious accident the previous day; *Eisenhauer v. Providence Washington Insurance Co.* (1887), 20 N.S.R. 48 (C.A.), in which the insured failed to inform the insurer of information to the effect that the vessel was overdue and might have encountered heavy weather.
[8]   [1991] 3 S.C.R. 622, [1992] 1 W.W.R. 217, rev'g. (1990), 72 D.L.R. (4th) 184, 48 B.C.L.R. (2d) 222 (C.A.), 37 C.C.L.I. 271 (S.C.).
[9]   *Ibid.*, at W.W.R. 228.

(2) Subject to this section, an agent who effects insurance for an insured must disclose to the insurer, before the contract is concluded,

(*a*) every material circumstance that is known to the agent, and

(*b*) every material circumstance that the insured must disclose, unless the insured learned of it too late to communicate it to the agent.

(3) A circumstance is material if it would influence the judgment of a prudent insurer in fixing the premium or determining whether to take the risk.

It is a question of fact whether any circumstance not disclosed is material or not.[10]

The consequence of non-disclosure, whether intentional or inadvertent, fraudulent or innocent, is that the underwriter is entitled to "avoid" the policy.[11] In an early Upper Canada case, *Perry v. British America Fire and Life Assurance Co.*,[12] Chief Justice Robinson, in instructing the jury, referred to it as a "well settled principle":

I told the jury also, that if either the assured or his agent knew any fact which it was plainly their duty to communicate, and they failed to do so, the concealment or omission would equally invalidate the policy, whether it arose from accident or design.[13]

4.2.1   The Meaning of "Disclose"

The ordinary meaning of "disclose" is to "inform" to "make known" or "reveal" — to communicate. In *Century Insurance Co. of Canada v. Case Existological Laboratories Ltd.*,[14] it was alleged that the insured had failed to disclose to the insurer that the "vessel", a rather unusual floating platform, would sink if certain valves were left open. After noting that in accordance with the "custom of the marine insurance business" the underwriters had requested a survey report from a specified surveyor, which had been supplied to them before they accepted the risk, Justice Ritchie adopted the reasons of Justice Lambert in the British Columbia Court of Appeal:

The assured is obliged to disclose every material circumstance. In my opinion, by describing the vessel accurately in the report of the marine surveyor, the assured discharged that obligation. In a report on a conventional vessel it is not a failure of disclosure if the report does not say that if the sea cocks are opened and enough water enters the interior of the vessel, it will sink. I think that the same is true in this case. Every material circumstance was disclosed. It was not the obligation of

---

[10]   *C.M.I.A.*, subs. 21(4).
[11]   *Ibid.*, subs. 21(7).
[12]   (1848), 4 U.C.Q.B. 330 (C.A.).
[13]   *Ibid.*, at 333.
[14]   (1980), 116 D.L.R. (3d) 199 (B.C.S.C.), rev'd. (1982), 35 B.C.L.R. 364, 144 D.L.R. (3d) 727 (C.A.), aff'd. [1983] 2 S.C.R. 47, 150 D.L.R. (3d) 9.

the assured to speculate about the various possibilities for improper operation of the vessel which would cause it to sink, including leaving the deck valves open, thereby permitting too much sea water to enter the hull.[15]

The underwriter had been supplied with sufficient accurate information to enable the risk to be fairly assessed. There was no obligation on the insured to interpret that information or to make sure that the underwriter understood its full import.

4.2.2 What Must Be Disclosed?

The *C.M.I.A.* is specific about what must be disclosed: "every material circumstance." A "circumstance" includes not merely facts but "any communication made to, or information received by, the insured".[16] In the *McFaul* case, the court held that even rumours must be disclosed:

> It is even held necessary to communicate everything the party knows as to rumours which he may have heard, even though such rumours should turn out to be unfounded, and the reason is, that the insurer may know everything which may affect his judgment in taking the risk.[17]

The *C.M.I.A.* contains its own definition of materiality. Subsection 21(3) provides that: "A circumstance is material if it would influence the judgment of a prudent insurer in fixing the premium or determining whether to take the risk."[18] At first blush, this definition is deceptively simple — one only need determine, according to the standard of the hypothetical "prudent insurer", whether the information or representation would "influence" the judgment of such an insurer in determining whether to accept the risk and in setting the premium. However, behind the simplicity of the definition lurk two questions which have been the subject of controversy in England and in Canada. These questions are:

(a) "What is the meaning of the word 'influence' in the definition of material?" Does it mean 'have a decisive effect on' or does it simply mean 'would be a serious factor to be taken into account when assessing the risk'? This has been referred to as the "decisive influence" test.

(b) "Is it necessary to show that the *actual* underwriter was induced to take the risk by the non-disclosure or misrepresentation, or is it enough to show that a "prudent" underwriter would have been?" This has been called the "actual inducement" test.

---

[15] [1983] 2 S.C.R. 47 at 56.
[16] *C.M.I.A.*, subs. 21(8).
[17] (1845), 2 U.C.Q.B. 59 (App. Div.), *per* McLean J. at 62.
[18] See also subs. 22(2): "A representation is material if it would influence the judgment of a prudent insurer in fixing the premium or determining whether to take the risk."

To rephrase the second question less elegantly, is the "imprudent" or reckless underwriter who actually incurred the risk without appropriate consideration, entitled to hide behind the better, after-the-fact judgment of the "prudent" underwriter?

These questions were addressed in the 1994 decision of the House of Lords in *Pan Atlantic Insurance Co. Ltd. v. Pine Top Insurance Co.*[19] The case involved the reinsurance of certain "long tail" American liability insurance business. While the insurance was non-marine, it was agreed that the principles were the same for both marine and non-marine insurance. When renewing the business for the 1982 year, Pan Atlantic's broker met with Pine Top's underwriter to discuss the premium. While the loss record for the years 1977 to 1979 (referred to as the "long record") was available to the underwriter for inspection, it was presented by the broker in such a way as to divert the underwriter's attention from examining it. It was accepted by the parties that the long record was so bad that a prudent underwriter would not have accepted the risk on the terms accepted by Pine Top's underwriter had he or she known of the record. The "short record", the loss record for the years 1980 and 1981, was available and was disclosed, but it contained a significant inaccuracy — the true losses for 1981 were about double the losses disclosed.

The losses under the reinsurance contract proved to be substantial and Pine Top sought to avoid the contract on the basis of material non-disclosure. All three levels of court, the trial judge, the Court of Appeal and the House of Lords held that it was entitled to do so, because of the misrepresentation of the "short record". They held that disclosure of the "long record" had been waived by the underwriter and that non-disclosure of that record was not an issue. Dealing with the "decisive influence" test, the majority in the House of Lords held that it is *not* necessary for the underwriter to show that the fact, if disclosed, would have had a "decisive" influence on the mind of the prudent insurer in determining whether to write the risk, on what terms and at what premium. It is sufficient that the fact "would have an effect on the thought-processes of the (prudent) insurer in weighing up the risk".[20] This aspect of the decision was very much in line with precedent.

The question of "actual inducement" was answered in a manner that departed from English precedent. The leading case up to that point had been *Container Transport International Inc. v. Oceanus Mutual Underwriting Association*,[21] ("*C.T.I.*") a decision of the English Court of Appeal in 1984. In *C.T.I.*, the Court of Appeal had held that the standard was the objective one of the hypothetical "prudent" insurer — the subjective thought processes of the actual underwriter were irrelevant, so it said. It was not necessary to show that the actual underwriter had been induced as long as a prudent underwriter would have been induced to take the risk by the fact misrepresented or by the non-disclosure. In *Pine Top*, this part of the reasoning of *C.T.I.* was overruled by the House of Lords. Their Lordships said that it is not enough to show that the fact not

---

[19]   [1994] 3 All E.R. 581 (H.L.).

[20]   *Ibid.*, at 587-88 and 600-601.

[21]   [1984] 1 Ll. L.R. 476.

disclosed or misrepresented was "material" by objective standards. It is necessary for the insurer to discharge the burden of proving not only materiality, but
also that he or she was actually induced by the misrepresentation or non-
disclosure to make the policy on the relevant terms and at the premium agreed.
After an extensive review of the law both before and after 1906, Lord Mustill
concluded:

> ...I conclude that there is to be implied in the 1906 Act a qualification that a mate-
> rial misrepresentation will not entitle the underwriter to avoid the policy unless the
> misrepresentation induced the making of the contract, using 'induced' in the sense
> in which it is used in the general law of contract.[22]

The *C.T.I.* case was considered in the Canadian case of *Amo Containers Ltd. v.
Drake Insurance Co. Ltd.*[23] in which the court appears to have applied the
"actual inducement" test to both the actual underwriter and the hypothetical
prudent underwriter. It did not accept the actual underwriter's evidence as to
inducement and it concluded that the underwriter had failed to establish that a
"prudent insurer" would have been induced by the misrepresentation.[24]

In an Ontario case, *Nuvo Electronics Inc. v. London Assurance,*[25] a cargo
insurer contended that a policy of insurance was void *ab initio* because the
insured, through its broker, had not accurately described its loss record. The
broker had told the insurer that there had been no "losses", when in fact there
had been losses of seven shipments sent by courier but claims had not yet been
made on the insurance policy at the time of the presentation of the loss record.
The insurer's witnesses defined "loss" to mean a claim made to the insurer and
paid by it. The judge stated that "[i]f [the insurer] had wanted any further
information, it could have followed up and asked about potential losses or
claims but it did not do so."[26] The judge went on to say:

> In my view, there was no obligation on Nuvo to advise [the insurer] of the UPS
> situation [the previous incidents] so far as it was aware before the policy attached
> in view of [the insurer's] own definition of 'loss'. Even if there were and [the un-
> derwriter] had been informed of all of the relevant circumstances pertaining to the
> UPS losses, I am satisfied on the evidence that he would have written the policy
> anyway without any adjustment either to premium or policy conditions, and in my
> view, he conceded as much to [counsel] during her very skillful cross-examination
> on this point. It is apparent that this was a competitive market, that [the under-
> writer] wanted this business, that the losses had all occurred within a very short
> time period, that the insured had taken every necessary precaution to insure that
> further like losses would not occur, and that the seven losses combined involved

---

22   [1994] 3 All E.R. 581 (H.L.) at 617.
23   (1985), 51 Nfld. & P.E.I.R. 55, 150 A.P.R. 55 (Nfld. S.C.).
24   See the annotation to *Laurentian Pacific Insurance Co. v. Halama* (1991), 7 C.C.L.I. (2d) 84, 60
     B.C.L.R. (2d) 190 (S.C.), which criticizes the court's reliance on the evidence of the actual
     underwriter, rather than on the test of the reasonable underwriter.
25   (2000), 49 O.R. (3d) 374, 19 C.C.L.I. (3d) 195 (S.C.J.), additional reasons at (2000), 23 C.C.L.I.
     (3d) 231 (S.C.J.), appeal withdrawn, Jan. 28, 2002, Ontario Court of Appeal.
26   (2000), 49 O.R. (3d) 374 (S.C.J.) at 386.

about $18,000. Perhaps most importantly, we know that during the currency of the London policy Nuvo suffered more losses having a far greater dollar value and in the face of a competing bid, London continued the coverage without change to premium or conditions.

In my view, it matters not what another prudent underwriter might have done given this information in the circumstances of this case where we know with a reasonable degree of certainty that in all likelihood it would have made no difference to the underwriter who accepted the risk.[27]

Counsel for the underwriter relied on *Pine Top*. The judge did not adopt the *Pine Top* tests, and said:

In my view the *Pine Top* decision does not reflect the law of this province and is contrary to the provisions of the *Marine Insurance Act*. Lord Mustill's definition of materiality flies in the face of the statutory definition.[28]

She went on to say:

What is material is a question of fact to be determined on an objective standard and that objective standard is set out in [subsection 3 of section 21] of the Act. For a successful defence on this basis it is expected that there would be evidence from the underwriter who wrote the policy to the effect that if the undisclosed facts had been revealed to him he would either have declined the risk or stipulated for a higher premium. But that underwriter's view is not sufficient and does not meet the requirement for an objective standard. There must be evidence from an independent 'prudent' underwriter to the same effect to void the policy.[29]

The judge concluded that notwithstanding the evidence of an independent expert underwriter, who said that he would have either increased the premium or modified the conditions, the fact that the actual underwriter would not have done anything was conclusive.

Respectfully, the judge in *Nuvo Electronics* may have misinterpreted Lord Mustill's statement in *Pine Top*:

Before embarking on this long analysis I suggested that the questions in issue were short. I propose the following short answers. (1) A circumstance may be material even though a full and accurate disclosure of it would not in itself have had a decisive effect on the prudent underwriter's decision whether to accept the risk and if so at what premium. But (2) if the misrepresentation or non-disclosure of a material fact did not in fact induce the making of the contract (in the sense in which that expression is used in the general law of misrepresentation) the underwriter is not entitled to rely on it as a ground for avoiding the contract.[30]

---

[27]   *Ibid.*, at 386-87.
[28]   *Ibid.*, at 388.
[29]   *Ibid.*
[30]   *Ibid.*, citing [1995] A.C. 501 at 550 (H.L.).

The judge in *Nuvo Electronics* appears to have agreed with point (2) but not with point (1), which is interesting to note, particularly in view of the statute's use of the word "influence".

The decision in *Nuvo Electronics* was followed a short time later by that of another Ontario judge in *1013799 Ontario Ltd. v. Kent Line International Ltd.*[31] In that case, the insured sued the insurer, the broker, the freight forwarder (which issued the insurance certificate) and the ocean carrier as a result of damage to a shipment of chocolate bars which had melted en route to Trinidad. The claims against the ocean carrier and the marine insurer were not pursued and the action continued against the freight forwarder, which arranged the insurance, and the insurance broker. The cargo was insured under the Institute Frozen Food Clauses (which only covered mechanical breakdown of more than 24 hours and which ceased five days after discharge). The insured stated that it told the forwarder that it wanted "all risks, warehouse to warehouse" coverage.

The judge found that the *contract* between the plaintiff and the forwarder was on the basis explained by the forwarder to the insured — that the insurance would be subject to the Frozen Foods 24 hour breakdown terms with coverage only up to 5 days after discharge.[32] However, the judge said:

> The case framed in negligence is a very different matter. The issue here is the duty that Can-Ship [the forwarder] and Nacora [the broker] owed to Multi-Foods [the plaintiff] and whether there was a breach of that duty that caused the loss complained of.[33]

The judge also found that there was coverage available in the marine insurance market which would have given broader coverage and that the defendants would be liable for failing to procure such insurance. The question remained, however, whether the insured had failed to disclose that the product was beyond its shelf life and that the manufacturer had expressed the opinion that it was not suitable for sale. The judge said that there was no evidence before him that these facts were material. Second, he said that this would merely make the contract *voidable*, not void, and that the insurer had not exercised any right to make it voidable:

> I do not see how Can-Ship and Nacora can assert the contract's avoidability in an attempt to show that Multi-Foods has suffered no loss because it could not have recovered from Maritime [the marine insurer].[34]

On the third issue, pertaining to non-disclosure, the judge referred to *Nuvo Electronics*:

> ...there was no evidence before me to suggest that *this* policy would not have been issued if the allegedly material information had been disclosed. The defendants led no evidence from the underwriter who actually authorized the policy or who would

---

[31] (2000), 21 C.C.L.I. (3d) 312, [2000] O.T.C. 635 (Sup. Ct.).

[32] (2002) 21 C.C.L.I (3d) 312 at 315-316.

[33] *Ibid.*, at 317.

[34] *Ibid.*, at 320.

have had to consider any request to incorporate the extension clauses, as to whether he would have regarded the undisclosed information sufficiently important to justify a refusal to underwrite the risk or, after the policy had been issued, to avoid it...

As I understand it, what MacFarland, J. [in *Nuvo Electronics*] was saying (and, respectfully, I agree) was that the insurer must show first that it did in fact regard the non-disclosure as material and, second, that a prudent independent underwriter takes the same view. The defendants did not lead such evidence.[35]

To summarize, the insured or the broker must disclose "material" facts or information — facts or information that would influence the judgment of a prudent insurer in determining whether to accept the risk or, if so, in fixing the premium. Since the acceptance of the risk and the setting of the premium sometimes depend on the insuring conditions that are offered (for example, all risks or named perils), this too would be a factor in the underwriter's decision. The materiality of the information may be a question for expert evidence, but it is not enough to show that the "prudent" underwriter's judgment would have been affected had the facts been disclosed. The actual underwriter must establish, to the satisfaction of the court, that he or she would have declined the risk, insisted on different terms or charged a higher premium.

4.2.3 Examples of Material Facts

Whether a particular circumstance is material or not is a question of fact. What is considered material in one case will not necessarily be material in another. As has been noted: "In cases of this sort, where the question is one of fact, decisions on other facts are only helps to a conclusion on the particular circumstances before the court."[36] With this caution, the following have been considered material in some Canadian cases:

- whether the ship was missing at the time the risk was placed;[37]

---

[35] (2000), 21 C.C.L.I. (3d) 312 at 320-21.

[36] *Brooks-Scanlon O'Brien Co. v. Boston Insurance Co.*, [1919] 2 W.W.R. 129, 47 D.L.R. 93 (C.A.), *per* Macdonald C.J.A. at 95.

[37] *Perry v. British America Fire and Life Assurance Co.* (1848), 4 U.C.Q.B. 330 (C.A.) where the court held that the fact that the vessel had already sailed at the time of placing the risk was not material unless the ship was a missing ship at the time the contract was made. However, the court said that if the underwriter asked that specific question, the answer would be material and an incorrect answer would entitle the underwriter to avoid the policy. Chief Justice Robinson stated at 333:

> If the defendant [underwriters] expressly inquired about that fact, then in my opinion it would be proper to conclude that they regarded it as material, and had therefore a right to the information in estimating the risk, whether it might appear to others to be material or not...

- that the ship had gone into port for repairs at the commencement of the voyage;[38]
- that the ship had gone aground and was leaking;[39]
- the age of the vessel;[40]
- that the vessel was to be towed up and down river;[41]
- that two scows were towed together, rather than singly;[42]
- that the vessel was generally weak and did not have a certificate required under the *Canada Shipping Act*;[43] and
- the unfavourable claims history of the insured.[44]

In *Seaman v. West*,[45] it was held that it was not material that the vessel was flying the Haitian flag. The Supreme Court of Canada found that there was nothing about the national character of the ship, to the knowledge of the insured, that would expose it to detention and capture. In *Fudge v. Charter Marine Insurance Co.*,[46] the insured placed insurance on his fishing vessel in the amount of $140,000. He believed that it had a market value of $120,000 to $125,000. He had bought it 10 years earlier for $156,000, but expert evidence at trial was to the effect that it had a market value of $50,000 to $70,000. The court found that the valuation of the vessel was "grossly excessive" and that "[n]o reasonable prudent insurer would consider an inflationary error of such proportions as immaterial."[47] It was held that "the behaviour of the plaintiff in putting forward

---

[38] *Boak v. Merchants' Marine Insurance Co.* (1876), 10 N.S.R. 288 (App. Div.), appeal quashed (1877), 1 S.C.R. 110. Mr. Justice Ritchie stated that it was material that the vessel's voyage commenced at a port to which she had put in for serious repairs of damage caused by rough weather. He stated at N.S.R. 288 at 294:

> I do not see how it could be otherwise than that the mind of any reasonable insurer would have been much influenced by these facts, if they had been communicated to him, and on this ground also I think there should be a new trial.

Justice Wilkins did not agree that the fact was material, but held:

> Nevertheless, ever since the decision of the case of *Haywood v. Rodgers*, 4 East 590, it has been clear law that the non-disclosure of such a fact as that last noticed, although the knowledge of it might and probably would have enhanced the premium, would not vacate a policy. The underwriter did not, as he might have done, ask for information on the subject. Had he done so, the assured would have been bound to disclose truly all that was within his knowledge.

[39] *Smith v. Royal Canadian Insurance Co.* (1884), Cout. S.C. 723, Cass. S.C. 386 (S.C.C.), rev'g. (1884), 17 N.S.R. 322 (C.A.).

[40] *Nova Scotia Marine Insurance Co. v. Stevenson* (1894), 23 S.C.R. 137, rev'g. (1889), 25 N.S.R. 210 (C.A.).

[41] *Bailey & Co. v. Ocean Mutual Marine Insurance Co.* (1891), 19 S.C.R. 153, aff'g. (1889), 22 N.S.R. 5 (C.A.).

[42] *Brooks-Scanlon O'Brien Co. v. Boston Insurance Co.*, [1919] 2 W.W.R. 129, 47 D.L.R. 93 (C.A.).

[43] *Atlantic Freighting Co. v. Provincial Insurance Co. Ltd.* (1956), 5 D.L.R. (2d) 164 (N.S.S.C.).

[44] *Neepawa Yacht Ltd. v. Laurentian P & C Insurance Co.* (1994), D.R.S. 95-04330 (S.C.).

[45] (1885), Cout. S.C. 723, Cass. S.C. 388 (S.C.C.) aff'g. (1884), 17 N.S.R. 207 (C.A.).

[46] (1992), 8 C.C.L.I. (2d) 252, 97 Nfld. & P.E.I.R. 91 (Nfld. S.C.T.D.).

[47] (1992), 97 Nfld. & P.E.I.R. 91 at 96 (Nfld. S.C.T.D.).

what was a speculative valuation of $140,000 in a valued policy was a material misrepresentation of the value that vitiates the policy."[48]

4.2.4 Insurance Placed Through Agent

The broker is the agent of the insured, and not of the underwriter.[49] The C.*M.I.A.* makes it clear that a broker acting on behalf of the insured has the same duties of disclosure as the insured and that the broker's failure to disclose material facts will make the policy voidable.[50]

4.3 WHEN MUST DISCLOSURE BE MADE?

4.3.1 Generally

Subsection 21(1) of the *C.M.I.A.* requires that the disclosure must be made "before the contract is concluded". Section 23 provides that: "A contract is deemed to be concluded when the proposal of the insured is accepted by the insurer, whether the marine policy is then issued or not..." It is typical that the policy will be issued some considerable time after the contract has actually been made. To determine when the contract was in fact made, it may be necessary to refer to the "slip", to notes or documents prepared by the broker and the underwriter, or to cover notes and "binders".[51]

4.3.2 Open Policies

It is also common for underwriters to issue an "open policy" permitting the policy holder to obtain binding insurance by making periodic "declarations" under the policy. Provided the risk to be insured falls within the terms of the open policy, the insured does not have to contact the underwriter to negotiate the terms of cover or the premium — the conditions of the open policy will instantly attach and the insured will report insurances falling within the policy on a periodic basis.[52]

The question arises as to whether, under an open policy, the insured has a duty to disclose material facts arising subsequent to the issuance of the policy itself, but prior to the declaration of a particular risk. In *Standard Marine Insurance Co. v. Whalen Pulp & Paper Mills Ltd.*,[53] the insurer had issued an open policy of cargo insurance to cover wood pulp during transportation between

---

[48]   (1992), 8 C.C.L.I. (2d) 252 at 258, 97 Nfld. & P.E.I.R. 91 at 96 (Nfld. S.C.T.D.). See also Chapter 6, *Insurable Value*.

[49]   See Chapter 23, *The Marine Insurance Broker*.

[50]   Subsection 21(2) and 22(8).

[51]   See *DeGroot v. J.T. O'Bryan & Co.* (1979), 15 B.C.L.R. 271, [1979] I.L.R. ¶1-1152 at 416 (C.A.), rev'g. [1977] I.L.R. ¶1-863 at 564 (S.C.) in which the trial court noted, at [1977] I.L.R. 566, that while only a cover note had been issued, a formal policy "would have followed as a matter of routine".

[52]   See Chapter 2, *The Marine Insurance Contract*.

[53]   (1922), 64 S.C.R. 90, 68 D.L.R. 269, aff'g. [1922] 1 W.W.R. 679, 68 D.L.R. 181 (C.A.).

certain terminals. The insured was bound to declare all shipments falling within the policy and to pay a premium. There was a provision in the policy by which seaworthiness of vessels was admitted between insurer and insured. The insured chartered a barge which sank during loading. The insurer paid the claim for the cargo loss, but later brought an action to recover the monies paid, alleging that the insured had been aware that the vessel was unseaworthy and had previously been refused insurance and that this was material non-disclosure. The Court of Appeal held that there was no duty of disclosure on the insured after the policy had been issued. The Supreme Court of Canada agreed, holding that the risk attached as soon as the conditions of the policy were complied with and that the insurer was bound to accept the risk. In the Supreme Court of Canada, Justice Duff stated:

> Such being the scope of the policy, was there any legal duty of disclosure resting on the respondent company? I think there was no such duty. The contract of insurance had been effected, the subject matter had been ascertained, the seaworthiness had been admitted of all craft within the contemplation of it; and the risk attached as soon as the conditions of the policy were complied with.[54]

One of the other judges, Mignault J., pointed out that there was insufficient evidence to show that the insured was aware that the vessel was unseaworthy. If the insured had actually been aware that the vessel was unseaworthy, the concealment of this fact would have been fraud; but the awareness that the vessel had previously been denied insurance was not a ground to avoid the policy.

This case was considered at trial in *C.C.R. Fishing v. British Reserve Insurance Co.*[55] The trial judge stated:

> Before embarking on an analysis of the alleged items of non-disclosure it is necessary to determine what constitutes the contract of insurance between the parties to this action. That determination is important because it fixes the time at which disclosure must be made.[56]

The judge noted that the plaintiff contended that the relevant time was the making of the "open cover" contract given to the broker. He stated:

> The cover provided by the open cover is to 'accept all business as may be declared by [the broker].' These words are plain and unambiguous and required the underwriters to accept all risks declared by [the broker] within the contemplation of the policy as to marine hulls. There was nothing for the underwriters to assess. They had already accepted the risk. There was nothing reserved to them and there was no information they needed and there was no information which would be of any assistance to them.[57]

---

[54] *Ibid.*, at S.C.R. 100.
[55] (1986), 21 C.C.L.I. 297 (S.C.), rev'd. on other grounds (1988), 34 B.C.L.R. (2d) 1, 55 D.L.R. (4th) 429 (C.A.), rev'd. [1990] 3 W.W.R. 501, 45 B.C.L.R. (2d) 145 (S.C.C.).
[56] *Ibid.*, at C.C.L.I. 311.
[57] *Ibid.*, at C.C.L.I. 313.

After reviewing the documentation, including endorsements and the cover note, the judge stated:

> In the result I have concluded that the policy of insurance in the present case is the open cover issued on January 2, 1982 and that any failures to disclose after that date are not effective to nullify the policy. Section 19(1) of the *Insurance (Marine) Act* only requires disclosure 'before the contract is concluded'. It does not require disclosure of material circumstances after the contract has been concluded.[58]

The trial judge distinguished *Berger v. Pollock*[59] on the basis that:

> ...the open cover in that case was much more narrow than the extremely broad provisions in the open cover in the case at Bar. In addition there were matters reserved to the underwriter in the *Berger* case. There is nothing reserved to the underwriters in the case at Bar. Unlike this case it was held in the *Berger* case that the open cover did not constitute a contract between the plaintiffs and the underwriters. On the facts of this case I have arrived at a different opinion. I have accordingly concluded that the defence of non-disclosure cannot succeed because the insurance was placed by declaration under an open cover with the result that in the broadest terms the underwriters agreed in advance to accept all risks declared by Tomenson Inc.[60]

Treating the date of the open policy as the key date for the purpose of disclosure is open to abuse and unfairness. An open policy avoids the administration and inconvenience of applying for new insurance each time a new shipment is made. It also has a commercial advantage to both parties. It allows the insured to have consistent rates and terms of coverage for its shipments, and it gives the underwriter the certainty of a volume of business and premium income. However, an open policy is not a blank cheque to the insured and it will invariably contain terms defining the type of risks that fall within it and to which insurance will automatically attach. If a particular risk does not fall within the policy, it would be normal for the insured or the broker to bring it to the attention of the underwriter and to request specific coverage, on terms to be arranged. If the insured becomes aware of material facts which would make a risk unusual or out of the ordinary, it seems reasonable to expect that those facts would be brought to the underwriter's attention as soon as they become known to the insured. This would permit the underwriter to determine whether an additional premium, or special terms, should be imposed.

---

[58]   *Ibid.*, at C.C.L.I. 316.

[59]   [1973] 2 Ll. L.R. 442. The judge also referred to *Standard Marine Insurance Co. v. Whalen Pulp and Paper Mills Ltd.* (1922), 64 S.C.R. 90, 68 D.L.R. 269, aff'g. [1922] 1 W.W.R. 679, 68 D.L.R. 181 (C.A.) and *Ionides v. Pacific Fire & Marine Insurance Co.* (1871) L.R. 6 Q.B. 674.

[60]   *C.C.R. Fishing v. British Reserve Insurance Co.* (1986), 21 C.C.L.I. 297 (S.C.), rev'd. on other grounds (1988), 34 B.C.L.R. (2d) 1, 55 D.L.R. (4th) 429, rev'd. [1990] 3 W.W.R. 501, 45 B.C.L.R. (2d) 145 (S.C.C.) at C.C.L.I. 318.

4.3.3 Renewals

Disclosure issues may arise in the case of renewals. In *Neepawa Yacht Ltd. v. Laurentian P. & C. Insurance Co.,*[61] the insurance policy on a valuable yacht was underwritten in 1990 and was renewed in 1991 and 1992 for one year terms. In February, 1993, while the policy was in effect, the yacht became a total loss as a result of a fire. On investigating the incident, the insurer discovered that there had been losses to the vessel, prior to the time that it came on risk in 1990, which had not been disclosed at the time of the original application for insurance. The issue was whether the non-disclosure in 1990, when the first contract of insurance was made, had any effect on the renewals of the policy of insurance in subsequent years. It was argued by the plaintiff that each renewal was a separate contract and that since the insurer did not request a claims history at the time of the later renewals, there was no need for disclosure of the previous losses. It was also argued that by the time of the last renewal, in 1992, the previous losses were sufficiently old that they would not have been considered material. The court rejected this contention. Justice Hall stated:

> In this case, either through inattention or lack of candor on the part of the agent, the defendant insurer did not obtain the true picture in the winter of 1990. To my mind, this non-disclosure taints that initial policy of insurance and the succeeding renewal contracts. I find on the evidence that there was a clear materiality as regards the previous losses going back to 1985 and that the failure to disclose the two additional incidents leads to the result that the defendant is properly entitled to avoid the claim advanced for the fire loss of February 1993.[62]

The court also stated:

> Insurance is a special type of contract. In the majority judgment in [*Coronation Insurance Co. v. Taku Air Transport Ltd.*] Cory J. reminds us of the judgment of Lord Mansfield in the leading case of *Carter v. Boehm*...where His Lordship noted that there is a high duty of disclosure cast upon an insured who is dealing with an underwriter. There are ample historical reasons and justification for this. In assessing the risk, the prudent underwriter needs to and wants to have the full picture before him or her. Much of the earlier law has been codified in our Act in sections 18 through 21. In short compass, an underwriter is entitled to what I suppose securities lawyers often refer to as true, full and plain disclosure in the context of securities law. Insurance is, of course, not a one way street. The courts have consistently held that insurers are not to be lightly absolved of their contractual obligations. The contra proferentem principle and the insistence by the courts that exclusionary language be given a strict construction are examples of the judicial attitude to the sanctity of insurance contracts...The other side of this coin is the principle that, to use the vernacular, the proposed insured has to be "up front' with

---

[61] (1994), D.R.S. 95-04330, p. 21 (B.C.S.C.).

[62] *Ibid.*, at 21-22.

the insurer. The principle or doctrine of uberrima fides is deeply ingrained in this branch of the law of contract.[63]

In *Laurentian Pacific Insurance Co. v. Halama*,[64] a policy on a yacht was issued in 1988 and was renewed in the two subsequent years. In 1989, the yacht was damaged in a collision and a claim under the policy was paid. The insurer subsequently discovered that the insured had failed to accurately complete its original application for insurance in 1998 which called for disclosure of losses within the previous five years. The insured had failed to disclose a loss in 1984. The court found that this was a misrepresentation which made the policy voidable and the insurer was entitled to recover the money it had paid out. The subsequent renewals of the policy were tainted by the non-disclosure on the original application.

It seems reasonable that at the time of a renewal, which is a new contract, the insured has an obligation to advise of any material change in circumstance, or any material fact which has come to his or her attention, since the previous contract was made. This should be the case whether or not the insurer requires a new application.

4.4 WHAT NEED NOT BE DISCLOSED?

The *C.M.I.A.* provides that there are certain things that the insured is not required to disclose.[65] These are:

4.4.1 Any Circumstance That Diminishes the Risk

Since the purpose of disclosure is to enable the underwriter to determine whether to accept the risk, a circumstance which diminishes the risk need not be disclosed since this could only operate so as to induce the acceptance of the risk or reduce the premium.[66]

4.4.2 Any Circumstance That Is Known By the Insurer

The insured is not required to disclose information or circumstances known to the insurer, either in the form of actual knowledge or information that the insurer is *presumed* to know. The *C.M.I.A.* provides that "an insurer is presumed to know circumstances of common notoriety and every circumstance that, in the ordinary course of an insurer's business, ought to be known by an insurer."[67]

---

[63] *Ibid.*, at 21.

[64] (1991), 7 C.C.L.I. (2d) 84, 60 B.C.L.R. (2d) 190 (S.C.).

[65] Subsection 21(5).

[66] Subsection 21(5)(*a*).

[67] Subsection 21(6)(*c*). For an application of this principle, see *Riverside Landmark Corp. v. Northumberland General Insurance Co.* (1984), 8 C.C.L.I. 119 (Ont. H.C.J.). The court found that there was a practice of lashing two vessels side by side for a period of time at the commencement of the tow, and that this practice should have been known to a competent marine underwriter. The insured's failure to disclose this fact was not a ground for avoidance of the

The Supreme Court of Canada considered this subject in a non-marine insurance case, *Canadian Indemnity Co. v. Canadian Johns-Manville Co.*[68] The insurer brought proceedings to avoid a comprehensive general liability policy, issued to Johns-Manville, an asbestos mining and manufacturing company. It was alleged that Johns-Manville should have disclosed reports in its possession dealing with the carcinogenic effects of asbestos. Johns-Manville alleged that the health risks of asbestos were well-known and relied upon provisions of the Quebec *Civil Code* that the insured was not obliged to disclose to the insurer "facts known to the insurer or which from their public character and notoriety he is presumed to know..."[69]

The Supreme Court made an extensive review of the law, noting that in *Carter v. Boehm*,[70] Lord Mansfield had indicated that the insured was not required to disclose facts which were known by the insurer. Justice Gonthier, giving the Court's judgment, characterized that case as illustrating "the dynamics involved in the gathering of material information by the insurer and the insured."[71] He stated:

> The pre-[Civil Code] codification authorities indicate that it is not a general principle of insurance that both insured and insurer must possess equal actual knowledge. On the contrary, it appears that if the insurer does not keep abreast of facts which are available and customary or well known in the field which it insures, then it ignores these facts at its peril, and the law does not require the insured to make up for the insurer's lack of diligence. Of course, the insurer is not actually engaged in the trade or activity which it insures, and there is a natural limit to that which should be well known to the insurer. In my view, art. 2486 [of the Civil Code] represents an attempt to define that limit. It appears to me to be quite clear that this limit includes but extends beyond that which is notorious to the general public or even to the well-informed individual. However, it stops short of information which is perhaps notorious to those within the trade, industry or activity which is being insured but not normally accessible or available to those who operate on the periphery.[72]

Jusice Gonthier held that an insurer has a duty to acquire a level of knowledge which is reasonable in the circumstances. He stated:

> In my opinion, the relevant standard by which the notoriety of the undisclosed fact must be assessed is that of the reasonably competent underwriter insuring similar

---

policy. See also *Macdonald v. Liverpool and London and Globe Insurance Co. Ltd.* (1978), 22 N.B.R. (2d) 172, 39 A.P.R. 172 (S.C.), in which the court, considering a different issue, stated that the insurer could be presumed to know that no one would sail a boat in the area in question in the month of April and that the boat would be out of commission at that time; and *Davis v. Scottish Provincial Insurance Co.* (1865), 16 U.C.C.P. 176.

[68] [1990] 2 S.C.R. 549, 72 D.L.R. (4th) 478, aff'g. [1988] R.J.Q. 2651, 54 D.L.R. (4th) 468 (Que. C.A.).

[69] S.Q. 1991, c. 64, art. 2486.

[70] (1706), 3 Burr. 1905.

[71] *Canadian Indemnity Co. v. Canadian Johns-Mansville Co.*, [1990] 2 S.C.R. 549, 72 D.L.R. (4th) 478 at 499, aff'g. [1988] R.J.Q. 2651, 54 D.L.R. (4th) 468 (Que. C.A.).

[72] *Ibid.*, at D.L.R. 505.

risks in the industry covered by the policy. Thus, art. 2486 [of the *Civil Code*] protects the insured against the ignorance of an insurer who enters a new market without the most basic, publicly available and generally known information about the risks covered by the policy.[73]

Later he continued:

The insurer will be presumed to know only those facts which are publicly available and which would be notorious to the reasonably competent underwriter insuring similar risks in that industry...

In the maritime insurance field of the nineteenth century, we have seen that courts expected that the insurer would be aware of certain facts which were notorious to those in the activity of shipping and trade. The insuring of shipping interests had by then gone on for over a century, and the information regarding the risks involved could be obtained by well-known means. A marine insurer ignored such information at its peril. In my opinion, the same would be true of an insurer of asbestos industry risks who ignored information which was publicly available and well known to insurers in that industry.[74]

The Supreme Court held that Johns-Manville was entitled to assume that the insurer had a basic professional knowledge of the risks associated with asbestos and that it was not obliged to disclose the reports which it had in its possession. The insured could assume that if the insurer required additional information, it would request it.

The law was taken one step farther by the Supreme Court of Canada in *Coronation Insurance Co. v. Taku Air Transport Ltd.*[75] The case dealt with the implications of misrepresentation and non-disclosure in the context of aviation insurance. Taku was a small commercial air carrier operating in northern British Columbia. In 1986, one of its aircraft crashed into a lake, killing four passengers. The liability insurer, Coronation, denied coverage and brought an application to have the policy declared void on the grounds of non-disclosure of Taku's rather dismal accident record and misrepresentation of the number of seats in the aircraft — on its application for insurance Taku had stated that there were four seats, when in fact there were five.

Justice Cory, giving the majority judgment of the Supreme Court of Canada, prefaced his reasons by noting:

This appeal...illustrates the difficulties that arise when principles of insurance law set forth by the courts in 1766 are strictly applied to policies of insurance mandated by statute or regulation and which are purportedly for the benefit of third parties (here passengers carried by commercial airlines) and not for the sole benefit of the insured party.[76]

---

[73]   *Ibid.*, at 506.

[74]   *Ibid.*, at 508-509.

[75]   [1991] 3 S.C.R. 622, [1992] 1 W.W.R. 217.

[76]   *Ibid.*, at 220-21.

He was referring to the mandatory liability insurance which Canadian licensed air carriers are required to procure. He cited *Carter v. Boehm* and made reference to the changes that had taken place in the insurance business, and in the types of insurance offered, since 1766:

> When Lord Mansfield set the principle governing insurance contracts the world was a little different. It was a simpler if not, in some respects, a gentler place. The business of insurance was very different. Then policies of insurance were issued most frequently to cover a vessel or its cargo. The contract was issued for the benefit of the insured. It was the owner as insured who would have the detailed knowledge of the vessel or its cargo. No one would know better than the owner of the incipient dry rot or the tendency of the ship to take on water in a fresh breeze. This was knowledge that the insurance company could not readily attain and it was appropriate to relieve the insurer of all responsibility for obtaining it. That principle held true in 1766. It can hold true today where the policy is for the exclusive benefit of the insured.[77]

In this case, however, the insurance was intended for the benefit of the public as well as for the insured. The loss record of Taku was available from two sources which were readily accessible by Coronation. First, an examination of its own files would have revealed that it had insured Taku for an earlier period, during which some of the previous undisclosed losses had occurred. Second, a review of the public files of the Canadian Transportation Accident Investigation and Safety Board would have revealed Taku's record. Mr. Justice Cory stated:

> I would think that where the policy of insurance required by statute or regulation is primarily for the benefit of members of the flying public and not just the insured the insurer must take some basic steps to investigate the flying record of the air carrier applying for insurance. At a minimum, it should review its own files on the applicant. Further the insurer should make a search of the public record of accidents of the air carrier.[78]

Referring to the *Johns-Manville* case, Justice Cory held that for these reasons, a reasonably competent aviation insurer would have known or could be presumed to have known, from its own records or easily available public records, the loss record of Taku. He concluded that the insurer had an active duty to investigate because the insurance was designed for the protection of the public and not just the insured. He described this as merely a "reasonable incremental change"[79] in the existing law.

The Supreme Court held, however, that the insurer was entitled to avoid the policy on the ground that Taku had misrepresented the number of passenger seats in the aircraft. This was a matter within the special and unique knowledge of Taku. Only it would know what modifications to the seating arrangements had been made and how many passengers it intended to carry; the insurer was entitled to rely on this representation without further inquiry.

---

[77] *Ibid.*, at 229.

[78] *Ibid.*, at 230.

[79] *Ibid.*, at 232.

Returning to subsections 21(5)(*b*) and 21(6)(*c*) of the *C.M.I.A.*, the insured will not be required to disclose any circumstance known to the insurer, including "circumstances of common notoriety and every circumstance that, in the ordinary course of an insurer's business, ought to be known by an insurer." The "prudent [marine] insurer" will appear at trial, in the form of an expert witness, to answer the question of what type of information and knowledge the under-writer can and should bring to bear in the assessment of a particular risk. As Justice Cory noted in *Taku*, there may be information peculiar to a particular risk which the insurer could have no way of knowing and which it would be reasonable to require the insured to disclose. After all, the insured should have the better knowledge of the business in which he or she operates. On the other hand, there is a general storehouse of knowledge which a competent underwriter should have and it is unreasonable to expect the insured to disclose information of this nature.

4.4.3 Any Circumstance As To Which Information is Waived By the Insurer

Waiver is a legal term to describe the voluntary surrender of a legal right. In this context, it refers to a situation where an insurer surrenders its right to the disclosure of material information. The doctrine of waiver has been successfully invoked in a number of cases; but, for the principle to apply, there must be evidence of some unequivocal act on the part of the insurer indicating an intention to waive further disclosure. Thus, in *Smith v. Royal Canadian Insurance Co.*,[80] it was argued that the insured had failed to disclose that the ship had been in an accident on the day before the placing of the insurance. The insurer became aware of the accident shortly thereafter, but proceeded to issue a policy. The Nova Scotia Court of Appeal had held that in issuing a policy with knowl-edge of the accident the insurer had waived its right to avoid the policy. However, the Supreme Court of Canada declined to apply the doctrine of waiver since "the appellant [insurer] could not waive that which he did not know" — at the time it issued the policy it did not know that the insured was aware of the previous accident. The insurer was contractually obliged to issue the policy, since it had bound itself to the risk, and the act of issuing the policy could not be considered a waiver of the insured's failure to disclose material information.

In *Central Native Fishermen's Co-op. v. Commonwealth Insurance Co.*,[81] the British Columbia Supreme Court rejected a non-disclosure defence. A survey report that had been requested from the broker by the underwriter turned out not to be particularly favourable, so it was not released to the underwriter. Subse-quently, a second, more favourable report was obtained from another surveyor. The court held that the underwriter had been "put on his inquiry" and had waived production of the earlier survey. With respect, this seems to adopt a rather low standard of disclosure from the insured. It condones the dangerous

---

[80] (1884), Cout. S.C. 723, Cass. S.C. 386 (S.C.C.), rev'g. (1884), 17 N.S.R. 322 (C.A.).
[81] [1979] I.L.R. ¶1-1091 (B.C.S.C.).

practice of the insured shopping around until he finds a survey report which suits his purposes.

In *Amo Containers Ltd. v. Drake Insurance Co. Ltd.*,[82] a non-disclosure case, the trial judge adopted the following statement from *Asfar and Co. v. Blundell and Others*:

> ...it is a well-settled principle of insurance law that underwriters are not entitled to be told what they waive all inquiry about. In this particular case they were told that there was a charter, and if they had wanted to learn the contents of that charter they had only to inquire. They chose to waive inquiry.[83]

In *Amo* the underwriter had knowledge that the insured containers were the subject of a lease, but did not make inquiry as to the terms of the lease. The court stated that the underwriter had waived further inquiry as to the terms of the lease and could not now assert that certain terms were material and should have been disclosed.

The trial judge in *Amo* also referred to *C.T.I.*,[84] which was then the leading case, in which Lord Justice Kerr stated:

> The principle is that if a certain fact is material for the purposes of ss. 18(2) and 20(2), so that a failure to draw the underwriter's attention to it distorts the fairness of the broker's presentation of the risk, then it is not sufficient that this fact could have been extracted by the underwriter from material to which he had access or which was cursorily shown to him. On the other hand, if the disclosed facts give a fair presentation of the risk, then the underwriter must enquire if he wishes to have more information.[85]

The judge concluded that since the insurer had made no inquiry of the terms of the lease of the containers, it was a "reasonable conclusion that that was not a matter that would influence its accepting the risk for it could scarcely be said to be influenced one way or the other by the existence of a one-year lease if it was unaware of the terms of the lease."[86]

In *Biggin v. British Marine Mutual Insurance Assn.*,[87] the insured claimed for a fire loss on a fishing boat. The insurer defended on a number of grounds, including the insured's failure to disclose his adverse claims history. The insured had signed an application which contained specific questions about claims on the vessel in the previous three years. The insured answered these truthfully, but did not disclose earlier losses. The form then had a space for "Any other material facts." This was left blank. The form concluded with the following "guidance note":

---

[82] (1985), 51 Nfld. & P.E.I.R. 55, 150 A.P.R. 55 (Nfld. S.C.).
[83] [1895] 2 Q.B. 196, *per* Matthews J. at 202.
[84] [1984] 1 Ll. L.R. 476.
[85] [1984] 1 Ll. L.R. 476 at 497.
[86] (1985), 51 Nfld. & P.E.I.R. 55 at 61, 150 A.P.R. 55 (Nfld. S.C.).
[87] (1992), 14 C.C.L.I. (3d) 66, D.R.S. 94-00148 (Nfld. S.C.).

DISCLOSURE OF MATERIAL FACTS

You must disclose all material facts, not only those covered by specific questions in the Form. Material facts are those which an insurer would regard as likely to influence the acceptance and assessment of your application. A good example is claims experience. If you fail to disclose a material fact, your insurance cover could become completely void. If you are in doubt as to whether any material fact is material, you should disclose it.

In spite of this language, the court concluded that the insurer had waived information respecting claims older than three years. If the insurer had wanted that information, said Justice Roberts, it should have said so: "Having asked specifically for losses within three years, one could rightly assume that losses beyond that were not relevant."[88] He found that the language of the application was ambiguous in this respect, and interpreted it against the insurer.

In the *Pine Top*[89] case, there was a complaint by the underwriter that there had been non-disclosure of the so-called "long record". On the evidence, that record was available at the time the risk was discussed between broker and underwriter, but it appears that the broker went out of his way to divert the underwriter's attention from this subject. The House of Lords held that the underwriter, being aware that the long record was available for his review, had waived any further disclosure of it. One might suggest, however, that there is a fine line between non-disclosure and "soft-pedaling" and that a broker does the latter at his or her peril. Obviously, in *Pine Top*, the House of Lords did not consider that the broker had crossed the line.

4.4.4 Any Circumstance the Disclosure of Which is Superfluous By Reason of Any Express Warranty or Implied Warranty

The insured is not required to disclose "any circumstance the disclosure of which is superfluous by reason of any express warranty or implied warranty."[90] A warranty is a promise by the insured that some thing will or will not be done or that some condition will be fulfilled. If that does not take place, the *C.M.I.A.* provides that, whether or not the warranty is material to the risk, the insurer is discharged from any liability for loss occurring after the date of the breach of warranty.[91]

It is common for marine policies to contain express warranties, for example, that the vessel will not sail in certain areas or at certain times of year, that it will not engage in certain kinds of trade or carry certain types of cargo or that it will be surveyed at particular times or by particular agencies. If there is a warranty in the policy with respect to a particular fact, the disclosure of the fact becomes superfluous, since the operation of the fact, while undoubtedly material, has the

---

[88]   *Ibid.*, at 78.
[89]   [1994] 3 All E.R. 581 (H.L.).
[90]   *C.M.I.A.*, s. 21 (5)(*d*). See also ss. 32 to 39 of the *C.M.I.A.* and Chapter 8, *Warranties.*
[91]   *C.M.I.A.*, s. 39.

effect of suspending the policy from the date of the breach of warranty, in any event.[92]

4.5 MISREPRESENTATION

Section 22 of the *C.M.I.A.* provides, in part:

> 22(1) Every material representation made by the insured or the insured's agent to the insurer during the negotiations for the contract and before the contract is concluded must be true.
>
> (2) A representation is material if it would influence the judgment of a prudent insurer in fixing the premium or determining whether to take the risk.

If a representation is material, and untrue, the underwriter is entitled to avoid the contract on becoming aware of it.[93]

4.5.1 Materiality

The provisions of the *C.M.I.A.* concerning the materiality of representations are similar to the disclosure provisions: "A representation is material if it would influence the judgment of a prudent insurer in fixing the premium or determining whether to take the risk."[94] It is a question of fact as to whether or not a representation is material.[95]

4.5.2 Types of Representations

The *C.M.I.A.* differentiates between representations of fact and representations of belief. Section 22 provides in part:

> 22(4) A representation may be as to a matter of fact or as to a matter of expectation or belief.
>
> (5) A representation as to a matter of fact is deemed to be true if the difference between what is represented and what is actually correct would not be considered material by a prudent insurer.
>
> (6) A representation as to a matter of expectation or belief is deemed to be true if it is made in good faith.

It is important to characterize the nature of the representation since different results will follow depending on whether the representation is considered to be one of fact or one of expectation or belief. The difference was considered in

---

[92] See Chapter 8 on *Warranties*.

[93] *C.M.I.A.*, subs. 22(8). See also *McDonald v. Doull* (1878), 12 N.S.R. 276 (C.A.), rev'd. Cass. S.C. 384.

[94] *Ibid.*, subs. 22(2).

[95] *Ibid.*, subs. 22(3).

Bailey & Co. v. Ocean Mutual Marine Insurance Co.[96] The plaintiff had made an application for insurance on a vessel which was in a foreign port at the time. In response to the question "Where is the vessel? When to sail", the answer given was "at Buenos Ayres or near port 3rd February bound up river, would tow up and back." In fact, while the vessel was towed up river, it was not towed back. The vessel was damaged coming down river, not in tow. It is interesting to note that the damage appears to have occurred before the placing of the insurance, but at a time when neither the insured nor the underwriter was aware of the damage to the vessel. The Supreme Court of Canada held that it was material that the return voyage was not under tow, since there would be less risk being towed. Chief Justice Ritchie said:

> I am of the opinion the representation was not a mere matter of expectation or belief, but a representation or affirmation of a positive fact that the ship would tow up and down, and I think all the surrounding circumstances show that the assured intended that assurers should so understand it...It was a positive representation of an existing or future fact material to the risk; there was no representation of belief or expectation, but a positive engagement that she should or would be towed up and down the river....I can really see no distinction between a promissory representation and a warranty.

> I think this was not a matter of expectation but the promissory representation of a material fact...[97]

Justice Gwynne stated:

> The language so used is capable of being construed, and reasonably so, as a positive representation of the plaintiffs made for the purpose of effecting the insurance through their agents; and the insurance company had reasonably a right so to understand the language, and as that representation was not fulfilled the policy is avoided.[98]

In *Nova Scotia Marine Insurance Co. v. Stevenson*,[99] the plaintiff, in answer to a question "when built?" in the application for insurance, answered "in 1890" the year in which the vessel had been extensively refurbished and rebuilt. The vessel had originally been built in 1868. The trial judge, and the Court of Appeal of Nova Scotia found that the representation was true in fact. Mr. Justice King in the Supreme Court of Canada disagreed:

> Where payment of a risk is resisted on the ground of misrepresentation it ought indeed to be made very clear that there has been such a misrepresentation...

> A representation is to be construed according to the fair and obvious import of words, and is equivalent to an express statement of all the inferences naturally and

---

[96] (1891), 19 S.C.R. 153, aff'g. (1889), 22 N.S.R. 5 (C.A.).
[97] *Ibid.*, at S.C.R. 155-156.
[98] *Ibid.*, at 157.
[99] (1893), 23 S.C.R. 137.

necessarily arising from it…It comprehends whatever would reasonably and necessarily be inferred by mercantile men from the language under the circumstances in which it was employed…[100]

He held that there had been a misrepresentation. As to its effect, he said:

> Then as to the effect of the misrepresentation. If made with intent to deceive the misrepresentation vitiates the policy however trivial or immaterial to the nature of the risk. If honestly made it vitiates only if material and if substantially incorrect. The test of materiality is the probable effect which the statement might naturally and reasonably be expected to produce on the mind of the underwriter in weighing the risk and considering the premium.[101]

He went on to state that if there is no intent to deceive, it is enough that there is "substantial compliance" with the representation. In this case, there was a difference in 20 years in the age of the vessel; and it was a reasonable conclusion that, had the truth been known, the underwriter would not have written the policy on the same terms. The court concluded, however, that the representation had been made with "intent to deceive".[102]

The case of *DeGroot v. J.T. O'Bryan & Co.*,[103] a decision of the British Columbia Court of Appeal, involved a policy of insurance on the yacht "Raven", which had been lost at sea. It was found that there had been a representation made by the insured's agent that a survey had been done on the vessel and that there were no recommendations made by the surveyor. In fact, no survey had been done. The court considered the difference between a representation as to an existing fact and a representation as to a matter of expectation or belief but noted that there could be a third type of representation — a promissory representation — a representation in the form of a promise to do something in the future. Taggart J.A., with whom Aikens J.A. concurred stated:

> Promissory representations appear to have survived in the law relating to contracts of marine insurance — at any rate, up to the time when the Marine Insurance Act was enacted. For cases in Canada relating to promissory representations, see *H.B.*

---

[100] *Ibid.*, at 139-40.

[101] *Ibid.*, at 141.

[102] *Ibid.*, at 142. While the insured's good faith is, according to s. 22 of the *C.M.I.A.*, only relevant in the case of representations as to expectation or belief, the courts appear to have been somewhat more lenient in the case of representations as to facts that are made in good faith, "true in letter and in spirit", or that have the "ring of truth": see *Amo Containers Ltd. v. Drake Insurance Co. Ltd.* (1984), 8 C.C.L.I. 97 at 107, 51 Nfld. & P.E.I.R. 55 (Nfld. S.C.); *Lyon v. Stadacona Insurance Co.* (1879), 44 U.C.Q.B. 472 at 484 (C.A.); and *Ewart v. Merchants' Marine Insurance Co.* (1879), 13 N.S.R. 168 (C.A.) where the vessel was described in the application for insurance as "A.1". The insurers contended that they understood that this meant that the ship was classified with the English Lloyd's, when in fact it was only in the American Lloyd's, which was not so high a rating. The court held that there was no evidence of misrepresentation of the classification or that the classification of the ship was not so inferior to English Lloyd's as to invalidate the insurance.

[103] (1979), 15 B.C.L.R. 271, [1979] I.L.R. ¶1-1152 (C.A.), rev'g. [1977] I.L.R. ¶I-863 (S.C.).

Bailey and Co. v. Ocean Marine Mutual Ins. Co. (1891), 19 S.C.R. 153, where at p. 155 Ritchie C.J. said of the representation there in issue:

> It was a positive representation of an existing or future fact material to the risk;

and *Brooks-Scanlon O'Brien Co. v. Boston Ins. Co.*, [1919] 2 W.W.R. 129, 47 D.L.R. 93 (B.C.C.A.).

However, the Marine Insurance Act was enacted in England in 1906 and in British Columbia in 1925 and no reference is made in it to promissory representations. Arnould...discusses the fact that the Act omits reference to promissory representations and concluded that, whatever foundation there may have been for the doctrine before the Act, it has ceased to exist since the Act came into force.[104]

Justice Taggart continued that unless the underwriter could show that the representation was either as to a matter of fact (in which case it had to be substantially correct or the underwriters were entitled to avoid the risk) or as to a matter of expectation (in which case it had to be made in good faith), then the underwriter would be bound, since:

> If it was something other than those two kinds of representations, such as a promissory representation, it was not a representation on which the appellants [underwriters] could rest a refusal to indemnify the respondent.[105]

The judge noted that the agent had said that a survey had been done and that there were no recommendations — as this was a representation of fact, and was not substantially correct, the underwriters were entitled to avoid the contract.

Justice Craig also found that there was a factual representation that a survey had been done, that this was untrue and that the underwriters were therefore entitled to avoid the contract. He considered, however, what the effect would have been if there had simply been a representation that a survey *would be* done. He said that this was a promissory representation. He stated:

> Were it not for the provision of the Marine Insurance Act, therefore, I would, on the authority of the *Bailey* case, hold that all the appellants [underwriters] were entitled to avoid the contract because it is incontrovertible that Mr. Williams represented to each of the agents of the underwriters either that the ship had been surveyed or that it would be surveyed, and that such a representation was untrue because an independent survey had not been done. However, I think that s. 22 of the Marine Insurance Act does not provide for a promissory representation. There are only two types of representation, namely, a representation as to an existing fact or past event and a representation as to a matter of expectation or belief. *If an in-*

---

[104] *Ibid.*, at B.C.L.R. 276.
[105] *Ibid.*, at 277.

surer wants to have the benefit of a promissory representation, he must insist that it be a warranty.[106]

[Emphasis added]

He went on to quote from Arnould to the effect that in marine insurance since the *M.I.A. 1906*, as in other contracts, the doctrine of promissory representations no longer has effect.[107]

From this discussion, it would appear that if the underwriter wishes a "promissory representation" to have contractual significance, it should be embodied in the policy in the form of a warranty.[108]

4.5.3 Misrepresentation By the Broker

The *C.M.I.A.* places specific obligations of disclosure on the broker[109] and the broker's representations, or misrepresentations, will bind the insured.[110] The principles expressed in the *C.M.I.A.* were applied in the case of *Perry v. British America Fire and Life Assurance Co.*,[111] in which Chief Justice Robinson stated:

> I stated to the jury, that whatever the person assured was informed of that was material to the risk, he was bound to communicate to his agent; that Mr. Heward [the agent] therefore must be assumed to have known what the principal knew in regard to the ship's sailing (whether he did in fact know it or not), for that the insurers are not to be prejudiced by the fact of his employing an agent, and giving him defective instructions; there is no doubt the law is so.[112]

It follows that the broker has a responsibility not only to communicate information which is disclosed by the principal, but also to actively search out from his or her client information which the broker knows, or should know, would be considered material by a prudent underwriter.

Where an insurer denies liability based on misrepresentation and non-disclosure, the broker may well find itself joined as a defendant in an action brought by the insured. For example, in *Central Native Fishermen's Co-op. v. Commonwealth Insurance Co.*,[113] both the broker and the insurer were sued. Similarly, in *DeGroot v. J.T. O'Bryan & Co.*,[114] the plaintiff sued both the underwriters and the broker, but succeeded only against the former. The court

---

[106] *Ibid.*, at 281.

[107] *Ibid.*, at 282.

[108] See *McKenzie v. Corbett* (1883), Cass. S.C. 385 (S.C.C.), rev'g. (1882), 16 N.S.R. 50 (C.A.); *Seaman v. West* (1885), Cout. S.C. 723, Cass. S.C. 388 (S.C.C.), aff'g. (1884), 17 N.S.R. 207 (C.A.).

[109] See subss. 21(2) and (6) quoted above.

[110] Subsection 22(1).

[111] (1848), 4 U.C.Q.B. 330 (C.A.).

[112] (1848), 4 U.C.Q.B. 330 at 333 (C.A.).

[113] [1979] I.L.R. ¶1-1091 (B.C.S.C.).

[114] (1979), 15 B.C.L.R. 271, I.L.R. ¶1-1152 (C.A.), rev'g. [1977] I.L.R. ¶564 (B.C.S.C.).

ordered, however, that the plaintiff could recover from the underwriter the costs awarded in favour of the broker.[115]

4.6 AVOIDANCE OF THE CONTRACT

Sections 20, 21(7) and 22(8) of the *C.M.I.A.* give the insurer the right to "avoid" the contract in the event of breach of the duty of good faith, material non-disclosure or material misrepresentation. The contract is not automatically void, it is voidable. The insurer has an *election* whether to treat the policy as subsisting or to set it aside — to rescind it. An insurer wishing to avoid the contract must do so reasonably promptly after becoming aware of the facts. The insurer must also avoid any conduct which could be construed as an affirmation of the contract or a waiver of the misrepresentation or non-disclosure. In *Smith v. Royal Canadian Insurance Co.*,[116] the following statement of Justice Weatherbe, who dissented in the Appeal Division, was approved in the Supreme Court of Canada:

> Any concealment of material fact puts it into the underwriter's power to repudiate the contract. But he may, with full knowledge of that fraudulent concealment, elect to continue it - or rather, as the law regards it, elect not to avoid it. If he delivers a policy with a view to carry out the contract, without the knowledge that anything was withheld, he is unquestionably not to be estopped by that act, and it is clear that he can never be bound under any circumstances short of disclosure of the fraud and waiver or election by him with full knowledge of everything.[117]

Where the insurer elects to avoid the contract, it is required to refund the premium, except in the case of fraud.[118]

In *McDonald v. Doull*,[119] the Supreme Court of Canada held that the insurers, by canceling the policy for misrepresentation as to the amount of "other insurance", but retaining the premium up to the date of cancellation, could not contend that the policy had been cancelled at an earlier date. The policy was cancelled on February 21, 1871, and the premium up to that date was retained. It was later determined that the vessel had sunk on February 20. Although the report is very brief, it appears to support the conclusion that the insurer was estopped from contending that the insurance was not in effect on the date of the loss.

In *Harold A. Berner and Bradley Finance Ltd. v. Sun Insurance Office Ltd.*,[120] the insurer alleged that the policy was voidable due to non-disclosure. The court

---

[115] See Chapter 23, *The Marine Insurance Broker*.

[116] (1884), Cout. S.C. 723, Cass. S.C. 386 (S.C.C.), rev'g. (1884), 17 N.S.R. 322 (C.A.).

[117] (1884), 17 N.S.R. 322 at 329 (C.A.).

[118] See, for example, *Neepawa Yacht Ltd. v. Laurentian P. & C. Insurance Co.* (1994), D.R.S. 95-04330 (B.C.S.C.). The report contains a reproduction of the "avoidance letter" sent by the underwriters.

[119] (1878), 12 N.S.R. 276 (C.A.), rev'd. Cass. S.C. 384.

[120] [1952] I.L.R ¶1-069 at 287 (Ont. S.C.J.).

held that the failure to return the premium was evidence that the insurer had not exercised its right to avoid the policy and it therefore remained bound:

> It follows that if the policy were void from the date of its issue by reason of lack of good faith or because of failure to disclose material circumstances, then the premium paid by the plaintiff should have been returned, pursuant to sec. 85 of *The Marine Insurance Act*, as I find that there was no fraud or illegality on the part of the plaintiff or his agents. Failure to return the premium on receiving the report of their adjuster is further evidence that the defendant did not rely on their rights, if any, under section 18 and 19(1) of *The Marine Insurance Act* and elect to avoid the contract of insurance.[121]

If the insurer has proper grounds to avoid the policy on the basis of non-disclosure, it follows that the policy has never been in effect, and the insured can be required to repay any losses which have been previously paid by underwriters.[122]

4.7 THE CONSEQUENCES OF FRAUD

Since even an innocent non-disclosure or misrepresentation will entitle the underwriter to avoid the policy, it is obvious that a fraudulent non-disclosure or misrepresentation will have the same effect. In *Intermunicipal Realty & Development Corp. v. Gore Mutual Insurance Co.*,[123] Mr. Justice Collier of the Trial Division of the Federal Court of Canada found that there had been a fraudulent misrepresentation as to the management of the vessel: "It was wilfully made to deceive an underwriter, in order to induce him to take on the risk."[124] The judge accepted that the standard of proof was on the balance of probabilities but said that "there are degrees of probability or proof within that standard."[125] After referring to leading cases in England and Canada on the subject,[126] he stated:

> To endeavour to pin the badge of fraud on the plaintiff here, is to make a serious allegation:
>
> > The more serious the allegation, the higher the degree of probability that is required; but it need not, in a civil case, reach the very high standard required by the criminal law.

---

[121] *Ibid.*, at 293.
[122] See *Neepawa Yacht Ltd. v. Laurentian P. & C. Insurance Co.* (1994), D.R.S. 95-04330 (B.C.S.C.).
[123] [1981] 1 F.C. 151, 112 D.L.R. (3d) 432 (T.D.).
[124] *Ibid.*, at 438.
[125] *Ibid.*, at 439.
[126] *Hanes v. Wawanesa Mutual Insurance Co.*, [1963] S.C.R. 154, 36 D.L.R. (2d) 718; *Bater v. Bater*, [1950] 2 All E.R. 458.

The defendants have, in my view, met the heavy onus required of them.[127]

Justice Collier then considered whether the underwriters were required to return the premium. After reviewing the law, he concluded that in a case of fraud the underwriters were entitled to retain the premium:

> Nevertheless, I propose to follow the traditional view: that in cases of fraud, in respect of a contract of marine insurance, the premium need not be returned. The cases discussed have stood for a very long time. Their authority and rationale have not heretofore been questioned. The marine industry, and the marine insurance field have, for many years, accepted the principle. The doctrine is implicit in the Marine Insurance Acts.[128]

The judge stated that if he had found the premium returnable, he would have deducted from it the costs incurred by the underwriters in investigating the claim, as those expenses would never have been incurred, but for the actions of the insured. He would not, however, have deducted the broker's commission, as this was a "matter arranged between the underwriter and the broker".[129]

4.8   BURDEN OF PROOF AND EVIDENCE

4.8.1   Burden of Proof

The burden of proof of misrepresentation or non-disclosure is on the underwriter who seeks to avoid the contract. It has been said that the burden is a heavy one:

> Where payment of a risk is resisted on the ground of representation it ought indeed to be made very clear that there has been such a misrepresentation.[130]

In *Central Native Fishermen's Co-op. v. Commonwealth Insurance Co.*,[131] it was admitted by counsel for the insurer that the onus was on the defendant to show that the insured or its agent failed to comply with the disclosure sections of the statute. Counsel for the broker submitted that the onus was on the insurer to prove "very clearly"[132] that there had been a misrepresentation or non-disclosure and this onus was admitted by counsel for the underwriter. The trial judge concluded.

---

[127] [1981] 1 F.C. 151, 112 D.L.R. (3d) 432 at 439 (F.C.T.D.), quoting from G. Spencer Bower and A. Turner, *Actionable Misrepresentation*, 3rd ed. (Markham: Butterworths, 1974), para. 187, pp. 210-11.

[128] *Ibid.*, at 141-42. A similar result was reached in Canada as early as *McFaul v. Montreal Inland Insurance Co.* (1845), 2 U.C.Q.B. 59 (App. Div.), in which it was stated at 61-62: "As to the return of the premium, it does not seem to have been claimed as an alternative at the trial; and if it had been, the more modern decisions seem to be against its return, where there has been actual fraud, as there seems to have been here."

[129] *Ibid.*, at 443.

[130] *Nova Scotia Marine Insurance Co. v. Stevenson* (1894), 23 S.C.R. 137, *per* King J. at 139, citing *Davies v. National Fire and Marine Insurance Co. of New Zealand*, [1891] A.C. 485.

[131] [1979] I.L.R. ¶1-1091 at 147 (B.C.S.C.).

[132] *Ibid.*, at 164, citing *Davies v. National Fire and Marine Insurance Co. of New Zealand*, [1891] A.C. 485.

...I am of the view that Commonwealth has failed to satisfy the onus of proving, by a preponderance of evidence, that neither the plaintiff nor its agent met the duty to disclose as imposed upon them by the *Marine Insurance Act.*[133]

In *Riverside Landmark Corp. v. Northumberland General Insurance Co.,*[134] it was accepted by all parties that the underwriters bore the onus of proof. The trial judge stated: "The onus is on the defendant to show that it is not liable to answer under the policy."[135]

4.8.2 Evidence

An important practical question in the trial of non-disclosure or misrepresentation cases is whether it is necessary to put the *actual underwriter* in the witness box or whether it is sufficient to simply call evidence of expert witnesses, to establish the standard of the "prudent underwriter". Clearly, the approach taken by the House of Lords in *Pine Top* requires that the *actual* underwriter give evidence. In Canada, the usual modern practice in misrepresentation and non-disclosure cases has been to have the underwriter testify, to explain what the effect of the information was or would have been on his or her thought process and to explain why the information was material.[136] It is also common for both parties to introduce expert evidence to establish the standard of behaviour of the "prudent underwriter".

Putting the actual underwriter in the witness box exposes him or her to cross-examination and requires the underwriter to show that he or she was not guilty of sloppy or speculative underwriting and is not attempting to hide behind the after-the-fact wisdom of the hypothetical "reasonable underwriter". In essence,

---

[133] *Ibid.,* at 166.

[134] (1984) 8 C.C.L.I. 118 (Ont. H.C.J.).

[135] [1979] I.L.R. ¶1-1091. It appears to be generally accepted that the underwriter bears onus of proof on all the issues, including, for example, the materiality of the information: see *Amo Containers Ltd. v. Drake Insurance Co. Ltd.* (1984), 8 C.C.L.I. 97, 51 Nfld. & P.E.I.R. 55 (Nfld. S.C.), *per* Goodridge J. at 60.

[136] See, for example, *James Yachts Ltd. v. Thames and Mersey Marine Insurance Co. Ltd.,* [1976] I.L.R. ¶1-751 at 141; *Central Native Fishermen's Co-op. v. Commonwealth Insurance Co.,* [1979] I.L.R. ¶1-1091 at 147 (B.C.S.C.); *DeGroot v. J.T. O'Bryan & Co.* (1979), 15 B.C.L.R. 271, [1979] I.L.R. ¶1-1152 at 416 (C.A.), rev'g. [1977] I.L.R. ¶1-863 at 564 (B.C.S.C.); *Century Insurance Co. of Canada v. Case Existological Laboratories Ltd.,* [1983] 2 S.C.R. 47, 150 D.L.R. (3d) 9, rev'g. (1980), 116 D.L.R. (3d) 199 (S.C.), aff'g. (1982), 35 B.C.L.R. 364; *Riverside Landmark Corp. v. Northumberland General Insurance Co.* (1984), 8 C.C.L.I. 119 (Ont. H.C.); *Biggin v. British Marine Mutual Insurance Assn.* (1992), 101 Nfld. & P.E.I.R. 156, 14 C.C.L.I. (2d) 66 (Nfld. S.C. T.D.); *Neepawa Yacht Ltd. v. Laurentian P. & C. Insurance Co.* (1994), D.R.S. 95-04330 (B.C.S.C.); *Nuvo Electronics Inc. v. London Assurance* (2000), 49 O.R. (3d) 374, 19 C.C.L.I. (3d) 195 (S.C.J.), additional reasons at (2000), 23 C.C.L.I. (3d) 231 (S.C.J.), appeal withdrawn, Jan. 28, 2002, Ontario Court of Appeal.

it prevents the unreasonable underwriter from benefiting from the wisdom and prudence of the "reasonable underwriter".[137]

In the British Columbia Supreme Court case of *Neepawa Yacht Ltd. v. Laurentian P. & C. Insurance Co.*,[138] the issue facing the court was the materiality of prior losses which had not been disclosed. The defendant insurer called expert evidence, which the trial judge described as "a considerable body of affidavit evidence in the nature of expert evidence from a number of underwriters not employed by the defendant company". These witnesses testified that the insured's claims record would have been considered material.[139] In addition, employees of the defendant, both the underwriter and the marine manager, deposed that full disclosure would have led the underwriter to either decline the risk, or to increase the premium and the deductible. In finding for the insurer, the court was particularly influenced by the evidence of the impartial underwriters, who considered that the undisclosed losses were material.

In light of the practice in Canada, and the persuasive reasoning of the majority of the House of Lords in *Pine Top*, the failure, without a good explanation, to call the actual underwriter could, at best, lead the court to conclude that the underwriter's evidence would not be helpful to the insurer. A judge would be entitled to draw an adverse inference from the underwriter's failure to testify. At worst, the court could conclude that the underwriter had failed to discharge the burden of proving that the information, or absence thereof, had made a difference to the underwriting decision.

Having said this, there remains an important place for the expert witness in such cases. The evidence of an expert will be of importance to the court in considering the materiality of the information, including whether or not it would have an "influence" (in whatever sense the term is used) on the decision to accept the risk and on what terms. An expert could also provide important evidence on other issues, such as whether the information in question would be the type of information a prudent underwriter would know or whether it is information that would be in the insured's ambit of special knowledge. The role of an expert is, of course, circumscribed by well-defined limits. It is not up to the expert to express conclusions of law or, as it is sometimes said, to answer the very question for the court to decide. In *Cleveland v. Sunderland Marine Mutual Insurance Co.*,[140] the expert evidence may have gone too far. The witness appears to have expressed an opinion, based on his experience as an underwriter, that the insured breached his contract. The court stated:

> Many of [the expert's] opinions in that regard were properly conclusions of law which were allowed into evidence on the restricted basis that they might be of

---

[137] See *Amo Containers Ltd. v. Drake Insurance Co. Ltd.* (1984), 8 C.C.L.I. 97, 51 Nfld. & P.E.I.R. 55 (Nfld. S.C.), where the court did not accept the evidence of the actual underwriter, although it appears that no expert evidence was called in that case.

[138] (1994), D.R.S. 95-04330 (B.C.S.C.).

[139] Extracts from two of the expert witness affidavits filed in that case are contained in the law report.

[140] (1987), 81 N.S.R. (2d) 1, 203 A.P.R. 1, 45 D.L.R. (4th) 340 (S.C.T.D.), additional reasons at (1987), 85 N.S.R. (2d) 42, 216 A.P.R. 42 (N.S.S.C.).

some help to the Court. However, the Court is quite capable of evaluating the evidence, ascertaining the applicable law, and reaching an appropriate decision without the help of an expert witness.[141]

4.9 CONCLUSION

The principle of the utmost good faith was designed primarily to ensure that the underwriter possessed the same information as the insured, so that a fair bargain could be struck between them. The strict consequences of non-disclosure or misrepresentation were intended as an inducement to candour. Considering the unique nature of insurance as a "contract on speculation", the principle and its consequences could be justified in an age when news travelled as slowly as ships. Can it be justified today?

There have been significant changes in the shipping and insurance businesses since 1766 when *Carter v. Boehm* was decided, and since the *M.I.A. 1906* was enacted. One of the most important changes is the proliferation of "information" and the speed at which information can be accessed and communicated. Insurers have at their fingertips an array of information concerning ships and cargos and they have an international intelligence network of agencies to serve as their eyes and ears in ports all around the world. Organizations such as the Salvage Association and Lloyd's Agents can provide on-the-spot information to underwriters.

One result of the technological revolution, therefore, is that some of the uncertainties and risks have gone out of the marine insurance business, but it remains fundamentally a business of risk-taking. When a risk is presented to the underwriter, his or her concerns are not simply whether to accept it, but what terms and conditions to offer, whether to impose a deductible, how much premium to charge and what percentage of the risk to accept. In reaching a decision on these important questions, the underwriter is required to assess or evaluate the risk.

This process involves the application of the underwriter's experience and knowledge to the set of facts presented on behalf of the insured. Sometimes it requires simply an analysis of the information submitted by the broker, but often it requires the collection and examination of other information obtained by the insured, the broker and the underwriter. It may happen, for example, that the insurer will require that the prospective insured complete some form of application, although this is not always the case in commercial marine insurance. The broker may present information to the insurer and the insurer may ask additional questions or raise concerns which the broker or the insured will attempt to address. The process is interactive. The insurer may request specific information, such as an up-to-date survey of the vessel to be insured. Finally, the insurer may consult sources of information such as texts, charts, meteorological records and the like, to obtain information concerning the voyage, the cargo and, generally, the risks to which the insured property may be exposed.

---

[141] *Ibid.*, at N.S.R. 13.

The process will work most efficiently and effectively if the insurer is able to obtain the most accurate and complete information concerning the risk, at the least cost. In theory, this will allow the insurer to fix a premium which best reflects the risks involved. In *Coronation Insurance Co. v. Taku Air Transport Ltd.*,[142] Justice Cory indicated that in private insurance contracts, including specifically marine insurance contracts, it is appropriate that detailed information concerning the particular characteristics of the vessel or cargo be provided by the insured, as these are most likely within the particular knowledge of the insured. In most cases, this is the most cost-effective and efficient means as well.

One of the difficulties facing the courts in non-disclosure cases is that avoidance is an all-or-nothing proposition. If the insured has breached the duty of "good faith" by misrepresentation or non-disclosure, the contract can be avoided — there is no middle ground. This drastic result has perhaps made judges understandably reluctant to give effect to the remedy in all but the clearest cases. Justice Gonthier of the Supreme Court of Canada in *Canadian Indemnity Co. v. Canadian Johns-Manville Co.* pointed out the considerations on both sides of the issue:

> The taking on of an insurance risk is made very difficult if the insurer cannot rely on the full and fair disclosure of the insured regarding facts material to the risk. Without such information, the insurer will be unable properly to decide whether to accept the risk and, if so, at what rate to set the premium. It would be unfair to require the insurer to take on the risk without all the relevant facts.
>
> Likewise, it must be said that the consequences of the annulment of an insurance contract are very serious for the insured. The insured has almost certainly relied on the validity of the contract and cannot at a later date acquire coverage for a risk which is now perhaps realised. Accordingly, it is in the interests of stability of such contracts that the insured be able to rely on the diligence and professionalism of the insurer so as to avoid having the insurance contract annulled on the basis of facts which were not disclosed but which should have been notorious to the insurer had it acquired the level of knowledge of a reasonably competent underwriter.
>
> ...
>
> Clearly, both parties are required by law to treat the contract of insurance as an *uberrimae fidei* contract. The insured will disclose fully and fairly or face the annulment of the contract, and the prudent insurer will ensure that it acquires a good knowledge of the industry which it insures or fail to do so at its peril.[143]

It should be noted as well that there is a difference between the communication of information by the insured and the assessment of that information by the underwriter. The insured has a duty to do the former, but it is the underwriter's

---

[142] [1991] 3 S.C.R. 622, [1992] 1 W.W.R. 217.
[143] [1990] 2 S.C.R. 549, 72 D.L.R. (4th) 478 at 529-30.

responsibility to do the latter. The difference is illustrated by *Century Insurance Company of Canada v. Case Existological Laboratories Ltd.*,[144] in which the trial judge had blamed the insured for failing to communicate the special risk to the underwriter: "The underwriter cannot be faulted for failing to provide the appropriate coverage when he was not made aware of the special risk inherent in the operation of this vessel."[145] In contrast, Justice Lambert in the British Columbia Court of Appeal blamed the underwriter for failing to properly assess the information which had been supplied to him:

> Following disclosure to him of every material circumstance, the underwriter is re-quired to assess the risk. In his own admission, Mr. Barber, for the lead under-writer in this case, reached an incorrect assessment of the risk. But that does not mean that the material circumstances were not disclosed to him. In my opinion any defect in the telephone communications between the underwriter and the marine surveyor was a defect in relation to the assessment of the risks by the underwriter and not a defect in relation to disclosure of a material circumstance by the as-sured.[146]

In dealing with "good faith" cases, the courts will try to strike a fair balance between the duties resting on the insured and the broker to make sure that information concerning the risk is fairly communicated to the underwriter and the duty resting on the underwriter to exercise reasonable care, in the discharge of its own business.

---

[144] [1990] 2 S.C.R. 549, 72 D.L.R. (4th) 478.

[145] (1980), 116 D.L.R. (3d) 199 at 206.

[146] (1982), 133 D.L.R. (3d) 727 at 739.

Chapter 5

Insurable Interest

5.1 INTRODUCTION

An insured must have an "insurable interest" in the subject-matter of the insurance at the time of the loss in order to recover under the policy. The insured must stand to lose something more than the premium if the property is lost or damaged. Without this requirement, insurance would be little more than a wager. In the early, more free-wheeling days of English marine insurance, some insurers engaged in a form of wagering, accepting premiums from gamblers who had no insurable interest in the insured "risk". Early marine insurance legislation was designed to prevent this dangerous and immoral activity.[1] With cheaper and more lucrative forms of gambling available today, this concern has diminished and a "wagering" contract of marine insurance would be unlikely. Cases on insurable interest, once the source of extensive litigation in England and Canada,[2] have become relatively rare. Moreover, the courts have adopted a broad definition of insurable interest, recognizing that it is in the interests of insurers and insureds to do so.

---

[1]   See the *Marine Insurance Act, 1745* (U.K.), 19 Geo. II, c. 37. This statute was repealed by the English *Marine Insurance Act ("M.I.A. 1906")*, (U.K.), 6 Edw. VII, c. 41, which contained its own prohibition against gaming contracts. Subsection 18(1) of the Canadian *Marine Insurance Act ("C.M.I.A")*, S.C. 1993, c. 22 provides that every contract by way of gaming or wagering is void; subs. 18(2) provides that a contract is deemed to be a contract by way of gaming or wagering if, among other things, the insured has no insurable interest and the contract is concluded with no expectation of acquiring such an interest.

[2]   See *Gerow v. Providence Washington Insurance Co.* (1889), 28 N.B.R. 435 (C.A.), aff'd. (1890), 17 S.C.R. 387; *Grant v. Aetna Insurance Co.* (1860), 11 Low. Can. R. 128 (S.C.), aff'd. on other grounds (1861), 11 Low. Can. R. 330 (C.A.), rev'd. (1862), 15 Moo. P.C. 516, 1 E.R. 589, 12 Low. Can. R. 386; *Browning v. Provincial Insurance Co. of Canada* (1873), 5 L.R.P.C. 263 (an agent can make an insurance contract for a principal and the principal is entitled to step in and sue in his or her own name); *Heard v. Marine Insurance Co.* (1873), 1 P.E.I. 428; *Lord v. Grant* (1875), 10 N.S.R. 120 (C.A.); *Moore v. Home Insurance Co.* (1873), 23 U.C.C.P. 383 (C.A.); *Scatcherd v. Equitable Fire Insurance Co.* (1859), 8 U.C.C.P. 415 (C.A.); *Wandlyn Motels Ltd. v. Commerce General Insurance Co.* (1968), 1 D.L.R. (3d) 392, 1 N.B.R. (2d) 213 (N.B.S.C. App. Div.), [1970] S.C.R. 992, 12 D.L.R. (3d) 605. In *Desrosiers v. Régime d'assurance des bateaux de pêche* (1994), 87 F.T.R. 101, it was held that the plaintiff, the daughter of the deceased, had an interest as heir and was entitled to sue on the policy; see also *Macaura v. Northern Assurance Co.*, [1925] A.C. 619.

The principle is set out in section 8 of the Canadian *Marine Insurance Act* ("*C.M.I.A.*"):[3]

8(1) Subject to this Act, a person who has an interest in a marine adventure has an insurable interest.

(2) A person has an interest in a marine adventure if the person has a legal or equitable relation to the adventure, or to any insurable property at risk in the adventure, and may benefit from the safety or due arrival of insurable property, may be prejudiced by its loss, damage or detention or may incur liability in respect of it.

The *C.M.I.A.* then lists a number of specific interests that are insurable, such as the interest of the master and crew in their wages,[4] the interest of a lender of money on the security of the ship or its cargo,[5] the interest of the mortgagor in the full value of the property and of the mortgagee in any sum due or to become due under the mortgage[6] and in the vessel to the amount of the mortgage.[7]

The insured has an insurable interest in the premium that it has paid for the insurance and may insure that premium.[8] It is usual for the seller under a cost insurance freight (C.I.F.) sale to insure the insurance costs as part of the sale price of the goods. The insurable value of a ship includes the value of insurance on the ship.[9]

The insurer has an insurable interest in the risk insured and may reinsure that risk and frequently does so.[10] The underlying insured has no interest in the reinsurance contract and no right to claim under it.

A partial interest of any nature is an insurable interest.[11]

The insured must have an insurable interest in the subject-matter insured at the time of the loss, but need not have such an interest at the time the contract is concluded.[12]

The leading Canadian case on the subject of insurable interest — a non-marine case — is the decision of the Supreme Court of Canada in *Kosmopolous*

---

[3] S.C. 1993, c. 22.

[4] *C.M.I.A.*, s. 11.

[5] *Ibid.*, s. 15; see *Clark v. Scottish Imperial Insurance Co.* (1879), 4 S.C.R. 192: the lender of money on a vessel in the course of construction on the faith of a verbal agreement that on completion of the vessel it would be placed in his hands for sale, out of which the loan would be repaid, had an equitable interest that was insurable. Any interest that would be recognized by a court of law or equity was an insurable interest.

[6] *C.M.I.A.*, s. 16. See *Pritchard v. Merchants Marine Insurance Co.* (1887), 26 N.B.R. 232 (C.A.); *Anchor Marine Insurance Co. v. Keith* (1884), 9 S.C.R. 483, aff'g. (1882), 15 N.S.R. 402 (C.A.); *Troop v. Mosier* (1876), 1 R.E.D. 189 (N.S.C.A.); *Richardson v. Home Insurance Co.* (1871), 21 U.C.C.P. 291 (C.A.); *Crawford v. St. Lawrence Insurance Co.* (1851), 8 U.C.Q.B. 135 (C.A.)

[7] *Crawford v. St. Lawrence Insurance Co.* (1851), 8 U.C.Q.B. 135 (C.A.).

[8] *C.M.I.A.*, s. 13.

[9] *Ibid.*, subs. 19(1)(*a*). See Chapter 6, *Insurable Value.*

[10] *Ibid.*, s. 14. See Chapter 17, *Reinsurance.*

[11] *Ibid.*, s. 10.

[12] *Ibid.*, subs. 7(1).

v. Constitution Insurance Co. of Canada.[13] Mr. Kosmopolous had for some years owned a leather goods business that he operated as a sole proprietorship under the name "Spring Leather Goods". On the advice of his lawyer, and in order to protect his personal assets, he incorporated a company, "Kosmopolous Leather Goods Limited", and transferred the assets of the business to the company. He obtained a fire insurance policy describing the insured as "Andreas Kosmopolous, O/A Spring Leather Goods". This was inaccurate, since it was the company and not Kosmopolous that owned the business, although Mr. Kosmopolous was the sole shareholder. A fire in the adjoining premises caused fire, water and smoke damage to the assets of the company and to its rented premises. Mr. Kosmopolous' claim under the policy was declined, on the basis that he had no insurable interest in the subject-matter of the insurance — the insured property was owned by the company and not by him. Under a long-standing line of authority in England and Canada he, as a shareholder, had no interest in the assets of the company.[14] Mr. Kosmopolous sued both his insurer and his insurance agent. He succeeded against the insurer in the Ontario High Court and in the Court of Appeal, but the insurers appealed to the Supreme Court of Canada.

The Supreme Court was faced with two principles of law that, on the facts of the case, resulted in an inequity. On the insurance law side, it had been settled law for at least two centuries that no one could claim under a policy of insurance unless he or she had an insurable interest in the subject-matter of the insurance.[15] On the company law side, it was well established by the House of Lords in *Salomon v. Salomon & Co.*[16] that a shareholder has no legal or equitable interest in the company's assets. Mr. Kosmopolous' lawyer asked the court to solve the problem by "lifting the corporate veil", that is, by looking behind the corporate structure of the company to find its true ownership — clearly Mr. Kosmopolous himself. The Supreme Court of Canada refused to "lift the corporate veil":

> Having chosen to receive the benefits of incorporation, he should not be allowed to escape its burdens. He should not be permitted to "blow hot and cold" at the same time...I would not lift the corporate veil in this case. The company was a legal entity distinct from Mr. Kosmopolous. It, and not Mr. Kosmopolous, legally owned the assets of the business.[17]

Instead, the Supreme Court of Canada decided to reform the law of insurable interest. Madam Justice Wilson stated:

---

[13]   [1987] 1 S.C.R. 2, 34 D.L.R. (4th) 208, aff'g. (1983), 42 O.R. (2d) 428, 149 D.L.R. (3d) 77 (C.A.), aff'g. [1981] I.L.R. ¶1-1449 at 539 (Ont. H.C.J.).

[14]   *Salomon v. Salomon & Co.*, [1897] A.C. 22.

[15]   *Lucena v. Crauford* (1806), 2 Bos. & Pul. (N.R.) 269.

[16]   [1897] A.C. 22.

[17]   *Kosmopolous v. Constitution Insurance Co. of Canada*, [1987] 1 S.C.R. 2 at 11-12, 34 D.L.R. (4th) 208, aff'g. (1983), 42 O.R. (2d) 428, 149 D.L.R. (3d) 77 (C.A.), aff'g. [1981] I.L.R. ¶1-1449 at 539 (Ont. H.C.J.).

In my view, there is little to commend the restrictive definition of insurable interest....It is merely a "technical objection...which has no real merit...as between the
assured and the insurer." The reasons advanced in its favour are not persuasive and
the policies alleged to underlie it would not appear to require it...if an insured can
demonstrate..."some relation to, or concern in the subject of the insurance, which
relation or concern by the happening of the perils insured against may be so affected as to produce a damage, detriment or prejudice to the person insuring", that
insured should be held to have sufficient interest. To "have a moral certainty of
advantage or benefit, but for those risks or dangers" or "to be so circumstanced
with respect to [the subject matter of the insurance] as to have benefit from its existence, prejudice from its destruction" is to have an insurable interest in it.[18]

The court rejected a more narrow definition of insurable interest that had
been applied in its earlier decisions.

The Supreme Court of Canada clearly felt that the requirement of insurable
interest was being raised as a technical defence and that reform of the law was
necessary to prevent injustice. Justice Wilson stated:

A broadening of the concept of insurable interest would, it seems to me, allow for
the creation of more socially beneficial insurance policies than is the case at present with no increase in risk to the insurer.[19]

On a practical level, what this means is that if someone takes out a policy of
insurance, and pays the premium, and has an "interest" in the property at the
time of the loss, such that he or she can demonstrate prejudice from the loss or
destruction of the property, the court will generally find that an insurable interest
exists.[20]

5.2 CARGO INSURANCE

A buyer of goods has an insurable interest even though he or she might have
elected to reject the goods or to treat them as being at the seller's risk.[21] A seller
has an insurable interest in the goods and may insure them, but in order to
recover must show that he or she had an insurable interest in the goods at the
time of the loss. If the seller has parted with all interest in the goods, and is

---

[18]   *Ibid.*, at 29-30.

[19]   *Ibid.*, at 17.

[20]   In *Guarantee Co. of North America v. Aqua-Land Exploration Ltd.*, [1966] S.C.R. 133, 54
D.L.R. (2d) 229, rev'g. [1964] 2 O.R. 181, 44 D.L.R. (2d) 645 (C.A.), aff'g. [1963] 1 O.R. 220,
36 D.L.R. (2d) 536 (H.C.J.), a case decided 20 years prior to *Kosmopolous v. Constitution
Insurance Co. of Canada*, the Supreme Court of Canada adopted a more restrictive approach to
insurable interest. The court held that the plaintiff, which had entered into an agreement to form
a company to purchase a drilling tower, did not have an insurable interest in the tower, which
had been destroyed while in the course of delivery by the seller to the buyer. The court said that
while a contractual right could give rise to an insurable interest, the plaintiff company did not
have such a right.

[21]   *C.M.I.A.*, subs. 9(2).

merely awaiting payment, he or she may have no insurable interest.[22] The consignee of goods may have an insurable interest in the goods, but only to the extent of his or her interest.[23]

In *Green Forest Lumber Ltd. v. General Security Insurance Co. of Canada*,[24] the plaintiff had entered into a contract with the Canadian International Development Agency to sell lumber to Tunisian purchasers. The terms of sale were C.I.F. Tunisian ports. The lumber was bought by the plaintiff from another Canadian company "F.O.B. ["free on board"] stowed ship". While the cargo was being loaded, the ship broke from its moorings and ran aground, sustaining damage and resulting in damage to the cargo by seawater. A claim was made under the cargo insurance policy. The insurer denied the claim on a number of grounds, including that the plaintiff had no insurable interest in the cargo at the time of the loss. While the plaintiff's claim was dismissed on other grounds, the trial judge also dealt with the issue of insurable interest. He noted that until the lumber was on board, it was at the risk of the suppliers, since the plaintiff's contract with them was "F.O.B. stowed ship". In dealing with the plaintiff's interest, the judge stated:

> In so far as the Tunisian consignees were concerned, the contract with them was c.i.f. (cost, insurance and freight). This allows risk to pass when shipment is ready and on transfer of the documents, the vendor being able to obtain payment of the goods before their arrival at their destination and even when they are lost in transit. The risk on shipment passes to the buyer even though he may still have the right to reject the goods on arrival, if they are not in accordance with the terms of the contract.
>
> In my view, however, there might in certain circumstances be a distinction drawn between the case of a purchaser contracting for a shipment of goods or of a specific cargo on a c.i.f. basis and that of a purchaser contracting to buy quantity of goods c.i.f., which may be sent in as many loads or shipments as the vendor might decide. In the former case, the risk does not pass to the buyer until the ship is completely loaded and the cargo contracted for complete, while in the latter, the risk might very well be held to pass as each part of the total amount of goods purchased is loaded aboard a ship for shipment to the purchaser.
>
> For the purpose of deciding the issue in the present case, it is not necessary to find when the property in the lumber passed to the purchaser for, although property and risk usually pass simultaneously, this does not apply to c.i.f. contracts and it has

---

[22] See *Outram v. Smith* (1876), 11 N.S.R. 187 (C.A.); *Pugh v. Wylde* (1876), 11 N.S.R. 177 (C.A.).

[23] See *Cusack v. Mutual Insurance Co.* (1862), 6 L.R. Jur. 97, 10 R.J.R.Q. 194; *Green Forest Lumber Ltd. v. General Security Insurance Co. of Canada*, [1977] 2 F.C. 351, [1977] I.L.R. 1-849 (T.D.), aff'd. [1978] 2 F.C. 773, [1978] I.L.R. 1-990 (C.A.), aff'd. [1980] 1 S.C.R. 176, 34 N.R. 303; *Merchants' Marine Insurance Co. of Canada v. Rumsey* (1884), 9 S.C.R. 577, aff'g. (1883), 16 N.S.R. 220 (C.A.); see also *Outram v. Smith* (1876), 11 N.S.R. 187 (C.A.); *Pugh v. Wylde* (1876), 11 N.S.R. 177 (C.A.).

[24] [1977] 2 F.C. 351, [1977] I.L.R. ¶1-849 (T.D.), aff'd. [1978] 2 F.C. 773, [1978] I.L.R. ¶1-990 (C.A.), aff'd. [1980] 1 S.C.R. 176, 34 N.R. 303.

been held that, where the policy has been assigned to him, the buyer may sue although he has no insurable interest in the goods at the time the damage occurred... The c.i.f. seller on the other hand cannot sue subsequently to shipment because he has no insurable interest in the goods...Where goods are not purchased afloat by the seller for shipment to the consignee, the seller must arrange for a contract of affreightment with the carrier and the cargo is shipped by the seller when loaded aboard the ship destined to carry it to the consignee, and the shipping documents are received from the carrier.[25]

The judge noted in this case that the contract with the Tunisian buyers called for the wood to be supplied "en deux tranches", which he held to mean "in two shipments". Since one shipment had already been shipped, until the balance of the lumber had been loaded on board the ship, "the lumber loaded aboard did not constitute a shipment and the risk did not pass to the purchaser. There, therefore, remained in the plaintiff until the entire cargo was loaded, an insurable interest in the lumber which had been stowed aboard and which was no longer at the risk of the mill owners...."[26] He held, therefore, that the plaintiff had an insurable interest in the cargo at the time of the loss.

The issue of insurable interest is most likely to arise in the case of cargo insurance and it becomes necessary to examine the terms of sale to determine the obligations and interests of the parties. The most common form of international sale contract is the "C.I.F." contract. The price paid by the buyer covers the invoice cost, the cost of insuring the goods in transit and the freight or transport charges. In practice, the seller usually fulfils its obligations to insure the goods either by declaring them under its open cargo policy (in the case of large exporters) or under an open policy held by the freight forwarder who arranged the shipment. In either case, the open policy will provide for the issuance of an insurance certificate, either by the seller or by the freight forwarder, to the buyer. The buyer then receives the shipping documents, generally consisting of the invoice, the insurance certificate and the bill of lading or other transport document. If the goods have become lost or damaged in transport, the buyer will then be able to make a claim under the insurance policy, which has, in legal terms, been "assigned" to it. The buyer can claim under the policy because it has an insurable interest in the goods, even though it did not have that interest when the insurance was taken out and because it holds the policy of insurance as "assignee". The seller could not claim under the policy for two reasons — he or she has parted with an interest in the goods and he or she has parted with the insurance policy, having assigned it to the buyer.

In the case of an "F.O.B." contract, on the other hand, the sale terms require the seller to deliver the goods on board the ocean vessel, at which time transfer of title and risk to the buyer generally takes place. The buyer becomes responsible for all costs and risks from that point onward. Generally, the buyer insures the goods, on its own behalf, from the point of loading on board ship to the point of delivery. The seller has an insurable interest in the goods to the point of

---

25   [1977] 2 F.C. 351 at 361-62 (T.D.).
26   *Ibid.*, at 362.

loading and the buyer has an insurable interest thereafter. If damage occurs prior to this point (for example, before or during loading onto the ship at the port of origin), the buyer may have no insurable interest, since title has not passed and the buyer is not at risk. In the case of a C.I.F. contract, although the seller procures the insurance policy, as was noted in *Green Forest Lumber Ltd. v. General Security Insurance Co. of Canada*, the seller has no further interest in the goods after the shipment and therefore no right to claim. It is invariably necessary, however, to examine the precise terms of sale and the contract between the parties, to determine their intentions and obligations with respect to the transfer of title and risk.

Some open cargo policies also provide seller's interest insurance, to protect the unpaid seller against the commercial risk that the buyer will not pay for the goods. In the absence of such specific insurance, the unpaid seller has no right to claim under the insurance policy, even if the goods are lost or damaged and the purchase price is unpaid.[27]

5.3 FREIGHT INSURANCE

"Freight" in maritime terminology refers to the money paid for the hire of a ship or for the carriage of goods. Normally, freight is paid to the owner of the ship or to the person who has the right to the use and possession of the ship, often referred to as the "charterer". The owner of a vessel has an insurable interest in the freight or earnings of the vessel. Proof of the ownership of the vessel has been held to be *prima facie* evidence of an insurable interest in the freight.[28] Similarly, where the ship is under charter, the charterer has an insurable interest in the freight.

A person who has paid freight in advance has an insurable interest in the freight payment, provided the freight is not repayable in the event of loss.[29] Normally, freight is payable by the shipper "vessel lost or not lost", meaning that if the ship fails to complete its voyage freight is nevertheless payable. Accordingly, it is common for the shipper of goods to insure the cost of the freight as part of the "insurable value" of the goods.[30]

5.4 PROOF OF INTEREST

There was at one time a practice of issuing so-called "P.P.I." ("policy proof of interest") policies, in which the policy itself was taken as evidence of the insured's interest. The *C.M.I.A.*, like the English *Marine Insurance Act* ("*M.I.A.*

---

27 Assuming that the seller has parted with the insurance policy and has no interest in the goods.

28 See *Driscoll v. Millville Marine and Fire Insurance Co.* (1883), 23 N.B.R. 160 (C.A.), rev'd. on other grounds (1884), 11 S.C.R. 183; *Wylde v. Union Marine Insurance Co.* (1874), 1 R.E.D. 203 (N.S.T.D.), aff'd. (1875), 10 N.S.R. 205 (C.A.); *Orchard v. Aetna Insurance Co.* (1856), 5 U.C.C.P. 445 (C.A.); but see *Heard v. Marine Insurance Co.* (1873), 1 P.E.I. 428 to the effect that the freight must be specifically insured.

29 *C.M.I.A.*, s. 12.

30 See Chapter 18, *Cargo Insurance*, and subs. 19(1)(*c*) of the *C.M.I.A.*

1906"),[31] deems such contracts to be by way of gaming and wagering and therefore void.[32]

There was also a practice requiring the filing of specific proof of interest as part of a marine insurance claim.[33] This is not part of modern practice and a proof of claim form, which is usually required in the general insurance field, is not required either by the *C.M.I.A.* or by most policies. In a claim under a hull and machinery policy, particularly a claim for total loss or constructive total loss, evidence will generally be provided to show that the insured has title to the vessel and whether or not there are any mortgagees or other encumbrancers entitled to part of the proceeds. In cargo insurance, the commercial invoice and customs documents will usually be submitted to the insurer to prove insurable interest.

5.5 INSURANCE FOR WHOM IT MAY CONCERN

A person may take out marine insurance "for whom it may concern".[34] Subsection 16(2) of the *C.M.I.A.* provides:

> 16(2)   A mortgagee, consignee or other person who has an insurable interest in the subject-matter insured may insure on the person's own behalf, on behalf and for the benefit of any other interested person or both on the person's own behalf and on behalf and for the benefit of any other interested person.

Thus, it is common for marine cargo policies to be taken out "for the benefit of whom it may concern" or "for the account of concerned"[35] or "as its interest may appear".[36] The reasons were stated by Chief Justice Hagarty in *McCollum v. Aetna Insurance Co.*:

> The insertion of this clause ["for himself and whom it may concern"], which is introduced into all our common printed forms of policy, is of great importance, as without it no one could take advantage of the policy except the party expressly named in it; but by the aid of this clause any party may avail himself of the policy who can prove that he was really interested in the subject matter of the insurance

---

[31] (U.K.), 6 Edw. VII, c. 41.

[32] *C.M.I.A.*, subs. 18(2)(*b*).

[33] See *McGhee v. Phoenix Insurance Co.* (1889), 28 N.B.R. 45 (C.A.), rev'd. (1890), 18 S.C.R. 61; *Grant v. Aetna Insurance Co.* (1860), 11 Low. Can. R. 128 (S.C.), aff'd. on other grounds (1861), 11 Low. Can. R. 330 (C.A.), rev'd. (1862), 15 Moo. P.C. 516, 1 E.R. 589, 12 Low. Can. R. 386 (J.C.P.C.); *Robertson v. New Brunswick Marine Assurance Co.* (1856), 8 N.B.R. 333 (C.A.); *Watson v. Summers* (1842), 4 N.B.R. 62.

[34] See *McGhee v. Phoenix Insurance Co.* (1889), 28 N.B.R. 45 (C.A.), rev'd. (1890), 18 S.C.R. 61; *Cunard v. Nova Scotia Marine Insurance Co.* (1897), 29 N.S.R. 409 (C.A.).

[35] See *McGhee v. Phoenix Insurance Co.* (1889), 28 N.B.R. 45 (C.A.), rev'd. on other grounds (1890), 18 S.C.R. 61, where it was held that insurance on a ship "on account of whom concerned" permitted evidence to be given that the person who took out the insurance did so on behalf of himself in respect of his interest in the ship (which was a one-half interest) as well as on behalf of the firm (of which he was a shareholder), owning the other one-half interest.

[36] *Canadian S.K.F. Co. v. Royal Bank*, [1936] 2 D.L.R. 40, 10 M.P.R. 325 (N.S.C.A.), aff'g. [1935] 4 D.L.R. 526 (N.S.S.C.).

during the risk and at the time of loss, and that he was the person upon whose account the insurance was *bona fide* intended to be made.[37]

Where the policy contains such a provision, the plaintiff is entitled to prove that he or she is a party for whose benefit the insurance was placed and that he or she had an insurable interest in the property at the time of the loss.[38] This principle has allowed various parties to insure for the benefit "of whom it may concern", such as a boat builder who had transferred the boat to the purchaser, but who had not been fully paid;[39] a ship's husband and mortgagee;[40] a part-owner on behalf of the interest of all owners;[41] and an agent on behalf of a principal.[42] It is, however, particularly important in the case of cargo insurance since, as we have seen, such insurance is frequently procured by the seller for the benefit of the buyer.

5.6 INTEREST AT THE TIME OF THE LOSS

The *C.M.I.A.* does not require that the insured have an insurable interest at the time the insurance is taken out; it simply requires that the insured must be interested in the subject-matter of the insurance at the time of the loss. Section 7(1) states:

> 7(1) In order to recover under a contract for a loss, the insured must have an insurable interest in the subject-matter insured at the time of the loss, but need not have such an interest when the contract is concluded.

Again, this is important in the case of cargo insurance, where the buyer may have no interest in the goods at the time the policy is procured but acquires the interest at a later time.

5.7 INSURANCE "LOST OR NOT LOST"

Marine insurance practice, confirmed by the *C.M.I.A.*, permits insurance of a subject-matter "lost or not lost", meaning that the insured may recover even though his or her interest was acquired after the loss, provided he or she was not

---

[37] (1870), 20 U.C.C.P. 289 at 291 (C.A.), citing *Arnould on Insurance*, Vol. 1, sec. 19.

[38] *Merchants Marine Insurance Co. v. Barss* (1888), 15 S.C.R. 185, aff'g. (1887), 26 N.B.R. 339 (C.A.), where the court held that a part-owner of the vessel could insure the shares of other owners together with his own under the "for whom it may concern" provisions of the policy; *McCollum v. Aetna Insurance Co.* (1870), 20 U.C.C.P. 289 (C.A.); *Queen Insurance Co. v. Hoffar-Beeching Shipyards Ltd.*, [1932] 3 W.W.R. 240, 46 B.C.R. 233 (S.C.); *Seaman v. West* (1885), Cout. S.C. 723, Cass. S.C. 388, aff'g. (1884), 17 N.S.R. 207 (C.A.); *Banks v. Wilson* (1872), R.E.D. 210 (N.S.C.A.); *Dimock v. New Brunswick Marine Assurance Co.* (1849), 6 N.B.R. 398 (C.A.); *Cunard v. Nova Scotia Marine Insurance Co.* (1897), 29 N.S.R. 409 (C.A.).

[39] *Queen Insurance Co. v. Hoffar-Beeching Shipyards Ltd.*, [1932] 3 W.W.R. 240, 46 B.C.R. 233 (S.C.).

[40] *Seaman v. West* (1885), Cout. S.C. 723, Cass. S.C. 388, aff'g. (1884), 17 N.S.R. 207 (C.A.).

[41] *Banks v. Wilson* (1872), R.E.D. 210 (N.S.C.A.).

[42] *Dimock v. New Brunswick Marine Assurance Co.* (1849), 6 N.B.R. 398 (C.A.).

aware of the loss at the time the insurance contract was concluded.[43] In the days when ships went to sea for months or even years at a time and communication was limited to the post or word of mouth from other vessels, it was common for insurance to be placed "vessel lost or not lost", since the parties often had no means of knowing whether the vessel was, in fact, lost at the time the insurance contract was made. It is still common to insure "lost or not lost", and as long as the insured is acting in good faith, and has no knowledge of the loss, the insurance will be valid.

---

[43]   *C.M.I.A.*, subs. 7(2).

Chapter 6

Insurable Value

6.1 INTRODUCTION

We have seen that because marine insurance is a contract of indemnity, an insured who has no interest in the property insured has lost nothing and therefore has no right to an indemnity. Applying the same principle, an insured should only be compensated for what he or she has actually lost. But how is that loss to be determined? If the insured was free to insure the property for any amount, the indemnity received could greatly exceed the true value of the loss sustained. Marine insurance deals with this by two related concepts. The first is "insurable value" — the value at which property may be insured. The second concept is "measure of indemnity" — the extent of indemnity the insured is entitled to receive. This chapter deals with the first concept. Chapter 10 deals with the *Measure of Indemnity*.

A policy may be valued or unvalued. Where the policy is valued, an agreed value of the property is stated in the policy and is treated as conclusive between the insurer and the insured, except in the case of fraud. Where the policy is unvalued, no value is stated, and the value is determined by the rules set out in the Canadian *Marine Insurance Act ("C.M.I.A.")*.[1]

The "insurable value" of the property should not be confused with the "sum insured", which is the amount of insurance effected on the property, or with the insured value, which is the value of the property specified in a valued policy. For example, the owner of a ship with a market value of $1,000,000 may value it

---

[1] S.C. 1993, c. 22. Section 30 reads:

    (1) A marine policy may be a valued policy or an unvalued policy.

    (2) A marine policy is a valued policy if it specifies the agreed value of the subject-matter insured.

    (3) A marine policy is an unvalued policy if it does not specify the value of the subject-matter insured and, subject to the limit of the sum insured, leaves the value to be determined in accordance with section 19.

    (4) Subject to this Act, and in the absence of fraud, the value specified by a valued policy is, as between the insurer and the insured, conclusive of the insurable value of the subject-matter intended to be insured, regardless of whether any loss is a total loss or a partial loss.

    (5) Unless a valued policy otherwise provides, the value specified by the policy is not conclusive for the purpose of determining whether there has been a constructive total loss.

at $750,000 for the purposes of the insurance, but the underwriter may only be prepared to insure it for $500,000. The insurable value is $1,000,000, the insured value is $750,000 and the sum insured is $500,000. The property is underinsured to the extent of one-third of its insured value and the insured will be required to bear that proportion of any loss.

The rules for the determination of insurable value of different types of property are contained in section 19 of the *C.M.I.A.*:

> 19(1) Subject to any express provision of, or any value specified in, the marine policy, the insurable value of the subject-matter insured is
>
> > (*a*) in the case of insurance on a ship, the aggregate of the value of the ship at the commencement of the risk and the charges of insurance;
> >
> > (*b*) in the case of insurance on freight, whether paid in advance or not, the aggregate of the gross amount of the freight at the risk of the insured and the charges of insurance;
> >
> > (*c*) in the case of insurance on goods, the aggregate of the prime cost of the goods, the expenses of and incidental to shipping and the charges of insurance on those goods and expenses; and
> >
> > (*d*) in the case of insurance on any other subject-matter, the aggregate of the amount at the risk of the insured when the policy attaches and the charges of insurance.
>
> (2) For the purposes of paragraph 1(*a*), the value of a ship includes money advanced for officers' and crew's wages and other disbursements incurred to make the ship fit for the marine adventure contemplated by the marine policy.

These rules for the determination of the "insurable value" of property are statements of general principle and are expressed to be "subject to any express provision of, or any value specified in, the marine policy...". They may therefore be modified by the express terms of the policy or by any value stated in the policy. For example, while subsection 19(1)(*c*) provides that the insurable value of goods is essentially their cost insurance freight (C.I.F.) value, with no element of profit included, marine cargo policies commonly provide that the insured value of the cargo is to be calculated based on a percentage (typically 10 per cent) above the C.I.F. value, to compensate the owner for some loss of profits if the cargo is lost or damaged. The value of a ship, on the other hand, may depend upon a number of factors, including its market value, its value to the owner as a going concern, or its replacement cost. The *C.M.I.A.* does not specify which of these values is to be used for the purpose of determining "value" if the policy is not a valued one.

6.2 VALUED AND UNVALUED POLICIES

A valued policy states an agreed value of the property insured, often by using the words "valued at..." after the description of the property. Most hull and machinery insurance in Canada is underwritten in this manner.[2] Valued cargo

---

[2] See, for example, *Shearwater Marine Ltd. v. Guardian Insurance Co. of Canada* (1997), 29 B.C.L.R. (3d) 13 (S.C.), aff'd. (1998), 60 B.C.L.R. (3d) 37 (C.A.).

policies are also the norm.[3] Unvalued policies are usual only in the case of freight insurance. If the policy is unvalued, the insured will be required to prove the amount of the loss by evidence of the value of the property insured, applying the principles set out in section 19 of the *C.M.I.A.*[4]

6.3 AMOUNT INSURED

An insurer may be unwilling to insure the property for its full insurable value and may want the insured to take some of the risk of loss. Thus, in hull and machinery insurance, a vessel may be insured for an amount less than its value stated in the policy. The policy will state both the agreed value of the property and the amount of insurance on the property. To the extent of the difference, the insured will be a co-insurer. In the case of cargo insurance, property may be insured for more or less than its insurable value.

6.4 Conclusiveness of Valuation

Subsection 30(4) of the *C.M.I.A.* provides that the value stated in the policy, agreed between the insurer and the insured, will be taken as conclusive unless there is evidence of fraud.[5] The mere fact that there is a difference, even a

---

[3] See *James Richardson & Sons Ltd. v. Standard Marine Insurance Co.*, [1936] S.C.R. 573, 3 D.L.R. 513.

[4] *Williams v. Canada.* (1984), 7 C.C.L.I. 198 (F.C.T.D.). See also *Williams v. Atlantic Assurance Co.* (1932), 43 Ll. L. Rep. 177 (C.A.). In *James Richardson & Sons Ltd. v. Standard Marine Insurance Co.*, [1936] S.C.R. 573 at 588, 3 D.L.R. 513, Mr. Justice Cannon adopted the following statement from *Halsbury's Laws of England* (2nd ed.):

> A valued policy is one which specifies the agreed value of the subject-matter insured: an unvalued, or as it is frequently called, an open policy is one which does not specify the value of the subject-matter but, subject to the limit of the sum insured, leaves it to be subsequently ascertained.
>
> . . . . .
>
> The difference in legal effect between the two policies is that in the case of an unvalued policy the value of the subject-matter insured is not admitted but has to be subsequently ascertained, whereas in the case of the valued policy, unless it be voidable on the ground of fraud or for some other reason, the value fixed in the policy is as between the insurer and assured conclusive of the value of the subject intended to be insured.

See also *Balix Furniture and Appliances Ltd. v. Maritime Insurance Co.*, [1978] O.J. No. 1514 (Ont. Co. Ct.) (QL), in which the court adopted the following statement from *British Shipping Laws, Vol. 9, The Law of Marine Insurance and Average*, at p. 394:

> The difference between an unvalued and a valued policy in form is solely this: that in a valued policy this blank [the statement of value in the Lloyds S.G. Policy] is filled up with the sum at which the parties agree to fix the amount of the insurable interest; in an unvalued policy it is left blank.
>
> The difference in effect between a valued and an unvalued policy is that under an unvalued policy, in case of loss, the assured must prove the actual value of the subject of insurance; under a valued policy he need not do so, the valuation in the policy being conclusive between the parties.

[5] See *Kenny v. Union Marine Insurance Co.* (1880), 13 N.S.R. 313 (C.A.).

substantial difference, between the value stated in the policy and the "market" value of the vessel will not justify setting aside the agreed valuation. In *Biggin v. British Marine Mutual Insurance Assn.*,[6] a vessel costing $275,000 was insured for $400,000. The court held that there was no evidence of fraud in fixing the value of the vessel and that the insurer was bound by it. The court referred with approval to a Nova Scotia case, *Kenny v. Union Marine Insurance Co.*:

> [W]here the value of the thing insured is stated in the policy in a manner to be conclusive between the insurer and the insured, then in respect of all rights and obligations which arise upon the policy of insurance the parties are estopped between one and other from disputing the value of the thing insured as stated in the policy.[7]

While not amounting to fraud, an excessive valuation may be treated as a misrepresentation. In *Fudge v. Charter Marine Insurance Co.*,[8] the plaintiff insured a fishing vessel for $140,000 under a valued policy. He thought that the vessel had a market value of between $120,000 and $125,000, and a replacement value of $140,000. The defendant insurer introduced expert evidence at trial putting the market value of the vessel at about one-half of the insured value, and no evidence was led by the plaintiff to support the valuation of the vessel. The court found that the valuation was "grossly excessive", that there had been a material misrepresentation of the value and that "[n]o reasonable prudent insurer would consider an inflationary error of such proportions as immaterial."[9] The over-valuation vitiated the policy. In this case, the vessel had been purchased 10 years earlier for $156,000, and although two-thirds of its working life had expired, the expert evidence indicated that it would have cost $200,000 to replace at the time of the loss. In the circumstances, the court's conclusion that there was a misrepresentation of the value seems debatable. The underwriters presumably knew the age of the vessel and chose to accept the insured's valuation, which was no doubt reflected in the premium received.

On the other hand, there may be such a gross over-valuation that fraud can be inferred. In the absence of fraud, however, courts should be cautious about treating high value as a ground for invalidating the insurance. There are many reasons why a shipowner might decide to insure its property for something more than its "market" value. Some purpose-built vessels are unique and their values very difficult to establish at any given time. It may be costly and expensive to search out a suitable replacement vessel and earnings may be lost while a search is underway. Underwriters are familiar with the costs of the vessels they insure and have ready access to ship appraisers should they require confirmation of values. The underwriter is paid a premium based on the value of the insured

---

[6]   (1992), 101 Nfld. & P.E.I.R. 156, 14 C.C.L.I. (2d) 66 (Nfld. S.C.T.D.).

[7]   (1880), 13 N.S.R. 313 at 318 (C.A.).

[8]   (1992), 97 Nfld. & P.E.I.R. 91, 8 C.C.L.I. (2d) 252 (Nfld. S.C.T.D.). See also the leading English cases of *Burnard v. Rodocanachi* (1882), 7 App. Cas. 333, 51 L.J.Q.B. 548 (H.L.) and *Ionides v. Pender* (1874), L.R. 9 Q.B. 531, the latter to the effect that significant over-valuation, if not disclosed, will be grounds to avoid the contract on the basis of material misrepresentation.

[9]   (1992), 97 Nfld. & P.E.I.R. 91 at 95-96, 8 C.C.L.I. (2d) 252 (Nfld. S.C.T.D.).

vessel and, having agreed to the value and accepted premiums based on that value, should find it difficult to later contend that the value was over-stated.[10] Fraud, of course, "vitiates all", but unless there is fraud, or such gross over-valuation as to amount to a misrepresentation, the value stated in the policy should be conclusive. As was stated in an old English case:

> ...nobody has been able to improve upon the practice as to valued policies which has been recognized and adopted by shipowners and underwriters, and has, at least amongst honest men, the advantage of giving the assured the full value of the thing insured, and of enabling the underwriters to obtain a larger amount of profit. It saves them both the necessity of going into an expensive and intricate question as to the value in each particular case; and its abandonment would in the end, as it seems to me, prove highly detrimental to the interests of the underwriters.[11]

6.5 CONSTRUCTIVE TOTAL LOSS

Subsection 30(5) of the *C.M.I.A.* provides:

> 30(5) Unless a valued policy otherwise provides, the value specified by the policy is not conclusive for the purpose of determining whether there has been a constructive total loss.

Most hull and machinery policy forms provide that the insured value is taken to be the repaired value for the purpose of determining whether there is a constructive total loss. In that case, if the cost of repairs exceeds the insured value, there is a constructive total loss.[12]

---

[10] See *General Shipping & Forwarding Co. v. British General Insurance Co.* (1923), 15 Ll. L. Rep. 175 (K.B.)

[11] Welles J. in *Lidgett v. Secretan* (1871), L.R. 6 C.P. 616 at 627; this statement was approved by Gorrell Barnes J. in *The "Main"*, [1894] P. 320 at 326-27; see also *Thames and Mersey Marine Insurance Co. Ltd. v. Gunford Ship Co. Ltd.*, [1911] A.C. 529 (H.L.).

[12] See Chapter 9, *Losses and Charges Recoverable*, on the subject of constructive total loss.

Chapter 7

Perils Insured

7.1 INTRODUCTION

Marine insurance is a contract of indemnity against losses incidental to a marine adventure.[1] A marine adventure occurs when insurable property is exposed to "maritime perils".[2] Most hull and machinery insurance policies are written on a "named perils" basis — the perils insured against are specified in the policy. Cargo insurance is written either on an "all risks" basis or on a named perils basis, depending on the nature of the cargo and the risk. Whatever the type of policy, the scope of the "perils clause" is purely a matter of contract. Policies frequently contain exclusions restricting the scope of the perils insured.

In Section 7.2 of this Chapter we will examine some of the "perils" traditionally covered by the Ship & Goods ("S.G.") form of policy, notably "perils of the seas", which have been the subject of considerable litigation in Canada, as well as some of the perils that are not covered, such as scuttling. The perils covered by various policies of marine insurance, cargo, hull, and protection and indemnity are examined in more detail in Chapters 18, 19 and 20, respectively. The insurance of other kinds of marine risks is discussed in Chapter 21, *Insurance of Particular Risks*.

---

[1] A "marine adventure" is defined by subs. 2(1) of the Canadian *Marine Insurance Act* ("*C.M.I.A.*"), S.C. 1993, c. 22 as:

    any situation where insurable property [ship, goods or moveables] is exposed to maritime perils, and includes any situation where

        (*a*)   the earning or acquisition of any freight, commission, profit or other pecuniary benefit, or the security for any advance, loan or disbursement, is endangered by the exposure of insurable property to maritime perils, and

        (*b*)   any liability to a third party may be incurred by the owner of, or other person interested in or responsible for, insurable property, by reason of maritime perils.

[2] "Maritime perils" are defined by subs. 2(1) of the *C.M.I.A.* as: "…the perils consequent on or incidental to navigation, including perils of the seas, fire, war perils, acts of pirates or thieves, captures, seizures, restraints, detainments of princes and peoples, jettisons, barratry and all other perils of a like kind and, in respect of a marine policy, any peril designated by the policy". See *Staples v. Great American Insurance Co.*, [1941] S.C.R. 213, [1941] 2 D.L.R. 1, in which it was held that the insurance of the vessel against fire did not make the policy one of fire insurance. It was a marine insurance policy.

The Canadian *Marine Insurance Act* ("*C.M.I.A.*")[3] identifies certain types of losses that are not insured against by a marine policy, unless the policy provides otherwise. These common exclusions from a marine insurance policy will be examined in Section 7.3.

It is a fundamental principle of marine insurance that the policy only covers a loss that is "proximately caused" by an insured peril. This requirement is discussed in Section 7.4.

Finally, the "burden of proof" or legal onus that rests on a claimant under a marine insurance policy is discussed in Section 7.5.

7.2 PERILS INSURED

Section 26 of the *C.M.I.A.* states that a marine policy must specify, among other things, the perils insured against. The broader the "perils clause", the broader the coverage afforded. The English *Marine Insurance Act* ("*M.I.A. 1906*")[4] had attached as a schedule the traditional Lloyd's S.G. form of policy which had been in use for many years, containing the time-honoured "perils" clause:

> Touching the adventures and perils which we, the assurers, are contented to bear and do take upon us in this voyage: they are of the seas, men-of-war, fire, enemies, pirates, rovers, thieves, jettison, letters of mart and countermart, surprisals, takings at sea, arrests, restraints and detainments of all kings, princes, and people, of what nation, condition, or quality soever, barratry of the master and mariners, and of all other perils, losses, and misfortunes, that have or shall come to the hurt, detriment, or damage of the said goods and merchandises, and ship, etc., or any part thereof.

This form was carried forward as a schedule to the marine insurance legislation of a number of the Canadian provinces,[5] but it was not included in the *C.M.I.A.* For many years in England and Canada it was common to write hull and cargo insurance using the S.G. Form, with relevant clauses attached. With the introduction of the "MAR" policy form in the English market in 1982, the use of the S.G. Form has largely ceased in the United Kingdom. It continues to be used, albeit with less frequency, in Canada.

7.2.1 Perils of the Seas

The essence of a maritime adventure is the exposure to "maritime perils", defined by section 2(1) of the *C.M.I.A.* as including "perils of the seas". This expression, which appears in the perils clause of the S.G. Form, is defined in the Schedule to the *C.M.I.A.* as "fortuitous accidents or casualties of the seas, but does not include ordinary action of the wind and waves".

This definition comes from the famous decision of the House of Lords in *Wilson, Sons & Co. v. Xantho (Cargo Owners)*, in which Lord Herschell stated:

---

[3]   S.C. 1993, c. 22.

[4]   6 Edw. VII, c. 41.

[5]   See, for example, the Ontario *Marine Insurance Act*, R.S.O. 1990, c. M.2, subs. 31(1), which provides: "A policy may be in the form in the Schedule."

I think it is clear that the term "perils of the sea" does not cover every accident or casualty which may happen to the subject-matter of the insurance on the sea. It must be a peril "of" the sea. Again, it is well settled that it is not every loss or damage of which the sea is the immediate cause that is covered by these words. They do not protect, for example, against that natural and inevitable action of the winds and waves, which results in what may be described as wear and tear. There must be some casualty, something which could not be foreseen as one of the necessary incidents of the adventure. The purpose of the policy is to secure an indemnity against accidents which may happen, not against events which must happen. It was contended that those losses only were losses by perils of the sea, which were occasioned by extraordinary violence of the winds or waves. I think this is too narrow a construction of the words, and it is certainly not supported by the authorities, or by common understanding. It is beyond question, that if a vessel strikes upon a sunken rock in fair weather and sinks, this is a loss by perils of the sea.[6]

One of the leading English cases on perils of the seas is *Canada Rice Mills Ltd. v. Union Marine and General Insurance Co.*,[7] a decision of the Judicial Committee of the Privy Council, on appeal from the Court of Appeal of British Columbia. A cargo of rice had sustained damage on a voyage from Rangoon to British Columbia. It was insured against "perils of the seas" and "all other perils losses and misfortunes that have or shall come to the hurt or damage of the subject-matter of the insurance". During the voyage, the ship's ventilators had to be closed due to heavy weather and the cargo heated and sustained damage. There was evidence that rice is likely to heat and ferment if not properly ventilated during carriage, and the insurers argued that the damage was not due to perils of the seas. The British Columbia Court of Appeal held that the loss was not recoverable since there was no evidence of perils of the seas and the weather encountered by the ship was no more than could have been expected on the voyage. The Judicial Committee of the Privy Counsel reversed, holding that there was a peril of the sea. Lord Wright referred to the judgment in *Wilson, Sons & Co. v. Xantho (Cargo Owners)* and stated:

> Where there is an accidental incursion of seawater into a vessel, at a part of the vessel, and in a manner, where seawater is not expected to enter in the ordinary course of things, and there is consequent damage to the thing insured, there is *prima facie* a loss by perils of the sea. The accident may consist in some negligent act, such as improper opening of a valve, or a hole made in a pipe by mischance, or it may be that seawater is admitted by stress of weather or some like cause bringing the sea over openings ordinarily not exposed to the sea or, even without stress of weather, by the vessel heeling over owing to some accident, or by the breaking of hatches or other coverings. These are merely a few amongst many possible in-

---

[6] (1887), 12 App. Cas. 503 at 509, 56 L.J.P. 116 (H.L.). See *Stad v. Fireman's Fund Insurance Co.*, [1979] I.L.R. ¶1-1070 (B.C.S.C.) to the effect that "perils of the seas" refers only to fortuitous accidents and not to the ordinary action of the winds and waves.

[7] [1941] A.C. 55, [1941] 1 D.L.R. 1 (J.C.P.C.), rev'g. [1939] 1 W.W.R. 450, [1939] 2 D.L.R. 306 (B.C.C.A.).

stances in which there may be a fortuitous incursion of seawater. It is the fortuitous entry of seawater which is the peril of the sea in such cases.[8]

The heavy weather encountered on the voyage, requiring the closing of the ventilators, was accidental. The loss was attributable to perils of the seas and the insured was entitled to recover.

In Canada, the leading case on perils of the seas is now *Century Insurance Co. of Canada v. Case Existological Laboratories Ltd.*[9] The insured vessel, a rather unique converted barge being used in underwater studies, sank because an employee negligently permitted valves to remain open, flooding the vessel. It was argued that there had to be some operative maritime peril in order to bring the claim within "perils of the sea" and that simple negligence was not sufficient. The Supreme Court of Canada agreed with the British Columbia Court of Appeal in rejecting this argument. Justice Ritchie, giving the judgment of the Supreme Court of Canada, stated:

> The effect of this section [the equivalent to section 53 of the *C.M.I.A.*, reproduced below in section 7.3.1] when read in conjunction with the "Rules for Construction of Policy" contained in the Schedule is that in order to succeed in a claim under the perils of the seas provision the insured must establish that the proximate cause of the loss was a "fortuitous accident or casualty of the seas", and furthermore, the claim may succeed even though the loss would not have happened "but for the misconduct or negligence of the master or crew".[10]

Justice Ritchie referred to Lord Wright's famous quotation in *Wilson, Sons & Co. v. Xantho (Cargo Owners)*, above, as well as to the judgment of Bailhache J. in *Cohen, Sons & Co. v. National Benefit Assurance Co.*,[11] in which a submarine sank because a workman left a valve open:

> In my view, the unintentional admission of sea water into a ship, whereby the ship sinks, is a peril of the sea. There is no warranty in this policy against negligence; there is no exception of negligence; and the fact that the unintentional admission of water into the ship is due to negligence is, in my opinion, totally and absolutely immaterial. There is a peril of the sea whenever a ship is afloat in the sea, and water from the sea is unintentionally admitted into her which causes a loss, either to the cargo or to the ship.[12]

The Supreme Court of Canada adopted the test applied by Mr. Justice Lambert in the British Columbia Court of Appeal:

---

[8]   *Ibid.*, at 68-69 A.C.; see also *Hamilton Fraser & Co. v. Pandorf & Co.* (1887), 12 App. Cas. 518, 57 L.J.Q.B. 24 (H.L.).

[9]   [1983] 2 S.C.R. 47, 2 C.C.L.I. 172, aff'g. (1982), 35 B.C.L.R. 364, [1982] I.L.R. ¶1-1567 (C.A.), rev'g. (1980), 116 D.L.R. (3d) 199, [1981] I.L.R. ¶1-1335 (B.C.S.C.). See also *C.C.R. Fishing Ltd. v. British Reserve Insurance Co.*, [1990] 1 S.C.R. 814, 43 C.C.L.I. 1, rev'g. (1988), 55 D.L.R. (4th) 429, 34 B.C.L.R. (2d) 1 (C.A.), rev'g. (1986), 21 C.C.L.I. 297 (B.C.S.C.).

[10] [1983] 2 S.C.R. 47 at 52.

[11] (1924), 18 Ll. L. Rep. 199 at 202.

[12] [1983] 2 S.C.R. 47 at 53, quoting from (1924), 18 Ll. L. Rep. 199 at 202.

... counsel for the insurers says that in addition to the negligence, there must be an operating peril of the seas of some category peculiar to marine operations, and counsel for the assured says that a sinking caused by a negligent act is a sufficient fortuitous accident of the sea.

· · · · ·

In my opinion, the resolution of this narrow issue rests on an analysis of the negligent act. An act is not negligent in itself but only in relation to a foreseeable risk of harm. If that foreseeable risk of harm is a peculiarly marine risk, then the act, coupled with its foreseeable consequence, is a fortuitous accident of the seas and a peril of the seas and a proximate cause of the loss.

That conclusion is sufficient to decide the first issue in this appeal. In this case there is no doubt that it was the risk of the *Bamcell II* sinking, and causing loss by that sinking, that made the failure to close the deck valves a negligent omission when there was a duty to act. When that negligent omission is coupled with its foreseeable consequence, the proximate cause of the loss in this case was a peril of the seas and, as such, covered by the policy.[13]

In the result, the Supreme Court of Canada confirmed the decision of the British Columbia Court of Appeal and held that there had been a loss through perils of the seas.

The decision in *Century Insurance Co. of Canada* clarified the law in Canada with respect to perils of the seas, but it was followed soon after by another case dealing with the same issue in the context of two operative causes of a loss. In *C.C.R. Fishing Ltd. v. British Reserve Insurance Co.*,[14] a vessel sank while at its berth as a result of the entry of water through two corroded screws and the failure to shut off a valve that would have prevented the flooding of the ship. It was argued that while there had been negligence, the sinking of the ship was not the foreseeable consequence of that negligence and that it should not therefore be regarded as a peril of the seas. It was also argued that the corrosion of the screws was not due to negligence but rather was the result of "ordinary wear and tear", an excepted peril. The Supreme Court of Canada, in a judgment dealing with a number of important issues, held that there was a loss by perils of the seas. Justice McLachlin (who later became Chief Justice of Canada), giving the judgment of the Supreme Court, stated:

The requirement that the cause of the loss be "fortuitous" excludes the natural and inevitable action of wind and waves, or ordinary wear and tear, inherent defects and intentionally caused losses. Events which are not fortuitous, as defined in the cases, are reflected in the exclusions found in s. 56 of the Act and the definition in the Act of "perils of the seas". In general, the word "fortuitous", as interpreted by

---

¹³ [1983] 2 S.C.R. 47 at 54, quoting from (1982), 133 D.L.R. (3d) 727 at 735 (B.C.C.A.).
¹⁴ [1990] 1 S.C.R. 814, 43 C.C.L.I. 1, rev'g. (1988), 55 D.L.R. (4th) 429, 34 B.C.L.R. (2d) 1 (C.A.), rev'g. (1986), 21 C.C.L.I. 297 (B.C.S.C.).

the cases, carries the connotation that the cause of the loss will not have been in-
tentional or inevitable. As Lord Herschell put it in *Thomas Wilson, Sons & Co. v.
The Owners of the Cargo per the "Xantho" (The "Xantho")* (1887), 12 A.C. 503
(H.L.) at p. 509:

> There must be some casualty, something which could not be foreseen as one
> of the necessary incidents of the adventure.

The second requirement, that the loss be "of the sea" excludes losses which could
have occurred in an accident on land: see *"The Bamcell II"*, *supra*. The sinking of
a ship as a result of the ingress of sea-water due to a fortuitous act has without exception been considered to be an accident which is "of the sea".[15]

As the Court noted, there is an interplay between "perils of the seas" and the
excluded causes under the *C.M.I.A.* and under most marine policies. These
exclusions are discussed in Section 7.4. They are, in general, designed to
exclude losses that are not "fortuitous". The term "perils of the seas" has been
held to include a number of maritime perils, such as striking a submerged
object,[16] the tearing of sails,[17] fire,[18] a vessel sinking at a dock,[19] a vessel sinking
in unexpected waves,[20] and a vessel sinking while being towed.[21]

---

[15]   [1990] 1 S.C.R. 814 at 819.

[16]   *Williams v. Canada* (1984), 7 C.C.L.I. 198 (F.C.T.D.): striking a submerged object, rather than
wear and tear or corrosion was found to be the cause of the loss.

[17]   *Hill v. Union Insurance Society of Canton Ltd.* (1927), 61 O.L.R. 201, [1927] 4 D.L.R. 718
(C.A.): tearing of the sails was not the "natural and inevitable action of the winds and waves". It
was not wear and tear, but it was a "casualty — something that could not be foreseen as one of
the necessary incidents of the adventure". The court noted that if the sails tear in an ordinary
wind, the loss would be due to deterioration by age and not a peril of the sea (at 723 D.L.R.).

[18]   *Stevenson v. Continental Insurance Co.*, [1973] 6 W.W.R. 316, [1973] I.L.R. ¶1-553 (B.C.S.C.),
in which it was held that a fire on board a work boat was a "fortuitous accident".

[19]   *Federal Business Development Bank v. Commonwealth Insurance Co.* (1983), 2 C.C.L.I. 200
(B.C.S.C.): a vessel sinking at a dock was a peril of the sea; there was no evidence of wilful
misconduct on the part of the insured and the negligence of the insured was not a factor.

[20]   *Cleveland v. Sunderland Marine Mutual Insurance Co.* (1987), 45 D.L.R. (4th) 340, 81 N.S.R.
(2d) 1 (S.C.T.D.), additional reasons at (1987), 85 N.S.R. (2d) 42, 216 A.P.R. 42 (S.C.T.D.): a
ship sinking in unexpected and unforeseen waves amounted to fortuitous circumstances and
perils of the seas.

[21]   *Central Native Fishermen's Co-op. v. Commonwealth Insurance Co.*, [1979] I.L.R. ¶1-1091
(B.C.S.C.). The insured vessel sank while being towed. It was held that it was not due to the
inevitable action of winds and waves but rather was due to a fortuitous accident or casualty of
the seas. In *Seattle Construction & Dry Dock Co. v. Grant, Smith & Co.*, [1918] 3 W.W.R. 703,
44 D.L.R. 90 (B.C.C.A.), aff'd. [1919] 3 W.W.R. 33, [1920] A.C. 162 (J.C.P.C.), it was stated
that it would be a mistake to give too precise a definition of "peril of the sea", but it is "some
condition of sea or weather or accident of navigation producing a result which but for these
conditions would not have occurred" (at p. 171 A.C.). In that case, the Judicial Committee of the
Privy Council stated (at p. 172 A.C.) that insurance against "perils of the sea" is "not a guarantee
that a ship will float" and does not cover losses caused by "the unfitness of the structure disasso-
ciated from any peril by wind or water". See also *Bohn v. Lloyd's of London*, [1988] B.C.J. No.
2721 (B.C. Co. Ct.) (QL); *Creedon & Avery Ltd. v. North China Insurance Co.*, [1917] 3

7.2.2 Scuttling

Scuttling is the intentional sinking of the insured vessel. In *Boyda v. Saxbee Insurance Agencies (1975) Ltd.*,[22] described by the trial judge as a "black farce about the efforts of three oddly assorted characters to rid themselves of an unwanted sailboat at the expense of the insurance company", it was found that the vessel had been deliberately sunk by the master with the connivance of the owner, and the claim was unrecoverable. The intentional sinking of the insured vessel by the insured would obviously be unrecoverable. The intentional sinking by a third party may or may not be recoverable, depending on the terms of the policy. For example, in *Miskofski v. Economic Insurance Co.*, the insured tug was found adrift with water leaking through an open seacock. The court found that "[t]he inference is overwhelming that some person or persons took the vessel, and abandoned it at sea after taking pains to insure that it was in a sinking condition."[23] There was no evidence that the owner was involved in the scuttling, but it was held, relying on the decision of the House of Lords in *Samuel v. Dumas*,[24] that scuttling by persons unknown, even without the involvement of the owner, was not a loss by perils of the seas and that the loss was not within the term "all other like perils, losses and misfortunes" in the S.G. Form. It is conceivable that another form of policy would be construed to cover the intentional scuttling of the vessel, without the involvement of the owner.

7.2.3 Barratry

"Barratry" includes "every wrongful act wilfully committed by the master or crew of the insured ship to the prejudice of the owner or charterer of the ship."[25] The term is said to derive from the Latin "barratrare", to cheat, but in marine insurance it extends to all wrongful acts committed by the crew.[26] It does not, however, include errors of judgment or negligence of the master or crew.[27] There

---

W.W.R. 33, 24 B.C.R. 33, 36 D.L.R. 359 (C.A.); *Federal Business Development Bank v. Commonwealth Insurance Co.* (1979), 13 B.C.L.R. 376, [1980] I.L.R. ¶1-1221 (S.C.).

[22] (1984), 4 C.C.L.I. 26, [1984] I.L.R. ¶1-1775 (B.C.S.C.).

[23] (1963), 45 W.W.R. 395, 43 D.L.R. (2d) 281 (B.C.C.A.), aff'g. (1962), 41 W.W.R. 309, 37 D.L.R. (2d) 536 at 537 (B.C.S.C.).

[24] [1924] A.C. 431, 93 L.J.K.B. 415.

[25] *C.M.I.A.*, Schedule, subs. 1(1). See *Crowell v. Geddes* (1862), 5 N.S.R. 184 (C.A.): "Barratry imports fraud; it must be something of a criminal nature against the owners of the ship by the master or mariners. . .The deviation of a vessel from the voyage insured, through the ignorance of the captain, or from any other motive not fraudulent, though it avoids the policy, does not constitute an act of barratry." In *Providence Washington Insurance Co. v. Corbett* (1884), 9 S.C.R. 256, it was held that the *bona fide* sale of a vessel by the master is not an insured peril. Barratry occurs only when the loss is done wilfully to the prejudice of the owner. See also *Cossman v. West*, (1887), 13 App. Cas. 160 (J.C.P.C.), rev'g. (1885), 18 N.S.R. 457 (C.A.), where the sale by the court for a salvage reward, after the barratrous scuttling of the ship by the master, was held to be covered by the policy.

[26] See F. Laverty, *The Insurance Law of Canada*, 2nd ed. (Toronto: Carswell, 1936), at 458.

[27] See *Wolff v. Merchants Insurance Co.* (1892), 31 N.B.R. 577 (C.A.), in which it was held that negligence or error in judgment on the part of the master, without criminal or fraudulent intent, is not barratry.

must be something of a criminal nature against the owners of the ship by the master or mariners.[28] Barratry is not a "peril of the sea" and is not covered by words insuring against perils of the sea.[29]

7.2.4 "All Risks" Policies

Marine cargo insurance is frequently written on an "all risks" basis. The Institute of London Underwriters[30] Cargo Clauses, All Risks (1/1/63) were in common use in Canada until the introduction of the Institute Cargo Clauses (1/1/82)(A), which essentially provide "all risks" coverage: "This insurance covers all risks of loss of or damage to the subject-matter insured except as provided in clauses 4, 5, 6 and 7 below."

It is well established, however, that "all risks" does not mean "all losses". It means losses caused by fortuitous circumstances, namely, accidental losses, as opposed to losses that are bound or certain to happen, given the nature of the property insured or the voyage in question. The leading case is *British & Foreign Marine Insurance Co. v. Gaunt*, in which Lord Birkenhead made his famous statement:

> The damage proved was such as did not occur, and could not be expected to occur, in the course of a normal transit. The inference remains that it was due to some abnormal circumstance, some accident or casualty. We are, of course, to give effect to the rule that the plaintiff must establish his case, that he must show that the loss comes within the terms of his policies; but where all risks are covered by the policy and not merely risks of a specified class or classes, the plaintiff discharges his special onus when he has proved that the loss was caused by some event covered by the general expression, and he is not bound to go further and prove the exact nature of the accident or casualty which, in fact, occasioned his loss.[31]

In *Holm v. Underwriters Through T.W. Rice & Co. Inc.*,[32] the plaintiff's yacht sank at its mooring in the Powell River in British Columbia after the plaintiff had removed a hose from an exhaust port. He left the vessel at its mooring, with no one to look after it, apparently relying on the bilge pump to discharge any accumulation of water. Two weeks later, the vessel sank. The policy insured the vessel against "all risks of physical loss of or damage from any external cause" and included an *"Inchmaree* clause"[33] covering "loss or damage...caused by the negligence of the master...provided such loss or damage has not resulted from want of due diligence by the owners or...the assured".[34] The court found that the plaintiff had not established coverage under the "all risks" cover, since he had

---

28   See also *Crowell v. Geddes* (1862), 5 N.S.R. 184 (C.A.).
29   *O'Connor v. Merchants Marine Insurance Co.* (1889), 16 S.C.R. 331.
30   Referred to as the "Institute" or the "I.L.U.", and now known as the International Underwriting Association or "I.U.A.".
31   [1921] All E.R. 447 at 450 (H.L.).
32   (1981), 124 D.L.R. (3d) 463, [1981] I.L.R. ¶1-1438 (B.C.S.C.).
33   See Section 7.3.7 of this Chapter on the subject of the *"Inchmaree* clause".
34   (1981), 124 D.L.R. (3d) 463 at 464, [1981] I.L.R. ¶1-1438 (B.C.S.C.).

not established loss by an external cause. The sinking resulted from the failure of the plaintiff, as "master" of his own boat, to plug the open exhaust port.[35]

Although all risks policies are common in the case of cargo insurance, they are unusual in hull and machinery insurance. As a basic proposition, if damage or loss occurs to cargo during transportation, and is of a kind that would not occur in the ordinary course of things, the loss will be covered by an "all risks" policy unless the insurer establishes that the loss was due to an excluded cause. The subject of burden of proof is discussed in more detail in Section 7.5 of this Chapter.

7.2.5 Mixed Sea, Air and Land Perils

The *C.M.I.A.* provides that a marine policy may insure against "losses arising from a land or air peril incidental to such an adventure if they are provided for in the contract or by usage of the trade".[36] A particular cargo may be carried by various modes of transportation, perhaps by road from the shipper's warehouse to a rail depot, by rail to the ocean port, by sea to an overseas port and then by rail or road to the consignee's premises. Part of the journey may be by air. A marine insurance contract can insure against losses on land or in the air if they are "incidental" to a marine adventure and marine open cargo policies frequently include coverage for the transportation of the insured's cargo by other conveyances.

Questions may arise as to whether transportation exclusively by a non-marine mode of transport can be covered by a marine insurance policy and whether that policy is subject to the *C.M.I.A.* For example, if there is a contract of insurance subject to the Institute Cargo Clauses (Air) (1/1/82) under a marine open cargo policy, is the contract subject to the *C.M.I.A.* when there is no marine component to the "adventure"? Is a so-called "Inland Marine" policy, covering transportation by road or rail with no marine transport, subject to the *C.M.I.A.*? In a Quebec case, *Model Furs Ltd. v. H. Lapalme Transport Ltée.*,[37] it was held that the principles applicable to marine insurance did not apply to a shipment of cargo by air and truck and that the use of a marine policy form did not make the contract one of marine insurance. As a matter of contract law, the use of a marine policy form is perfectly appropriate, even for a non-marine risk, since there is nothing to prevent the parties from using any contractual agreement they choose. On the other hand, since the *C.M.I.A.* applies only to contracts covering losses "incidental to a marine adventure", as defined, an adventure that is not marine would not be subject to its terms.

---

[35] For an example of a form of all risks cargo insurance, see *Richardson & Sons Ltd. v. Standard Marine Insurance Co.*, [1936] S.C.R. 573, [1936] 3 D.L.R. 513, in which a cargo of grain was insured against "loss or damage by any external cause".

[36] *C.M.I.A.*, subs. 6(1)(*a*). See *Richardson v. Canadian Pacific Railway* (1914), 7 O.W.N. 458, 20 D.L.R. 580 (H.C.); new trial ordered (1915), 8 O.W.N. 221 (Div. Ct.).

[37] (1995) D.R.S. 95-20092, [1995] R.R.A. 611 (Que. C.A.).

7.2.6 Inland Waters

Marine insurance policies in Canada frequently insure property on inland waters, including cargo travelling on inland waterways, cargo and passenger ships, ferries and pleasure boats. Marine policies also insure the liabilities of owners and operators of vessels operating on lakes and inland rivers. While the *C.M.I.A.* does not expressly refer to inland waters, the case law suggests that the scope of Canadian maritime law, including the common law and statute law relating to marine insurance, would extend to inland waterways.[38]

7.3 EXCLUSIONS

Unless the policy provides otherwise, there are certain losses for which the marine insurer is not liable. These will be considered in this section and include: (1) losses attributable to the wilful misconduct of the insured; (2) loss under a hull or cargo policy proximately caused by delay; (3) ordinary wear and tear; (4) ordinary leakage or breakage; (5) inherent vice; (6) loss proximately caused by vermin; and (7) loss or damage to machinery not proximately caused by maritime perils.[39]

7.3.1 Wilful Misconduct of the Insured

Subsection 53(2) of the *C.M.I.A.* provides that the insurer is not liable for a loss attributable to the insured's wilful misconduct. This exception must be read in conjunction with subsection 53(1), which provides that the insurer *will* be liable for a loss which would not have occurred but for the misconduct or negligence of the master or crew, provided that the loss was caused by an insured peril:

> 53(1) Subject to this Act and unless a marine policy otherwise provides, an insurer is liable only for a loss that is proximately caused by a peril insured against, including a loss that would not have occurred but for the misconduct or negligence of the master or crew.
>
> (2) Without limiting the generality of subsection (1), an insurer is not liable for any loss attributable to the wilful misconduct of the insured . . .

If the "proximate cause" of the loss is an insured peril, the fact that the negligence of the captain or crew contributed to the loss will not prevent recovery.[40] However, where the loss is "attributable" to the wilful misconduct *of the insured*, the insurer will not be liable.[41]

---

[38]   See Chapter 1, *Overview of Marine Insurance.*

[39]   *C.M.I.A.*, subs. 53(1).

[40]   For an early example of this principle, see *Cross v. Allan* (1880), 3 L.N. 47 (Que.), in which it was observed that "perils" of the sea can include a loss caused or peril made operative through the negligence of the captain or crew.

[41]   See *P. Samuel & Co. v. Dumas* (1924), 18 Ll. L. Rep. 211, [1924] All E.R. 66 (H.L.).

In the case of hull and machinery insurance, this exception must also be considered in light of the "*Inchmaree* clause", discussed in Section 7.3.7, extending the insurance to a loss proximately caused by the negligence of the master, officer or crew of the vessel, "provided such loss or damage has not resulted from want of due diligence by the Assured, the Owners or Managers of the Vessel".

"Wilful misconduct" means something more than simple negligence, error in judgment or mistake of the insured. One purpose of insurance is to protect people against the consequences of their own mistakes. If insurers were not liable because the "fault" of their insured caused or contributed to the loss, many losses would be uninsured. In *Williams v. Canada*, the Court stated:

> In the absence of express stipulations to the contrary, negligence on the part of the assured or of a person for whom he is or may be responsible does not exempt the insurer from liability though the loss is caused thereby, for one of the main objects of insurance is to protect the assured against the consequences of negligence.[42]

When does conduct cross the borderline between negligence and "wilful misconduct"? Negligence is the failure to exercise reasonable care — the care a reasonable and prudent person would take in the conduct of his or her own affairs. Wilful misconduct is different from negligence. The word "wilful" implies either a deliberate act intended to cause the harm, or such blind and uncaring conduct that one could say that the person was heedless of the consequences. The judgment of Chief Justice Duff of the Supreme Court of Canada, in *McCulloch v. Murray*, has been cited in several cases:

> All these phrases, gross negligence, wilful misconduct, wanton misconduct, imply conduct in which, if there is not conscious wrongdoing, there is a very marked departure from the standards by which responsible and competent people in charge of motor cars habitually govern themselves.[43]

The distinction between negligence and wilful misconduct was discussed in an Ontario case, *Russell v. Canadian General Insurance Co.*[44] The insured's yacht sustained water damage during storage, and the insurer argued that the insured's failure to inspect the yacht during storage amounted to wilful misconduct because reasonable inspection would have prevented the damage. The court referred to the statement of Chief Justice Duff in *McCulloch v. Murray*, above, and continued:

> This statement does not stand for the proposition that the phrases "gross negligence, wilful misconduct, wanton misconduct" all amount to the same thing. The courts have made a distinction between negligence, gross negligence and wilful misconduct or wilful neglect.

---

[42]   (1984), 7 C.C.L.I. 198 at 211 (F.C.T.D.).
[43]   [1942] S.C.R. 141 at 145. See *Atwood v. Canada* (1985), 10 C.C.L.I. 62 (F.C.T.D.).
[44]   (1999), 11 C.C.L.I. (3d) 284, [1999] I.L.R. ¶1-3674 (Ont. Gen. Div.).

A finding of negligence on the part of an insured does not preclude a finding that damages were caused by an accident ...

Even a finding of gross negligence will not necessarily preclude a determination that damages were caused by an accident.

In *Stats v. Mutual of Omaha Insurance Co.* [(1978), 87 D.L.R. (3d) 169 (S.C.C.)] a woman was killed as a result of driving while intoxicated and the issue was whether her death was caused by an accident. The Ontario Court of Appeal concluded that, while the woman's driving was dangerous and grossly negligent, she did not voluntarily "look for" or "court" the risk of collision, therefore it was an accident.

The phrase "wilful neglect" implies an intentionality on the part of the insured. There is no evidence presented by the Defendants that the Plaintiff had an intention to have damage occasioned to his sailboat. Even if the damage was caused by a negligent act, in that he did not act as a prudent and reasonable boat owner, and even if the damage might have been foreseeable, the damage is still considered to be accidental so long as the damage was not intended.[45]

The judge concluded:

Based on the evidence before the court, I find that the loss was not intended by the Plaintiff nor did the Plaintiff court the risk of the loss. It cannot be said that damage to the boat was the natural and direct consequence of any failure to properly inspect the sailboat.[46]

The effect of subsection 53(1) of the *C.M.I.A.* is that the negligence of the master or crew of the insured ship does not necessarily preclude recovery under the policy, provided that the proximate cause of the loss was a peril insured against. For example, in the case of *Century Insurance Co. of Canada v. Case Existological Laboratories Ltd.*, discussed in Section 7.2.1 above, the failure of a crew member to close a valve, allowing seawater to enter and ultimately sink the ship, was attributable to a marine peril notwithstanding that the negligence of the crew member was a contributing factor.[47]

In *Atwood v. Canada*,[48] a decision of the Federal Court of Canada, the policy contained an exclusion for "wrongful or reckless acts". The insured attempted to start the vessel's motor by using a screwdriver to bridge two points on the starter, producing a spark that in turn caused a fire. In holding that the insured was entitled to recover, the court found that there was no evidence of recklessness to bring the

---

[45] *Ibid.*, at 293 C.C.L.I.

[46] *Ibid.*, at 295.

[47] [1983] 2 S.C.R. 47, 2 C.C.L.I. 172, aff'g. (1982), 35 B.C.L.R. 364, [1982] I.L.R. ¶1-1567, rev'g. (1980), 116 D.L.R. (3d) 199, [1981] I.L.R. ¶1-1335 (B.C.S.C.). See also *C.C.R. Fishing Ltd. v. British Reserve Insurance Co.*, [1990] 1 S.C.R. 814, 43 C.C.L.I. 1, rev'g. (1988), 55 D.L.R. (4th) 429, 34 B.C.L.R. (2d) 1 (C.A.), rev'g. (1986), 21 C.C.L.I. 297 (B.C.S.C.).

[48] (1985), 10 C.C.L.I. 62 (F.C.T.D.).

policy exclusion into play. The insured was undoubtedly negligent, but not so "reckless" as to prevent recovery.[49]

In *Federal Business Development Bank v. Commonwealth Insurance Co.*,[50] the insured vessel grounded and became partially submerged after breaking away from its moorings at what the court found was an "old, improvised flimsy float", rather than at a more substantial government wharf. The insurer argued that the owner or master was so negligent in securing the vessel or in failing to right the vessel that the loss was inevitable. The trial judge referred to the provision of the British Columbia *Insurance (Marine) Act*,[51] which is comparable to subsection 53(1) of the *C.M.I.A*, and said:

> The defendants contend the loss is not a result of the "perils of the sea". It is submitted there was a physical inevitability the vessel would be torn away from its mooring and therefore it was not a peril of the sea. The owner created conditions that made the sinking inevitable. The defendants say the owners were negligent and the negligence was the cause of the loss.[52]

The judge continued:

> Thus the defendants are not liable for wilful misconduct of the assured. That, however, has not been proven in the evidence before me. The insurer is liable, unless otherwise provided, against loss proximately caused by a peril of the sea even though the loss would not have happened but for the misconduct or negligence of the master or the crew. This policy contained no provision excluding loss arising from the negligence of the master or the crew. What the defendants are contending is that the owners or the master was so negligent in securing the vessel or in failing to right the vessel that the sinking was inevitable and the insurer is not liable. The statute, however, says otherwise.
>
> . . .
>
> If negligence is irrelevant, it is then only a matter of determining whether the proximate cause of the loss was a peril of the sea. There is no doubt the loss happened on the sea. What occurred to the vessel is that it became stranded and the master did not take adequate steps to secure the vessel. The mooring arrangement failed when a rope chafed or broke and, when offshore, the vessel keeled to the port. The damage occurred when the vessel took on water.
>
> . . .

---

[49] See also the early Upper Canada case of *Gillespie v. British America Fire & Life Assurance Co.* (1849), 7 U.C.Q.B. 108 at 109, in which the policy did "otherwise provide": there was an exception of losses caused "from want of ordinary care or skill, such as is necessary and proper on such voyages and in said navigation".

[50] (1983), 2 C.C.L.I. 200 (B.C.S.C.).

[51] R.S.B.C. 1979, c. 203.

[52] (1983), 2 C.C.L.I. 200 at 206 (B.C.S.C.).

Similar circumstances were considered in Baxendale v. Fane (1940), 66 Lloyd's L.L.R. 174 at 181:

> I have come to the conclusion that whether the damage was caused by the vessel sitting on the block or on the uneven bottom of the dock or on the seven baulks of timber or by a combination of these things in each case, the plaintiff has established a loss due to a peril *ejusdem generis* with a peril of the sea, namely, stranding.
>
> I find the loss occurred at sea. It was not intentional. It was fortuitous. Accordingly, the insurer is liable.[53]

The exclusion of losses caused by the wilful misconduct of the insured refers to conduct *before* the loss occurs. Negligence or misconduct of the insured *after* a loss may preclude recovery under the policy or may reduce the amount of recovery if it is a breach of the insured's duty to "sue and labour".[54] This subject is discussed in Chapter 11, *Duties of the Insured: Sue and Labour.*

7.3.2   Loss Caused by Delay

Unless the policy provides otherwise, in the case of insurance on a ship or cargo, the insurer is not liable for loss proximately caused by delay, including delay caused by a peril insured against.[55] Delay can cause deterioration of perishable cargo, loss of market value and other consequential losses that insurers are unwilling to assume and, as a result, most cargo policies exclude liability for delay.

Occasionally goods go missing in transportation, a claim is made under the cargo insurance policy and it is paid on the assumption that the goods have been lost. The goods are later recovered in sound condition. Is the insured obliged to take delivery of the goods and refund the insurance payment? This depends on the terms of the policy and any agreement made at the time the loss was paid. In *Federation Insurance Co. of Canada v. Coret Accessories Inc. and Hirsh,*[56] the underwriter paid a claim for goods apparently lost in transit, but the goods were later recovered. It was held that the insurer could recover the money paid to the

---

[53]   *Ibid.*, at 210.

[54]   See *Suo v. Openshaw Simmons Ltd.* (1978), 5 B.C.L.R. 370, [1978] I.L.R. ¶1-982 (S.C.), in which the distinction was discussed; see also Chapter 11, *Duties of the Insured: Sue and Labour* with respect to the insured's duty to take reasonable measures, after a loss has occurred, to mitigate the loss.

[55]   *C.M.I.A.*, subs. 53(2)(*a*). In *Jordan v. Great Western Insurance Co.* (1886), 14 S.C.R. 734, rev'g. (1885), 24 N.B.R. 421 (C.A.), it was held that the loss of freight caused by the detention of the ship due to the lateness of the season, with the result that it could not get out of the river due to ice, was not a loss by the perils of the seas. It was a natural result of the lateness of the season and the ordinary and inevitable course of nature. See *Continental Insurance Co. v. Almassa International Inc.*, unreported (24 March 2003), Toronto (Ont. Sup. Ct. of Justice), where the trial judge held that the proximate cause of damage to a cargo of lumber was the failure of the ship to properly ventilate the cargo and not the delay of the ship in making delivery of the cargo. Although the damage became worse the longer the ship was delayed, there would have been no damage had there been proper ventilation.

[56]   [1968] 2 Ll. L.R. 109 (Que. S.C.).

insured because the policy did not cover goods delayed or lost temporarily. In the British Columbia case of *Phoenix Assurance PLC v. Golden Imports Ltd.*,[57] however, cargo lost during air shipment was later recovered. Based on the language of the policy and the documentation executed at the time of the loss, the court came to the conclusion that the underwriter was not entitled to recoup the money paid. Presumably, the insurer was entitled to retain the goods for salvage.

To prevent disputes in cases of delay, some cargo insurers require that their insured sign a "loan receipt" promising to take delivery of the missing goods and to refund the insurance payment should the goods ultimately be delivered. An example of a loan receipt is contained in Appendix L.[58]

7.3.3 Ordinary Wear and Tear

"Ordinary wear and tear" — the ordinary aging or deterioration of the vessel or cargo — is not insured under a policy of marine insurance in the absence of specific language.[59] The principle was expressed in an early Ontario case, *Coons v. Aetna Insurance Co.*,[60] where the insured vessel began to leak soon after leaving port and later sank in good weather. The court held that the circumstances raised a presumption that the loss did not arise by perils of the seas. The court quoted Chief Justice Cockburn in *Patterson v. Harris* that,

> ...the purpose of insurance is to afford protection against contingencies and damages which may or may not occur: it cannot properly apply to a case where the loss or injury must take place in the ordinary course of things. The wear and tear of a ship, the decay of her sheathing, the action of worms on her bottom, have been properly held not to be included in the insurance against perils of the sea, as being unavoidable consequences of the service to which the vessel is exposed: the insurer cannot be understood as undertaking to indemnify against losses which in the nature of things must necessarily happen.[61]

Where the loss or injury "must take place in the ordinary course of things", there is no fortuity, but rather a certainty. In each case it will be a matter of determining whether the proximate cause of the loss was a fortuity or ordinary wear and tear.[62]

---

[57] (1989), 43 C.C.L.I. 313, [1990] I.L.R. ¶1-2562 (B.C. Co. Ct.).

[58] In cases other than missing goods, there are potential problems related to the use of a loan receipt in lieu of a subrogation receipt. These are discussed in Chapter 12, *Subrogation*.

[59] *C.M.I.A.*, subs. 53(2)(*b*). Many policies do contain specific exclusions for wear and tear. See *Miller v. Elite Insurance Co.*, [1987] B.C.J. No. 89 (B.C. Co. Ct.) (QL).

[60] (1868), 18 U.C.C.P. 305.

[61] *Ibid.*, at 309-10, quoting (1861), 7 Jur. N.S. 1279, 1 B & S. 336.

[62] See, for example, *Hill v. Union Insurance Society of Canton Ltd.* (1927), 61 O.L.R. 201, [1927] 4 D.L.R. 718 (C.A.), where it was held that damage to the sails of a ship was not a result of wear and tear, but was a casualty that could not be foreseen as one of the usual incidents of the voyage. The court noted that if the sails tear in an ordinary wind, the loss would be due to deterioration by age and not a peril of the sea. See also *Seattle Construction & Dry Dock Co. v. Grant, Smith & Co.*, [1918] 3 W.W.R. 703, 44 D.L.R. 90 (B.C.C.A.), aff'd. [1919] 3 W.W.R. 33, [1920]

In the Federal Court of Canada decision, *Williams v. Canada*, referred to above, the Court adopted the suggestion in a leading text that in modern times, at least in the case of hull and machinery insurance, the "wear and tear" exception will be limited to those cases where there is a "general debility of the vessel":

> It is submitted that the better view is probably that a defence of wear and tear or inherent vice is applicable to cases where the loss is attributable to a general debility of the vessel such as to make it plain that the loss was a certainty, whatever the state of the weather or the sea, but that the defence is unlikely to prevail in cases where there is a sudden failure of a part of the structure, even though this may have long-standing causes, or be due merely to metal fatigue and though the weather and sea conditions may be in no way unusual or extreme . . .[63]

This statement should be applied with caution, since the court concluded that the loss was due to a collision with a submerged object rather than wear and tear or metal fatigue.

7.3.4   Ordinary Leakage or Breakage

Certain commodities are susceptible to leakage or breakage as a result of their nature and the manner in which they are usually shipped. When wine is shipped in casks or flour in bags, a certain amount of loss is to be expected. Losses of this nature are inevitable rather than fortuitous and for this reason they are not covered, even under an "all risks" policy. The loss or damage is not a "risk", but rather a "certainty". Loss due to "ordinary wear and tear, ordinary leakage or breakage or inherent vice" are excluded by section 53(2)(*b*) of the *C.M.I.A.* This exception was perhaps more relevant in the days before sophisticated shipping techniques. Today, most cargos, properly packaged, should be able to reach their destination undamaged. The failure to prepare or package a cargo to withstand the ordinary stresses of transportation is a form of "inherent vice" and is discussed in the next section.

A.C. 162 (J.C.P.C.). See *C.C.R. Fishing Ltd. v. British Reserve Insurance Co.*, [1990] 1 S.C.R. 814, 43 C.C.L.I. 1, rev'g. (1988), 55 D.L.R. (4th) 429, 34 B.C.L.R. (2d) 1 (C.A.), rev'g. (1986), 21 C.C.L.I. 297 (B.C.S.C.) at 43 C.C.L.I. 1 at 10, where the court adopted the definition of "ordinary wear and tear" contained in M.J. Mustel and J.C.B. Gilman, eds., *Arnould's Law of Marine Insurance and Average*, vol. 2, 16th ed. (London: Stevens, 1981): ordinary wear and tear is "merely the result of ordinary service conditions operating upon the hull or machinery, as for example when the relevant part wears out". The Supreme Court stated that while ordinary corrosion might fall within this definition, it did not apply to corrosion caused by the negligent use of the wrong materials.

[63]   (1984), 7 C.C.L.I. 198 at 209 (F.C.T.D.), quoting from M.J. Mustel and J.C.B. Gilman, eds., *Law of Marine Insurance and Average*, 16th ed. (London: Stevens, 1981), para. 798 at 659.

7.3.5 Inherent Vice or Nature of the Subject-Matter Insured

Unless the policy otherwise provides, the insurer is not liable for loss caused by "inherent vice or nature of the subject-matter insured".[64] The term "inherent vice" refers to a loss "stemming from qualities inherent in the thing lost".[65] One of the most frequent applications of the term is in cargo insurance, where it refers to the inherent tendency of the cargo, shipped as it is, to sustain damage. The insurer does not agree to insure against damage that is bound to happen as a result of the natural tendency of the cargo to deteriorate or sustain damage. This may occur because of the nature of the cargo, or the manner in which it is shipped, or a combination of the two. For example, fresh produce will gradually age and inevitably deteriorate, no matter how it is shipped. Damage due to the inherent tendency of produce to decay is inherent vice. On the other hand, if it is shipped in a refrigerated container that breaks down due to the operation of an insured peril, this is a fortuity and the resultant damage to the cargo is not attributable to inherent vice.

Inherent vice is also used to describe a loss that, due to the manner in which the cargo is shipped, is regarded as inevitable. For example, fresh eggs shipped without any packing or protection are likely to sustain damage no matter how carefully they are handled. Chocolates shipped in an ordinary container in the summer are bound to melt. Damage that occurs in the course of ordinary handling and transportation of cargos, without the intervention of a fortuity, is due to inherent vice.[66]

In *Star-Rite International Food Inc. v. Maritime Insurance Co.*,[67] a cargo of ginger root had been shipped in an unrefrigerated container from the tropics to Canada. It deteriorated in transit as a result of build-up of moisture within the container and on the surface of the product. The shipment was insured on an "all risks" basis, but the marine insurer pleaded inherent vice, arguing that the loss was bound to happen given the manner in which the cargo was shipped. The court referred to the famous statement of Lord Sumner in *British and Foreign Marine Insurance Co. v. Gaunt*:

> There are, of course, limits to "all risks". There are risks and risks insured against. Accordingly the expression does not cover inherent vice or mere wear and tear or British capture. It covers a risk, not a certainty; it is something which happens to the subject-matter from without, not the natural behaviour of that subject-matter, being what it is, in the circumstances under which it is carried. Nor is it a loss

---

[64] For a case in which the policy provided otherwise, see *Soya GmbH Mainz KG v. White*, [1983] 1 Ll. Rep. 122 (H.L.).

[65] *C.C.R. Fishing Ltd. v. British Reserve Insurance Co.*, [1990] 1 S.C.R. 814, 43 C.C.L.I. 1, rev'g. (1988), 44 D.L.R. (4th) 429, 34 B.C.L.R. (2d) 1 (C.A.), rev'g. (1986), 21 C.C.L.I. 297 (B.C.S.C.).

[66] See *Gee and Garnham Ltd. v. Whittall*, [1955] 2 Ll. R. 562 (Q.B.D.); *F.W. Berk & Co. v. Style*, [1955] 2 Ll. Rep. 382 (Q.B.D.); *Soya GmbH Mainz KG v. White*, [1983] 1 Ll. Rep. 122 (H.L.).

[67] (December 12, 1984), (Ont. Co. Ct.), appeal dismissed [1986] O.J. No. 542 (Ont. C.A.) (QL).

which the assured brings about by his own act, for then he has not merely exposed the goods to the chance of injury, he has injured them himself.[68]

With reference to inherent vice, the trial judge in the *Star-Rite* case stated:

> This phrase (generally shortened to "inherent vice"), where it is used in s. 55(2)(c) [of the Ontario *Marine Insurance Act*] refers to a peril by which a loss is proximately caused; it is not descriptive of the loss itself. It means the risk of deterioration of the goods shipped as a result of their natural behaviour in the ordinary course of the contemplated voyage without the intervention of any fortuitous external accident or casualty.[69]

The plaintiff contended that it had given specific instructions to the ocean carrier to leave the doors of the container open during the ocean voyage to allow ventilation and to prevent the build-up of moisture, and that it had shipped similar cargos in this manner in the past, without sustaining damage. The court accepted this evidence and held that the failure of the ocean carrier to follow the shipper's instructions was a fortuity, taking the case out of the "inherent vice" exception.

In *Equipements de Ferme Lambo (1980) Inc. v. Royal Insurance Canada*,[70] goods being carried on a truck were damaged when they hit a bridge overpass. The insurer pleaded inherent vice based on the alleged failure of the shipper to advise the carrier that the goods were over-height. The Federal Court of Canada rejected this contention, holding that the negligence of the carrier was a fortuity.

One of the most troublesome issues in marine cargo insurance has been the question of damage attributable to insufficient packing of the cargo. Goods transported internationally are subject to the rolling of ships, bumping of rail cars and trucks, and handling by stevedores and others. Goods must be packed in such a way as to withstand these ordinary incidents of transport. Based on the leading English authorities,[71] it is clear that damage attributable to the failure of the shipper to properly pack the cargo so as to enable it to withstand the "ordinary rigours" of the intended transportation is a form of inherent vice and unrecoverable. This line of authority has been followed in an Ontario case, *Balix Furniture & Appliances Ltd. v. Maritime Insurance Co.*, in which the plaintiff claimed for damage to a shipment of paintings. The trial judge found that the paintings had been inadequately packed:

> [D]amage resulting from improper or inadequate packing is an "inherent vice" in the goods which relieves the insurer from liability even under an "all risks" policy, as here, unless expressly excluded. Authority for this proposition may be found in several cases, of which *Gee and Garnham Ltd. v. Whittall* (1955) 2 Lloyd's Rep. 562, is one.

---

68   [1921] 2 A.C. 41 at 57.
69   (December 12, 1984), (Ont. Co. Ct.).
70   [1986] F.C.J. No. 290 (F.C.T.D.) (QL).
71   See *Gee and Garnham Ltd. v. Whittall*, [1955] 2 Ll. R. 562 (Q.B.D.); *F.W. Berk & Co. v. Style*, [1955] 2 Ll. Rep. 382 (Q.B.D.).

Accordingly, I dismiss the plaintiff's claim arising from the damage to the paintings. . . ."[72]

The issue of insufficiency of packing has been addressed by the Institute Cargo Clauses (1/1/82),[73] which contain an exclusion for:

> 4.3 loss damage or expense caused by insufficiency or unsuitability of packing or preparation of the subject-matter insured (for the purpose of this Clause 4.3 "packing" shall be deemed to include stowage in a container or liftvan but only when such stowage is carried out prior to attachment of this insurance or by the Assured or their servants).

The intent of the first part of this clause is clear enough and confirms the exclusion of loss caused by insufficient packing — that is, damage occurring without the intervention of any negligent or fortuitous event due to the failure to package the cargo so as to withstand the foreseeable rigours of transport. The second part of the clause, dealing with containerized cargo, is intended to exclude damage attributable to either (a) bad packing carried out by the insured or its *servants*; or (b) bad packing carried out before the insurance attaches which, in the case of "warehouse to warehouse coverage", usually means before the goods have left the shipper's premises. The reference to the insured's *servants* is noteworthy since this would normally refer to employees, as opposed to *agents* or third parties contracted by the insured.

Clause 4.3 of the Institute Cargo Clauses (1/1/82) was considered by the Federal Court of Canada in *Rainbow Technicoloured Wood Veneer Ltd. v. Guardian Insurance Co. of Canada.*[74] The insurer alleged, based on the expert evidence of marine surveyors, that the packing of a machine within the ocean container was inadequate because appropriate methods of securing the cargo had not been employed. The packing of the container had been carried out in Italy by a subcontractor at the premises of the supplier. Mr. Justice Dubé held that the loss was not covered. Referring to the "duration clause" (8.1) and to the "exclusion clause" (4.3) of the Institute Cargo Clauses (1/1/82) (A), he said:

> It seems to me that the language of those clauses is clear. Under clause 4.3, damage incurred by insufficiency of packing into a container leads to exclusion from insurance coverage if packing is carried out prior to the attachment of the insurance or is carried out by the assured. In the instant case, packing was not carried out by the assured but it was carried out prior to the attachment. Under clause 8.1, the insurance attaches from the time the cargo leaves the place of storage. And when the guillotine left the place of storage of Emme Elle the [packing] had already been carried out and, as it turned out, not properly carried out.

> There is no jurisprudence directly on point because the purpose of those two clauses is crystal clear. Insufficiency of packing and clause 4.3 are discussed in

---

[72] [1978] O.J. No. 1514 (Ont. Co. Ct.) (QL) at paras. 8-9.
[73] See Appendices B, C and D.
[74] (2000), 184 F.T.R. 304, [2000] I.L.R. ¶1-3838, aff'd. (2002), 288 N.R. 17, [2002] I.L.R. ¶1-4083 (F.C.A.).

Arnould's Law of Marine Insurance and Average [footnote omitted], and more precisely at paragraph 215 (p. 215) as follows:

> 215. As has already been noted, insufficiency or unsuitability of packing is treated as a separate *exclusion from cover* under this sub-clause, and the exclusion is qualified by providing that stowage in a container or liftvan shall be deemed to be included in "packing", but only *when such stowage is carried out prior to attachment of the insurance or by the assured or their servants*. This provision appears to be drafted on the assumption that damage due to defective packing in containers will not be excluded, under the wider provisions of the inherent vice exceptions at Clause 4.4, in the circumstances contemplated in Clause 4.3 in which the container is not to be treated as "packing".[75] (emphasis added)

The judge went on to state:

> In the case at bar, the insufficiency of packing occurred prior to attachment of the insurance. That condition by itself results in the exclusion of coverage, whether or not the packing was carried out by the assured or his servants.[76]

The trial judgment was affirmed by the Federal Court of Appeal.[77]

In theory, a policy could provide coverage for "inherent vice",[78] although it would be unusual that an insurer would agree to provide coverage for something that was truly inevitable.

7.3.6   Loss Caused by Vermin

The *M.I.A. 1906* contained an exclusion for any loss proximately caused by "rats or vermin", whereas the *C.M.I.A.* only carried forward the exclusion for "vermin". The exclusion for rats dates back to the days of sailing ships, when rats were a common problem and a source of inevitable damage to cargo as well as a peril to the ship itself.[79] With the advent of steel ships and modern rodent control methods, the drafters of the Canadian legislation may have been content to leave the exclusion of vermin only. The term "vermin" may, however, include rats which begs the question — are rats, therefore, covered within the definition of "vermin" within the *C.M.I.A.*, or did the drafters consider that in the modern world rats are a peril?

7.3.7   Loss or Damage to Machinery
Not Caused By Insured Perils

Section 53(2)(*d*) of the *C.M.I.A.* excludes liability for "any loss or damage to machinery not proximately caused by maritime perils", unless the policy

---

[75]   *Ibid.*, at 307 F.T.R.

[76]   *Ibid.*, at 308 F.T.R.

[77]   (2002), 288 N.R. 17, [2002] I.L.R. ¶1-4083 (F.C.A.).

[78]   *Soya GmbH Mainz KG v. White*, [1983] 1 Ll. Rep. 122 (H.L.).

[79]   See *Hamilton v. Pandorf* (1887), 12 App. Cas. 518 (H.L.) to the effect that rats causing a leak that allows ingress of seawater and damages cargo constitutes a peril of the sea.

otherwise provides. Hull and machinery policies invariably contain a clause, known as the *"Inchmaree* clause", that does "otherwise provide". The clause was incorporated into such policies as a result of a case involving the ship *Inchmaree*: *Thames & Mersey Marine Insurance Co. v. Hamilton, Fraser & Co.*[80] In that case, the House of Lords held that a sailor's negligent closing of a valve, causing damage to a pump, was not a "peril of the sea", nor did it fall within the term "all other perils, losses and misfortunes..." in the S.G. policy form.[81] Following this case, hull and machinery policies were amended by adding an *Inchmaree* clause covering:

> loss of, or damage to hull or machinery through the negligence of master, mariners, engineers or pilots, or through explosion, bursting of boilers, breakage of shafts, or through any latent defect in the machinery or hull; provided such loss or damage has not resulted through want of due diligence by the owners of the ship or any of them, or by the manager . . .

The *Inchmaree* clause extends the hull and machinery policy to cover various accidents arising in the operation of the ship. Among other things, this clause covers damage to machinery and damage to the ship caused by negligence of the crew, provided that the loss or damage has not resulted from the negligence of the insured shipowner. The intent of the clause is that underwriters agree to insure the ship and its machinery against the consequences of certain types of "accidental" damage, including damage caused by operational negligence of shipboard employees, provided that it is not attributable to the failure of the owner to act responsibly in the upkeep of the ships or the training of the crew. This includes taking reasonable care to engage a competent crew, as well as to providing the necessary training, instruction and supervision to ensure that the crew members are capable of carrying out their duties in a responsible manner. In one of the leading U.S. cases, *Allen N. Spooner & Son Inc. v. Connecticut Fire Insurance Co.*, the clause was described as extending to:

> seagoing or operational negligence of the master (whether or not he is also the charterer or owner) [but as excluding damage] due to the shoreside failure of the shipowner's managerial staff properly to prepare or equip the vessel for the voyage or service she is about to perform.[82]

The Canadian Board of Marine Underwriters Great Lakes Hull Clauses (Sept. 1, 1971) and Canadian Hulls (Pacific) Clauses (Sept. 1/91) contain *Inchmaree* clauses, with slight differences in language.[83]

The leading Canadian case on the *Inchmaree* clause is the decision of the Supreme Court of Canada in *Coast Ferries Ltd. v. Century Insurance Co. of*

---

[80]   (1887), 12 App. Cas. 484, 6 Asp. M.L.C. 200 (H.L.), rev'g. (1886), 17 Q.B.D. 195 (C.A.).

[81]   In legal terminology, this is referred to as the *ejusdem generis* principle of interpretation.

[82]   [1963] A.M.C. 859 (United States Court of Appeals, 2nd Cir.).

[83]   The Canadian Board of Marine Underwriters Great Lakes Hull Clauses (Sept. 1, 1971) are reproduced in Appendix G; the Canadian Hulls (Pacific) Clauses (Sept. 1/91) are reproduced in Appendix E. See generally Chapter 19, *Hull and Machinery Insurance.*

Canada.[84] That case concerned the capsizing of a converted automobile ferry that was being used as a freighter. The vessel rolled over and lost its cargo off the British Columbia coast as a result of negligent loading by the master. It was found that the ship was in an unseaworthy condition for which the master was to blame. The issue before the court, however, was whether the master's negligence occurred without "want of due diligence by the Assured" so as to bring the claim within the *Inchmaree* clause. The trial judge had found that there was no lack of due diligence, but the British Columbia Court of Appeal reversed. Mr. Justice Davey stated:

> But when the owner left full responsibility for the loading to the master it became its duty to furnish the master with sufficient information about minimum freeboard and trim for the vessel (among other data) to enable the master to exercise sound judgment in loading in the light of his skill and experience. The owner did not do so. Therein lay its want of due diligence. That information was especially necessary because the owner's standing instructions required the master to load the cargo on the vessel (mostly on the deck for which the vessel was well suited) in the inverse order to which it was to be unloaded according to the order of ports of call. Such procedure on occasion required heavier items of deck cargo to be placed well forward, which would depress the bow. On some occasions the owner, not the master, changed the usual order of ports of call to avoid excessive draught at the stem.[85]

The Court of Appeal noted that the owner had a naval architect's report concerning the stability of the ship but had failed to make it available to the master or to discuss its implications with him, and had failed to give him proper loading instructions.

The owner appealed to the Supreme Court of Canada, which confirmed the decision of the Court of Appeal. The Supreme Court found that the owner had not taken basic precautions to verify the master's conduct, had failed to furnish the master with appropriate information and had not put appropriate safety systems in place. Mr. Justice de Grandpré stated:

> The duty of due diligence imposed upon the owner is not satisfied if for years he closes his eyes and does nothing. His obligation is to act reasonably in the circumstances and the evidence in the present case discloses that the appellant's main competitor maintains a much better procedure.[86]

It was held that the owner had not exercised due diligence and the insured was not entitled to recover under the *Inchmaree* clause.

"Due diligence" is a legal term used in a variety of contexts, including marine insurance. It essentially means "reasonable care in the circumstances". In determining "due diligence", the court will consider all the surrounding circumstances, including those known or reasonably to be expected. In setting a

---

[84]   [1975] 2 S.C.R. 477, 48 D.L.R. (3d) 310, aff'g. B.C.C.A., rev'g. (1971), 23 D.L.R. (3d) 226, [1971] I.L.R. ¶1-439 (B.C.S.C.).

[85]   Quoted at 481 S.C.R.

[86]   [1975] 2 S.C.R. 477 at 483.

standard of due diligence, the court will consider the practice of others involved in the same industry, although a court may find that the industry practice is itself negligent.[87] In *Charles Goodfellow Lumber Sales Ltd. v. Verreault*,[88] the Supreme Court of Canada considered the concept of "due diligence" in relation to the carriage of goods by water and adopted the following definition in *Maxine Footwear v. Canadian Government Merchant Marine Ltd.*:

> "Due diligence" seems to be equivalent to reasonable diligence, having regard to the circumstances known, or fairly to be expected, and to the nature of the voyage, and the cargo to be carried. It will suffice to satisfy the condition if such diligence has been exercised down to the sailing from the loading port. But the fitness of the ship at that time must be considered with reference to the cargo, and to the intended course of the voyage; and the burden is upon the shipowner to establish that there has been diligence to make her fit.[89]

While *Goodfellow* was a case under the *Carriage of Goods by Water Act*,[90] the test of "due diligence" under the *Inchmaree* clause is likely the same.[91] Unlike in the case of carriage of goods by water, however, the shipowner has no burden of proving the exercise of due diligence. The legal burden or *onus* will be on underwriters to establish a lack of due diligence.[92]

The due diligence of the owner is only a consideration where the insured makes a claim under the *Inchmaree* clause as opposed to some other provision of the policy, such as the "perils of the seas" clause in the S.G. Form or some other "named peril" in other forms of policy. In *Atwood v. Canada*,[93] referred to above, a fishing vessel insured under a policy issued by the Canadian Fishing Vessel Insurance Plan was destroyed in a fire. The insurer claimed that the

---

[87] See, for example, *Hatfield v. Canada* (1984), 5 C.C.L.I. 276, [1984] I.L.R. ¶1-1781 (F.C.T.D.), aff'd. (1984), 10 C.C.L.I. 280, [1984] I.L.R. ¶1-1838 (F.C.A.), supplementary reasons [1984] I.L.R. ¶1-1781, in which Mr. Justice Urie, giving the judgment of the Federal Court of Appeal, stated: "I agree with counsel for the defence that a time-honoured practice is not 'due diligence', if it is a bad practice."

[88] [1971] S.C.R. 522, 17 D.L.R. (3d) 56.

[89] [1952] Ex. C.R. 569, aff'd. [1956] Ex. C.R. 234, aff'd. [1957] S.C.R. 801, 10 D.L.R. (2d) 513, rev'd. [1959] A.C. 589, 21 D.L.R. (2d) 1 (P.C.), at 808 S.C.R., quoting from *Carver's Carriage of Goods by Sea*, 9th ed. (1952) at 182.

[90] S.C. 1993, c. 21 [repealed, 2001, c. 6, s. 130].

[91] This was confirmed in *Hatfield v. Canada* (1984), 5 C.C.L.I. 276 at 282, in which Mr. Justice Collier adopted the statement in *Goodfellow* that due diligence means "reasonable diligence, having regard to the circumstances known, or fairly to be expected, and to the nature of the voyage and the cargo to be carried".

[92] *Hatfield v. Canada* (1984), 5 C.C.L.I. 276, [1984] I.L.R. ¶1-1781 (F.C.T.D.), aff'd. (1984), 10 C.C.L.I. 280, [1984] I.L.R. ¶1-1838 (F.C.A.). In *Morris v. Canada (Minister of Fisheries and Oceans)* (1991), 47 F.T.R. 271, [1992] I.L.R. ¶1-2807, the plaintiff's fishing vessel was insured under the Fishing Vessel Insurance Plan. It capsized and sank as a result of the negligence of the engineer in the operation of the pumping system. The insurer defended on various grounds, including the allegation that the insured had not exercised due diligence in hiring the engineer, the master or the crew. The court was not prepared to find that these individuals were incompetent generally or that the owners had failed to exercise due diligence in hiring them.

[93] (1985), 10 C.C.L.I. 62 (F.C.T.D.).

vessel had been sent to sea in an unseaworthy state and that there was a lack of due diligence on the part of the insured in attempting to start the engine using a screwdriver. The court stated that the defence of due diligence becomes available only where the insured invokes coverage under the *Inchmaree* clause:

> That coverage is set out in cl. 4 of the plaintiff's policy. The plaintiff here did not put his loss under that coverage. The question of due diligence does not, therefore, arise."[94]

Similarly, in *Century Insurance Co. of Canada v. Case Existological Laboratories Ltd.*,[95] also discussed above, both the British Columbia Court of Appeal and the Supreme Court of Canada said that the insurer's allegations of unseaworthiness were really allegations of lack of due diligence that would only have been relevant to a claim under the *Inchmaree* clause. Since there was no claim under that clause, the allegations were not relevant.

Interesting questions have arisen under the *Inchmaree* clause in cases where the owner is also the master of the vessel. Is the negligence of the master to be treated as a lack of due diligence as an owner, so as to preclude coverage under the clause? In *Holm v. Underwriters Through T.W. Rice & Co. Inc.*,[96] the plaintiff's yacht sank at its mooring in the Powell River in British Columbia after he had removed a hose from an exhaust port. He left the vessel at its mooring with no one to look after it, apparently relying on the bilge pump to remove any accumulation of water. Two weeks later the vessel sank. The policy insured the vessel against "all risks of physical loss of or damage from any external cause" and included an *Inchmaree* clause.

The court found that the plaintiff had not established coverage under the "all risks" cover, since he had not established loss by an external cause, other than the normal movements of wind and water. The court also found that the sinking resulted from the failure of the plaintiff, as "master" of his own boat, to plug the open exhaust port. The question then became whether there might be coverage under the *Inchmaree* clause. Since the assured was both the owner and the "master" of the boat, could his obvious negligence as "master" be separated from his conduct as "owner"? Expressed another way, could he have exercised "due diligence" as owner when he had obviously failed to do so as master? Referring to another Canadian decision dealing with the role of an owner-master of a pleasure vessel in the context of limitation of liability,[97] the judge concluded that in cases of this kind it is possible to make a distinction between acts of the

---

[94]   *Ibid.*, at 68, referring to *H.B. Nickerson & Sons Ltd. v. Insurance Co. of North America*, [1984] 1 F.C. 575, 49 N.R. 321 (C.A.), leave to appeal refused (1984), 54 N.R. 80*n* (S.C.C.); *Williams v. Canada* (1984), 7 C.C.L.I. 198 (F.C.T.D.); *Hatfield v. Canada* (1984), 5 C.C.L.I. 276, [1984] I.L.R. ¶1-1781 (F.C.T.D.), aff'd. (1984), 10 C.C.L.I. 280, [1984] I.L.R. ¶1-1838 (F.C.A.). See also *Suo v. Openshaw Simmons Ltd.* (1978), 5 B.C.L.R. 370, [1978] I.L.R. ¶1-982.

[95]   [1983] 2 S.C.R. 47, 2 C.C.L.I. 172, aff'g. (1982), 35 B.C.L.R. 364, [1982] I.L.R. ¶1-1567, rev'g. (1980), 116 D.L.R. (3d) 199, [1981] I.L.R. ¶1-1335 (B.C.S.C.).

[96]   (1981), 124 D.L.R. (3d) 463, [1981] I.L.R. ¶1-1438 (B.C.S.C.).

[97]   See *Walithy Charters Ltd. v. Doig* (1979), 15 B.C.L.R. 45 (S.C.).

individual in his or her capacity as master and acts in his or her capacity as owner. The judge stated:

> ...I must ask whether exercise of due diligence by the plaintiff as owner would have saved the vessel. Ought the plaintiff, in his capacity as owner, to have done something which would have removed the peril in which he placed the vessel by his negligence as master?[98]

The judge concluded that in his capacity as owner the plaintiff ought to have taken steps to have someone look after his boat:

> I find myself obliged in the circumstances to say that the loss occurred as a result of "want of due diligence" on the plaintiff's part in his capacity as owner. While the problem which resulted in the sinking was caused by the plaintiff's negligence as master, no damage would have flowed from it had the plaintiff shown due diligence as owner. Simply put, the plaintiff had to have some knowledgeable person look at the boat within a reasonable time if he wished to protect his coverage.[99]

There was, therefore, no coverage under the *Inchmaree* clause.

Other Canadian cases on the *Inchmaree* clause have evidenced a judicial reluctance to place too heavy a responsibility on the owners of small commercial vessels.[100] For example, in *Cleveland v. Sunderland Marine Mutual Insurance Co.*,[101] the Nova Scotia Supreme Court found that the sinking of a fishing vessel was due to perils of the seas, and that modifications to the vessel carried out by the owner, and even the operation of the vessel without government inspection and certification, were not indicative of a want of due diligence. These cases suggest that if the court is satisfied that the owner has made a reasonable and responsible effort to conduct a safe operation, it will be reluctant to find a failure to exercise due diligence.

The *Inchmaree* clause extends to losses caused by latent defects. In *J.L. Fisheries Ltd. v. Boston Insurance Co.*,[102] a hull and machinery policy on a scallop dragger contained an *Inchmaree* clause insuring against "damage ...directly caused by...breakage of shafts or any latent defect in the machinery". While the vessel was engaged in normal operations there was a breakage of a shaft resulting in damage to the main propulsion machinery. The insurer argued that the loss was caused by a defect in the design of the machinery rather than a latent defect, and that therefore it was not covered under the *Inchmaree* clause. The trial judge traced the evolution of the *Inchmaree* clause and, quoting from *Arnould*, pointed out that "The clause contains the agreement between the

---

[98] (1981), 124 D.L.R. (3d) 463 at 470 (B.C.S.C.).

[99] *Ibid.*

[100] *Hatfield v. Canada* (1984), 5 C.C.L.I. 276, [1984] I.L.R. ¶1-1781 (F.C.T.D.), aff'd. (1984), 10 C.C.L.I. 280, [1984] I.L.R. ¶1-1838 (F.C.A.); *Morris v. Canada (Minister of Fisheries and Oceans)* (1991), 47 F.T.R. 271, [1992] I.L.R. ¶1-2807; see also *Graystone v. Sun Alliance*, [1994] B.C.J. No. 3266 (B.C. Prov. Ct.) (QL).

[101] (1987), 45 D.L.R. (4th) 340, 81 N.S.R. (2d) 1 (S.C.T.D.), additional reasons at (1987), 85 N.S.R. (2d) 42 (S.C.T.D.).

[102] (1968), 69 D.L.R. (2d) 18, [1969] I.L.R. ¶1-227 (N.S.T.D.).

parties, defining the liability of underwriters for damage to hull or machinery in cases where the damage cannot be said to be the direct consequence of a maritime peril."[103] He also quoted from the Judgment of Lord Justice Scrutton in *Hutchins Brothers v. Royal Exchange Assurance Corp.*:

> The Inchmaree Clause is, in my view, an extension of the list of perils insured against in an ordinary Lloyd's policy, and only the actual loss or damage to hull from the named perils is recoverable. Loss to the shipowner's pocket is only recoverable as the measure of the actual loss of or damage to hull.
>
> . . . . .
>
> In my view what is recoverable under this part of the Inchmaree Clause is: (1) Actual total loss of a part of the hull or machinery, through a latent defect coming into existence and causing the loss during the period of the policy. This was the kind of latent defect alleged in the *Inchmaree* case. (2) Constructive total loss under the same circumstances, as where, though the part of the hull survives, it is by reason of the latent defect of no value and cannot be profitably repaired. (3) Damage to other parts of the hull happening during the currency of the policy, through a latent defect, even if the latter came into existence before the period of the policy. The pre-existing latent defect itself is not damage, indemnity for which is recoverable, even if by wear and tear it becomes visible during the policy.[104]

The judge found that there was in fact a breakage of shafts that brought the case within the *Inchmaree* clause. He would also have found that there was a latent defect in the machinery rather than a weakness in design, and there would have been coverage under this branch of the clause as well.

In *Atlantic Freighting Co. v. Provincial Insurance Co. of Canada*,[105] a vessel began to leak shortly after leaving port, sank and ultimately was declared a constructive total loss. The owner alleged that the damage was caused by a latent defect in the hull and that the claim fell within the *Inchmaree* clause. The court found that there was no latent defect, but even if there was one, the owners were precluded from recovery due to a failure to exercise due diligence to become aware of the defect and to rectify it before the vessel sailed. It was found that the owners knew that the vessel was in a weakened condition before it sailed and they should have taken measures to detect and correct the situation. Since a latent defect is one that cannot be discovered through the exercise of ordinary diligence, it is difficult to imagine a situation in which a true claim for the consequences of "latent defect" under the *Inchmaree* clause could be defeated by a failure to exercise due diligence. Merchant ships are required to be inspected periodically by their classification societies, and after the ship reaches a certain age the inspection usually includes a test of the integrity and thickness of the ship's hull plating. The failure to conduct such inspections and testing could be considered a lack of due diligence.

---

[103] *Arnould on Marine Insurance*, 13th ed., Vol. 2, at 783.
[104] [1911] 2 K.B. 398 at 405 and 406.
[105] (1956), 5 D.L.R. (2d) 164, [1956] I.L.R. ¶1-245 (N.S.S.C.).

7.4 PROXIMATE CAUSE

Section 53(1) of the *C.M.I.A.* mandates that, unless the policy otherwise provides, an insurer is only liable for a loss "proximately caused" by a peril insured against, including a loss which would not have occurred "but for the misconduct or negligence of the master or crew". This means that it is usually necessary to determine the "proximate cause" of the loss in order to ascertain whether the loss is covered by the policy.

The principle embodied in section 53(1) was expressed by Mr. Justice Ritchie of the Supreme Court of Canada in *John C. Jackson Ltd. v. Sun Insurance Office Ltd.*: "It has now long been recognized that the liability of a marine underwriter is limited to losses caused by the direct operation of one of the perils insured against..."[106] In practice, the application of this apparently simple principle has given rise to debates about causation that at times sounded more like philosophical dialogues than discussions of commercial insurance issues.[107]

Fortunately, in the leading case of *C.C.R. Fishing Ltd. v. British Reserve Insurance Co.*,[108] mentioned in section 7.2.1 of this Chapter, the Supreme Court of Canada explained the principle in plain and straightforward terms. The fishing vessel *LaPointe* was laid up at its berth when it sank as a result of the ingress of seawater due to two causes: (1) the failure of corroded screws that permitted seawater to enter the engine room; and (2) the failure of a crew member to close a valve that would have stopped the entry of water. The insurance policy was on the S.G. Form and insured against "perils of the sea". The trial judge had found that the loss was the result of negligence, was fortuitous and was a peril of the sea, resulting in coverage. The British Columbia Court of Appeal, with one judge dissenting, reversed, holding that there was no fortuitous accident or casualty of the sea. The insured appealed to the Supreme Court of Canada.

The Supreme Court stated that the issue was whether the sinking was a loss "proximately caused" by a peril of the sea. That depended on whether the cause of the sinking was a "fortuitous accident or casualty of the sea" as defined in the British Columbia *Insurance (Marine) Act*.[109] After concluding that it was, Justice McLachlin stated:

> I have approached the matter thus far on the assumption made in the Court of Appeal below that there can only be one proximate cause of the loss, concluding that even on that basis, there is coverage. However, I am of the view that it is wrong to place too much emphasis on the distinction between proximate and remote cause

---

[106] [1962] S.C.R. 412 at 416, 33 D.L.R. (2d) 513, aff'g. (1960), 25 D.L.R. (2d) 604, 33 W.W.R. 420 (B.C.C.A.), rev'g. (1960), 24 D.L.R. (2d) 53, 31 W.W.R. 660 (B.C.S.C.).

[107] See *H.B. Nickerson & Sons Ltd. v. Insurance Co. of North America*, [1984] 1 F.C. 575, 49 N.R. 321 (C.A.), leave to appeal refused (1984), 54 N.R. 80*n* (S.C.C.); *Case Existological Laboratories v. Foremost Insurance Co.* (1982), 133 D.L.R. (3d) 727, 35 B.C.L.R. 364 (C.A.), aff'd. [1983] 2 S.C.R. 47, 150 D.L.R. (3d) 9; *Williams v. Canada* (1984), 7 C.C.L.I. 198 (F.C.T.D.).

[108] [1990] 1 S.C.R. 814, 43 C.C.L.I. 1, rev'g. (1988), 55 D.L.R. (4th) 429, 34 B.C.L.R. (2d) 1 (C.A.), rev'g. (1986), 21 C.C.L.I. 297 (B.C.S.C.).

[109] R.S.B.C. 1979, c. 203, Schedule, s. 7.

in construing policies such as this. Generally speaking, the authorities do not follow such a course. I do not read s. 56 of the *Insurance (Marine) Act* as limiting the cause of the loss to a single peril. Realistically speaking, it must be recognized that several factors may combine to result in a loss at sea. It is unrealistic to exclude from consideration any one of them provided it has contributed to the loss. What is essential in order to establish that the loss is "fortuitous" is an accident caused by the intervention of negligence, or adverse or unusual conditions without which the loss would not have occurred. This is the shared idea which underlies the exclusion from coverage of damage due to ordinary wear and tear or inherent vice.[110]

She concluded:

In summary, it is my view that the following procedure should be followed in determining whether a loss was proximately caused by a peril of the sea. First, the cause or causes of the loss should be ascertained. It should then be asked whether the loss is fortuitous in that it would not have occurred but for an accident or unforeseen event brought about by negligence or adverse or unusual conditions. The loss will not be fortuitous if the exclusions in s. 56(2) or in the definition of "perils of the seas" in the schedule to the Act are established. If the loss is fortuitous in this sense then the policy applies.

I am of the view that regardless of how the cause of the loss is analyzed, the loss here was the result of a "fortuitous accident" related to or "of the sea", and hence within the coverage for perils of the sea. Having said that, it is my view that in determining whether a loss falls within the policy, the cause of the loss should be determined by looking at all the events which gave rise to it and asking whether it is fortuitous in the sense that the accident would not have occurred "but for" or without an act or event which is fortuitous in the sense that it was not to be expected in the ordinary course of things. This approach is preferable, in my view, to the artificial exercise of segregating the causes of the loss with a view to labelling one as proximate and the others as remote, an exercise on which the best of minds may differ. On this approach, the loss here at issue falls within the policy because it would not have occurred but for the negligent act of leaving open the valve.[111]

The Supreme Court's decision was clearly intended to lay down a test that would be clear and simple to apply, and would help resolve rather than foster insurance disputes. Justice McLachlin stated:

The question of whether insurance applies to a loss should not depend on metaphysical debates as to which of various caused contributing to an accident was proximate. Apart from the apparent injustice of making indemnity dependent on such fine and contestable reasoning, such a test is calculated to produce disputed claims and litigation. It should be sufficient to bring the loss within the risk if it is established that, viewed in the entire context of the case, the loss is shown to be

---

[110] [1990] 1 S.C.R. 814 at 822-23.
[111] *Ibid.*, at 825-26.

fortuitous in the sense that it would not have occurred save for an unusual event not ordinarily to be expected in the normal course of things.[112]

While the case was concerned with a policy insuring against perils of the sea, the Supreme Court's observations suggest that the determination of whether or not a cause is the "proximate cause" of the loss, within the meaning of subsection 53(1) of the *C.M.I.A.*, is to be based on broad common-sense principles. The cause or causes of the loss must first be determined and it must then be asked whether the loss would not have occurred "but for" the insured peril. If so, the loss was proximately caused by the peril.

Difficult issues may arise where the loss can be said to have two or more causes, one being an insured peril and the other being an excluded peril. In *Sin Mac Lines Ltd. v. Hartford Fire Insurance Co.*,[113] it was held that in appropriate cases the court can apportion the damage caused by the insured peril, but this may not be possible where the damage is not divisible. Arguably, if an excluded peril is a proximate cause of the loss, there should be no coverage, notwithstanding that another insured peril was also operative.[114]

7.5 BURDEN OF PROOF

The "burden of proof" is a legal term referring to the legal onus of establishing a fact to the satisfaction of the court, which in civil cases is "on a balance of probabilities". In a named perils policy, the insured bears the burden of proving that the loss was proximately caused by an insured peril.[115] If the insured discharges this burden, the insurer bears the burden of proving that the loss falls within an exception.[116] Thus, In *Williams v. Canada*, Mr. Justice McNair of the Federal Court of Canada stated:

---

[112] *Ibid.*, at 823. See *MacMillan Bloedel Ltd. v. Youell* (1993), 95 B.C.L.R. (2d) 130, in which the British Columbia Court of Appeal held that the costs of removing, storing and reloading the ship's cargo were not proximately caused by the peril insured against — they were not the direct result of the steps taken to prevent fire loss of the vessel and cargo.

[113] [1937] S.C.R. v (J.C.P.C.), [1936] S.C.R. 598, [1936] 3 D.L.R. 412, aff'g. (1935), 2 I.L.R. 597 (Que. C.A.), aff'g. (1934), 72 Que. S.C. 213, 1 I.L.R. 308.

[114] See *Charterhouse Properties Ltd. v. Laurentian Pacific Insurance* (1991), 56 B.C.L.R. (2d) 329, 4 C.C.L.I. (2d) 299 (S.C.), rev'd. (1993), 75 B.C.L.R. (2d) 299, 14 C.C.L.I. (2d) 299 (C.A.); *Lizotte v. Traders General Insurance Co.* (1986), 20 C.C.L.I. 320, [1986] 3 W.W.R. 546 (B.C.C.A.), aff'g. [1985] 1 W.W.R. 595, [1985] I.L.R. ¶1-1874 (B.C.S.C.). In *Continental Insurance Co. v. Almassa International Inc.*, unreported (24 March 2003), Toronto (Ont. Sup. Ct. of Justice), the court held that whether or not an exclusion clause ousts coverage where an insured peril operates concurrently with an excluded peril is a matter of construction of the policy. In that particular case, it was held that the language of the exclusionary clause was not sufficiently clear to exclude coverage.

[115] See *Stad v. Fireman's Fund Insurance Co.*, [1979] I.L.R. ¶1-1070 (B.C.S.C.); *Marion Logging Co. v. Utah Home Fire Insurance Co.* (1956), 5 D.L.R. (2d) 700, [1957] I.L.R. ¶1-250, (B.C.S.C.); *J.L. Fisheries Ltd. v. Boston Insurance Co.* (1968), 69 D.L.R. (2d) 18, 2 N.S.R. 856 (S.C.T.D.); *Russell v. Aetna Insurance Co.*, [1975] I.L.R. ¶1-699 (Ont. C.A.).

[116] *Russell v. Aetna Insurance Co.*, [1975] I.L.R. ¶1-699 (Ont. C.A.).

The affirmative burden of proof of [perils of the sea] rests with the plaintiff. In short, the plaintiff must make out a *prima facie* case that the loss was occasioned by a peril of the sea. The defendant has the burden of establishing the defences alleged to exclude the risk. One of these is ordinary wear and tear.[117]

A *prima facie* case is one where the plaintiff has proven all the necessary ingredients of its claim and will succeed unless the defendant is able to introduce evidence of facts rebutting the claim.

When a ship sinks in unexplained circumstances, the insured may find itself in the difficult position of attempting to identify loss through an insured peril without any evidence as to why the loss occurred. The insurer, on the other hand, may argue that the very fact that the ship sank in apparently benign conditions is evidence of its unseaworthiness. In *Gould v. Cornhill Insurance Co.*,[118] the insurer argued that the failure of the ship to have a Steamship Inspection certificate was conclusive proof that it was unseaworthy. The court held that this was simply one piece of evidence to be taken into consideration and that there was evidence of rough weather and heavy seas that made loss by perils of the seas a more probable conclusion.[119]

---

[117]   (1984), 7 C.C.L.I. 198 at 205 (F.C.T.D.).

[118]   (1983), 1 D.L.R. (4th) 183, 2 C.C.L.I. 148 (Nfld. C.A.), leave to appeal refused (1983), 1 D.L.R. (4th) 183*n*, 52 N.R. 70*n* (S.C.C.).

[119]   See *Dawson v. Home Insurance Co.* (1870), 21 U.C.C.P. 20 to the effect that if there is evidence that the vessel is seaworthy and in good condition at the commencement of the voyage, and there is evidence of bad weather, it is appropriate to put the case to the jury. For other cases on the burden of proof, see *Myles v. Montreal Insurance Co.* (1870), 20 U.C.C.P. 283 (C.A.): there is a presumption that a ship is unseaworthy if it founders in good weather shortly after leaving port; *Ewart v. Merchants' Marine Insurance Co.* (1879), 13 N.S.R. 168 (C.A.), where evidence that the vessel was in good condition prior to sailing led to the conclusion that it was seaworthy; *Climie v. Western Assurance Co.*, [1938] O.W.N. 333 (Masters Chambers), where it was held that the plaintiff who alleges that loss occurred by perils of the seas is not required to plead how the sinking came about; *Coons v. Aetna Insurance Co.* (1868), 18 U.C.C.P. 305 (C.A.); *Murray v. Nova Scotia Marine Insurance Co.* (1875), 10 N.S.R. 24 (C.A.): perils of the seas do not cover all losses happening on the sea; *Steinoff v. Royal Canadian Insurance Co.* (1877), 42 U.C.Q.B. 307 (C.A.); *Pacific Coast Coal Freighters Ltd. v. Westchester Fire Insurance Co. of New York*, [1926] 3 W.W.R. 356, 38 B.C.R. 20, [1926] 4 D.L.R. 963 (S.C.), aff'd. [1927] 1 W.W.R. 878, 38 B.C.R. 315, [1927] 2 D.L.R. 590 (C.A.): presumption that foundering was the cause of the loss; *Cross v. Allan* (1880), 3 L.N. 47 (Que.); *Creedon & Avery Ltd. v. North China Insurance Co.*, [1917] 3 W.W.R. 33, 24 B.C.R. 335, 36 D.L.R. 359 (C.A.): where goods are shipped in good condition and the ship encounters a sudden storm causing the seas to wash over the hatches and the goods on destination are found to be damaged by seawater, held, that the inference is that water got down the hatches during the storm and the onus on the insured is satisfied; *Musgrave v. Mannheim Insurance Co.* (1899), 32 N.S.R. 405 (C.A.); *Morrison v. Nova Scotia Marine Insurance Co.* (1896), 28 N.S.R. 346 (C.A.); *Western Assurance Co. v. Scanlan* (1886), 13 S.C.R. 207, 33 L.C. Jur. 301, rev'g. (1885), 15 R.L.O.S. 449 (Que. Q.B.): where a vessel sank due to the entry of water as a result of the loss of a plug that had been placed in a hole in the hull, the court held, among other conclusions, that the loss was due to "inherent defects and other unseaworthiness" and not due to a peril of the sea.

In *H.B. Nickerson & Sons Ltd. v. Insurance Co. of North America*,[120] the plaintiff's fishing boat sank at its berth and a claim was made under an insurance policy insuring the vessel against "perils of the seas". The plaintiff and defendant offered different theories of the loss, the plaintiff contending that the ship had most likely snagged on a spike on the wharf and the insurer arguing that the loss was most likely due to a shifting of ballast water. The trial judge was unable to accept either theory and concluded that the plaintiff had failed to discharge the onus of proving a *prima facie* case of loss through an insured peril. Only after the insured had done so, said the judge, did the onus shift to the underwriters to establish one of the policy exclusions. The judge quoted with approval from the judgment of Justice MacFarlane in *Marion Logging Co. v. Utah Home Fire Insurance Co.*:

> Considering the evidence in this case, I am unable to find the means by which the water, which eventually caused the sinking of the boat, entered it. As I have already said, no explanation of the sinking of the ship was found in the evidence. It seems then to me to be a case which must be decided according to where the onus of proof lies. On the question of the onus of proof, the ordinary rule is where upon the evidence the Court is left in doubt whether the loss was due to a peril insured against or to a cause not covered by the policy, then the plaintiff having failed to discharge the burden which lies upon him of proving his case, there must be judgment for the defendant underwriter . . .[121]

The Federal Court of Appeal in *H.B. Nickerson & Sons Ltd.* agreed with the trial judge and pointed out that the onus is on the insured to establish, on the balance of probabilities, that the loss was due to a peril of the sea and that if the loss is attributable to unseaworthiness, the insurer is not liable if the ship was sent to sea in an unseaworthy state with the privity of the insured. In some cases, the owner will establish a precise fortuity, but, said the court, if the insurer is able to establish that unseaworthiness, with the privity of the insured, "was a parallel and primary cause of the loss", the insurer may avoid liability. In those cases where the insured is unable to point to a precise cause of the loss, he or she is not without recourse. As Justice Marceau put it:

> The onus is of establishing that a peril of the sea was at the origin of the loss, not of identifying the exact cause, and the standard of proof applicable is only that of a balance of probabilities. If the owner, although unable to put his finger on the precise cause of the loss, can nevertheless demonstrate on a balance of probabilities that, because of the circumstances of the case and the clear seaworthiness of his vessel, most of the events that could not be included into the concept of peril of the sea have to be disregarded as possible causes, he may very well satisfy the onus that rested upon him. This is so, obviously, because proof by inference or pre-

---

[120] [1984] 1 F.C. 575, 49 N.R. 321 (C.A.), leave to appeal refused (1984), 54 N.R. 80*n* (S.C.C.).

[121] (1956), 5 D.L.R. (2d) 700 at 703-04 (B.C.S.C.). In the *Marion Logging* case, a moored ship sank. The insured was not able to explain the reason for the sinking and it was held that the insured had not discharged the onus of proving that there had been a loss through perils of the seas and was not entitled to recover under the policy.

sumption is a perfectly valid means of evidence and the inference relied upon here may be quite reasonable in view of the great extension given by the case law to the concept of peril of the sea (see, in relation to this last point, the recent judgment of the Supreme Court in *Century Insurance Company of Canada, et al. v. Case Existological Laboratories Ltd. et al. . . .*[122]

The Federal Court of Appeal agreed with the trial judge that, on the facts of this case, with the vessel simply sinking at its berth, the weight of the evidence did not support a loss through perils of the sea.

While it is clear that under a named perils policy the initial onus is on the insured to establish that the loss was caused by a named peril,[123] it is equally clear that under an "all risks" policy the insured need only prove that the loss was fortuitous or of a kind not likely to occur in the circumstances, without identifying the specific peril that caused the loss. The onus of proof then shifts to the insurer to establish that the loss was due to an excluded peril.[124] The practical reality, however, is that few marine insurance cases turn on the burden of proof. Each party usually introduces whatever evidence it can, including expert evidence, to support its theory of causation or to refute the other party's theory, and it would be a rare case where the court would throw up its hands and decide the case on the burden of proof.[125]

Where the insurer contends that the insured itself was responsible for the loss, for example, by scuttling, arson or other fraudulent means, the burden of proof, while still on the civil standard of "balance of probability", is a heavy one and must be clearly met. Nevertheless, it may be established by circumstantial evidence.[126]

---

[122] [1984] 1 F.C. 575 at 591-92, 3 C.C.L.I. 78 (C.A.).

[123] See *Dueck (c.o.b. Peter P. Dueck & Son) v. Manitoba Mennonite Mutual Insurance Co.*, [1993] 4 W.W.R. 531 at 534, 13 C.C.L.I. (2d) 155 (Man. C.A.), *per* Scott C.J.M., aff'g. (1992), 80 Man. R. (2d) 173, 11 C.C.L.I. (2d) 87 (Q.B.).

[124] *British and Foreign Marine Insurance Co. v. Gaunt*, [1921] All E.R. 447 (H.L.); *Re National Benefit Assurance Co.* (1993), 45 Ll. L.R. 147 (Ch. Div.); *British Columbia Ferry Corp. v. Commonwealth Insurance Co.* (1985), 66 B.C.L.R. 295 (S.C.), rev'd. on other grounds (1987), 40 D.L.R. (4th) 766, 27 C.C.L.I. 281 (C.A.); *Bevan v. Gartside Marine Engines Ltd.*, [2000] B.C.J. No. 528 (B.C. Co. Ct.) (QL).

[125] For just such a case, see *Rhesa Shipping Co., S.A. v. Edmunds*, [1985] 2 Lloyd's Rep. 1, the famous "yellow submarine" case, in which the ship developed an unexplained leak and sank. The House of Lords, rejecting the insured's theory that the ship must have hit a submarine, overruled the Court of Appeal and the trial judge and held that the insured had not discharged the burden of proof.

[126] See *Lady Tanya Fisheries Ltd. v. Sunderland Mutual Insurance Co.*, [1993] F.C.J. No. 261 (F.C.T.D.) (QL). In a claim on a fishing vessel allegedly lost as a result of fire, the court rejected the evidence of the crew and found that the owner's financial condition was a strong motive to deliberately destroy the vessel. The insurance claim was disallowed. To the same effect, see *Poirier v. Laurentian Casualty Co.* (November 5, 1995) (Ont. Gen. Div.).

Chapter 8

Warranties

8.1 INTRODUCTION

In marine insurance, a warranty is a contractual promise — that some state of affairs exists or that the insured will do or refrain from doing something.[1] It is a promise of such significance that it must be exactly complied with and its breach relieves the insurer from further obligations under the policy.[2] The policy is no longer operative, and any subsequent loss is unrecoverable, even though it was not caused by the breach of warranty.[3]

The Canadian *Marine Insurance Act* ("*C.M.I.A.*") recognizes express warranties and implied warranties.[4] An express warranty is written in the policy. An implied warranty is engrafted onto the policy by operation of law. An implied warranty may be overruled by the terms of the policy.

---

[1] The *Canadian Marine Insurance Act*, S.C. 1993, c. 22 ("*C.M.I.A.*"), subs. 32(1) provides:

32(1) In this section and sections 33 to 39, "warranty" means a promissory warranty by which the insured

    (*a*)   undertakes that some particular thing will or will not be done or that some condition will be fulfilled; or

    (*b*)   affirms or negates the existence of particular facts.

[2] *C.M.I.A.*, subs. 39(1) provides:

39(1) Subject to this section, a warranty must be exactly complied with, whether or not it is material to the risk.

(2) Subject to any express provision in the marine policy or any waiver by the insurer, where a warranty is not exactly complied with, the breach of the warranty discharges the insurer from liability for any loss occurring on or after the date of the breach, but does not affect any liability incurred by the insurer before that date.

See *Shearwater Marine Ltd. v. Guardian Insurance Co. of Canada* (1997), 29 B.C.L.R. (3d) 13 (B.C.S.C.), aff'd. (1998), 60 B.C.L.R. (3d) 37 (C.A.).

[3] The subject of warranties is dealt with in ss. 32 to 39 of the *C.M.I.A.*

[4] S.C. 1993, c. 22. *C.M.I.A.* subs. 32(2) provides: "A warranty may be an express warranty or an implied warranty." Subsection 33(1) provides:

33(1) An express warranty may be in any form of words from which the intention to warrant may be inferred.

(2) An express warranty must be included in, or written on, the marine policy or be contained in a document incorporated by reference into the policy.

(3) An express warranty does not exclude an implied warranty, unless they are inconsistent.

The *C.M.I.A.* provides that a breach of warranty is excused if, because of a change in circumstances, the warranty has ceased to be applicable to the circumstances contemplated by the contract, or if compliance with the warranty is rendered unlawful by any subsequent law.[5]

A breach of warranty relieves the insurer of any liability under the policy from the date of the breach, whether or not the warranty was material to the risk and whether or not the breach caused the loss.[6] The policy remains valid up to the time of the breach and the insurer remains liable for losses up to that point, but has no liability for losses after the breach. It is no excuse that a breach of warranty has been remedied prior to the event causing a loss.[7] A breach of warranty may be waived or forgiven by the insurer, either by an express provision of the policy or by the insurer's conduct.

Notwithstanding some suggestions in the case law that a breach of warranty gives rise to an election on the insurer's part to "avoid" the warranty, the insurer is not required to "avoid" the policy where there has been a breach of warranty.[8] The operation of the policy is suspended from the time of the breach, unless the insurer waives the breach and demonstrates an intention to treat the policy as operative. To prevent any uncertainty about the insurer's intentions, it is prudent for the underwriter to advise the insured that it considers that a warranty has been breached and that the policy is no longer operative.

As we shall see in this chapter, the case law on the subject of warranties evidences a reluctance on the part of the courts to find a breach of warranty unless the warranty has been clearly expressed and clearly breached. If there is any ambiguity in the language of the warranty, it will be interpreted in the way most favourable to the insured. The courts have drawn a distinction between a warranty and a "description of the risk",[9] and between a warranty and a "suspensive condition"[10] that suspends the operation of the policy during the breach but reinstates it afterward. In some cases, the courts have erroneously required that there be a direct connection between the breach of warranty and the loss,[11] apparently due to a reluctance to permit coverage to be denied as a result of a "technical" breach of the policy.

---

[5]   *C.M.I.A.*, subs. 32(2); see *DeGroot v. J.T. O'Bryan & Co.* (1979), 15 B.C.L.R. 271, [1979] I.L.R. ¶1-1152 (C.A.), rev'g. [1977] I.L.R. ¶1-863 (B.C.S.C.).

[6]   See *Beacon Life & Fire Assurance Co. v. Gibb* (1862), 1 Moo. P.C. N.S. 73 (P.C.), 15 E.R. 630 (C.A.).

[7]   *C.M.I.A.*, subs. 39(5) provides: "It is no defence to a breach of a warranty that the breach was remedied and the warranty complied with before any loss was incurred."

[8]   See section 8.6, "Consequences of Breach of Warranty".

[9]   See *Staples v. Great American Insurance Co. of New York*, [1941] S.C.R. 213, [1941] 2 D.L.R. 1; see also *Tulloch v. Canada (Dept. of Fisheries and Oceans)* (1988), 21 F.T.R. 72, 32 C.C.L.I. 36, aff'd. (1989), 96 N.R. 51, 37 C.C.L.I. 229 (F.C.A.).

[10] See *Century Insurance Co. of Canada v. Case Existological Laboratories Ltd.* (1980), 116 D.L.R. (3d) 199, [1981] I.L.R. ¶1-1335 (B.C.S.C.), rev'g. (1982), 133 D.L.R. (3d) 727, 35 B.C.L.R. 364 (C.A.), aff'd. [1983] 2 S.C.R. 47, 150 D.L.R. (3d) 9; *Federal Business Development Bank v. Commonwealth Insurance Co.* (1983), 2 C.C.L.I. 200 (B.C.S.C.).

[11] See *Elkhorn Developments Ltd. v. Sovereign General Insurance Co.* (2000), 18 C.C.L.I. (3d) 203, [2000] I.L.R. ¶1-3840 (B.C.S.C.), rev'd. (2001), 87 B.C.L.R. (3d) 290, 26 C.C.L.I. (3d) 23 (C.A.).

8.2 DISTINCTION BETWEEN A WARRANTY, REPRESENTATION, DESCRIPTION OF RISK AND SUSPENSIVE CONDITION

A warranty differs from a representation. A representation is a statement of fact, expectation or belief that occurs before the contract is made. A representation must be "substantially correct".[12] A warranty, on the other hand, is a promise contained in the contract and must be exactly complied with. A misrepresentation entitles the insurer to treat the contract as void from the outset,[13] whereas a breach of warranty suspends the operation of the contract from the time of the breach.

For this reason, the courts often distinguish between a "true" promissory warranty and a statement that simply describes the risk. Marine insurers have historically used the term "warranty" or "warranted" in different ways, and the language used to impose warranties in marine policies has not always been as clear as it might have been.[14] The term "warranted" is sometimes used as a form of shorthand to describe the nature of the risk, for example, "warranted free from particular average" to show that the policy is intended to cover total losses only, or "warranted free from capture" to exempt the insurer from loss by capture. In contrast, a true warranty is a separate promise; for example, the statement "warranted not to be used for commercial purposes" in a policy of insurance on a pleasure craft is a promise that the boat will not be used for commercial purposes. An examination of some of the cases will illustrate the distinctions drawn by Canadian courts.

In *Riverside Landmark Corp. v. Northumberland General Insurance Co.*,[15] the policy covered two old ships being towed from Quebec City to Mexico. Under the heading in the policy entitled "description of risk", they were described as being "covered whilst being towed in tandem". The insurer argued that there had been a breach of warranty because, at the commencement of the tow, the two ships were lashed together side-by-side rather than one ahead of the other or on separate tow lines. The court found that the practice in tows of this kind was to lash the two vessels together until such time as they could be strung out on separate tow lines and that the words "towed in tandem" should be interpreted in light of this practice. The court also found that the words "towed in tandem" were merely descriptive of the risk and were not a true warranty.

In *Century Insurance Co. of Canada v. Case Existological Laboratories Ltd.*,[16] a leading decision of the Supreme Court of Canada, the insured vessel

---

[12] See Chapter 4, *Good Faith: Misrepresentation and Non-Disclosure.*
[13] *Ibid.*
[14] See *Britsky Building Movers Ltd. v. Dominion Insurance Corp.*, [1981] I.L.R. ¶1-1470, 7 Man. R. (2d) 402 (Co. Ct.), rev'd. [1981] I.L.R. ¶1-1345, 7 Man. R. (2d) 397 (C.A.), in which the court was influenced by the fact that the word "warranty" had been used in the policy in several senses, some of which were clearly not true warranties.
[15] (1984), 8 C.C.L.I. 118 (Ont. H.C.J.).
[16] [1983] 2 S.C.R. 47, 150 D.L.R. (3d), aff'g. (1982), 35 B.C.L.R. 364, 133 D.L.R. (3d) 727 (C.A.), rev'g. (1980), 116 D.L.R. (3d) 199, [1981] I.L.R. ¶1-1335 (B.C.S.C.).

sank because some valves had been inadvertently left open, flooding the ship. The policy contained a "warranty":

> WARRANTED that a watchman is stationed on board the BAMCELL II each night from 2200 hours to 0600 hours with instructions for shutting down all equipment in an emergency.

In the British Columbia Court of Appeal, Mr. Justice Lambert stated that the clause was not a true warranty but was a "warranty delimiting the risk":

> [T]he nature of the matter covered by the clause must be considered to determine whether the parties intended to create a warranty or whether they intended to create a "suspensive condition" or "warranty delimiting the risk"...[T]he parties can not have intended that if the watchman was late one night, or even missed a night, then the insurers should be discharged from liability for the remainder of the term of the policy...[I]t is my opinion that the clause in this case under the heading "Special Conditions" is a clause which limits the risk and not a true warranty which discharges the insurer. The limitation on the risk has no effect in this case.[17]

On appeal to the Supreme Court of Canada, that court noted that although there was no watchman on board the vessel during the hours described in the clause, it had nothing to do with the loss, which occurred in mid-afternoon. The Supreme Court agreed with the Court of Appeal that the clause was a "limitation of the risk insured against" but it was not a warranty — it would only have been applicable if the loss had occurred during the night and it was established that there had been no watchman aboard during that time.

In *Tulloch v. Canada (Department of Fisheries and Oceans)*,[18] a policy on a fishing vessel contained the following warranty:

> Warranted free from any claim for loss, damage or expense where anyone other than the Assured is Master of the insured vessel...without the prior approval of the [Fishing Vessel Insurance] Plan.

The insured left the vessel in the charge of someone who was not an approved master. This individual moved the vessel from the place where he had been instructed to stay with it and the vessel sank. The Federal Court of Appeal held that the fact that someone other than the owner had been master at another time did not permanently invalidate the policy. Justice Stone, speaking for the court, stated:

> The legal distinction that must be borne in mind here is between an 'express' form of promissory warranty provided for in s. 34(10) of the [British Columbia] *Insurance (Marine) Act*, and a warranty that merely delimits and is part of the description of the risk. Non-compliance with the former renders the insurance contract voidable as from the time of the breach regardless whether the loss had any connection with the breach, whereas non-compliance with the latter merely exempts the insurer from liability for the specific loss only. All of the leading text-writers

---

[17]   (1982), 35 B.C.L.R. 364 at 379-80 (C.A.).
[18]   (1988), 32 C.C.L.I. 36, 21 F.T.R. 72, aff'd. (1989), 37 C.C.L.I. 229, 96 N.R. 51 (Fed. C.A.).

agree on this point, which is carefully explained by Donaldson, J. (now Lord Donaldson M.R.) in *De Maurier (Jewels) Ltd. v. Bastion Insurance Company Ltd. et al.*, [1967] 2 Lloyd's 550 (Com. Ct.) at pages 558-59:

> I also hold, as was ultimately conceded, that the warranty delimits and is part of the description of the risk and is not of a promissory character. By a warranty of a promissory character I mean a warranty by the assured that a particular state of affairs will exist, breach of which destroys a substratum of the contract and entitles the underwriter to decline to come on risk or, as the case may be, to terminate the risk as from the date of a breach. In the marine field, "warranted free from capture and seizure" is a warranty of the former character leaving the contract effective in respect of loss by other perils. "Warranted to sail on or before a particular date" is, however, of a promissory character, breach of which renders the contract voidable. The commercial reasoning behind this legal distinction is clear, namely, the breach of the former type of warranty does not affect the nature or extent of the risks falling outside the terms of the warranty; breach of a promissory warranty may, however, materially affect such risks.[19] (footnotes omitted)

Justice Stone continued:

> The words "warranted free" in the cl[ause] 12 warranty indicate to me that it was intended to operate as an exemption from liability for losses of the nature specified therein rather than as an "express warranty". This follows from the opinion expressed by Donaldson J., and is in line with the view of the learned editors of *Halsbury's Laws of England*, 4th ed., Vol. 25, para. 58 (note 2), at p. 45 where they stated:
>
> > The word "warranted" when followed by the word "free" as in "free from capture", "free of particular average" etc., is used in a very different sense from the use of the word "warranty" in the *Marine Insurance Act, 1906* . . . In these cases it only has the effect of exempting the underwriter from liability for losses of the nature specified in the warranty.
>
> The question for this court is one of construing the cl[ause] 12 warranty as an exempting provision and, more specifically, in discovering the true meaning of the word "Master" appearing therein.[20]

The Federal Court of Appeal held that the individual was not acting as "master" of the vessel at the material time.

For reasons that will be mentioned below, the Court of Appeal's comment that the contract was "voidable" on the occurrence of a breach of warranty, relying on the comments of Justice Donaldson, is open to question. Neither the *C.M.I.A.* nor the English *Marine Insurance Act, 1906* ("*M.I.A. 1906*") uses[21] this expression in relation to a breach of warranty, and both statutes state that "the breach of the warranty discharges the insurer from liability for any loss occur-

---

[19] (1989), 37 C.C.L.I. 229 at 235 (F.C.A.).
[20] *Ibid.*, at 235-36.
[21] (U.K.), 6 Edw. VII, c. 4.1.

ring on or after the date of the breach"[22] unless that breach is waived or forgiven by the insurer.

In *Elkhorn Developments Ltd. v. Sovereign General Insurance Co.*,[23] there was a warranty in a policy on a barge that any movements of the vessel were to be subject to the underwriter's prior approval. While the policy was in effect, and without the knowledge of either the broker or the insurer, the barge was moved on two separate occasions, ultimately to the location at which it sank and became a total loss. The underwriters took the position that there had been a breach of warranty. The chambers judge, on a motion for summary judgment, held that in order for a clause to be construed as a true warranty it was necessary that there be a "substantial relationship" between the warranty and the loss incurred and that evidence would be required to determine whether or not the towing of the vessel had been causative of the loss.

The British Columbia Court of Appeal overruled, holding that the determination of whether or not a clause is a warranty is not a retrospective question. It is not determined by asking the question, after a loss has occurred, "was the loss caused by the breach?" If that was the case, neither insurer nor insured would know, before the fact, whether or not a term was a warranty. The Court of Appeal held that the prior approval of the insurer was a condition precedent to continued coverage and was a promissory warranty the breach of which discharged the insurer from further liability, regardless of the ultimate cause of the loss. The court appears to have been influenced by the facts that the clause was clearly described as a warranty, the parties were sophisticated and were advised by professionals, and the policy of insurance was not a standard form but had been negotiated between the insurer and the broker to fit the particular circumstances.

The threshold question in warranty cases, therefore, is whether one is dealing with a "true" warranty, a "representation", a "description of the risk" or a "suspensive condition". The use of the term "warranty" or "warranted" is not determinative, but the use of the expression "warranted free from ..." would suggest that losses of the kind described are excluded from the policy. On the other hand, the description of the consequences of the breach of the condition — the loss of coverage — may be the clearest possible indication that the condition is intended to be a warranty. In the middle ground are those situations where the terms "warranty" or "warranted" are used but the consequences are not described. In those cases, it may become necessary to examine the circumstances to determine the nature of the promise being made by the insured and the reasons why the insured and insurer might have agreed to the inclusion of such a promise. If the intent was to limit the risk being taken on by the insurer, it seems reasonable to treat the condition as a true warranty. If, on the other hand, the clause is reasonably capable of the interpretation that it was simply intended to suspend coverage during the occurrence of certain events, then, in accordance with the *contra proferentem* rule, it should be construed in the insured's favour.

---

[22]   *C.M.I.A.*, subs. 39(2).

[23]   (2000), 18 C.C.L.I. (3d) 203, [2000] I.L.R. ¶1-3840 (B.C.S.C.) rev'd. (2001), 87 B.C.L.R. (3d) 290, 26 C.C.L.I. (3d) 23 (C.A.).

The solution may lie in brokers and underwriters learning to express their intentions in clearer more explicit language, rather than relying on shorthand that may have particular meaning to them, but not necessarily to others. Given the severe consequences of a breach of warranty, it behooves insurers to express themselves in the clearest possible terms.[24]

8.3 EXPRESS WARRANTIES

An express warranty is often used as an underwriting tool to limit the extent of the risk accepted. The underwriter may insist upon the inclusion of one or more warranties, depending on the nature of the risk presented to him or her, but it is not uncommon for the broker to propose a warranty. He or she may do this with the expectation that there is a better chance that the underwriter will accept the risk if it is limited by a warranty. The broker or insurer may suggest the warranty as a loss prevention measure or as a means of reducing the premium or expanding the insuring terms proposed by the underwriter. For example, in a cargo policy the insurer might require a warranty that the stowage of the cargo be approved by a marine surveyor, whose recommendations must be complied with prior to the vessel sailing. In a hull and machinery policy, the insurer might require that the vessel's navigation be confined to a particular location or time of year. The warranty limits the nature of the risk that the insurer accepts and the premium reflects the reduced risk.

An express warranty must be included in or written on the policy or contained in a document incorporated by reference into the policy.[25] It is not possible to have a verbal warranty.[26]

Courts have distinguished between a true warranty as used in section 32 of the *C.M.I.A.* and a mere statement of intent. In *Grant v. Aetna Insurance Co.*,[27] the policy insured a vessel "now lying in Tate's Dock, Montreal and intended to Navigate the St. Lawrence and lakes". The vessel never left the dock and burnt about one year later. The Judicial Committee of the Privy Council, noting that the question of whether or not the words were a warranty was a matter of

---

[24]   The drafters of the British Columbia Builders' Risks Clauses (1/1/89) (Appendix I) were clearly cognizant of the Canadian case law when they drafted the policy. Clause 1 states:

> This policy contains warranties and general conditions none of which are to be interpreted as suspensive conditions, The Underwriters have agreed to accept the risk of insuring the Vessel on the condition precedent that the Assured will comply strictly and literally with these warranties and conditions. If the Assured breaches any of these warranties or conditions, the Underwriters at their option will not pay any claim arising thereafter, regardless of whether or not such breach is causative or in any way connected to such claim.

[25]   *C.M.I.A.*, s. 33.

[26]   But see *DeGroot v. J.T. O'Bryan & Co.* (1979), 15 B.C.L.R. 271, [1979] I.L.R. ¶1-1152 (C.A.), rev'g. [1977] I.L.R. ¶1-863 (B.C.S.C.).

[27]   (1862), 15 Moo. P.C. 516, 6 L.C. Jur. 224 (P.C.), revg. (1861), 5 L.C. Jur. 285, 11 Low. Can. R. 330 (C.A.).

construction, held that the words were not a contractual warranty but merely a statement of intent.[28]

Some of the more common forms of express warranties are discussed in the next seven subsections of this chapter.

8.3.1 Navigation Limits

The risks to which a vessel is exposed can vary substantially depending on where it is navigated. Ocean waters usually present greater risks than inland waters. Certain areas are notoriously dangerous at particular times of year, due to stormy weather or ice conditions. The insurer may therefore require a warranty to ensure that the vessel does not sail beyond certain defined points, generally or without previous approval or at certain times of year.[29] For example, the C.B.M.U. Great Lakes Hull Clauses (Sept. 1, 1971) (reproduced in Appendix G) contain a warranty that the vessel's navigation is to be confined to the waters of the Great Lakes, not east of a specified location, and that navigation is to be confined to the period March 31 to December 15. Navigation outside these dates is "held covered" provided "(a) prompt notice is given to Underwriters (b) any amended terms of cover and any additional premium required by the Underwriters are agreed to by the Assured and (c) prior approval of each sailing is obtained from Underwriters Surveyor".[30] In practice, this "trading warranty" is frequently overridden by the insertion of broader trading limits when insuring modern Great Lakes vessels.

In *Britsky Building Movers Ltd. v. Dominion Insurance Corp.*,[31] a pleasure craft policy provided: "Warranted confined to the navigable waters of the Province of Manitoba." In fact, the vessel had been navigated in British Columbia on one occasion and it was destroyed by fire while parked on a trailer in Calgary, Alberta. It was held at trial that the words were not a true warranty and were merely descriptive of the risk. The court observed that the word "warranty" was used elsewhere in the policy to describe something other than a true warranty and there was no permanent prejudice to the insurer by the breach

---

[28] In contrast, in *Great Northern Transit Co. v. Alliance Insurance Co.* (1898), 25 O.A.R. 393 (C.A.), the court held that the insurance never attached because the ship never left the dock.

[29] *Grant v. Aetna Insurance Co.* (1860), 11 Low. Can. R. 128 (S.C.), aff'd. on other grounds (1861), 5 L.C. Jur. 285, 11 Low. Can. R. 330 (C.A.), rev'd. (1862), 15 Moo. P.C. 516, 6 L.C. Jur. 224, 12 Low. Can. R. 386 (P.C.); *Grant v. Equitable Fire Insurance Co.* (1863), 8 L.C. Jur. 13, 9 R.J.R.Q. 320; *Richard S.S. Co. v. China Mutual Insurance Co.* (1907), 4 E.L.R. 269 (N.S.S.C.), aff'd. (1907), 42 N.S.R. 240 (C.A.); *Taylor v. Moran* (1885), 11 S.C.R. 347 ("warranted not to enter or attempt to enter or to use the Gulf of St. Lawrence prior to the 10th day of May, nor after the 30th day of October"); *Robertson v. Stairs* (1875), 10 N.S.R. 345 (C.A.); *Owen v. Ocean Mutual Marine Insurance Co.* (1885), 18 N.S.R. 495 (C.A.) ("prohibited from the River and Gulf of St. Lawrence and Ports in Newfoundland including St. Pierre and Miquelon between the 5th Dec and the 15th April without payment of additional premium or leave first obtained"); *O'Leary v. Pelican Insurance Co.* (1889), 29 N.B.R. 510 (C.A.).

[30] This second paragraph is a form of "held covered" clause, which is discussed in Section 8.7.1.

[31] [1981] I.L.R. ¶1-1470, 7 Man. R. (2d) 402 (Co. Ct.), new trial ordered [1981] I.L.R. ¶1-1345, 7 Man. R. (2d) 397 (C.A.).

of the so-called warranty. The requirement that there be "permanent prejudice" is, respectfully, not dictated either by the *C.M.I.A.* or by the case law. The fact that the insured has flouted a promise made to the underwriter should be sufficient to permanently suspend the operation of a policy. The *C.M.I.A.* itself provides that it is no excuse that a breach of warranty has been remedied prior to the loss.[32]

8.3.2 Laid Up and Out of Commission Warranty

Due to the condition of the vessel, the insurer may only be prepared to insure it while it is out of operation or ashore, where the risks are obviously reduced. The insurer may require a warranty that the vessel be "laid up and out of commission", either during a defined period of time[33] or generally, perhaps while awaiting repairs.[34] In *MacDonald v. Liverpool and London and Globe Insurance Co. Ltd.*,[35] the policy provided that a yacht would be "laid up and out of commission from Oct. 1". The yacht was burnt on October 6 while in the water waiting to be stored on land. The Court held that "out of commission" did not require the yacht to be ashore. It simply meant that navigation had to terminate on the specified date and that removal from the water had to take place within a reasonable time thereafter. If the insurer wanted more, the warranty should have stipulated "laid up *ashore* and out of commission".

In *Federal Business Development Bank v. Commonwealth Insurance Co.*,[36] there was a provision in a hull and machinery policy warranting that the vessel would be laid up at the "north foot of Columbia Street", where there was a large, modern wharf. The vessel was laid up not in this location, but in the waters north of Columbia Street and north of Carrall Street. The court construed the warranty *contra proferentem*:

> If there be any doubt as to what the parties intended when they included the warranty in the form set out in the second endorsement, the court should invoke the *contra proferentem* rule and interpret the words against the insurer.[37]

The "north foot of Columbia street" was held to be merely descriptive of the general geographic area where the vessel was to be laid up. If the insurer wanted the vessel to be laid up at a particular dock, said the court, the policy should have been more specific. The underwriters argued that there had been a breach of the "laid up" aspect of the warranty because the vessel had been moved to another dock. The court found that this was not a promissory warranty within

---

[32] See *C.M.I.A.*, subs. 39(5).

[33] For example, the winter months, when navigation is either impossible or much more dangerous due to weather and ice conditions.

[34] For an example of the latter, see *Marler v. Schmucki*, [1961] O.J. No. 3865 (Ont. Gen. Div.) (QL); see also *Dolbec v. United States Fire Insurance Co. of New York*, [1963] B.R. 153 (C.A.), [1963] B.R. 170; *Daneau v. Laurent Gendron Ltée*, [1964] 1 Ll. L.R. 220 (Exch. Ct. Can.).

[35] (1978), 22 N.B.R. (2d) 172, 39 A.P.R. 172 (Q.B.).

[36] (1983), 2 C.C.L.I. 200 (S.C.).

[37] *Ibid.*, at 204.

the meaning of the British Columbia marine insurance statute. Justice MacKinnon stated:

> The parties never intended the warranty of laying up at the north foot of Columbia Street to be an undertaking or condition that must be exactly complied with. Probably if a loss occurred whilst the vessel was tied up at Terminal Docks or at False Creek there would be no coverage. In *Provincial Insurance Co. v. Morgan*, [1932] K.B. 70, affirmed [1933] A.C. 240, [1932] All E.R. Rep. 899 (H.L.), Lord Justice Scrutton stated [at pp. 79-80 K.B.]:
>
>> No doubt a great deal turns upon the language of the particular policy; but it must be remembered that in contracts of insurance the word "warranty" does not necessarily mean a condition or promise the breach of which will avoid the policy. A warranty that a marine policy is free from particular average certainly does not mean that if there is a partial loss to the insured ship the whole policy is avoided. It merely describes the risk, and means that the only risk being insured against is the risk of a total loss and that a partial loss is not the subject of the insurance. Again, if a time policy contains the clause "warranted no St. Lawrence between October 1 and April 1," and the vessel was in the St. Lawrence on October 2, but emerged without a loss, and during the currency of the policy in July a loss happens, the underwriters cannot avoid payment on the ground that between October 1 and April 1 the vessel was in the St. Lawrence: *Birrell v. Dryer* (1884), 9 App. Cas. 345. This is an example of a so-called warranty which merely defines the risk insured against.
>
> Applying the same principles, I find that even though the vessel may have been moored at Terminal Dock or at False Creek, it was not so moored at the time of the risk. The vessel was taken outside the geographical limits contained in the trading warranty; however, it was returned to the area described in the warranty. Taking the vessel outside the warranted limits, the owners have not committed a breach of a condition or promise that would allow the insurers to avoid the policy.[38]

On the Great Lakes, most commercial vessels are laid up for the winter due to ice conditions that make navigation impractical. The C.B.M.U. Great Lakes Hull Clauses (Sept. 1, 1971) contain a warranty to this effect.[39]

---

[38]   *Ibid.*, at 205-06. On the other hand, in *Marler v. Schmucki*, [1996] O.J. No. 3865 (Ont. Gen. Div.) (QL), a yacht policy contained a warranty that it be "laid up and out of commission" because, due to its deteriorated condition, the insurers were not prepared to cover the vessel for navigation risks. The vessel had been surveyed by a marine surveyor, who noted a number of deficiencies in its condition and who made recommendations for repairs. The underwriters made further coverage conditional on compliance with the surveyor's recommendations and an additional survey. In breach of the warranty contained in the policy, the insured moved the vessel to a dock where it was ultimately damaged in a storm. The court found that the insured fully understood the terms of the warranty and he was not entitled to recover under the policy.

[39]   Lines 87-88:
       WINTER MOORINGS:
       Warranted that the Vessel be properly moored in a safe place and under conditions satisfactory to the Underwriter's Surveyor during the period the Vessel is in Winter lay-up.

8.3.3 Identity of Master

In the case of smaller commercial vessels, the underwriter may require a warranty that a named individual be the captain or "master", to ensure that it is operated by a competent person with a real interest in the vessel's safety. There has been some litigation in Canada in connection with such warranties under a federal program (since discontinued) known as the Fishing Vessel Insurance Plan. Policies issued by that Plan typically contained a warranty stipulating that the insured was required to be the master of the vessel and that there could be no change in the master without the approval of the administration. In *Tulloch v. Canada (Department of Fisheries and Oceans)*,[40] referred to above, the Federal Court of Appeal declined to find a breach of a "warranty" to this effect. On the other hand, in *Lewis v. Canada (Department of Fisheries and Oceans)*,[41] the plaintiff's claim was dismissed for failure to have the master approved by the Plan. In *Morris v. Canada (Minister of Fisheries and Oceans)*,[42] after evaluating conflicting evidence, the court found that the administration had approved the substitution of a new master.

8.3.4 Towing Warranties

Ships may be towed by other ships in a variety of circumstances. Towage may be required when the ship has been in an accident or has suffered a breakdown. Larger ships are frequently assisted by tugboats in port, in going to anchor or in berthing at a dock, where confined waters may necessitate assistance in manoeuvring. Towing usually involves greater risk to the vessel being towed, since it relies on the towing vessel for motive power and manoeuvring assistance. For this reason, the commonly used hull and machinery clauses provide that the insured vessel may not be towed except when customary or when it is in need of assistance.[43] Tugs themselves are usually insured under the American Institute Tug Form (August 1, 1976) or similar insurance that does not limit the vessel's towing activities. When unpowered vessels, such as barges, are insured, prohibitions or restrictions on towage are usually deleted.

Due to the enhanced risks of towage, when underwriters are requested to insure the tow of a vessel they usually insist on a warranty requiring prior approval of the tow by an independent marine surveyor. The surveyor may

---

[40] (1988), 32 C.C.L.I. 36, 21 F.T.R. 72, aff'd. (1989), 37 C.C.L.I. 229, 96 N.R. 51 (Fed. C.A.).

[41] (1995), 98 F.T.R. 278.

[42] (1991), 47 F.T.R. 271, [1992] I.L.R. ¶1-2807.

[43] See, for example, the C.B.M.U. Great Lakes Hull Clauses (Sept. 1, 1971), which provide at lines 92-94: "but the Vessel may not be towed, except as is customary or when in need of assistance, nor shall the Vessel render assistance or undertake towage or salvage services under contract previously arranged by the Assured, the Owners, the Managers or the Charterers of the Vessel". The Canadian Hulls (Pacific) Clauses (Sept. 1/91) at Appendix E provide:

> 5. The Vessel is covered subject to the provisions of this insurance at all times and has leave to sail or navigate with or without pilots, to go on trial trips and to assist and tow vessels or craft in distress, but it is warranted that the Vessel shall not otherwise tow or be towed, except as is customary, or to the first safe port or place when in need of assistance.

stipulate conditions that must be satisfied by the vessel carrying out the tow. The surveyor or underwriter may also stipulate the number of tugs required for the move.[44]

8.3.5   Warranties Regarding Surveys or Inspections

Hull and machinery policies frequently contain a warranty requiring that the vessel be inspected by a marine surveyor, whose recommendations must be complied with before the insurance attaches.[45] In the case of cargo insurance, for a particularly large, valuable or cumbersome cargo, the insurer may include a warranty that the packing, stowage or securing arrangements be inspected and approved by a designated marine surveyor.

8.3.6   Private Pleasure Use

In the insurance of pleasure craft, it is common to include a warranty that the vessel is to be used for private pleasure purposes only, since the carriage of passengers increases the risk to which the underwriter is exposed.[46] In *Staples v. Great American Insurance Co. of New York*,[47] a policy contained a warranty that the boat "shall be used solely for private pleasure purposes and not to be hired or chartered unless approved and permission endorsed hereon". There was evidence that during the term of the policy, the boat had been used for commercial purposes. The Supreme Court of Canada held that there was no breach of warranty: the intention of the insured was that the boat would be used solely for pleasure purposes, this was the normal use of the boat, and the boat was never hired or chartered during the currency of the policy. On the other hand, in *Billings v. Zurich Insurance Co.*,[48] the plaintiff's boat was broken into by thieves and property was stolen. The insurer denied liability on the ground that the insured had breached a "special condition" of the policy, stipulating that the policy would be "null and void" if the boat was "used for carrying passengers or goods for payment". The court found that the insured had been carrying passengers for payment and declared that the policy was null and void. The policy was on a "plain language" form and left the insured in no doubt of his obligations and of the consequence of a breach of those obligations.

---

[44] See *Riverside Landmark Corp. v. Northumberland General Insurance Co.* (1984), 8 C.C.L.I. 118 (Ont. H.C.); *J.P. Porter & Sons Ltd. v. Western Assurance Co.* (1938), 12 M.P.R. 469, [1938] 1 D.L.R. 619 (N.S.C.A.); *Provincial Insurance Co. of Canada v. Connolly* (1879), 5 S.C.R. 258 ("vessel to go out in tow"). On the other hand, in *Brooks-Scanlon O'Brien Co. v. Boston Insurance Co.* (1919), 47 D.L.R. 93, [1919] 2 W.W.R. 129 (B.C.C.A.), a representation with respect to towing was binding on the insured.

[45] See *Silva v. British Columbia* (1992), 67 B.C.L.R. (2d) 75 (C.A.).

[46] See *Phil Whittaker Logging Ltd. v. British Columbia Hydro & Power Authority* (1985), 65 B.C.L.R. 384, 5 C.P.C. (2d) 71 (S.C.).

[47] [1941] S.C.R. 213, [1941] 2 D.L.R. 1.

[48] [1987] I.L.R. ¶1-2250, 27 C.C.L.I. 60 (Ont. Dist. Ct.).

8.3.7 No Other Insurance

Prior to the *M.I.A. 1906*, insurers occasionally inserted a "No other insurance" warranty to prevent the insured from profiting from double insurance.[49] That statute, and its modern successors such as the *C.M.I.A.*, preclude the insured from recovering more than a full indemnity where there is double insurance,[50] so the warranty is not of modern significance.

8.4 CONSTRUCTION OF EXPRESS WARRANTIES

Reference has been made to the reluctance of the courts to find a "true" warranty and to the use of the concepts of "suspensive condition" or "warranty delimiting the risk" as less drastic alternatives. In addition to these techniques, the *contra proferentem* principle has been applied with particular vigour in the case of warranties.[51] For example, in *Shearwater Marine Ltd. v. Guardian Insurance Co. of Canada*,[52] the policy contained a warranty: "Vessel inspected daily basis and pumped as necessary". The court held that the warranty would be construed *contra proferentem* and that it did not require that the vessel actually be boarded on a daily basis. It was sufficient that it be looked at from a distance.[53] Similarly, in *Federal Business Development Bank v. Commonwealth Insurance Co.*,[54] referred to above in connection with the "laid up and out of commission" warranty, the trial judge construed the warranty *contra proferentem* against the underwriter.[55]

Whether the stipulation is a true warranty or merely a condition may be a matter of construction. For example, in *Stevenson v. Continental Insurance Co.*,[56] it was held that the failure of the plaintiff to have his compass set in accordance with the recommendations of a survey made after insurance coverage was issued was not a breach of warranty entitling the insurer to avoid liability.

Where a true warranty has been identified, Canadian courts have followed the injunction of the House of Lords in *Provincial Insurance Co. v. Morgan*[57] that "a warranty or condition...though it must be strictly complied with, must be strictly though reasonably construed." The Supreme Court of Canada did so in *Staples v. Great American Insurance Co. of New York*,[58] referred to above, holding that

---

[49]   *Butler v. Merchants' Marine Insurance Co.* (1884), 17 N.S.R. 301 (C.A.), aff'd. (1885), Cass. Dig. 390 (S.C.C.).

[50]   See Chapter 13, *Double Insurance*.

[51]   See Chapter 3, *Construction of the Marine Policy*.

[52]   (1997), 29 B.C.L.R. (3d) 13 (S.C.), aff'd. without reasons (1998), 60 B.C.L.R. (3d) 37 (C.A.).

[53]   See also *J.P. Porter & Sons Ltd. v. Western Assurance Co.* (1938), 12 M.P.R. 469, [1938] 1 D.L.R. 619 (N.S.C.A.), citing *Metropolitan Life Insurance Co. v. Montreal Coal & Towing Co.* (1904), 35 S.C.R. 266 at 271.

[54]   (1983), 2 C.C.L.I. 200 (B.C.S.C.).

[55]   *Ibid.*, at 204.

[56]   [1973] 6 W.W.R. 316, [1973] I.L.R. ¶1-553 (B.C. Dist. Ct.).

[57]   [1933] A.C. 240 at 253-5, [1932] All E.R. Rep. 899.

[58]   [1941] S.C.R. 213, [1941] 2 D.L.R. 1.

the words "not to be hired or chartered" were to be used to construe "private pleasure purposes", and that the statement was merely descriptive of the risk and did not mean that if the yacht was ever used for other than pleasure purposes the policy was terminated.

In *Butler v. Merchants Marine Insurance Co.*,[59] there was a "no other insurance" warranty in the policy. After the policy had been issued, the plaintiff asked a third party to take out insurance on the vessel to cover a debt owed to that party. The plaintiff argued that the warranty meant that there should be no other insurance in effect at the time the insurance was taken out, but that it did not preclude future insurance. This submission was rejected by the trial judge, the Nova Scotia Court of Appeal and the Supreme Court of Canada. The Court of Appeal pointed out that "it was the duty of the defendants [insurers] to use apt words for their own protection" and that "a warranty cannot be created by construction".[60] The Court cited *Arnould on Insurance* to the effect that "No particular form of words is necessary to constitute an express warranty, not any special words such as 'warranty' or 'warranted'".[61] The court held that the words "no other insurance" and "warranted no other insurance" meant that there should be no other insurance on the vessel during the continuance of the risk.

8.5 IMPLIED WARRANTIES

An implied warranty is one attached to the policy by operation of law even though it is not specifically stated in the policy. The Act mentions several.[62]

8.5.1 Legality

Section 34 of the *C.M.I.A.* provides: "There is an implied warranty in every marine policy that the marine adventure insured is lawful and, in so far as the insured has control, will be carried out in a lawful manner." A comparable provision in the British Columbia statute was considered in *James Yachts Ltd. v. Thames & Mersey Marine Insurance Co.*,[63] where it was held that using the

---

[59] (1884), 17 N.S.R. 301 (C.A.), aff'd. (1885), Cass. Dig. 390 (S.C.C.).

[60] (1884), 17 N.S.R. 301 at 305 (C.A.).

[61] *Arnould on Insurance*, 544.

[62] Section 35 of the *C.M.I.A.* provides: "There is no implied warranty in any marine policy as to the nationality of a ship or that the nationality of a ship will not be changed during the risk." Subsection 36(1) provides:

    36(1) Where in any marine policy insurable property is expressly warranted to be neutral, there is an implied condition in the policy

    (a) that the property will have a neutral character at the commencement of the risk and that, in so far as the insured has control, that character will be preserved during the risk; and

    (b) where the property is a ship, that, in so far as the insured has control, the papers necessary to establish the neutrality of the ship will be carried on the ship and will not be falsified or suppressed and no simulated papers will be used.

    (2) If any loss occurs through a breach of the implied condition referred to in paragraph (1)(b), the insurer may avoid the contract.

[63] [1976] I.L.R. ¶1-751 (B.C.S.C.).

insured's premises for boat building, contrary to a municipal building by-law, was a breach of the implied warranty of legality. In that case, there was a failure to carry out the adventure insured in a lawful manner. The use of unapproved premises obviously created an enhanced risk.

Is a technical breach of a statute, not causative of the loss, a breach of the warranty of legality? In *Federal Business Development Bank v. Commonwealth Insurance Co.*,[64] the underwriter alleged that there had been a breach of the British Columbia *Ministry of Forests Act.*[65] The court stated that there may have been, at most, a technical breach of the statute, but it was remote from the adventure insured and there was no public policy that required enforcement.[66]

Borderline cases may present more difficulty. Consider the situation where a Canadian registered vessel fails to obtain inspection certificates from the Coast Guard, but the vessel is in all respects seaworthy. A loss occurs that has nothing to do with the vessel's condition or the absence of the required certificates. Is there a breach of the warranty of legality and is the insurer entitled to avoid liability? It is suggested that the court should focus on the requirement of section 34 of the *C.M.I.A.* that the *adventure* must be lawful and that it must be lawfully carried out. Operating a ship for the purposes of smuggling would be unlawful. So would entry into a port in contravention of a government-ordered embargo. Both these actions would involve an enhanced risk for the insurer and in both cases the "adventure" would be unlawful. On the other hand, the failure of the vessel owner to obtain a radio certificate would not, in and of itself, make the *adventure* unlawful and, provided the vessel's radios were properly functioning, would not involve an enhanced risk.

In *Conohan v. Cooperators*,[67] there was a collision between two boats. The operator of one of the boats was later charged with operating the vessel while his ability was impaired by alcohol and the insurer denied liability coverage on the ground, among others, that there had been a breach of section 34 of the *C.M.I.A.* It was also asserted that the insured had breached a warranty against drunken operation of the vessel. The trial court held, for reasons that, respectfully, are not particularly clear, that the negligent operation of the vessel was not a maritime peril within the meaning of the *C.M.I.A.* and that the implied warranty of legality had no application. Unfortunately, the Federal Court of Appeal did not find it necessary to deal with the trial judge's conclusion on this issue, as it dismissed the appeal on other grounds.

---

[64] (1979), 13 B.C.L.R. 376, [1980] I.L.R. ¶1-1221 (S.C.).

[65] R.S.B.C. 1990, c. 300.

[66] See *Atlantic Freighting Co. v. Provincial Insurance Co.* (1953), 32 M.P.R. 180 (N.S.C.A.), where it was held that the failure to have a Canadian Certificate of Inspection did not make a voyage wholly outside Canadian waters an illegal voyage, although there is a suggestion that a voyage within Canadian waters would have been illegal.

[67] [2002] 3 F.C. 421, 286 N.R. 364 (C.A.), aff'g. 2001 FCT 658.

8.5.2 Seaworthiness

There is an implied warranty in a voyage policy that the ship will be seaworthy at the commencement of the voyage for the purpose of the adventure insured.[68] "Seaworthy" is defined by section 37(5) of the *C.M.I.A.* to mean "reasonably fit in all respects to encounter the ordinary perils of the seas of the marine adventures insured".[69] Seaworthiness refers not only to the hull of the ship and its machinery and equipment, but also to the competence, training and experience of its officers and crew. The ship must be reasonably fit to encounter the particular perils of the *contemplated* voyage.

In a time policy, on the other hand, there is no implied warranty of seaworthiness, but the *C.M.I.A.* provides that where, with the *privity of the insured*, the ship is sent to sea in an unseaworthy state, the insurer is not liable for any loss attributable to that unseaworthiness.[70]

In *Laing v. Boreal Pacific*,[71] the plaintiff claimed for the loss of an excavator from his barge in heavy weather. The insurer claimed that the barge had been sent to sea in an unseaworthy state with the privity of the insured. The Federal Court of Appeal, affirming the trial judge, held that there was no coverage. The appeal court agreed with the trial judge's conclusion that the vessel was unseaworthy because it was too heavily laden for the sea conditions expected to be encountered and the excavator, which was not secured, was not stowed in a safe manner for those conditions. The Court of Appeal adopted the trial judge's definition of seaworthiness:

> Seaworthiness is a relative term and varies with the nature of the voyage to be undertaken: its location, whether in a river, or canal, or on the ocean; the type of weather to be expected on the voyage, summer conditions or winter storms. Improperly stowed cargo will make a vessel unseaworthy, if the improper stowage endangers the safety [of] the ship. When the policy covers both the vessel and the cargo, however, a vessel will not be seaworthy if in order to save the ship the cargo must be jettisoned. If a vessel is overloaded it is not seaworthy.[72]

The trial judge held that the insured owner not only knew of the facts that rendered the vessel unseaworthy but that he had turned a "blind eye" to those

---

[68] *C.M.I.A.*, s. 37.

[69] See *Quebec Marine Insurance Co. v. Commercial Bank of Canada* (1869), 13 L.C. Jur. 267, rev'd. (1870), 17 E.R. 1, L.R. 3 P.C. 234; *Reed v. Philps* (1870), 13 N.B.R. 171 (C.A.); *Leduc v. Western Assurance Co.* (1880), 25 L.C. Jur. 55, 3 L.N. 124; *Lemelin v. Montreal Assurance Co.* (1873), 1 Q.L.R. 337 (Que. S.C.); *Coons v. Aetna Insurance Co.* (1868), 18 U.C.C.P. 305; *Cleveland v. Sunderland Marine Mutual Insurance Co.* (1987), 45 D.L.R. (4th) 340, 81 N.S.R. (2d) 1 (S.C.T.D.).

[70] *C.M.I.A.*, subs. 37(4): "There is no implied warranty in any time policy that the ship will be seaworthy at any stage of the marine adventure, but where, with the privity of the insured, the ship is sent to sea in an unseaworthy state, the insurer is not liable for any loss attributable to unseaworthiness."

[71] (1999), 163 F.T.R. 226, 12 C.C.L.I. (3d) 66, aff'd. (2000), 264 N.R. 378, 25 C.C.L.I. (3d) 189 (F.C.A.).

[72] *Ibid.*, at 380 N.R.

facts and was therefore privy to the unseaworthiness. The Court of Appeal adopted the test of "privity" applied by Lord Denning M.R. in *The "Eurysthe-nes"*, in which he stated:

> To disentitle the shipowner, he must, I think, have knowledge not only of the facts constituting the unseaworthiness but also knowledge that those facts rendered the ship unseaworthy, that is, not reasonably fit to encounter the ordinary perils of the sea. And, when I speak of knowledge, I mean not only positive knowledge but also the sort of knowledge expressed in the phrase "turning a blind eye". If a man, suspicious of the truth, turns a blind eye to it, and refrains from inquiry — so that he should not know if for certain — then he is to be regarded as knowing the truth. This "turning a blind eye" is far more blame-worthy than mere negligence. Negligence in not knowing the truth is not equivalent to knowledge of it.[73]

Because the barge had been sent to sea in an unseaworthy state with the privity of the insured, the insured was not entitled to recover.[74]

In *Atwood v. Canada*,[75] a claim was made under the Fishing Vessel Insurance Plan for the loss of a vessel by fire after the insured attempted to start it using a screwdriver to bridge a gap between the battery and the engine. It was argued that the vessel was unseaworthy when sent to sea and that the insured was privy to its unseaworthiness. The insurer invoked the marine insurance sections of the Nova Scotia *Insurance Act*[76] (which incorporated the *M.I.A. 1906*) to the effect that there is no implied warranty of seaworthiness in a time policy, but where the ship is sent to sea in an unseaworthy state the insurer is not liable for any loss attributable to unseaworthiness. Justice Collier of the Federal Court of Canada held that it was not intended that the insurer could invoke a specific portion of a provincial statute, without a stipulation to that effect in the policy or in the regulations. The judge did not consider the point that the statutory provisions were no more than a codification of the common law and that the

---

[73] [1976] 2 Ll. L.R. 171 at 179.

[74] In *Coast Ferries Ltd. v. Century Insurance Co. of Canada*, [1975] 2 S.C.R. 477, 48 D.L.R. (3d) 310, affg. (B.C.C.A.), rev'g. (1971), 23 D.L.R. (3d) 226, [1971] I.L.R ¶1-439 (B.C.S.C.), the court dealt with the *Inchmaree* clause. The court referred to s. 41(5) of the British Columbia statute (dealing with the warranty of seaworthiness) but did not have to deal with it, in view of its finding that the loss did not fall within the *Inchmaree* clause. See *Federal Business Development Bank v. Commonwealth Insurance* (1979), 13 B.C.L.R. 376, [1980] I.L.R. ¶1-1221 (S.C.); *Woodhouse v. Provincial Insurance Co.* (1871), 31 U.C.Q.B. 176, where the plea of knowingly sending the ship to sea in an unseaworthy state was not made out; *Pacific Coast Coal Freighters Ltd. v. Westchester Fire Insurance Co. of New York*, [1926] 3 W.W.R. 356, 38 B.C.R. 20, [1926] 4 D.L.R. 963 (S.C.), aff'd. [1927] 1 W.W.R. 878, 38 B.C.R. 315, [1927] 2 D.L.R. 590 (C.A.), where it was held that the assured who had chartered the vessel to a third party was not privy to the vessel's unseaworthiness and was entitled to recover; *Graystone v. Sun Alliance*, [1994] B.C.J. No. 3266 (B.C. Prov. Ct.) (QL), where the court found that the plaintiff's boat sank due to a combination of fortuitous circumstances, not due to unseaworthiness or a failure to exercise due diligence.

[75] (1985), 10 C.C.L.I. 62 (F.C.T.D.).

[76] R.S.N.S. 1967, c. 148.

application of the common law would have produced the same result as the statute. The judge concluded that the vessel was seaworthy in any event.

8.5.3   No Implied Warranty That Goods Are Seaworthy

Subsection 38(1) of the *C.M.I.A.* provides: "There is no implied warranty in any marine policy on insurable property, other than a ship, that the insurable property is seaworthy." However, subsection 38(2) stipulates:

> There is an implied warranty in every voyage policy on insurable property, other than a ship, that, at the commencement of the voyage, the ship is seaworthy and reasonably fit to carry the insurable property to the destination contemplated by the policy.

To avoid this provision, cargo policies generally contain a term whereby seaworthiness of the carrying vessel is admitted. The reasoning is that in most cases the insured cargo owner is unable to control the seaworthiness of the vessel on which the goods are shipped.[77]

8.5.4   Time of Sailing

In *Spinney v. Ocean Marine Mutual Insurance Co.*,[78] the Supreme Court of Canada confirmed that there is an implied "understanding" in a voyage policy that:

> the voyage shall be commenced and completed with all reasonable expedition, that is, with all reasonable and ordinary diligence, and that any unreasonable or unexcused delay, either in commencing or prosecuting the voyage insured, alters the risk and absolves the underwriter from his liability for any subsequent loss.

In a time policy there may be an express warranty as to the time of sailing.[79]

---

[77]   The Institute Cargo Clauses (1/1/63) contained a "seaworthiness admitted" clause whereby the underwriters admitted, as between themselves and the insured, the seaworthiness of the carrying vessel and agreed that as long as the insured was not privy to any misconduct on the part of the vessel owner, its right of recovery would not be prejudiced. In the Institute Cargo Clauses (1/1/82) (reproduced in Appendices B, C and D), a similar clause is placed among the exclusions but was expanded to encompass unseaworthy vessels and unfit craft, conveyances, containers and lift vans. The text of the clause, entitled "Unseaworthiness and Unfitness Exclusion Clause", is as follows:

>   5.1   In no case shall this insurance cover loss damage or expense arising from
>   unseaworthiness of vessel or craft,
>   unfitness of vessel craft conveyance container or liftvan for the safe carriage of the subject-matter insured,
>   where the Assured or their servants are privy to such unseaworthiness or unfitness, at the time the subject-matter insured is loaded therein.
>   5.2   The Underwriters waive any breach of the implied warranties of seaworthiness of the ship and fitness of the ship to carry the subject-matter insured to destination, unless the Assured or their servants are privy to such unseaworthiness or unfitness.

[78]   (1890), 17 S.C.R. 326 at 329.

[79]   *Robertson v. Pugh* (1888), 15 S.C.R. 706; *Royal Canadian Insurance v. Pugh* (1887), 20 N.S.R. 133 (C.A.).

8.6 CONSEQUENCES OF BREACH OF WARRANTY

As noted above, subsection 39(2) of the *C.M.I.A.* provides that a breach of warranty "discharges the insurer from liability for any loss occurring on or after the date of the breach". This means that losses occurring prior to the breach are fully covered by the policy, but losses after the breach are not covered, unless the insurer has waived the breach. It has been stated in some of the cases, and even suggested by some writers, that on a breach of warranty the insurer is entitled to "avoid" or cancel the policy.[80] This implies that the insurer is required to take some positive action to give consequences to a breach of warranty. It is submitted that this is not required by the *C.M.I.A.*, nor is it necessary from the case law. The *C.M.I.A.*, like the *M.I.A. 1906*, simply says that a breach of warranty "discharges" the insurer from liability. There is no requirement (as there is in the case of non-disclosure or misrepresentation) that the insurer take positive action to avoid the policy. While the *C.M.I.A.* contemplates that the insurer may "waive" or forgive a breach of warranty,[81] there is no statutory requirement that positive action be taken following a breach of warranty. In fact, the insurer may be unaware that the breach of warranty has taken place until some time long after its occurrence. The term "avoid", used in the context of non-disclosure or misrepresentation,[82] refers to a situation where the insurer is required to take some positive act to render the contract void, on becoming aware of facts entitling him or her to do so. Upon the insurer declaring the policy void, it becomes of no effect *ab initio* — from the outset. The use of the term is inappropriate in the case of a breach of warranty, because the policy remains effective from its inception to the time of the breach, but its operation is automatically suspended from the time of the breach.

8.7 AVOIDING THE CONSEQUENCES OF A BREACH OF WARRANTY

Subsection 39(2) of the *C.M.I.A.* provides that a breach of warranty may be remedied in two ways. First, there may be an express relieving provision in the policy. Second, an insurer who knows of the breach may demonstrate an intention not to rely on its strict legal rights — this is known as "waiver" of the breach. These are discussed in the following subsections.

---

[80] See R.H. Brown, *Marine Insurance, Vol. 1: Principles and Basic Practice*, 6th ed. (London: Witherby & Co., 1998) at p. 85: "There is a popular misconception in the marine insurance market that in the event of a breach of warranty the insurer is entitled to avoid the contract." For a Canadian example, see the decision of the Federal Court of Appeal in *Tulloch v. Canada (Department of Fisheries and Oceans)* (1988), 32 C.C.L.I. 36, 21 F.T.R. 72, aff'd. (1989), 37 C.C.L.I. 229, 96 N.R. 51 (Fed. C.A.), which in turn relied on English authority.

[81] See Section 8.7.2, "Waiver of Breach of Warranty".

[82] See Chapter 4, *Good Faith: Misrepresentation and Non-Disclosure*; *C.M.I.A.* subss. 21(7) and 22(8) provide that where there is non-disclosure of material facts or a material misrepresentation by the insured or its agent, the insurer is entitled to "avoid" the contract.

8.7.1 "Held Covered" Clauses

A breach of warranty can occur without any fault of the insured and results in the insured being without insurance. To mitigate this effect, the *C.M.I.A.* envisages that the policy may contain an express provision forgiving a breach of warranty.[83] Policies frequently include a "held covered" clause, whereby the insurer agrees in advance to waive breaches of certain warranties, provided prompt notice is given, and an additional premium to cover the increased risk is paid, if required by the underwriter.

The Institute Cargo Clauses (1/1/82) contain a "held covered" provision where the destination is changed:

> Where, after attachment of this insurance, the destination is changed by the Assured, *held covered at a premium and on conditions to be arranged, subject to prompt notice being given to the Underwriters.* [Emphasis added.]

Open cargo policies normally contain a classification clause placing limits on the types of vessels acceptable to the insurer in accordance with the rates set in the policy. There is normally a "held covered" provision to cover the contingency of the insured using a vessel falling outside this clause. For instance, the Institute Classification Clause (13/4/92) incorporates the following:

> Cargos and/or interests carried by mechanically self-propelled vessels not falling within the scope of the above are held covered subject to a premium and on conditions to be agreed.

Hull and machinery policies usually contain "held covered" clauses to permit breach of certain warranties, such as a breach of the navigation limits, subject to payment of an additional premium.[84]

8.7.2 Waiver of Breach of Warranty

The insurer may forgive or "waive" a breach of warranty by the insured. In order for the waiver to be effective, the insurer must have knowledge of the

---

[83]   *C.M.I.A.*, subs. 39(2) begins with the words *"Subject to any express provision in the marine policy or any waiver by the insurer..."*. This contemplates that the policy may contain a provision waiving a breach or otherwise qualifying the usual rule that a breach of warranty discharges the insurer from the date of the breach. In *Atlantic Freighting Co. v. Provincial Insurance Co.* (1953), 32 M.P.R. 180 at 190, [1954] 1 D.L.R. 235 at 242 (N.S.C.A.), the court pointed out that it is necessary to look at the entire policy to determine whether there is any provision mitigating the effects of a breach of warranty.

[84]   The Canadian Hulls (Pacific) Clauses (Sept. 1/91) contain a similar provision at lines 81-85, although it does not use the words "held covered":

>   6. The Vessel is covered in case of any breach of warranty as to cargo, employment, towage, salvage services or date of sailing, provided notice be given to the Underwriters immediately after receipt of advices and any amended terms of cover and any additional premium required by them be agreed.

The C.B.M.U. Great Lakes Hull Clauses (Sept. 1, 1971) contain similar wording, although the words "held covered" are used and the terms are referred to as conditions rather than warranties.

breach and must demonstrate, through words or conduct, an intention to treat the contract as valid and subsisting. It is not necessary that the insurer expressly waive the breach of warranty or affirm the continuation of the contract. It is enough that the insurer conducts itself in a manner consistent with the continued operation of the contract. In *Daneau v. Laurent Gendron Ltée.*,[85] the insurer alleged that the insured was in breach of a "laid up and out of commission" warranty requiring that the insured scow be "laid-up and out of commission between the 16th of November and the 30th of April, both inclusive, unless otherwise specifically agreed". Although the scow had been laid up at the beginning of November, it was later moved from its berth, and across a small bay, where it was moored for the winter. Arguably, this was a breach of the warranty. During the winter months the scow sustained damage due to ice. The insurers were advised of the damage and of the location of the lay-up, and temporary repairs were carried out with the approval of the underwriters' surveyor. The vessel subsequently encountered damage on a voyage and was abandoned. The insurers argued that the breach of warranty had terminated the insurance, but it was held that they had waived any breach of warranty by agreeing to repair the vessel on the approval of the surveyor. The judge stated:

> It is noteworthy that the policy contains no non-waiver clause and that...[the surveyor] actively participated in, and in some respects actually directed and approved the arrangements made for the attempted repairs of the scow...

> At no time did the [insurer] act to cancel the policy or in any way indicate that it considered that the insured had forfeited its right to claim thereunder. It was only by its statement of defence filed in October, 1963 that it for the first time offered to tender back to the defendant the insurance premium paid by him.

> In the Court's opinion, the proof justifies the conclusion that the [insurer], with full knowledge of the circumstances of which it now complains of as constituting a violation of the conditions of the policy, nevertheless so acted and dealt with the defendant that it must be deemed to have waived compliance with these conditions, if a violation there was.[86]

It was the action of the insurer in taking measures that it would only be required to do under a subsisting contract that amounted to a waiver.[87] The court's language implies that the insurer was required to take some action to cancel the

---

[85] [1964] 1 Ll. L.R. 220 (Exch. Ct. Can.).
[86] *Ibid.*, at 224.
[87] The court referred to one of the leading American cases, *Titus v. Glens Falls Insurance Co.* (1880), 81 N.Y. 410 (1880), and to the headnote in *Reliance Insurance Co. v. The Escapade*, [1961] A.M.C. 2410 (5th Cir. Fla. 1960):
> An insurer was estopped from asserting forfeiture of a marine policy upon a yacht because of breach of the private pleasure warranty, when with full knowledge of the breach, and without denying liability, it demanded that the assured incur liability for salvage by a salvor of its choice, for preservation at a repair yard, and for cleaning up in order to permit a survey; by such action the policy was revived.

policy. It is submitted that this is not required. The insurer must take care to avoid the argument that it has affirmed the continued existence of the policy, but it has no obligation to cancel the policy since it has been discharged of liability thereunder from the date of the breach.

These authorities suggest that an insurer faced with a potential breach of warranty must be careful to avoid conduct that could amount to waiver of the breach. While the judge in *Daneau v. Laurent Gendron Ltée* pointed out that the insurer did not cancel the policy, even the act of cancellation of the policy may amount to a waiver of a breach of warranty, since the cancellation of the policy affirms its continued existence up to the time of cancellation. If there has been a breach of warranty, the insurer is discharged from liability from the time of the breach and there is really no need to terminate the contract. The insurer may be best advised to write to the insured (and the broker) stating that there has been a breach of warranty and that the policy has ceased to be operative from the date of the breach. This appears to have been the course followed in *Elkhorn Developments Ltd. v. Sovereign General Insurance Co.*[88] After the sinking of a barge, the underwriters advised the broker that there had been a breach of warranty, discharging them from liability under the policy. At a later date, the broker and the insurer agreed to the cancellation of the policy and the return of a *pro rata* proportion of the premium.

8.8   EFFECT OF BREACH OF WARRANTY ON PREMIUM

There is no provision in the *C.M.I.A.* requiring the insurer to refund any part of the premium where there has been a breach of warranty. Unlike misrepresentation or non-disclosure, where the policy is treated as void from the outset and the premium is returned to the insured because the underwriter has incurred no risk, in the case of breach of warranty the policy has been effective but the insurer is discharged from liability from the date of the breach. While insurers confronted with a breach of warranty sometimes cancel the policy and refund a *pro rata* portion of the premium covering the balance of the term, they have no statutory obligation to do so.

---

[88]   (2000), 18 C.C.L.I. (3d) 203, [2000] I.L.R. ¶1-3840, rev'd. (2001), 87 B.C.L.R. (3d) 290, 26 C.C.L.I. (3d) 23 (C.A.).

Chapter 9

Losses and Charges Recoverable

9.1 INTRODUCTION

This chapter deals with the types of losses and expenses recoverable under a policy of marine insurance. Chapter 10 will discuss the compensation or "measure of indemnity" the insured is entitled to receive in the event of a loss. The Canadian *Marine Insurance Act* ("*C.M.I.A.*")[1] speaks of two types of loss: total loss and partial loss. A total loss can be further divided into "actual total loss" and "constructive total loss". Where there is an actual total loss, the insured property is beyond *physical* retrieval. Where there is constructive total loss, the insured property is beyond *economic* retrieval. A partial loss is any loss that is not a total loss, and has four forms: a particular average loss, a general average loss, a salvage charge and a particular charge. A particular average loss is borne by the *particular* property affected, whereas a general average loss is borne *generally* by all the interests in the marine adventure. A salvage charge is a charge incurred in "saving" the insured property and a particular charge is an expense incurred by the insured in preserving the property.

9.2 TOTAL LOSS

A total loss may be either an actual total loss or a constructive total loss.[2] Unless the policy provides otherwise, insurance against total loss includes a constructive total loss.[3] The measure of indemnity in the case of a total loss is the full sum insured specified in the policy. As pointed out in Chapter 6, *Insurable Value*, the sum insured may be different from either the insurable value and the insured value.

9.2.1 Actual Total Loss

An actual total loss occurs when the property insured is lost beyond retrieval. Subsection 56(1) of the *C.M.I.A.* defines it as follows:

---

[1]   S.C. 1993, c. 22.

[2]   *C.M.I.A.*, subs. 55(1).

[3]   *Ibid.*, subs. 55(2); see *O'Leary v. Stymest* (1865), 11 N.B.R. 289 (C.A.).

56(1) A loss is an actual total loss if the subject-matter insured is destroyed or is so damaged as to cease to be a thing of the kind insured or if the insured is irretrievably deprived of the subject matter.

A total loss does not require the complete extinction or annihilation of the subject-matter insured.[4] It can occur where a ship or cargo are beyond physical recovery. In *McGhee v. Phoenix Insurance Co.*, Mr. Justice Strong of the Supreme Court of Canada stated:

> Cases of high and unimpeachable authority have established that to constitute a total loss in the case of a ship the subject of insurance must be either such an entire wreck as to be reduced, as it is said, to a mere 'congeries of planks' or if it still subsists in specie it must, as a result of perils insured against, be placed in such a situation that it is totally out of the power of the owner or the underwriter at any labor, and by means of any expenditure, to get it afloat and cause it to be repaired and used again as a ship.[5]

An actual total loss includes cases where a ship is sunk, cargo is lost overboard, or property is destroyed by fire, as well as cases in which the property is put out of the reach of the owners, such as capture by pirates.

If damage to cargo is so great that the goods, even though continuing to exist in form, are unmarketable and of no value, there is a total loss. In *Almon v. British American Assurance*,[6] a cargo of potatoes arrived at their destination damaged by seawater, and were unfit for consumption and unmarketable. They were considered to be a total loss, even though a small portion was capable of being separated out from the cargo and sold, much below the market price.

In an action for total loss (whether actual or constructive) the insured who does not establish a total loss can still recover for a partial loss[7] unless the policy

---

4   *Cossman v. West* (1887), 13 App. Cas. 160 (P.C.), rev'g. (1885), 18 N.S.R. 457 (C.A.).
5   (1890), 18 S.C.R. 61 at 70-71, rev'g. (1889), 28 N.B.R. 45 (C.A.); see Sir Barnes Peacock in *Cossman v. West* (1887), 13 App. Cas. 160 at 169-70 (P.C.), rev'g. (1885), 18 N.S.R. 457 (C.A.):
> To constitute a total loss within the meaning of a policy of marine insurance, it is not necessary that a ship should be actually annihilated or destroyed; it may, as in the case of capture and sale upon condemnation, remain in its original state and condition; it may be capable of being repaired if damaged; it may be actually repaired by the purchaser or it may not even require repairs. If it is lost to the owner by an adverse valid and legal transfer of his right of property and possession to a purchaser by a sale under a decree of a Court of competent jurisdiction in consequence of a peril insured against, it is as much a total loss as if it had been totally annihilated.
6   (1882), 16 N.S.R. 43 (C.A.).
7   See *The Merchants' Marine Insurance Co. v. Ross* (1884), 10 Q.L.R. 237 (C.A.); *Hart v. Boston Marine Insurance Co.* (1894), 26 N.S.R. 427 (C.A.); *Harkley v. Provincial Insurance Co.* (1868), 18 U.C.C.P. 335 (C.A.); *Troop v. Union Insurance Co.* (1893), 32 N.B.R. 135 (C.A.); *Dimock v. New Brunswick Marine Assurance Co.* (1849), 6 N.B.R. 398 (C.A.); *Phoenix Insurance Co. v. McGee* (1890), 18 S.C.R. 61, rev'g. (1889), 28 N.B.R. 45 (C.A.). In *Western Assurance Co. v. Scanlan* (1886), 13 S.C.R. 207 at 215, Mr. Justice Strong stated:
> According to English practice...a plaintiff suing on a marine policy for constructive total loss may, if it turns out that he is disentitled to recover for the loss suffered as a total loss, fall back on his right to recover as for a partial or average loss.

otherwise provides. A policy written on "total loss only" ("T.L.O.") terms would be an example of one where recovery for partial loss would not be permitted.

In the case of actual total loss, the insured is required to provide satisfactory evidence of the loss to underwriters, but there is no requirement of "abandonment", as there is in constructive total loss.

Subsection 56(2) of the *C.M.I.A.* provides that where a ship is missing and no news of it has been received within a reasonable time, an actual total loss may be presumed. With advances in technology, the definition of "reasonable time" has obviously diminished since the days of sail.

9.2.2 Constructive Total Loss

A "constructive total loss", often abbreviated to "C.T.L.", occurs where the insured property exists in form, but has no economic value because the cost of retrieving and repairing it exceeds its insured value. For example, if a ship runs aground in a remote location, it may cost more than the insured value to carry out temporary repairs, remove the ship from its location, tow it back to port and repair it. It is considered to be a constructive total loss. To take another example, the costs of repairing a cargo of machinery damaged by seawater may exceed its insured value — it is a constructive total loss because, although it exists in form, it has no commercial value.

Section 57 of the *C.M.I.A.* defines constructive total loss:

57(1) Unless a marine policy otherwise provides, a loss is a constructive total loss if the subject-matter insured is reasonably abandoned because the actual total loss of the subject-matter appears unavoidable or the preservation of the subject-matter from actual total loss would entail costs exceeding its value when the costs are incurred.

(2) Without limiting the generality of subsection (1), a loss is a constructive total loss if

(a) in the case of a ship or goods, the insured is deprived of possession of the ship or goods by reason of a peril insured against and either the insured is unlikely to recover the ship or goods or the cost of recovery would exceed the value of the ship or goods when recovered;

(b) in the case of a ship, the ship is so damaged by a peril insured against that the cost of repairing it would exceed the value of the ship when repaired; or

(c) in the case of goods, the goods are so damaged that the cost of repairing them and forwarding them to their destination would exceed the value of the goods on arrival.

Section 57 of the *C.M.I.A.* contemplates two situations that may give rise to a constructive total loss: (a) the insured property is "abandoned" because its total loss appears unavoidable; or (b) the preservation of the property from actual total loss entails costs in excess of its value. The section allows the parties to the insurance contract to define constructive total loss and the circumstances in which it arises.

No subject has spawned more litigation in Canadian marine insurance law than constructive total loss.[8] In the years before the English *Marine Insurance Act ("M.I.A. 1906")*[9], the Canadian courts, including, on a regular basis, the Supreme Court of Canada, wrestled with the concepts of constructive total loss and abandonment.[10] This was probably because in those times policies were often written on "total loss only" terms and when a vessel sustained serious damages but was not completely lost, the only way the insured could recover under the policy was to make a claim for constructive total loss.

In *Providence Washington Insurance Co. v. Corbett*,[11] one of the leading Canadian cases, Mr. Justice Gwynne in the Supreme Court of Canada stated:

> An absolute total loss entitles the assured to claim the whole amount. A constructive total loss gives him the like right upon condition only of his giving such notice [of abandonment]. Absolute total loss occurs only when in the progress of the voyage, the vessel becomes totally destroyed or annihilated, or placed, by reason of

---

8   *Hart v. Boston Marine Insurance Co.* (1894), 26 N.S.R. 427 (C.A.); *Rourke v. Union Insurance Co.* (1894), 23 S.C.R. 344, aff'g. (1893), 32 N.B.R. 191; *Heard v. Marine Insurance Co.* (1871), 1 P.E.I. 381, Peters 252; *O'Leary v. Pelican Insurance Co.* (1889), 29 N.B.R. 510; *O'Leary v. Stymest* (1865), 11 N.B.R. 289 (C.A.); *Western Assurance Co. v. Scanlan* (1886), 13 S.C.R. 207, 33 L.C. Jur. 301, rev'g. (1885) 15 R.L.O.S. 449 (Que. Q.B.); *Providence Washington Insurance Co. v. Almon* (1885), Cass. S.C. 390 (S.C.C.), rev'g. (1883), 16 N.S.R. 533 (C.A.); *Anchor Marine Insurance Co. v. Keith* (1884), 9 S.C.R. 483, aff'g. (1882), 15 N.S.R. 402 (C.A.); *Anchor Marine Insurance Co. v. Phoenix Insurance Co.* (1881), 6 O.A.R. 567, aff'g. (1880), 30 U.C.C.P. 570 (C.A.); *Meagher v. Aetna Insurance Co.* (1861), U.C.Q.B. 607 (C.A.); *Meagher v. Home Insurance Co.* (1860), 11 U.C.C.P. 313 (C.A.); *Stalker v. Weir* (1854), 2 N.S.R. 248 (C.A.); *Crawford v. St. Lawrence Insurance Co.* (1851), 8 U.C.Q.B. 135 (C.A.); *Davis v. St. Lawrence Inland Marine Assurance Co.* (1846), 3 U.C.Q.B. 18 (C.A.); *Kenny v. Halifax Marine Insurance Co.* (1840), 1 N.S.R. 141 (C.A.); *Cobequid Marine Insurance Co. v. Barteaux* (1875), L.R. 6 P.C. 319 (On appeal from N.S.S.C.); *King v. Western Assurance Co.* (1858), 7 U.C.C.P. 300; *Cunningham v. St. Paul Fire & Marine Insurance Co.* (1914), 5 W.W.R. 1098 (B.C.S.C.); *Morrison Mill Company Inc. v. Queen Insurance Co. of America* (1925), 34 B.C.R. 509 (C.A.); *Churchill & Co. v. Nova Scotia Marine Insurance Co.* (1895), 28 N.S.R. 52 (C.A.), aff'd. (1896), 26 S.C.R. 65.

9   (U.K.) 6 Edw. VII, c. 41.

10 *Buck v. Knowlton* (1891), 31 N.B.R. 417 (C.A.), aff'd. on other grounds (1892), 21 S.C.R. 371; *Fairbanks v. Union Marine Insurance Co.* (1856), 3 N.S.R. 67 (C.A.); *Sedgwick v. Montreal Light, Heat & Power Co.* (1909), 41 S.C.R. 639 (S.C.C.), rev'g. (1908) 34 Que. S.A.C. 127 (C.A.), rev'd. on other grounds [1910] A.C. 598 (J.C.P.C.); *Watson v. Mercantile Marine Insurance Co.* (1873), 9 N.S.R. 396 (C.A.) (constructive total loss of cargo); *McGhee v. Phoenix Insurance Co.* (1890), 18 S.C.R. 61; *Wilson v. Merchants' Marine Insurance Co.* (1872), 9 N.S.R. 81 (freight); *Barss v. Merchants' Marine Insurance Co.* (1887), 26 N.B.R. 339, aff'd. (1888), 15 S.C.R. 185; *Gallagher v. Taylor* (1881), 5 S.C.R. 368, rev'g. (1879), 13 N.S.B. 279 (C.A.); *Rumsey v. Providence-Washington Insurance Co.* (1880), 13 N.S.R. 393 (C.A.); *Nova Scotia Marine Insurance Co. v. L.P. Churchill & Co.* (1896), 26 S.C.R. 65; *Gerow v. British American Insurance Co.* (1889), 16 S.C.R. 524; *Meagher v. Aetna Insurance Co.* (1873), 20 Gr. 354 (Ont. H.C.); *Troop v. Merchants Marine Insurance Co.* (1886), 13 S.C.R. 506 (loss of freight following C.T.L. of vessel); *Millville Mutual Marine & Fire Insurance Co. v. Driscoll* (1884), 11 S.C.R. 183, rev'g. on other grounds (1883), 23 N.B.R. 160 (C.A.).

11 (1884), 9 S.C.R. 256; see also *Harkley v. Provincial Insurance Co.* (1868), 18 U.C.C.P. 335 (C.A.).

the perils against which the underwriter insures, in such a position, that it is wholly out of the power of the assured, or of the underwriter, to extricate her from her peril, or that she was in such imminent danger of destruction that a sale appeared to afford the only reasonable hope of saving any part of her value....Constructive total loss occurs when, by some of the perils insured against, the vessel has become of so little value, that a prudent owner uninsured, would decline any further expense in putting the vessel in a state of repair to pursue her voyage; and if the expense of repairing her, so as to pursue her voyage, be greater than the value of the vessel when repaired, he is justified in declining to incur that expense, and he is allowed to abandon her and to treat the loss as total.[12]

In *Green Forest Lumber Ltd. v. General Security Insurance Co. of Canada*,[13] a shipment of lumber from Quebec to Tunisia was damaged by seawater. The plaintiff, claiming that the cargo was a constructive total loss, gave notice of abandonment to its underwriters. This notice was rejected and an action was commenced claiming a total loss. Mr. Justice Addy of the Federal Court of Canada stated:

> Unlike actual total loss, which is a loss in law and in fact, constructive total loss is a total loss in law, although not a total loss in fact. A proper notice of abandonment given under conditions, which warrant it, entitles the insured to claim a total loss against his insurer.

> It is clear, however, that the conditions must warrant the notice and if the circumstances are not such that it is unlikely that the assured can recover the goods, or if the property is not so badly damaged that the cost of repairing would exceed the value of the goods, or if the absolute destruction or irretrievable loss would not appear to be unavoidable, the insured cannot elect to turn what at the time of abandonment is only an average loss into a total loss merely by giving a notice of abandonment.

> Constructive total loss occurs where such circumstances exist, where a prudent uninsured owner, in the exercise of the soundest judgment, would have sold the cargo as she lay rather than try to save or repair it. The cost of saving and repairing must however exceed the full repaired value. There must be such a preponderating excess of expense that no reasonable man could hesitate as to the propriety of selling under the circumstances rather than repairing.[14]

As Justice Addy noted, the test of constructive total loss is whether a reasonable owner would have sold the insured property rather than attempt to repair it. This test is well-established by the Canadian case law.[15] In this case, the evidence

---

[12] *Ibid.*, at 273-74. This case is also discussed in Chapter 5, *Insurable Interest.*

[13] [1977] 2 F.C. 351, 34 N.R. 308 (T.D.), aff'd. [1978] 2 F.C. 773, 34 N.R. 306 (C.A.), aff'd. [1980] 1 S.C.R. 176, 34 N.R. 303.

[14] [1977] 2 F.C. 351 at 363-64.

[15] See *Cunningham v. St. Paul Fire & Marine Insurance Co.* (1914), 5 W.W.R. 1098, 16 D.L.R. 39 (B.C.S.C.); *Sedgwick v. Montreal Light, Heat & Power Co.* (1909), 41 S.C.R. 639 (S.C.C.),

established that the shipment was later sold at market prices. The judge noted that the "burden of proof is of course on the insured to establish affirmatively that there existed in the circumstances a constructive total loss".[16] He concluded:

> I therefore find as a fact that the plaintiff either incorrectly assumed that the entire cargo was unfit for shipping and made that assumption without taking the normal precautions that a careful and prudent uninsured owner would be expected to take of having it examined on the spot by a knowledgeable person or that the plaintiff recklessly, and because it considered itself insured, arbitrarily chose to condemn and abandon the entire cargo. The conclusion seems obvious: the plaintiff has completely failed to establish a constructive total loss.[17]

In *Allarco Developments Ltd. v. Continental Insurance Co.*,[18] the insured vessel sank and was seriously damaged. It proved capable of salvage, however, and two years later the insured obtained an estimate of repair. The policy was limited to total loss (including constructive total loss, defined to exist when the expense of repairing and recovering the vessel was greater than the insured value). The court pointed out that whether a vessel is a constructive total loss is often to be determined by expert evidence:

> A difficulty encountered in these cases is that the vessel at issue is never repaired and so the cost of repairs and the value of the vessel as repaired are always determined by the Court on the basis of estimates and opinion evidence and not by sales or transactions on the open market.[19]

It was held that the plaintiff had not established that the repair costs would have exceeded the insured amount. The plaintiff should have repaired the vessel because the value of the vessel after repair would have exceeded the costs of repair.[20]

In practice, the surveyor appointed "in the interest of whom it may concern" will assist both the insurer and the insured in the determination of whether the property insured is a constructive total loss. In cases where agreement is not reached, or where the issue may become contentious, the parties may be well-advised to appoint their own surveyors or other experts for the purpose of determining whether the property is in fact beyond economic recovery and repair.[21]

---

rev'g. (1908), 34 Que. S.A.C. 127 (C.A.), rev'd. on other grounds, [1910] A.C. 598 (J.C.P.C.): In order to determine whether a ship is a constructive total loss, the value of the hull when broken up should be added to the cost of repairs. This principle is overridden by most policy forms; *Providence Washington Insurance Co. v. Corbett* (1884), 9 S.C.R. 256, rev'g. (1882), 15 N.S.R. 109 (C.A.); *Meagher v. Aetna Insurance Co.* (1873), 20 Gr. 354 (Ont. H.C.).

[16]   [1997] 2 F.C. 351 at 364.

[17]   *Ibid.*, at 366.

[18]   [1980] I.L.R. ¶1-1281 (Alta. Q.B.).

[19]   *Ibid.*, at 1077.

[20]   See *Baker v. Brown* (1872), 9 N.S.R. 100 at 105 (C.A.):

> Did a probable loss then, founded on the judgment of competent surveyors, and on the bona fide opinion, as we must assume of the insured, justify an abandonment and sale of the vessel, and impose a liability as for total loss on the defendant?

[21]   See Chapter 24, *The Marine Surveyor.*

United States cases on the subject of constructive total loss must be read with caution, since in that country the usual rule is that if the ship or goods sustain damage which is more than 50 per cent of their value, they may be abandoned and a claim may be made for constructive total loss. It is common for policies issued in the United States to contractually alter this rule.

9.2.2.1 ABANDONMENT

An insured faced with a constructive total loss has two options: he or she may either treat the loss as a partial loss, or may "abandon" the property to the insurer and treat the loss as an actual total loss. The insurer then has the right, but not the obligation, to accept the notice of abandonment and take over the property.

The *C.M.I.A.* sets out the rights and obligations of the parties with respect to abandonment:

58(1) An insured may treat a constructive total loss as a partial loss or may abandon the subject-matter insured to the insurer and treat the constructive total loss as an actual total loss.

(2) Subject to this section and section 59, an insured who elects to abandon the subject-matter insured to the insurer must give a notice of abandonment to the insurer with reasonable diligence after the insured receives reliable information of the loss.

(3) An insured who receives doubtful information of a loss is entitled to a reasonable time to make inquiries before giving notice of abandonment.

(4) An insured may give notice of abandonment orally or in writing, or partly orally and partly in writing, and in any terms that indicate the insured's intention to abandon unconditionally the insured interest in the subject-matter to the insurer.

(5) If an insured fails to give a notice of abandonment as required by this section, the constructive total loss may be treated only as a partial loss.

Subsection 60(4) provides:

60(4) On acceptance of an abandonment, the insurer

    (*a*) conclusively admits liability for the loss and the sufficiency of the notice of abandonment; and

    (*b*) is entitled to acquire the interest of the insured in whatever remains of the subject-matter insured, including all proprietary rights incidental thereto.

It has been held that notice of abandonment is "indispensably necessary" in all cases in which the insured elects to abandon[22] and the underwriter will not be liable for a constructive total loss where a notice of abandonment has not been given[23] unless the case falls within one of the exceptions discussed below. The insurer may, however, be liable for the loss as a partial loss, provided the policy covers such losses.[24] Abandonment is another example of the principle of indemnity in operation. The insured who claims that the property is a constructive total loss must be prepared to give up the property to the insurers.

In *Rose v. Weekes*,[25] a Newfoundland "longliner" fishing vessel insured for $100,000 was holed by ice and abandoned by the master and crew, who left it barely afloat amongst the ice floes. The insured gave notice of abandonment to the insurers. The vessel was later recovered and taken to shore. Surveyors were engaged by the parties to examine and report on its condition. Two conflicting repair estimates were given, one being for $142,000 and the other for $59,000. The trial judge stated that the issue was whether the vessel was a constructive total loss and made the following comments:

> A constructive total loss is one which entitles the assured to claim the whole amount of the insurance, on giving due notice of abandonment. A constructive total loss exists when the subject-matter insured is not in fact totally lost, but is likely to become so from the improbability of recovery or the impracticability of repair. The doctrine is peculiar to marine insurance. The assured must give notice of abandonment to justify constructive total loss recovery. But the notice of abandonment is not conclusive and the underwriters may refuse to accept it. It then becomes necessary to determine under the circumstances whether the abandonment should remain operative. One of these circumstances is whether the destruction or loss of the thing insured appears to be 'unavoidable'. Notice of abandonment must be justified by the facts as they exist at the time it is given and at the time of action brought. The first and basic test is: Is the recovery of the vessel unlikely? Another necessary test in the case of a vessel not totally destroyed is whether a prudent owner, who is uninsured, would have abandoned the vessel because of the probable likelihood of the cost of repair or restoration exceeding its value.[26]

He pointed out that in most cases, constructive total loss is a question of fact.[27] On the facts of this case, the insured had acted reasonably in abandoning the

---

[22]   See *Harkley v. Provincial Insurance Co.* (1868), 18 U.C.C.P. 335 (C.A.).

[23]   *Wood v. Stymest* (1862), 10 N.B.R. 309 (C.A.).

[24]   *Gallagher v. Taylor* (1881), 5 S.C.R. 368, rev'g. (1880), 13 N.S.R. 279 (C.A.); but see *Patch v. Pitman* (1886), 19 N.S.R. 298 (C.A.), aff'd. (1885), Cass. S.C. 389 (S.C.C.) to the effect that where there is nothing to abandon, notice of abandonment is not required.

[25]   (1984), 7 C.C.L.I. 287 (F.C.T.D.): the insured was entitled to recover for constructive total loss.

[26]   *Ibid.*, at 294-95.

[27]   *Taylor v. Smith* (1868), 12 N.B.R. 120 at 121 (C.A.), to the effect that where the vessel is abandoned but the abandonment is not accepted and the vessel is later recovered and can be repaired for less than its value, the loss is only a partial loss and the insured can only recover for a partial loss: "The right to recover depends upon the state of things existing at the time the action is brought"; *Providence Washington Insurance Co. v. Corbett* (1884), 9 S.C.R. 256, rev'g. (1882), 15 N.S.R. 109 (C.A.); *Marstrand Shipping Co. v. Beer* (1936), 56 Ll. L.R. 163; *Kalten-*

vessel. Noting that for the purpose of determining whether there was a constructive total loss the insured value should be taken as the repaired value, the judge found that the reasonable cost of repair was $142,000. On this basis, the vessel was a constructive total loss since the insured value was $100,000.

Subsection 58(4) of the *C.M.I.A.* confirms that notice of abandonment may be given orally or in writing or by a combination of the two. No special language is required as long as the insured's intention to make an unconditional abandonment of the property is made clear.[28] In *Baker v. Brown*,[29] the Nova Scotia Court of Appeal stated:

> ...But whatever strictness of construction might have been applied to notices of abandonment in former times, it could never have been absolutely necessary to use the technical word "abandon" - any equivalent expressions which informed the underwriters that it was the intention of the insured to give up to them the property insured upon the ground of its having been totally lost must always have been sufficient.[30]

For reasons of proof, it is usual to give underwriters a written notice of abandonment.

Many of the early Canadian "constructive total loss" cases were ones in which the captain had sold the vessel following a casualty. In cases of "urgent necessity" or "imperative necessity" the captain was entitled to do so to prevent further damage or deterioration and the courts held that in such case notice of abandonment to underwriters could be dispensed with. The onus was on the insured to establish necessity and that the sale was *bona fide*.[31] In *Rumsey v. Providence Washington Insurance Co.*,[32] a vessel was wrecked on the Labrador coast and it would have been hazardous to leave the goods on board during the winter. It was held that the captain was entitled to sell the goods without notice to the underwriters. The court observed that the purpose of notice of abandonment is to give the underwriters the opportunity to sell or save the cargo, but held that in all the circumstances it was reasonable for the master to sell the cargo without notice to the underwriters.[33] This line of authority is probably of

---

bach v. McKenzie (1878), 3 C.P.D. 467; *Irvin v. Hind*, [1950] 1 K.B. 555; *Barlett v. Western Marine Insurance Co.*, [1927-31] N.L.R. 170, aff'd. N.L.R. 217; *Cunningham v. St. Paul Fire and Marine Insurance Co.* (1914), 16 D.L.R. 39, 19 B.C.R. 33 (B.C.S.C.).

28 *C.M.I.A.*, subs. 58(4).

29 (1872), 9 N.S.R. 100 (C.A.).

30 (1872), 9 N.S.R. 100 at 104.

31 See, for example, *Morton v. Patillo* (1872), 9 N.S.R. 17 (C.A.); *Nova Scotia Marine Insurance Co. v. L.P. Churchill & Co.* (1895), 26 S.C.R. 65, aff'g. (1895), 28 N.S.R. 52 (C.A.).

32 (1880), 13 N.S.R. 393 (C.A.).

33 See: *Nova Scotia Marine Insurance Company v. L.P. Churchill & Co.* (1895), 26 S.C.R. 65, aff'g. (1895), 28 N.S.R. 52 (C.A.); *Hart v. Boston Marine Insurance Co.* (1894), 26 N.S.R. 427 (C.A.); *O'Leary v. Pelican Insurance Co.* (1889), 29 N.B.R. 510 (C.A.); *Merchants' Marine Insurance Co. v. Ross* (1884), 10 Q.L.R. 237 (C.A.); *Providence Washington Insurance Co. v. Corbett* (1884), 9 S.C.R. 256, rev'g. (1882), 15 N.S.R. 109 (C.A.); *Gallagher v. Taylor* (1881), 5 S.C.R. 368, rev'g. (1880), 13 N.S.R. 279 (C.A.); *Codequid Marine Insurance Co. v. Barteaux* (1875), L.R. 6 P.C. 319; *Heard v. Marine Insurance Co.* (1873), 1 P.E.I. 428; *Watson v. Mer-*

historical interest only. It is difficult to imagine circumstances in the twenty-first century in which the captain or owners would be entitled to sell the vessel or cargo without giving prior notice to the underwriters.

9.2.2.2 ACCEPTANCE OF ABANDONMENT BY INSURER

Whether or not the insurer has accepted abandonment is a question of fact.[34] The acceptance of abandonment by the insurer may take the form of some unequivocal words or conduct.[35] The insurer's acceptance of abandonment may, of course, be by express words, such as a letter written to the insured or the broker. Underwriters seldom expressly accept abandonment, out of concern for the liabilities arising from possession of the vessel. However, the insurer's conduct may be taken to be an acceptance of abandonment. For example, in *McLeod v. Insurance Co. of North America*,[36] the insurer took possession of the vessel, carried out repairs and then allowed the vessel to be sold. The Nova Scotia Court of Appeal found that this conduct was an acceptance of the abandonment. Similarly, in the Ontario case of *Berner v. Sun Insurance Office Ltd.*,[37] the insurer sent a marine surveyor to inspect the damage to the insured's yacht. He advised the insured to abandon the vessel and gave assistance in the preparation of a letter of abandonment. It was held that through the actions of the surveyor the insurer had accepted the abandonment. In *Provincial Insurance Co. v. Leduc*,[38] the Privy Council stated that if, after receiving notice of abandonment, the insurer does nothing, it cannot be concluded that it has accepted the abandonment; however, if the insurer takes possession of the property, repairs it, and does not repudiate the notice of abandonment, it will be held to have accepted it. Insurers should therefore exercise extreme caution following a loss to ensure that their actions, or the actions of their representatives, are not taken to be acceptance of abandonment or a waiver of the requirement of notice of abandonment.[39]

Some policies contain a provision to the effect that no act of the underwriter or the assured in recovering or saving the property will be considered an acceptance or waiver of abandonment. Where notice of abandonment is given by the insured and declined by underwriters, it is common to include a statement to this effect in the insurer's letter declining to accept abandonment.

---

cantile Marine Insurance (1873), 9 N.S.R. 396 (C.A.); *Wood v. Stymest* (1862), 10 N.B.R. 309 (C.A.).

[34] *Cates Tug & Wharfage Co. v. Franklin Insurance Co.*, [1927] 3 W.W.R. 43, [1927] A.C. 697, 3 D.L.R. 1025 (P.C.), aff'g. [1926] 4 D.L.R. 638, 3 W.W.R. 362 (C.A.), rev'g. [1926] 2 D.L.R. 434, 1 W.W.R. 901 (S.C.).

[35] In *O'Leary v. Pelican Insurance Co.* (1889), 29 N.B.R. 510 (C.A.) it was held that the statements of the agent of the insured to the effect that he would forward the notice of abandonment to the insurers and that he believed that they would pay the claim, did not amount to an acceptance of the abandonment by underwriters; see also *Troop v. Jones* (1884), 17 N.S.R. 230 (C.A.).

[36] (1901), 34 N.S.R. 88 (C.A.).

[37] [1952] I.L.R. ¶1-069 (Ont. H.C.J.).

[38] (1874), L.R. 6 P.C. 224, 19 L.C. Jur. 281, 5 R.L.O.S. 579, 20 R.J.R.Q. 203, aff'g. 14 L.C. Jur. 273 (Que.).

[39] *King v. Western Assurance Co.* (1858), 7 U.C.C.P. 300 (C.A.).

Acceptance of abandonment by the insurer has important consequences, set out in the *C.M.I.A.* First, the insurer is deemed to have conclusively admitted liability for the loss. The insurer acknowledges that there has been a total loss and is unable to contend that there has been a breach of a condition or warranty in the policy. This is one reason why an insurer would be unlikely to accept notice of abandonment, particularly in the initial stages of the claim, while the facts are under investigation. A second consequence of acceptance of abandonment is that the insurer is entitled to "acquire the interest of the insured in whatever remains of the subject-matter insured, including all proprietary rights incidental thereto."[40] The effect of the acceptance of notice of abandonment is to vest in the insurer all the insured's rights in the property.[41] Due to a reluctance to assume ongoing responsibility for the abandoned property and because of the liabilities that may be attached to it, hull and machinery underwriters are usually reluctant to accept notice of abandonment. Normally, therefore, these underwriters decline to accept abandonment and will generally confirm their declination in writing.[42]

The insurer to whom notice of abandonment is tendered is not *required* to accept the abandonment, but the *C.M.I.A.* provides that if the underwriter refuses to accept the abandonment, the rights of the insured are not prejudiced.[43]

9.2.2.3 POLICY PROVISIONS REGARDING CONSTRUCTIVE TOTAL LOSS[44]

The Institute Cargo Clauses (1/1/82) essentially reflect the provisions of the *C.M.I.A.* with respect to constructive total loss.[45] It should be noted, however, that in determining constructive total loss, the costs of recovering the goods, reconditioning them and forwarding them to the destination specified in the policy are to be taken into account.

---

[40] *C.M.I.A.*, s. 60(4)(*b*).

[41] *King v. Western Assurance Co.* (1858), 7 U.C.C.P. 300 (C.A.) where it was stated that the effect of acceptance of notice of abandonment is to vest ownership in the underwriters.

[42] The letter contains a provision to the effect that underwriters agree to place the insured in the same position as if a writ had been issued on the date of the letter. L.J. Buglass, *Marine Insurance and General Average in the United States*, 3rd ed. (Centreville, Maryland: Cornell Maritime Press, 1991) pp. 111-113, notes that the reason for this provision is that in English law, the determination of whether a vessel is a constructive total loss is made as of the date the action against underwriters is commenced, not as of the date that notice of abandonment is given. To avoid immediate litigation, underwriters will agree that the insured need not issue a writ, but will treat the date of underwriters' letter as the effective date for determining whether a C.T.L. exists: "Underwriters decline to accept abandonment but agree to place the assured in the same position as if a writ had been issued this day."

[43] Subsection 60(1).

[44] See also Chapter 18, *Cargo Insurance* and Chapter 19, *Hull and Machinery Insurance.*

[45] Institute Cargo Clauses (A), cl. 13:
No claim for Constructive Total Loss shall be recoverable hereunder unless the subject-matter insured is reasonably abandoned either on account of its actual total loss appearing to be unavoidable or because the cost of recovering, reconditioning and forwarding the subject-matter to the destination to which it is insured would exceed its value on arrival.

With regard to hull and machinery insurance, the C.B.M.U. Great Lakes Hull Clauses (Sept. 1, 1971) provide at lines 174-182:

TOTAL LOSS

There shall be no recovery for a constructive Total Loss hereunder unless the expense of recovering and repairing the vessel shall exceed the Agreed Value. In making this determination, only expenses incurred by reason of a single accident or a sequence of damages arising from the same accident shall be taken into account.

In ascertaining whether the Vessel is a constructive Total Loss the Agreed Value shall be taken as the repaired value and nothing in respect of the damaged or break-up value of the Vessel or wreck shall be taken into account.

In the event of Total Loss (actual or constructive), no claim to be made by the Underwriters for freight, whether notice of abandonment has been given or not.

In no case shall the Underwriters be liable for unrepaired damage in addition to a subsequent Total Loss sustained during the period covered by this Policy.

The Canadian Hulls (Pacific) clauses (Sept. 1/91) contain a provision which is substantially the same. The "Unrepaired Damage" clause means that underwriters are not required to pay for damage the insured has not repaired if a total loss has intervened. If it were otherwise, the insured would receive a windfall — a benefit to which he or she was not entitled.[46]

9.3 PARTIAL LOSSES

A partial loss is "any loss that is not a total loss".[47] It is any loss of or damage to the property which does not result either in its complete physical loss or destruction or which is not a constructive total loss.[48] A total loss of a *part* of the property insured is nevertheless a partial loss. If 10 packages out of a shipment of 20 are lost overboard, this is a partial loss even though part of the insured property is totally lost. This was more significant when it was common to insure certain kinds of property on "Free of Particular Average" ("F.P.A.") terms, since the total loss of a part of the shipment was considered "particular average" and not recoverable.[49] While at one time there was a standard form of cargo insur-

---

[46] The Institute Cargo Clauses (1/1/82) can be found at Appendices B, C and D. The C.B.M.U. Great Lakes Hull Clauses are reproduced at Appendix G and The Canadian (Hulls) Pacific Clauses can be found at Appendix E.

[47] *C.M.I.A.*, subs. 61(1).

[48] In *James Richardson & Sons Ltd. v. Standard Marine Insurance Co. Ltd.*, [1936] S.C.R. 573, 3 D.L.R. 513, an entire cargo of wheat became tough due to excessive moisture and was downgraded, losing some of its value. The majority of the Supreme Court of Canada found that this was a 'partial loss' under the provisions of the Quebec *Civil Code*, S.Q. 1991, c. 64. Mr. Justice Cannon, who agreed with the result, stated at S.C.R. 589, perhaps erroneously: "This is not, strictly speaking, a partial nor a total loss of the cargo but rather a deterioration of the whole cargo causing damage for only part of the sum insured." This is incorrect, since "partial" refers not to the quantity of the property affected but to the extent of the loss.

[49] But see *Singer Manufacturing Co. v. Western Assurance Co.* (1896), 10 Que. S.C. 379 (C.A.): where each sewing machine was separately valued, the insured was entitled to abandon the ones

ance on F.P.A. terms, this has been dropped from the Institute Cargo Clauses (1/1/82).

Sections 61 and 62 of the *C.M.I.A.* provide:

61(1) A partial loss is any loss that is not a total loss.

(2) Where insured goods reach their destination in specie but cannot be identified by reason of obliteration of marks or otherwise, the loss, if any, is a partial loss.

(3) Unless a marine policy otherwise provides, an insured who brings an action for a total loss, but establishes only a partial loss, may recover for a partial loss.

62. A partial loss may be a particular average loss, a general average loss, salvage charges or particular charges.

Section 62 identifies four types of partial loss: a particular average loss, a general average loss, salvage charges and particular charges. We will examine these different losses in the following sections. In the case of a partial loss, the amount the insured is entitled to recover — the "measure of indemnity" — will be "adjusted" according to the rules set out in the *C.M.I.A.* and in the policy of insurance.[50]

9.3.1 Particular Average Loss

A particular average loss is a type of partial loss. The *C.M.I.A.* definition is as follows:

63(1) A particular average loss is a loss of the subject-matter insured that is caused by a peril insured against and is not a general average loss, but does not include particular charges.

This language is repeated in section 2(*c*) of the Schedule to the *C.M.I.A.*[51]

A particular average loss is best understood as a partial loss of or damage to the property insured which affects that *particular* property only and is borne by the owner (or perhaps ultimately the insurer) of *that particular property only*. It is contrasted with a general average loss, which is a loss borne by all the parties to the adventure *generally*, even though the property of only one of those parties may have suffered the loss. Examples of a particular average loss include damage by seawater, damage to the insured property caused by collision or other accident, fire damage, or any other physical damage resulting in partial destruction

---

that were a constructive total loss, even though the policy was on F.P.A. terms. See also *Moore v. Provincial Insurance Co.* (1873), 23 U.C.C.P. 383, to the effect that where the policy insures goods in packages, free from average unless general, and some of the packages are a total loss, the insurers are not liable for the loss unless it is expressed that the packages are separately insured; *Mowat v. Boston Marine Insurance Co.* (1895), 33 N.B.R. 109 (C.A.), rev'd. (1896), 26 S.C.R. 47.

[50] The subject of *Measure of Indemnity* is discussed in Chapter 10.

[51] Schedule to *C.M.I.A*, s. 2: "In a marine policy, a reference...(c) to "average unless general" means a partial loss of the subject-matter insured, other than a general average loss, but does not include particular charges..."

of the property or a loss of part of the property. Marine insurance policies usually insure against particular average losses, unless the policy is "F.P.A.".

9.3.2 General Average Loss

A general average loss is a loss caused by an extraordinary sacrifice or expenditure voluntarily and reasonably made in time of peril to preserve the property in a common maritime adventure.[52] While general average losses fall, in the first instance, on the owner of the property who suffers the loss or the expense, maritime law requires that this type of loss be shared by the several parties to the marine adventure. The theory is that since all the parties to the adventure receive a benefit from the expense or sacrifice, all should share the burden, in proportion to the value of their property saved. Examples of general average losses or sacrifices include jettison of cargo overboard to keep the ship from sinking,[53] damage incurred by the ship or its cargo in extinguishing a fire,[54] and the costs incurred at a "port of refuge" in order to permit the continuation of the voyage after a ship has sustained an accident at sea.[55]

Maritime law defines the circumstances giving rise to general average losses and how they are to be shared amongst the parties to the adventure. Marine insurance policies typically insure against general average sacrifices and expenditures and also insure the owner of the property against any general average contribution his or her property may be called upon to make. The provisions of the *C.M.I.A.* dealing with the treatment of general average losses and contributions under marine insurance policies are discussed in Chapter 22, *General Average*.

9.3.3 Salvage Charges

Salvage charges are the third type of partial loss. Salvage is a concept unique to maritime law and refers to services rendered to maritime property, in time of peril, which save the property, or part of it, from loss. The person providing the services is referred to as a "salvor" and is entitled to a "reward" for the services, provided they were wholly or partially successful. Salvage services are sometimes rendered voluntarily and without any contract. In that event, the salvor is entitled to a payment intended to provide not only compensation, but also a premium for meritorious action as an inducement to others to preserve and protect property in distress at sea.

Salvage is frequently rendered by professional salvors pursuant to a contract. When salvage is rendered contractually, the salvor may be entitled to compensation, calculated in accordance with the contract. Some salvage contracts, such

---

[52] *C.M.I.A.*, subs. 65(1). General average is discussed in Chapter 22.

[53] *Grouselle v. Ferrie* (1843), 6 O.S. 454.

[54] See, for example *Century Insurance Co. of Canada v. N.V. Bocimar, S.A.*, [1987] 1 S.C.R. 1247, 39 D.L.R. (4th) 465, rev'g. (1984), 53 N.R. 383, 7 C.C.L.I. 165 (F.C.A.).

[55] See, for example: *Singer Manufacturing Co. v. Western Assurance Co.* (1896), 10 Que. S.C. 379 (C.A.).

as the *Lloyd's Open Form* (known as the "L.O.F.") preserve the salvor's right to a reward rather than simply compensation based on *quantum meruit*.

If the insured property is "salved" a claim will be made against it by the salvor. Under maritime law, the claim can be exercised against the property itself, by means of an action *in rem* in the Federal Court of Canada.[56] Since the salvage works to the benefit of the marine insurer, saving the insured property from damage or perhaps total loss, most insurance policies stipulate that the insurer will pay for salvage charges incurred in respect of the property.

Section 64 of the *C.M.I.A.* deals with salvage charges as follows:

> 64(1) Salvage charges are charges recoverable under maritime law by a salvor, independently of any contract, but do not include expenses incurred for services in the nature of salvage rendered by the insured or the insured's agent, or any person hired by the insured or the insured's agent, for the purpose of averting a loss by a peril insured against.

> (2) Subject to any express provision in the marine policy, salvage charges incurred for the purpose of averting a loss by a peril insured against may be recovered from the insurer as a loss by such peril.

> (3) The expenses referred to in subsection (1) that are not salvage charges may, when properly incurred, be recovered from the insurer as particular charges or as a general average loss, according to the circumstances under which they were incurred.

Under the *C.M.I.A.*, salvage charges are regarded as a form of "partial loss", since the property itself is saved from total loss. If there has been a total loss, nothing has been salved and therefore no salvage can be payable. The *C.M.I.A.* provides that "pure" or non-contractual voluntary salvage charges, incurred for the purpose of averting a loss by a peril insured against, are recoverable from the insurer as a loss by such peril.[57] It should be noted, however, that the peril averted must have been an insured peril — if the peril was not insured under the policy, then regardless of how meritorious the services were, the salvage charges are not recoverable. It should also be noted that the cost of this type of salvage is not recoverable in addition to the policy amount.[58]

The *C.M.I.A.* deals separately with expenses incurred "for services in the nature of salvage rendered by the insured or the insured's agent, or any person hired by the insured or the insured's agent, for the purpose of averting a loss by a peril insured against."[59] It provides that these charges may be recoverable from the insurer as particular charges or as a general average loss, depending on the circumstances in which they were incurred.

---

[56] *Federal Court Act*, R.C.S. 1985, c. F-7, subss. 22(2)(*j*) and 43(2).

[57] C.M.I.A., subs. 64(2).

[58] See *Aitchison v. Lohre* (1879), 4 App. Cas. 755, 28 W.R. 1 (H.L.) to the effect that "pure salvage" is not recoverable under the "sue and labour" clause and is not recoverable in addition to the amount specified in the policy.

[59] *C.M.I.A.*, subs. 64(1). See also subs. 64(3).

It appears to be well-accepted that a "pure", non-contractual salvage on the one hand and salvage under a contract on the other hand, are treated differently. In the first case, the insurer has no obligation to pay anything more than the total amount insured under the policy. Thus if a vessel insured for $1,000,000 is saved by voluntary salvors, not operating under a contract, who receive a salvage award of $500,000 and there is particular average damage to the vessel of $900,000, the limit of the insurer's obligations is $1,000,000, even though the "loss" to the insured is $900,000 in particular average as well as a salvage reward of $1,400,000. On the other hand, if the salvage is made pursuant to a contract, the salvors are regarded as the servants or agents of the insured and the charge is recoverable under the sue and labour clause in the policy. In modern times, the distinction is difficult to appreciate, since "pure" salvage is rare, at least in the case of major maritime salvage operations, which are usually done under *Lloyd's Open Form* or some similar contract which preserves the "voluntariness" requirement of salvage but contains provisions with respect to the determination of the salvage reward and other matters.

The Institute Cargo Clauses (1/1/82) provide:

> 2. This insurance covers general average and salvage charges, adjusted or determined according to the contract of affreightment and/or the governing law and practice, incurred to avoid or in connection with the avoidance of loss from any cause except those excluded in Clauses 4, 5, 6 and 7 or elsewhere in this insurance.

The C.B.M.U. Great Lakes Hull Clauses (Sept. 1, 1971) provide at lines 269-297:

> General Average and Salvage shall be payable as provided in the contract of affreightment, or failing such provision or there be no contract of affreightment payable in accordance with the Rules of Practice for the Great Lakes of the Association of Average Adjusters of Canada.
>
> ...
>
> In the event of salvage, towage or other assistance being rendered to the Vessel by any vessel belonging in part or in whole to the same Owners or Charterers, the value of such services (without regard to the common ownership or control of the vessels) shall be ascertained by arbitration in the manner provided for under the Collision Liability clause in this Policy, and the amount so awarded so far as applicable to the interest hereby insured shall constitute a charge under this Policy.
>
> When the contributory value of the Vessel is greater than the Agreed Value herein, the liability of the Underwriters for General Average Contribution (except in respect to amounts made good to the Vessel), or Salvage, shall not exceed that proportion of the total contribution due from the Vessel which the amount insured hereunder bears to the contributory value; and if, because of damage for which the Underwriters are liable as Particular Average, the value of the Vessel has been reduced for the purpose of contribution, the amount of such Particular Average damage recoverable under this Policy shall first be deducted from the amount insured hereunder, and the Underwriters shall then be liable only for the proportion which such net amount bears to the contributory value.

The purpose of the third clause is to ensure that underwriters' share of the salvage reward is proportionate to the amount they have agreed to insure. Part of the calculation of the salvage reward requires the court or arbitrator to make an assessment of the value of the insured vessel. If that assessment produces a value greater than the insured value, the underwriters are only required to pay a proportionate amount of the salvage reward. If the vessel has sustained damage recoverable as particular average under the insurance policy, that amount must be deducted from the insured value for the purpose of determining the value of the vessel under the policy.[60]

9.3.4 Particular Charges

Particular charges are the fourth and final type of partial loss. They are defined by subsection 63(2) of the *C.M.I.A.*:

> 63(2) Particular charges are expenses incurred by or on behalf of an insured for the purpose of preserving the subject-matter insured from a peril insured against, but do not include a general average loss or salvage charges.

Particular charges are distinguishable from general average charges because they are incurred solely with respect to a *particular* interest insured, for example the hull, cargo or freight insured, rather than in respect of the entire adventure. They include expenses incurred in preserving the cargo, such as warehousing, drying and packing charges[61] as well as charges in connection with the sale of cargo.[62] Survey fees to ascertain the nature and extent of damage to insured property, and to quantify the loss, may also be a form of particular charge.[63]

---

[60] For example: Salvage services are rendered to a vessel valued at $10 million for insurance and which has sustained $1 million in damage. For the purposes of the salvage award, the court assesses the damaged value of the vessel at $12 million and grants a salvage reward of 25 per cent or $3 million. The insured is required to pay $3 million to the salvor. It makes a claim under its hull and machinery policy for the particular average damage of $1,000,000 and for salvage. The underwriters pay the particular average claim of $1,000,000. For the purpose of contributing to the salvage reward, the insured value of the vessel is therefore $9 million ($10 million minus $1 million) and the underwriters share of the salvage is 9/12 of $3 million or $2,250,000.

[61] See *Ultramar Canada Inc. v. Mutual Marine Office Inc.*, [1995] 1 F.C. 341, 82 F.T.R. 1 (T.D.).

[62] See R.H. Brown, *Marine Insurance, Volume One: Principles and Basic Practice*, 6th ed. (London: Witherby & Co. Ltd., 1998) at pp. 114, 238-39.

[63] This may be indirectly confirmed by subs. 77(4) of the *C.M.I.A.*:

> 77(4) Where the subject-matter insured under a marine policy is warranted free from particular average under a specified percentage, for the purpose of determining whether the percentage has been attained, only the actual loss incurred in respect of the subject-matter may be considered, and no particular charges or expenses incurred in establishing the loss may be included.

9.3.5   Sue and Labour Charges

The insured has a duty to "sue and labour" to take reasonable measures to avert or minimize a loss.[64] The subject of sue and labour is discussed in Chapter 11.

The duty to sue and labour is imposed by law, but most insurance policies on cargo, hull and machinery and freight include a sue and labour clause obliging the insured to take such measures and providing that the underwriters will pay reasonable expenses incurred in so doing. Charges incurred in the exercise of this duty are referred to as "sue and labour charges" and are a form of particular charge. They are, in general, recoverable under the policy in addition to a payment for a partial or total loss.

9.3.6   Special Charges

Special charges are a form of particular charge. Technically, they are charges incurred by a ship owner on behalf of a cargo owner for the safety and preservation of the cargo.[65] In *Ultramar Canada Inc. v. Mutual Marine Office Inc.*[66] an oil barge was stranded and the cargo was heated so that it could be pumped off. The costs of so doing were treated as "special charges on cargo" and were recovered under the cargo insurance policy.

---

[64]   See *James Richardson & Sons, Ltd. v. Standard Marine Insurance Co.*, [1936] S.C.R. 573. The duty to sue and labour is confirmed by s. 80 of the *C.M.I.A.*

[65]   *See Western Assurance Co. v. Baden Marine Assurance Co.* (1902), 22 Que. S.C. 374; see L.J. Buglass, *Marine Insurance and General Average in the United States*, 3rd ed. (Centreville, Maryland: Cornell Maritime Press, 1991) at p. 263.

[66]   [1995] 1 F.C. 341, 82 F.T.R. 1.

Chapter 10

The Measure of Indemnity

10.1 INTRODUCTION

We have examined in Chapter 6 how the insurable value of property is determined and in Chapter 9 the types of losses and charges recoverable under a marine policy. This chapter deals with the final step in the process of adjusting a claim under a marine policy — the determination of the compensation or "measure of indemnity" the insured is entitled to receive. Determining the measure of indemnity can be a complex exercise, requiring a careful examination of the policy, knowledge of the provisions of the Canadian *Marine Insurance Act ("C.M.I.A.")*[1] and an appreciation of marine insurance practice. It is often undertaken by experienced average adjusters or claims adjusters. There may be little legal precedent to guide the adjuster and he or she may have reference to legal and insurance texts and commentaries and to the practices of other adjusters. In some cases, these are codified in rules of practice of professional organizations, such as the Association of Average Adjusters of Canada.

Section 66 of the *C.M.I.A.* sets out the general principle:

> 66. The measure of indemnity in respect of a loss under a marine policy is the amount that the insured can recover in respect of the loss under the policy, such amount not exceeding
>
> (*a*) in the case of an unvalued policy, the insurable value of the subject-matter insured; or
>
> (*b*) in the case of a valued policy, the value of the subject-matter insured specified by the policy.

The sections following section 66 deal with the principles applicable to different kinds of losses of various types of insured property. We will review these provisions when considering the different types of losses. In most cases, the rules in the *C.M.I.A.* for determining the measure of indemnity are expressed to be "subject to any express provision in the policy" and marine insurance policies frequently contain express terms modifying the principles expressed in the *C.M.I.A.*

Where the policy is unvalued, a relatively rare phenomenon these days, it is necessary to apply the rules of the *C.M.I.A.* to ascertain the insured value in

---

[1] S.C. 1993, c. 22.

order to determine the measure of indemnity.[2] Where the policy is valued, the insured value stated in the policy is taken to be conclusive, unless the insurer can establish that the value is so overstated as to amount to fraud.[3]

The policy may contain a deductible or a franchise. A deductible is an amount borne by the insured and deducted from the claim. Some policies provide that there is no deductible in the case of total losses or for certain other types of loss. A "franchise" clause, on the other hand, provides that the under-writer will not be liable for losses below a specified percentage — for example, a franchise of 5 per cent, means that losses below 5 per cent are not covered. However, any loss in excess of 5 per cent is fully covered. Thus, a 4 per cent loss would not be covered at all, whereas a 6 per cent loss would be fully covered.[4]

10.2 TOTAL LOSS

Section 67 of the *C.M.I.A.* deals with total loss:

> Subject to this Act and any express provision in the policy, the measure of indem-nity in respect of a total loss of the subject-matter insured is
> (a) in the case of an unvalued policy, the insurable value of the subject-matter; and
> (b) in the case of a valued policy, the value of the subject-matter specified by the policy.

The calculation of the measure of indemnity in the case of total loss does not present difficulties. Where the policy is valued, the value specified in the policy is conclusive, in the absence of fraud and the insured is entitled to recover the insured value, or the sum insured if the property is underinsured. Where the policy is unvalued, the measure of indemnity is the insurable value calculated in accordance with the *C.M.I.A.*[5]

10.3 PARTIAL LOSS

10.3.1 Partial Loss of Ship

Subject to any contrary provision in the policy,[6] where there is damage to a ship amounting to a partial loss, the measure of indemnity is the "reasonable cost of the repairs", regardless of whether the policy is valued or unvalued and whether

---

[2] *C.M.I.A.*, s. 19. See Chapter 6, *Insurable Value*.

[3] See *Kenny v. Union Marine Insurance Co.* (1880), 13 N.S.R. 313 (C.A.); *Biggin v. British Marine Mutual Insurance Assn. Ltd.* (1992), 101 Nfld. & P.E.I.R. 156, 14 C.C.L.I. (2d) 66 (Nfld. S.C. T.D.); *Fudge v. Charter Marine Insurance Co.* (1992), 8 C.C.L.I. (2d) 252, 97 Nfld. & P.E.I.R. 91 (Nfld. S.C.), where misrepresentation of the value may entitle the insurer to avoid the policy.

[4] This is sometimes expressed as a warranty: for example, "Warranted free from average under 5%."

[5] *C.M.I.A.*, s. 19.

[6] Obviously if the policy is "total loss only" or "T.L.O." there is no recovery for a partial loss.

or not the ship was insured for its full insurable value.[7] This rule is expressed in Section 68 of the *C.M.I.A.*:

> 68. Subject to any express provision in the marine policy the measure of indemnity in respect of a partial loss of a ship is
>
> (*a*) where the ship is repaired, the reasonable cost of the repairs, less the customary deductions, but not exceeding the sum insured in respect of any one casualty.

Subsection 68(*b*) provides that where there have been partial repairs, the insured is entitled to receive the reasonable cost of those repairs, plus an amount for depreciation of the unrepaired damage, provided that the total may not exceed the reasonable cost of repairing all the damage.[8]

Subsection 68(*c*) allows recovery for "unrepaired damage" where the ship has not been repaired. The insured can recover a reasonable amount for the depreciation of the ship if the damage is unrepaired and the ship is not sold prior to the expiry of the policy term.[9]

10.3.2 Partial Loss of Goods

Section 70 of the *C.M.I.A.* states the measure of indemnity in the case of a partial loss of goods:

> 70(1) Subject to any express provision in the policy, the measure of indemnity in respect of a partial loss of goods or movables is
>
> (*a*) where part of the goods or movables insured by an unvalued policy is totally lost, the insurable value of the part lost, ascertained as in the case of a total loss;
>
> (*b*) where part of the goods or movables insured by a valued policy is totally lost, that proportion of the value of the goods or movables specified in the policy that the insurable value of the part lost bears to the insurable value of all the goods or movables, ascertained as in the case of an unvalued policy; and
>
> (*c*) where the whole or any part of the goods or movables is delivered damaged at its destination, that proportion of the insurable value of all the goods or movables, in the case of an unvalued policy, or the value of all the goods or mov-

---

[7]   The emphasis is on "reasonableness": in *Lockwood v. Moreira* (1995), 28 C.C.L.I (2d) 290 (Ont. Ct. Gen. Div.), the plaintiff's boat was damaged by soot as a result of vandalism. He claimed the cost of restoring the boat to its previous "immaculate" condition, even though this would have resulted in additional expenses of over $100,000. The court held that the insurer was only required to restore the boat to a condition reasonably comparable to its pre-accident condition. The extraordinary repairs requested by the plaintiff would have resulted in a recovery of more than the boat was worth at the time of the vandalism.

[8]   *C.M.I.A.*, s. 68(*b*):

> 68(*b*) where the ship is partially repaired, the aggregate of the reasonable cost of the repairs, as determined under paragraph (*a*), and the reasonable depreciation, if any, arising from the unrepaired damage, the aggregate not exceeding the cost, as determined under paragraph (*a*), of repairing the whole damage...

[9]   *Ibid.*, s. 68(*c*):

> 68(*c*) where the ship is not repaired and is not sold in a damaged state during the risk, the reasonable depreciation arising from the unrepaired damage, but not exceeding the cost, as determined under paragraph (*a*), of repairing the damage.

ables specified by the policy, in the case of a valued policy, that the difference between the gross value of all the goods or movables in a sound condition at that destination and their gross value in their damaged condition at that destination bears to the gross value of all the goods or movables in a sound condition at that destination.[10]

Where there is a partial loss of goods, in the case of a shipment containing different types of goods, the value of the part lost or damaged must be ascertained by reference to its insurable value, in proportion to the insurable value of the entire shipment. The resulting proportion must be applied to the insured value of the shipment to determine the insured value of the part affected. The measure of indemnity with respect to that part can then be calculated according to whether it has been lost or damaged.

When the goods are all of the same type, the calculation is simpler, and it is a matter of determining either: (a) the insured value of the part lost or, (b) where there is damage, the extent of the damage to the part affected. Using the formula set out in subsection 70(1)(c) of the *C.M.I.A.*, it is necessary to make the following calculation, where gross sound market value ("GSMV") is equal to the "arrived" sound market value of the goods, and gross damaged market value ("GDMV") is equal to the arrived damaged market value of the goods:

$$\text{Measure of indemnity} = \frac{\text{GSMV} - \text{GDMV}}{\text{GSMV}} \times \text{Insured Value}$$

In some cases, the damaged market value of the goods will be established by a salvage sale. In other cases, a surveyor will recommend a depreciation factor to be applied to the insured value and the insured will often agree to retain the damaged goods, subject to being indemnified for the depreciation.

In *James Richardson & Sons, Ltd. v. Standard Marine Insurance Co.*,[11] a cargo of 98,099 bushels of wheat was insured under a "floating policy" pursuant to a marine insurance certificate which valued the wheat at sixty-five cents per bushel. The entire cargo was damaged by moisture and with the involvement of marine surveyors, bids for the purchase of the downgraded cargo were received. Ultimately, the insured agreed to keep the cargo, notionally buying it for forty-six and a quarter cents per bushel, the amount of the highest bid. Later, the insured was able to dry the wheat and ultimately sold it for a greater price. The Court of Appeal had taken this sale into account in determining the claim under the insurance policy, but the Supreme Court of Canada held that this was not correct. The case was decided under the former article 2535 of the Quebec *Civil Code*,[12] which was in substantially the same form as section 70(1)(c) of the

---

[10]   See the definition of "gross value" contained in subss. 70(2) and (3).

[11]   [1936] S.C.R. 573, [1936] 3 D.L.R. 513.

[12]   S.Q. 1991, c. 64:

2535. The amount for which the insurer is liable on a partial loss is ascertained by comparing the gross produce of the damaged sales with the gross produce of the sound sales and applying the percentage of difference to the value of the goods as specified in the policy, or established in the manner provided for by the last preceding article.

C.M.I.A. The Supreme Court held that the amount of the claim should be established as follows:

> The insured value of the cargo was $63,852.84...the gross produce of the damaged sales was $44,352.84. The sound value of the grain on September 1st, 1931, the first day of unloading at Montreal, was 52 1/8 cents per bushel...The total sound value of the cargo is therefore $51,205.08. The difference between the sound and damaged values is $6,852.24 which is 13.382% of the sound value. This percentage of the insured value of the total quantity of wheat delivered at Montreal, $63,852.84, amounts to $8,544.79 which is the loss for which the [insurer] is liable.[13]

Had it not been for the agreement to settle the insurance claim based on the tender, the "sue and labour" clause in the insurance policy would have required the plaintiff to bring the profit into account.

In *Balix Furniture and Appliances Ltd. v. Maritime Insurance Co.*,[14] a shipment of paintings arrived with some missing and others damaged. The goods were insured under an open policy issued to the insured's customs broker, containing a "valuation clause" insuring the cargo at "Invoice Cost plus Freight and Charges and 10% added thereto." Applying the provisions of the Ontario *Marine Insurance Act*[15] (which was, at the time, the only applicable marine insurance statute in Ontario, the *C.M.I.A.* not being law until 1993), the judge calculated the "insurable value" of the missing paintings determined according to the Act, in proportion to the insurable value of the total shipment, and multiplied this by the insured value of the whole calculated in accordance with the policy. A similar approach was taken to the calculation of the measure of indemnity in relation to the damaged paintings, using the "market value" of the paintings to determine their sound value. The court dismissed the claim for this damage because it found that the paintings had not been properly packed for transportation.[16]

10.3.3   Partial Loss of Freight

The carrier may insure the freight at risk. The shipper's liability to pay freight will be determined by the contract of carriage, whether it is a bill of lading, a charterparty or some other form of contract of affreightment and is often payable "goods lost or not lost", meaning that even if the goods are lost or damaged, the shipper remains liable to the carrier for the costs of transportation. Freight is customarily insured under an unvalued policy.

Section 69 of the *C.M.I.A.* states:

---

[13]   [1936] S.C.R. 573 at 580-81.
[14]   [1978] O.J. No. 1514 (QL).
[15]   R.S.O. 1990, c. M.2, am. S.O. 1993, c. 27, Sched.
[16]   See Chapter 7, *Perils Insured*, with respect to the exclusion of losses caused by insufficiency of packing.

69. Subject to any express provision in the policy, the measure of indemnity in respect of a partial loss of freight is that proportion of the insurable value of the freight, in the case of an unvalued policy, or the value of the freight specified by the policy, in the case of a valued policy, that the part of the freight lost by the insured bears to the whole freight at the risk of the insured under the policy.

10.3.4 General Average Contribution

The measure of indemnity in respect of general average contribution is discussed in Chapter 22.[17]

10.3.5 Salvage Charges

The measure of indemnity for salvage charges is similar to the measure of indemnity for general average.[18] In the absence of contrary policy terms, if the property is insured to its full contributory value, the insurer pays the full salvage contribution. If the property is insured for less than its contributory value (the value at which it is assessed for the purposes of the salvage reward), the insurer pays a proportionate contribution.[19] In the latter case, where there has been a particular average loss of the property that has been deducted from its contributory value and paid by the insurer, the amount of such loss is deducted from the insured value to determine the insurer's contribution. Provisions reflecting these statutory principles are contained in the C.B.M.U. Great Lakes Hull Clauses (Sept. 1, 1971)[20] and the Canadian Hulls (Pacific) Clauses (Sept. 1/91).[21]

10.3.6 Sue and Labour Expenses

The sue and labour clause is treated as a supplementary contract and the insured is entitled to recover sue and labour expenses in addition to a total or partial loss of the property insured.[22] The subject of sue and labour is discussed in Chapter 11.

10.3.7 Particular Average

Section 77 of the *C.M.I.A.* deals with policies written on "free of particular average" or "F.P.A." terms.[23] Such policies are less common since the withdrawal by the English market of the Institute Cargo Clauses — F.P.A. (1963) in

---

[17] See *C.M.I.A.*, s. 72.
[18] *Ibid.*, subs. 72(3).
[19] *Ibid.*, subs. 72(1)(*a*) and (*b*).
[20] Appendix G, lines 167-173.
[21] Appendix E, lines 140-150.
[22] Subsection 79(1). This subsection makes specific reference only to a total loss, but it is clear that sue and labour charges may be recovered, in addition to a payment for either partial or total loss, up to the amount insured.
[23] See Chapter 9, *Losses and Charges Recoverable*.

1982 and of F.P.A. hull clauses in 1983, but they are still used by some brokers and underwriters in Canadian markets.

10.4 OTHER LOSSES

Section 74 of the *C.M.I.A.* provides that "the measure of indemnity in respect of a loss not provided for in any of sections 67 to 73 is to be determined, as much as possible, in accordance with those sections."

10.5 SUCCESSIVE LOSSES

Section 78 of the *C.M.I.A.* provides that the insurer is liable for successive losses, even though the total exceeds the sum insured. If there is a partial loss of a ship, which is repaired, followed by either a total loss or a partial loss, the insurer remains liable for the subsequent loss, even though the total of the two losses exceeds the sum insured. However, where there is an unrepaired partial loss, followed by a total loss, the insurer is liable only for the total loss.[24]

10.6 LIABILITY INSURANCE

Section 73 of the *C.M.I.A.* provides:

> 73. Subject to any express provision in the policy, the measure of indemnity in respect of any liability to a third party that is expressly insured against by a marine policy is the amount paid or payable by the insured to the third party in respect of the liability.

Subject to any deductible and limit of liability expressed in the policy, the insurer is obliged to indemnify the insured for any amount for which it is found liable to the third party.[25]

10.7 PROPORTIONAL LIABILITY

Marine insurance policies are often written on a subscription basis, with a number of insurers subscribing to different percentages of the risk. Each insurer becomes liable for its own percentage of the indemnity payable under the policy. Section 75 of the *C.M.I.A.* confirms the proportionate liability of each insurer:

> 75. Where a loss is recoverable under a marine policy, the insurer, or each insurer if there is more than one, is liable for that proportion of the measure of indemnity in respect of the loss that the amount subscribed by the insurer is of

---

[24] *C.M.I.A.*, subs. 78(2).

[25] Liability insurance offered by "P. & I." Clubs was at one time unlimited. In light of the liabilities faced by shipowners, particularly liability for pollution, protection and indemnity insurance is now subject to limits which are, nevertheless, substantial: see Chapter 20, *Protection and Indemnity Insurance*.

(*a*) in the case of an unvalued policy, the insurable value of the subject-matter; and

(*b*) in the case of a valued policy, the value of the subject-matter specified by the policy.

The additional effect of this provision is that if the property is insured for less than its full value, the insured is its own insurer for a proportionate amount of the loss. In the case of a single insurer, liability is proportionate to either the insurable value of the subject-matter (in the case of an unvalued policy) or the value stated in the policy (in the case of a valued policy). To take the example given at the outset of Chapter 6, if under a valued policy a vessel valued at $750,000 is insured for $500,000, the insured would bear one third of any loss. If there were ten insurers, each bearing ten percent of the loss, each would be responsible for one tenth of any loss, or $50,000 in the event of a total loss.

10.8 PARTICULAR POLICY PROVISIONS

10.8.1 Cargo Insurance

The measure of indemnity in marine cargo insurance is usually left to general principles, subject to specific provisions in the policy itself. For example, the Institute Cargo Clauses (1/1/82) (reproduced in Appendices B, C and D) provide for the payment of forwarding charges where the transit of the goods is terminated prior to their destination as a result of an insured peril.[26] Open cargo policies may contain provisions with respect to a deductible as well as other clauses concerning particular types of losses, such as the relabeling or reconditioning of cartons, removal of debris, and cleaning and repacking charges.

10.8.2 Hull and Machinery Insurance

The C.B.M.U. Great Lakes Hull Clauses (September 1, 1971) and the Canadian Hulls (Pacific) Clauses (Sept. 1, 1991) contain detailed provisions with respect to deductibles, the supervision of repairs, the appointment of surveyors and the adjustment of claims, including claims for general average, salvage and sue and labour charges. The subject of hull and machinery insurance is discussed in Chapter 19.

---

[26] Institute Cargo Clauses (A), cl. 12:

Where, as a result of the operation of a risk covered by this insurance the insured transit is terminated at a port or place other than that to which the subject-matter is covered under this insurance, the Underwriters will reimburse the Assured for any extra charges properly and reasonably incurred in unloading storing and forwarding the subject-matter to the destination to which it is insured hereunder.

Chapter 11

Duties of the Insured: Sue and Labour

11.1 INTRODUCTION

After an accident has occurred, the insured has an obligation to take reasonable measures to minimize the resultant loss — in the technical language of marine insurance, to "sue and labour". Since such measures benefit the insurer, policies on hull and machinery and cargo usually provide that, in addition to indemnifying the insured against the loss itself, the insurer will also pay the costs of such measures, known as "sue and labour charges". Sue and labour charges are a form of "particular charge". That is, they are incurred in relation to a *particular* interest: the property that is the subject of the insurance. They differ from general average charges, which are incurred on behalf of the several interests making up the marine adventure. Other forms of particular charges, known as "salvage charges" and "special charges"[1] are not recoverable under the sue and labour clause.[2] It is said that sue and labour charges differ from other forms of particular charges in that they are incurred prior to destination, whereas particular charges are incurred at destination.

Section 80 of the Canadian *Marine Insurance Act* ("*C.M.I.A.*") states the duty on the insured to sue and labour:

> 80. It is the duty of an insured and an insured's agent to take such measures as are reasonable for the purpose of averting or diminishing a loss under the marine policy.

Subsection 79(1) provides that the "sue and labour" clause in a policy is a "supplementary contract" and that the insured can recover expenses incurred under that clause even where the insurer has paid for a total loss of the property insured:

> 79(1) Where a marine policy contains a sue and labour clause, the engagement thereby entered into is supplementary to the contract and the insured may recover from the insurer any expenses properly incurred under the clause, even if the insurer has paid for a total loss of the subject-matter insured or the subject matter

---

[1] See Chapter 9, *Losses and Charges Recoverable*.

[2] Subsection 79(2) of the Canadian *Marine Insurance Act*, S.C. 1993, c. 22 ("*C.M.I.A.*"). See *Western Assurance Co. v. Baden Marine Assurance Co.* (1902), 22 Que. S.C. 374 for a discussion of the distinction between "special charges" and "particular charges".

insured is warranted free from particular average, either wholly or under a specified percentage.

(2) General average losses, general average contributions, salvage charges and expenses incurred for the purpose of averting or diminishing a loss by a peril not insured against are not recoverable under a sue and labour clause.

Thus, the insured is entitled to recover under the sue and labour clause in addition to the payment for a total loss where the insured has incurred expenses in attempting to avert such a loss.[3] Subsection 79(2) confirms that sue and labour charges are only recoverable if they are incurred to preserve the property from a peril insured by the policy. If the loss sought to be averted or minimized is not covered by the policy, neither are the expenses incurred to avoid it.

Sue and labour expenses are recoverable even if the sue and labour effort is not successful, as long as the expenses were reasonably incurred. Expenses incurred after a casualty that are simply part of the ordinary costs of the insured's operations and not incurred for the purpose of minimizing the loss are not recoverable as sue and labour charges.[4]

11.2   THE DUTY TO SUE AND LABOUR

In *James Richardson & Sons, Ltd. v. Standard Marine Insurance Co.*, Mr. Justice Davis of the Supreme Court of Canada described the purpose of the sue and labour clause:

> Sue and labour clauses in marine insurance have for their object the encouragement of the insurer and the insured to do work to preserve, after an accident, the property covered by the policy and to make the best of a bad state of affairs. Should they do so, the waiver clause provides that their respective rights shall be in no wise prejudiced by any acts done in pursuance of such object and that the insured shall be entitled to obtain his expenses consequent on the work from the insurers. Under such a clause it is the duty of the insured to take reasonable measures to avert loss.[5]

---

[3]   Where the policy insures on F.P.A. ("free of particular average") terms it must be shown that the expenses claimed as sue and labour were incurred to avert a total loss. See *Glen Falls Insurance Co. v. Montreal Light, Heat and Power Consolidated* (1928), 45 Que. K.B. 304, where it was noted that the insured has an independent duty to sue and labour and is entitled to recover the costs of salvaging the insured property and preventing a total loss, notwithstanding that the policy insures on F.P.A. terms. In *Porter & Son Ltd. v. Western Assurance Co.*, [1938] 1 D.L.R. 619, 12 M.P.R. 469 (N.S.C.A.), it was held that the act of beaching a laden scow was a general average act for the benefit of the entire adventure but that expenses incurred thereafter for the purposes of saving the scow were recoverable under the sue and labour clause.

[4]   See *McLeod v. Insurance Co. of North America* (1901), 34 N.S.R. 88: the wages of the master and crew of the ship, who stayed with the ship after a casualty, were not incurred as a result of services rendered pursuant to the sue and labour clause.

[5]   [1936] S.C.R. 573 at 595-96, 3 D.L.R. 513. See also *Toron Construction Ltd. v. Continental Insurance Co.* (1982), 34 A.R. 456 (Q.B.) as to the effect of the sue and labour clause.

The *C.M.I.A.* provides that the insured, or its agent, must take "reasonable" measures to "avert or diminish" a loss.[6] The touchstone is "reasonableness". Whether the insured has acted reasonably depends on all the surrounding circumstances and on the court's assessment of what a reasonable and prudent person would have done in similar circumstances. It is sometimes said that the insured must act as though he or she had no insurance — to act "as a prudent uninsured". This means that when the loss occurs the insured cannot simply turn the problem over to the insurer, but must take purposeful and reasonable measures to mitigate the loss.

11.3 CONSEQUENCES OF THE FAILURE TO SUE AND LABOUR

Section 80 of the *C.M.I.A.* speaks of a duty to do two things — to "avert" and to "diminish" a loss. The word "avert" suggests that there is a duty to "avoid" a loss, but the term is not used in this manner. The insured's negligence in incurring the loss or in failing to avoid it, will not necessarily deprive the insured of coverage. This subject is discussed in more detail in Chapter 7, *Perils Insured.*

But what of the failure of the insured to take reasonable measures to diminish or reduce the loss after the loss has occurred? Several Canadian cases have held that the insured's failure to "sue and labour" after a loss will reduce the recovery under the policy or may even preclude recovery if the damages could have been mitigated or altogether avoided by reasonable measures. For example, in *Oswald v. Anglo-Scottish Insurance Co.,*[7] the insured's boat was stolen and burnt. The insured recovered it, but failed to move it to a place of safety and it suffered further damage in a storm. It was held that the insured's failure to take anything more than the most superficial measures after the loss limited his recovery to the damages caused by the original loss. Similarly, in *Fudge v. Charter Marine Insurance Co.,*[8] the court held that the failure of the plaintiff to take "reasonable and obvious measures" after a fire broke out on his fishing vessel, including sending a "mayday", using the fire extinguishers and towing the boat to a place of safety, was a breach of the duty to sue and labour and precluded recovery.[9]

On the other hand, in *Suo v. Openshaw Simmons Ltd.,*[10] the court held that the plaintiff had done "everything possible" after his vessel began to take on water to get it to a place of safety and had acted reasonably as required by the British

---

[6] *C.M.I.A.,* s. 80.
[7] [1961] I.L.R. ¶1-020 (B.C.S.C.).
[8] (1992), 97 Nfld. & P.E.I.R. 91, 8 C.C.L.I. (2d) 252 (Nfld. S.C.).
[9] The court referred to *Stad v. Fireman's Fund Insurance Co.,* [1979] I.L.R. ¶1-1070 (B.C.S.C.), in which the trial judge had stated that the failure of the plaintiff to stand by the vessel after the casualty, to keep a spotlight on it and to note its location, could have been a bar to recovery. The court also referred to *Stephen v. Scottish Boat Owners' Mutual Insurance Association* (1989), 104 N.R. 63 (H.L.).
[10] (1978), 5 B.C.L.R. 370, [1978] I.L.R. ¶1-982.

Columbia *Insurance (Marine) Act*[11] and by the Canadian Hulls (Pacific) Clauses (Sept. 1/91).[12] The trial judge described the sue and labour clauses as a "contract within a contract" and said that the duty to sue and labour only occurred once an actual peril had created a potential loss. There was no conflict between the sue and labour provisions of the B. C. *Insurance (Marine) Act*[13] and the provisions of the Act under which the insurer is liable even though the loss would not have occurred but for the negligence or misconduct of the master or crew.[14]

In determining whether the insured has taken such measures "as are reasonable" after a loss, it is important to recognize that the touchstone is "reasonableness" and not perfection. After the fact and with the benefit of hindsight, it is always possible to suggest some course of action that might have reduced the claim, however, the test is not hindsight but rather the circumstances that existed at the time. When a marine loss occurs, the insured may be called upon to make decisions promptly when the options and resources are limited. A reasonable insured will take advice from suitable experts including, quite possibly, a marine surveyor appointed under the policy, and will consider the range of alternatives available; but if the insured acts in a reasonable and responsible manner, the Court will not likely second-guess his or her decisions simply because the insurer, after the fact, can suggest a way that would have reduced the claim under the policy.

11.4   STANDARD POLICY TERMS

Most cargo and hull and machinery policy forms contain a "sue and labour" clause confirming the insured's obligation to sue and labour and the underwriter's agreement to pay sue and labour charges. The S.G. (Ship and Goods) form provides:

> And in he case of any loss or misfortune it shall be lawful to the assured, their factors, servants and assigns, to sue, labour and travel for, in and about the Defence, Safeguard and Recovery of the said Goods and Merchandise, and Ship, etc., or any Part thereof, without Prejudice to this Insurance; to the Charges whereof we, the Assurers, will contribute, each one according to the Rate and Quantity of his sum herein assured.

11.4.1   Cargo Insurance

The Institute Cargo Clauses (1/1/82) (reproduced in Appendices B, C and D) have a "plain language" sue and labour clause under the heading "Minimising Losses":

---

[11]   R.S.B.C. 1996, c. 230.

[12]   Appendix E.

[13]   Section 80.

[14]   The relevant provision of the *C.M.I.A.* is subs. 53(1). The provision of the British Columbia *Insurance (Marine) Act* was (then) subs. 57(2).

16. It is the duty of the Assured and their servants and agents in respect of loss recoverable hereunder

16.1 to take such measures as may be reasonable for the purpose of averting or minimizing such loss, and

16.2 to ensure that all rights against carriers, bailees or other third parties are properly preserved and exercised and the Underwriters will, in addition to any loss recoverable hereunder, reimburse the Assured for any charges properly and reasonably incurred in pursuance of these duties.

Unlike most forms of hull and machinery insurance, the Institute Cargo Clauses do not call for the apportionment of sue and labour charges to the extent of any underinsurance.

Cargo policies usually state that the insured must give proper and timely notice to carriers and other third parties who may be responsible for the loss and against whom the insured or its underwriters may have a right of recovery. The insured must also ensure that rights of actions against such parties are properly preserved.[15] The failure to do so may result in the disallowance of the claim, either in whole or to the extent underwriters have been prejudiced.

11.4.2 Hull and Machinery Insurance

The principle forms of hull and machinery insurance contain a sue and labour clause. For example, the C.B.M.U. Great Lakes Hull Clauses (Sept. 1, 1971)[16] contain a sue and labour clause at lines 183-196:

SUE AND LABOR

And in case of any Loss or Misfortune, it shall be lawful and necessary for the Assured, their Factors, Servants and Assigns, to sue, labor and travel for, in, and about the defense, safeguard and recovery of the Vessel, or any part thereof, without prejudice to this insurance, to the charges whereof the Underwriters will contribute their proportion as provided below. And it is expressly declared and agreed that no acts of the Underwriters or Assured in recovering, saving or preserving the Vessel shall be considered as a waiver or acceptance of abandonment.

In the event of expenditure under the Sue and Labor clause, the Underwriters shall pay the proportion of such expenses that the amount insured hereunder bears to the Agreed Value, or that the amount insured hereunder, less loss and/or damage payable under this Policy, bears to the actual value of the salved property, whichever proportion shall be less.

If claim for Total Loss is admitted under this Policy and sue and labor expenses have been reasonably incurred in excess of any proceeds realized or value recovered, the amount payable under this Policy will be the proportion of such excess that the amount insured hereunder (without deduction for loss or damage) bears to the Agreed Value or to the sound value of the Vessel at the time of the accident, whichever value was greater. The foregoing shall also apply to expenses reasonably incurred in salving or attempting to salve the vessel and other property to the

---

[15] See Chapter 12, *Subrogation.*

[16] Appendix G.

extent that such expenses shall be regarded as having been incurred in respect of the Vessel.[17]

The second of these three clauses means that if the amount of insurance (*i.e.*, "the amount insured hereunder") is less than the agreed value stated in the policy, the insured is a co-insurer in respect of sue and labour charges. In Canadian marine insurance practice it is common to add an endorsement removing this provision.

A sue and labour clause in a hull and machinery policy was interpreted by the Federal Court of Canada in *Ultramar Canada Inc. v. Mutual Marine Office Inc.*,[18] a complex action against three sets of insurers — hull, cargo and P. & I. — after a barge carrying oil stranded in the St. Lawrence River off Matane, Quebec. Substantial sums of money were spent by the shipowner (which also owned the cargo) to get the barge and its cargo removed and to avoid a massive oil spill. The costs incurred substantially exceeded the value of the property at risk, it having been determined that the hull was a constructive total loss. An average adjuster prepared an adjustment in general average, calling for some of these expenses to be borne by the cargo insurers as "excess general average" and some to be paid by the hull and machinery insurer as sue and labour charges. One of the issues before the court was how much of the costs should be borne by the hull and machinery underwriters as sue and labour charges, considering that the vessel itself was ultimately a constructive total loss. The trial judge had this to say:

> In the allocation of the excess general average under the sue and labour clause, scholarly authority and the testimony of ... [an average adjuster and expert witness] indicates the proper solution to the valuation of the barge is to be found in the use of values which existed when the expenditure was incurred. While there is little in the way of either case law or legal commentary dealing with the valuation of a ship for the purposes of the sue and labour clause, credible authority for the proposition that actual as opposed to estimated values are to be employed is found in Lowndes and Rudolph, *The Law of General Average and the York-Antwerp Rules*, 10th ed., wherein the authors state, at page 430:
>
> > The insurers are to pay such proportion of the expenses in that class 'as may reasonably be regarded as having been incurred in respect of the vessel'. How is the apportionment to be made? It cannot be on arrived values, since *ex hypothesi* the vessel has none, or almost none. The choice lies between sound values, and actual values at the time when the expenditure was incurred (but without discount for the contingency that the interests would be lost). It is submitted that the latter is the more plausible solution.
>
> In the eleventh and most recent edition of the text the authors acknowledge, at page 610 that

---

[17] The Canadian Hulls (Pacific) Clauses (Sept. 1/91) contain a similar provision, although the wording is somewhat different.

[18] [1995] 1 F.C. 341, 82 F.T.R. 1 (T.D.).

...although the clause gives no precise guide, it is submitted that the abortive expenses — (or the excess over any proceeds) — should be apportioned over approximate values of the property sought to be saved, *and in the condition it was likely to be saved.* [Emphasis added.][19]

The judge went on to apply this methodology in the calculation of the amount of the "sue and labour" falling on the hull underwriters. The remaining expenses, which were not recoverable from the P. & I. Club, fell on the insured shipowner as uninsured costs of the operation.

11.4.3 Protection and Indemnity Insurance

The rules of P. & I. associations[20] invariably include a provision such as the following:

Obligation to sue and labour
Upon the occurrence of any casualty, incident or other event which may give rise to a claim by a Member upon the Club, it shall be the duty of the Member and his agents to take and continue to take such measures as may be reasonable for the purpose of averting or minimising any loss, damage, expense or liability in respect whereof he may be insured by the Club. In the event that a Member commits any breach of this obligation, the Board may in its discretion reject any claim by the Member against the Club arising out of the casualty, incident or event, or reduce the sum payable by the Club in respect thereof by such amount as the Board may determine.[21]

The rules of the association may also provide that costs and expenses, including legal expenses incurred by the member in avoiding or attempting to avoid an insured liability, will be payable by the "club". There may, however, be a requirement that such expenses be approved in advance by the managers or determined by the managers or the board to have been reasonably incurred.[22]

In *MacMillan Bloedel Ltd. v. Youell*,[23] the British Columbia Court of Appeal held that in the absence of express language, sue and labour charges were not recoverable under a protection and indemnity policy. In that case, hull and machinery insurance on a vessel had been effected under a policy containing a standard form of "sue and labour" clause. A form of charterer's liability insurance was attached to the policy. The court found that the liability policy did not incorporate the sue and labour clause and that, as a matter of principle,

---

[19] [1995] 1 F.C. 341 at 372.

[20] See Chapter 20, *Protection and Indemnity Insurance*. As noted in that chapter, a large proportion of shipowners' protection and indemnity insurance is effected on a mutual basis, through associations known as "P & I Clubs".

[21] Rules of the Standard Steamship Owners' Protection and Indemnity Association (Bermuda) Limited, 2002-2003.

[22] See Rule 20.33 ("Costs of Sue and Labour") of the Standard Steamship Owners' Protection and Indemnity Association (Bermuda) Limited, 2002-2003.

[23] (1991), 2 C.C.L.I. (2d) 241, 79 B.C.L.R. (2d) 326 (S.C.), var'd (1993), 95 B.C.L.R. (2d) 130 (C.A.), leave to appeal refused (1994), 23 C.C.L.I. (2d), 18*n* (S.C.C.).

expenses incurred to avert a liability are not recoverable, unless specifically provided for in the policy.[24] Thus, while there may be a duty to sue and labour under P. & I. insurance, as there is with all marine insurance, the costs incurred by the insured in so doing are not recoverable in the absence of an agreement in the policy.

The SP-23 Protection and Indemnity Form (Rev'd. 1/56), which is sometimes used to provide P. & I. insurance for a vessel not covered by the clubs, does not have a specific sue and labour clause, nor does it expressly indemnify against sue and labour expenses. It does, however, provide for the payment for "Costs, charges and expenses, reasonably incurred and paid by the Assured, in defense against any liabilities insured against hereunder, in respect of the vessel named herein..." subject to the policy deductible. The Canadian (Pacific) Protection and Indemnity Clauses (1/1/83)[25] contain similar provisions.

Other forms of marine liability policies, such as stevedore's liability, charterer's liability and wharfinger's liability policies may contain provisions confirming the obligation of the insured to take reasonable measures to protect the insurer's interests in the event of an occurrence likely to give rise to a claim under the policy and to give prompt notice to the insurer of any potential claim. Most such policies provide that the insurer will pay legal costs and expenses of defending any claim brought against the insured and covered by the policy, provided the insurer has been given appropriate notice.

---

[24] A different conclusion was reached by the New South Wales Supreme Court in *Goldmining Co. Ltd. v. Switzerland General Insurance Co. Ltd.*, [1964] 1 Ll. Rep. 348, where the court held that sue and labour expenses were recoverable under a cargo insurance policy, notwithstanding the absence of a sue and labour clause.

[25] See Appendix N.

Chapter 12

Subrogation

12.1 INTRODUCTION

Subrogation is one of the basic principles of marine insurance. It is the right of the insurer, having paid a claim under the policy, to exercise the rights of the insured against any third party responsible for the loss. The insurer "steps into the shoes" of the insured and is entitled to take legal proceedings, using the insured's name, to recover the loss from the responsible party. The principle was expressed in the leading English case of *Castellain v. Preston*:

> ...as between the underwriter and the assured the underwriter is entitled to the advantage of every right of the assured, whether such right consists in contract, fulfilled or unfulfilled, or in remedy for tort capable of being insisted on or already insisted on, or in any other right, whether by way of condition or otherwise, legal or equitable, which can be, or has been exercised or has accrued, and whether such right could or could not be enforced by the insurer in the name of the assured by the exercise or acquiring of which right or condition the loss against which the assured is insured, can be, or has been, diminished.[1]

The rationale for subrogation is that insurance is a contract of indemnity — a contract requiring that the insured be "made whole", but no more. To permit the insured to recover under the policy and also to recover from the third party would permit double recovery. There is no right of subrogation unless the policy is one of indemnity. Thus "P.P.I." (policy proof of interest) policies do not give rise to a right of subrogation.[2] Since all modern marine insurance contracts are contracts of indemnity, this is not a significant issue.

Some authorities consider that the right of subrogation arises as a result of an "implied term" of the contract of indemnity. Others consider that subrogation has equitable underpinnings.[3] Whatever its doctrinal basis, subrogation is a

---

[1] (1883), 11 Q.B.D. 380 at 388 (C.A.).

[2] *John Edwards & Co. Ltd. v. Motor Union Insurance Co. Ltd.*, [1922] 2 K.B. 249. See Chapter 5, *Insurable Interest*.

[3] *National Fire Insurance Co. v. McLaren* (1886), 12 O.R. 672. This case has been followed in a number of other Canadian decisions: see *Ledingham v. Ontario (Hospital Services Commission)*, [1975] 1 S.C.R. 332, 46 D.L.R. (3d) 699, rev'g. [1973] 1 O.R. 291, 31 D.L.R. (3d) 18 (C.A.), rev'g. [1972] 1 O.R. 785, 24 D.L.R. (3d) 257 (H.C.J.); *Globe & Rutgers Fire Insurance Co. v. Truedell* (1927), 60 O.L.R. 227 (C.A.), rev'g. (1926), 59 O.L.R. 444 (S.C.J.); *Gibson v. Sun Life*

creation of the common law, and does not depend upon contractual confirmation, although some marine insurance contracts expressly provide for the insurer's rights of subrogation.

Section 81 of the Canadian *Marine Insurance Act* ("*C.M.I.A.*")[4] confirms the principle of subrogation:

> 81(1)   On payment by an insurer for a total loss of the whole of the subject-matter insured or, if the subject-matter insured is goods, for any apportionable part of the subject-matter insured, the insurer becomes entitled to assume the interest of the insured in the whole or part of the subject-matter and is subrogated to all the rights and remedies of the insured in respect of that whole or part from the time of the casualty causing the loss.

> (2) On payment by an insurer for a partial loss of the subject-matter insured, the insurer acquires no title to the subject-matter but is subrogated to all the rights and remedies of the insured in respect of the subject-matter from the time of the casualty causing the loss to the extent that the insured is indemnified, in accordance with this Act, by the payment for the loss.

12.2   DIFFERENCE BETWEEN RIGHT OF OWNERSHIP AND RIGHT OF SUBROGATION

A unique feature of marine insurance, expressed in subsection 81(1), is that, on the payment of a *total* loss, the insurer becomes entitled to take over the insured's rights in the *property*. The insurer's right to take over the property is separate and distinct from its right of subrogation.[5] Hull and machinery underwriters usually decline to accept the insured's interest in the wrecked ship due to the liabilities attaching to it. In the case of cargo insurance, having paid a constructive total loss, the underwriters may sell the property for salvage (if it has residual value) and retain the proceeds.[6]

12.3   DIFFERENT RIGHTS FOR PARTIAL AND TOTAL LOSS

As mentioned above, and as section 81 of the *C.M.I.A.* indicates, there is a difference between the insurer's rights in the case of a total loss and in a partial loss. In the former, the insurer acquires the right "to assume the interest of the insured" in the subject-matter, whereas in the case of a partial loss, the insurer acquires "no title to the subject-matter". If the vessel or goods are an actual total

---

    Assurance Co. of Canada (1984), 45 O.R. (2d) 326, 6 D.L.R. (4th) 746 (S.C.J.); *Ontario Health Insurance Plan v. United States Fidelity & Guaranty Co.* (1986), 57 O.R. (2d) 459 (H.C.J.), 33 D.L.R. (4th) 439, aff'd. (1989), 68 O.R. (2d) 190, 57 D.L.R. (4th) 640 (C.A.), leave to appeal to SCC refused (1989), 68 O.R. (2d) 190*n*, 57 D.L.R. (4th) 640*n*.

[4]   S.C. 1993, c. 22.

[5]   See, however, *Stalker v. Wier* (1854), 2 N.S.R. 248 (C.A.) in which it was held that the insurer could bring action in the name of the insured (who was described as a "trustee" for underwriters), to assert other causes of action against third parties.

[6]   See Chapter 9, *Losses and Charges Recoverable.*

loss — for example, irretrievably sunk or consumed by fire — the acquisition of the insured's interest in the property is of little significance.[7] Where there is a "constructive total loss", that is, the property continues to exist in form but is damaged beyond repair, the insurer has the right, but not the obligation, to take over the property.[8]

In the case of a total loss, according to section 81, the insurer is subrogated to "all the rights and remedies of the insured", whereas in a partial loss, the underwriter's right of subrogation is limited to "the extent that the insured is indemnified in accordance with this Act". This means that in the case of a partial loss the insurer is not allowed to profit from the subrogation and that any recovery in excess of the indemnity paid to the insured, after allowing for interest and the costs of recovery, should be for the benefit of the insured. In the case of a total loss, however, there is an argument that the insurer, having become entitled to "all" the rights and remedies of the insured, may claim and retain the full value of the property, even where it exceeds the insured value. In the case of total loss, if the sum insured is less than the insured value of the property stated in the policy, the insured is treated as his or her own insurer of the property and is entitled to share with the insurer in the recovery, on a *pro rata* basis.

While there are no Canadian authorities directly on point, it seems probable that a Canadian court would follow English precedent in holding that where property is insured for less than the value stated in the policy, the insured and the underwriter are entitled to share *pro rata* in any recovery, on the theory that the insured is its own insurer in respect of the balance.[9] This should not, however, be confused with a situation in which the property is insured to its full value stated in the policy, in which case the insurer is entitled to full recovery, up to the amount it has paid.[10] Even if it is established in the subrogated action that the property has a market value in excess of the value stated in the policy, the insurer is nevertheless entitled to all the fruits of subrogation, up to the amount it has paid, together with interest and costs.[11] Only if the insurer recovers more than the sum insured, interest and its costs (which might occur in the rather unusual situation where the insurer makes a recovery based on a market value substantially in excess of the sum insured stated in the policy) would the insured be entitled to the excess.

Robert H. Brown, a respected English insurance writer,[12] suggests that it is only in the case of underinsurance in an unvalued policy that the insured is entitled to share in the recovery. Where the property is undervalued in a valued policy, he

---

[7]   Unless, however, the property is later recovered, in which event the insurer who has paid for a total loss is entitled to the property: *Houstman v. Thornton* (1816), Holt. N.P. 242.

[8]   See Chapter 9, *Losses and Charges Recoverable*.

[9]   See *The Commonwealth*, [1907] P. 216.

[10]   *Goole and Hull Steam Towing Co. Ltd. v. Ocean Marine Insurance Co. Ltd.*, [1928] 1 K.B. 589.

[11]   *Thames and Mersey Marine Insurance Co. v. British & Chilian Steamship Co.*, [1916] 1 K.B. 30 (C.A.); but see *Yorkshire Insurance Co. v. Nisbet Shipping Co. Ltd.*, [1962] 2 Q.B. 330 (Q.B.D.).

[12]   R.H. Brown, *Marine Insurance, Vol 1: Principles and Basic Practice*, 6th ed. (London: Witherby & Co. Ltd., 1998) at p. 253.

suggests the insured has no right to participate in the recovery until the amount of the insurance claim paid by the insurer has been reached. Where, however, there is underinsurance in an unvalued policy, the insured is entitled to be considered his or her own insurer and is entitled to participate proportionately in recoveries.[13] Brown also suggests that under English practice, co-insurance is not considered to apply to the deductible, so that recoveries go directly to the insurer, even though the insured has borne a part of the loss under the deductible.

In non-marine insurance law, the principle seems to be that until such time as the insured has been fully indemnified, the insurer's right of subrogation does not take effect.[14] Thus, if an insured suffers a loss that is not fully covered by the policy, he or she is entitled to pursue the third party and, subject to any provisions of the policy, is entitled to retain the fruits of recovery until a full indemnity for the loss has been reached, at which point the insurer is entitled to the excess.

The difference in marine insurance is that hull and cargo policies are invariably valued policies and the valuation of the property contained in the policy is taken to be conclusive as between the parties, so that underwriters pursuing subrogation are entitled to retain the recovery until that value, net of costs and interest, has been reached. In marine insurance, therefore, it would appear that a distinction should be made between the effect of undervaluation (*i.e.*, insurance of property for less than its market value) and the effect of insurance for less than its insurable value as defined by the *C.M.I.A.* under a valued policy. In the former case, the insured has no right to participate in recoveries until such time as the amount paid by underwriters has been recovered. In the latter case, where the sum insured under a valued policy is less than the insured value stated in the policy, the insured is deemed to be self-insured for the difference and is entitled to participate on a proportionate basis in any recoveries.[15]

The question of policy deductibles raises interesting legal questions and potentially troublesome practical ones concerning the right of the insured to share in recoveries in respect of its deductible. In principle, one could make the argument that the insured is a co-insurer in respect of its deductible and that, like

---

[13] See *The Welsh Girl* (1906), 22 T.L.R. 475, aff'd. *sub nom. The Commonwealth*, [1907] P. 216, (1907), 10 Asp. M.L.C. 538 (C.A.). On the other hand, where the amount insured and the valuation are the same, the insured has no right to share in any recovery: *Thames & Mersey Marine Insurance Co. v. British and Chilian Steamship Co.*, [1916] 1 K.B. 30; *Goole and Hull Steam Towing Co. v. Ocean Marine Insurance Co. Ltd.*, [1928] 1 K.B. 589.

[14] See, for example, *Confederation Life Insurance Co. v. Causton*, [1989] B.C.J. No. 1172 (B.C.C.A.); *National Fire Insurance Co. v. McLaren* (1886), 12 O.R. 672; *Globe & Rutgers Fire Insurance Co. v. Truedell* (1927), 60 O.L.R. 227 (C.A.), rev'g. (1926), 59 O.L.R. 444 (S.C.J.); *Ledingham v. Ontario (Hospital Services Commission)*, [1975] 1 S.C.R. 332, rev'g. 46 D.L.R. (3d) 699, rev'g. [1973] 1 O.R. 291, 31 D.L.R. (3d) 18 (C.A.), rev'g. [1972] 1 O.R. 785, 24 D.L.R. (3d) 257 (H.C.J.).

[15] C.M.I.A., s. 88:

> 88. Where an insured is insured for a sum that is less than the insurable value of the subject-matter insured, in the case of an unvalued policy, or less than the value of the subject-matter insured specified by the policy, in the case of a valued policy, the insured is deemed to be self-insured in respect of the uninsured difference.

any other co-insurer, it is entitled to its proportionate share of recoveries, provided it shares the costs and risks of legal proceedings to collect the claim. In practice, in the case of cargo insurance where deductibles are generally low, underwriters generally retain all the recovery, unless there has been a special agreement with the insured at the outset to share the costs and proceeds of recovery. English law and practice holds that in the absence of specific agreement, the insured is not entitled to recover its deductible until the insurer's subrogated claim has been fully satisfied, although this may be dictated in part by common forms of hull and machinery policy.[16] Canadian practice is generally the same, although certain policy forms may dictate other outcomes.[17] To avoid doubt, particularly in the case of larger recoveries, it would be prudent for the insured and the underwriter to discuss the issue before the claim is put in subrogation and to reach an agreement concerning the sharing of costs and recoveries.

12.4 NO SUBROGATION UNLESS PAYMENT UNDER POLICY

The right of subrogation only arises under section 81 of the *C.M.I.A.* where the insurer has *paid* "for a...*loss* of the...subject-matter insured". Where the insurer has denied liability under the policy, but has made an *ex gratia* payment in settlement of the claim, without acknowledging a liability *under the policy*, there is no right of subrogation. In *Wellington Insurance Co. v. Armac Diving Services Ltd.*,[18] the insurer initially disputed liability to its insured but later, after legal proceedings had been taken against it, made a payment as a "public relations" gesture. The insured later recovered against the third party for its loss and the insurer claimed a share of the recovery. The British Columbia Court of Appeal held that since the insurer had not paid the insured pursuant to the policy, but had made a payment wholly outside it, there was no right of subrogation and no right to share in the recovery. The case is a warning to insurers making *ex gratia* payments on settlements of contentious claims. They should be prepared to either forego their subrogation rights or reach a specific written agreement with the insured, perhaps by way of an assignment of rights, to enable the insurer to make a recovery against the third party.

---

[16] See R.H. Brown, *Marine Insurance, Vol. 1: Principles and Practice*, 6th ed. (London: Witherby & Co. Ltd., 1998) at p. 253. The Institute Time Clauses Hulls (1/11/95) confirm this: "12.3 Excluding any interest comprised therein, recoveries against any claim which is subject to the above deductible shall be credited to the Underwriters in full to the extent of the sum by which the aggregate of the claim unreduced by any recoveries exceeds the above deductible."

[17] See, for example, the Canadian Hulls (Pacific) Clauses (Sept. 1/91), which give the insured the option, prior to commencement of suit, of entering into an agreement with the insurer to participate jointly in recoveries, sharing the costs in proportion to its uninsured deductible or undervaluation. In the absence of such an agreement, underwriters are entitled to the full recovery (excluding interest) up to the amount of the claim.

[18] (1987), 37 D.L.R. (4th) 462, 24 C.C.L.I. 1 (C.A.), aff'g. *sub. nom. Firemen's Fund Insurance Co. of Canada v. Armac Diving Services Ltd.* (1986), 18 C.C.L.I. 221, [1986] I.L.R. 1-2067 (B.C. Co. Ct.)

On the other hand, it seems reasonable that an insurer who has denied a claim and is then sued under the policy by the insured, should have the right to bring third party proceedings against the party responsible for the insured's loss, on the theory that if found liable to the insured, the insurer will be subrogated to the insured's rights against that party.[19] Third party proceedings enable the defendant insurer to bring the party responsible for the loss into the litigation so that the rights of all parties can be determined in the same litigation. Since there will likely be common issues of fact and law in both proceedings, it makes sense that they be heard together, and this course of action has been permitted in several Canadian cases.[20]

12.5   NO RIGHT OF SUBROGATION UNTIL PAYMENT

The right of subrogation does not arise until payment by the insurer and the insurer has no right to commence suit in the name of the insured until the claim has been paid.[21] Once the claim has been paid, the insurer's rights relate back to the time of the casualty causing the loss. It is common for the insurer and the insured to agree to the commencement of legal proceedings against the third party "for the benefit of whom it may concern", pending the settlement of the claim.

12.6   INSURED MUST NOT PREJUDICE INSURER'S RIGHT OF SUBROGATION

The insured must not prejudice the insurer's rights of subrogation and, if it does so, it may lose the right to recovery under the policy. This could arise in two ways. First, the insured might release the third party from liability either before

---

[19]   *Welded Tube v. Hartford Fire*, [1973] A.M.C. 555; see also *Nuvo Electronics Inc. v. London Assurance* (2000), 49 O.R. (3d) 374, 19 C.C.L.I. (3d) 195 (S.C.J.), additional reasons at (2000), 23 C.C.L.I. (3d) 231 (Ont. S.C.J.), appeal withdrawn, Jan. 28, 2002, Ontario Court of Appeal, in which the insurer denied liability under a cargo policy. The insured sued both the third party air carrier and the insurer. The court held that the insured could recover against both. Although the judge's reasons do not deal with the issue of subrogation, presumably there are two possibilities: (i) either the carrier pays the full amount to the insured and there is nothing to claim under the policy, or (ii) the insurer pays the insured and is entitled to "step into the shoes" of the insured in the exercise of the judgment against the carrier.

[20]   See *Manning v. Boston Insurance Co.* (1962), 34 D.L.R. (2d) 140 (P.E.I.S.C.), where the insured was entitled to do so; *Chatham Motors Ltd. v. Fidelity & Casualty Insurance Co. of New York* (1983), 42 O.R. (2d) 464, 149 D.L.R. (3d) 94 (Ont. H.C.J.), rev'g. (1982), 38 O.R. (2d) 180 (Master), where third party proceedings by the insurer were permitted in a non-marine action.

[21]   In *Pacific Coyle Navigation Co. v. Ruby General Insurance Co.* (1954), 12 W.W.R. 715 (B.C.S.C.), the insured alleged that the loss of a barge was due to insured perils, but the insurer contended that it was not. The insurer wanted to add the tortfeasor as a third party on the basis that in certain contingencies it would be entitled to recover against the third party. The court held that the right to subrogation did not arise until the claim had been paid and refused to permit the third party to be added. This case was distinguished in *Chatham Motors Ltd. v. Fidelity & Casualty Insurance Co. of New York* (1983), 42 O.R. (2d) 464, 149 D.L.R. (3d) 94 (Ont. H.C.J.), rev'g. (1982), 38 O.R. (2d) 180 (Master).

or after a loss. Second, the insured might take some action, or fail to take some action, preventing a recovery against the third party.[22]

Dealing with the first situation, the insured must not enter into an agreement with a third party, without the insurer's consent, either before or after a loss, which is prejudicial to the insurer's right of subrogation. Where the insured has done so, the insurer may be relieved of liability under the policy. Clauses in contracts between the insured and the third party having the effect of barring subrogation or reducing recovery, may prejudice the insurer's subrogation rights. This can be significant in the marine context where many standard contracts with carriers or bailees contain exclusions or limitations of liability. Arguably, underwriters should be aware of, and impliedly consent to, contracts that are customary in the business in which their insureds operate. For example, the insurers of vessels should know that contracts for the engagement of tugs typically contain a release by the owner of the towed vessel in favour of the tug.[23] Assuming the policy permits the vessel to be towed[24] (for instance, where tugs are used to dock vessels in port) the insurer should be aware that its insured's contracts will contain such standard conditions. The limits on the underwriter's rights of subrogation in such circumstances should not be grounds for refusing to indemnify the insured for a loss arising out of the tow.

The second situation is when the actions of the insured after the loss prejudice the insurer's recovery rights. Such actions may be a bar to recovery under the policy. For example, the insured might settle with the third party and then make a claim on the policy of insurance for any unrecovered balance of its loss or sometimes for the whole loss. In cargo insurance, this occasionally happens when the insured puts a carrier on notice and then files a claim with its cargo insurer. In the meantime, the carrier might send a cheque to the insured, paying its contractual limitation of liability, and the insured might sign the carrier's standard form of release document. The insurer will then pay the insured's claim and commence action against the carrier, only to discover that the insured has released the carrier. Does the execution of the release by the insured bar its recovery under the policy? While it is clear that the insured must pay over to the insurer any amount recovered from the third party, it is equally clear that the release is a bar to the insurer's right of subrogation against the carrier. Whether the release is a breach of the contract of insurance, entitling the insurer to recover the amounts paid under the policy, will depend upon whether the insurer

---

[22] See *Maryland Casualty Co. v. Blue Sparrow Industries Ltd.*, [1980] I.L.R. ¶1-299 (Ont. H.C.J.), a trucking case, in which the owner of the cargo agreed with the trucking company, before the loss, to procure cargo insurance and to hold the trucker harmless against any loss or damage. The insurer paid a cargo claim and then subrogated against the trucker, who successfully raised this agreement as a defence. It was held that the insurer was entitled to recover the money paid to the insured, since the insured had prejudiced its subrogation rights.

[23] See Chapter 21, *Insurance of Particular Risks*, with respect to insurance in relation to towage.

[24] Standard hull and machinery insurance clauses permit a vessel to be towed only where customary or when in need of assistance. See, for example, the American Institute Hull Clauses (June 2, 1977), lines 61-62: "...but the Vessel may not be towed, except as is customary or when in need of assistance..."; the C.B.M.U. Great Lakes Hull Clauses (Sept. 1, 1971) contain identical wording at lines 92-93.

had any reasonable prospect of recovering more than the limitation amount from the carrier. Often the carrier's limit of liability, while substantially less than the insured value of the property, will be all that is available to the insurer on subrogation and it would be unreasonable to say that the insurer can avoid all liability under the policy simply because the insured has accepted the carrier's limitation amount.[25]

The insured must not allow the insurer's rights of subrogation to lapse or become stale.[26] The insured is required to take reasonable measures to protect the insurer's rights of recovery against third parties. This may require the insured to give appropriate notice of claim to carriers or bailees[27] or even to commence suit within the relevant limitation period if the claim has not been paid. This obligation is confirmed by the sue and labour clause, clause 16, in the Institute Cargo Clauses (1/1/82).[28]

The failure to properly preserve the insurer's subrogation rights could reduce the insured's recovery under the policy, at least to the extent of any amount the insurer might reasonably have expected to recover from the third party. Due to carriers' contractual and statutory limitations of liability, recoveries are sometimes very limited, and, once again, it would not be reasonable to wholly deprive the insured from recovery under the policy for failing to protect the insurer's right to a nominal recovery. At most, the recovery under the policy should be reduced by the amount of the carrier's liability.

The insured's duty to preserve the insurer's subrogation rights is an adjunct of its duty to sue and labour. It is entitled to recover its reasonable expenses of so doing.[29]

12.7   SUIT IN THE NAME OF THE INSURED

In the common law provinces, a suit by the subrogated insurer must be brought in the name of the insured. There is no right to bring action in the insurer's own name.[30] In Quebec, the practice has been to sue in the name of the insurer and it has been held that this is the only proper procedure in that province.[31] The

---

[25]   See *Globe & Rutgers Fire Insurance Co. v. Truedell* (1927), 60 O.L.R. 227 (C.A.), rev'g. (1926), 59 O.L.R. 444 (S.C.) in which the court held that where the insured pursues the third party, it must advance the claim in good faith and must not settle the claim unreasonably at the expense of the insurer's rights.

[26]   *Moryoussef v. Maritime Insurance Co.*, [1982] C.P. 22 (Que. Prov. Ct.).

[27]   Some insurers require that notice of damage be given to the primary contracting carrier as well as to the delivering carrier.

[28]   See Appendices B, C and D and see Chapter 11, *Duties of the Insured: Sue and Labour*, Section 11.4.1, "Cargo Insurance".

[29]   See Chapter 11, *Duties of the Insured: Sue and Labour*.

[30]   *Northern Elevator Co. v. Richelieu & Ontario Navigation Co.* (1907), 11 Ex. C.R. 25, aff'd. *sub nom. Ogilvie Flour Mills Co. v. Richelieu & Ontario Navigation Co.* (1908), 11 Ex. C.R. 231.

[31]   *Model Furs Ltd. v. H. Lapalme Transport Ltee.*, [1995] R.R.A. 611, [1995] A.Q. No. 554 (Que. C.A.). In this case, an action was commenced in Quebec by the insurer in the name of the insured, following the practice in marine insurance in common law jurisdictions. It was held that because the transaction in question involved non-marine transportation — by truck and then by

different practices have engendered debate about the correct procedure where an action is brought in the Federal Court of Canada. In *Switzerland General Insurance Co. v. Logistec Navigation Inc.*,[32] a case that arose in Quebec, the insurer brought action in the Federal Court of Canada in its own name, relying on the Quebec practice. The defendant argued that as maritime law is "federal" in nature, the Quebec procedure was inapplicable. The Federal Court of Canada held that while marine insurance is a matter under federal jurisdiction, as part of maritime law, subrogation is a matter of property and civil rights falling under provincial jurisdiction by virtue of the *Constitution Act*.[33] Accordingly, the insurer was entitled to bring the action in its own name, as permitted by Quebec law.[34] This decision may be subject to reconsideration in light of the decision of the Supreme Court of Canada in *Ordon Estate v. Grail*,[35] confirming the uniform nature of Canadian maritime law. In the provinces other than Quebec, which have legal systems based on English common law, the correct practice, whether the action is brought in the provincial superior court or in the Federal Court of Canada, is to sue in the name of the insured.

In *Al-Qahtani-Shaw-Leonard Ltd. v. Crossworld Freight Ltd.*,[36] the issue arose as to whether underwriters were permitted to maintain a subrogated action in the name of a corporation that had been deleted from the commercial registry in Saudi Arabia. At trial, the plaintiff moved to add the underwriters as plaintiffs in the action. The defendant argued that since the plaintiff no longer had any corporate existence, the action should be dismissed. At the time the insurance claim was settled, the insured had signed a proof of loss assigning its right of action to its underwriters. The trial judge held that it was not necessary to add the underwriters because, as assignees of the cause of action, they were entitled to bring the action in the name of the assignor and their right to do so did not depend on the continued existence of the assignor. The Court of Appeal, without disagreeing with the result at trial, held that the judge should have permitted the insurers to be joined as plaintiffs, presumably because there would be no prejudice to the defendant, the action having been properly constituted at the time it was commenced. While the defendant's technical objection was defeated because, fortuitously, there had been an assignment of the claim, would the

---

air — the practice in marine matters did not apply. The Court held that the Quebec civil law procedure should have been followed and the action should have been brought by the insurers in their own name. The fact that a marine insurance form of policy had been used did not make it a contract of marine insurance. See also: *Forage Mercier Inc. v. Societe de Construction Maritime Voyageurs Ltee.*, [1998] A.Q. No. 2190 (Que. C.A.); *Martel v. Fortier* (1995), 116 F.T.R. 246 (T.D.).

32   (1986) 7 F.T.R. 196, [1987] 22 C.C.L.I. 243 (T.D.).
33   Schedule B to the *Canada Act 1982* (U.K.), 1982, c. 11.
34   The *Switzerland General* case was followed in a subsequent decision of the Federal Court of Canada: *Porto Seguro Companhia de Seguros Gerais v. Belcan S.A.*, [1997] 3 S.C.R. 1278, 153 D.L.R. (4th) 577, rev'g. [1996] 2 F.C. 751, 195 N.R. 241 (C.A.), aff'g. (1994), 82 F.T.R. 127 (T.D.).
35   [1998] 3 S.C.R. 437, 166 D.L.R. (4th) 193, aff'g. (1996), 30 O.R. (3d) 643, 140 D.L.R. (4th) 52 (C.A.). See generally Chapter 1, *Overview of Marine Insurance*.
36   (1988), 66 O.R. (2d) 256, 54 D.L.R. (4th) 192 (C.A.), var'g. (1987), 60 O.R. (2d) 565, 40 D.L.R. (4th) 656 (Ont. H.C.J.).

result have been different if the underwriter relied solely on the common law of subrogation? Arguably, in such a case, the court should permit the insurer to be added as a plaintiff to prevent the third party from avoiding its liabilities.

The derivative nature of subrogation can sometimes lead to unintended results. In the case of a collision between two ships, owned by the same insured but insured with different underwriters, the underwriters could have difficulty enforcing their right of subrogation, since the insured owner would not, technically, be entitled to sue itself for damages.[37] To avoid this problem, hull and machinery policies usually contain a "sister-ship clause" permitting subrogation against ships in the same ownership.[38]

12.8 OBLIGATIONS OF THE INSURED

Having received an indemnity under the policy, the insured has an obligation to assist the insurer in the exercise of its right of subrogation. This right is sometimes spelled out in the policy itself and is sometimes confirmed in a "subrogation receipt" which the insurer may ask the insured to execute prior to payment.[39] This express language is unnecessary since the insured's duty of assistance springs from the payment itself. The insured must allow its name to be used by the insurer in the prosecution of the suit. The suit itself will likely require the cooperation of the insured, to collect relevant documents, to attend pre-trial discovery and to provide evidence at trial if required.

Where the insured makes a recovery against a third party, having previously been indemnified by the insurer, the principle of indemnity requires that any surplus must be held for the benefit of the insurer.[40]

12.9 OBLIGATIONS OF THE INSURER

The insurer usually reimburses the insured for any necessary out-of-pocket expenses incurred in prosecuting the subrogated claim — for example, transportation and hotel charges and other expenses which are reasonably necessary so that the insured can attend to give evidence at examination for discovery or trial. It is not usual to pay the insured a fee for such assistance, although a fee is occasionally requested. The time and inconvenience suffered by the insured is simply part of the price to be paid for the indemnity that it has received.

Since suit is brought in the insured's name, the insured is legally liable for the costs of the litigation, should it prove unsuccessful. In Canada, the losing party generally pays a portion of the victor's legal costs[41] and the insured could find

---

[37] This was the result in the English case of *Simpson v. Thompson* (1877), 3 App. Cas. 279 (H.L.).

[38] See Chapter 19, *Hull and Machinery Insurance.*

[39] For a form of subrogation receipt, see Appendix K; for loan receipt, see Appendix L.

[40] *Ledingham v. Ontario (Hospital Services Commission)*, [1975] 1 S.C.R. 332, rev'g. 46 D.L.R. (3d) 699, rev'g. [1973] 1 O.R. 291, 31 D.L.R. (3d) 18 (C.A.), rev'g. [1972] 1 O.R. 785, 24 D.L.R. (3d) 257 (H.C.); *Co-operative Fire and Casualty Co. v. Levesque* (1976), 13 A.P.R. 399 (N.B.C.A.), a non-marine case. See the English case of *Goole & Hull Steam Towing Co. Ltd. v. Ocean Marine Mutual Insurance Co. Ltd.*, [1928] 1 K.B. 589.

[41] See Chapter 25, *Practice and Procedural Issues.*

itself exposed, after an unsuccessful subrogation action, to significant legal costs. Although there is no Canadian authority on this point, it seems clear that as the insurer has chosen to pursue subrogation, it has an obligation to indemnify its insured against any such costs. It will also have an obligation to provide security for costs where its insured is an out-of-jurisdiction litigant.[42]

By virtue of its right of subrogation, the insurer is generally entitled to control the litigation and to settle it as it sees fit.

12.10 ALTERNATIVES TO SUBROGATION

There may be some cases where the insured has a legal right of action[43] against the third party but there is an impediment to the insurer exercising that right of action. One example is where the policy of insurance waives subrogation[44] against affiliated companies of the insured. Another example is where the contract between the insured and the third party contains a "benefit of insurance" clause.[45] There may be circumstances in which the insurer and the insured wish to avoid these limitations, perhaps because it will have an impact on the insured's loss record or future premiums. Can the insurer avoid these problems by taking an assignment of the insured's rights against the third party or, in the case of cargo insurance, by taking the bills of lading by endorsement?

In principle, at least in the case of a contractual claim, the insurer can take an assignment of the insured's cause of action and sue in its own name.[46] Case law in Canada suggests that even a claim in tort, such as a negligence claim, may be assigned.[47]

In *Insurance Co. of North America v. Colonial Steamships Ltd.*,[48] the underwriter of cargo, apparently in an attempt to avoid defences that the carrier might have raised against the insured, sued not by way of subrogation but rather in its own name, allegedly having taken over the bills of lading by endorsement. The Exchequer Court of Canada held that as an endorsee of the bills of lading, having had notice of the terms of the contract between the insured and the carrier, the insurer would be subject to any defences that might have been raised

---

[42] See *St. Lawrence Underwriters' Agency of the Western Assurance Co. v. Fewster and Marchiori* (1922), 69 D.L.R. 351.

[43] In legal terms, known as a "cause of action".

[44] See Section 12.11 "Waiver of Subrogation".

[45] See Section 12.13 "Benefit of Insurance Clauses".

[46] See *King v. Victoria Insurance Co. Ltd.*, [1896] A.C. 250 (P.C.) to the effect that the insurer may sue in its own name. See the interpretation of this case by Middleton J.A. in *Royal Exchange Assurance v. Grimshaw Brothers Ltd.* (1928), 52 O.L.R. 25 at 26. Suit under an assignment was recognized in *Al-Qahtani-Shaw-Leonard Ltd. v. Crossworld Freight Ltd.* (1987), 60 O.R. (2d) 565, aff'd. (1988), 66 O.R. (2d) 256 (C.A.). See also *Compania Columbiana de Seguros v. Pacific Steam Navigation Co.*, [1965] 1 Q.B. 101.

[47] The case of *Fredrickson v. Insurance Corp. of British Columbia*, [1988] 1 S.C.R. 1089, 49 D.L.R. (4th) 160, aff'g. (1986), 28 D.L.R. (4th) 414 (B.C.C.A.), 15 C.C.L.I. 249, aff'g. [1985] 5 W.W.R. 342 (B.C.S.C.) suggests that even in tort an insurer may take an assignment of the insured's cause of action.

[48] [1942] Ex. C.R. 79 (Ex. Ct.), aff'd. [1942] S.C.R. 357, 3 D.L.R. 225.

against the insured. The court held that there was no consideration for the endorsement, since the insurer had acquired its rights under the policy of insurance. On appeal, the Supreme Court of Canada held that the *Bills of Lading Act*[49] did not avail the insurer, since it acquired an interest in the cargo not by virtue of the endorsement but by virtue of its rights under the policy of insurance. The court held, however, that the insurer was subject to the shipowner's counterclaim for general average, since it had become the owner of the cargo.

12.11 WAIVER OF SUBROGATION

It is usually no defence to a subrogated action that the insured has been indemnified by insurance or that the "true" plaintiff is the subrogated insurer. Where, however, the defendant claims that there has been a waiver of subrogation[50] or that the insurance has been taken out for its benefit,[51] the plaintiff's insurance may be very relevant. The insurer is entitled to waive its right to subrogation and while it would be unusual for the insurer to entirely relinquish its right, it is common to waive subrogation against specific parties. For example, the insured may not want its insurers to pursue subrogation against affiliated companies or others with which it has a close corporate or commercial relationship.[52]

In *Fraser River Pile & Dredge Ltd. v. Can-Dive Services Ltd.*,[53] the plaintiff chartered a crane and a barge to the defendant. The barge was lost in a storm, allegedly due to the negligence of the charterer. The plaintiff's insurance policy contained a waiver of subrogation against the charterer. The plaintiff agreed with its insurer to relinquish any rights it might have under the waiver of subrogation clause and the insurer, having paid the plaintiff's claim, brought subrogation proceedings against the charterer.

The British Columbia Supreme Court held that the agreement between the plaintiff and the defendant charterer did not include an agreement that the plaintiff would insure the barge for the benefit of the charterer and that the

---

[49] Presently R.S.C. 1985, c. B-5.

[50] *Fraser River Pile & Dredge Ltd. v. Can-Dive Services Ltd.*, [1999] 3 S.C.R. 108, 176 D.L.R. (4th) 257, aff'g. (1997), 39 B.C.L.R. (3d) 187, 47 C.C.L.I. (2d) 111, rev'g. (1995), 9 B.C.L.R. (3d) 260, 33 C.C.L.I. (2d) 9 (S.C.).

[51] *St. Lawrence Cement Inc. v. Wakeham & Sons Ltd.*, [1995] S.C.C.A. No. 553, leave to appeal ref'd. (1995), 26 O.R. (3d) 321, 86 O.A.C. 182 (C.A.), rev'g. (1992), 8 O.R. (3d) 340, 9 C.C.L.I. (2d) 211, leave to appeal ref'd.

[52] It is common for hull and machinery policies to contain waivers of subrogation against affiliated companies. For example, the American Institute Hull Clauses (June 2, 1977) provide at lines 6-8:
     Underwriters waive any right of subrogation against affiliated, subsidiary or interrelated companies of the Assured, provided that such waiver shall not apply in the event of a collision between the Vessel and any vessel owned, demise chartered or otherwise controlled by any of the aforesaid companies, or with respect to any loss, damage or expense against which such companies are insured.
     An identical clause is found in lines 6 to 9 of the C.B.M.U. Great Lakes Hull Clauses (Sept. 1, 1971).

[53] *Fraser River Pile & Dredge Ltd. v. Can-Dive Services Ltd.*, [1999] 3 S.C.R. 108, 176 D.L.R. (4th) 257, aff'g. (1997), 39 B.C.L.R. (3d) 187, 47 C.C.L.I. (2d) 111, rev'g. (1995), 9 B.C.L.R. (3d) 260, 33 C.C.L.I. (2d) 9 (S.C.).

charterer, being a stranger to the insurance contract, could not enforce it. It was accepted that had there been an agreement between the parties that the barge owner would insure for the benefit of both parties, it would have been a good defence to the subrogated action.

In the Court of Appeal and the Supreme Court of Canada it was held that where the policy expressly extended the waiver of subrogation to a third party it was appropriate to relax the doctrine of privity of contract where the parties intended the benefit to apply to the third party and where the activities of the third party were specifically contemplated by the contract. Justice Iacobucci, giving the unanimous decision in the Supreme Court of Canada stated:

> I conclude that the circumstances of this appeal nonetheless meet the requirements established in *London Drugs* for a third-party beneficiary to rely on the terms of a contract to defend against a claim initiated by one of the parties to the contract. As a third-party beneficiary to the policy, Can-Dive is entitled to rely on the waiver of subrogation clause whereby the insurers expressly waived any right of subrogation against Can-Dive as a 'charterer' of a vessel included within the policy's coverage.[54]

He held that the provisions of the insurance contract were clearly intended to benefit Can-Dive and that the rights of Can-Dive had "crystallized" at the time of the agreement made by the parties to try to take it away:

> Having contracted in favour of Can-Dive as within the class of potential third party beneficiaries, Fraser River and its insurers cannot revoke unilaterally Can-Dive's rights once they have developed into an actual benefit. At the point at which Can-Dive's rights crystallized, it became for all intents and purposes a party to the initial contract for the limited purpose of relying on the waiver of subrogation clause. Any subsequent alteration of the waiver provision is subject to further negotiation and agreement among all the parties involved, including Can-Dive.[55]

He also held that the activities of the charterer were clearly contemplated in the insurance contract. Finally, he held that there were sound policy reasons for relaxing the doctrine of privity of contract in this particular context:

> ...Fraser River in the course of this appeal has been unable to provide any commercial reason for failing to enforce a bargain entered into by sophisticated commercial actors. In the absence of any indication to the contrary, I must conclude that relaxing the doctrine of privity in these circumstances establishes a default rule that most closely corresponds to commercial reality as is evidenced by the inclusion of the waiver of subrogation clause within the contract itself.

> A plain reading of the waiver of subrogation clause indicates that the benefit accruing in favour of third parties is not subject to any qualifying language or limiting conditions. When sophisticated commercial parties enter into a contract of insurance which expressly extends the benefit of a waiver of subrogation clause to

---

[54] [1999] 3 S.C.R. 108 at 132-33.
[55] *Ibid.*, at 128.

an ascertainable class of third-party beneficiary, any conditions purporting to limit the extent of the benefit or the terms under which the benefit is to be available must be clearly expressed. The rationale for this requirement is that the obligation to contract for exceptional terms most logically rests with those parties whose intentions do not accord with what I assume to be standard commercial practice. Otherwise, notwithstanding the doctrine of privity of contract, courts will enforce the bargain agreed to by the parties and will not undertake to rewrite the terms of the agreement.[56]

12.12   AGREEMENTS TO INSURE

In some commercial relationships it may be most cost-effective for one party to insure the property in question for the benefit of both parties. A charterparty, where the owner of a vessel leases it to another party, is one example.[57] Another example is a contract of towage, where a tug owner agrees to tow a barge or ship owned by another party.[58] In such cases, it may be prudent for the contract to provide that:

(a) the insurance is intended for the benefit of both parties;
(b) the property owner will hold the other harmless for damage to the insured property; and
(c) the property owner will obtain a waiver of subrogation from its insurer in favour of the other party.

At the same time, the property owner should make sure that its insurer consents to the arrangement, and includes a waiver of subrogation in the policy, since any "hold harmless" agreement without the insurer's consent, while binding on the insurer vis-à-vis the third party, could invalidate the owner's insurance. This could put the property owner in the unenviable position of having no insurance

---

[56]   *Ibid.*, at 131.
[57]   See *Brynjolfson v. Clay's Wharf*, [1975] F.C. 319, 7 N.R. 614 (C.A.): where there was an "insurance clause" in a charterparty whereby the owner of the vessel agreed to pay for insurance and the charterer agreed to pay for damages not covered by insurance. The court held at 322 that this was an implied release from liability for damages covered by insurance:

> In these circumstances, with some doubt, I have concluded that the 'insurance' clause is to be construed as impliedly exonerating the appellant from any liability to the respondent in respect of loss of, or damage to, the vessel during the time of the charterparty other than the liabilities expressly set out therein.

See also *L. & B. Construction Ltd. v. Northern Canada Power Commission*, [1984] 6 W.W.R. 598, 28 B.L.R. 100, [1984] N.W.T.R. 324 (S.C.), rev'd. N.W.T. C.A., June 28, 1983, unrept'd.
[58]   See *St. Lawrence Cement Inc. v. Wakeham & Sons Ltd.*, [1995] S.C.C.A. No. 553, leave to appeal ref'd. (1995), 26 O.R. (3d) 321, 86 O.A.C. 182 (C.A.), rev'g. (1992), 8 O.R. (3d) 340, 9 C.C.L.I. (2d) 211; *J. Clark & Son v. Finnamore* (1972), 32 D.L.R. (3d) 236, 5 N.B.R. (2d) 467 (N.B.S.C.). In a different context, see also *Rose v. Borisko Bros.*, [1981] I.L.R. 1-1455, aff'd. [1983] I.L.R. 1-1704, (1983), 147 D.L.R. (3d) 191 (Ont. C.A.), dealing with the liability of a warehouse, in which the court held that there was no special relationship between the parties or contractual term which would restrict the insurer's rights of subrogation.

and also having no right of recourse against the third party whom he or she has released.

In *St. Lawrence Cement Inc. v. Wakeham & Sons Ltd.*,[59] the plaintiff's barge went aground while being towed by the defendant's tug. The contract between the parties provided that the towing operation was to be done "at the sole risk of the vessel to be towed and its owners". The contract also provided that the plaintiff barge owner was to be "responsible for insurance on the barge and its cargo". The trial judge found that the defendant had been negligent in towing the barge, and held that the agreement to insure, coupled with the "sole risk" clause, did not relieve the tug operator from its negligence. The Ontario Court of Appeal reversed the trial judge's decision. Chief Justice Dubin, giving the court's judgment, stated:

> In my opinion, the respondent's [plaintiff's] agreement to be responsible for in-suring the [barge] and its cargo could have no purpose other than to relieve the ap-pellant [tug owner] from liability for losses caused by its negligence. Because of the towing agreement, the only way in which the appellant could be liable to the respondent was by way of negligence. The insurance must be taken to address that contingency. The agreement to be responsible for insurance would, as it is said, 'otherwise lack subject-matter'.[60]

Referring to a number of other Canadian decisions in which an agreement to insure has been held to place the risk of loss through negligence on the shoulders of the party procuring insurance,[61] the Court of Appeal held that the insurance was for the benefit of both the plaintiff and the defendant, and the plaintiff and its subrogated insurers were precluded from making a claim against the defendant.[62]

12.13 BENEFIT OF INSURANCE CLAUSES

Sometimes carriers attempt to prevent subrogation by including a clause in their contracts of carriage purporting to give them the benefit of the cargo owner's insurance. A typical clause might provide as follows:

---

[59] *St. Lawrence Cement Inc. v. Wakeham & Sons Ltd.*, [1995] S.C.C.A. No. 553, leave to appeal ref'd. (1995), 26 O.R. (3d) 321, 86 O.A.C. 182 (C.A.), rev'g. (1992), 8 O.R. (3d) 340, 9 C.C.L.I. (2d) 211.

[60] *St. Lawrence Cement Inc. v. Wakeham & Sons Ltd.*, [1995] S.C.C.A. No. 553, leave to appeal ref'd. (1995), 26 O.R. (3d) 321 at 327, 86 O.A.C. 182 (C.A.), rev'g. (1992), 8 O.R. (3d) 340, 9 C.C.L.I. (2d) 211.

[61] See, for example, *Agnew-Surpass Shoe Stores Ltd. v. Cummer-Yonge Investments Ltd.*, [1976] 2 S.C.R. 221, 55 D.L.R. (3d) 676, rev'g. [1972] 2 O.R. 341, 25 D.L.R. (3d) 501 (C.A.), rev'g. [1970] I.L.R. ¶1-380 (Ont. H.C.J.); *T. Eaton Co. v. Smith*, [1978] 2 S.C.R. 749, 92 D.L.R. (3d) 425, aff'g. [1972] I.L.R. ¶1-485 (Ont. H.C.J.).

[62] In *Martel v. Fortier* (1995), 116 F.T.R. 246 (T.D.), it was argued that an agreement for the transportation of a houseboat, pursuant to which the boat owner agreed to pay for insurance, prevented its subrogated insurer from pursuing recovery. The Court distinguished *St. Lawrence Cement Inc. v. Wakeham & Sons Ltd.* and held that the agreement with respect to insurance did not prevent the insurer from pursuing subrogation.

> Upon payment of the premium, the carrier shall have the benefit of any insurance
> taken out by the owner of the goods.

The intent of such a clause is to make the carrier a beneficiary of the cargo
owner's insurance. In *C.N.R. v. Canadian Industries Ltd.*,[63] the defendant
railway relied on a condition in its bill of lading that the carrier was entitled to
the benefit of the cargo owner's insurance, provided it reimbursed the premium
"so far as this shall not avoid the policies or contracts of insurance." The insured
cargo owner had signed a "loan receipt" in favour of its insurer, which then
pursued subrogation. In holding that the benefit of insurance clause did not
prevent subrogation, Justice Hudson stated:

> If the plaintiffs or their successors entered into any contract which would impair
> this right of subrogation, the insurance company would be relieved from liability...
>
> Under the terms of the loan receipt the insurance company would, I think, be enti-
> tled to a return of the money advanced if it were found that they had been deprived
> of the fruit of subrogation because of some action by the insured. There is no sug-
> gestion here that the insurance company had been advised of any condition such as
> that set up; in fact, it is entirely improbable that they knew anything about it. Un-
> der these circumstances, it would seem clear that the condition relied upon could
> not in any way cover the circumstances here.[64]

In contracts of carriage by water, covered by the *Marine Liability Act*,[65] a benefit
of insurance clause is automatically invalid as being in contravention of the
legislation, which prevents the carrier from contracting out of certain minimum
responsibilities and liabilities. In principle, however, there is no reason why such
clauses may not be valid in respect of other means of carriage or forms of
bailment. For this reason it is common for policies of cargo insurance to contain
a "not to inure" clause, such as that contained in the Institute Cargo Clauses
(1/1/82):

> BENEFIT OF INSURANCE: 15. This insurance shall not inure to the benefit of
> the carrier or other bailee.

12.14   SUBROGATION PRACTICE

Subrogation is an important right for marine insurers. It helps in the recovery of
some of the money paid out by the insurer in claims and ultimately reduces the
cost of insurance. From the insured's perspective, successful subrogation by its
insurer reduces its overall loss record and its premiums. Some marine insurers
have their own "recoveries" departments specializing in the recovery of paid
claims from the responsible third parties, typically carriers and other bailees.

---

[63]   [1941] S.C.R. 591, 4 D.L.R. 561, aff'g. [1940] O.W.N. 452, 4 D.L.R. 629 (Ont. C.A.) aff'g.
       [1940] 3 D.L.R. 621 (Ont. H.C.J.).

[64]   [1941] S.C.R. 591 at 598-99.

[65]   S.C. 2001, c. 6; formerly the *Carriage of Goods by Water Act*, S.C. 1993, c. 21.

There are, as well, several Canadian and international recovery agencies specializing in collecting subrogated claims on behalf of insurers.

Once the insurance claim has been adjusted and the funds paid to the insured, the recoveries department (if there is one) or the outside recovery agent will collect relevant information, such as commercial documents and survey reports, and will present the claim to the third party or its insurers. In the case of cargo insurance, the claim will often be presented to the claims department of the ocean carrier, airline, trucking company, warehouse or other bailee responsible for the loss. In the case of hull and machinery insurance, if the damage can be traced to the fault of a third party, the claim will be presented to that party or its insurer. Very often, the case will be settled directly between the insurers without recourse to legal proceedings.

Marine insurers frequently require their insureds to sign a form of "subrogation receipt" on payment of the insurance claim. While not strictly required, since the right of subrogation arises by operation of law and not as a matter of contract, the subrogation receipt is often a useful confirmation of the insurer's rights and a reminder to the insured of its responsibility to provide assistance to the insurer, even after the claim has been paid. As well, the subrogation receipt provides useful evidence to the third party that the insurer has paid an insurance claim and has the right to pursue recovery and to give a release for the claim. Some carriers insist on production of a subrogation receipt or other evidence of release of the insured's rights as a condition of any settlement with the subrogated insurer. At the time of paying the claim, the prudent insurer will make certain that it has obtained from the insured a signed subrogation receipt as well as copies of all relevant documents, witness statements and other information that may be necessary for the prosecution of the subrogated action.

Some insurers, like the cargo insurer in *C.N.R. v. Canadian Industries Ltd.*, follow the practice of obtaining a "Loan Receipt" rather than a subrogation receipt. A form of this document, which is more common in United States practice, is included in Appendix P. The loan receipt describes the payment to the insured as a "loan", repayable out of any net recovery from a third party. A primary objective of the loan receipt is to prevent the third party from taking advantage of any provision in its contract with the insured which might give it the "benefit of insurance" taken out by the insured.

The loan receipt has other functions. It may be used in the case of missing goods that the insurer suspects may ultimately be delivered. The standard forms of marine cargo insurance do not insure against delay in delivery. If the goods are eventually delivered, even though late, the insured is required to take delivery of them and has no claim under the policy. In the case of goods that have gone missing for a considerable period of time, and are presumed to be lost, some insurers require the insured to execute a loan receipt, pursuant to which the insurer pays the claim under the policy, but obliges the insured to take delivery of the goods and repay the "loan" in the event the goods are ultimately recovered.[66] The Quebec Superior Court upheld the validity of such a provision in *Federation Insurance Co. of Canada v. Coret Accessories Inc.*[67] Since the policy in question did not cover loss through delay, and since the goods were recovered *in specie*, the insurer was entitled to recoup the money it had paid to its insured.[68]

A loan receipt may also be used when the insurer agrees to make an advance payment on a claim pending the proper quantification of the loss, allowing the insurer to recover some of the payment if it is ultimately determined that the claim is less than the advance.

There is some risk attached to the use of a loan receipt. In the Quebec case of *Chubb Insurance Co. of Canada v. Cast Line Ltd.*,[69] an ocean carrier being sued on a subrogated cargo claim argued that the insurance company, which had paid a claim in exchange for a "loan receipt" had no right to sue in its own name, since the action should have been brought in the name of the insured, to whom the loan had been made. Fortunately for the insurer, the court concluded that the amount paid "was essentially an insurance indemnity, reimbursable by the insured only in the event that it should obtain indemnification from another source. The contractual arrangement between the parties was clearly not a loan, and it cannot be said that Plaintiff has clearly no interest in the amount claimed by the present proceedings".[70]

It has been held that an insurer prosecuting a subrogated claim is entitled to prejudgment interest only from the date of payment to its insured.[71] In view of the fact that the insurer stands in the shoes of its insured, and asserts the insured's right of action not its own, this decision is debatable and results in a windfall for the third party.

12.15   PARTICULAR POLICY PROVISIONS

The Canadian Hulls (Pacific) Clauses (Sept. 1/91) contain the following provision at lines 102-112 with respect to recoveries from third parties:

---

[66]   Such a clause might provide: "If at any time non-delivered goods be found, in whole or in part, the undersigned undertakes to accept such goods and to reimburse the said insurance company to the extent of the insured value of the goods."

[67]   [1968] 2 Ll. L.R. 109 (Que. S.C.).

[68]   For a case in which the underwriters settled a claim for missing goods but failed to make provision for a refund in the event they were later found, see *Phoenix Assurance PLC v. Golden Imports Ltd.* (1989) 43 C.C.L.I. 313, [1990] I.L.R. ¶1-2562 (B.C. Co. Ct.). The court noted that there was nowhere in the settlement a reservation or exception by the insurer in the event that the goods were later found. The court distinguished the *Coret* case by noting that in that case there was an acknowledgment by the insured that if the goods were later located, the insured would accept them and reimburse the insurer.

[69]   [2001] Q.J. No. 2363 (Que. Sup. Ct.) (Q.L.).

[70]   *Ibid.*, at para. 21.

[71]   *Switzerland General Insurance Co. v. Logistec Navigation Inc.* (1986), 22 C.C.L.I. 243, 7 F.T.R. 196.

Unless the Assured and Underwriters shall have agreed in writing prior to commencement of suit to participate jointly in recoveries and concomitant legal costs, then net recoveries (excluding interest comprised therein) made against any claim subject to the above deductible, or any other deductions by reason of the difference between the insured and sound values, shall first be credited to the Underwriters up to the amount of the claim paid by them and then to the Assured.

Interest comprised in recoveries shall be apportioned between the Assured and the Underwriters, taking into account the sums paid by Underwriters and the dates when such payments were made.

A similar provision regarding the deductible is contained in the Institute Hull Clauses (1/11/95),[72] apparently reflecting English practice that the insurer is entitled to the proceeds of the recovery (net of recovery expenses and interest) up to the amount paid, at which point the insured becomes entitled to any excess.[73] There is no comparable provision in the C.B.M.U. Great Lakes Hull Clauses (Sept. 1, 1971), but the practice followed by brokers and underwriters under those clauses is similar.

---

[72] Clause 12.3:

> 12.3 Excluding any interest comprised therein, recoveries against any claim which is subject to the above deductible shall be _____ credited to the Underwriters in full to the extent of the sum by which the aggregate of the claim unreduced by any _____ recoveries exceed the above deductible.

[73] See R.H. Brown, *Marine Insurance, Vol. 1: Principles and Basic Practice*, 6th ed. (London: Witherby & Co. Ltd., 1998), at pp. 252-53.

Chapter 13

Double Insurance

13.1 INTRODUCTION

Double insurance occurs where two or more policies of insurance cover the same subject-matter, the same risk and the same interest.[1] It offends the principle of indemnity to permit the insured to recover more than the compensation permitted by the Canadian *Marine Insurance Act* (*"C.M.I.A."*), so equity requires the apportionment of the loss between the two policies. Equity also entitles the insured to a refund of the portion of the premium for which he or she has obtained no benefit. The principle behind double insurance is similar to subrogation — to ensure that the insured obtains an indemnity, but no more.

While not common (at least intentionally) today, double insurance was at one time used to hedge against the risk of an insolvent or irresponsible underwriter. It may also have been used at times as an instrument of fraud. Today, double insurance can arise inadvertently where two or more parties, uncertain as to who is responsible for taking out insurance, procure policies covering the same risks.[2] Double insurance may also arise where policies taken out by a single insured overlap. While it is commonly thought of in relation to property insurance, double insurance can also arise where the insured's liabilities are insured under more than one policy. There is nothing unlawful about double insurance unless the policies have been procured for fraudulent reasons.

---

[1] Canadian *Marine Insurance Act*, S.C. 1993, c. 22 (*"C.M.I.A."*), s. 86:

> 86(1) An insured is over-insured by double insurance if two or more marine policies are effected by or on behalf of the insured on the same marine adventure and interest or part thereof and the sums insured exceed the indemnity allowed by this Act.

See *Bank of British North America v. Western Assurance Co.* (1884), 7 O.R. 116 at 169-70:

> For the law of Canada is the same as that in England, that in case of a double insurance the insured may sue any of the insurers, leaving them to recover contribution from the others.

For recent examples in Canada, see *Dominion of Canada General Insurance Co. v. Wawanesa Mutual Insurance Co.* (1985), 64 B.C.L.R. 122, 16 C.C.L.I. 69, [1986] I.L.R. ¶1-1990 (S.C.); *Tinmouth v. Groupe Desjardins, Assurances Générales* (1986), 57 O.R. (2d) 187, 32 D.L.R. (4th) 621 (H.C.J.), aff'd. (1988), 64 O.R. (2d) 352, 49 D.L.R. (4th) 768 (C.A.), leave to appeal ref'd. (1988), 65 O.R. (2d) x.

[2] This could occur, for example, where both the buyer and seller of goods take out insurance on the goods which are the subject-matter of their contract. It may also occur where a freight forwarder insures goods on behalf of a customer, unaware of insurance effected by another party.

A distinction must be made between insurance of the same *interest* and insurance of the same *property*. Two or more persons with different interests in the same property may take out insurance of their separate interests without giving rise to double insurance.[3]

Determining whether or not there is double insurance requires the examination of the policies to answer the following questions:

(a)   Is the insurance effected by or on behalf of the same insured?
(b)   Is the subject-matter or property insured under each policy the same?
(c)   Is the interest insured the same?
(d)   Is the risk insured against the same?

A simple test for double insurance is to ask whether the insured could recover for the loss under either policy.[4]

13.2   RIGHTS OF THE INSURED

Where there is double or "multiple" insurance, the insured is entitled to claim the entire amount from any insurer who is in turn entitled to contribution from the other insurer(s) for their proportionate shares.[5] Alternatively, the insured may claim a proportionate part of the loss from each insurer. These rights are set out in *C.M.I.A.*, section 86(2):

> 86(2) An insured who is over-insured by double insurance
>
> (*a*)   may claim payment from the insurers in any order, unless the marine policy under which the claim is made provides otherwise, but may not receive more than the indemnity allowed by this Act;
>
> (*b*)   if claiming under a valued policy, shall give credit, as against the value specified in the policy, for any sum received by the insured under any other policy without regard to the actual value of the subject-matter insured;
>
> (*c*)   if claiming under an unvalued policy, shall give credit, as against the full insured value, for any sum received by the insured under any other policy; and
>
> (*d*)   is deemed to hold any sum received in excess of the indemnity allowed by this Act in trust for the insurers, according to their right of contribution among themselves.

---

[3]   See *North British and Mercantile Insurance Company v. London, Liverpool and Globe Insurance Co.* (1877), 5 Ch. D. 569. Where different persons, for example a mortgagor and a mortgagee, have different interests in the same property, they are entitled to insure those interests.

[4]   See D. O'May, *O'May on Marine Insurance*, J. Hill, ed. (London: Sweet & Maxwell, 1993), at p. 496.

[5]   See *Bank of British North America v. Western Assurance Co.* (1884), 7 O.R. 116.

13.3 RIGHTS OF INSURERS AGAINST EACH OTHER

The rights of the insurers between themselves in a case of double insurance are set out in *C.M.I.A.*, section 87:

> 87(1) Where an insured is over-insured by double insurance, each insurer is liable, as between the insurer and the other insurers, to contribute ratebly to the payment of a loss in proportion to the amount for which the insurer is liable under the insurer's contract.
>
> (2) An insurer who contributes more to the payment of a loss than required by subsection (1) is entitled to bring an action against the other insurers for contribution and to such other remedies as a surety is entitled to for paying more than the surety's proportion of a debt.

Thus, an insurer who has indemnified the insured against the whole loss, or against a greater portion of the loss than it is required to bear, has a direct right of action against the other insurer(s) to recover the amount of the overpayment.[6]

13.4 REFUND OF PREMIUM

The general rule in double insurance cases is that a proportionate part of both premiums is returnable to the insured.[7] Where two policies have attached at different times, and one policy has borne the entire risk up to the time of the loss, no part of the premium on the policy first in time is refundable. Where the insured has knowingly taken out double insurance, no part of the premium is refundable.[8]

13.5 "OTHER INSURANCE" CLAUSES

Marine insurance policies frequently contain double insurance clauses. Such provisions may take different forms:

---

[6] *C.M.I.A.*, subs. 87(2).

[7] *Ibid.*, s. 85:

> 85(10) Subject to subsections (2) to (9), where an insured is over-insured by double insurance, a proportionate part of the premiums is returnable.
>
> (11) Subsection (10) does not apply
>
> (a) where the double insurance is knowingly effected by the insured, in which case none of the premiums is returnable, and
>
> (b) where the policies are effected at different times and either the earlier policy has at any time borne the entire risk or a claim has been paid on the earlier policy in respect of the full sum insured by it, in which case the premium for the earlier policy is not returnable and the premium for the later policy is returnable.

[8] See *ibid.*, subs. 85(11)(a).

(a) a provision that there be "no other insurance";[9] or

(b) a provision that in the event of other insurance the provisions of the policy will not apply; or

(c) a provision that in the event of other insurance the policy will only respond to the extent of any deficiency.[10]

The policies must be examined to determine what is permitted by their terms. It is essentially a matter of contract interpretation (aided by the principles of the *C.M.I.A.*) to see which policy or policies apply.[11] In the Canadian case of *Kenny v. Union Marine Insurance Co.*,[12] the court gave effect to an "other insurance" clause in a marine policy and held that where the insured had been fully indemnified by one insurer, he was not entitled to recover under the second policy. The insured was, however, entitled to a return of premium on the second policy.

It has been said that the courts do not favour a result in which one insurer, through the existence of a "no other insurance clause", can avoid a liability which would otherwise exist under the policy.[13] Since double insurance is usually fortuitous, neither insurer should be able to avoid its responsibilities due to the coincidence that there is another policy (of which the insurer was unaware) covering the loss. The equitable thing to do, usually, is to require that both insurers share the loss. On the other hand, the court should also ask whether one insurer has a legitimate reason to provide coverage only when there is "no other insurance". A protection and indemnity (P. & I.) insurer, for example, may be prepared to cover certain liabilities where there is no other coverage under a hull and machinery policy. This has always been one of the useful functions of P. & I. insurance, as a backstop to potential gaps in other policies. Similarly, in a "seller's risk" insurance policy, the intent of the insurer is to provide coverage only in the unusual situation where the seller is unpaid. It is not intended to provide a second policy against loss or damage to the cargo.

---

9   See, for example, the C.B.M.U. Great Lakes Hull Clauses (Sept. 1, 1971), Appendix G, lines 245-277:

   It is a condition of this Policy that no additional insurance against the risk of Total Loss of the Vessel shall be effected to operate during the currency of this Policy by or for account of the Assured...except on the interests and up to the amount enumerated in the following Sections...

10   See *Union Marine Insurance Co. v. Metzler* (1873), 9 N.S.R. 331 (C.A.) where there was a clause in the policy which provided that if there was other insurance the policy would only respond to the extent of any deficiency.

11   In the non-marine context, see *Trenton Cold Storage Ltd. v. St. Paul Fire & Marine Insurance Co.* (1999), 11 C.C.L.I. (3d) 127, [1999] I.L.R. I-3656 (Ont. Gen. Div.), rev'd. (2001), 199 D.L.R. (4th) 654, 28 C.C.L.I. (3d) 177 (Ont. C.A.). The trial judge had found that the two policies, one a "Warehouseman or Bailee Liability" policy and the other an "Umbrella Excess Liability Policy", created a double insurance situation. The Ontario Court of Appeal reversed, holding that the first policy was primary and the second policy provided excess coverage.

12   (1880), 13 N.S.R. 313 (C.A.).

13   See R. Colinvaux, *Colinvaux's Law of Insurance*, 7th ed., R. Merkin, ed. (London: Sweet & Maxwell, 1997) at p. 190.

Where two policies each contain a prohibition against double insurance, and purport to exclude losses covered by other policies, it is reasonable to conclude that the provisions cancel each other out, leaving it to both policies to contribute.

13.6 PARTICULAR POLICY PROVISIONS

13.6.1 Cargo Insurance

In a typical (Cost insurance freight) "C.I.F." sale, it is the responsibility of the seller to insure the goods and to provide the buyer with a certificate of insurance as part of the sale documentation. If the goods are lost or damaged during transport, the buyer will make a claim under that policy of insurance. In the unlikely event that the buyer also has its own policy covering the loss, a double insurance situation will probably exist. A careful review of the policies may be required to determine whether there is in fact double insurance or whether there are provisions in one policy which make it applicable only in the event that there is no other insurance. An insurer may be prepared to give a buyer contingent coverage, if no other policy is available, as part of a broader package of insurance and it might be unfair to treat this as a true "double insurance" situation. Similarly, the seller may have a "seller's interest" policy which is designed to apply only in the event that the buyer does not pay.

It is typical for marine open cargo policies to contain an "Other Insurance" clause such as the following:

> If any property included herein shall at the time of any loss or damage be also covered by any other insurance this insurance shall not insure the same except only as regards any excess of value beyond the amount of any other insurance.

Another example of a form is as follows:

> 1. If an interest insured hereunder is covered by other insurance which attached prior to the coverage provided by this policy then this company shall be liable only for the amount in excess of such prior insurance, the company to return to the insured premium equivalent to the cost of the prior insurance at this company's rates.

> 2. If an interest insured hereunder is covered by other insurance which attached subsequent to the coverage provided by this policy, then this company shall nevertheless be liable for the full amount of the insurance without right to claim contribution from the subsequent insurers.

> 3. Other insurance upon the property of same attaching date as the coverage provided by this policy shall be deemed simultaneous and this company will be liable only for a rateable contribution to the loss or damage in proportion to the amount for which this company would otherwise be liable under this policy and will return to the assured an amount of premium proportionate to such reduction of liability.

13.6.2 Hull and Machinery Insurance

Standard forms of hull and machinery insurance, including the C.B.M.U. Great Lakes Hull Clauses (1/9/71) and the Canadian Hulls (Pacific) Clauses (Sept. 1/91) ("C.H.P.") contain prohibitions against additional insurances, except as specifically allowed. The C.B.M.U. clauses prohibit additional insurance against the risk of total loss of the vessel except in respect of certain specified interests. The C.H.P. clauses (reproduced in Appendix G) are less restrictive.

13.6.3 Liability Insurance

The rules of double insurance also apply to liability insurance. In *Dominion of Canada General Insurance Co. v. Wawanesa Mutual Insurance Co.*,[14] based on double insurance principles, two liability insurers were required to indemnify the insured who was responsible for a water-skiing accident. In an Ontario non-marine case, involving accountants' errors and omissions insurance, *Tinmouth v. Groupe Desjardins, Assurances Générales*,[15] the court was faced with the issue of whether there was double insurance. In addressing the question, the court adopted the submissions of one of the parties (which was largely agreed upon by the other party):

> Each case depends upon the language of the policies involved. The reasonable expectations of the insured should prevail over any absurdity in the literal application of contractual provisions but contractual provisions should otherwise govern.[16]

This referred to the potential absurdity of both policies being interpreted so as to leave the insured without any coverage. The court then looked to the wordings of the two policies and the "sensible commercial meaning" of the policies to determine whether there was double insurance. The judge concluded:

> It is my conclusion that the insured intended to be covered by an insurer for claims presented during specified times and not to have two policies with combined limits applying to the same loss. In the circumstances, I find that from the sensible commercial meaning and the 'reasonable expectations' principle, the General policy is not valid and collectible other insurance so that the Lloyd's policy exclusion does not apply. The result of all of this is that the claims made are made during the terms of the Lloyd's policy and are not excluded and there is not the application of another policy and there is not *pro rata* contribution.[17]

The Ontario Court of Appeal affirmed the decision, with brief reasons:

---

[14] (1985), 64 B.C.L.R. 122, 16 C.C.L.I. 69, [1986] I.L.R. ¶1-1990 (S.C.).

[15] (1986), 57 O.R. (2d) 187, 32 D.L.R. (4th) 621, (H.C.J.), aff'd. (1988), 64 O.R. (2d) 352, 49 D.L.R. (4th) 768 (C.A.), leave to appeal ref'd. (1988), 65 O.R. (2d) x.

[16] (1986), 57 O.R. (2d) 187 at 190-91, referring to *Seagate Hotel Ltd. v. Simcoe & Erie* (1980), 22 B.C.L.R. 374, [1980] I.L.R. 1098 (S.C.). aff'd. (1981) 27 B.C.L.R. 89, [1982] I.L.R. 1-1470 (B.C.C.A.).

[17] (1986), 57 O.R. (2d) 187 at 192.

We find no error in the reasons or conclusion of the trial judge. The appellant [Lloyd's] must have been aware of the exclusion clause of the General insurance policy which made it clear that it would not provide coverage after the policy term if there was another applicable policy in force.[18]

These reasons are somewhat at odds with those of the trial judge as they import a consideration of whether the "other" insurer had actual or imputed knowledge of the policy which was first in time.

In a Quebec case, *West of England Shipowners Mutual Insurance Association (Luxembourg) v. Laurentian General Insurance Co. Inc.,*[19] a dredging company which had damaged an underwater pipeline, sought indemnity from its liability insurers. The Quebec Superior Court treated the "other insurance" clauses in the two liability insurance policies as having no effect and required the two insurers to share the loss in proportion to their policy limits.

P. and I. Club Rules frequently contain a prohibition against double insurance, the following clause being typical:

> Where a Member is insured elsewhere in any manner whatsoever against any of the liabilities, costs or expenses enumerated which would otherwise have been recoverable under these Rules, no contribution shall be made by the Club to such liabilities, costs or expenses, on the basis of double insurance or otherwise, to the extent to which the Member is so insured; nevertheless, with the approval of the Board, a Member may be insured by special agreement with the Club, made either directly with himself or with other insurers upon the terms that certain liabilities, costs or expenses shall be borne by the Club, notwithstanding such other insurance.[20]

---

[18] (1988), 64 O.R. (2d) 352.

[19] [1993] R.J.Q. 122, [1993] R.R.A. 213 (C.S.) For a comment on this case, see A. Ness, "Double Insurance in Quebec", 5 C.I.L.R. 203.

[20] Rules of the Standard Steamship Owners' Protection and Indemnity Association (Bermuda) Limited, 2002-03, Rule 17.3. See also the SP-23 form of Protection and Indemnity Insurance (Rev. 1/56), which provides:

> Provided that where the Assured is, irrespective of this insurance, covered or protected against any loss or claim which would otherwise have been paid by the Assurer, under this policy, there shall be no contribution by the Assurer on the basis of double insurance or otherwise.

Chapter 14

Underinsurance and Overinsurance

14.1 INTRODUCTION

Underinsurance occurs where property is insured for less than its insurable value.[1] In an unvalued policy, it occurs where the property is insured for an amount less than its insurable value as defined by the Canadian *Marine Insurance Act ("C.M.I.A.")*. In a valued policy, it occurs where the property is insured for an amount less than the agreed valuation in the policy. There may be various reasons for underinsurance. It may be more economical to insure for less than the full market value of the property and the insured may be prepared to retain some of the risk in order to save on insurance costs. For its part, the insurer may want the insured to retain some of the risk as a loss prevention measure.

Overinsurance, on the other hand, only applies to an unvalued policy. It occurs where the property is insured for an amount *more* than its insurable value. Where there is overinsurance, the *C.M.I.A.* provides that the insured is entitled to a return of a proportionate part of the premium. The reason why overinsurance does not apply in a valued policy is that in the case of a valued policy, the valuation stated in the policy is conclusive, unless there is fraud or misrepresentation permitting the insurer to avoid the policy.

The statutory rule with respect to underinsurance is set out in section 88 of the *C.M.I.A.*:

> 88. Where an insured is insured for a sum that is less than the insurable value of the subject-matter insured, in the case of an unvalued policy, or less than the value of the subject-matter insured specified by the policy, in the case of a valued policy, the insured is deemed to be self-insured in respect of the uninsured difference.

The rule as to overinsurance is found in subsection 85(8):

> 85(8) Where an insured is over-insured under an unvalued policy, a proportionate part of the premium is returnable.

Unvalued policies are rare in Canadian insurance practice today and they are seldom used in either hull and machinery or cargo insurance. Over the years, market forces and competition between insurers have led to the removal of some of the consequences of underinsurance. An example of this is found in the

---

[1] For the meaning of "insurable value" see the Canadian *Marine Insurance Act*, S.C. 1993, c. 22 ("*C.M.I.A.*"), s. 19 and Chapter 6, *Insurable Value*.

modern open cargo policy, which is invariably a valued policy. The open policy usually contains a valuation clause, with a formula for determining the value of any shipment insured under the policy.[2] The open cargo policy usually contains a limit on the amount of financial liability an insurer will accept, as in the following instances:

(a) cargo shipped on deck of any one vessel (and connecting conveyance) and subject to an "on deck" bill of lading;
(b) cargo shipped on any one vessel (and connecting conveyance) and subject to an under deck bill of lading; and
(c) cargo shipped on board any one aircraft and connecting conveyance.

If these limits are exceeded, either inadvertently or otherwise, and a loss occurs, the insurer is entitled to prorate the loss in accordance with the percentage that the applicable limit bears to the actual insured value of the shipment, and the insured will become a co-insurer for the difference. To partly overcome this situation, most insurers have introduced the following "Limits of Liability Exceeded" clause:

> If the total value at risk exceeds the applicable policy limit, the insured shall nevertheless report to these insurers the full amount at risk and shall pay full premium thereon. The acceptance by these insurers of such reports and premium shall not alter or increase the limits of liability of these insurers, but these insurers shall be liable for the full amount of loss (without applying co-insurance) up to but not exceeding the applicable limit of liability.

The effect of this clause is that, in return for being permitted to keep the entire premium whenever a limit is exceeded by an insured, the insurer agrees not to prorate any losses at or below the level of that particular limit. Thus, the insurer does not have to go to the trouble of refunding part of the premium for the shipment in question and the insured enjoys full protection up to the limit for partial losses, but not for more than the limit.

14.2 ADJUSTMENT OF LOSSES

Where the insured is considered self-insured for the underinsured difference between the insured value and the value either stated in the policy or determined in accordance with the *C.M.I.A.*, the insured is required to bear a proportionate share of any loss. If the loss is total, then subject to any provisions in the policy, the insurers pay their proportion of the insured value. If the loss is partial, the insurers pay in proportion to the amount they have agreed to insure and the insured bears a proportionate share, in the absence of a limits of liability exceeded clause.

For example, if the value stated in the policy is $1,000,000 and the property is insured for $750,000, the *C.M.I.A.* provides that there is underinsurance and the insured is self-insured for the uninsured difference. A claim for damage to

---

[2] For example, the cost insurance freight ("C.I.F.") value of the goods, plus 10 per cent.

the property will be adjusted on the basis of the underwriters bearing 75 per cent of any loss and the insured bearing the remaining 25 per cent.

14.3 APPORTIONMENT OF RECOVERIES

Where the property is undervalued, and the insurer pays a claim and then pursues subrogation against a third party, is the insured entitled to a share in the recovery?[3] In principle, where there is underinsurance, any recovery from a third party should be apportioned between the insurer and the insured in proportion to their respective interests. Some policy forms contain specific provisions in this regard, and, in practice, particularly in the case of small deductibles under cargo policies, insurers frequently pursue recoveries without reference to the insured's deductible. This subject is discussed in more detail in Chapter 12, *Subrogation*.

---

[3] See Chapter 12, *Subrogation*. See also *Attorney-General v. Glen Line, Ltd.* (1930), 37 Ll. L. Rep. 55.

Chapter 15

Assignment of the Marine Policy

15.1 INTRODUCTION

Assignment is the transfer by one of the parties to a contract of its rights and obligations under that contract. The person transferring the contract is referred to as the "assignor" and the recipient is referred to as the "assignee". In marine insurance, assignment refers to the transfer by the insured of its right to indemnity under the policy. The Canadian *Marine Insurance Act* (*"C.M.I.A."*) provides that a marine policy may be assigned,[1] provided it takes place at a time when the insured retains an interest in the subject-matter of the insurance.[2] At common law, the assignee of a policy was not entitled to sue the insurer in his or her name but instead had to obtain the assistance of the original policy holder, the assignor, to sue. This is now unnecessary because subsection 51(3) of the *C.M.I.A.* permits the assignee to sue in his or her own name.[3] The insurer may raise all defences against the assignee that would have been available to it in a suit brought by the original insured.[4] The policy may expressly prohibit its assignment or may require that the insurer's previous consent be given.

---

[1] Canadian *Marine Insurance Act*, S.C. 1993, c. 22 (*"C.M.I.A."*), s. 51:

> 51(1) A marine policy is assignable either before or after a loss, unless it expressly prohibits assignment.
>
> (2) A marine policy may be assigned by endorsement on the policy or in any other customary manner.

[2] *C.M.I.A.*, s. 52:

> 52(1) Where an insured transfers or loses an interest in the subject-matter insured and does not, before or at the time of so doing, expressly or impliedly agree to assign the marine policy, no subsequent assignment of the marine policy is operative.
>
> (2) Subsection (1) does not apply in respect of an assignment of a marine policy after a loss.

[3] *Ibid.*, subs. 51(3):

> 51(3) Where a marine policy is assigned so as to transfer the beneficial interest in the policy, the assignee of the policy is entitled to sue on it in the assignee's name and, in any such action, the defendant is entitled to raise any defence arising out of the contract that the defendant would have been entitled to raise if the action had been brought in the name of the person by or on behalf of whom the policy was effected.

[4] See *C.M.I.A.*, subs. 51(3).

15.2   TRANSFER OF THE INSURED PROPERTY

There is a distinction between the assignment of the policy and the transfer of the property insured. An insurance policy is a personal contract between the insurer and the insured and, unless otherwise stated in the policy, the contract contained in the policy does not pass to a purchaser of the insured property. In order for the purchaser of the property to acquire benefits under the policy, there must be an assignment of the policy. Subsection 17(1) of the *C.M.I.A.* provides that in order for the transferee of the property to receive the benefit of the insurance on it, it must have been expressly or impliedly agreed, *at or before the time of the transfer of the insured property*, that the insurance policy would also be assigned. Once the property has been transferred, the transferor loses an insurable interest in it, and any subsequent transfer of the insurance conveys nothing.

15.3   RIGHTS OF THE INSURER

Subsection 51(3) of the *C.M.I.A.* entitles the insurer to raise against the assignee any defence that could have been raised against the assignor. The assignee cannot enforce a policy which the assignor would have been unable to enforce[5] and the assignee's claim under the policy will be defeated by the assignor's misrepresentation, non-disclosure, breach of warranty or other breach of contract.[6]

15.4   MARINE INSURANCE PRACTICE

The *C.M.I.A.* provides that a policy may be assigned by endorsement thereon or in any other customary manner.[7] In practice, policies are often assigned by physical transfer, usually accompanied by the insured's endorsement on the back of the policy.

15.4.1   Cargo Insurance

Assignment is of great importance in cargo insurance, since the seller under a cost insurance freight ("C.I.F.") contract is obliged to procure insurance on the goods and to assign the insurance to the buyer. A cargo insurer usually does not allow the underlying open policy to be assigned, and most open policies contain a prohibition against assignment without the insurer's consent. The insurer does

---

[5]   See *Re S.S. Dorin (The)*, [1935] 4 D.L.R. 526 (N.S.S.C.), aff'd. (*sub nom. Canadian S.K.F. Co. v. Royal Bank*), [1936] 2 D.L.R. 40, 10 M.P.R. 325 (N.S.C.A.); *Anchor Marine Insurance Co. v. Phoenix Insurance Co.* (1880), 30 U.C.C.P. 570 (C.P.), aff'd (1881), 6 O.A.R. 567 (C.A.): the assignee of the policy receives only what the assignor has to assign and can stand in no higher position than the assignor. The assignee is subject to all defences that the insurer could raise against the assignor.

[6]   See *Federal Business Development Bank v. Commonwealth Insurance Co.* (1980), 13 B.C.L.R. 376, 2 C.C.L.I. 200 (S.C.).

[7]   Subsection 51(2).

contemplate, however, that particular shipments under an open policy will be covered as required by the insured's terms of sale with its buyer and that the right to claim under the insurance will be assigned to the buyer. The certificate of insurance assigned to the buyer provides evidence of the insurance contract and the buyer is entitled to enforce the contract if the goods are lost or damaged. The certificate generally contains reference to the insuring conditions, the procedure to be followed in the event of a claim, requirements for the appointment of a surveyor in the event of loss of or damage to the goods and the name of the insurer's local agent for the settlement of claims. In an Ontario case, *Ronald A. Chisholm Ltd. v. Agro & Diverses Souscriptions Internationale— A.D.S.I.-S.A.*[8] it was held that a jurisdiction clause[9] in the underlying open policy was not binding on the purchaser of goods who received an assignment of the insurance certificate containing no reference to the clause. The court considered that if the insurer regarded the jurisdiction clause as important, it should have been included in the certificate.

15.4.2 Hull and Machinery Insurance

The ownership and management of the insured vessel is usually an important consideration for hull and machinery insurers, and their policies typically provide that the insurance terminates automatically in the event of change of the vessel's ownership or flag.[10] For example, the Canadian Board of Marine Underwriters Great Lakes Hull Clauses (Sept. 1, 1971) provide at lines 229-232:

> In the event of any change, voluntary or otherwise, in the ownership or flag of the Vessel, or if the Vessel be placed under new management, or be chartered on a bareboat basis or requisitioned on that basis, or if the Classification Society of the Vessel or her class therein be changed, cancelled or withdrawn, then, unless the Underwriters agree thereto in writing, this Policy shall automatically terminate...

The Canadian Hulls (Pacific) Clauses (Sept. 1/91) and the Institute Time Clauses (Hulls) (1/11/95) contain similar provisions.[11]

15.4.3 Protection and Indemnity Insurance

Like hull insurers, protection and indemnity insurers are vitally interested in the ownership and operation of the vessels they insure. P. & I. Club rules invariably include a clause prohibiting assignment of the insurance without the written consent of the Managers. The SP-23 (Rev'd. 1/56) form contains a similar

---

[8] (1991), 2 C.P.C. (3d) 120 (Master), aff'd (1991) 4 O.R. (3d) 539 (S.C.).

[9] A clause requiring that suit under the policy must be taken in a particular country — in this case, in the country where the insurer had its place of business.

[10] The ship's "flag" refers to the country in which the ship is registered.

[11] Canadian Hulls (Pacific) Clauses (Sept. 1/91), Appendix E, lines 239-251; Institute Time Clauses (Hulls) (1/11/95), clauses 5 and 21.

provision[12] as do the Canadian (Pacific) Protection and Indemnity Clauses (1/1/83).[13]

15.5 LOSS OF INTEREST

Subsection 52(1) of the *C.M.I.A.* provides that an assignment of the insurance after the insured has lost its interest in the property is ineffectual. Obviously, the insured cannot assign a contract where it no longer has an insurable interest in the property.

---

[12]   No claim or demand against the Assured under this policy shall be assigned or transferred, and no person, excepting a legally appointed receiver of the property of the Assured, shall acquire any right against the Assurer by virtue of this insurance without the expressed consent of the Assurer.

[13]   This insurance shall be void in case the vessel or any part thereof, shall be sold, transferred or mortgaged, or if there be any change of management or charter of the vessel, or if this policy be assigned or pledged, without the previous consent in writing of the Assurer(s).

Chapter 16

The Premium

16.1 INTRODUCTION

A premium is the sum of money paid, in a lump sum or periodically, to purchase an insurance contract. In Canada, as in England, the marine insurance broker is regarded as the agent of the insured and is the debtor of the underwriter for the payment of the premium.

Where insurance is effected on the terms that a premium is to be arranged, and no arrangement has yet been made, the Canadian *Marine Insurance Act* ("*C.M.I.A.*") provides that a reasonable premium is payable.[1] Where the insurance is effected on terms that an additional premium is to be paid "on the happening of a given event", and the event happens without an arrangement having been made, a reasonable additional premium is payable.[2]

The *C.M.I.A.* also identifies circumstances in which the premium, or part of it, must be refunded to the insured.[3] There are a number of other provisions of the *C.M.I.A.* that deal with the premium.[4] These will be identified and discussed in the course of this Chapter.

---

[1] Canadian *Marine Insurance Act*, S.C. 1993, c. 22 ("*C.M.I.A.*"), subs. 47(1).

[2] *C.M.I.A.*, subs. 47(2).

[3] See *McLarty v. Eagle Star Insurance Co.*, [1944] 2 D.L.R. 266 (Que. C.A.) to the effect that the premium cannot be divided or apportioned unless there is a clear indication from the policy that the risks were intended to be divided; *Palmer v. Ocean Marine Insurance Co.* (1890), 29 N.B.R. 501 (C.A.); *Dickie v. Blenkorn* (1882) 15 N.S.R. 38 at 287 (C.A.); *Harold A. Berner and Bradley Finance Ltd. v. Sun Insurance Office Ltd.*, [1952] I.L.R. 1-069 (Ont. S.C.J.); *Intermunicipal Realty Corp. v. Gore Mutual Insurance Co.*, [1981] 1 F.C. 151, 112 D.L.R. (3d) 432 (T.D.).

[4] The following sections of the *C.M.I.A.* include provisions dealing with the premium:
Section 13: The insured has an insurable interest in the premium.
Section 47: Reasonable premium payable.
Section 48: Duty to pay premium and to issue policy are concurrent conditions.
Section 49: Policy effected through broker.
Section 50: Acknowledgment of receipt conclusive as between insurer and insured.
Sections 82-85: Return of premium.
Section 91: Reasonable premium a question of fact.

16.2   LIABILITY FOR PREMIUM

The custom in marine insurance, codified in subsection 49(1)(*a*) of the *C.M.I.A.*, is that the broker, not the insured, is the debtor of the underwriter for the payment of premium:

> 49(1) Unless otherwise agreed, where a broker effects a marine policy on behalf of the insured,
>
> > (*a*)   the broker is directly responsible to the insurer for the premium;
> >
> > (*b*)   the broker has, as against the insured, a lien on the policy for the amount of the premium and the broker's charges in effecting the policy; and
> >
> > (*c*)   the insurer is directly responsible to the insured for any amount that may be payable in respect of losses or a returnable premium.
>
> (2) Unless otherwise agreed, where a broker effects a marine policy on behalf of a person who employs the broker as a principal, the broker has a lien on the policy in respect of any balance on any insurance account that may be due to the broker from that person, unless, when the debt was incurred, the broker had reason to believe that the person was only an agent.[5]

In *O'Keefe and Lynch of Canada Ltd. v. Toronto Insurance and Vessel Agency Ltd.*,[6] an Ontario case decided prior to the enactment of that province's *Marine Insurance Act*,[7] the court held, based on the ordinary law of agency, that the broker was liable to the underwriter for the premium. Justice Rose referred to the custom in England:

> In England, by custom which was proved so often that the courts took judicial notice of it, when marine insurance was effected through a broker, the broker and not the assured was liable to the underwriter for the premium, while the underwriter was directly responsible to the assured for the loss; and this was the case even when the policy recited an undertaking on the part of the assured to pay the premium.[8]

Subsection 49(1)(*b*) of the *C.M.I.A.* gives the broker a lien on the policy for the premium. Since the policy must be presented at the time a claim is made, the broker's possession of the policy enables it to recover its payment of the premium out of the claim. It has been held in Canada that the broker has a right

---

[5]   See *Mowat v. Goodall Bros.* (1914), 31 W.L.R. 537, 21 B.C.R. 394, 24 D.L.R. 781 (C.A.); *Ranney v. Gregory* (1868), 12 N.B.R. 152 at 156 (C.A.), *per* Wilmot J.: "In England the premium on a marine policy is due from the assured to the broker, and from the latter to the underwriter. The broker has his action against the assured for the premium, and the underwriter against the broker."

[6]   (1926), 59 O.L.R. 235, [1926] 4 D.L.R. 477 (Ont. H.C.J.).

[7]   R.S.O. 1990, c. M.2.

[8]   (1926), 59 O.L.R. 235 at 240.

in rem against the insured vessel for premium paid on behalf of the owner — that is, it can sue the insured ship itself to recover the premium.[9]

The obligation of the insured or the broker to pay the premium and the obligation of the insurer to issue the policy are concurrent conditions. Unless the policy provides otherwise, the insurer is not required to issue the policy until the premium has been paid or tendered.[10]

16.3   ACKNOWLEDGMENT OF PREMIUM

Section 50 of the *C.M.I.A.* provides:

> 50. Where a broker effects a marine policy on behalf of an insured, an acknowledgment in the policy of the receipt of the premium is, in the absence of fraud, conclusive as between the insurer and the insured, but not as between the insurer and the broker.

This means that if the policy states that the premium has been paid, even if it has not in fact been paid, the insurer is not entitled to claim it from the insured, although it may claim the premium from the broker.

16.4   PREMIUM TO BE ARRANGED — REASONABLE PREMIUM

Sometimes the insurance contract does not specify the premium but leaves it to be arranged at a later time. The *C.M.I.A.* states that where insurance is effected at a premium to be arranged, and no arrangement is made, a reasonable premium is to be paid.[11] The policy may also provide that on the happening of a particular event, an additional premium will be arranged. In such cases, where no additional premium is arranged, the *C.M.I.A.* stipulates that a "reasonable additional premium is payable".[12] This may occur where the policy confirms that the insured will be "held covered" in the event of a breach of warranty. A hull and machinery policy, for example, may include a "held covered" provision in the case of a breach of the trading limits requiring the insured to pay an additional premium. A cargo policy may call for an additional premium in the event of the employment of a vessel older than permitted by the classification clause or deviation from the agreed voyage.[13] The determination of the amount of the

---

[9]   *Fairway Life & Marine Insurance Ltd. v. "Susan Darlene" (The)*, [1987] 2 F.C. 547, 21 C.C.L.I. 83 (T.D.).

[10]   *C.M.I.A.*, s. 48:

> 48. Unless otherwise agreed, the duty of the insured or the insured's agent to pay the premium and the duty of the insurer to issue the marine policy to the insured or the insured's agent are concurrent conditions, and the insurer is not required to issue the policy until the premium is paid or tendered.

See *Walker v. Provincial Insurance Co.* (1860), 8 Gr. 217 (U.C.C.A.).

[11]   *Ibid.*, subs. 47(1).

[12]   *Ibid.*, subs. 47(2).

[13]   See: *Chartered Bank of India v. Pacific Marine Insurance Co.*, [1923] 1 W.W.R. 1136, [1923] 2 D.L.R. 612 (S.C.); aff'd. [1924] 1 W.W.R. 114, [1923] 4 D.L.R. 942 (C.A.); *Peters v. Canada Sugar Refining Co.* (1886), 321 L.C. Jur. 72, M.L.R. 2 Q.B. 420 (Que. C.A.) to the effect that the

additional premium is a question of fact[14] to be ascertained by reference to reasonable underwriting practice.[15]

16.5 RETURN OF PREMIUM

The *C.M.I.A.* identifies a number of circumstances in which the insured is entitled to a refund of all or a portion of the premium.[16]

16.5.1 Failure of Consideration

Where the consideration for a premium fails, or a part of the consideration fails, and there is no fraud or illegality on the part of the insured or its agent, then the premium or a proportionate part thereof is returnable to the insured.[17] This could occur, for example, where an insured takes out insurance on a vessel that has already been lost. Since the insurer assumes no risk (and has no possibility of liability under the policy) he or she gives no value in exchange for the premium — there is said to be "no consideration" given by the underwriter and the premium is returnable.

16.5.2 Avoiding the Policy Due to Misrepresentation or Non-Disclosure

Where the policy is void *ab initio* (from its inception), or where the insurer has avoided the policy for misrepresentation or non-disclosure, and there is no fraud or illegality, the premium is returnable. However, this does not apply where the risk is not apportionable and has attached.[18] Where there has been fraud by the insured, the premium is not returnable.[19]

16.5.3 Where There is Illegality

If the adventure is illegal, the policy does not attach and the premium must be refunded.

---

additional premium paid by the cargo owner as a result of the deviation of the vessel from the agreed voyage may be recovered in an action in damages against the shipowner who was responsible for the unlawful deviation.

[14] *C.M.I.A.*, s. 91: "Any question as to what constitutes a reasonable time, a reasonable premium or reasonable diligence for the purposes of this Act is a question of fact."

[15] See *Chartered Bank of India v. Pacific Marine Insurance Co.*, [1923] 1 W.W.R. 1136, [1923] 2 D.L.R. 612 (S.C.); aff'd. [1924] 1 W.W.R. 114, [1923] 4 D.L.R. 942 (C.A.).

[16] *C.M.I.A.*, ss. 82 to 85.

[17] *Ibid.*, subss. 84(1) and (2).

[18] *Ibid.*, subss. 85(2) and (3).

[19] *Intermunicipal Realty Corp. v. Gore Mutual Insurance Co.*, [1981] 1 F.C. 151, 112 D.L.R. (3d) 432 (T.D.).

16.5.4 Where the Property Was Never Imperiled

Where the subject-matter insured has never been exposed to any peril the premium is returnable because there is no consideration — the insurer has not incurred any risk.[20]

16.5.5 Where the Insured Has No Insurable Interest

The *C.M.I.A.* provides that "where the insured has no insurable interest throughout the period of the risk, the premium is returnable".[21]

16.5.6 Where the Risk Never Attaches

In a voyage policy where the contracted voyage never takes place, or where goods to be shipped are never committed to transportation, it is said that the risk did not attach and therefore no premium is payable.

16.5.7 Double Insurance

Where the insured is "overinsured by double insurance, a proportionate part of the premiums is returnable"[22] unless the insured knowingly took out double insurance.[23] Where the policies have been effected at different times and either the earlier policy has borne the entire risk or has paid a claim in respect of the full sum insured, the premium on the earlier policy is treated as fully earned and is not recoverable, but the premium on the later policy is returnable.[24]

16.5.8 Overinsurance

Where the insured is overinsured under an unvalued policy, a proportionate part of the premium is returnable. The insured has paid a greater premium than necessary.[25]

16.6 WAIVER AND ESTOPPEL

When the insurer has the right to avoid the policy, and does so, it is required to return the premium or the unearned portion thereof. The failure to do so, combined with the subsequent retention of the premium by the insurer, will be regarded as an affirmation of the contract and a waiver of the insurer's right to

---

[20] *C.M.I.A.*, subs. 85(4); but see subs. 85(5):

> 85(5) Where the subject-matter is insured 'lost or not lost' and has arrived at its destination safely before the contract is concluded, subsection (4) does not apply and the premium is not returnable unless, at the time the contract is concluded, the insurer knows of the safe arrival.

[21] *Ibid.*, subs. 85(6); but see subs. 85(7) in respect of gaming or wagering.
[22] *Ibid.*, subs. 85(10); see also Chapter 13, *Double Insurance*.
[23] *Ibid.*, subs. 85(11)(*a*).
[24] *Ibid.*, subs. (11)(*b*).
[25] *Ibid.*, subs. 85(8); see also Chapter 14, *Underinsurance and Overinsurance*.

treat the policy as void. For this reason, an insurer exercising its right to avoid the policy should do so promptly and unequivocally upon becoming aware of the circumstances and should tender return of the premium.[26]

16.7   CANCELLATION FOR NON-PAYMENT OF PREMIUM

Where the policy provides for cancellation for non-payment of premiums, the insurer cannot avoid liability under the policy if (a) the insured's default did not occur until after the loss;[27] (b) the insured has provided the insurer with a guarantee for the payment of the premium;[28] or (c) the insured has promised to pay the premium and this promise has been expressly or impliedly accepted by the insurer.[29]

16.8   HELD COVERED CLAUSES

Many marine insurance policy forms, both cargo and hull, contain "held covered clauses", permitting a breach of warranty but calling for the payment of an additional premium to compensate the underwriter for the increased risk.[30] "Held covered" clauses provide a protection for both the insurer and the insured. The insured is protected against events occurring during the voyage due to circumstances beyond its control and the insurer is protected by obtaining an additional premium to cover the enhanced risk. In the case of hull and machinery insurance, for example, the Institute Time Clauses — Hulls (1/11/95) contain a "Breach of Warranty" clause as follows:

> Breach of Warranty:
>
> Held covered in case of any breach of warranty as to cargo, trade, locality, towage, salvage services or date of sailing, provided notice be given to the Underwriters immediately after receipt of advices and any amended terms of cover and any additional premium required by them be agreed.

The Canadian Hulls (Pacific) Clauses (Sept. 1/91) provide:

> 6. The vessel is covered in case of any breach of warranty as to cargo, employment, towage, salvage services or date of sailing, provided notice be given to the Underwriters immediately after receipt of advices and any amended terms of cover and any additional premium required by them be agreed.[31]

---

[26] For a more detailed discussion of this subject, see Chapter 4, *Good Faith: Misrepresentation and Non-Disclosure*. The insurer is entitled to a reasonable amount of time to investigate the facts.

[27] See *Meagher v. Home Insurance Co.* (1860), 10 U.C.C.P. 313 (C.A.).

[28] *Anchor Marine Insurance Co. v. Corbett* (1882), 9 S.C.R. 73, aff'g. (1881), 14 N.S.R. 375 (C.A.) in which the guarantee of payment of a premium was held to be equivalent to the payment of the premium.

[29] *Osborne v. R.*, [1984] I.L.R. ¶1-1724 (F.C.T.D.).

[30] See Chapter 8, *Warranties*.

[31] Appendix E, lines 76-80. See also C.B.M.U. Great Lakes Hull Clauses (Sept. 1, 1971), Appendix G, at lines 95-97:

16.9 MARINE PREMIUMS — INSURANCE PRACTICE

Industry practice in Canada with regard to the issuing of policies and the payment of premiums often departs from what a strict reading of the *C.M.I.A.* would indicate. This occurs for two reasons. First, the industry is small and there are few brokerage firms specializing exclusively in marine insurance. Brokers have tended to be influenced by the business practices of the much larger fields of property and casualty insurance. In addition, the accounting systems developed for the payment of premiums to underwriters and the collection of return premiums have tended to ignore the subtle differences between marine and non-marine insurance legislation. At the same time, multi-line insurers in Canada have welcomed this efficient way of dealing with the funds that pass back and forth between themselves and the brokers. Insurers also grant premium payment terms to the brokers of up to 60 days from the end of the month in which the inception date of any policy falls before they expect payment.

A second reason for the divergence between the law and marine practice in Canada is that marine insurers and brokers in Canada tend not to deal with international business, as in the case of a large insurance centre such as London. The industry is intensely competitive, with brokers and insurers striving to retain their clients on a long-term basis. The emphasis is very much on service. Thus, although section 48 of the *C.M.I.A.* provides that the insurer need not issue the policy until the premium has been paid, the usual practice is that policies are issued very soon after the coverage has been bound, and often before the premium has been paid. Where a broker is unfamiliar with the payment habits of a new insured, it might initially present the client with a binder or cover note and delay the issuance of the policy until payment has been received.

Underwriters and brokers have, however, taken certain measures to protect themselves against default by the insured. Open cargo policies typically contain a cancellation notice clause enabling an insurer who has not received the premium to give notice of cancellation to a delinquent insured. In some policies, this cancellation notice provision is extended to the broker of record who has not been paid a premium. The notice of cancellation is usually accompanied by a demand for payment of the premium earned up to the cancellation date.

A difficult problem occasionally arises for a broker who places a hull and machinery policy for a client but fails to collect the premium immediately, and the broker's accounting department pays the insurers as a matter of course. Most hull and machinery policies are non-cancellable and will run their full term (usually one year) if the premium has been paid to the insurer. This can put the broker in a difficult position if the insured fails to remit the premium. To prevent this situation, brokers often insert a clause in the hull policy (which, in Canada, they, themselves invariably, issue) known as a Broker's Cancellation Clause, such as the following:

The Vessel is held covered in case of any breach of conditions as to towage or salvage activities, provided (a) notice is given to the Underwriters immediately following receipt of knowledge thereof by the Assured, and (b) any amended terms of cover and any additional premium required by the Underwriters are agreed to by the Assured.

It is hereby agreed between the underwriters hereon and the insured that in the event of the insured failing to pay to [broker] the premium including any install-ment thereof on the due date(s) this policy may forthwith be cancelled by [broker] giving to underwriters notice in writing. The underwriters will thereupon tender ten days' notice of cancellation to the insured and following the expiry of this no-tice period they will return to [broker] pro rata return premium following the ef-fective date of such cancellation.

As a last resort, the broker may be obliged to take legal action against its customer for recovery of the unpaid premium, in which event the right *in rem* against the vessel may prove to be a particularly useful remedy.[32]

---

[32] *Fairway Life & Marine Insurance Ltd. v. "Susan Darlene" (The)*, [1987] 2 F.C. 547, 21 C.C.L.I.
    83 (T.D.).

Chapter 17

Reinsurance

17.1 INTRODUCTION

From earliest times, marine insurance has been a form of risk-spreading, with the risk undertaken by the owner of the ship or cargo being shared with the insurer. Insurers themselves have traditionally spread the risk by sharing it amongst a number of underwriters. Reinsurance is another form of risk-sharing: having accepted a part of the risk, an insurer commonly reinsures all or some of it with other insurers. This keeps the insurer's liabilities at a level consistent with its assets and reduces its exposure to catastrophic losses. Reinsurance also provides an insurer with additional "capacity" — the ability to take on more risks and more substantial risks. While reinsurance is a common practice, there have been few Canadian cases on the subject.[1]

Section 14 of the Canadian *Marine Insurance Act* ("C.M.I.A.")[2] confirms the right of an insurer to reinsure the risk:

> 14. The insurer under a contract has an insurable interest in the risk insured and may reinsure in respect of it, but, unless the marine policy provides otherwise, the original insured has no right or interest in the reinsurance.

The section provides that the underlying insured has no rights against the reinsurer. If the original insurer denies the claim, or becomes insolvent[3] and unable to pay the claim, the insured has no right of action against the reinsurer.[4]

---

[1] See, for example: *Western Assurance Co. v. Baden Marine Assurance Co.* (1902), 22 Que. S.C. 374; *Provincial Insurance Co. v. Aetna Insurance Co.* (1858), 16 U.C.Q.B. 135, concerning the limitation of time for suit under a reinsurance contract; *Canadian International Marine Underwriters Ltd. v. Symons General Insurance*, [1986] I.L.R. ¶1-2042, aff'd. Ont. C.A., March 11, 1998, unrept'd., for a discussion of reinsurance practice and terminology; *Canada Fire & Marine Insurance Co. v. Western Insurance Co.* (1879), 26 Gr. 264, aff'd. (1880), 5 O.A.R. 244 (C.A.): the application and acceptance of the reinsurance risk were sufficient to create a binding contract notwithstanding that a policy had not been issued.

[2] S.C. 1993, c. 22.

[3] See, however, *Charter Reinsurance Co. Ltd. v. Fagan*, [1997] A.C. 313, [1996] 2 Ll. Rep. 113 (H.L.), where it was held that in the case of an insolvent reinsured, it was not necessary to establish that the reinsured had paid the underlying claim before being able to collect from its reinsurers. The House of Lords appeared to be influenced by the consideration that to hold otherwise would result in prejudice to the underlying insured.

[4] See *Kungl v. Great Lakes Reinsurance Co.*, [1969] S.C.R. 342, aff'g. [1967] B.R. 717 (Que. C.A.).

The relationship between insurer (referred to as the "cedant", "ceding company" or "reinsured") and reinsurer is one of insured and insurer. All the provisions of the *C.M.I.A.* applicable to marine insurance contracts are applicable to the reinsurance contract. Thus, non-disclosure or misrepresentation by the cedant or the reinsurance broker allows the reinsurer to avoid the contract. The principle of indemnity also applies to reinsurance contracts. The cedant is not entitled to recover more from its reinsurers than it has actually paid out on the claim or claims.

Reinsurance can be obtained on an *ad hoc* basis or through a contract by which the original insurer agrees to reinsure particular types of risks, or part of those risks, with another insurer. "Facultative reinsurance" offers the insurer the opportunity to reinsure particular risks on a case-by-case basis. The insurer has the option, but not the obligation, to submit a particular risk for reinsurance and the reinsurer has the right, but not the obligation, to accept that particular risk. "Treaty reinsurance", on the other hand, is an agreement by a reinsurer to reinsure part or all of a class of business underwritten by the ceding company. All business falling within the defined class will be automatically reinsured, subject to the terms of the reinsurance contract. The portion of each loss retained by the ceding company is referred to as its "retention" and may be a specific amount or a percentage.

The reinsurer itself frequently reinsures risks which it has already reinsured. This process is referred to as "retrocession" and the reinsurer accepting the reinsured risk is referred to as the "retrocessionaire". There are standard forms of reinsurance contracts in common use, as well as "tailor-made" forms for specific types of business.

Is the reinsurer entitled to raise as a defence to a claim by the reinsured the fact that the claim does not fall within the terms of the underlying insurance? Can the reinsurer contend that the reinsured should not have paid the claim? In *Western Assurance Co. of Toronto v. Poole*, the court stated:

> The reinsurer, when called upon to perform his promise, is entitled to require the reassured first to shew that a loss of the kind reinsured has in fact happened; and secondly, that the reassured has taken all proper and businesslike steps to have the amount of it fairly and carefully ascertained. That is all. He must then pay... He has promised 'to pay as may be paid thereon.' Such is in my opinion the meaning and effect of these reinsurance policies...[5]

While earlier cases suggested that the reinsurer was entitled to insist on strict proof of the loss and of the liability of the reinsured,[6] modern reinsurance contracts contain "follow the settlements" clauses obliging reinsurers to follow settlements made by the reinsured.[7] A settlement can only be challenged if the

---

[5]   [1903] 1 K.B. 376 at 386.

[6]   *Firemen's Fund Insurance Co. v. Western Australian Insurance Co.* (1927), 28 Ll. L. Rep. 243, 33 Com. Cas. 36.

[7]   For example: "...the reinsurer shall pay as may be paid thereon and shall follow the settlements of the reassured subject always to the limits, terms and conditions of the contract", or "The reassured shall have full discretion in the settlement or compromise or investigation of claims

claim did not legally fall within the terms of the underlying insurance contract, or within the reinsurance contract.[8]

---

and the reinsurer agrees to pay to the reassured its proportional share of all settlements, compromises ...including *ex gratia* payments made by the reassured..."

[8] *Insurance Co. of Africa v. Scor (U.K.) Reinsurance Co.*, [1985] 1 Ll. Rep. 312 (C.A.); *Hill v. Mercantile and General Reinsurance Co. plc*; *Berry v. Same*, [1996] Ll.L.R. 341.

PART II

PARTICULAR TYPES OF MARINE INSURANCE

Chapter 18

Cargo Insurance

18.1 INTRODUCTION

While an individual shipper of goods may be prepared to run the risk of loss or damage to the goods in transit, most would prefer to obtain insurance, if it can be done at a reasonable cost. Without insurance, the shipper faces the risk of serious personal loss, often with limited recourse against the parties responsible.[1] The seller also wants to ensure that the buyer will not be able to reject the goods if they arrive damaged. Buyers are not usually prepared to pay for goods (and their banks are not prepared to lend them money to do so) unless loss of or damage to the goods during transportation is covered by insurance. Marine insurance plays a vital role by ensuring that the buyer will be compensated if the goods are lost or damaged and that the seller will be paid for the goods regardless.

Marine cargo insurance covers goods and commodities in transit. While it originally applied to cargo on marine voyages, it can also cover inland (rail or road) or aviation transit incidental to a marine voyage.[2] In practice, marine policies often insure aviation cargo shipments unconnected with maritime voyages.[3]

Most Canadian cargo insurance is underwritten by branch offices of American, British or continental companies and by Managing General Agents ("M.G.A.s"). In the case of substantial risks, it is sometimes necessary for a broker to place a subscription policy with a group of insurers. Some Canadian cargo business has traditionally been placed in London (with Lloyds and/or insurance companies) and foreign markets, but this has become less common

---

[1]   Contracts for the carriage of goods by sea, air, road or rail, frequently contain limitations of the carrier's liability, often depending on the weight of the goods shipped. Similar limitations are contained in domestic legislation, such as the Ontario *Truck Transportation Act*, R.S.O. 1990, c. T.22, as amended; the Canadian *Marine Liability Act*, S.C. 2001, c. 6, Part 5, "Liability for Carriage of Goods by Water" (which replaced the *Carriage of Goods by Water Act*, S.C. 1993, c. 21), incorporating the *Hague-Visby Rules*; and the *Carriage by Air Act*, R.S.C. 1985, c. C-26, incorporating the *Warsaw Convention*.

[2]   See the Canadian *Marine Insurance Act* ("*C.M.I.A.*"), S.C. 1993, c. 22, subs. 6(1)(*a*).

[3]   See *Model Furs Ltd. v. H. Lapalme Transport Ltée.* (1995) D.R.S. 95-20092 (Que. C.A.) where the Quebec Court of Appeal held that the use of a marine insurance policy form in the insurance of an air cargo shipment did not necessarily make the law of marine insurance applicable if the risk insured was not in fact a marine one.

due to the increased capacity, flexibility and competitiveness of Canadian insurers.

18.2 POLICY FORMS

For many years, it was common to insure both cargo and hull risks under the Lloyd's "S.G." form.[4] Over time, special clauses were developed for different types of cargo risks, and the Institute of London Underwriters eventually introduced the "Institute Cargo Clauses", a set of standardized clauses dealing with different types of insurance. The original clauses were known as the Institute Cargo Clauses (F.P.A.) ("free of particular average") and (W.A.) ("with average"). In 1963, the Institute Cargo Clauses "All Risks" (1/1/63) were introduced. As the name implies, these latter clauses provided broader cargo insurance coverage on "all risks" terms. In some instances, the Institute Clauses were simply attached to the "S.G." form, while in other cases, they were incorporated into an open policy. A move for reform, partly driven by a desire for simpler policy language, led in 1982 to the adoption in London of a new overriding policy form, known as the MAR Form[5] as well as three sets of cargo clauses for use with the form. The clauses are known as the Institute Cargo Clauses (A), (B) and (C), (1/1/82), (referred to in this chapter as "I.C.C. (1/1/82)") with (A) being the widest form of cover (comparable to all risks) and (C) being the most restrictive. Copies of these clauses are reproduced in the Appendices B, C and D.

18.3 OPEN POLICIES

While marine insurance is occasionally provided on a shipment-by-shipment basis under a "single shipment" policy, an importer or exporter of goods, with frequent shipments from or to foreign buyers, may find it more convenient to obtain an "open policy" of cargo insurance covering all shipments received by the importer or made by the exporter falling within the terms of the insurance.[6] An insured selling to customers on "C.I.F." ("cost insurance freight") terms must obtain insurance to comply with the terms of sale. As evidence of the insurance, the seller will provide the buyer with a "certificate" of insurance, on the insurer's form, which attests to the fact that the goods have been insured and identifies the conditions of the insurance and the open policy number. The open policy facilitates these arrangements. The insured files a monthly or quarterly "declaration" with the insurer, listing all shipments made under the policy; provides the insurer with copies of the certificates, where applicable; and pays a

---

[4]   "Ship and Goods", see Chapter 2, *The Marine Insurance Contract*, Section 2.10, "Marine Insurance Forms".

[5]   In England, the MAR form became mandatory for cargo insurance in 1982 and for hull and machinery insurance in 1983. It is not in common use in Canada.

[6]   For the difference between an open policy and a floating policy, see Chapter 2, *The Marine Insurance Contract*. Floating policies are not used in modern Canadian marine insurance practice.

premium based on the value of the shipments. When the policy is issued, the insured will be provided with insurance certificates, which it can complete with respect to each insured shipment and forward to its buyer. The certificate identifies the goods sold, the method of shipment, the insured value and the insuring conditions. If the goods are lost or damaged in transit, the buyer will be entitled to make a claim on the insurance certificate. The certificate will identify the insurer's local claims agent for the presentation of claims, so that the consignee knows who to contact in the event of a claim.[7]

A typical open cargo policy should contain the following provisions:

- a description of the property insured — usually a defined commodity or range of products, manufactured or sold by the insured;
- the geographic limits — the countries between which the goods will be shipped;
- the limits of liability — the insurer will likely limit its exposure to a defined amount on any one vessel;
- a method of valuation — typically, the merchandise will be valued on a C.I.F. basis, with an uplift of 10 per cent to 30 per cent to cover loss of profits, inconvenience, cost of replacement and so on;
- the insuring conditions — the terms and conditions on which the goods will be insured, which usually includes insurance against war and strikes risks;[8]
- the rates at which the cargo will be insured and the premium calculated;
- a classification clause;[9] and
- a "held covered" clause.[10]

In Canada, it is common for open policies to be issued to freight forwarders who arrange for transportation on behalf of shippers and receivers and who often provide marine insurance as part of their service to customers.[11] The customer pays a marine insurance charge as part of the forwarder's fee and the forwarder undertakes to make the insurance arrangements. This is often done by means of an open policy issued to the forwarder, pursuant to which the forwarder is permitted to declare shipments made on behalf of its customers.

An open policy is an example of "good faith" at work in the modern marine insurance market. The insurer relies on the integrity of the insured to declare and pay a premium on all shipments coming within the terms of the policy, even though declarations are often filed with the insurer after the shipments have arrived at which time the insured knows whether or not the goods have arrived safely.

---

[7] An importer buying on F.O.B. ("free on board") or C. & F. ("cost and freight") terms that do not require the buyer to provide transportation insurance may wish to obtain an open policy as a simple and cost-effective way of procuring insurance, on a repetitive basis, for its imports.

[8] See Chapter 21, *Insurance of Particular Risks*, Section 21.12, "War & Strikes Insurance".

[9] See below, Section 18.4.6.2.

[10] See Chapter 8, *Warranties*.

[11] See Chapter 21, *Insurance of Particular Risks*.

18.4   CARGO INSURANCE FORMS

18.4.1   The Pre-1983 Forms

Prior to 1983, there were three standard forms of cargo insurance issued by the Institute of London Underwriters in general use in Canada and the United Kingdom. The broadest form was the Institute Cargo Clauses All Risks (1/1/63). All risks cargo insurance covers direct physical loss or damage to the goods caused by fortuitous accidents during transportation, subject to specific exclusions. It does not cover consequential damages, nor does it cover damage caused by delay or by the "inherent vice" or condition of the goods themselves. It does not cover loss due to war, strikes, riots and civil commotions, although separate coverage for these risks is usually procured.[12] While the "All Risks" Clauses were withdrawn by the I.L.U. when the I.C.C. (1/1/82) (A) clauses were issued, they remain in use in some Canadian policies.

The second form of cargo insurance was known as "with average" (W.A.), and was designed to cover certain types of losses, subject to a requirement that the loss exceed a specified percentage of the insured value, typically 3 per cent, referred to as a "franchise". The franchise is different from a deductible, which is borne by the insured regardless of the size of the loss. When the amount of the franchise is exceeded, the full amount of the loss falls on the insurer. The insurer is not liable for small losses falling below the franchise but is fully liable for losses where the franchise is exceeded.

The third form of cargo insurance commonly available prior to 1982 was on "Free of Particular Average" or "F.P.A." terms. Under this form, "particular average" losses (such as partial damage or partial losses) were excluded from the cover, but total losses as well as salvage and general average charges were covered.

18.4.2   The I.C.C. (1/1/82) (A), (B) and (C)

The I.C.C. (1/1/82) were introduced to provide simple, "plain language" cargo insurance. The basic structure of the I.C.C. (1/1/82) (A), (B) and (C) is similar, but they offer markedly different coverages. The broadest coverage is provided by the (A) clauses, which essentially provide "all risks" insurance, with some exclusions discussed below. The (B) clauses offer "named perils" coverage against a narrower range of risks and the "C" clauses offer similar coverage against still narrower risks. There are exclusions common to all three sets of clauses and some additional exclusions in the (B) and (C) clauses which are not found in the (A) clauses.[13]

---

12   See below, Section 18.4.6.1.

13   Exclusion 4.7: "deliberate damage to or deliberate destruction of the subject-matter insured or any part thereof by the wrongful act of any person or persons." Exclusion 6.2: "capture seizure arrest restraint or detainment..." without excepting piracy, which is excepted in the (A) clauses.

18.4.2.1 THE (A) CLAUSES

The main risks covered by the "A" clauses[14] are:

- all risks of loss or damage to the insured property with certain specific exclusions set out below;
- general average[15] and salvage charges in relation to the cargo;
- any liability of the insured under a "both to blame collision" clause in the contract of affreightment.[16]

The principle exclusions under the "A" clauses (and also under the "B" and "C" clauses), are:

- loss caused by the wilful misconduct of the insured;
- ordinary wear and tear;
- loss attributable to insufficiency of packing or preparation of the subject-matter insured;
- loss damage or expense caused by the inherent vice of the insured property;
- damage proximately caused by delay;
- loss due to the financial default of the owners or operators of the vessel;
- loss from any weapon of war employing atomic fission;
- loss caused by war and strike risks; and
- loss arising from unseaworthiness of the vessel or craft where the insured or their servants are privy to the unseaworthiness.

Some of these exclusions are discussed below as well as in Chapter 7, *Perils Insured*.

18.4.2.2 THE (B) CLAUSES

The I.C.C. (1/1/82) (B) and (C) clauses provide "named perils" cover, which is considerably more restrictive than the "all risks" cover under the (A) clauses.

---

[14] For a detailed discussion of the risks insured under the (A), (B) and (C) clauses, see *Marine Insurance: The Silent Export*, 2nd ed. (Canadian Board of Marine Underwriters, 1994).

[15] Institute Cargo Clauses (A), cl. 2:

> This insurance covers general average and salvage charges, adjusted or determined according to the contract of affreightment and/or the governing law and practice, incurred to avoid or in connection with the avoidance of loss from any cause except those excluded in Clauses 4, 5, 6 and 7 or elsewhere in this insurance.

See Chapter 22, *General Average*.

[16] Institute Cargo Clauses (A), cl. 3:

> This insurance is extended to indemnify the Assured against such proportion of liability under the contract of affreightment 'Both to Blame Collision' Clause as is in respect of a loss recoverable hereunder. In the event of any claim by shipowners under the said Clause the Assured agree to notify the Underwriters who shall have the right, at their own cost and expense, to defend the Assured against such claim.

The difference is significant and generally reflects an insurer's assessment of the degree of risk attached to the goods or the voyage as well as the price which the insured is prepared to pay for the coverage. Underwriters are generally not prepared to insure certain commodities on an all risks basis (used machinery is a common example) because it is often difficult to separate transit damage from pre-shipment damage. In other cases, the insured may not require "all risks" cover because the nature of the cargo is such that particular average losses are unlikely (for example, bulk shipments of ore).

In addition to covering general average and salvage charges and the insured's liability under a "both to blame collision" clause, the coverage provided by the (B) clauses is against:

1.1	loss of or damage to the subject-matter insured reasonably attributable to:
1.1.1	fire or explosion;
1.1.2	vessel or craft being stranded[17] grounded sunk[18] or capsized;
1.1.3	overturning or derailment of land conveyance;
1.1.4	collision or contact of vessel craft or conveyance with any external object other than water;
1.1.5	discharge of cargo at a port of distress;
1.1.6	earthquake volcanic eruption or lightning;

as well as:

1.2	loss of or damage to the subject-matter insured caused by:
1.2.1	general average sacrifice;
1.2.2	jettison or washing overboard;
1.2.3	entry of sea lake or river water into vessel craft hold conveyance container liftvan or place of storage;[19]
1.3	total loss of any package lost overboard or dropped whilst loading on to, or unloading from, vessel or craft.

Both the (B) clauses and the (C) clauses have more extensive exclusions than the (A) clauses, including deliberate damage.[20]

18.4.2.3   THE (C) CLAUSES

Like the (B) clauses, the (C) clauses provide coverage against major casualties, such as fire, stranding, sinking, capsizing and collision. They do not include the coverage afforded in clause 1.1.6 (earthquake or volcano), 1.2.2 ("jettison" is

---

[17] With reference to the meaning of the word "stranding", see *Rudolf v. British and Foreign Marine Insurance Co.* (1898), 30 N.S.R. 380, aff'd. without written reasons (1898) 28 S.C.R. 607, where it was taken to mean the vessel running aground due to an accidental or extraneous cause.

[18] As to the meaning of "sinking", see *John C. Jackson Ltd. v. Sun Insurance Office Ltd.*, [1962] S.C.R. 412 at 416, aff'g. (1961), 25 D.L.R. (2d) 604, 33 W.W.R. 420 (B.C.C.A.).

[19] For some reason of drafting style, the policy form itself does not include commas in this clause or in other clauses.

[20] Exclusion 4.7: "deliberate damage to or deliberate destruction of the subject-matter insured or any part thereof by the wrongful act of any person or persons".

covered, but "washing overboard" is not), 1.2.3 (entry of sea lake or river water) or 1.3 ("total loss of any package lost overboard or dropped whilst loading on to, or unloading from, vessel or craft").

18.4.3 Both to Blame Collision Clause

All three of the I.C.C. (1/1/82) clauses cover the insured's liability under a "both to blame collision" clause in a contract of affreightment in respect of a loss recoverable under the policy. This liability arises due to a difference between United States law on the one hand, and the law of Canada and the United Kingdom on the other hand, concerning liability of a shipowner for damage to cargo caused by a collision between the carrying ship and another ship. Under Canadian law (as in English law), where two ships are to blame for a collision which results in damage to the cargo, the cargo owner is entitled to recover from each of the ships in proportion to their fault for the collision. Thus, if the carrying ship is 25 per cent to blame for the accident and the other ship is 75 per cent to blame, the cargo owner is, in theory, entitled to recover 25 per cent of its loss from the carrying ship and 75 per cent from the other ship. The words "in theory", refer to the fact that under Canadian carriage of goods by water law, the owner and operator of the carrying vessel may have a defence to the cargo owner's claim, based on "error of navigation".[21] That being the case, the cargo owner's recovery, in Canada, is reduced to the percentage of damages (in this example, 75 per cent) that it can recover from the owner of the non-carrying ship. Where the goods are insured, this normally means that the cargo insurer pays out 100 per cent of the claim to its insured and then pursues the "non-carrying" ship in subrogation and, in the best of circumstances, recovers from that ship according to its degree of fault. Under United States law, however, the cargo owner has the right to sue either the carrying ship or the non-carrying ship for 100 per cent of its damages, regardless of how much at fault that ship may have been. The ship paying damages is entitled to recover a proportion of those damages (in accordance with the degree of fault) from the other ship. If the cargo owner were to sue the carrying ship in the United States it would be met with the "error in navigation" defence. However, if it sued the non-carrying ship, there is no such defence and the cargo owner would be entitled to recover 100 per cent of its loss from the non-carrying ship. That ship will, in turn, sue the carrying ship for its proportion of the damages, thereby indirectly depriving the carrying ship of its "error in navigation" defence. To avoid this possibility, carriers' bills of lading frequently contain the so-called "both to blame collision" clause whereby the cargo owner agrees to indemnify the shipowner against the carrying ship's of collision-related cargo damages.[22] The "both to blame

---

[21] Canadian *Marine Liability Act*, S.C. 2001, c. 6, Part 5, "Liability for Carriage of Goods by Water": The shipowner is not liable if it can establish that it exercised "due diligence" prior to and at the commencement of the voyage to make the ship seaworthy and that (among other defences) the loss or damage to cargo occurred as a result of an error in the "navigation or management" of the vessel.

[22] The following example of the clause comes from L. J. Buglass, *Marine Insurance and General Average in the United States*, 3rd ed. (Centreville, MD: Cornell Maritime Press, 1991) at p. 367:

collision" clause in a marine cargo policy is a promise by the cargo underwriters to indemnify their insured in the event a claim of this nature is made by the carrying ship. It protects the insured from the possibility that it will recover 100 per cent of the loss from its cargo insurer, but could lose a portion of that in the event the insurer pursues subrogation against the non-carrying vessel, which in turn pursues the carrying vessel for its proportionate share of the loss. In that event, the insured could find itself being sued by the carrying vessel for that vessel's "share" of the claim.

18.4.4 General Average Clause

The I.C.C. (1/1/82) clauses all contain the following clause 2:

> This insurance covers general average and salvage charges, adjusted or determined according to the contract of affreightment and/or the governing law and practice, incurred to avoid or in connection with the avoidance of loss from any cause except those excluded in Clauses 4, 5, 6 and 7 or elsewhere in this insurance.

The concluding words of this clause incorporate the effect of subsection 65(6) of the Canadian *Marine Insurance Act* (*"C.M.I.A."*) which states that, unless the policy otherwise provides "an insurer is not liable for a general average loss or a general average contribution, unless the loss was incurred for the purpose of averting, or in connection with the avoidance of, a peril insured against".

18.4.5 Exclusions Under the ICC (1/1/82) (A), (B) and (C) Clauses

There are some exclusions which are common to the I.C.C. (1/1/82) (A), (B) and (C) clauses. Several of these exclusions are also excluded by the *C.M.I.A.* and are discussed in Chapter 7, *Perils Insured*.

18.4.5.1 WILFUL MISCONDUCT

The clause 4.1 exclusion of "loss damage or expense attributable to wilful misconduct of the Assured" reflects the legal position, codified by the *C.M.I.A.*,[23] that insurers are not liable for such losses.

If the ship comes in collision with another ship as a result of the negligence of the other ship and any act, neglect or default of the master, mariner, pilot or the servants of the carrier in the navigation or in the management of the ship, the owners of the goods carried hereunder will indemnify the carrier against all loss or liability to the other or non-carrying ship or her owners insofar as such loss or liability represents loss of, or damage to, or any claim whatsoever of the owners of said goods, paid or payable by the other or non-carrying ship or her owners to the owners of said goods and set-off recouped or recovered by the other or non-carrying ship or her owners as part of their claim against, the carrying ship or carrier. The foregoing provisions shall also apply where the owners, operators or those in charge of any ship or ships or objects other than, or in addition to, the colliding ships or objects are at fault in respect of a collision or contact.

[23] Subsection 53(2).

18.4.5.2 ORDINARY WEAR AND TEAR

There is an exclusion in clause 4.2 for: "ordinary leakage, ordinary loss in weight or volume, or ordinary wear and tear of the subject-matter insured." The insurer does not insure losses that are inevitable and do not involve an element of fortuity. Although packaging methods have improved since the days when wine was shipped in wooden casks and flour in jute bags, certain cargos are subject to an ordinary and expected loss in weight or volume and the underwriter does not agree to insure these losses. Nor does the underwriter insure against the ordinary deterioration of the insured property through wear and tear.[24]

18.4.5.3 UNSUITABILITY OF PACKING

The I.C.C. (1/1/82) contain an exclusion for:

> 4.3 loss, damage or expense caused by insufficiency or unsuitability of packing or preparation of the subject-matter insured (for the purpose of this Clause 4.3 'packing' shall be deemed to include stowage in a container or liftvan but only when such stowage is carried out prior to attachment of this insurance or by the Assured or their servants.)

Prior to the adoption of the I.C.C. (1/1/82), it was generally accepted that poor packing was a form of "inherent vice" because it meant that the goods were unfit to withstand the ordinary rigours of the contemplated voyage, and losses attributable to bad packing were not recoverable because they lacked the necessity of fortuity.[25] In the case of goods packed in a container supplied by the shipping company, the question sometimes arose as to whether damage caused from "within" the container as a result of bad packing or bad stowage in the container itself, rather than by some external fortuitous accident, was recoverable. The I.C.C. (1/1/82) have resolved this issue by providing that if the packing in the container is carried out after the commencement of transit, by someone other than the insured or its servants,[26] the exclusion will not apply and the poor packing will be regarded as a transit fortuity. If the insured carried out the stowage in the container, or if the stowage in the container was done prior to the commencement of transit, damage attributable to poor stowage would not be recoverable.[27]

---

[24] See Chapter 7, *Perils Insured*.

[25] See *Gee and Garnham Ltd. v. Whittall*, [1955] 2 Ll. R. 562 (Q.B.D.); *F.W. Berk & Co. Ltd. v. Style*, [1955] 2 Ll. Rep. 382 (Q.B.D.), discussed in Chapter 7, *Perils Insured*.

[26] The term "servants" is narrower than "agents" and arguably refers only to the insured's immediate employees and not to third party agents engaged to pack or "stuff" the goods into the container.

[27] This subject is discussed in Chapter 7, *Perils Insured*, Section 7.3.5, "Inherent Vice or Nature of the Subject-Matter Insured". See in particular: *Rainbow Technicoloured Wood Veneer Ltd. v. Guardian Insurance Co. of Canada* (2000), 184 F.T.R. 304, aff'd. (2002), 288 N.R. 17, [2002] I.L.R. ¶1-4083 (F.C.A.).

18.4.5.4　Inherent Vice

The I.C.C. (1/1/82) contain an exclusion for:

> 4.4 loss, damage or expense caused by inherent vice or nature of the subject-matter insured.

This same provision, which reflects subsection 53(2)(*b*) of the *C.M.I.A.*, is found in the Institute Cargo Clauses (All Risks) 1/1/63.

18.4.5.5　Delay

There is an exclusion for:

> 4.5 loss damage or expense proximately caused by delay, even though the delay be caused by a risk insured against.[28]

Delay and its consequences are simply beyond the scope of a marine insurance policy, even though the delay may result in physical damage to the goods.[29]

18.4.5.6　Insolvency or Financial Default

The clauses exclude:

> 4.6 loss damage or expense arising from insolvency or financial default of the owners managers charterers or operators of the vessel.

18.4.5.7　Atomic Weapons

There is an exclusion for:

> 4.8 loss damage or expense arising from the use of any weapon of war employing atomic or nuclear fission and/or fusion or other like reaction or radioactive force or matter.

18.4.5.8　Unseaworthiness with the Privity of the Insured

The I.C.C. (1/1/82) clauses contain the following exclusion:

> 5.1　In no case shall this insurance cover loss damage or expense arising from
>
> > unseaworthiness of vessel or craft,
> > unfitness of vessel craft conveyance container or liftvan for the safe carriage of the subject-matter insured,
>
> where the Assured or their servants are privy to such unseaworthiness or unfitness, at the time the subject-matter insured is loaded therein.

---

[28]　See also *C.M.I.A.*, subsection 53(2)(*a*).

[29]　See Chapter 7, *Perils Insured*, Section 7.3.2, "Loss Caused by Delay".

5.2 The underwriters waive any breach of the implied warranties of seaworthiness of the ship and fitness of the ship to carry the subject-matter insured to destination, unless the Assured or their servants are privy to such unseaworthiness or unfitness.

It would be an unusual situation, in modern day cargo insurance, that the insured would be privy to any unseaworthiness of the vessel.

18.4.6 Other Clauses

18.4.6.1 WAR AND STRIKES

War and Strikes insurance is a specialized form of insurance covering the risk of loss of or damage to the property insured as a result of war and strikes. Most of the principal cargo, hull and liability clauses exclude war, strikes and incidental perils.[30] The I.C.C. (1/1/82) contain a "war exclusion clause" (clause 6) and a "strikes exclusion clause" (clause 7) excluding these risks, but it is common for the insured to obtain coverage for these excluded risks by purchasing additional cover under the Institute War Clauses (Cargo) (1/1/82).

18.4.6.2 CLASSIFICATION

Underwriters are vitally interested in ensuring that the cargos they insure are carried on suitable vessels — typically, vessels "in class" (regularly inspected by a recognized classification society) and not beyond a certain age. Open cargo policies typically contain a "classification clause" or incorporate the Institute Classification Clause 13/4/92. These clauses contain requirements with respect to the classification and age of vessels, but also provide that cargos carried on vessels which do not meet these requirements are "held covered subject to a premium and on conditions to be agreed".[31]

18.5 PARTICULAR ISSUES IN CARGO INSURANCE

18.5.1 Insurable Interest

We have seen in Chapter 5 that in order to recover under a policy of marine insurance, the insured must have an insurable interest in the goods at the time of the loss, although the insured need not have such an interest at the time the contract was made.[32] This is confirmed in the I.C.C. (1/1/82).[33] Due to the complexity of international trade, disputes occasionally arise as to whether a claimant has the requisite insurable interest. The issue seldom arises in the case of C.I.F. shipments, where the seller is obliged to take out insurance for the

---

[30] Referred to as an "F.C.& S." clause ("free of capture and seizure").

[31] See Chapter 8, *Warranties*, with respect to "held covered" clauses.

[32] *C.M.I.A.*, subs. 7(1); see Chapter 5, *Insurable Interest*.

[33] Each of the clauses contains a provision in clause 11.1 that "In order to recover under this insurance the Assured must have an insurable interest in the subject-matter insured at the time of the loss."

benefit of the buyer and assigns the certificate of insurance to the buyer as part of the sale documentation. The insurer contemplates that an assignment will take place, and that if the goods are lost or damaged during transit, a claim will be made by the purchaser under the policy. As the buyer has opened a letter of credit which must be honoured on presentation of the requisite commercial documents, the sale is completed regardless of the loss or damage to the cargo.

Problems can arise, however, where, for one reason or another, the buyer refuses to take delivery of the goods, and refuses to pay the seller, who then makes claim under the policy of insurance. If a "sale" has taken place, and the documents assigned to the buyer, with only the price remaining to be paid, it is arguable that the seller has no insurable interest and simply suffered an unin-sured commercial loss. The seller can avoid this difficulty by purchasing "seller's interest insurance", which is triggered by the buyer's refusal to pay for the goods. Similarly, where the sale is on F.O.B.[34] or C.F.R.[35] terms, with no responsibility on either party to procure insurance, who has an insurable interest and at what times? The usual rule in the case of F.O.B. and C.F.R. contracts is that the seller is responsible for the goods until they are loaded on board the vessel at the time of shipment, at which time the risk of loss passes to the buyer. If the goods are lost or damaged after title and risk have passed to the buyer, the seller has no insurable interest in the goods and no claim under a cargo policy unless it is a seller's interest policy.

18.5.2 Valuation

Open cargo policies invariably contain a "valuation clause" stipulating how cargo is to be valued for the purpose of the insurance. The insurer agrees to insure the cargo at some percentage (typically 10 per cent) over the importer's actual cost or invoice price to cover the loss of profits, inconvenience and replacement costs which the importer will incur if the goods are lost or damaged. In the absence of such a clause, the provisions of the *C.M.I.A.* will be applied to determine the insured value.[36]

18.5.3 Commencement and Duration of Transit

The I.C.C. (1/1/82) contain a provision known as the "transit clause" providing "warehouse to warehouse" coverage.[37] The goods are covered in the ordinary

---

[34]   Free on Board.

[35]   Cost and Freight, often referred to as "C. & F."

[36]   *C.M.I.A.*, subs. 19(1)(*c*): "… in the case of insurance on goods, the aggregate of the prime cost of the goods, the expenses of and incidental to shipping and the charges of insurance on those goods and expenses…" See Chapter 6, *Insurable Value.*

[37]   Clause 8:

      8.1   This insurance attaches from the time the goods leave the warehouse or place of storage at the place named herein for the commencement of the transit, contin-ues during the ordinary course of transit and terminates either

course of transit from the time they leave the seller's warehouse until delivery at the receiver's warehouse. Other provisions in the clauses protect the insured if the goods are shipped to a destination other than that named in the contract, if there is a deviation or variation of the voyage or if the voyage is terminated prematurely. In the latter case, the insured may be entitled to obtain coverage for the "new" voyage if prompt notice is given to the underwriters and an additional premium paid if necessary. The clause also deals with the consequences of delay during transportation or the termination of the contract of carriage at some point prior to the contemplated destination. Where the transit is terminated at a place other than the one named in the policy, the underwriters agree to reimburse the insured for the costs of temporary storage of the goods and forwarding them to destination.

The object of the transit clause (or, as it is sometimes known, the "warehouse to warehouse" clause) is to provide coverage for the goods throughout their transportation. The insurance does not take effect or "attach" until such time as transit has commenced and it terminates once transit has been completed. It sometimes happens that, for reasons of its own, the insured delays the commencement of the transit or postpones taking delivery of the goods. If a loss occurs during such delay, a dispute may arise as to whether or not the policy was in force at the time of the loss.[38] This will be a question of fact, to be determined by the language of the policy and the circumstances of the loss, keeping in mind that the insurer has agreed to insure transit risks and not risks to which the goods are exposed before the transit begins or after it has been completed.

18.5.4 Deck Cargo

Cargo carried on the deck of a vessel is exposed to greater risks than cargo carried below deck and cargo policies frequently contain restrictions on the coverage applicable to deck cargo. Such restrictions are generally removed in the case of goods shipped in containers, which may or may not be stowed on deck depending on circumstances outside the shipper's control.

8.1.1 on delivery to the Consignees' or other final warehouse or place of storage at the destination named herein,

8.1.2 on delivery to any other warehouse or place of storage, whether prior to or at the destination named herein, which the Assured elect to use either

8.1.2.1 for storage other than in the ordinary course of transit or

8.1.2.2 for allocation or distribution,

    or

8.1.3 On the expiry of 60 days after completion of discharge overside of the goods hereby insured from the oversea vessel at the final port of discharge,

    whichever shall first occur.

A predecessor to this clause was known as the "warehouse to warehouse" clause.

[38] See: *Savroche Enterprises Inc. v. Great Atlantic Insurance Co. of Delaware*, unreported (18 April 1995), Montreal Docket No. A-221-84 (F.C.A.); *Fiske v. Hartford Insurance Co. of Canada*, [1994] I.L.R. ¶1-3009 (Ont. Gen. Div.), aff'd. (July 17, 1995) Doc. C.A. C176-22 (Ont. C.A.); *Barer Engineering & Machinery Co. Ltd. v. Garfield Container Transport Inc.*, unreported (18 November 1998), (Que. S.C.), rev'd. (19 March 2002), Montreal (C.A.); *Crow's Transport Ltd. v. Phoenix Assurance Co. Ltd.*, [1965] 1 All E.R. 596; *Sadler Bros. Co. v. Meredith*, [1963] 2 Ll. Rep. 208.

18.5.5   Constructive Total Loss

The I.C.C. (1/1/82) provide:

> 13. No claim for Constructive Total Loss shall be recoverable hereunder unless the subject-matter insured is reasonably abandoned either on account of its actual total loss appearing to be unavoidable or because the cost of recovering, reconditioning and forwarding the subject-matter to the destination to which it is insured would exceed its value on arrival.

The subject of constructive total loss is discussed in Chapter 9, *Losses and Charges Recoverable.*

18.5.6   Benefit of Insurance

The I.C.C. (1/1/82) contain a provision, known as the "Not to Inure" clause:

> 15. This insurance shall not inure to the benefit of the carrier or other bailee.

The purpose of this clause is to negate provisions in some bills of lading purporting to give the transportation company (the "carrier or other bailee") the benefit of any insurance taken out by the owner of the cargo. Under the international carriage of goods by sea conventions known as the *Hague Rules* or the *Hague-Visby Rules*,[39] a benefit of insurance clause would be invalid, but this does not prevent other carriers, such as truckers, or bailees, such as warehousemen, from attempting to insert such clauses in their contracts.

18.5.7   Minimizing Losses

The I.C.C. (1/1/82) contain a "sue and labour clause" which is similar to the provisions of the *C.M.I.A.* and requires the insured to take reasonable measures to avert or minimize a loss and to protect rights against third parties. The underwriter agrees that in addition to any loss recoverable under the policy, it will "reimburse the Assured for any charges properly and reasonably incurred in pursuance of these duties". The duty of the insured to sue and labour is discussed in Chapter 11.

18.5.8   Avoidance of Delay

The I.C.C. (1/1/82) provide:

> 18. It is a condition of this insurance that the Assured shall act with reasonable despatch in all circumstances within their control.

18.5.9   Law and Practice

In clause 19, the I.C.C. (1/1/82) provide that "[t]his insurance is subject to English law and practice." The clause is invariably left in the form, even though

---

[39]   *Marine Liability Act*, Part 5.

the policy is issued in Canada. As a practical matter, Canadian law and practice are generally the same as in England.

18.6 INSURANCE OF PARTICULAR COMMODITIES AND TRADES

For almost as long as there has been cargo insurance there have been specialized insurance forms for particular types of commodities which are subject to unique risks. There are special clauses for air cargo, frozen foods, timber, logs, frozen meats, oils, seeds and fats, jute, rubber and coal, to mention a few.[40] Experienced cargo underwriters and brokers will know the particular characteristics of a wide range of commodities, and the risks to which they are exposed in transportation, and will negotiate the coverage, and the premium, accordingly.

18.7 REJECTION INSURANCE

Importers of foodstuffs may want to insure against the risk that apparently undamaged goods are rejected by the authorities of the importing country due to contamination or impurity, even though there is no "physical" damage to the goods. Since this risk is not covered by a standard cargo insurance policy, it will be necessary for the importer to purchase rejection insurance for this risk. Rejection coverage typically includes stringent conditions to ensure that the goods are properly prepared, packed and inspected at the country of origin before transportation.

18.8 INCREASED VALUE INSURANCE

All of the I.C.C. (1/1/82) clauses contain a provision dealing with increased value insurance. This may be obtained by a cargo owner (typically an owner of a commodity which is subject to significant price fluctuations) who purchases goods on C.I.F. terms and becomes entitled to an assignment of the insurance policy. The buyer may increase the insured value of the cargo to insure against anticipated profits on the sale of the goods by purchasing an additional policy, known as an "increased value" policy. The I.C.C. (1/1/82) provide that where this is done, the agreed value of the cargo is deemed to be increased to the sum of the values in the two policies and each insurer will contribute to a claim in proportion to the amount insured under its policy.[41]

---

[40] See, for example, the Institute Frozen Meat Clauses (A) (1/1/86), the Institute Jute Clauses (1/1/84), the Institute Natural Rubber Clauses (1/1/84) and the Institute Trade Federation Clauses (1/4/86).

[41] Clause 14.1:

> If any Increased Value insurance is effected by the Assured on the cargo insured herein the agreed value of the cargo shall be deemed to be increased to the total amount insured under this insurance and all Increased Value insurances covering the loss, and liability under this insurance shall be in such proportion as the sum insured herein bears to such total amount insured. In the event of claim the Assured shall provide the Underwriters with evidence of the amounts insured under all other insurances.

18.9　INSTITUTE THEFT, PILFERAGE AND NON-DELIVERY CLAUSE 1/12/82

As theft and pilferage are not covered by the (B) and (C) clauses, the market has provided a form of coverage for "theft or pilferage, or by non-delivery of an entire package" permitting the insured to "buy back" this exclusion.

18.10　LIABILITIES

With the very limited exceptions of general average contributions and the cargo owner's liability under a "both to blame collision" clause, marine cargo insurance does not insure the cargo owner's liabilities. It is property insurance, not liability insurance and the liability of the cargo owner for damage caused by the cargo is not insured. Thus, if the cargo is not sufficiently packed and breaks loose during transportation causing damage to other property, the cargo owner's liability to the owner of the other property is not insured under a standard cargo policy. Nor is the cargo owner's liability in the event a pollutant cargo escapes, causing damage to private property or to the environment.

18.11　SURVEYS

There is no provision in the I.C.C. (1/1/82) requiring that the insured appoint a surveyor to inspect the damaged goods or to investigate the loss, but this is typically provided in open policies or in insurance certificates issued under such policies.[42]

---

[42]　See Chapter 24, *The Marine Surveyor.*

Chapter 19

Hull and Machinery Insurance

19.1 INTRODUCTION

Hull and machinery insurance covers physical loss of or damage to the structure of the ship. While such policies commonly provide limited coverage for the shipowner's liability for collision, it is not full liability insurance and separate protection and indemnity (P. & I.) cover is invariably necessary.[1] Separate insurance is also required if coverage is desired for loss of earnings if the vessel is taken out of service due to an accident.

Voyage and time clauses were developed in the London insurance market for use with the S.G. (Ship and Goods) form. These clauses contained terminology that would be considered antiquated by modern standards, but they were used until 1983 when the I.L.U.'s (Institute of London Underwriters') "plain language" time and voyage clauses for hulls were introduced.[2] In 1995 these clauses were replaced with clauses that, in many respects, resembled the earlier ones but with some important revisions.[3] The Institute Time Clauses Hulls — Restricted Perils (1/11/95) were also introduced in 1995.

Most North American hull and machinery insurers did not follow London's lead to "plain language" clauses. The policy forms used in Canada to insure commercial hulls vary to some extent from one region to another, not only because of variations in the types of risks encountered, but also due to the individual preferences of insureds, brokers and underwriters. On the Canadian west coast, the preferred clauses are the Canadian Hulls (Pacific) Clauses (Sept. 1/91) (the "C.H.P." clauses which are reproduced in Appendix E). Brokers on the east coast seem to favour the Institute Time Clauses Hulls (1/11/95). Great Lakes fleets are generally insured under either the Canadian Board of Marine Underwriters Great Lakes Hull Clauses (Sept. 1, 1971) (the "C.B.M.U." clauses) or the American Institute Great Lakes Hull Clauses (9/3/78). Ocean-going and coastal vessels are often insured under the American Institute Hull Clauses (2/6/77). Where insurance for a single voyage is required, the clauses usually chosen are the Institute Voyage Clauses — Hulls (1/11/95).

---

[1]   See Chapter 20, *Protection and Indemnity Insurance*.

[2]   The Institute Time Clauses — Hulls (1/10/83) and the Institute Voyage Clauses — Hulls (1/10/83).

[3]   The Institute Time Clauses — Hulls (1/11/95) and the Institute Voyage Clauses — Hulls (1/11/95).

While these standard industry forms usually provide the basic terms of hull and machinery insurance, they are frequently supplemented in Canada by the addition of the broker's manuscript clauses which expand the scope of the standard form and tailor the coverage to the specific requirements of the insured.

This chapter will examine the principle features of hull and machinery insurance, beginning with time policies and with particular reference to the C.B.M.U. and C.H.P. clauses. At the end of this chapter there will be a brief discussion of voyage policies on hulls.

19.2   TIME POLICIES

19.2.1   The Insured

Every policy of insurance must identify the insured. The C.B.M.U. clauses contain a space for the insertion of the name of the insured. There is a provision at lines 4-5 that:

> If claim is made under this Policy by anyone other than the Owner of the Vessel, such person shall not be entitled to recover to a greater extent than would the Owner, had claim been made by the Owner as an Assured named in this Policy.

The form provides at line 6 for waiver of subrogation against "affiliated, subsidiary or interrelated companies of the Assured".[4] The intent is that underwriters should not be able to pay a loss to the insured and recoup their payment from a related company of the insured. However, exceptions exist in the case of:

(a) collision between the insured vessel and a vessel owned, demise chartered or controlled by affiliated companies; and

(b) loss, damage and expense in respect of which the affiliate is insured.

In the case of collision with a vessel in the same ownership, the C.B.M.U. clauses provide for the liability of the vessels to be determined by arbitration, to overcome the procedural problem that, in law, the insured would be unable to sue itself for the damage caused to its vessel by another vessel it owns.[5] The intent of the second exception is to recognize that there is no harm to the insured where the affiliate is insured against the claim in question.

The C.H.P. clauses do not contain a waiver of subrogation against affiliated and related corporations, although in most cases such a clause would be added by the broker's manuscript wording. The C.H.P. clauses contain a provision that in the event of a collision with a ship in related ownership, the insured's rights

---

[4]   The form continues at lines 6-9:

> ...provided that such waiver shall not apply in the event of a collision between the Vessel and any vessel owned, demise chartered or otherwise controlled by any of the aforesaid companies, or with respect to any loss, damage or expense against which such companies are insured.

[5]   See C.B.M.U. clauses, Appendix G, lines 211-216.

are not to be affected but the liability for the collision is to be determined by arbitration.[6]

Most policy forms provide that the insurance automatically terminates in the event of a transfer of the vessel to a new owner or any other change in ownership. The policy may also provide for termination in the event of changes affecting the quality of the vessel, such as a change in its "flag" or classification society.

19.2.2 Duration of the Risk

Time policies necessarily contain a statement of the time period during which the insurance is in force. Typically, the policy will identify the precise time, down to the minute, at which coverage commences and ends. The C.B.M.U. clauses state that "In the event of payment by the Underwriters for Total Loss of the Vessel this policy shall thereupon automatically terminate."

The C.H.P. clauses contain a provision to the effect that, "[S]hould the vessel at the expiration of this insurance be at sea, or in distress, or at a port of refuge or of call, she shall, provided previous notice be given to the Underwriters, be held covered at a pro rata monthly premium, to her port of destination."[7] This provision is a throwback to earlier times when communication between owners and their ships was difficult and when a policy might expire while the ship was still at sea. It seems difficult to justify in modern times when it should be possible to arrange new insurance irrespective of the location of the ship. In fact, the new version of the Institute Time Clauses — Hulls (1/11/95) restricted the "held covered" provision to cases in which the vessel was both at sea *and* in distress. There is no comparable "held covered" provision in the C.B.M.U. clauses.

19.2.3 Agreed Value and Amount Insured

Hull and machinery insurance policies invariably specify an agreed valuation of the vessel. The sum insured under the policy, which may be less than the agreed value, is also inserted into the policy. As noted in Chapter 6, *Insurable Value*, the agreed valuation may be more or less than the market value, for a variety of reasons. In the case of the C.B.M.U. clauses, there is a provision as follows:

AGREED VALUE

The Vessel, for so much as concerns the Assured, by agreement between the Assured and the Underwriters in this Policy, is and shall be valued at____Dollars.

The agreed value of the vessel will be inserted in the blank. A few lines below in the form there is a provision entitled:

---

[6]   Lines 203-210.
[7]   Lines 342-345.

AMOUNT INSURED HEREUNDER

followed by a space for the insertion of the sum insured. If the sum insured is less than the agreed value, the insured becomes a co-insurer for the difference.

19.2.4   Deductible

The deductible is a tool commonly used by the insurer to reduce its exposure and by the insured to reduce its insurance costs. Hull and machinery policies typically contain one or more deductibles. There is usually a standard deductible, in a stated amount, with respect to all claims from any one accident, other than in the case of a total loss or a constructive total loss in which case the policy may stipulate that there is no deductible.[8] In addition to a standard deductible to be inserted in the policy form, the C.B.M.U. clauses contain a deductible of $50,000 or 10 per cent of the insured value, whichever is less, for claims arising from damage by ice. The C.B.M.U. clauses also provide that, in the case of claims arising under the *Inchmaree* clause[9] for damage attributable to crew negligence, there will be, in addition to the standard deductible, a deductible equal to 10 per cent of the balance of the claim, not to exceed $50,000, but not applicable in the case of actual or constructive total loss. This provision is intended to be an inducement to shipowners to exercise careful supervision over their crews. Some policies, particularly policies covering a fleet of vessels, may contain an annual aggregate deductible, which must be exceeded before the policy responds to any claim.

Both the C.H.P. clauses and the C.B.M.U. clauses provide that there is no deductible applicable to claims under the sue and labour clause, nor to claims for salvage or general average.[10] Under both sets of clauses there is no deductible applicable to claims for actual or constructive total loss or to claims for sue and labour charges, salvage expenses or general average. The C.B.M.U. clauses also contain a separate deductible for ice damage (except in the case of actual or constructive total loss) of the lesser of $50,000 or 10 per cent of the insured value. There is also a separate deductible under the C.B.M.U. clauses applicable to claims for machinery damage recoverable under the *Inchmaree* clause and attributable to the negligence of the crew.

Both sets of clauses provide that damage due to heavy weather on a single sea passage will be subject to only one deductible, even though there may have been a number of different occurrences of damage during that passage. The C.B.M.U. clauses provide that a sequence of damage from the same accident shall be treated as due to that one accident. Both contain a penalty of 15 per cent in the event that the insured fails to comply with the claims clause — for

---

[8]   The C.H.P. clauses provide at lines 91-92 that the deductible is not applicable to claims for total loss or constructive total loss. The C.B.M.U. clauses contain the same provision at lines 30-31. The C.H.P. clauses and the C.B.M.U. clauses also provide that there is no deductible applicable to sue and labour, salvage expenses and general average.

[9]   See Chapter 7, *Perils Insured*, Section 7.3.7, "Loss or Damage to Machinery not Caused by Insured Perils".

[10]   C.H.P. clauses, lines 91-92; C.B.M.U. clauses, lines 40-41.

example, by failing to give proper notice to underwriters so that they can appoint their own surveyor.

Interesting questions can arise as to whether one or more deductibles is applicable in the event of successive accidents. A careful analysis of the policy wording and of the facts surrounding the accidents will be required to determine whether one or more deductibles should be applied.

19.2.5 The Perils Clause

Hull and machinery policies are invariably "named perils" policies, with the perils insured specifically identified in the policy. The description of the perils can vary. At one end of the range is a derivation of the "S.G." form perils clause found in the C.H.P. and C.B.M.U. clauses:

> Touching the Adventures and Perils which we, the Underwriters, are contented to bear and take upon us, they are of the Seas, Men-of-War, Fire, Enemies, Pirates, Rovers, Thieves, Jettisons, Letters of Mart and Counter-Mart, Surprisals, Takings at Sea, Arrests, Restraints and Detainments of all Kings, Princes and Peoples, of what nation, condition or quality soever, Barratry of the Master and Mariners and of all other like Perils, Losses and Misfortunes that have or shall come to the Hurt, Detriment or Damage of subject matter insured (hereafter the "Vessel") or any part thereof; excepting, however, such of the foregoing Perils as may be excluded by provisions elsewhere in these clauses or by endorsement.[11]

On the other hand, the Institute Time Clauses Hulls 1/11/95 provide as follows:

6. PERILS

6.1 This insurance covers loss of or damage to the subject-matter insured caused by

6.1.1	perils of the seas rivers lakes or other navigable waters
6.1.2	fire, explosion
6.1.3	violent theft by persons from outside the Vessel
6.1.4	jettison
6.1.5	piracy
6.1.6	contact with land conveyance, dock or harbour equipment or installation
6.1.7	earthquake volcanic eruption or lightning
6.1.8	accidents in loading discharging or shifting cargo or fuel.

6.2 This insurance covers loss of or damage to the subject-matter insured caused by

6.2.1	bursting of boilers breakage of shafts or any latent defect in the machinery or hull
6.2.2	negligence of Master Officers Crew or Pilots

---

[11] This language comes from the C.H.P. clauses, lines 1-11. The language of the C.B.M.U. clauses, lines 98-103, is substantially the same. As to "perils of the sea" and other perils covered by the perils clause, see Chapter 7, *Perils Insured*.

6.2.3   negligence of repairers or charterers provided such repairers or charterers are not an Assured hereunder

6.2.4   barratry of Master Officers or Crew

6.2.5   contact with aircraft, helicopters or similar objects, or objects falling therefrom
provided that such loss or damage has not resulted from want of due diligence by the Assured, Owners, Managers or Superintendents or any of their onshore management.

6.3 Masters Officers Crew or Pilots not to be considered Owners within the meaning of this Clause 6 should they hold shares in the Vessel.

19.2.6   Additional Perils (Inchmaree) Clause

All the common hull and machinery insurance forms contain an *Inchmaree* clause, variously worded but usually extending the cover to include, among other things, accidents in loading, discharging or shifting cargo, bursting of boilers, breakage of shafts or latent defect in the machinery or hull, negligence of master, officers, crew or pilots, negligence of repairers or charterers, and barratry of the master, officer or crew, "provided the loss or damage has not resulted from the want of due diligence of the insured or the owners or managers". The C.H.P. clauses have a somewhat modified *Inchmaree* clause which omits accidents to the vessel while on, or going on or off drydocks, graving docks and so forth, and breakdown of motor generators or other electrical machinery.[12] The Institute Time Clauses Hulls (1/11/95), quoted above, do not have a separate *Inchmaree* clause. Instead, there is simply one perils clause which incorporates the traditional *Inchmaree* coverage.

The subject of the *Inchmaree* clause is discussed in Chapter 7, *Perils Insured*.

19.2.7   Restricted Perils

The Association of Marine Underwriters of British Columbia (now the Marine Insurance Association of British Columbia) has published a set of clauses referred to as the Canadian (Pacific) Total Loss and Excess Liabilities Clauses (December 31, 1991), reproduced in Appendix L. These clauses, which are a form of increased value insurance, cover only actual or constructive total loss of the vessel caused by certain named perils, including the standard S.G. perils as well as perils covered under the *Inchmaree* clause. The purpose of the clauses is to provide total loss cover in addition to the insured value specified in the hull and machinery policy. The form also covers general average, salvage and sue and labour charges not recoverable in full under the hull and machinery policy due to differences in valuation.

---

[12]   C.H.P. clauses, lines 49-62.

19.2.8 Pollution

The shipowner's liability for pollution is insured under its P. & I. insurance. However, what coverage is available should the vessel become a pollution hazard and is destroyed by the authorities in order to prevent further pollution?[13] The C.H.P. clauses contain an express provision covering loss of or damage to the vessel "directly caused by any governmental authority acting under the powers vested in them to prevent or mitigate a pollution hazard or threat thereof" provided that the pollution results from damage to the vessel for which the underwriters are liable and provided that it has not resulted from a lack of due diligence on the part of the insured.[14] There is a similar provision in the Institute Time Clauses — Hulls, both (1/10/83) and (1/11/95),[15] but not in the C.B.M.U. clauses. One would expect that a broker's manuscript wording would contain a provision to this effect in order to reflect legal developments since the C.B.M.U. clauses were first introduced.

19.2.9 Collision Liability

One of the unusual features of hull and machinery insurance, in most forms, is that it may provide liability insurance in respect of collision.[16] Before the widespread availability of P. & I. insurance, it was common for hull and machinery underwriters to provide limited collision liability coverage under the so-called "three-fourths running down clause". Under this clause, underwriters agreed to pay up to three-quarters of the insured value of the vessel to indemnify the shipowner against certain liabilities arising from collision with another vessel. The remaining one-fourth was borne by the insured, as an incentive to safe navigation. The London market standard hull clauses have traditionally incorporated this three-fourths collision liability coverage. The expectation is that if the shipowner is liable in the event of a collision, the hull and machinery underwriters will provide an indemnity for three-quarters of the liability and the P. & I. club will respond for the remainder.

---

[13] Under Part XVI of the *Canada Shipping Act*, R.S.C. 1985, c. S-9, the authorities have the power to order the removal or destruction of a vessel which is discharging a pollutant or which they have reasonable grounds to believe is likely to discharge a pollutant.

[14] Lines 211-220.

[15] The language of the clause in the Institute Time Clauses — Hulls (1/11/95) is:

7. This insurance covers total (actual or constuctive) loss of the Vessel caused by any governmental authority acting under the powers vested in it to prevent or mitigate a pollution hazard or damage to the environment, or threat thereof, resulting directly from damage to the Vessel for which the Underwriters are liable under this insurance, provided that such act of governmental authority has not resulted from want of due diligence by the Assured, Owners or Managers to prevent or mitigate such hazard or damage or threat thereof. Master, Officers, Crew or Pilots not to be considered Owners within the meaning of this Clause 7 should they hold shares in the Vessel.

[16] In hull and machinery insurance, the word "collision" has a very narrow meaning. It is defined as a physical impact between two or more vessels. It does not encompass a vessel contacting a dock or other fixed or floating object. Liabilities arising out of such incidents are insured under protection and indemnity insurance.

The text of the three-fourths Collision Liability Clause was updated when the plain language clauses were introduced, but there is very little difference in coverage offered by the Institute collision clause when compared with the North American versions. An exception is that the Institute clauses (1/1/95) make provision in clause 8.4.5 for the hull and machinery underwriter to make payment to salvors under the 1989 International Convention on Salvage when their skills and efforts are used to prevent or minimize damage to the environment in connection with pollution resulting from a collision incident.[17] This provision, which reflects a compromise between hull and machinery underwriters on the one hand, and protection and indemnity insurers on the other, as to liability for certain salvage charges, is not reflected in either the C.B.M.U. or the C.H.P. Clauses. Again, one would expect that the provision might be incorporated into a policy through a broker's manuscript wording.

A further slight difference, but not one impacting on the extent of coverage, is the provision in the North American collision clause for the appointment of an arbitrator or arbitrators when two vessels which are the property of the same owners or charterers are involved in a collision. The arbitrator is appointed to determine the division of responsibility between the two vessels.

Included in the collision liability clause, typically, are the following:

(a) an agreement by each subscribing underwriter (in the case of a subscription policy) to pay its proportionate share (*i.e.*, the subscribing underwriter's proportionate share of the sum insured in relation to the insured value) of any damages which the insured may be required to pay to another party as a result of collision, including the legal and related costs of defending such a claim and any costs which may be payable by the insured to the other party;

(b) an agreement to settle claims on the basis of cross-liabilities, in the case where both ships are to blame. The underwriters agree to pay the balance, if any, owing by their insured;

(c) a so-called "sister ship" clause, which provides that where there is a collision between two ships in the same ownership, the responsibility

---

[17]   In the Institute Time Clauses — Hulls (1/11/95) the coverage is introduced by way of an exclusion to an exclusion, as follows:

> 8.4 Provided always that this Clause 8 shall in no case extend to any sum which the Assured shall pay for or in respect of
>
> ...
>
> 8.4.5. pollution or contamination, or threat thereof, of any real or personal property or thing whatsoever (except other vessels with which the insured Vessel is in collision or property on such other vessels) or damage to the environment, or threat thereof, save that this exclusion shall not extend to any sum which the Assured shall pay for or in respect of salvage remuneration in which the skill and efforts of the salvors in preventing or minimising damage to the environment as is referred to in Article 13 paragraph 1(b) of the International Convention on Salvage, 1989 have been taken into account.

See also Chapter 22, *General Average.*

between them will be resolved either by arbitration or by some other acceptable method;[18]

(d) certain exceptions to the coverage provided, including: (i) removal of wreck; (ii) injury to persons or property (other than the other vessel); (iii) pollution; and (iv) damage to cargo.[19]

19.2.10 Removal of Wreck

The term "removal of wreck" refers to a situation in which the insured vessel has been in an accident, such as a stranding or sinking, resulting in a legal requirement that it be removed, perhaps because it is blocking a channel or berth or is a hazard to navigation. If the shipowner and the hull and machinery underwriters have determined that they do not wish to salvage the vessel, and if the hull and machinery underwriters have not accepted the abandonment of the vessel as being a constructive total loss,[20] the issue arises as to who has the responsibility to remove the wreck. This is a risk that normally falls on protection and indemnity insurers, who undertake to indemnify the ship owner against wreck removal expenses, where the removal is required by law.

19.2.11 Differences Between the London and North American Collision Clauses

The collision liability clause in all of the standard North American wordings (including the C.B.M.U. and C.H.P. Clauses) covers four-fourths or 100 per cent of the insured vessel's collision liability subject to the policy limit which is identical to the insured value of the vessel. For example, a policy that insures a ship for $10 million physical damage, also provides a collision liability limit of $10 million (as opposed to the Institute collision clause which would provide a limit of $7.5 million). If that ship were to collide with another and sink, the policy would pay out $10 million for the loss of the ship, and, in addition, pay up to an additional $10 million towards the damages to the second ship, assuming the insured vessel was 100 per cent at fault.

If an amount of collision liability coverage in excess of the hull insured value (or three-fourths of its value in the case of the Institute clause) is required, this can be obtained by direct purchase of an excess collision liability cover from an excess insurer or by purchasing a P. & I. policy incorporating collision liability coverage in excess of the basic (or underlying) coverage of the hull and machinery policy. If the vessel is entered in a P. & I. club, the club will readily grant this type of excess cover.

---

[18] With respect to collision, see C.H.P. clauses, clauses 14 and 15, and lines 166-210; C.B.M.U. clauses, lines 197-228.

[19] The exclusions are stated in the C.H.P. clauses, lines 191-202 and in the C.B.M.U. clauses, lines 217-228.

[20] See Chapter 9, *Losses and Charges Recoverable.*

19.2.12   Navigation Warranties

Hull and machinery policies typically state the areas within which the ship is entitled to operate, known as "navigation limits" or "trading warranties". This may be identified in terms of a specific geographic area or it may specify areas where the vessel is not permitted to navigate, either generally or during defined time periods. In the case of the C.B.M.U. clauses, there is a line for identification of the eastern limits of navigation, whereas west coast underwriters have published four different trading warranties, and descriptive charts, restricting navigation to the particular waters identified therein.

The American Institute Hull Clauses (2/6/77) and the Institute Time Clauses — Hulls (1/11/95) were designed principally for insuring ocean-going and coastal vessels and it is necessary to incorporate trading limits whenever using these forms. These can consist of standard navigating warranties, such as the Institute Warranties, published by the I. L. U. or the American Institute Trade Warranties, or navigating limits specifically tailored to suit the trading pattern of the particular ship. It is possible to use the C.H.P. clauses for ocean-going or coastal vessels provided the proper navigating limits are added and any other necessary modifications are made.

The two standard broad form hull time clauses for the Great Lakes, the C.B.M.U. clauses and the American Institute Great Lakes Hull Clauses (9/3/79) have navigating limits incorporated in the printed forms. These limits are frequently overridden, however, because they are usually not suitable for the trading patterns of modern Great Lakes vessels, which extend to the St. Lawrence Seaway and sometimes to the Canadian east coast.

19.2.13   Season of Navigation

The C.B.M.U clauses contain a limitation on the navigations season to the period between midnight March 31st and midnight December 15th, subject to a "held covered" provision discussed below. There is a warranty that the vessel will be laid up in a safe place during the winter, under conditions satisfactory to the underwriter's surveyor.[21]

19.2.14   Towage and Salvage

Towage or salvage services rendered to or by the insured vessel can expose the vessel to risks beyond those normally contemplated by underwriters. On the other hand, some towage, such as the use of tugs for manoeuvring in port, is customary and is contemplated by underwriters. As well, a need to render or receive towage services occasionally can arise in an emergency without any opportunity to contact underwriters for permission. For this reason, most hull and machinery policies (including the C.B.M.U. and C.H.P. clauses) contain a

---

[21]   Lines 87-88:

Warranted that the Vessel be properly moored in a safe place and under conditions satisfactory to the Underwriter's Surveyor during the period the Vessel is in Winter lay-up.

prohibition against certain towage coupled with a "held covered" or "tow and assist" clause permitting the insured to have coverage for a breach of the towage prohibition, provided an additional premium is paid.[22]

Both the C.B.M.U. and the C.H.P. clauses contain a "sister ship" clause with respect to salvage services which provides that if salvage has been rendered to the insured vessel by another ship belonging to the same owners, the salvage reward will be determined by arbitration, as if the vessels were in separate ownership.

19.2.15 Held Covered Clauses

The "tow and assist" clause is an example of a "held covered" clause, designed to permit certain breaches of warranty provided the underwriter receives an additional premium to cover the enhanced risk.[23] The policy may contain other held covered clauses, such as a clause providing coverage in the event of a breach of the navigation limits, or providing coverage if the ship is at sea or in distress on the termination of the insurance, to enable the ship to remain insured, at a *pro rata* premium, until it reaches port.

19.2.16 Sue and Labour[24]

A sue and labour clause is an integral part of a hull and machinery policy. The clause typically has four components:

  (a) an obligation of the insured to "sue, labour and travel for, in, and about the defence, safeguards and recovery" of the Vessel or any part thereof;[25]
  (b) a statement that no act of the underwriters or the insured in attempting to save the vessel is to be construed as a waiver or acceptance of abandonment;
  (c) an agreement by underwriters to pay sue and labour charges in proportion to the relationship between the amount insured under the policy and the insured value;

---

[22] See for example, the C.H.P. clauses at lines 76-80:

> 5. The Vessel is covered subject to the provisions of this insurance at all times and has leave to sail or navigate with or without pilots, to go on trial trips and to assist or tow vessels or craft in distress, but it is warranted that the Vessel shall not otherwise tow or be towed, except as is customary or to the first safe port or place when in need of assistance.

> The held covered clause, sometimes known as the "tow and assist" clause, follows immediately after:

> 6. The vessel is covered in case of any breach of warranty as to cargo, employment, towage, salvage services or date of sailing, provide notice be given to the Underwriters immediately after receipt of advices and any amended terms of cover and any additional premium required by them be agreed.

[23] See Chapter 8, *Warranties*.

[24] See Chapter 11, *Duties of the Insured: Sue and Labour*.

[25] The language derives from the original S.G. policy form, attached as a schedule to the *M.I.A. 1906*.

(d) an agreement by underwriters to pay, in addition to a total loss, sue and labour charges reasonably incurred in excess of the proceeds received from the sale of the wreck. Underwriters agree to pay a proportionate amount of such sue and labour charges, in proportion to either the relationship between the amount insured and the agreed value, or to the sound market value of the vessel at the time of the incident, whichever value was greater. The same agreement is made with respect to salvage charges.[26]

Underwriters also agree to pay sue and labour expenses reasonably incurred to avoid a total loss in proportion to the relationship between the amount insured and the insured value.[27] Under both the C.H.P. and the C.B.M.U. clauses, if the vessel is not insured for its full value, as stated in the policy (*i.e.*, if there is underinsurance), underwriters agree to pay a proportionate amount of sue and labour expenses.[28]

As noted above, under the C.B.M.U. clauses and the C.H.P. clauses, there is no deductible applicable to sue and labour expenses.

19.2.17 The Premium

The amount of the premium, sometimes expressed as a percentage rate, will be specified in the policy. The policy may stipulate, as does the C.B.M.U. form, that if the premium is not paid by a specified date, the policy will be automatically terminated, with the premium up to that date being due and payable. The C.H.P. clauses provide that if the premium has not been paid within 30 days after attachment, underwriters are entitled to cancel the policy. The policy may also contain provisions with respect to return of premium on the happening of

---

[26] See *Ultramar Canada Inc. v. Mutual Marine Office Inc. (The "Pointe Lévy")*, [1995] 1 F.C. 341, 82 F.T.R. 1 (T.D.).

[27] C.B.M.U. clauses, lines 191-196.:

> If claim for Total Loss is admitted under this Policy and sue and labor expenses have been reasonably incurred in excess of any proceeds realized or value recovered, the amount payable under this Policy will be the proportion of such excess that the amount insured hereunder (without deduction for loss or damage) bears to the Agreed Value or to the sound value of the Vessel at the time of the accident, whichever value was greater. The foregoing shall also apply to expenses reasonably incurred in salving or attempting to salve the Vessel and other property to the extent that such expenses shall be regarded as having been incurred in respect of the vessel.

[28] The C.H.P. clauses provide, at lines 24-33:

> When expenses are incurred pursuant to this clause, the liability under this insurance shall not exceed the proportion of such expenses that the amount insured hereunder bears to the value of the Vessel as stated herein, or to the sound value of the Vessel at the time of the occurrence giving rise to the expenditure if the sound value exceeds that value. Where the Underwriters have admitted a claim for total loss and subject matter insured by this insurance is saved, the foregoing provisions shall not apply unless the expenses of suing and labouring exceed the value of such property saved and then shall apply only to the amount of the expenses which is in excess of such value.

certain events, such as a change in ownership, cancellation of the policy or lay up of the vessel.

19.2.18 Classification

The Institute Time Clauses — Hulls (1/11/95) require that the insured vessel be classed with a classification society agreed upon by underwriters and that class be maintained throughout the term of the insurance. The clauses also require that any recommendations of the classification society be complied with and that in the event of the owner's failure to comply with these requirements, the underwriters will be discharged of liability under the policy. The C.B.M.U. clauses require that in the event of a change in classification society or class of the vessel, the policy is to terminate.

19.2.19 Underwriters' Surveyor

Underwriters occasionally specify a surveyor to be appointed to inspect damage and to assess the claim on their behalf. The C.B.M.U. form contains a space for the identity of the underwriter's surveyor. The C.H.P. clauses provide that in the event of an accident, notice is to be given to underwriters so they can appoint their surveyor. The London Salvage Association, a traditional choice of London underwriters, has an office in Canada with resident surveyors in several major ports, but specialist independent surveyors are available on both the east and the west coasts of Canada as well as on the Great Lakes.

19.2.20 Claims

The adjustment of hull and machinery claims is a technical subject carried out by specialist average adjusters and is beyond the reach of this book. Policies typically contain provisions with respect to claims, often giving underwriters the right to specify where the vessel is to be repaired in the event of a casualty. The C.H.P. clauses provide that "unless this insurance otherwise provides, claims for partial loss recoverable hereunder shall not be subject to depreciation." The C.B.M.U. clauses contain a provision that general average and particular average will be payable "without deduction new for old". These provisions mean that underwriters are responsible for the full cost of repair, even though the result is that old material or machinery is replaced with new.

The C.B.M.U. clauses require that "prompt notice" be given to underwriters "of any accident or occurrence which could give rise to a claim "under the policy."[29] In the event of a failure to comply with the clause, 15 per cent is to be deducted from the amount of the ascertained claim.[30] There is a similar provision in the C.H.P. clauses.[31]

---

[29] C.B.M.U. clauses, lines 119-120.

[30] *Ibid.*, lines 150-151.

[31] Lines 225-238.

19.2.21   General Average, Salvage and Special Charges

One of the important features of hull and machinery insurance is coverage for general average, salvage and special charges. The policy provides for payment of the ship's share of general average, either as provided by the contract of affreightment or by the York-Antwerp rules.[32] The C.B.M.U. clauses and the C.H.P. clauses provide that in the event of a difference between the insured value of the vessel stated in the policy and the "contributory value" of the vessel determined for the purposes of general average or salvage, a proportionate payment will be made.[33] This means that underwriters' payments for general average or salvage charges are to be prorated based on the proportion between the insured value and the contributory value. In the case of adjustments under the Rules of Practice (Great Lakes) of the Association of Average Adjusters of Canada, the insured value of the vessel (less any particular average damage) is taken to be its contributory value, whereas in adjustments other than Great Lakes, the value is based on the actual net value of the ship at the termination of the adventure.

If the vessel has sustained particular average damage which has reduced its value, the amount paid by underwriters for particular average is to be deducted from the insured value for the purpose of determining underwriters' contribution.[34]

19.2.22   Additional Insurances

Underwriters frequently stipulate that the insured must not have other insurance against total loss, but they may permit the insured to take out additional insurances against risks not covered by the policy, including disbursements insurance, increased value insurance, loss of freight or hire, and war and strikes risks. Both the C.B.M.U. and C.H.P. clauses contain a provision to this effect.

---

[32]   The C.B.M.U. clauses stipulate, instead of the *York-Antwerp Rules*, the *Rules of Practice for the Great Lakes* of the Association of Average Adjusters of Canada.

[33]   The C.H.P. clauses state at lines 140-150:

> 10…When the contributory value of the Vessel is greater than the valuation herein, the liability of these Underwriters for General Average contribution (except in respect to amount made good to the Vessel) or Salvage shall not exceed that proportion of the total contribution due from the Vessel that the amount insured hereunder bears to the contributory value. If because of damage for which these Underwriters are liable as partial loss, the value of the Vessel has been reduced for the purpose of contribution, the net amount of the partial loss under this insurance shall be deducted from the amount insured hereunder and these Underwriters shall be liable only for the proportion which such amount bears to the contributory value.

The C.B.M.U. clauses contain a similar provision at lines 167-173.

[34]   See *Ultramar Canada Inc. v. Mutual Marine Office Inc. ("The Pointe Levy")*, [1995] 1 F.C. 341, (1994), 82 F.T.R. 1 (T.D.).

19.2.23 Exclusions — War and Strikes

Standard hull and machinery insuring forms typically contain an exclusion of loss, damage or expense resulting from capture and seizure, requisition, mines, war, civil war, rebellion, riots, strikes and related risks. An insured wishing to purchase such cover can obtain it as an add-on to the policy at an additional premium. The C.H.P. clauses specifically exclude damages arising from the detonation of an explosive or weapon of war caused by any terrorist or any person acting from a political motive. The C.B.M.U. clauses, on the other hand, do not specifically refer to terrorists although certain exclusions (such as bombs) could apply to terrorist acts.

In Canada, the Canadian Shipowners Mutual Assurance Association provides war and strikes cover for hull and machinery, as well as war and strikes cover supplementary to protection and indemnity insurance.

19.2.24 Recoveries

The C.H.P. clauses recognize that the insured may have an interest in recoveries by virtue of its deductible or the difference between the insured and market value, but stipulate that if the insured wishes to pursue that interest, it must first reach an agreement with underwriters to share in the legal costs. Under the C.B.M.U. clauses, where there is a significant deductible, or where there have been uninsured losses such as the loss of earnings while the vessel is being repaired, the practice is for underwriters and the insured to enter into an agreement for the sharing of the recovery, provided the insured bears its share of the costs.[35]

19.2.25 Law and Practice

Some policies contain a stipulation that the policy is to be interpreted according to a specific legal system. For example, the C.H.P. clauses provide:

> This insurance is subject to Canadian law and usage as to liability for and settlement of any and all claims.[36]

There is no comparable provision in the C.B.M.U. clauses, although the broker's manuscript wording would likely contain a similar provision. The Institute Time Clauses — Hulls (1/11/95) begin with a statement "This insurance is subject to English law and practice." These provisions mean that claims under the policy are to be interpreted according to the law of the specified country. There are no "jurisdiction clauses" requiring that suits under the policy must be brought in the courts of a particular country.[37] While Canadian marine insurance law and practice is modeled on and similar to English law, it would be prudent to include

---

[35] See Chapter 12, *Subrogation*.
[36] Lines 369-370.
[37] As to jurisdiction clauses, see Chapter 25, *Practice and Procedural Issues.*

a stipulation in any policy issued in Canada that it is to be subject to Canadian law.

The precise scope of the "Canadian law and usage" clause is uncertain. Either the underwriter or the insured would be entitled to introduce evidence that particular usages or practices in the Canadian market would affect the indemnity provided by the contract.

19.3 VOYAGE POLICIES

While voyage policies can apply to all forms of marine risks — hull and machinery, cargo or freight — we are concerned here with hull and machinery insurance. Some of the principles expressed in this section, however, are applicable to voyage policies on cargo or freight.

Hulls are usually insured on a time basis, but occasionally an insured requires insurance for a particular voyage, for example, if the ship is being towed for repair or scrapping. From the insurer's perspective, the voyage to be insured is a matter fundamental to the assessment of the risk.[38] If the ship sails from or to a different place than those named in the policy, the risk will not attach and the insurance will have no effect.[39] A change in the voyage (known as a "deviation"), without the insurer's consent, will generally discharge the insurer from liability, even though the cause of the loss was unconnected with the deviation.[40] Voyage policies often permit certain types of deviation, and in some cases call for the payment of an additional premium when a deviation occurs. "Deviation" refers not only to the geographic voyage insured, but also to the risks insured against. A material departure from that risk will vitiate the insurance.[41] In a time policy, on the other hand, subject to any express restrictions in the policy, which

---

[38] See *Reed v. Weldon* (1869), 12 N.B.R. 460 (C.A.), *per* Ritchie J.:

It cannot be doubted that the meaning of the contract of insurance for a voyage from one port or place to another, and thence to another...is that they shall be performed with reasonable diligence and without unnecessary delay, that is, with all safe, convenient and practicable expedition, and in the regular and customary track, and any unjustifiable deviation or delay discharges the underwriter from subsequent losses, because, if voluntary or without necessity, it is the substitution of another risk and determines the contract.

See also *Taylor v. Moran* (1885), 11 S.C.R. 347, rev'g. (1884), 24 N.B.R. 39 (C.A.); *Spinney v. Ocean Mutual Marine Insurance Co.* (1890), 17 S.C.R. 326, aff'g. (1889), 21 N.S.R. 244 (T.D.); *Quebec Marine Insurance Co. v. Commercial Bank of Canada* (1870), L.R. 3 P.C. 234, 19 R.J.R.Q. 372, rev'g. (1869) 13 L.C. Jur. 267 (Que. C.A.).

[39] Canadian *Marine Insurance Act* ("*C.M.I.A.*"), S.C. 1993, c. 22, s. 41.

[40] See *Rodgers v. Jones* (1883), 16 N.S.R. 96 (C.A.); *Boak v. Merchants' Marine Insurance Co.* (1876), 10 N.S.R. 288 (C.A.), appeal quashed (1877), 1 S.C.R. 110; *Mannheim Insurance Co. v. Atlantic & Lake Superior Railway* (1900), 11 Que. K.B. 200 (C.A.), rev'g. (1899), 15 Que. S.C. 476, aff'g. on other grounds (1899), 15 Que. S.C. 469; *McGivern v. Provincial Insurance Co. of Toronto* (1856), 8 N.B.R. 311 (S.C.), aff'd. (1858), 9 N.B.R. 64 (C.A.).

[41] *Reed v. Weldon* (1869), 12 N.B.R. 460 (C.A.); *James Duncan & Co. v. British American Insurance Co.* (1871), 1 P.E.I. 370. (*sub nom. Duncan, Hodgson & Robertson v. Montreal Assurance Co.*), Peters 243; *Dimock v. New Brunswick Marine Assurance Co.* (1849), 6 N.B.R. 398 (S.C.).

are common, there is no qualification to the geographic area in which the vessel may trade.[42]

The courts have shown some flexibility, however in determining the precise scope of the port named in the policy.[43] Moreover, if it is shown that there is a usage or custom that is invariably followed, and which the parties could be said to have contracted with reference to, there may be some flexibility in the description of the place of loading.[44] On the other hand, in a time policy, subject to any provisions in the policy restricting the geographic limits, there is no such limit.[45]

There is an implied condition in a voyage policy that the adventure will begin within a reasonable time. Deviation or delay in the prosecution of the voyage agreed in the policy will discharge the insurer from liability from and after that time.[46] But where there is a partial loss prior to the deviation, the insurer will be responsible as deviation does not affect a prior loss.[47] The marine adventure insured by a voyage policy must be carried out with reasonable dispatch, and failure to do so without lawful excuse will discharge the insurer from liability

---

[42] See *Avon Marine Insurance Co. v. Barteaux* (1871), 8 N.S.R. 195 at 197 (C.A.), *per* Young C.J.:
...a time policy, unless there be special restrictions, confers the power of sailing from any port, domestic or foreign, and in our own Province, whose ships are to be found in every sea, and where the ship, once launched, often instantly embarks in foreign commerce, and never returns, perhaps, to her home port, foreign employment must be understood to be as much in the contemplation of the ship owner and insurer as domestic use.

[43] See *Central Native Fishermen's Co-op. v. Commonwealth Insurance Co.*, [1979] I.L.R. ¶1-1091 at 147 (B.C.S.C.); *St. Paul Fire & Marine Insurance Co. v. Troop* (1896), 26 S.C.R. 5, aff'g. (1895), 33 N.B.R. 105 (C.A.) to the effect that the word "port" when used in a marine policy does not have a fixed meaning and has to be understood in its popular and commercial sense; *Hyndman v. Montreal Insurance Co.* (1876), 2 P.E.I. 132 (C.A.): "When clear of the ice was not confined to ice" at the originating port, but meant that before the risk would attach the ship would have to arrive at a point when the risks of the voyage would not be increased due to ice.

[44] *Fisher v. Western Assurance Co.* (1854), U.C.Q.B. 255 (C.A.).

[45] *Avon Marine Insurance Co. v. Barteaux* (1871), 8 N.S.R. 195 (C.A.).

[46] *C.M.I.A.*, s. 43:
43(1) A deviation without lawful excuse from the voyage contemplated by a marine policy discharges the insurer from liability for any loss occurring on or after the time when the deviation occurs, regardless of the intention to deviate and whether or not the ship returns to its course of voyage before the loss occurs.
(2) There is a deviation from the voyage contemplated by a marine policy where
    (*a*)   the course of the voyage is specified by the policy and is departed from; or
    (*b*)   the course of the voyage is not specified by the policy but the usual and custom-ary course is departed from.
(3) Where a marine policy specifies the ports of discharge, the ship may proceed to any or all of them, but if, in the absence of any usage or sufficient cause, the ship does not proceed to them, or such of them as it goes to, in the order specified, there is a deviation from the voyage contemplated by the policy.
See *Taylor v. Moran* (1890), 11 S.C.R. 347 where there was a clause in the policy prohibiting entry into the Gulf of St. Lawrence prior to a certain date. The court held that an unnecessary delay in the prosecution of the voyage will vitiate the policy.

[47] See *Fairbanks v. Union Marine Insurance Co.* (1854), 2 N.S.R. 271 (C.A.).

for any loss occurring on or after the time when the delay becomes unreasonable.[48]

A change of the voyage will discharge the insurer from any loss occurring on or after the time when the intention to change is manifested, whether or not the ship has actually left the course of voyage contemplated by the policy.[49] An intention to deviate may be inferred from the circumstances of the loss.[50]

A voyage policy may contain a "held covered clause" permitting deviation in certain circumstances. The clause may require that underwriters must be notified as soon as possible after the deviation and that an additional premium be paid, if required.[51]

The *C.M.I.A.*[52] provides that deviation or delay can be excused for a variety of reasons:

(a) a special term in the policy permits it — for example, a "held covered" clause;

(b) it is beyond the control of the master and the master's employer;

(c) it was reasonably necessary in order to comply with an express or implied warranty;

(d) it was reasonably necessary for the safety of the ship or the subject-matter insured;[53]

(e) it was made for the purpose of saving human life or aiding a ship in distress where human life may be in danger;

---

48 *C.M.I.A.*, s. 44:

> The marine adventure insured by a voyage policy must be carried out with reasonable dispatch and a delay, without lawful excuse, in carrying it out discharges the insurer from liability for any loss occurring on or after the time when the delay becomes unreasonable.

49 *Ibid.*, s. 42(1):

> 42(1) Unless a marine policy otherwise provides, a change of voyage discharges the insurer from liability for any loss occurring on or after the time when the intention to change is manifested, whether or not the ship has in fact left the course of voyage contemplated by the policy when the loss occurs.
>
> (2) There is a change of voyage where, after the commencement of the risk, the destination of the ship is voluntarily changed from that contemplated by the marine policy.

50 *Boak v. Merchants' Marine Insurance Co.* (1876), 10 N.S.R. 288 (C.A.), aff'd. (1877), 1 S.C.R. 110.

51 The Institute Voyage Clauses — Hull (1/10/83) contain the following held covered provision: Change of Voyage

> Held covered in case of any deviation or change of voyage or any breach of warranty as to towage or salvage services, provided notice be given to the underwriters immediately after receipt of advices and any amended terms of cover and any additional premium required by them be agreed.

See *Chartered Bank of India v. Pacific Marine Insurance Co.*, [1924] 1 W.W.R. 114, [1923] 4 D.L.R. 942 (C.A.), aff'g. [1923] 1 W.W.R. 1136, [1923] 2 D.L.R. 612 (S.C.).

52 Subsection 45(1).

53 See, for example, *Eisenhauer v. Nova Scotia Marine Insurance Co.* (1892), 24 N.S.R. 205 (C.A.), aff'd. (1894), Cout. S.C. 811 (S.C.C.); *Fairbanks v. Union Marine Insurance Co.* (1854), 2 N.S.R. 271 (C.A.).

(f) it was reasonably necessary for the purpose of obtaining medical aid for any person on board the ship; or

(g) it was caused by the barratrous[54] conduct of the master or crew, if barratry is one of the perils insured against.

Once the "excuse for deviation or delay ceases, the voyage must be resumed with reasonable dispatch".[55]

As well, a deviation can be excused by the underwriter either expressly or impliedly waiving it.[56] For this to occur, the underwriter must have knowledge of the conduct amounting to a deviation and must by word or conduct show an intention to keep the policy in effect.

Section 46 of the *C.M.I.A.* provides:

> 46. Where the voyage contemplated by a marine policy is interrupted, by a peril insured against, at an intermediate port or place in such circumstances as, apart from the contract of affreightment, justify the master in landing and reshipping, or transshipping, the goods or moveables and sending them to their destination, the insurer continues to be liable for a loss occurring on or after the landing or transshipment.

In *Fairbanks v. Union Marine Insurance Co.*,[57] the court stated that all the surrounding circumstances would have to be taken into account in determining whether it was appropriate to forward the goods to an intermediate port for further forwarding.

---

[54] See *O'Connor v. Merchants Marine Insurance Co.* (1889), 16 S.C.R. 331.

[55] *C.M.I.A.*, subs. 45(2); see also *Fairbanks v. Union Marine Insurance Co.* (1854), 2 N.S.R. 271 (C.A.).

[56] *Gerow v. Providence Washington Insurance Co.* (1889), 28 N.B.R. 435 (C.A.), aff'd. (1890), 17 S.C.R. 387.

[57] *Fairbanks v. Union Marine Insurance Co.* (1854), 2 N.S.R. 271 (C.A.).

Chapter 20

Protection and Indemnity Insurance

20.1 INTRODUCTION

The Canadian *Marine Insurance Act* (*"C.M.I.A."*) recognizes a form of insurance known as "mutual insurance" — an agreement by two or more persons to insure each other against marine losses.[1] It originated in the eighteenth century when groups of shipowners formed "Hull Associations" to mutually insure their ships. While mutual hull insurance is rare today, these associations were the forerunners of another form of mutual insurance known as protection and indemnity ("P. & I.") insurance. P. & I. insurance developed in the nineteenth century, partly due to the inability of shipowners to obtain full coverage for their "collision" liability in the English insurance market. Collision liability — the liability arising from a physical impact between two or more ships — was originally insured under the "running down clause" in the hull and machinery policy, whereby the insurer agreed to accept three-fourths of the insured vessel's liability for damages to another ship in collision, up to the insured value of the hull. The remaining one-fourth fell to be self-insured by the shipowner itself, as an inducement to careful navigation. Eventually shipowners, reluctant to shoulder this one-fourth liability on their own and perhaps hoping to reduce their insurance costs, banded together to share the risk. Another factor leading to the development of P. & I. insurance was the expansion of shipowners' liabilities by the courts and legislatures, making it necessary for them to obtain appropriate insurance coverage.[2] To procure this coverage, a number of shipowners agreed

---

[1] Canadian *Marine Insurance Act* (*"C.M.I.A."*), S.C. 1993, c. 22, s. 89(1):

> 89(1) Mutual insurance is insurance whereby two or more persons mutually agree to insure one another against marine losses.
>
> (2) Subject to subsections (3) and (4), this Act applies in respect of mutual insurance.
>
> (3) The provisions of this Act relating to premiums do not apply in respect of mutual insurance, but a guarantee, or such other arrangement as may be agreed on, may be substituted for the premium for mutual insurance.
>
> (4) The provisions of this Act may, in the case of mutual insurance effected by an association, be modified by a marine policy issued by the association, or by the rules and regulations of the association, to the extent that the provisions may be modified by agreement of the parties to the insurance.

[2] For example, the enactment of *Lord Campbell's Act*, 14 & 15 Vict. c. 100, in England in 1846 made it possible for the spouses and children of deceased crew members to take legal action against the shipowner for damages arising from wrongful death.

to mutually insure their liabilities and the first P. & I. association or "club" was formed in 1855. Initially, the clubs provided "protection" insurance, covering collision liability, damage to fixed objects and certain death and injury claims. As time went by, various forms of "indemnity" cover were added to provide insurance against risks such as the shipowner's liability for the carriage of goods by water.

The operation of a modern shipping fleet requires an investment of millions, if not hundreds of millions, of dollars. Yet, the liabilities from a single accident — for example, a collision with another ship resulting in loss of life, substantial damage to property and environmental pollution, could wipe out the shipowner's investment. No shipowner can afford to operate (and no lender would permit the owner to operate) without insurance against these liabilities. Shipowners today have the alternative of joining a P. & I. club or insuring their shipowning liabilities in conventional insurance markets under protection and indemnity clauses at a fixed premium and subject to stated limits and deductibles.[3] The majority of smaller commercial vessels obtain coverage in this latter manner. The liabilities of most large cargo and passenger vessels are insured by a member club of the International Group of Protection and Indemnity Associations. These "clubs" offer very substantial liability insurance to their insureds (known as "members"), by means of interlocking pooling and reinsurance arrangements. In fact, it is the incorporated association that provides the insurance and not the members themselves.[4] The majority of the world's large ocean-going ships are entered in the International Group of P. & I. Clubs, many of which are based in the United Kingdom, with others operating in Scandinavia, Bermuda, Japan, and the United States. The Protection and Indemnity Clubs insure a significant number of vessels in Canada, including cargo vessels, tug and barge fleets, passenger and tour boats, fishing boats and ferries.

There have been few Canadian cases dealing with P. & I. insurance, probably because disputes are infrequent. However, when they do occur, they are resolved directly between the member and the club, by arbitration if necessary.[5]

---

[3]　A.I.M.U. (American Institute of Marine Underwriters) Protection and Indemnity Clauses (2/6/83) or the Protection and Indemnity SP-23 form (revised 1/56). The A.I.M.U. Protection and Indemnity Clauses (2/6/83) do not insure the shipowner's liability for damage to cargo. In order to procure this coverage, there is a companion form, the American Institute of Marine Underwriters Protection and Indemnity Clauses Cargo Liability Endorsement (2/6/83).

[4]　See J.P. Bolger, "Marine Insurance Terms and Conditions" (Canadian Maritime Law Association Seminar, December 1, 1995).

[5]　For examples of protection and indemnity insurance, see *Catherwood Towing Ltd. v. Commercial Union Assurance Co.* (1996), 26 B.C.L.R. (3d) 57, 35 C.C.L.I. (2d) 124 (C.A.), aff'g. (1995), 30 C.C.L.I. (2d) 135, [1955] I.L.R. ¶1-3245 (B.C.S.C.) and *Burrard Towing Co. v. Reed Stenhouse Ltd.* (1996), 19 B.C.L.R. (3d) 391, 35 C.C.L.I. (2d) 145 (C.A.), rev'g. (1994), 100 B.C.L.R. (2d) 92, 29 C.C.L.I. (2d) 29 (S.C.) which deal with important issues of liability for cargo under tower's liability policies. See also: *Nanaimo Shipyards (1985) Ltd. v. Underwriters, Lloyds* (1990), 6 C.C.L.I. (2d) 161 (B.C.S.C.); *Western Assurance Co. v. Desgagnés*, [1976] 1 S.C.R. 286, 57 D.L.R. (3d) 410 (the policy insured the carrier against liability for loss or damage to cargo); *Driftwood Lands & Timber Ltd. v. United States Fire Insurance Co. of New York*, [1954] O.R. 733, [1955] 1 D.L.R. 176 (H.C.), aff'd. [1954] O.W.N. 935, [1955] 1 D.L.R. 176 at

20.2 OVERVIEW OF P. & I. INSURANCE

P. & I. clubs do not issue policies of insurance. Instead, they publish "Rule Books" containing the terms of insurance provided to their members. The rules are, in effect, the insurance policy. The clubs issue "certificates of entry" to confirm that members are insured under the club's rules and identify any variations from the normal club rules such as higher deductible(s) and additional exclusions or extensions.

The provisions of the *C.M.I.A.* with respect to premiums do not apply to mutual insurance.[6] P. & I. associations have traditionally operated by assessing a premium, known as a "call" or "advance call" at the commencement of the year and imposing "supplementary calls" on the members for additional premiums if these advance calls do not meet the claims and expenses of running the club. One of the risks of insurance through P. & I. Clubs, therefore, has been that a member with a good loss record may find itself paying higher premiums at a later date as a result of the bad loss record of other members or the poor management of the association. This has led to the emergence of a limited number of "fixed premium" P. & I. insurers who guarantee a fixed premium with defined limits of liability.

P. & I. policies typically contain a deductible to be absorbed by the member on each claim. This is a means of reducing the club's exposure and reducing the cost of insurance for the member.

Until fairly recently, one of the unique features of P. & I. insurance through the clubs was that there were no limits to the coverage provided, except for oil pollution. The shipowner was insured against the covered liabilities, no matter how great the amount of the claim. In response to the enormous potential liabilities facing shipowners, clubs have placed limits on the insurance they provide — for both oil pollution liabilities and for other liabilities. In 1990, the International Group of P. & I. Clubs reduced their coverage limits for oil pollution liability to US$500 million per occurrence. This was increased in 2001 to US$1 billion.[7] In 1997, the Clubs reduced their limits for other liabilities to approximately US$4.25 billion.

---

183 (C.A.); *Ocean Fisheries Ltd. v. Pacific Coast Fishermen's Mutual Marine Insurance Co.*, [1998] 1 F.C. 586, 220 N.R. 68 (C.A.), aff'g. (1997), 128 F.T.R. 232, rev'g. (1997) 125 F.T.R. 20; *Terra Nova Mutual Marine Insurance Co. Ltd. v. Blackwood* (1952), 32 M.P.R. 277, [1952] I.L.R. ¶1-074 (Nfld. S.C.); *Ultramar Canada Inc. v. Mutual Marine Office Inc. (The "Pointe Levy")*, [1995] 1 F.C. 341, 82 F.T.R. 1 (T.D.); *Gulf Canada Resources Ltd v. Merlac Marine Inc.* (1994), 18 O.R. (3d) 239 (S.C.J.).

6   Section 89(3).

7   Part 6 of the Canadian *Marine Liability Act*, S.C. 2001, c. 6, incorporates two important international conventions dealing with pollution from oil tankers: The 1969 *International Convention on Civil Liability for Oil Pollution Damage*, as amended by Protocols of 1976 and 1992, and the 1971 *International Convention on the Establishment of an International Fund for Compensation for Oil Pollution*, as amended by 1972 and 1992 Protocols. These conventions, which have been broadly adopted around the maritime world, impose a regime of very strict civil liability of oil tankers for pollution, subject to limits of liability. They also provide for a compensation fund to ensure that those affected by oil pollution from tankers are properly compensated. Under s. 60 of the *Marine Liability Act*, a ship is required to have a Certificate of Financial

The Board of Directors of a P. & I. Club is made up of representatives of shipowning members who oversee the operation of the club, but the day-to-day management of the club is entrusted to a specialist management company with expertise in underwriting, reinsurance, claims handling and loss prevention. Each club has a network of "correspondents" around the world who represent the club and its members and who provide on-the-spot assistance in the event of an incident.

20.3   RISKS INSURED BY P. & I. CLUBS

The following, while not exhaustive, is a list of the principal liabilities covered by P. & I. Clubs:

(a) *Collision Liability:* This cover insures the liability of the vessel and the shipowner as a result of a collision between the ship and one or more other ships, to the extent not covered by the vessel's hull and machinery policy. Generally, the clubs insure the one-fourth collision liability for damage to the other vessel and all of the liability for death and injury, which is not insured under the hull and machinery policy. If there is no such coverage under the hull and machinery policy, up to four-fourths collision coverage can be obtained from the clubs. In addition, the clubs will insure the shipowner's excess liability, over and above the coverage provided by the hull policy, which is usually the insured value of the hull.

(b) *Damage Caused by the Ship:* There are two main liabilities covered under this heading. First, there is the liability of the ship or the shipowner for damage to third parties caused by the operation of the ship, other than by collision, sometimes called "non-contact" or "wash" damage. This includes damage to ships without actual contact, such as "crowding" a ship off its course and into another vessel or aground as well as damage to other vessels or structures as a result of the ship's wake or "wash". Second, there is damage to movable and immovable structures other than ships, including marine structures (buoys, rigs) and land-based structures (docks, wharves, bridges, boathouses) through the negligent operation of the ship.

(c) *Cargo Liability:* P. & I. insurance provides indemnity against the liability of the shipowner for loss of or damage to cargo being carried. Typically, the shipowner is obliged to carry cargo pursuant to a contract of carriage incorporating the *Hague* or *Hague-Visby Rules.*[8]

Responsibility as required by the *Civil Liability Convention.* That convention permits a direct right of action against the insurer.

[8]   The *Hague Rules* and *Hague-Visby Rules* are international conventions relating to the carriage of goods by water, given effect in Canada by Part 5 of the *Marine Liability Act,* which in turn repealed the former statute, the *Carriage of Goods by Water Act,* S.C. 1993, c. 21. The statute imposes minimum responsibilities and liabilities on carriers of goods by water and, in turn, gives them certain immunities and limitations of liability.

(d) *Liability to Passengers:* P. & I. insurance provides coverage for personal injury, illness or death of passengers through the negligence of the carrying vessel as well as loss of or damage to passengers' baggage or personal effects.[9]

(e) *Crew Liabilities:* A traditional function of P. & I. insurance has been to cover the owner's liability for personal injury, loss of life or illness of crew members. P. & I. insurance of Canadian flag vessels does not cover the shipowner's liability for personal injury or death of crew members where these exposures are covered under provincial workers' compensation legislation. The P. & I. entries for Canadian vessels usually carry the following exclusion: "Excluding any and all liability to crew and/or others on or about the vessel under any and all workers compensation acts or equivalent legislation applicable under Canadian federal or provincial law." Some Canadian shipowners insure their workers' compensation act exposure with a mutual specifically formed for this purpose — The Standard Compensation Act Liabilities Association or "S.C.A.L.A.". The P. & I. Clubs do, however, insure other liabilities of the shipowner resulting from illness, injury or death of a crew-member where not covered by the workers' compensation boards.

(f) *Personal Injury/Death of Third Parties:* P. & I. insurance provides coverage for physical injuries or death of third parties as a result of the operation of the insured ship — for example, injuries to stevedores or longshore workers, visitors to the ship and other shore workers.

(g) *Pollution:* The clubs insure liability as a result of pollution from the entered ship and the costs of measures taken after a pollution incident in order to minimize the effect of pollution. They also insure the special compensation which may be payable to a salvor under the *Salvage Convention* where the salvor has prevented or minimized environmental pollution and has either failed to earn a reward or has not earned a sufficient reward.

(h) *General Average:* The clubs insure the vessel's contribution to general average expenses not recoverable under the hull and machinery policy and they also insure the inability of the shipowner to collect the share of general average falling on the owners of the cargo as a result of the ship's breach of the contract of carriage.[10]

(i) *Wreck Removal Expenses:* When a vessel is wrecked, and damaged beyond repair, the insured may tender notice of abandonment to its hull and machinery underwriters, but those underwriters have no obligation to accept the abandonment and generally refuse to do so.[11] In such a case, they would pay a claim for constructive total loss of the vessel, but title to the vessel and responsibility for it remains with the owner. If the

---

[9] Part 4 of the *Marine Liability Act*, gives effect to the *Athens Convention on the Carriage of Passengers and their Luggage by Sea, 1974*, permitting carriers to limit their liability for death or personal injury to passengers or for loss of or damage to their luggage.

[10] See Chapter 22, *General Average*.

[11] See Chapter 9, *Losses and Charges Recoverable*.

vessel is wrecked in a location where it is a hazard to navigation, or a pollution or safety risk, the authorities may insist that the owner remove it. P. & I. Clubs insure costs and expenses incurred as a result of a legal requirement that the wreck of the entered ship be raised, removed, destroyed or marked as well as liabilities incurred as a result of such operations. They also insure the cost of the removal of any other vessel wrecked as a result of collision with the entered ship.

(j) *Towing Indemnities:* The clubs insure the liabilities incurred by the shipowner as a result of an indemnity in a contract of towage, provided that the towage is considered customary.[12]

(k) *Sue and Labour Expenses:* Many clubs provide coverage for costs and expenses incurred in avoiding or minimizing any liability for which the member may be insured, if incurred with the consent of the managers or approved by the board. These expenses, known as "sue and labour expenses", may be unrecoverable under P. & I. policies in the absence of express provision in the rules.[13] P. & I. Club rules invariably require the member to give prompt notice of any incident that could give rise to a claim. The failure of the member to comply with these requirements, or to "sue and labour", could result in a decision by the club to deny coverage or to limit its indemnity to the extent that the member's default has increased the claim.[14]

(l) *Legal and Investigation Expense:* Legal and other costs incurred in the defence of claims against the member are generally covered.

(m) *Miscellaneous:* P. & I. insurance provides coverage for a number of other specific liabilities, including fines and penalties, crew repatriation expenses, stowaways and refugees, quarantine expenses, and enquiry expenses.

(n) *Expenses Incidental to Shipowning:* The P. & I. Clubs provide a catch-all form of coverage, sometimes referred to as "expenses incidental to shipowning" or the "omnibus rule", covering liabilities approved by the Board.[15] This discretion, which would never be found in a traditional commercial liability insurance policy, is an important feature of the mutual nature of P. & I. insurance. It permits the Board to consider and

---

[12] Many standard forms of towing agreements, such as the Eastern Canada Towing Conditions of the Eastern Canada Tug Owners Association, require the owner of a vessel being towed to indemnify the tug owner against loss or damage to the "tow" as well as against third party liabilities arising from collision between the tow and other property.

[13] See Chapter 11, *Duties of the Insured: Sue and Labour*. See also *MacMillan Bloedel Ltd. v. Youell* (1991), 2 C.C.L.I. (2d) 241, 79 B.C.L.R. (2d) 326 (S.C.), var'd. (1993), 95 B.C.L.R. (2d) 130 (C.A.), leave to appeal to S. C. C. refused (1994), 23 C.C.L.I. (2d) 18*n*.

[14] See Chapter 11, *Duties of the Insured: Sue and Labour* with respect to the payment of "sue and labour charges" under P. & I. policies.

[15] For example, the 2002-03 Rules of the Standard Steamship Owners' Protection and Indemnity Association (Bermuda) Limited (the "Standard Club") provide coverage for:
     20.32 Liabilities, costs and expenses incidental to the business of owning, operating or managing ships which the Board may decide to be within the scope of the Club, but only to the extent that the Board may decide that the Member shall recover from the Club.

to approve any particular claim, not covered by the express language of its rules, which could reasonably be considered to be within the spirit of protection and indemnity insurance.

20.4   OTHER SERVICES PROVIDED BY P. & I. CLUBS

P. & I. Clubs provide claims handling services for the defence and resolution of claims against members. In the event of an incident that may be covered by their insurance, the club or its local correspondent can provide emergency response and assistance to a member. They will assist the member in appointing surveyors, lawyers and other experts to investigate a casualty and in the evaluation and settlement of claims.

When a ship is involved in a maritime accident resulting in damage to third parties and potential claims against the owners and the ship, a third party is entitled to "arrest" the ship in order to obtain security for its claims. This security is referred to as "bail" and requires that a bond be posted with the court to ensure that the claim will be paid if the court grants judgment in favour of the third party. As a rule of thumb, bail is usually requested for 150 per cent of the claim amount, to cover the claim, interest and costs. Since most such claims will ultimately be borne by the P. & I. Club, the clubs frequently agree to assist their members by providing a form of security to the third party instead of bail. This is known as a "letter of undertaking" or "L.O.U." and is a written promise by the club to honour any judgment against the member.[16] There is usually nothing in the club's rules obliging it to provide such security, but in the case of a member in good standing, that has paid its "calls", the club will generally provide a letter of undertaking when requested.[17] A plaintiff has no legal obligation to accept a letter of undertaking, and is entitled to insist upon his or her strict legal rights by requiring a bail bond or other security, as required by the rules of the Federal Court of Canada. There are some risks in accepting a letter of undertaking, which is only as good as the club giving it, and it is good practice to make enquiries concerning the credit position of the club itself before accepting one. The letter of undertaking gives the third party a direct enforceable claim for judgment against the club and is an exception to the club's usual requirement (discussed in section 20.6) that the member must pay the third party's claim

---

[16]   The letter of undertaking usually contains an agreement to submit to the jurisdiction of a Canadian court, typically the Federal Court of Canada. In *Methanex New Zealand Ltd. v. "Kinugawa" (The)*, [1998] 2 F.C. 583, 142 F.T.R. 81 (Prothonotary) such a provision was enforced. See also *Atlantic Lines & Navigation Co. Inc. v. "Didymi" (The)* (1987), 39 D.L.R. (4th) 399, 78 N.R. 99 (F.C.A.). For a specimen form letter of undertaking, see Appendix M.

[17]   The rules of the Standard Club provide:
> 25.1 The Club is under no obligation to provide bail or other security on behalf of a Member, but where the same is provided, it shall be on such terms as the Managers may consider appropriate and shall not constitute any admission of liability by the Club for the claim in respect of which the bail or other security is given.

In cases where three-fourths collision liability coverage is provided by the hull and machinery policy, the Club may provide a letter of undertaking but will require counter-security from the hull underwriters.

before seeking indemnity from the club. To avoid having to pursue the club in a foreign jurisdiction, it may be prudent to include a provision in the letter of undertaking that the parties submit to the jurisdiction of the Federal Court of Canada for the purpose of enforcement or interpretation of the LOU.

The liability policies issued by marine insurance companies seldom contain a provision requiring the insurer to post security for a claim, and in the absence of a contractual obligation, the insurer has no duty to do so, although it is sometimes done in practice.

20.5 QUALITY CONTROL

All insurers are concerned about the quality of the risks they insure. P. & I. Clubs, perhaps because they are based on the principle of mutuality, take this issue very seriously. To ensure that entered vessels comply with certain minimum standards of quality, the clubs invariably require that the vessel be "in class" — that is, regularly inspected and certified by a recognized classification society. They also require that entered vessels comply with legislation and standards of the country of their registry. P. & I. Clubs often employ in-house shipping experts who can provide advice on loss prevention to their members. Shipowners who fail to meet the club's standards, or whose claims record is indicative of sloppy management or operations, will soon find themselves looking for other insurance.

20.6 THE "PAY-TO-BE-PAID" PRINCIPLE

The principle of indemnity finds expression in a rule of all P. & I. Clubs: the member must first discharge its liability to the third party before claiming indemnity from the club.[18] This so-called "pay-to-be-paid" rule means that a third party has no direct right of action against the P. & I. Club. The principle has been upheld in the United Kingdom and in Canada.

In *Conohan v. Cooperators*,[19] it was held by the Federal Court of Appeal, following the decision of the House of Lords in *Firma C-Trade S.A. v. Newcastle Protection and Indemnity Assn.*,[20] that the liability insurer of a pleasure craft had no obligation to indemnify an injured party since its own insured had not paid the claim of the plaintiff. In that case, its policy only required it to indemnify the insured if the insured had "become liable to pay and *shall pay* by way of damages to any other person or persons any sum".[21] [emphasis added] It was

---

[18] For example, in the rules of the Standard Club, it is provided that:
> 16.7 Unless the Board shall in its discretion otherwise determine, it is a condition precedent of a Member's right to recover from the funds of the Club in respect of any liabilities, costs or expenses that he shall first have paid the same out of funds belonging to him unconditionally and not by way of loan or otherwise.

The latter language was added to prevent the third party arranging a "loan" to the member to satisfy the liability and obtaining an assignment of the member's claim against the Club.

[19] [2001] 2 F.C. 238, 197 F.T.R. 239 (T.D.), aff'd. (2002), 286 N.R. 364 (F.C.A.).

[20] [1991] 2 A.C. 1, [1990] 3 W.L.R. 78 (H.L.).

[21] [2001] 2 F.C. 238 at 251.

held that payment to the third party was a condition precedent to recovery by the insured under the policy.

In practice, the clubs may not insist upon compliance with the "pay-to-be-paid" principle in every case, and the directors or managers of the clubs frequently pay claims which have not been previously paid by the member, provided the member is solvent and in good standing.

Legislation in most Canadian provinces allows direct action by third parties against insurers where the insured has failed to satisfy a judgment against him or her[22] but there is no such provision in the *C.M.I.A.*, and it is unlikely that the provincial statutory provisions would be interpreted to apply to marine insurance claims.

An exception to the pay-to-be-paid rule exists in the case of oil tankers and other vessels over a certain size carrying pollutants, which are required by international convention and the laws of some states to carry pollution liability insurance and to file proof of such insurance (known as a "Certificate of Financial Responsibility") with the authorities. The legislation gives parties and governments affected by pollution from a tanker a direct right of action against the insurer issuing the insurance certificate.[23]

20.7 DISPUTES

P. & I. Club rules generally provide that disputes between members and the club are to be submitted first to the Board and, if not resolved, are to be referred to binding arbitration, generally in the country in which the club operates. While this may make it inconvenient for a foreign shipowner to advance a dispute with the club, such provisions are undoubtedly enforceable.

Due to the broad nature of liability coverage afforded by P. & I. Clubs, and the discretion of the Board to extend coverage with respect to claims coming within the spirit if not the letter of the club rules, disputes as to coverage rarely arise. If they do, they should be addressed before a defence is provided or pursuant to a reservation of rights agreement between the club and the member. Under Canadian law, if an insurer provides a defence to the insured without such a reservation of rights, it will be barred or "estopped" from raising coverage issues at a later date.[24]

20.8 FREIGHT, DEMURRAGE AND DEFENCE INSURANCE

P. & I. Clubs also provide a separate class of insurance, known as "Freight, Demurrage and Defence Cover" (or "F.D.& D." or "Defence" cover) which insures against legal costs and expenses incurred by shipowners in prosecuting or defending certain commercial disputes. While the underlying claims are not themselves insured, the club provides advice and assistance to the member and

---

[22] See, for example, the British Columbia *Insurance Act*, R.S.B.C. 1996, c. 226, s. 24(1); Ontario *Insurance Act*, R.S.O. 1990, c. I.8, s. 132; Nova Scotia *Insurance Act*, R.S.N.S. 1989, c. 231.

[23] See Canadian *Marine Liability Act*, Part 6.

[24] See, for example, *Snair v. Halifax Insurance* (1995), 145 N.S.R. (2d) 132 (S.C.).

pays the costs of retaining lawyers to handle the claims. As the name suggests, these include claims by the shipowner for freight and demurrage[25] and breaches of charterparties, as well as the defence of other commercial claims.[26]

20.9 WAR RISKS

P. & I. Clubs do not insure war risks as part of their standard cover, although they do offer additional war risks cover with limits of US$50 million in excess of the hull and machinery war risks P. & I. cover. Shipowners frequently obtain war risks P. & I. cover as an adjunct to their hull and machinery war risks insurance. In Canada, the Canadian Shipowners Mutual Assurance Association provides hull and machinery and protection and indemnity war risks coverage.

20.10 P. & I. INSURANCE OUTSIDE THE CLUBS

There is no requirement that a shipowner insure its liabilities with a P. & I. Club, and, in fact, some of the larger marine insurers do offer liability insurance, but because of their insuring "capacity" and their expertise, the P. & I. Clubs have historically been the largest insurers of shipowners' liabilities. A shipowner who is unable or unwilling to insure through the P. & I. Clubs has the option of seeking coverage in the commercial insurance market. The policy form most frequently used in Canada is the SP-23 form (revised 1/56) covering many of the risks insured by P. & I. Clubs, including cargo, with some exceptions. While it covers removal of the wreck of the insured vessel, it does not cover removal of the wreck of a third party vessel that has been in a collision with the insured vessel. The Canadian (Pacific) Protection and Indemnity Clauses (1/1/83) provide coverage for many aspects of shipowner's liability, with the notable exception of liability for loss of or damage to cargo on the insured vessel.[27]

The SP-23 form contains a "pay to be paid" provision in its opening words:

> The Assurer hereby undertakes to make good to the Assured or the Assured's executors, administrators and/or successors, all such loss and/or damage and/or expense as the Assured shall as owners of the vessel named herein have become liable to pay *and shall pay* on account of the liabilities, risks, events and/or happenings herein set forth. [Emphasis added.]

---

25 Demurrage is a form of damages for the delay of the ship by the charterer. The charterparty generally allows the charterer a defined amount of time, known as "laytime" for the loading or discharging of the ship. If the charterer takes more time to do so, it must pay damages, usually in a stated amount per day, for the detention of the ship beyond the allowed time.

26 Disputes with suppliers, ship repairers, insurance disputes, inquiry and investigation expenses.

27 The Canadian (Pacific) Protection and Indemnity Clauses (1/1/83) provide coverage for: liability for loss of life and bodily injury; hospital, medical or other expenses; repatriation expenses; liability for damage to other vessels by collision and otherwise; liability for damage to fixed or movable objects; pollution; removal of the wreck of the insured vessel, where compulsory by law; fines; extraordinary expenses in the case of quarantine; prosecution expenses with respect to mutiny; and legal and defence costs. There is a twelve month suit time limitation and a pay-to-be-paid provision (lines 3 to 5).

The form also requires that proof of loss be filed with the insurer within six months of payment by the insured and that any action against the insurer be brought within one year of any judgment against the insured or payment of the claim by the insured.

Chapter 21

Insurance of Particular Risks

21.1 INTRODUCTION

Canadian marine insurers cover a variety of risks connected with transportation by water. This chapter gives an overview of the exposures arising from some of those risks and of the insurance available in the market to insure them.

21.2 INLAND MARINE INSURANCE

The rather oddly-named "inland marine insurance" has long been recognized as a class of business underwritten by Canadian marine insurers. It refers to insurance, other than marine insurance, against loss or damage to property while in transit or during delay incidental to such transit.[1] This refers to inland transport by road or rail and is sometimes distinguished from "ocean marine" or "wet marine" insurance. As well as insuring the cargo itself, marine insurers commonly cover the liabilities of inland carriers, warehouses and other storage facilities.

21.3 FREIGHT FORWARDERS

Freight forwarders handle a very substantial percentage of Canadian import and export shipments and play a vital role in the country's international trade. The Canadian International Freight Forwarders Association ("C.I.F.F.A.") was established in 1948 and since that time the profession has undergone an explosive growth. A freight forwarder is a transportation intermediary whose functions and responsibilities are defined by its contractual agreement with its customer.

In its most limited role, the forwarder acts purely as an "agent" on behalf of the customer, making contractual arrangements for the transportation of goods on behalf of the customer, but it is the customer and not the forwarder, who actually contracts with the service provider. In its broadest role, the forwarder assumes a direct contractual obligation to move the client's goods from origin to destination and to carry out a myriad of incidental services, such as storage and packing, preparation of import and export documents and obtaining permits or licenses. In this latter situation, the freight forwarder may be the only party with

---

[1]   See *Staples v. Great American Insurance Co. of New York*, [1941] S.C.R. 213, 2 D.L.R. 1.

whom the client contracts and the client receives a forwarder's "house bill of lading" evidencing a contract of carriage directly with the forwarder or the forwarder's transportation "line". In point of fact, the forwarder does not usually operate the ship or other means of carriage but enters into sub-contracts with transportation companies and others for the carriage of its customer's goods.[2]

The freight forwarder's important connection with marine insurance arises because marine insurers frequently issue open cargo policies to forwarders, allowing them to declare customers' shipments under the policy, thereby providing their customers with standard marine cargo insurance at a competitive price.[3] This enables a customer, selling on cost insurance freight ("C.I.F.") terms, to have access to a policy of cargo insurance in order to satisfy its contractual obligation to provide such insurance to its buyer. The forwarder will typically provide the customer with a certificate of insurance which can then be passed on to the buyer. If the goods are lost or damaged during transit, the customer notifies the forwarder who assists in the notification of a surveyor and the preparation of a claim under the insurance policy. The insurer usually pays the claim to the forwarder's customer and generally subrogates against responsible parties. Because the forwarder is the "named insured" under the cargo policy, the insurer cannot pursue subrogation against it, even though it may be legally liable to its customer for the loss of or damage to the cargo.

The extensive involvement of freight forwarders in the cargo insurance business is not without controversy. The premium for marine insurance to the customer may be bundled together with the overall fee charged by the forwarder to its customer and may not necessarily be made explicit in the forwarder's invoice. The customer will not have access to the open policy issued to the forwarder and will generally receive only a certificate of insurance, making reference to the policy and to the insuring terms (for example, Institute Cargo Clauses (A) 1/1/82 which is reproduced in Appendix B) under which the cargo is insured. In the event of a dispute concerning a claim, the customer may have to make inquiries to determine exactly what insurance it obtained and what exclusions or conditions are contained in the open policy. Finally, in providing advice and guidance to its client concerning marine insurance, the freight forwarder is effectively acting as an insurance broker.

In the absence of nationwide standards or licensing requirements for forwarders, there is a risk associated with unqualified forwarders providing marine insurance advice. As was discussed in Chapter 18, marine cargo insurance is a complicated area, and there are a range of coverage options available, each with particular exclusions and limitations on coverage. If the insuring terms provided by the forwarder prove to be inadequate, or if the insurer denies coverage due to policy exclusions, the forwarder may find itself responsible for failing to adequately protect the client's foreseeable insurance needs or for failing to fully

---

[2]   For a discussion of the functions and responsibilities of freight forwarders, see P. Jones, *FIATA Legal Handbook on Forwarding*, 1st ed. (Zurich: FIATA, 1993); W. Tetley, *Marine Cargo Claims*, 3rd ed. (Montreal: Blais International Shipping Publications, 1988), chapter 33, "Responsibility of Freight Forwarders".

[3]   See Chapter 18, *Cargo Insurance*, Section 18.3, "Open Policies".

advise the client of the limitations on coverage or the insurance options available.[4]

The freight forwarder's liabilities depend on the obligations it has contractually assumed. The C.I.F.F.A. has published a set of standard contractual terms and conditions for use by its members, defining the forwarder's duties and responsibilities and, in certain cases, limiting its liabilities. These terms and conditions do not have the force of law and must be incorporated in the forwarder's contract with its customer. Like any professional, a forwarder is required to exercise reasonable care and diligence in the performance of its calling[5] and in addition to cargo insurance covering loss or damage to the customer's goods, a forwarder generally needs liability insurance to cover its errors and omissions liability to its customer. The extent of insurance required will vary, depending on the obligations assumed by the forwarder. If the forwarder acts solely as an agent, without assuming contractual responsibility to its customer for the transportation of goods, its insurance requirements may be narrower than the forwarder who issues a "house" bill of lading or "NVOCC"[6] bill of lading and assumes the direct obligation to the client for the safe transportation of goods from origin to destination.

Freight forwarder's liability insurance is available internationally through a specialty P. & I. Club and domestically in the Canadian marine insurance market by several insurers writing this class of business. Such insurance generally provides liability coverage for the forwarder's errors and omissions and, where assumed, its contractual liability for the delivery of cargo.

---

[4] This was precisely the situation in the Ontario case of *1013799 Ontario Ltd. v. Kent Line International Ltd.* (2000), 21 C.C.L.I. (3d) 312, [2000] O.T.C. 635 (S.C.J.), where the freight forwarder and insurance broker were held liable for failing to advise the customer that an extension to the Institute Frozen Foods clauses was available which could have provided coverage for a loss that was excluded by the coverage actually provided.

[5] See *Al-Qahtani-Shaw-Leonard Ltd. v. Crossworld Freight Ltd.* (1988), 66 O.R. (2d) 256, 54 D.L.R. (4th) 192 (C.A.), var'g. (1987), 60 O.R. (2d) 565, 40 D.L.R. (4th) 656 (H.C.J.): forwarder held liable for failing to procure necessary documentation and permits. The obligations of the forwarder as agent were discussed in *J. Morgan Forwarding v. Jupiter Developments* (1980), 3 A.C.W.S. (2d) 319, referring to *Jones v. European & General Express Co.* (1920), 90 L.J.K.B. 159 at 160. For a discussion of the distinction between the forwarder's various roles, see *Nabob Food Ltd. v. Harry W. Hamacher Spediteur GmbH & Co.*, [1988] B.C.J. No. 250 (B.C. Co. Ct.) (QL); *Raith v. Worldwide Overseas Moving Service (B.C.) Inc.*, [2000] B.C.J. No. 1385 (B.C. Prov. Ct.) (QL); *Interpayment Services Ltd. v. Brinks Canada Ltd.* (1996), 4 O.T.C. 279 (Ont. Ct. Gen. Div.); *Canusa Systems Ltd. v. "Canmar Ambassador" (The)*, (1998), 146 F.T.R. 314 (T.D.); *Ocean Transportation Services Freight Forwarding Inc. v. JNL Transport Inc.*, [2001] O.J. No. 1676 (Ont. S.C.J.) (QL). In *Crompton Saage Enterprises Inc. v. Lep International Inc.*, [1994] B.C.J. No. 333 (B.C.S.C.) (QL), the freight forwarder, which the court found had breached its contract to properly pack the plaintiff's goods, was held entitled to limit its liability based on the C.I.F.F.A. terms and conditions.

[6] Non-Vessel-Operated Common Carrier.

21.4   CUSTOMS BROKERS

A customs broker provides advice and assistance to its client concerning customs tariffs or rates and the documentation and procedures necessary to import or export the client's goods. The broker's services generally include the preparation of customs documents, the payment of customs duties and charges on behalf of its client, the clearance of the goods through customs and, in some cases, eventual delivery to the client.

Most goods shipped internationally are insured from "warehouse to warehouse" and this generally includes the time the goods are awaiting customs clearance. However, the customs broker may be liable for the safe custody of the goods if it actually takes possession of them. It may, therefore, require insurance to cover its own responsibility for the goods while they are in its possession.

The customs broker also needs insurance for liability arising from its errors and omissions. This liability insurance is provided in the Canadian market, either through manuscript wording prepared by brokers or by specialized cover of certain marine insurers. It generally provides coverage against the broker's errors and omissions as well as the broker's liability for fines or penalties imposed upon its customer due to the broker's negligence. While the broker's potential exposure in the case of an individual shipment is usually fairly low, it may face significant liabilities in the event of the repetition of the same error over a large number of shipments. In such circumstances, interesting questions could arise as to whether or not each shipment gives rise to a distinct "error" and is subject to a deductible, or whether all errors of the same kind, repeated over time, are subject to a single deductible.

21.5   STEVEDORES

Stevedores provide cargo-handling services, including loading onto or discharging from the ship, stowage on board the ship and removal after discharge. The stevedore may also provide its own terminal or warehouse for storage of goods prior to loading or after discharge from the ship. The stevedore is a "bailee" in law and has an obligation to take reasonable care of the cargo while in its possession.[7] The stevedore also has a duty to take reasonable care not to damage other property, such as the ships on which it works or other cargo on board such ships. Where the stevedore provides other services, such as loading or securing of the cargo onboard the ship, it will be liable if damage results from its failure to use reasonable care and diligence. Like most contractors, stevedores are entitled to limit or exclude their liability by contract, provided that the terms are clear and unambiguous and have been agreed to by the other contracting party. Stevedores sometimes attempt to include such provisions in their standard "tariffs" and it becomes a question of proof as to whether such terms

---

[7]   See *Mitsui & Co. (Canada) v. Y.O.W. Shipping Co. S.A.*, [1991] B.C.J. No. 3308 (B.C.S.C.) (QL); *Canadian General Electric Co. v. Pickford & Black Ltd.*, [1971] S.C.R. 41, 14 D.L.R. (3d) 372, rev'g. [1969] 2 Ex. Cr. 392.

have been accepted by the customer.[8] It has been held in Canada that a stevedore is entitled to shelter under a "Himalaya clause" contained in an ocean carrier's bill of lading, extending the carrier's limitations and immunities to the stevedore.[9]

Stevedores face very substantial legal liabilities, not only for loss of or damage to the cargo they handle, but also for damage to third party property, such as the ships on which they work. Stevedores can also be held liable if their negligent workmanship results in damage to others. For example, if the stevedore negligently stows cargo on the ship and the cargo breaks loose and damages the ship or other cargo, the stevedore can be held legally liable for the consequences. Stevedore's liability insurance covering these liabilities is available in the Canadian market and internationally. It may provide coverage for the stevedore's liability for loss of or damage to cargo in its care, custody and control; loss of or damage to third party property; and bodily injury or property damage arising out of the stevedoring operations. It should also provide coverage for the consequences of negligent workmanship carried out by the stevedore after the cargo has left its possession or control.

Liability insurance will only be a part of the stevedore's insurance package. The stevedore requires insurance to cover its other property and liabilities arising from the use of such property, such as vehicles, warehouses, and other equipment, as well as comprehensive general liability insurance to cover risks not insured by its stevedoring liability insurance. Part of the task of the stevedore's insurance broker is to ensure that appropriate coverage is provided for all the property and liability exposures of its customer, in the most cost-effective manner possible.

21.6 PORT AND HARBOUR AUTHORITIES

The owners and operators of ports have duties and responsibilities for the safety of ships using their docks,[10] for the safe care and custody of cargo landed at, handled in or stored at the port and for the safety of persons making use of their facilities. In general, port and harbour authorities have a duty to exercise reasonable care to provide a "safe berth" for ships using the facility, and to ensure that the docks and its approaches are navigable and safe.[11] They may have

---

[8]   See *Braber Equipment Ltd. v. Fraser Surrey Docks Ltd.* (2000), 130 B.C.A.C. 307, aff'g. (1998), 59 B.C.L.R. (3d) 108, 42 B.L.R. (2d) 314 (S.C.); see also *ITO-International Terminal Operators Ltd. v. Miida Electronics Inc.*, [1986] 1 S.C.R. 752, 28 D.L.R. (4th) 641, aff'g. [1982] 1 F.C. 406, 124 D.L.R. (3d) 33 (C.A.), aff'g. [1979] 2 F.C. 283, 96 D.L.R. (3d) 518 (T.D.); *Calkins & Burke Ltd. v. Empire Stevedoring Co. Ltd.*, [1976] 4 W.W.R. 337 (B.C.S.C.).

[9]   See *(I.T.O.) International Terminal Operators Ltd. v. Miida Electronics Inc.*, [1986] 1 S.C.R. 752, 28 D.L.R. (4th) 641, aff'g. [1982] 1 F.C. 406, 124 D.L.R. (3d) 33 (C.A.), aff'g. [1979] 2 F.C. 283, 96 D.L.R. (3d) 518 (T.D.).

[10] See *Greater Vancouver Water District v. "Sparrow's Point" (The)*, [1951] S.C.R. 396, [1951] 2 D.L.R. 785, rev'g. in part [1950] Ex. C.R. 279.

[11] See, however *Cleveland-Cliffs Steamship Co. v. R.*, [1957] 1 S.C.R. 810, 10 D.L.R. (2d) 673, aff'g. [1956] Ex. C.R. 255; *Algoma Central & Hudson Bay Railway Co. v. Manitoba Pool Elevators Ltd.*, [1966] S.C.R. 359, aff'g. [1964] Ex. C.R. 505.

a responsibility to remove wrecked vessels or other obstructions preventing access to the port or to berths within the port and for this reason they may also require insurance against this liability.

Under section 30(4) the *Marine Liability Act*, the owner of a dock, canal or port is entitled to limit its liability for damage to ships, cargo or to other property on board a ship, unless the damage resulted from "the personal act or omission of that owner [or person for whose act the owner is responsible]...committed with intent to cause the loss or recklessly and with knowledge that the loss would probably result". The limitation is based on the greater of $2 million or $1,000 multiplied by the tonnage of the largest ship to have been within the area of the dock, canal or port in the preceding five years.[12]

Marine insurers provide owners or operators of ports, harbour commissions and dock and wharf owners with insurance against their marine liability exposures arising from the operation of their facilities as well as against their liability for cargo entrusted to their safe keeping.[13]

21.7 STORERS

A storer or "warehouser", undertakes the storage of goods for compensation. As a "bailee", the storer will be liable, subject to any contractual limitation or defence, if the goods are lost or damaged as a result of its fault.[14] In *W. Carsen & Co. Ltd. v. Eastern Canada Stevedoring Co. Ltd.*, the Ontario High Court

---

[12] *Marine Liability Act*, S.C. 2001, c. 6, s. 30:

> 30(1) The maximum liability of an owner of a dock, canal or port, for a claim that arises on any distinct occasion for loss caused to a ship, or to any cargo, or other property on board a ship, is the greater of
>
> (a) $2,000,000 and
>
> (b) the amount calculated by multiplying $1,000 by the number of tons of the gross tonnage of the largest ship that is at the time of the loss, or had been within a period of five years before that time, within the area of the dock, canal or port over which the owner had control or management.
>
> . . .
>
> (3) The maximum liability specified in subsection (1) also applies to any person for whose act or omission the owner is responsible. (4) This section does not apply to an owner, or to a person for whose act or omission the owner is responsible, if it is proved that the loss resulted from the personal act or omission of that owner or that person, as the case may be, committed with intent to cause the loss or recklessly and with knowledge that the loss would probably result. (5) For the purpose of this section,
>
> . . .
>
> (b) 'owner of a dock, canal or port' includes any person or authority having the control or management of the dock, canal or port and any ship repairer using the dock, canal or port.

[13] *Braber Equipment Ltd. v. Fraser Surrey Docks Ltd.* (2000), 130 B.C.A.C. 307, aff'g. (1998), 59 B.C.L.R. (3d) 108, 42 B.L.R. (2d) 314 (S.C.).

[14] One of the leading Canadian cases is *London Drugs Ltd. v. Kuehne & Nagel International Ltd.*, [1992] 3 S.C.R. 299, 97 D.L.R. (4th) 261, aff'g. (1990), 70 D.L.R. (4th) 51, [1990] 4 W.W.R. 289 (B.C.C.A.), rev'g. (1986) 2 B.C.L.R. (2d) 181, [1986] 4 W.W.R. 183 (S.C.), a decision of the Supreme Court of Canada. The court held that the employees of the warehouse were entitled to the benefit of a limitation of liability contained in the storage contract.

adopted the following statement from *Halsbury's Law of England*, as to the duty of a bailee:[15]

> A custodian for reward is bound to use due care and diligence in keeping and preserving the article entrusted to him on behalf of the bailor. The standard of care and diligence imposed on him is higher than that required of a gratuitous depositary, and must be that care and diligence which a careful and vigilant man would exercise in the custody of his own chattels of a similar description and character in similar circumstances.
>
> He is therefore bound to take reasonable care to see that the place in which the chattel is kept, including the tackle used in connexion with it, is fit and proper for the purpose, to see that the chattel is in proper custody, to protect it against unexpected danger should that arise, to recover it if it is stolen, and to safeguard the bailor's interest against adverse claims...The obligation to take due care exists independently of contract and an action based on breach of the obligation is an action founded on tort.
>
> The bailee is not, apart from special contract, an insurer, and therefore, in the absence of negligence on his part he is not liable for the loss or damage to the chattel due to some accident, fire, the acts of third parties, or the unauthorized acts of his servants acting outside the scope of their employment....
>
> The custodian is further responsible to the owner of the chattel entrusted to him, both for the negligence of his agents or servants, and for their acts of fraud or other wrongful acts, provided that such acts were committed by them within the apparent scope of their authority, either in the supposed interest of their principal or master or in the course of their employment.

Storers commonly attempt to contractually limit or exclude their heavy common law liabilities and it has been held that they are entitled to do so without offending provincial legislation governing their liabilities.[16]

A storer requires insurance against the consequences of its negligence in the provision of its services and for loss of or damage to cargo in its possession.

---

[15] [1961] O.R. 872 at 875 (H.C.J.), citing 2 *Halsbury's Law of England*, 3rd ed., pp. 114-117.

[16] *Evans Product Co. v. Crest Warehousing Co.*, [1980] 1 S.C.R. 83, 100 D.L.R. (3d) 1, aff'g. [1978] 1 W.W.R. 648, 95 D.L.R. (3d) 631 (B.C.C.A.), rev'g. [1976] 5 W.W.R. 632, 69 D.L.R. (3d) 575 (B.C.S.C.). See the British Columbia *Warehouse Receipt Act*, R.S.B.C. 1996, c. 481, subs. 2:

> (4) A warehouser may insert in a receipt issued by the warehouser any other term or condition that
>
> (a) is not contrary to any provision of this Act, and
>
> (b) does not impair the warehouser's obligation to exercise the care and diligence in regard to the goods as a careful and vigilant owner of similar goods would exercise in the custody of them in similar circumstances.

The Ontario *Warehouse Receipts Act*, R.S.O. 1990, c. W.3, subs. 2(4)(b) is to the same effect.

Such insurance, known as "warehouseman's legal liability" insurance, is available under standard form policies offered by a number of insurers.

21.8 SHIP REPAIRERS

As a bailee of the property of others, a ship repairer is liable if it negligently causes damage to that property. As well, it may be liable if its negligent workmanship subsequently causes damage to the owner of the property.[17] A ship repairer needs marine insurance to protect the property of its customer entrusted to it for construction or repair. It also needs liability insurance to protect it against liability for pollution caused by its activities as well as for property damage and personal injury and death caused by negligence, either during the work or as a result of negligent performance of the work.

A ship repairer's legal liability policy, like virtually all liability policies, typically contains a limit of liability and a deductible. The insuring terms are a matter of negotiation, but such policies generally cover the legal liability of the ship repairer, its employees and agents for damage to vessels or other property in its "care custody or control"; loss of or damage to vessels or other property at sea — property or vessels which the insured's employees are working on; loss of or damage to other property on the vessel, including cargo and the property of others; damage to property removed from a vessel for work; wreck removal expenses; personal injury or death caused to third parties; and costs of defence, legal fees and other expenses. The policy may also insure the ship repairer's legal liability for pollution caused by its operations.[18] Where the ship repairer is engaged in shipbuilding operations, it will generally be necessary to purchase separate insurance covering that risk. There may be exclusions to coverage, such as losses arising from faulty design, losses in relation to vessels accepted for storage only; losses arising from collision or towage liability, and certain consequential losses such as demurrage and loss of profits.

The policy only responds to the legal liability of the repairer. If the repairer's liability is limited in some manner, either contractually or by statute, the insurer defending the claim is entitled to invoke such limitation. While ship repairers in Canada do not have any general limitation of liability, the limitation of liability contained in the *Marine Liability Act* and applicable to owners of docks, ports and canals also extends to "any ship repairer using the dock, canal or port".[19]

Ship repairer's liability coverage frequently stipulates that the policy only responds to claims discovered and reported to the insurer within a specific time

---

[17] See *Burrard Drydock Co. v. Canadian Union Line Ltd.*, [1954] S.C.R. 307, [1954] 3 D.L.R. 561, aff'g. [1953] 2 D.L.R. 828, 9 W.W.R. 13 (B.C.C.A.), additional reasons at (1952), 7 W.W.R. 94 (B.C.S.C.), where a repair firm was held liable to indemnify a shipowner for damages that it had to pay to an owner of cargo which was damaged as a result of water leaking through a valve which had not been properly tightened by the repair firm. See also *Nanaimo Shipyard (1985) Ltd. v. Underwriters, Lloyds* (1992), 12 B.C.A.C. 179, 66 B.C.L.R. (2d) 162 (C.A.), leave to appeal to S.C.C. refused (1992) 70 B.C.L.R. (2d) xxxiii*n*.

[18] See, for example, *Skaarup Shipping Corp. v. Hawker Industries Ltd.*, [1980] 2 F.C. 746, 111 D.L.R. (3d) 343 (C.A.), rev'g. [1978] 2 F.C. 361, 81 D.L.R. (3d) 101 (T.D.).

[19] *Marine Liability Act*, subs. 30(5)(*b*).

after the completion of the work. Premiums under ship repairer's liability policies are usually charged based on a percentage of the gross revenues of the business, thus reflecting the extent of the ship repairer's activities and the risks assumed by the insurer.

21.9 LOG INSURANCE

There is a very substantial timber industry on the Canadian west coast, serving the lumber and pulpwood businesses. Due to limited road and rail access to the forests of the British Columbia interior, marine transportation has proven to be a particularly cost-effective method of moving timber to the mills. One of the most common methods is the collection of logs in massive "booms", which are then towed by tugs to destination. Another method is the use of specially-designed log barges. These are capable of self-loading through onboard cranes and self-discharging their log cargo by filling "tipping tanks" with ballast, producing a list, and allowing the cargo to slide off. The cargo is then boomed for further transportation by tug. Because of the high value of logs, the west coast logging business has generated its own unique maritime law issues, including claims for log salvage and log piracy.[20]

The Association of Marine Underwriters of British Columbia has approved a form of open policy of insurance for logs transported by boom or barge, known as the "Marine Insurance – Logs Form 1/1/93". The form insures "logs whilst waterborne (including piling, boomsticks and swifters), but excluding Alder, Maple, Cottonwood, Aspen and Birch logs, unless otherwise specifically agreed upon prior to the attachment of risk." The insurance is against "all risks" for either total loss of an entire boom or log barge shipment, or, if the insurer is prepared to accept the risk, "total loss of part of a boom or barge shipment or of logs in storage". There is an exclusion of loss caused by sinking. The form includes a sue and labour clause as well as an agreement to pay general average, salvage and special charges. It also contains a reporting clause, requiring that shipments be reported at the end of each month, with full particulars of logs in transit and in storage. There are also many standard provisions in the form, typical of other marine cargo insurance forms.

21.10 TUG AND TOW RISKS

Towage is the employment of one vessel to expedite the voyage of another. The towing vessel is generally referred to as the "tug" and the vessel being towed is referred to as the "tow". Tugs are used to assist ships in docking or undocking and in confined waters, rivers and canals. They also assist vessels that are incapacitated or in distress. Tugs frequently engage in cargo transportation, by pulling barges or ships laden with cargo. Tug companies are also involved in salvage operations, although for most companies this is an occasional, albeit

---

[20] See R. Sheret, *Tugs Booms & Barges: The Story of the Tugs and Crews in British Columbia and Puget Sound* (Washington: Robert Hale & Co., 1999).

remunerative, sideline to their regular business. Tug companies operate on all Canadian coasts, in the St. Lawrence River, and in the Great Lakes.

A distinction should be made between the insurance of tugs and their operations and the insurance of other vessels while being towed. The first type of insurance will be discussed in Section 21.10.1 and the insurance of other ships whilst under tow will be discussed in Section 21.10.2.

21.10.1 Insurance of Tug Operations

The towage business is risky, both financially and physically. It involves a large outlay of capital to purchase tugs, particularly large ocean-going tugs used for long tows or salvage operations. The towing activity itself is also risky — tugs operate in close quarters alongside massive ships, often in difficult weather and sea conditions. These risks affect the way tug companies do business and the way in which insurers underwrite towage related risks.

In one of the earliest, and still leading, Canadian cases, *Sewell v. British Columbia Towing and Transportation Co.*, the Supreme Court of Canada expressed the legal relationship between tug and tow in this manner:[21]

> ...it is difficult to see how there can be any doubt as to the duties of a tug under circumstances like those in evidence here. In [The *"Julia"* , 14 Moo. P.C. 210]. Lord Kingsdown lays it down that:
>
>> 'The law implies an engagement that each vessel would perform its duty in completing the contract, that proper skill and diligence would be used on board of each, and that neither vessel by neglect or misconduct would create unnecessary risk to the other, or increase any risk which would be incidental to the service undertaken.'

The judge went on to quote from another case to the effect that "The contract [of towage] requires no more than that he who undertakes to tow shall carry out his undertaking with that degree of caution and skill which prudent navigators usually employ in similar services."[22]

---

[21] (1883), 9 S.C.R. 527 at 544.

[22] *Ibid.*, at 543, *per* Ritchie C.J., citing *Webb*, 14 Wall. 406. See also (1883), 9 S.C.R. 527 at 543, *per* Strong J.: "...the authorities establish that the defendants [tug owners] were bound to use reasonable care and skill in the performance of their undertaking".
   See also *Canada Steamship Lines Ltd. v. Montreal Trust Co.*, [1940] Ex. C.R. 220, *per* Angers J. at 234-35:
   > In the absence of definite and express limitation of the tug's responsibility such as is established in the present case, a contract of towage implies an engagement that each vessel will fulfil its duty in executing it; that proper skill and diligence will be used on board tug and tow and that neither vessel, by neglect or misconduct, will create unnecessary risk to the other or increase any risk incidental to the services undertaken.
   See also *McKenzie Barge & Derrick Co. v. Rivtow Marine Ltd.* (1969), 7 D.L.R. (3d) 96*n* (S.C.C.), aff'g. (1968), 70 D.L.R. (2d) 409 (Exch. Ct.), *per* Sheppard D.J.A. at 70 D.L.R. (2d) 409 at 414, where the court adopted the following extract from *Halsbury's Laws of England*:
   > In an ordinary contract of towage the owner of the tug contracts that the tug shall be efficient for the purpose for which she is employed and that her crew, tackle and equip-

The tug company is not, however, a "bailee" of the vessel being towed. In *Gatti v. The Queen*, the Federal Court of Canada accepted the following statement from Parks' *The Law of Tug, Tow and Pilotage* (2nd ed.):

> It is of great comfort to towboat companies that under a straight towage contract, where the tug is towing a barge or other object belonging to another person or entity, the law does not impose liability on the towboat company as if it were an insurer or bailee. It has been repeatedly held by the courts that a tug is neither a bailee nor an insurer of the tow. The tug is obliged to use only reasonable and ordinary care and skill and the burden of proving a lack of it is on the one who asserts such liability. Negligence must therefore be proved.[23]

In the absence of express contractual terms to the contrary, the court will imply that the tug, the crew and the equipment will be reasonably fit for the towage service, in the circumstances reasonably to be expected,[24] and that reasonable skill and diligence will be used in the performance of the towage contract.[25]

In order to protect tug owners against the financial risk of damage to the tow, towage contracts frequently place the risk of loss or damage on the towed vessel. There is nothing improper about tug owners contracting on terms whereby the risks of the tow are borne by the owner of the towed vessel and such contracts are common in Canada. This is simply a matter of allocation of risk and it is one of the commercial considerations that determines the price to be paid for the services and the arrangements that will be made for insurance. There are a

---

ment shall be equal to the work to be accomplishes in the weather and under the circumstances reasonably to be expected.

See also *"Champlain" (The) v. Canada Steamship Lines Ltd.*, [1939] Ex. C.R. 89 at 95, *per* Maclean J.:

> The obligation to carry out a towage contract requires nothing more than that degree of caution and skill which prudent navigators usually employ in such services. The occurrence of an accident raises no presumption against the tug and the burden is on the complaining party to prove a lack of ordinary care. A tug is not an insurer and I think this is particularly true of a "named' tug...

As was stated in *Hamilton Marine & Engineering Ltd. v. C.S.L. Group Inc.* (1995), 95 F.T.R. 161 at 171 (F.C.T.D.), *per* Nadon J.:

> In determining the [legal] duties and obligations between a tugboat and the vessel being towed, it is important to determine which was in control at the time of the incident...the determination of which vessel is in control is a question of fact to be determined in every case. As the rule now stands, there is a general presumption that it is the tow which is in control of the tug. As stated by Sir Robert Phillimore in *The Mary* (1879), 5 P.P. 14 at 16...'the tug is the servant of the tow'.

[23] [1984] F.C.J. No. 243 (QL); see also *Hamilton Marine & Engineering Ltd. v. C.S.L. Group Inc.* (1995), 95 F.T.R. 161 (T.D.); *Wire Rope Industries of Canada (1966) Ltd. v. B.C. Marine Shipbuilders Ltd.*, [1981] 1 S.C.R. 363, 121 D.L.R. (3d) 517, rev'g. (1978), 20 N.R. 486 (F.C.A.).

[24] *Pointe Anne Quarries Ltd. v. "M.F. Whalen" (The)*, [1923] 1 D.L.R. 45 (P.C.), aff'g. (1921) 63 S.C.R. 109, var'g. (1921) 21 Ex. C.R. 99.

[25] See *Wire Rope Industries of Canada (1966) Ltd. v. B.C. Marine Shipbuilders Ltd.*, [1981] 1 S.C.R. 363, 121 D.L.R. (3d) 517, rev'g. (1978), 20 N.R. 486 (F.C.A.); see also *Hamilton Marine & Engineering Ltd. v. C.S.L. Group Inc.* (1995), 95 F.T.R. 161 (T.D.).

number of cases which have considered such clauses. Provided the language of the clause is clear and unambiguous,[26] and provided the parties have clearly made it a part of their contract, there is no reason why it will not be upheld by the court, as other such contracts frequently have been.[27]

In Canada, there are several forms of standard towing contract in use. These include the Eastern Canada Towing Conditions, adopted by the Shipping Federation of Canada and the Eastern Canada Tug Owners Association (the "ECTOW" conditions); the standard towing conditions of the British Columbia Tugboat Owners Association; and the "Towcon" and "Towhire" conditions which are used internationally. Some Canadian cases have made it clear that towing conditions can become part of the contract, even without a formal written contract.[28]

There is a significant difference between the ECTOW conditions and the Towcon or Towhire Conditions. While both attempt to allocate to the owners of the towed vessel all risk of loss or damage to that vessel, the "Towcon" and

---

[26] In *Engine & Leasing Co. v. Atlantic Towing Ltd.* (1992), 51 F.T.R. 1, var'd. (1993), 157 N.R. 292 (F.C.A.), the Federal Court of Appeal held that the exculpatory provisions in a towage contract did not apply to negligent repair work carried out by the tug company prior to the commencement of the tow. The result was that the tug company was found liable for its negligence, even though the towing contract would have exonerated it from negligence in the performance of the tow. See *Meeker Log & Timber Ltd. v. "Sea Imp VIII" (The)* (1996), 21 B.C.L.R. (3d) 101 (C.A.), aff'g. (1994) 1 B.C.L.R. (3d) 320, leave to appeal ref'd. Jan. 30, 1997, in which the British Columbia Court of Appeal held that the tug company's towing conditions were so inconsistent and ambiguous that they could not be given any reasonable meaning. The Court of Appeal agreed with the trial judge at (1996), 21 B.C.L.R. (3d) 101 at 103 that "A clause relied upon to obtain an exemption from liability that is not clear and unambiguous is no exemption at all", and that the towing contract was so ambiguous that "there is no telling what was agreed".

[27] See *Wakeham & Sons Ltd. v. St. Lawrence Cement Inc.* (1995), 26 O.R. (3d) 321, 86 O.A.C. 182 (C.A.), rev'g. (1992), 8 O.R. (3d) 340, 9 C.C.L.I. (2d) 211 (Gen. Div.), leave to appeal ref'd. (1996), 29 O.R. (3d) xvn; *Mitsubishi Canada Ltd. v. Rivtow Straits Ltd.* (12 May 1977), Vancouver (B.C.S.C.); *Plumper Bay Sawmills Ltd. v. Jericho Towing Ltd.*, [1980] F.C.J. No. 406; *McKenzie Barge & Derrick Co. v. Rivtow Marine Ltd.* (1969), 7 D.L.R. (3d) 96n (S.C.C.), aff'g. (1968), 70 D.L.R. (2d) 409 (Exch. Ct.); *Gravel & Lake Services Ltd. v. Bay Ocean Management Inc.* (2001), 204 F.T.R. 225 (F.C.T.D.), var'd. [2002] F.C.J. No. 1646. In *Wire Rope Industries of Canada (1966) Ltd. v. B. C. Marine Shipbuilders Ltd.*, [1981] 1 S.C.R. 363, 121 D.L.R. (3d) 517, rev'g. (1978), 20 N.R. 486 (F.C.A.), it was held that the tug owner had exercised due diligence to make the tug seaworthy and that the defect in the towline was latent and something that could not have been discovered with reasonable diligence.

[28] See, for example, *Misener Transportation Ltd. v. "George N. Carlton"(The)*, [1980] F.C.J. No. 404; see also *Wakeham & Sons Ltd. v. St. Lawrence Cement Inc.* (1995), 26 O.R. (3d) 321, 86 O.A.C. 182 (C.A.), rev'g. (1992), 8 O.R. (3d) 340, 9 C.C.L.I. (2d) 211 (Gen. Div.), leave to appeal ref'd. (1996) 29 O.R. (3d) xvn, where towing conditions, which had been incorporated into purchase orders and correspondence, were held to be a valid contract; *McKenzie Barge & Derrick Co. v. Rivtow Marine Ltd.* (1969), 7 D.L.R. (3d) 96 (S.C.C.), aff'g. (1968), 70 D.L.R. (2d) 409 (Exch. Ct.) in which the plaintiff, unsuccessfully, attempted to rely on an exemption clause in its invoice; *A.I.M. Steel Ltd. v. Gulf of Georgia Towing Co. Ltd.* (1964), 50 W.W.R. 476, 48 D.L.R. (2d) 549 (B.C.S.C.); *Gravel & Lake Services Ltd. v. Bay Ocean Management Inc.* (2001), 204 F.T.R. 225 (T.D.), var'd. [2002] F.C.J. No. 1646.

"Towhire" terms provide that each party is required to insure its own property against the risk of loss or damage and to hold the other party harmless for such insured loss or damage. This is sometimes referred to as a "knock for knock" provision. The Towcon and Towhire terms also require a pre-tow survey of the towed vessel, and a certificate of a surveyor certifying that the vessel is fit to be towed and that the tug and towing connections are suitable for the job. In practice, the surveyor's certificate will be given to the master of the tug, and will impose conditions or limitations on the voyage. The certificate may stipulate, for example, that the tug cannot travel in excess of a certain speed or must seek refuge in the event that high winds or heavy seas are in the forecast. Thus, although the insurers of the tow may lose the right of subrogation against the tug owner, their interests are protected by the surveyor's approval of the tow and the imposition of towage warranties.

The insurance of tugs presents particular challenges. One starting point may be to ask the question, "What is being insured?" Is it the physical property involved in the operation, that is, the tug, the tow or the cargo (if any) on board the tow? Is it the liability of the tug to the tow, including liability to the cargo (if any) on board the tow? An equally important, but different, question is "For whose benefit is the insurance being taken out?" Is the insurance for the benefit of only one of the parties to the adventure, or is it taken out for the benefit of more than one party?

The failure to properly identify the risk being insured can lead to unfortunate consequences. For example, in *Burrard Towing Co. v. Reed Stenhouse Ltd.*,[29] a barge laden with scrap metal capsized while being towed by the plaintiff's tug. The policy of insurance on the tug excluded liability for damage to the vessel being towed or its cargo, but an additional premium had been paid to obtain extended coverage for a vessel in tow and its "freight". A claim was made under this extended coverage for the value of the lost cargo. The British Columbia Court of Appeal held that the policy did not cover the tug's liability for the loss of cargo under what was essentially a contract of affreightment or carriage. Ironically, in a very similar case, occurring near the same time but involving somewhat different policy language and different facts, the British Columbia Court of Appeal held that a tower's liability endorsement did provide coverage for the tug owner's liability for loss of cargo on board the towed vessel and held that the exclusion of liability in respect of "cargo" only referred to cargo on board the insured tug.[30]

---

[29] (1996), 19 B.C.L.R. (3d) 391, 35 C.C.L.I. (2d) 145 (C.A.), rev'g. (1994), 100 B.C.L.R. (2d) 92, 29 C.C.L.I. (2d) 29 (S.C.).

[30] *Catherwood Towing Ltd. v. Commercial Union Assurance Co.* (1996), 26 B.C.L.R. (3d) 57, 35 C.C.L.I. (2d) 124 (C.A.), aff'g. (1995), 30 C.C.L.I. (2d) 135, [1995] I.L.R. ¶1-3245 (B.C.S.C.). For a case involving similar problems of construction, see *Driftwood Lands & Timber Ltd. v. United States Fire Insurance Co. of New York*, [1954] O.R. 733 (H.C.J.), aff'd. [1955] 1 D.L.R. 176 at 183 (C.A.), where a marine liability insurance policy insured the plaintiff "in respect of a barge" and indemnified the plaintiff "as owner of the vessel". It was held that this did not provide indemnity to the plaintiff for its liability to the owner of a dock that was damaged when the barge ran into it due to the negligence of those operating the plaintiff's tug. The liability was presumably that of the tug, not of the barge.

Since towage contracts, such as the Towcon and Towhire forms, often involve undertakings by one party to take out insurance for the benefit of both parties coupled with waiver of subrogation provisions to prevent the insurer of one party from subrogating against another, it may be important for the insurer to know the terms of the actual towage contract. This is one example of a situation in which the tug owner's lawyer and its insurance broker may work together to ensure that the desired allocation of risk has been properly achieved through a combination of contractual and insurance protection.

The American Institute Tug Form (August 1, 1976) is specifically designed to provide standard hull insurance for tugs as well as to provide liability insurance in respect of the tug's owing operations. The relevant provisions are:

And it is further agreed that:

(a) If the Vessel hereby insured shall come into collision with any other vessel, craft or structure, floating or otherwise (including her tow); or shall strand her tow or shall cause her tow to come into collision with any other vessel, craft or structure, floating or otherwise, or shall cause any other loss or damage to her tow or the freight thereof or to the property on board, and the Assured, or the Surety, in consequence of the Insured Vessel being at fault, shall become liable to pay and shall pay by way of damages to any other person or persons any sum or sums, we, the Underwriters, will pay the Assured or Surety, whichever shall have paid, such proportion of such sum or sums so paid as our subscriptions hereto bear to the value of the vessel hereby insured; provided always that our liability in respect of any one such casualty shall not exceed our proportionate part of the value of the vessel hereby insured.

(b) In cases where the liability of the Vessel has been contested or proceedings have been taken to limit liability with the consent in writing, of a majority (in amount) of the Underwriters on hull and machinery, we will also pay a like proportion of the costs which the Assured shall thereby incur or be compelled to pay.[31]

There are, however, exclusions to this coverage, including in particular: loss, damage or expenses to vessels in tow which are owned; bareboat chartered or operated by the assured or its affiliates; cargo owned by the assured or its affiliates onboard the vessel in tow; removal of obstructions, wrecks or their cargos under statutory powers or otherwise pursuant to law; and cargo, baggage or engagements of the insured vessel.

21.10.2 Insurance of Ships Under Tow

Different considerations apply to the insurance of ships under tow. Since the towage of a vessel affects the risks to which it is exposed, the fact that the vessel is being towed, as opposed to being under its own power, materially affects the risk. Most time policies therefore provide that the vessel is not to be towed

---

[31] See *Bailey & Co. v. Ocean Mutual Marine Insurance Co.* (1891), 19 S.C.R. 153, aff'g. (1889), 22 N.S.R. 5 (C.A.); *Brooks-Scanlon O'Brien Co. Ltd. v. Boston Insurance Co.*, [1919] 2 W.W.R. 129, 47 D.L.R. 93 (B.C.C.A).

except where customary or where in distress or in need of assistance.[32] In the case of a voyage policy, the failure to disclose that the insured vessel is being towed could be grounds to avoid the policy. Underwriters are sometimes asked to insure the tow of a disabled vessel from one place to another, in which case it is common to insert a warranty requiring prior approval of the tow by an independent marine surveyor or stipulating that the tow must be carried out by one or more approved tugs.[33]

Most standard hull clauses permit the insured vessel to be towed "when customary or in distress". The American Institute Great Lakes Hull Clauses (March 9, 1978) provide at lines 81-84, under the description of the "Adventure":

> ...with leave to sail or navigate with or without pilots, to go on trial trips and to assist and tow vessels or craft in distress, but the Vessel may not be towed, except as is customary or when in need of assistance, nor shall the Vessel render assistance or undertake towage or salvage services under contract previously arranged by the Assured, the Owners, the Managers or the Charterers of the Vessel...

There is, however, a "held covered" provision in the same clauses at lines 85-87:

> The Vessel is held covered in case of any breach of conditions as to towage or salvage activities, provided (a) notice is given to the Underwriters immediately following receipt of knowledge thereof by the Assured, and (b) any amended terms of cover and any additional premium required by the Underwriters are agreed to by the Assured.

There is an identical provision in the C.B.M.U. Great Lakes Hull Clauses (Sept. 1, 1971) at lines 89-97, and a similar provision in the Canadian Hulls (Pacific) Clauses (Sept. 1/91) at lines 76-85.[34]

---

[32] See, for example, the C.B.M.U. Great Lakes Hull Clauses (Sept. 1, 1971), which provide at lines 92-94:

> ...but the Vessel may not be towed, except as is customary or when in need of assistance, nor shall the Vessel render assistance or undertake towage or salvage services under contract previously arranged by the Assured, the Owners, the Managers or the Charterers of the Vessel.

[33] The subject of towing warranties has generated some litigation in Canada. See: *Riverside Landmark Corp. v. Northumberland General Insurance Co.* (1984), 8 C.C.L.I. 118 (Ont. S.C.J.); *J.P. Porter & Sons Ltd. v. Western Assurance Co.*, [1938] 1 D.L.R. 619, 12 M.P.R. 469 (N.S.C.A.), aff'g. [1938] 1 D.L.R. 619 (N.S.S.C.). See also: *Provincial Insurance Co. of Canada v. Connolly* (1879), 5 S.C.R. 258 ("vessel to go out in tow") and *Brooks-Scanlon O'Brien Co. Ltd. v. Boston Insurance Co.*, [1919] 2 W.W.R. 129, 47 D.L.R. 93 (B.C.C.A.).

[34] Canadian Hulls (Pacific) Clauses:

> 5. The Vessel is covered subject to the provisions of this insurance at all times and has leave to sail or navigate with or without pilots, to go on trial trips and to assist and tow vessels or craft in distress, but is warranted that the Vessel shall not otherwise tow or be towed, except as is customary or to the first safe port or place when in need of assistance.

> 6. The vessel is covered in case of any breach of warranty as to cargo, employment, towage, salvage services or date of sailing, provided notice be given to the Underwriters

21.11 FREIGHT INSURANCE

The term "freight" is sometimes used to describe the cargo itself, but in marine insurance "freight" refers to the compensation payable for the carriage of cargo.[35] The term "hire" refers to the compensation paid by a charterer to an owner for the use of the vessel during the charter period. At common law, freight is only payable on the delivery of the goods and if the goods are not delivered for some reason, freight is not payable. To override this principle, shipowners and charterers usually include a provision in the contract of carriage that freight is payable "vessel and/or cargo lost or not lost". Nevertheless, shipowners often wish to procure insurance to protect themselves against the possibility that freight is unrecoverable and for this purpose the freight will be separately insured.

The Canadian *Marine Insurance Act*, like the *M.I.A. 1906*,[36] has little to say about the insurance of freight. Subsection 19(1)(*b*) confirms that the insurable value of freight is "the aggregate of the gross amount of the freight at the risk of the insured and the charges of insurance". Section 69 deals with the measure of indemnity in the event of a partial loss of freight:

> Subject to any express provision in the policy, the measure of indemnity in respect of a partial loss of freight is that proportion of the insurable value of the freight, in the case of an unvalued policy, or the value of the freight specified by the policy, in the case of a valued policy, that the part of the freight lost by the insured bears to the whole freight at the risk of the insured under the policy.

The two main forms available for the insurance of freight are the Institute Time Clauses Freight and the Institute Voyage Clauses Freight (1/11/95). These cover the shipowner's loss of freight due to named perils as well as the liability to pay damages for three-fourths of the lost freight of another vessel as a result of a collision with that vessel. The policy also insures against general average and salvage charges in relation to freight. The measure of indemnity in case of partial loss of freight is not to exceed the gross freight actually lost, whereas in the case of actual total loss or constructive total loss, the insured is entitled to recover the amount stated in the policy whether or not the vessel was earning freight at the time of the loss. The policy form excludes claims "consequent on loss of time", referring to periods when the vessel is out of service as a result of an accident and unable to earn revenues.

---

immediately after receipt of advices and any amended terms of cover and any additional premium required by them be agreed.

The C.B.M.U. Great Lakes Hull Clauses (Sept. 1, 1971) can be found in Appendix G and the Canadian Hulls (Pacific) Clauses (Sept. 1/91) can be found in Appendix E.

[35] Canadian *Marine Insurance Act*, S.C. 1993, c. 22, s. 2(1): "freight includes the profit derivable by a shipowner from the use of the shipowner's ship to carry the shipowner's goods or movables and freight payable by a third party, but does not include passenger fares."

[36] 6 Edw. VII, c. 41.

21.12   WAR AND STRIKES INSURANCE

The risks of war and strikes are excluded by most standard marine insurance forms and it is usually necessary to purchase separate coverage for these risks. For example, the Institute Cargo Clauses (A), (B) and (C), 1/1/82 contain a "war exclusion clause" and a "strikes exclusion clause". The Institute Time Clauses Hulls (1/11/95) contain similar exclusions. While the C.B.M.U. Great Lakes Hull Clauses (Sept. 1, 1971) exclude both war and strikes, the Canadian Hulls (Pacific) Clauses (Sept. 1/91) excludes war risks but there is express coverage for strikes, riots and civil commotions as well as destruction of or damage to the vessel caused by persons acting maliciously.

In the case of cargo insurance, using the Institute Cargo Clauses (1/1/82), it is necessary to purchase separate coverage for war risks (the Institute War Clauses (Cargo) 1/1/82) and for strikes (the Institute Strikes Clauses (Cargo) 1/1/82). In the case of hull and machinery insurance, on the other hand, the two coverages are combined in one form — for example, the Institute War and Strikes Clauses Hulls — Time 1/11/95.

The form of the Institute Strikes Clauses (Cargo) 1/1/82 is similar in content and structure to the (A), (B) and (C) clauses 1/1/82, but the risks covered are loss or damage caused to the subject-matter insured caused by:

1.1   strikers, locked-out workmen, or persons taking part in labour disturbances, riots or civil commotions

1.2   any terrorist or any person acting from a political motive.

The insurance covers general average charges "incurred to avoid or in connection with the avoidance of loss from a risk covered under these clauses". (Clause 2) The exclusions in the Institute Strikes Clauses (Cargo) are similar to the exclusions in the Cargo Clauses (1/1/82) and exclude "loss damage or expense proximately caused by delay". (Clause 3.5) This is important because one of the greatest risks of strikes in relation to cargo is that the cargo will lose its value — either due to deterioration or due to loss of market.

The Institute War Clauses (Cargo) (1/1/82) cover loss or damage to the subject matter insured caused by:

1.1   war civil war revolution rebellion insurrection or civil strife arising therefrom, or any hostile act by or against a belligerent power

1.2   capture seizure arrest restraint or detainment, arising from risks covered under 1.1 above, and the consequences thereof or any attempt threat

1.3   derelict mines, torpedoes or other derelict weapon of war.

Like the strikes clauses, the war clauses cover general average and salvage charges incurred to avoid a loss from a risk covered by the insurance. The war clauses cover the cargo until it arrives at the discharge port and for a further 15 days in the port, but the cover ceases once the goods are transported on land.

In the case of hull and machinery insurance, it is common to purchase combined war and strikes coverage using, for example, the Institute War and Strikes

Clauses Hulls — Time 1/11/95. This form insures loss or damage to the vessel caused by:

1.1 War civil war revolution rebellion insurrection, or civil strike arising therefrom, or any hostile act by or against a belligerent power

1.2 Capture seizure arrest restraint or detainment, and the consequences thereof or any attempt thereat

1.3 derelict mines torpedoes bombs or other derelict weapons of war

1.4 strikers, locked-out workmen or persons taking part in labour disturbances, riots or civil commotions

1.5 Any terrorist or any person acting maliciously or from a political motive

1.6 Confiscation or expropriation.

There is a specific provision that if, as a result of capture, seizure, arrest, restraint, detainment, confiscation or expropriation, the insured has lost "the free use and disposal of the Vessel for a continuous period of 12 months", then "for the purpose of ascertaining whether the Vessel is a constructive total loss, the Assured shall be deemed to have been deprived of the possession of the Vessel without any likelihood of recovery". (clause 3)

There are a number of exclusions at clause 5, including: damage caused by atomic or nuclear weapons; outbreak of war between any of the United Kingdom, the United States, France, the Russian Federation and the People's Republic of China; requisition or pre-emption; capture or detention or confiscation by order of the state in which the Vessel is registered.

In the case of Canadian vessels, hull and machinery and protection and indemnity war risks and strikes insurance can be obtained through a mutual insurance association, the Canadian Shipowners Mutual Assurance Association, which offers several types of insurance. The coverage is complex, but the following is a brief summary of the insurance:

- so-called "Canada engaged risks", which are the risks reinsured by the Government of Canada pursuant to a reinsurance agreement with the association under the *Marine and Aviation War Risks Act*,[37] and include war risks arising from war or other hostilities in which Canada is involved;

- hull and machinery war risks insurance in respect of hostilities other than those involving Canada;

- detention and diversion expenses arising from hostilities;

- protection and indemnity coverage in respect of war and strikes risks;

- sue and labour expenses in respect of insured risks; and

- claims which the directors may, in their discretion, determine to be within the scope of the coverage provided by the association.

---

[37]   R.S.C. 1970, c. W-3.

In the case of P. & I. insurance, the P. & I. Clubs invariably exclude war risks from their general coverage, but provide separate insurance which can be purchased against such risk. The standard forms of P. & I. insurance outside the Clubs typically contain an exclusion for war risks. For example, the SP–23 form excludes liability:

> For any loss, damage or expense sustained by reason of capture, seizure, arrest, restraint or detainment, or the consequence thereof, or of any attempt thereat, or sustained in consequence of military, naval or air action by force of arms, including mines and torpedoes or other missiles or engines of war...

The Canadian (Pacific) Protection and Indemnity Clauses (1/1/83)[38] also exclude war risks.

21.13 PLEASURE CRAFT

Boating is said to be the fastest-growing recreational activity in Canada, involving over 3 million boats with nearly 10 million Canadians enjoying the waterways each year. The boats range from canoes and rowboats, to small fishing and sailboats, to exotic and expensive sailing yachts and cabin cruisers. There is an infinite variety of unique vessels in this range, including high-powered ski boats, jet boats, personal watercraft, antique boats, technology-laden fishing boats and ocean-going sail and power boats. The variety and complexity of these vessels, coupled in many cases with their high values and unusual uses, present particular challenges for insurance brokers and for insurers.

Like owners of commercial vessels, pleasure boat owners need insurance to protect their asset against loss or damage. As well, they need insurance for third party liabilities, which is not generally covered by other insurance policies, in the absence of a specific endorsement. Under Canadian maritime law, the operator of a pleasure craft is liable for damage done to third parties as a result of his or her negligence in the operation of the vessel. However, unlike the case in motor vehicles, the owner of a yacht or motor boat is not by statute "vicariously liable" for the negligence of the operator. Thus, the owner of a boat who entrusts the "care and control" of the boat to another, is not *necessarily, for that reason alone*, liable to a third party who is injured as a result of the operator's negligence. The owner may be held liable if the accident was caused as a result of his or her *personal* negligence — for example, if the boat was unseaworthy, not properly equipped, or otherwise unfit for operation, or if the owner of the boat knew that the operator was unskilled, unfit to operate the vessel, or was impaired as a result of the consumption of alcohol or drugs. Similarly, if the operator of the boat could be regarded as the "agent" of the owner, it is possible that the owner might be liable for the operator's negligence. In the absence of these circumstances, however, the owner would not, as such, be liable for the negligence of the operator.[39]

---

[38] Appendix N.
[39] See, however, *Leggat Estate v. Leggat*, [2001] O.J. 1301 (S.C.J.).

A unique feature of Canadian maritime law is that the owner of a vessel and a person operating the vessel are entitled to limit their liability for damage caused by the vessel in a maritime accident, unless the accident was caused by the "personal act or omission [of the owner or operator of the vessel] committed with the intent to cause such loss, or recklessly and with knowledge that such loss would probably result".[40] This provision applies both to pleasure craft and commercial vessels.[41] In the case of vessels less than 300 tons, which would include most pleasure craft other than the most substantial yachts, the limitation is fixed at $1 million for claims in respect of loss of life or personal injury and at $500,000 in respect of any other claims, such as claims for property damages. It has been held that these provisions are constitutionally valid and applicable to both pleasure craft and commercial vessels.[42]

The owner of a pleasure craft will need liability insurance to cover his or her liability as an operator and owner of the vessel as well as the liability of family members and others operating the vessel with the owner's consent. Notwithstanding the absence of statutory "vicarious liability" and the limitation of liability available to boat owners and operators, the owner may wish to have the comfort of coverage for operator-related liabilities as well as insurance in excess of the statutory limitation.

In Canada, many standard homeowner's, condominium owner's and tenant's insurance policies permit watercraft to be added to the insurance policy, either by a specific endorsement or by stand-alone policy wording. Some homeowner's policies may automatically include protection for personal watercraft liability exposures, subject to limitations as to the size or power of the vessel, at no additional cost. Vessels of a greater size or horsepower may require additional premium to cover the enhanced risk. The policy may contain limitations in terms of horsepower, above which it will be necessary for the insured to purchase a separate policy. The policy may also cover medical expenses incurred as a result of an accident, including hospital treatment, rehabilitation and so on.

For larger and more expensive pleasure craft, or for unique vessels, the broker may recommend a stand-alone policy of marine insurance. Several of the leading Canadian marine insurers have crafted special policies designed for pleasure craft, which may provide "all risks" or "named perils" insurance for physical loss or damage to the boat, trailer and auxiliary equipment, third party liability coverage, coverage for defence costs, sue and labour expenses, removal of wreck as well as emergency medical expenses and death benefits. Most policy forms have exclusions with respect to wear and tear and inherent vice as

---

[40] Canadian *Marine Liability Act*, S.C. 2001, c. 6, Schedule 1, Convention on Limitation of Liability for Maritime Claims, 1976, as amended by the Protocol of 1996, Article 4.

[41] *Whitbread v. Walley*, [1990] 3 S.C.R. 1273, [1991] 2 W.W.R. 195, aff'g. (1988), 51 D.L.R. (4th) 509, [1988] 5 W.W.R. 313 (B.C.C.A.), rev'g. (1987), 45 D.L.R. (4th) 729, 19 B.C.L.R. (2d) 120 (S.C.).

[42] *Whitbread v. Walley*, [1990] 3 S.C.R. 1273, [1991] 2 W.W.R. 195, aff'g. (1988), 51 D.L.R. (4th) 509, [1988] 5 W.W.R. 313 (B.C.C.A.), rev'g. (1987), 45 D.L.R. (4th) 729, 19 B.C.L.R. (2d) 120 (S.C.).

well as damage caused by war risk and nuclear incident. Most policies also exclude coverage for damage or liabilities resulting from dishonest or illegal acts committed by the insured or the operator. Some policies also exclude coverage if the operator's abilities were impaired by alcohol or drugs at the time of the accident.

The insurer of a pleasure craft, like the insurer of a commercial vessel, may be concerned enough to impose limitations on the manner in which the vessel is operated. It is common for such policies to contain warranties that the vessel will be used for private pleasure purposes only,[43] that it will not be used for racing, that it will be operated only within a designated area,[44] and that, depending on the area of operation, it will be "laid up and out of commission" during the winter months.[45] The policy may also impose obligations on the insured to keep the vessel licensed, to operate it in accordance with law, and to maintain it in a seaworthy condition. These are important considerations for the insurer, as the failure to comply with them will materially affect the risk to which the insurer is exposed. The subject of warranties is discussed in detail in Chapter 8, *Warranties*.

In principle, the law of marine insurance applies equally to commercial vessels and to pleasure craft. Canadian maritime law is considered to be uniform across the country and there is generally no difference in the application of that law as between commercial vessels and pleasure craft.[46] The *C.M.I.A.* does not make a distinction between commercial vessels and pleasure craft, nor is there any such distinction in the case law. There are numerous cases in which the law of marine insurance and Canadian marine insurance legislation have been found to be applicable to the insurance of pleasure craft.[47] While there is little doubt that the *C.M.I.A.* applies to a stand-alone policy of insurance covering a pleasure craft, it would be interesting to question whether it would apply to the "marine" risks covered by a homeowner's policy that included coverage, either generally or by way of endorsement, for private watercraft.

21.14 MARINAS

The thousands of inland lakes and rivers in Canada and the country's vast ocean coastline support numerous businesses catering to the needs of recreational boaters. Marinas, for example, provide facilities for the storage, docking, fueling and repair of pleasure craft. Unless protected by contractual limitations or exclusions, the bailee will be liable for any loss or damage to its customers'

---

[43] See Chapter 8, *Warranties*, Section 8.3.6, "Private Pleasure Use".

[44] See Chapter 8, *Warranties*, Section 8.3.1, "Navigation Limits".

[45] See Chapter 8, *Warranties*, Section 8.3.2, "Laid up and Out of Commission".

[46] See *Whitbread v. Walley*, [1990] 3 S.C.R. 1273, [1991] 2 W.W.R. 195, aff'g. (1988), 51 D.L.R. (4th) 509, [1988] 5 W.W.R. 313 (B.C.C.A.), rev'g. (1987), 45 D.L.R. (4th) 729, 19 B.C.L.R. (2d) 120 (S.C.); *Ordon Estate v. Grail*, [1998] 3 S.C.R. 437, 166 D.L.R. (4th) 193, aff'g. (1996), 30 O.R. (3d) 643, 140 D.L.R. (4th) 52 (C.A.), leave to appeal allowed (1997), 225 N.R. 238*n* (S.C.C.).

[47] See for example: *Marler v. Schmucki*, [1996] O.J. No. 3685 (Ont. Gen. Div.); *Staples v. Great American Insurance Co. of New York*, [1941] S.C.R. 213, 2 D.L.R. 1.

property unless it establishes that it exercised "due care for the safety of the article entrusted to him by taking such care of the goods as would a prudent man of his own possessions".[48] The marina will also be liable for personal injuries suffered by those using or visiting its premises, if caused by its negligence.[49]

A properlyworded contract may allow a marina to exclude or limit liabilities which it would otherwise have.[50] As with any such contract, the court will ask whether the customer actually agreed to its terms either by signing the contract or by implicitly accepting its terms. Some marinas attempt to exclude liability by posting signs on their premises such as "Boats and motors stored at owner's risk" or "Marina has no liability for loss or damage to boats, however caused." While the case law in this area is very fact-driven, it is probably safe to say that such signage offers little protection in the absence of written contract.[51]

Some marinas attempt to place the risk of loss on their customers by requiring them to take out insurance and contractually stipulating that the marina is entitled to have the benefit of such insurance. As a risk management measure, provided the contractual documentation is sound, this approach is perfectly acceptable, since the boat owner will generally have hull and machinery insurance and since the cost of marina operator's legal liability insurance may be expensive. As with any such exemption clause, the court will carefully examine the underlying contractual documentation to determine whether the parties did in fact agree that any loss or damage to the insured boat, even if caused by the negligence of the marina, would be covered by the boat owner's insurer without recourse to the marina or its liability insurer.[52]

Where the boat owner has entered into such an agreement without the express or implied agreement of its own insurer, there is an argument that its hull insurance could be invalidated since the owner has released a third party from liability without the insurer's consent, thus impairing the insurer's subrogation rights.[53] Most small boat owners would not think to obtain their insurer's permission before signing a marina storage contract and one would expect that most Canadian insurers know that marinas commonly contractually limit or exclude their liability. It could be argued that insurers impliedly consent to their insured's entering into such customary forms of storage contracts.

---

[48] *Punch v. Savoy's Jewellers Ltd.* (1986), 54 O.R. (2d) 383 at 389, 26 D.L.R. (4th) 546 (C.A.), *per* Cory J. (as he then was), cited with approval in *Neff v. St. Catharines Marina Ltd.* (1998), 37 O.R. (3d) 481, 155 D.L.R. (4th) 647 (C.A.). In the Neff case, the Court of Appeal found that a fire in the marina was "accidental" and of unknown origin, and that the marina operator had therefore established that the fire occurred without its fault.

[49] See *Weller v. Keswick Marine Ltd.*, [1978] O.J. No. 609.

[50] *Dryburgh v. Oak Bay Marina (1992) Ltd.* (2001), 206 F.T.R. 255 (T.D.).

[51] For a case in which the marina's mooring contract was upheld, see *Dryburgh v. Oak Bay Marina (1992) Ltd.* (2001), 206 F.T.R. 255 (T.D.).

[52] See Chapter 12, *Subrogation*, Section 12.11, "Waiver of Subrogation"; see also *Wakeham & Sons Ltd. v. St. Lawrence Cement Inc.* (1995), 26 O.R. (3d) 321, 86 O.A.C. 182 (C.A.), rev'g. (1992), 8 O.R. (3d) 340, 9 C.C.L.I. (2d) 211 (Gen. Div.), leave to appeal ref'd. (1996), 29 O.R. (3d) xvn.

[53] See Chapter 12, *Subrogation*.

There are various forms of marina operator's liability insurance offered in the Canadian market. The policy may include: coverage for legal liability for loss or damage to vessels including motors and other fittings while in the care, custody and control of the insured; liability for loss or damage to other property; liability arising out of the use of non-owned vessels in the operation of the marina; and liability for death or personal injury (although this may be covered by other policies, such as a comprehensive general liability policy). Common exclusions in marina operators' liability policies are: liability for faulty workmanship; liabilities assumed under contract; liability for damage or loss of property owned or leased by the insured; and liability for pollution. Some insurers provide an endorsement pursuant to which the marina can purchase "P. & I." liability insurance covering liabilities of the marina arising out of the operation of vessels either owned by the marina or being operated by the marina's personnel in the course of their duties.[54] Others offer this coverage as part of their standard policy wording. The insurance of marinas can be a complex matter and the broker will need to consider the various risks to which its client is exposed, its contractual obligations to its customers and the other marine and non-marine insurance which it has, or should have, to cover its operations.

21.15 BUILDER'S RISK

Subsection 6(1)(*b*) of the *C.M.I.A.* provides that a contract of marine insurance may insure against "losses that are incidental to the building, repair or launch of a ship", and it is common to insure a ship during construction under a "Builder's Risk" policy. This type of insurance may be effected by a shipyard pursuant to an open policy, to insure each new vessel as construction begins or by the ship owner itself, to cover the ship while under construction. The Association of Marine Underwriters of British Columbia has published the British Columbia Builders' Risks Clauses (1989), reproduced in Appendix I. The policy contains four sections. The first section deals with general matters including the description and duration of the risk; the premium; the amount insured as well as provisions dealing with subrogation;[55] assignment; cancellation; and suit time limitation.[56] The subrogation clause provides that the insured and the insurer will participate jointly in recoveries. There is a "plain language" warranty in section 1 of the clauses, apparently designed to avoid the tendency of Canadian courts to "read down" warranties:

> This policy contains warranties and general conditions none of which are to be interpreted as suspensive conditions. The Underwriters have agreed to accept the risk of insuring the Vessel on the condition precedent that the Assured will comply strictly and literally with these warranties and conditions. If the Assured breaches

---

[54] See Chapter 20, *Protection and Indemnity Insurance*. See also, for example, *Pillgrem v. Cliff Richardson Boats Ltd.*, [1976] I.L.R. ¶1-742 (Ont. H.C.J.), where the claim for the loss of the plaintiff's boat was held to come under a marina operator's liability policy but not under the protection and indemnity endorsement to the policy.

[55] The policy provides that the insurer and the insured will jointly participate in recoveries.

[56] The time for suit is twelve months.

any of these warranties or conditions, the Underwriters at their option will not pay any claim arising thereafter, regardless of whether or not such breach is causative or in any way connected to such claim.

The next section of the policy is entitled "Hull Section" and insures against all risks of physical loss or damage to the Vessel from any external cause while under construction and/or fitting out and while on trial trips. It also insures materials on the premises of the insured and in transit within 100 miles of the construction site.

The third section provides collision liability and protection and indemnity insurance for the vessel. The final section contains exclusions, amongst them war and strikes; liability under Workers Compensation Act legislation; claims for loss of earnings of the vessel; and claims arising from defects in material or design.

The Institute of London Underwriters also publishes the Institute Clauses for Builder's Risks, (1/6/88), as well as associated war and strikes clauses.

21.16   CHARTERER'S LIABILITY INSURANCE

A charterer can be thought of as a hirer of a vessel. Charters can be obtained for a single voyage, known as a "voyage charter", or for a period of time, known as a "time charter". The charterer will usually require "charterer's liability insurance" to cover its liability for: loss of or damage to cargo when it acts as a carrier of goods; damage to third parties including, in some jurisdictions, damage to the environment or others caused by oil pollution; breach of its duty to nominate a safe port or safe berth; damage to the ship caused by the operations of loading or discharging cargo as well as damage caused to the ship or to others by the carriage of dangerous cargo; and the charterer's duty to indemnify the shipowner against liability to third parties caused by the fault of the charterer. This is a specialized form of insurance, which usually requires careful scrutiny of the relevant charterparty and contracts of carriage. It can be procured in the domestic and international marine insurance markets.

21.17   POLLUTION

Pollution liability presents a potentially vast exposure for an insurer and for this reason many of the standard forms of marine insurance specifically exclude this liability. The subject of pollution is discussed in Chapter 20, *Protection and Indemnity Insurance*, as it relates to this class of marine insurance. It is worth noting, however, that both cargo insurance and hull and machinery insurance are *property* insurance and do not normally cover the liability of the owner of the property for damage caused by pollution emanating from that property. Thus, the insurer of a pollutant cargo, insured under a standard marine cargo insurance form, such as the Institute Cargo Clauses (1/1/82) does not insure the cargo owner's potential liability if the cargo escapes and causes damage to third parties or to the environment. The insurer does, of course, insure against the financial consequences of damage *to* the cargo as well as the financial consequences of the *loss of the cargo* as a result of an insured peril. As well, the insurance covers the consequences of damage to the cargo caused by pollution due to an insured peril. For example, if oil or another contaminant leaks from the ship or other cargo onto the insured cargo, the damage will generally be covered by the cargo insurance policy.

As well, the standard forms of hull and machinery insurance do not cover pollution, other than pollution liability that may be insured under the limited coverage of the collision liability clause, or coverage for loss or damage due to the actions taken by a governmental authority to prevent a pollution hazard as a result of an insured peril.[57]

The shipowner's liability for pollution is generally covered by protection and indemnity policies. This subject is discussed in Chapter 20. The Canadian (Pacific) Protection and Indemnity Clauses (1/1/83) cover the shipowner's liability for pollution, where caused by the fault of the assured, but specifically exclude coverage for punitive or exemplary damages.

21.18 CONCLUSION

One of the unique features of marine insurance has been its adaptability and responsiveness to the business needs of its customers. As this chapter indicates, the insurance needs of a particular business involves an interplay between the physical and financial risks associated with the business, the legal regime under which it operates, and the contractual arrangements between the business person and his or her customers. The challenge for the client and its broker is to tailor an insurance program that gives the client the protection it needs at a cost which it can afford. The challenge for the insurer is to underwrite that program at a cost which will reflect the risk to which it is exposed.

Insurance is only one level of protection for the client. As many of the above examples indicate, the client's business contracts are frequently designed to provide a level of protection for the business by allocating risks to some other parties. Frequently, therefore, the client's lawyer and insurance broker work together to make sure that the client's insurance program is in harmony with the way it structures its business and does business with its customers.

---

[57] See Chapter 19, *Hull and Machinery Insurance*.

PART III

GENERAL AVERAGE

Chapter 22

General Average[1]

22.1 INTRODUCTION

The term "general average" refers to a maritime loss that is *shared generally* amongst the parties to the maritime adventure. It is distinguished from a particular average loss which is borne, initially, by the *particular* party on whom it falls. The definition of general average in the early English case of *Birkley v. Presgrave*, has been cited with approval in numerous Canadian cases:

> All loss which arises in consequence of extraordinary sacrifices made or expenses incurred for the preservation of the ship and cargo come within general average, and must be borne proportionably by all who are interested. Natural justice requires this.[2]

General average is often thought of as a form of insurance because it is one of the earliest examples of the sharing of maritime losses. The parties to the "common adventure" were taken to have impliedly agreed to share "extraordinary" sacrifices and expenditures on the theory that since their "common adventure" has been completed (albeit with some unforeseen sacrifices or expenses) all the participants in that adventure should share in the sacrifices or expenses. While general average sacrifices and expenses, as well as the liability to make general average contributions, are typically covered by insurance, it is important to recognize that general average exists quite independently of insurance and that rights and obligations in general average are adjusted without reference to whether or not the parties are insured.[3] In most cases, the fact that

---

[1] This chapter is based on a self-published booklet by George R. Strathy, *The Law and Practice of General Average in Canada* (1995), written to mark the end of his 1994-95 term as Chair of the Association of Average Adjusters of Canada.

[2] (1801), 1 East 220, *per* Lawrence J. at 228-29. See, for example, *Northland Navigation Co. Ltd. and Northland Shipping (1962) Co. Ltd. v. Patterson Boiler Works Ltd.*, [1983] 2 F.C. 59 (T.D.); *Dancey v. Burns* (1880), 31 U.C.C.P. 313 (Ont. C.A.); *Chaffey v. Schooley* (1876), 40 U.C.Q.B. 165 (Ont. C.A.). For a discussion of the history of general average, see *Edward and Charles Gurney v. Aeneas D. MacKay* (1875), 37 U.C.Q.B. 324 at 340 (C.A.); see also N.G. Hudson, *The York-Antwerp Rules*, 2nd ed. (London: Witherby & Co. Ltd., 1991) at pp. 7-13; Lowndes & Rudolf, *General Average and the York-Antwerp Rules*, 11th ed., D.J. Wilson & J.H.S. Cooke, eds. (London: Sweet and Maxwell, 1990) at pp. 39-59.

[3] In *Ultramar Canada Inc. v. Mutual Marine Office Inc. (The "Pointe Levy")* (1994), 82 F.T.R. 1 at 8 (T.D.), the trial judge stated: "General average exists quite independently of marine insurance."

the interests are insured will have no bearing on the way in which the general average is adjusted.[4] However, the common forms of hull, cargo and freight marine insurance policies insure against both particular average and general average losses and also against the *contribution* the property owner is required to make in general average. Protection and indemnity (P. & I.) policies usually contain provisions dealing with aspects of the shipowner's liability in general average.

This chapter will examine the treatment of general average under marine insurance policies. In order to properly understand the issues, an explanation of the basics of general average is required.

22.2 THE PRINCIPLES OF GENERAL AVERAGE

General average is part of maritime law and exists independently of the contract of carriage.[5] In practice, however, most such contracts, whether bills of lading or charterparties, incorporate a set of internationally-accepted rules for general average, known as the *York-Antwerp Rules*. Sections from the 1994 version of these rules, known as the "*YAR 1994*", are reproduced in this chapter, with the permission of the Comité Maritime Internationale, the custodian of the *YAR*.

Subsection 65(2) of the Canadian *Marine Insurance Act* ("*C.M.I.A.*")[6] defines general average:

> 65(2) A general average act is any extraordinary sacrifice or expenditure, known as a general average sacrifice and a general average expenditure, respectively, that is voluntarily and reasonably incurred in time of peril for the purpose of preserving the property from peril in a common adventure.

The requirements of general average, as defined by the *C.M.I.A.* and the case law, are therefore:

    (a) a common maritime adventure;[7]

---

[4]   See *Ultramar Canada Inc. v. Mutual Marine Office Inc. (The "Pointe Levy")* (1994), 82 F.T.R. 1 at 8 (T.D.).

[5]   In *Ultramar Canada Inc. v. Mutual Marine Office Inc. (The "Pointe Levy")* (1994), 82 F.T.R. 1 at 8 (T.D.), the trial judge stated: "The obligation to contribute in general average does not depend upon any contract between the parties."

[6]   S.C. 1993, c. 22

[7]   The practice of average adjusters in Canada is to treat ballast voyages as though the vessel had cargo on board, for the purpose of adjusting a general average loss under the hull and machinery policy. This practice is confirmed in the *Rules of Practice* (Other than Great Lakes) of the Association of Average Adjusters of Canada. The Canadian Hulls (Pacific) Clauses (Sept. 1/91), Appendix E, contain a specific provision to this effect at clause 10, lines 131-139. See L.A. Buglass, *Marine Insurance and General Average in the United States*, 3rd ed. (Centreville, MD: Cornell Maritime Press, 1991) at pp. 214-217 for a detailed discussion of the treatment of ballast voyages under United States law and practice. With respect to the situation in which the ship and cargo are owned by the same person, see *C.M.I.A.*, subs. 65(7) and *Montgomery v. Indemnity Mutual Marine Insurance Company*, [1901] 1 K.B. 147, [1902] 1 K.B. 734. The principle in this subsection was applied in *Ultramar Canada Inc. v. Mutual Marine Office Inc. (The "Pointe*

(b) an extraordinary sacrifice or extraordinary expenditure;

(c) made for the preservation from a common peril which is extraordinary in nature and not one of the ordinary incidents of the voyage;[8]

(d) voluntarily made or incurred;[9]

(e) and reasonably made or incurred;[10]

(f) for the purpose of preserving the adventure;[11] and

(g) resulting in the successful preservation of the adventure, or part of it.[12]

22.3 TYPES OF SACRIFICES AND EXPENDITURES RECOVERABLE

The requirements of general average can best be understood by examining the types of losses and charges recoverable in general average. These are of two broad types, *sacrifices* and *expenditures*, and can be further divided into losses affecting the *cargo* and losses affecting the *ship*. *Sacrifices* of cargo can include: jettison — the "sacrifice" of cargo by throwing it overboard in order to lighten

---

Levy") (1994), 82 F.T.R. 1 (T.D.), in which the plaintiff owned both the vessel and the cargo. General average was adjusted as though the two interests were separately owned, and the resulting contributions were apportioned as between the hull and cargo underwriters. With respect to tug and tow and general average, see the addresses "General Average and the Community of Tug and Tow", given by Mr. A.H. Platt, Chairman of the Association of Average Adjusters of Canada, at the 7th annual meeting of the association in 1973; "Tugs, Tows and Extraordinary Charges", by K. Hext, Chairman, at the association's 18th annual meeting in 1984; "Tug and Tow: General Average Situations", by T.G. Stradling, Chairman, at the 26th annual meeting in 1992. See also *Northland Navigation Co. Ltd. and Northland Shipping (1962) Co. Ltd. v. Patterson Boiler Works Ltd.*, [1983] 2 F.C. 59 (T.D.); the decision of the United States Supreme Court in *The "J.P. Donaldson"*, 167 U.S. 599 (1897); Rule 15 of the *Rules of Practice* (Other than Great Lakes) of the Association of Average Adjusters of Canada and Rule B of the *YAR 1994*. With respect to maritime activities that are not "adventures", see *Insurance Co. of North America v. Colonial Steamships Ltd.*, [1942] Ex. C.R. 79 (Ex. Ct.), aff'd. [1942] S.C.R. 357, 3 D.L.R. 225.

8   See *Edward and Charles Gurney v. Aeneas D. MacKay* (1875), 37 U.C.Q.B. 324 at 341 (C.A.); *Kidd v. Thomson* (1899), 26 O.A.R. 220 (C.A.). The peril need not be immediate, as long as it is "actual or impending": *St. Lawrence Construction Ltd. v. Federal Commerce & Navigation Co. Ltd.*, [1985] 1 F.C. 767, 56 N.R. 174 (C.A.), leave to appeal refused (1985), 58 N.R. 236. With respect to so-called "artificial general average", see *Ellerman Lines Ltd. v. Gibbs, Nathaniel (Canada) Ltd.* (1983), 4 D.L.R. (4th) 645, (F.C.T.D.), aff'd. (1986), 66 N.R. 81 (F.C.A.).

9   *Ainsworth v. Cusack* (1858), 4 Nfld. L.R. 236.

10   See, for example, *Singer Manufacturing Co. v. Western Assurance Co.* (1896), 10 Que. S.C. 379 (C.A.), where the court quoted with approval from the English case of *Svendsen v. Wallace* (1884), 13 L.R. Q.B. 69 (C.A.), aff'd. 10 A.C. 404 (H.L.); see also *Federal Commerce and Navigation Co. Ltd. v. Eisenerz-GmbH*, [1974] S.C.R. 1225. See *Canadian Transport Co. Ltd. v. Hunt, Leuchars Hepburn (The "City of Alberni")* (1947), 63 B.C.L.R. 262 at 264 (B.C.S.C.), to the effect that general average applies to expenditures, with the proviso that they must be reasonable. See also the "Rule Paramount" in the *YAR 1994*.

11   *Dancey v. Burns* (1881), 31 U.C.C.P. 313 (C.A.).

12   *Western Assurance Co. v. Ontario Coal Co.* (1890), 19 O.R. 462, (Q.B.), aff'd. (1892), 19 O.A.R. 41 (C.A.), aff'd. (1892), 21 S.C.R. 383; *Ultramar Canada Inc. v. Mutual Marine Office Inc. (The "Pointe Levy")* (1994), 82 F.T.R. 1 (T.D.).

the ship in time of peril;[13] burning cargo for fuel;[14] and damage to cargo in fire extinguishing.[15] Sacrifices of the ship can include: its intentional grounding or stranding;[16] damage to engines in getting off the ground;[17] the burning of ship's

---

[13] See *YAR 1994*, Rule 1, Jettison of Cargo: "No jettison of cargo shall be made good as general average, unless such cargo is carried in accordance with the recognised custom of the trade." The *Rules of Practice* (Other than Great Lakes) of the Association of Average Adjusters of Canada are to a similar effect. Rule 22, Deckload Jettison provides: "Where cargo is in accordance with a custom of trade, carried on and under deck, that portion of the cargo loaded on deck shall be subject to the same rules of adjustment in case of jettison and expense incurred as if the same were laden under deck." The address of Mr. Ralph A. Lyons, Chairman of the Association of Average Adjusters of Canada, at the association's annual meeting in 1970, entitled "Thoughts on General Average in the Container Age", discussed among other things, the allowance in general average for containers stowed on deck. He stated: "It is my opinion that cargo carried on deck and which is containerised and jettisoned, can be the subject of an allowance in General Average and dealt with accordingly." He also discussed the subject of jettison of empty containers. The issue of deck carriage was discussed in a number of early cases, including *Grouselle v. Ferrie* (1843), 6 O.S. 454; *Marks v. Watson* (1843), 4 N.B.R. 211 (C.A.); *Johnston and Kaye v. Crane* (1841), 3 N.B.R. 356 (C.A.); *Paterson v. Black* (1849), 5 U.C.Q.B. 481 (C.A.); and *Sellars v. Grand Bank Fisheries Ltd.* (1938), 14 Nfld. L.R. 206.

[14] *YAR 1994*, Rule IX, Cargo, Ship's Materials and Stores used for Fuel:

> Cargo, ship's material and stores, or any of them, necessarily used for fuel for the common safety at a time of peril shall be admitted as general average, but when such an allowance is made for the costs of ship's materials and stores the general average shall be credited with the estimated cost of the fuel which would otherwise have been consumed in prosecution of the intended voyage.

See also Rule 16 of the *Rules of Practice* (Other than Great Lakes) of the Association of Average Adjusters of Canada.

[15] See *Century Insurance Co. of Canada v. N.V. Bocimar, S.A. (The "Hasselt")* (1987), 39 D.L.R. (4th) 465 (S.C.C.), rev'g. (1984), 53 N.R. 383 (F.C.A.) as an example of a modern Canadian case involving extensive water damage to the ship in the course of firefighting efforts. *YAR 1994*, Rule III, Extinguishing Fire on Shipboard provides:

> Damage done to a ship and cargo, or either of them, by water or otherwise, including damage by beaching or scuttling a burning ship, in extinguishing a fire on board the ship, shall be made good as general average, except that no compensation shall be made for damage by smoke however caused or by heat of the fire.

See also Rule 20 of the *Rules of Practice* (Other than Great Lakes) of the Association of Average Adjusters of Canada.

[16] *YAR 1994*, Rule V, Voluntary Stranding:

> When a ship is intentionally run on shore for the common safety, whether or not she might have been driven on shore, the consequent loss or damage to the property involved in the common maritime adventure shall be allowed in general average.

See *Dancey v. Burns* (1880), 31 U.C.C.P. 313 (C.A.); *Gibb v. McDonnell* (1850), 7 U.C.Q.B. 356 (C.A.). In *Grover v. Bullock* (1849), 5 U.C.Q.B. 297, it was pointed out that while a stranding may be originally involuntary or fortuitous, and the damages caused by stranding regarded as particular average, the stranding itself may put the vessel and cargo in a condition of peril such that expenses subsequently incurred may fall into general average.

[17] *YAR 1994*, Rule VII, Damage to Machinery and Boilers:

> Damage caused to any machinery and boilers of a ship which is ashore and in a position of peril in endeavouring to refloat, shall be allowed in general average when shown to have arisen from an actual intention to float the ship for the common safety at the risk of

materials or stores for fuel;[18] and damage in fire extinguishing.[19] Freight, the payment made to the shipowner for the carriage of cargo, can also be the subject of a general average sacrifice.

Expenditures recoverable in general average can also be categorized by those relating to cargo and those relating to ship. Expenditures relating to cargo can include: expenses of discharging cargo;[20] and salvage charges.[21] Expenditures relating to the ship include: salvage charges;[22] port of refuge expenses;[23]

---

such damage; but where a ship is afloat no loss or damage caused by working propelling machinery and boilers shall in any circumstances be made good as general average.

[18] *YAR 1994*, Rule IX.

[19] *YAR 1994*, Rule III.

[20] *YAR 1994*, Rule VIII, Expenses lightening a Ship when Ashore and Consequent Damage. When a ship is ashore and cargo and ship's fuel and stores or any of them are discharged as a general average act, the extra cost of lightening, lighter hire and reshipping (if incurred), and any loss or damage to the property involved in the common maritime adventure in consequence thereof, shall be admitted as general average.

See also Rule 18 of the *Rules of Practice* (Other than Great Lakes) of the Association of Average Adjusters of Canada and *YAR 1994*, Rule XII, Damage to Cargo in Discharging etc.:

Damage to or loss of cargo, fuel or stores sustained in consequence of their handling, discharging, storing, reloading and stowing shall be made good as general average, when and only when the cost of those measures respectively is admitted as general average.

See also Rule 28 of the *Rules of Practice* (Other than Great Lakes) adopted by the Association of Average Adjusters of Canada; and *Federal Commerce and Navigation Company Limited v. Eisenerz-GmbH*, [1974] S.C.R. 1225.

[21] *YAR 1994*, Rule VI, Salvage Remuneration:

(a) Expenditure incurred by the parties to the adventure in the nature of salvage, whether under contract or otherwise, shall be allowed in general average, provided that the salvage operations were carried out for the purpose of preserving from peril the property involved in the common maritime adventure.

The balance of Rule VI deals with compensation payable in relation to environmental damage. For a discussion of salvage in the context of general average, see the address of John A. Cantello, Chairman, Association of Average Adjusters of Canada, at the 24th annual meeting of the Association in 1990.

[22] See *Ultramar Canada Inc. v. Mutual Marine Office Inc. (The "Pointe Levy")* (1994), 82 F.T.R. 1 (T.D.) for an example of contract salvage in relation to the vessel and cargo, where the salvage expenses were adjusted in general average. See also *Edward and Charles Gurney v. Aeneas D. MacKay* (1875), 37 U.C.Q.B. 324 (C.A.).

[23] See *YAR 1994*, Rule X, Expenses of Port of Refuge, etc., and Rule XI, Wages and Maintenance of Crew and other expenses bearing up for and in a port of refuge etc. See also, for example: *Ainsworth v. Cusack* (1858), 4 Nfld. L.R. 236, in which it was held that where a ship is obliged to go into port for the benefit of the whole concern, the charges of unloading and reloading the cargo and taking care of it, and the wages of the workmen hired for repairs, were recoverable in general average; *Canadian Transport Company Ltd. v. Hunt, Leuchars Hepburn (The "City of Alberni")*, [1947] Ex. C.R. 83, 63 B.C.L.R. 262 (S.C.), but see *Edward and Charles Gurney v. Aeneas D. MacKay* (1875), 37 U.C.Q.B. 324 (C.A.) where the court said: "By the law of England, after the cargo is in safety, the benefit it may derive from being carried in the ship to its place of destination is not a ground for making it contribute towards the cost of repairing the ship, nor of placing the ship in a position in which she can be repaired." In *Singer Manufacturing Co. v. Western Assurance Co.* (1896), 10 Que. S.C. 379 (C.A.), the court quoted with approval from the English case of *Svendsen v. Wallace* (1884), 13 L.R. Q.B. 69 (C.A.), aff'd. 10 A.C. 404 (H.L.):

expenses in getting off the bottom;[24] and expenses lightening ship when ashore.[25] An additional category of expense, known as "substituted expenses",[26] can be recovered if incurred to avoid expenses which would have been recoverable in general average.

22.4   APPORTIONMENT OF GENERAL AVERAGE

The preceding sections have examined the essential elements of general average and the typical situations in which general average occurs. This section deals with the principles upon which general average losses are adjusted. The basic concept is that general average losses and expenses are apportioned between surviving interests in proportion to their surviving values. To carry out this apportionment, the adjuster must answer certain questions:

(1)   What losses are to be included in general average?
(2)   How are these losses to be valued?
(3)   What interests will contribute to the general average?
(4)   How are the interests to be valued?
        and
(5)   How is the loss to be apportioned over the interests?

22.4.1   Losses To Be Included In General Average

In Section 22.3 we identified the types of sacrifices and expenses recoverable in general average. Such sacrifices or expenditures must be the direct consequence of the general average act.[27] The adjuster's task begins with the identification of

---

> If there is danger to both ship and cargo from destruction if the ship remains at sea, the act of putting into a port to repair is an extraordinary act which may well be called a general average act. If in order to do that act an expenditure is reasonably incurred, that expenditure is a general average expenditure. If in order to do that act, towage, pilotage or inward dues, must be paid, those expenditures are all and each general average expenditures.

24   *Grover v. Bullock* (1849), 5 U.C.Q.B. 297.

25   *YAR 1994*, Rule VIII, Expenses lightening a Ship when Ashore, and Consequent Damage:
> When a ship is ashore and cargo and ship's fuel and stores or any of them are discharged as a general average act, the extra cost of lightening, lighter hire and reshipping (if incurred), and any loss or damage to the property involved in the common maritime adventure in consequence thereof, shall be admitted as general average.

See *Montreal Trust Co. v. Canadian Surety Co.* (1937), 75 R.J.Q. 278 (Que. S.C.), aff'd. [1939] 4 D.L.R. 614 (Que. C.A.).

26   *YAR 1994*, Rule F; See also Rule 27 of the *Rules of Practice* (Other than Great Lakes) of the Association of Average Adjusters of Canada. Rule 7 of the Rules of Practice of the Association of Average Adjusters of Canada allows for the recovery of the cost of air-freighting parts where shipment by other means would cause unreasonable delay. See *Western Canada Steamship Co. Limited v. Canadian Commercial Corp.*, [1960] S.C.R. 632 at 649, *per* Ritchie J.

27   *YAR 1994*, Rule C (in part):
> Only such losses, damages or expenses which are the direct consequence of the general average act shall be allowed as general average.

...

the general average sacrifices or expenses incurred. In some cases, this may require a careful examination of the damage, and discussions with the general average surveyor, to distinguish between particular average damage to property and general average damage. For example, where there has been a fire on the ship, damaging ship and cargo, the damage to that property caused by *extinguishing* the fire is general average damage, but the damage caused by the fire itself is not — it is particular average damage. In examining the property and assessing the losses, the surveyor must distinguish between damage from different causes.

22.4.2 Valuing the General Average Losses

The *YAR 1994* contain provisions for the valuation of losses of freight;[28] loss or damage to cargo;[29] and loss or damage to the ship, its machinery and gear.[30]

Demurrage, loss of market and any loss or damage sustained or expense incurred by reason of delay, whether on the voyage or subsequently, and any indirect loss whatsoever, shall not be admitted as general average.

[28] *YAR 1994*, Rule XV, Loss of Freight:

Loss of freight arising from damage to or loss of cargo shall be made good as general average, either when caused by a general average act, or when the damage to or loss of cargo is so made good. Deduction shall be made from the amount of gross freight lost, of the charges which the owner thereof would have incurred to earn such freight but has, in consequence of the sacrifice, not incurred.

[29] *YAR 1994*, Rule XVI, Amount to be made good for Cargo Lost or Damaged by Sacrifice:

The amount to be made good as general average for damage to or loss of cargo sacrificed shall be the loss which has been sustained thereby based on the value at the time of discharge, ascertained from the commercial invoice rendered to the receiver or if there is no such invoice from the shipped value. The value at the time of discharge shall include the cost of insurance and freight except insofar as such freight is at the risk of interests other than the cargo.

When cargo so damaged is sold and the amount of the damage has not been otherwise agreed, the loss to be made good in general average shall be the difference between the net proceeds of sale and the net sound value as computed in the first paragraph of this Rule.

Under English common law, claims in general average for loss or damage to cargo are based on market values, whereas under the *YAR*, for the sake of convenience and efficiency, they are based on invoice values.

[30] *YAR 1994*, Rule XVIII, Damage to Ship:

The amount to be allowed as general average for damage or loss to the ship, her machinery and/or gear caused by a general average act shall be as follows:

(a) When repaired or replaced,

The actual reasonable cost of repairing or replacing such damage or loss, subject to deductions in accordance with Rule XIII;

(b) When not repaired or replaced,

The reasonable depreciation arising from such damage or loss, but not exceeding the estimated cost of repairs. But where the ship is an actual total loss or when the cost of repairs of the damage would exceed the value of the ship when repaired, the amount to be allowed as general average shall be the difference between the estimated sound value of the ship after deducting therefrom the estimated cost of repairing damage which is not

22.4.3 Interests Contributing to General Average

The ship, the cargo and the freight, where freight is at risk, contribute to general average. Bunkers (fuel) owned by charterers may be called upon to contribute. The owners of empty containers may be required to contribute. Some interests, although technically benefiting from the general average act, may be excluded for convenience — for example, passengers' luggage.

22.4.4 Valuing the Interests

The interests saved as a result of the general average act contribute to general average based on their surviving values, that is, their values at the time and place of the termination of the adventure. To these values must be added any amounts "made good" in general average.[31] This refers to the amount of loss or damage

---

general average and the value of the ship in her damaged state which may be measured by the net proceeds of sale, if any.

[31] This principle is set out in *YAR 1994*, Rule XVII, Contributory Value, which provides:

The contribution to a general average shall be made upon the actual net values of the property at the termination of the adventure except that the value of cargo shall be the value at the time of discharge, ascertained from the commercial invoice rendered to the receiver or if there is no such invoice from the shipped value. The value of the cargo shall include the cost of insurance and freight unless and insofar as such freight is at the risk of interests other than the cargo, deducting therefrom any loss or damage suffered by the cargo prior to or at the time of discharge. The value of the ship shall be assessed without taking into account the beneficial or detrimental effect of any demise or time charterparty to which the ship may be committed.

To these values shall be added the amount made good as general average for property sacrificed, if not already included, deduction being made from the freight and passage money at risk of such charges and crew's wages as would not have been incurred in earning the freight had the ship and cargo been totally lost at the date of the general average act and have not been allowed as general average; deduction being also made from the value of the property of all extra charges incurred in respect thereof subsequently to the general average act, except such charges as are allowed in general average...

...

In the circumstances envisaged in the third paragraph of Rule G, the cargo and other property shall contribute on the basis of its value upon delivery at original destination unless sold or otherwise disposed of short of that destination, and the ship shall contribute upon its actual net value at the time of completion of discharge of cargo.

...

Mails, passenger's luggage, personal effects and accompanied private motor vehicles shall not contribute in general average.

See also Rule 8 of the *Rules of Practice* (Great Lakes) of the Association of Average Adjusters of Canada and Rule 31 of the *Rules of Practice* (Other than Great Lakes) of the Association of Average Adjusters of Canada. There are detailed discussions of these *Rules of Practice* in addresses given at several of the annual meetings of the Association of Average Adjusters of Canada. See the address entitled "Proposed Rules of Practice for the Great Lakes" given by C. Nicolson, at the 5th annual meeting of the association in 1971; also the address of J. Cantello at the 24th annual meeting in 1990 — referring to Rule 8, he stated: "The strong feature of the Rules of Practice for the Great Lakes is their emphasis on simplicity. This applies to Rule 8 Valuation of Contributing Interests in General Average."

sustained by the property and recoverable in general average, the intent being that all property contributes to the loss on an equal basis.

Rule G of the *YAR 1994* provides in part:

> General average shall be adjusted as regards both loss and contribution upon the basis of values at the time and place when and where the adventure ends.

In *Ultramar Canada Inc. v. Mutual Marine Office Inc. (The "Pointe Levy"),*[32] a case referred to in more detail below, the trial judge found that the average adjuster had failed to deduct "special charges"[33] from the contributory value of the cargo. This resulted in the cargo being given a greater contributory value than was appropriate, and a correspondingly greater share of the general average expenses. The court pointed out that under Rule XVII of the *YAR* (Contributory Value), contribution is to be based on "actual net values" at the termination of the adventure. In the case of cargo, this requires the deduction of any loss or damage suffered by the cargo prior to or at the time of discharge, as well as any "special charges" incurred solely in respect of that cargo. The trial judge noted that the purpose of such deductions is to ensure that "contribution is made only on the 'net' value of the property saved".[34]

22.4.5 Apportionment of the General Average Loss Over the Contributing Interests

Having determined the losses recoverable in general average, and having identified and valued the contributing interests, the determination of each interest's contribution in general average is a mathematical exercise. Essentially, each interest contributes to the general average sacrifice and expenditures based on its contributory value, with the result that each interest bears an equal percentage of the loss. As exemplified by the *Ultramar* case, new and troublesome issues can present themselves. In that case, there had been a massive salvage operation attempting to save a barge laden with bunker fuel which was in danger of breaking up and damaging the sensitive coastline near the Matane shrimp fishery in Quebec. At the end of the day, the costs of the operation substantially exceeded the surviving values of the interests, ship and cargo. The average adjuster described this as "excess general average". The issue of "excess general average" (general average losses in excess of contributory values) had been discussed by average adjusters, but this appears to have been the first case to address the issue directly. The trial judge stated:

> With respect to the extent of cargo's liability for the expenses incurred in the general average act, I am satisfied cargo's liability is limited to its properly calculated

---

[32] (1994), 82 F.T.R. 1 (T.D.).

[33] "Special charges" are expenses incurred by the shipowner on behalf of the owner of cargo for the preservation and safety of the cargo. They are not recoverable in general average because they are incurred at a time when the "common adventure" is not in peril.

[34] (1994), 82 F.T.R. 1 at 14 (T.D.).

contributory value. The evidence before the court demonstrates this is the practice followed by average adjusters around the world.

...

To the extent there are 'excess' general average expenses after contributory values are exhausted, those expenses fall on the shipowner, who may or may not have insurance coverage for them under its various policies, depending on the policies taken out and the wording thereof.[35]

22.5   GENERAL AVERAGE AND INSURANCE

22.5.1   Overview

In considering the subject of general average and insurance, one must keep in mind the distinction between the insurance of general average *losses* on the one hand, and the insurance of general average *liabilities* on the other. The insurance of general average *losses* refers to the obligation of an insurer to indemnify the insured for a loss that, although ultimately recoverable in general average, falls in the first instance on the insured.[36] An example in the case of cargo insurance is jettison which is typically an insured peril under an all-risks cargo policy. The owner of the cargo jettisoned is entitled to recover its loss from its cargo insurer, who, in turn, is entitled to exercise rights of subrogation to claim recovery in general average of the proportion of the loss falling on other interests — the ship and the owners of other cargo. Similarly, to take an example from hull and machinery insurance, the damage caused by the intentional grounding of a ship to prevent it from sinking as a result of an accident is usually covered by a hull and machinery policy. The owner of the ship is entitled to recover the costs of repairing the hull from its hull insurer, who can, in turn, claim general average contribution from the other interests (or their respective insurers).

The insurance of general average *liabilities*, on the other hand, refers to the insurer's obligation to indemnify its insured against its legal liability to *contribute* in general average.[37] In the jettison example, the insurers of the vessel and the cargo saved are required to indemnify their insureds against their obligations to "make good" the loss of the jettisoned cargo.

Subject to the policy wording, the insurer is not liable to compensate the insured for general average losses or contributions unless the loss or expense was incurred for the purpose of avoiding an insured peril.[38]

---

[35]   *Ibid.*, at 11.

[36]   Canadian *Marine Insurance Act* ("*C.M.I.A.*"), S.C. 1993, c. 22, subs. 65(4).

[37]   *Ibid.*, subs. 65(5).

[38]   *Ibid.*, subs. 65(6).

22.5.2 Insurance of General Average Sacrifices and Expenditures

Subsection 65(4) of the Canadian *Marine Insurance Act* *("C.M.I.A.")* provides:

65(4) Subject to any express provision in the marine policy,

(*a*) an insured who incurs a general average expenditure may recover from the insurer in respect of the proportion of the loss falling on the insured; and

(*b*) an insured who incurs a general average sacrifice may recover from the insurer in respect of the whole loss, without having enforced the insured's right to contribution from other persons.

It is to be noted that the section distinguishes between sacrifices and expenditures. In the case of a general average expenditure, the insured may only recover the *proportion* falling on it. Unless the policy provides otherwise, the insured is left to collect the balance of the expenditure (for example, cargo's share) from other interests. In the case of general average sacrifice, by contrast, the insured is entitled to recover the entire loss. On payment, the insurer becomes subrogated to the insured's right to contribution from the other parties.

22.5.3 Insurance of General Average Contributions

Subsection 65(5) of the *C.M.I.A.* provides that "an insured who has paid, or is liable to pay, a general average contribution in respect of the subject-matter insured may recover the contribution from the insurer". Most policies in common use in Canada insure general average contributions falling on the insured. These are discussed below.

22.5.4 The Measure of Indemnity

As discussed in Section 22.4.4, in order to determine the extent of liability of an interest in general average, one must first determine the contributory value of that interest. That is, the value on which its contribution to general average is assessed. The contributory value may be greater than the insured value, and where this is the case, there may be underinsurance. If the property is not fully insured, the insured will not be entitled to recover a full indemnity for general average expenses or contributions, unless the policy otherwise provides. This is confirmed by section 72 of the *C.M.I.A.*:

72(1) Subject to any express provision in the marine policy, the measure of indemnity in respect of a general average contribution that an insured has paid or is liable to pay is:

(*a*) where the subject-matter of the contribution is fully insured for its contributory value, the full amount of the contribution; and

(*b*) where the subject-matter of the contribution is not fully insured for its contributory value or only part of it is insured, that proportion of the full amount of the contribution that the insured value of the subject-matter bears to its contributory value.

(2) In order to determine the measure of indemnity under paragraph 1(*b*) in a case where a particular average loss that is to be deducted from the contributory value has been incurred and is payable by the insurer, the amount of the loss must be deducted from the insured value of the subject-matter.

The section is prefaced by the words "subject to any express provision in the policy." The policy may well include a provision designed to protect the insured from underinsurance. In the *Ultramar* case, the cargo policy contained a clause stating:[39]

> 26A. General Average, Salvage and Special Charges, as per foreign custom, payable according to foreign statement and/or per York Antwerp Rules and/or in accordance with the contract of affreightment, if and as required; or, failing any provision in or there being no contract of affreightment, payable in accordance with the Laws and Usages of the Port of New York.

> 26B. General Average Contributions, Salvage and Special Charges and Sue and Labour Charges will be *payable in full, irrespective of insured and contributory values.*
> [Emphasis added.]

The plaintiff argued that the wording at the end of subclause B obliged the cargo insurer to pay the "full" general average as adjusted, which included so-called "excess general average", in excess of the contributory value of the interests saved. The trial judge rejected this contention, stating that "the sole purpose of [the clause] is to protect the assured against the consequences of an underinsurance situation which would arise by virtue of s. 73 of the Marine Insurance Act, 1906."[40]

22.5.5   Interests in Common Ownership

While general average is, in principle, adjusted without reference to the existence of insurance, an exception occurs where two or more "interests" in the adventure are owned by the same party. In such case, the interests are treated as though they were owned by different persons. This is mandated by subsection 65(7) of the *C.M.I.A.*:

> 65(7) Where any ship, freight, and goods or any two of them, are owned by the same insured, the liability of the insurer for a general average loss or a general average contribution shall be determined as if they were owned by different persons.

In the absence of this provision, the entire loss would fall on the party who incurred the loss or expense, since he or she could not sue himself or herself for recovery of the loss. This is not a concern in the absence of insurance, but where the interests are insured, it would create the inequitable result that one insurer

---

[39]   (1994), 82 F.T.R. 1 at 12 (T.D.).
[40]   *Ibid.*; s. 73 of the English *Marine Insurance Act*, 6 Edw. VII, c. 41 corresponds to s. 72 of the *C.M.I.A.*

would bear all the loss, since it could not pursue subrogation against its own insured.[41] The *C.M.I.A.* overcomes this impediment by creating the fiction, that the interests are separate. This principle was applied in *Ultramar*, in which both the barge and its cargo of bunker fuel were owned by the same party.

22.5.6 Application of General Average to Particular Forms of Marine Insurance

22.5.6.1 HULL AND MACHINERY INSURANCE

Hull and machinery policies invariably provide coverage for general average. The General Average and Salvage clause contained in the Canadian Board of Marine Underwriters Great Lakes Hull Clauses (September 1, 1971) provides as follows:

GENERAL AVERAGE AND SALVAGE

General Average and Salvage shall be payable as provided in the contract of af-freightment, or failing such provision or there be no contract of affreightment pay-able in accordance with the Rules of Practice for the Great Lakes of the Association of Average Adjusters of Canada. Provided always that when an ad-justment according to the laws and usages of the port of destination is properly demanded by the owners of the cargo, General Average shall be paid accordingly.

In the event of salvage, towage or other assistance being rendered to the Vessel by any vessel belonging in part or in whole to the same Owners or Charterers, the value of such services (without regard to the common ownership or control of the vessels) shall be ascertained by arbitration in the manner provided for under the Collision Liability clause in this Policy, and the amount so awarded so far as ap-plicable to the interest hereby insured shall constitute a charge under this Policy.

When the contributory value of the Vessel is greater that the Agreed Value herein, the liability of the Underwriters for General Average contribution (except in re-spect to amounts made good to the Vessel), or Salvage, shall not exceed that pro-portion of the total contribution due from the Vessel which the amount insured hereunder bears to the contributory value; and if, because of damage for which the Underwriters are liable as Particular Average, the value of the vessel has been re-duced for the purpose of contribution, the amount of such Particular Average dam-age recoverable under this Policy shall first be deducted from the amount insured hereunder, and the Underwriters shall then be liable only for the proportion which such net amount bears to the contributory value.[42]

---

[41] See, however, *Montgomery v. Indemnity Mutual Marine Insurance Co.*, [1901] 1 K.B. 147, [1902] 1 K.B. 734; and see *Ultramar Canada Inc. v. Mutual Marine Office Inc. (The "Pointe Levy")* (1994), 82 F.T.R. 1 (T.D.).

[42] Appendix G, lines 159-173. The American Institute Great Lakes Hull Clauses (March 9, 1978), in common use in Canada, contain an almost identical provision regarding general average and

The second part of this clause is a "sister ship" clause, designed to deal with the fact that in law, a claim for salvage cannot be made where the salving vessel and the salved vessel are in the same ownership — the shipowner could not sue itself for a salvage reward. To encourage vessels in common ownership to render assistance to one another, the hull and machinery underwriters agree to pay salvage remuneration in spite of the common ownership.

The third part of the clause confirms that underwriters only contribute proportionately where the vessel is underinsured (where the contributory value is greater than the insured value). It also states that any particular average damage for which underwriters are liable must be first deducted from the insured value.

In *Ultramar*, the court had occasion to consider the liability of the hull underwriter in circumstances in which it had paid a constructive total loss, and where there was substantial "excess general average" in relation to the salvage costs incurred in an effort to save the vessel and cargo. The trial judge noted that, absent a provision in the policy, the shipowner would have had no further recourse against its hull insurer:

> Having paid the insured value of the hull in the amount of $3,000,000 the hull underwriters have discharged their liability to indemnify Ultramar for general average contribution. The plaintiff therefore has no recourse against its hull underwriters unless the latter has assumed greater liabilities in its policy of insurance than those imposed by law. As stated above, it is well-settled that excess general average falls on the shipowner alone, subject to collection under its various policies of insurance.[43]

The judge went on to state:

> In the allocation of the excess general average under the Sue and Labour Clause, scholarly authority and the testimony of [expert witness] indicates that the proper solution to the valuation of the barge is to be found in the use of values which existed when the expenditure was incurred. While there is little in the way of either case law or legal commentary dealing with the valuation of a ship for the purposes of the Sue and Labour Clause, credible authority for the proposition that actual as opposed to estimated values are to be employed is found in Lowndes and Rudolf.[44]

He then found that the vessel was a constructive total loss and that the value to be used for the purpose of general average contribution was the amount made good rather than the estimated values.

22.5.6.2 CARGO INSURANCE

The Institute Cargo Clauses (1/1/82) (reproduced in Appendices B, C and D) insure general average and salvage charges assessed against the cargo, unless the loss sought to be avoided by the general average act is excluded by the provisions of clauses 4, 5, 6 and 7. Clause 2 provides:

---

salvage. See also the Canadian Hulls (Pacific) Clauses (Sept. 1/91) of the Association of Marine Underwriters of British Columbia, Appendix E, lines 124-150.

[43] (1994), 82 F.T.R. 1 at 14 (T.D.).

[44] *Ibid.*, at 17.

This insurance covers general average and salvage charges, adjusted or determined according to the contract of affreightment and/or the governing law and practice, incurred to avoid or in connection with the avoidance of loss from any cause except those excluded in Clauses 4, 5, 6, and 7 or elsewhere in this insurance.

The words "from any cause", found in this clause mean that the policy insures general average charges even if the cause of the loss might be excluded under the more restricted cover of the (B) and (C) clauses. Loss of or damage to cargo caused by general average sacrifice is expressly covered under section 1.2.1 of the (B) and (C) clauses and by the "all risks" provisions of the (A) clauses.

22.5.6.3 INSURANCE OF FREIGHT

The insurance of freight typically insures the freight's general average liability.[45]

22.5.6.4 PROTECTION AND INDEMNITY INSURANCE

As noted in Section 22.3, general average is concerned with sacrifices and expenses pertaining to property. With the exception of the "special compensation" payable to salvors under Lloyd's Open Form ("L.O.F.") salvage contracts and under Article 14 of the 1989 *Salvage Convention*, expenses incurred for the purpose of avoiding liabilities do not fall within general average. While the P. & I. Clubs have agreed to insure the shipowner's liability for this special compensation, they do not otherwise cover the shipowner's general average sacrifices or expenditures. P. & I. insurance does, however, typically indemnify the shipowner for the cargo's share of general average which is unrecoverable by the shipowner solely due to a breach of its contract of carriage.[46] The clubs may also

---

[45] See the Institute Time Clauses Freight 1/11/95, clause 11, General Average and Salvage which provides:

> 11.1 This insurance covers the proportion of general average, salvage and/or salvage charges attaching to freight at risk of the Insured, reduced in respect of any over-insurance.
> 11.2 Adjustment to be according to the law and practice obtaining at the place where the adventure ends, as if the contract of affreightment contained no special terms upon the subject; but where the contract of affreightment so provides the adjustment shall be according to the *YAR*.
> 11.3 No claim under this Clause 11 shall in any case be allowed where the loss was not incurred to avoid or in connection with the avoidance of a peril insured against.

[46] The rules of most P. & I. Clubs indemnify the ship owner for cargo's proportion of general average, including special charges and salvage, not legally recoverable solely by reason of a breach of the contract of carriage. Other P. & I. insurance is written under specific policies, such as the "SP-23" form (revised 1/56). Under that form, the insurer agrees to cover, among other things:

> (13) Liability for, or loss of, cargo's proportion of general average, including special charges, in so far as the Insured cannot recover same from any other source; subject, however, to the exclusion of section (8) and provided, that if the Charter Party, Bill of Lading or Contract of Affreightment does not contain the quoted clause under Section 8(bb) the Assurer's liability hereunder shall be limited to such as would exist if such clause were contained therein.

be prepared to advance to the shipowner a proportion of cargo's share of general average, after the adjustment has been prepared, subject to the execution and delivery of appropriate documentation. P. & I. Clubs also afford coverage for the ship's proportion of general average unrecoverable under the hull and machinery policy by virtue of the contributory value of the ship being assessed at an amount greater than its insured value. The P. & I. Club pays the shipowner's uninsured contribution unless the ship has been unreasonably underinsured.

22.6 SUBROGATION

Where the policy insures general average losses, the insured is entitled to demand payment of the full amount from underwriters. The underwriters are obliged to pay that amount, unreduced by general average recoverable from the other parties. The insurer may then exercise the insured's general average rights against third parties.[47] For example, if a ship is deliberately grounded to prevent a total loss, the hull and machinery insurer pays for the damage thus incurred, and is entitled to exercise the rights of the shipowner to require the other parties to the adventure to share in the loss through general average. An insurer who pays a general average claim is entitled to pursue subrogation against the party responsible.

22.7 GENERAL AVERAGE AND FAULT

The *YAR* are not concerned with fault, and the adjustment of general average is carried out regardless of whether the shipowner was at fault.[48] However, the shipowner's fault may prevent it from recovering the cargo's general average contribution. A detailed discussion of this subject is beyond the scope of this text,[49] but in principle, where the general average event has arisen because of the shipowner's legal fault, such as the failure of the shipowner to fulfill its obligations under the Canadian *Marine Liability Act*[50] (to exercise due diligence to make the ship seaworthy), cargo interests may have a defence to a claim by

---

The reference to section 8(bb) is to a New Jason clause (see note 53). Effectively, the insurer agrees to assume no greater liability than the insured would have incurred had a New Jason clause been included in the contract of carriage.

[47] *Steinhoff v. Royal Canadian Insurance Co.* (1877), 42 U.C.Q.B. 307 (C.A.); see also *Phoenix Insurance Co. v. Anchor Insurance Co.* (1884), 4 O.R. 524 (H.C.).

[48] See Rule D of the *YAR 1994* which is unchanged from the 1974 rules:

> Rights to contribution in general average shall not be affected, though the event which gave rise to the sacrifice or expenditure may have been due to the fault of one of the parties to the adventure; but this shall not prejudice any remedies or defences which may be open against or to that party in respect of such fault.

What this rather convoluted language means is that the adjustment is to be carried out without reference to the question of fault between the parties, but that the claimant's fault may be a defence to a claim for general average.

[49] The subject is discussed in more detail in chapter 7 of George R. Strathy, *The Law and Practice of General Average in Canada* (privately published, 1995).

[50] S.C. 2001, c. 6.

the shipowner for contribution to general average.[51] For example, in *Century Insurance Co. of Canada v. N.V. Bocimar, S.A. ("The Hasselt")*,[52] the shipowner claimed general average damage to the ship caused by water used to extinguish a fire. It was admitted that the shipowner was not at fault in relation to the cause of the fire itself, but it was found that the owner had failed to exercise due diligence to train the crew of the ship to fight a fire at sea. The incompetence of the crew prolonged the fire and substantially contributed to the general average damage caused by the firefighting. The shipowner's failure to exercise due diligence to properly train the crew was causally related to the damage caused by the great quantities of water used in the firefighting exercise, and the Federal Court of Canada dismissed the shipowner's attempt to recover the cargo interests' share of the general average.

Most bills of lading and charterparties contain a clause known as the "New Jason" clause,[53] designed to achieve this result. In a leading Canadian case, *Ellerman Lines v. Gibbs, Nathaniel (Canada) Ltd.*, the wording of the clause was as follows:[54]

> In the event of accident, danger, damage or disaster, before or after the commencement of the voyage resulting from any cause whatsoever, whether due to negligence or not, for which or for the consequence of which the Carrier is not responsible, by statute, contract or otherwise, the goods, Shippers, Consignees and/or Owners of the goods shall contribute with the Carrier in general average to the payment of any sacrifices, losses, or expenses of a general average nature that may be made or incurred and shall pay salvage or special charges incurred in respect of the goods.

The effect of the "New Jason" clause is to bring United States law into harmony with Anglo-Canadian law. The shipowner is entitled to general average contribution where the event giving rise to general average occurred without the fault

---

[51] This topic, and the liability of hull underwriters for general average where an accident has resulted from the unseaworthiness of the vessel (possibly with the privity of the shipowner), was the subject of an address given by Mr. R. Lyons, Chairman of the Association of Average Adjusters of Canada, at the third annual meeting of the association in 1969. He noted that, "Under English law, if the ship sails in an unseaworthy condition with the privity of the owners, Underwriters would not be liable for any general average contribution on ship." The subject of unseaworthiness as a defence to claims for general average against cargo was the topic of an address entitled "Unseaworthiness, Due Diligence and Onus of Proof", given by D.L.D. Beard, Q.C., Chairman of the Association of Average Adjusters of Canada at the 19th annual meeting in 1985.

[52] (1987), 39 D.L.R. (4th) 465 (S.C.C.), rev'g (1984), 53 N.R. 383 (F.C.A.). For other cases on the subject of general average and "fault", see: *St. Lawrence Construction Ltd. v. Federal Commerce and Navigation Co. Ltd.*, [1985] 1 F.C. 767, 56 N. R. 174 (C.A.); *Western Canada Steamship Co. Ltd. v. Canadian Commercial Corp.*, [1960] S.C.R. 632; *Canadian Transport Company Ltd. v. Hunt, Leuchars Hepburn (The "City of Alberni")*, [1947] Ex. C.R. 83, 63 B.C.L.R. 262 (S.C.); *Montreal Trust Co. v. Canadian Surety Co.*, [1939] 4 D.L.R. 614 (Que. C.A.), aff'g. (1937), 75 R.J.Q. 278.

[53] The name comes from *"Jason" (The)* (1912), 225 U.S. 32 (U.S.S.C.), in which the Supreme Court of the United States upheld the clause.

[54] (1983), 4 D.L.R. (4th) 645 at 650 (F.C.T.D.), aff'd. (1986), 26 D.L.R. (4th) 161 (F.C.A.).

of the carrier or in one of the circumstances in which the carrier would be exonerated from liability under the *Hague-Visby Rules* as embodied in the Canadian *Marine Liability Act*. While the "New Jason" clause is not required when Canadian law applies, it is invariably included in Canadian bills of lading, charterparties and other contracts of affreightment, to cover the possibility of general average being adjusted under U.S. law. The clause has been discussed and approved in several Canadian cases.[55]

22.8 GENERAL AVERAGE AND ENVIRONMENTAL ISSUES

General average is concerned with expenses incurred or sacrifices made in the preservation of property — the ship and its cargo. As a general rule expenses incurred to avoid or minimize liabilities, including expenses incurred to avoid pollution or to mitigate its effects, are not recoverable in general average because they are not made or incurred for the purpose of preserving *property* from peril. Having said this, the fact that expenses properly incurred for the purpose of saving property also have the effect of avoiding pollution does not disqualify them from being recoverable in general average.[56]

The increasing international concern with respect to oil pollution, particularly from oil tankers, has led to some significant changes in the maritime law of salvage and general average. The *YAR 1994* introduced an important new provision dealing with the adjustment of certain expenses incurred to avoid pollution. The basic rule, expressed in Rule C, is that damages or expenses resulting from pollution do not fall within general average:

> In no case shall there be any allowance in general average for losses, damages or expenses incurred in respect of damage to the environment or in consequence of the escape or release of pollutant substances from the property involved in the common maritime adventure.

However, Rule XI(d) of the *YAR 1994* contains an exception to this in the case of certain measures to prevent or minimize damage to the environment:

> (d) The cost of measures undertaken to prevent or minimise damage to the environment shall be allowed in general average when incurred in any or all of the following circumstances:
>
> > (i)   as part of an operation performed for the common safety which, had it been undertaken by a party outside the common maritime adventure would have entitled such party to a salvage reward;
> >
> > (ii) as a condition of entry into or departure from any port or place in the circumstances prescribed in Rule X(a);

---

[55] See *St. Lawrence Construction Ltd. v. Federal Commerce & Navigation Company Ltd.*, [1985] 1 F.C. 767, 56 N.R. 174 (C.A.), leave to appeal refused (1985), 58 N.R. 236; *Drew Brown Ltd. v. "Orient Trader" (The)*, [1974] S.C.R. 1286, 34 D.L.R. (3d) 339 at 368.

[56] *Ultramar Canada Inc. v. Mutual Marine Office Inc. (The "Pointe Levy")* (1994), 82 F.T.R. 1 (T.D.).

(iii) as a condition of remaining at any port or place in the circumstances prescribed in Rule X(a), provided that when there is an actual escape or release of pollutant substances the cost of any additional measures required on that account to prevent or minimise pollution or environmental damage shall not be allowed as general average;

(iv) necessarily in connection with the discharging, storing or reloading of cargo whenever the cost of those operations is admissible as general average.

Also relevant to this subject are the provisions of Rule VI, dealing with salvage remuneration. This rule was introduced in 1990 to take into account the effect of the *Salvage Convention* of 1989. The rule provides:

(a) Expenditure incurred by the parties to the adventure in the nature of salvage, whether under contract or otherwise, shall be allowed in general average provided that the salvage operations were carried out for the purpose of preserving from peril the property involved in the common maritime adventure.

Expenditure allowed in general average shall include any salvage remuneration in which the skill and efforts of the salvors in preventing or minimising damage to the environment such as is referred to in Article 13 paragraph 1(b) of the International Convention on Salvage, 1989 have been taken into account.

(b) Special compensation payable to a salvor by the shipowner under Article 14 of the said Convention to the extent specified in paragraph 4 of that Article or under any other provision similar in substance shall not be allowed in general average.

Salvage expenses are recoverable in general average. This applies to "pure salvage" not rendered under contract and to salvage services provided under a contract such as the Lloyd's Open Form. Traditionally, salvage awards were based on the value of the property saved. The *Salvage Convention* of 1989, taking into account concerns with respect to the salvage of oil tankers in particular, provided that in fixing a salvage award one of the factors to be considered would be "the skill and efforts of the salvors in preventing or minimizing damage to the environment." The 1989 *Salvage Convention* also made an exception to the "no cure, no pay" requirement of salvage by providing for an award to be made to an unsuccessful salvor who nevertheless prevented or minimized environmental damage. The object of this was to encourage salvors to go to the assistance of stricken vessels without the fear that their "prize" might be lost, either through the forces of nature or through government intervention.[57]

---

[57] See the address of John A. Cantello, Chairman, Association of Average Adjusters of Canada, at the association's 24th annual meeting in 1990. The address dealt with the subject of salvage and discussed the then proposed amendments to the *YAR* to reflect the amendment of the *Salvage Convention* dealing with pollution.

The 1990 amendments to the *YAR* provided that the salvage award, including the component reflecting the skill and effort of the salvor in preventing environmental damage, would be shared in general average. But, if the vessel and cargo were lost, there would be no sharing because there would be no surviving values to contribute. Any special compensation payable to the salvor in those cases would presumably be paid solely by the P. & I. insurer.

The changes introduced by the *YAR 1994* to deal with pollution were a compromise between hull and cargo insurers on the one hand, who did not wish to accept any liability for pollution, and P. & I. insurers on the other hand, who felt that some provision should be included. The compromise excluded environmental damage generally from general average (by virtue of Rule C) but allowed limited recovery of the cost of measures to *prevent* or *minimize* damage to the environment in the circumstances described in Rule XI(d). It will presumably be in the interests of shipowners and their P. & I. insurers to encourage the authorities to issue a form of order which would give rise to the operation of Rules XI (d) (ii) and (iii).[58]

22.9   GENERAL AVERAGE PRACTICE

The general average adjustment process usually begins with the shipowner "declaring" general average and appointing an average adjuster. While any party is entitled to make a claim for general average and to appoint an adjuster, it is usually the shipowner who does so because the shipowner is usually the party who has incurred the general average expense. In Canada, the adjuster will invariably be a full member of the Association of Average Adjusters of Canada.[59]

One of the first concerns of the average adjuster is to obtain security for any general average contribution cargo interests may be required to make. The right to security arises because a carrier has a "possessory" lien against cargo to secure that cargo's liability for general average contribution.[60] Typically, the shipowner, through the average adjuster, will require that cargo interests provide security before the cargo will be released. Where the cargo is insured by a reputable marine insurer, the average adjuster will normally require a general average bond from the consignee together with a general average guarantee

---

[58]   The fact that the language of the *YAR 1994* may be open to debate or interpretation is evidenced by the fact that when the proposed rules were debated, the United States delegation at Sydney, Australia was so concerned that the rules might be misunderstood that it issued a statement to the effect that it "understands" that the rules exclude allowances in general average "in respect of liability in consequence of the escape or release of pollutants from the property".

[59]   This Association has adopted *Rules of Practice* to provide uniformity in adjusting practice.

[60]   *"Annie M. Allen" (The)* (1881), 3 C.L.T. 108 (Exch. Ct.); see also *Ellerman Lines Ltd. v. Gibbs, Nathaniel (Canada) Ltd.* (1983), 4 D.L.R. (4th) 645 (F.C.T.D.), aff'd. (1986), 26 D.L.R. (4th) 161 (F.C.A.). For a detailed discussion of the lien and of lien procedure, see *Castle Insurance Co. v. Hong Kong Shipping Co.*, [1984] A.C. 226; see also *Edward and Charles Gurney v. Aeneas D. MacKay* (1875), 37 U.C.Q.B. 324 (C.A.); and *Federal Court Act*, R.S.C. 1985, c. F-7, sections 22(2)(*q*) and 43(2).

from the cargo insurer. Where the cargo is not insured, the carrier may demand more substantial security, such as a bank letter of credit or even a cash deposit.

The marine insurance industry has established standard form general average guarantees. A new form of guarantee was approved at the British Association of Average Adjusters in May of 1995. The wording of the bond or guarantee should stipulate that the party giving the bond is liable to pay only such general average "as may properly be found owing", or words to that effect. This language has been incorporated in the new English form of guarantee. The authorities suggest that such language may be implied.[61]

Bills of lading or charterparties sometimes provide for the payment of a cash deposit prior to the release of the cargo.[62] The adjuster may want to obtain a cash deposit, in addition to a guarantee, for several reasons. He or she may want to ask for a "payment on account" from cargo interests to provide interim funding of the expenses pending the preparation of the adjustment. There may be a concern regarding the solvency of underwriters or the enforceability of a guarantee, or the security of cash may simply be preferred to a guarantee. In Anglo-Canadian law, cargo interests have no liability to pay general average until such time as the adjustment has been completed.[63] The shipowner has the right to require reasonable security, but where this has been provided, it has no right, in principle, to insist on a cash deposit as well.[64] Nevertheless, it would appear that this has been sanctioned by practice and by the *YAR* themselves.[65] In practice, cash deposits are demanded only when the cargo is uninsured.

The average adjuster may request that parties make a "payment on account" of the general average contribution which is ultimately payable, and some general average guarantees contain wording obliging the guarantor to make a payment on account.[66] It is generally accepted that payments on account are

---

[61]   *Western Assurance Co. v. Ontario Coal Co.* (1890), 19 O.R. 462 (Q.B.), aff'd. (1892), 19 O.A.R. 41 (C.A.), aff'd. (1892), 21 S.C.R. 383.

[62]   *Ellerman Lines Ltd. v. Gibbs, Nathaniel (Canada) Ltd.* (1983), 4 D.L.R. (4th) 645 (F.C.T.D.), aff'd. (1986), 26 D.L.R. (4th) 161 (F.C.A.). The carrier's bill of lading provided:

> Such deposit as the Carrier or his Agents may deem sufficient to cover the estimated contribution of the goods and any salvage and special charges thereon shall, if required, be made by the Shippers, Consignees and/or owners of the goods to the Carrier before delivery.

[63]   *Brandeis, Goldschmidt & Co. v. Economic Insurance Co. Ltd.* (1922), 11 Ll. L.R. 42.

[64]   See *Leggett v. Italia-America Shipping Corp.* (1926), 26 Ll. L. R. 108 (U.S. 2d cir.). In that case, the shipowner's bill of lading provided that the consignee deposit with the shipowner the amount required by it as a guarantee for the amount due in general average. The carrier refused to deliver the cargo except on payment of the estimated amount of general average due. The court held that the bill of lading clause was unreasonable because it bound the shipper to pay any amounts that the carrier demanded, and put the shipper's money at risk of the carrier's solvency. The carrier had the right to insist on reasonable security, but did not have the right to insist on payment in advance.

[65]   *YAR 1994*, Rule XXII, Treatment of Cash Deposits, requires that the cash deposit is to be paid into a special account and shall accrue interest. If the deposit proves to be more than sufficient to pay the contribution, the balance, with interest, is to be returned.

[66]   For example: "We further agree to make a prompt payment on account to the average adjusters if required by you as soon as such a payment may be certified to by the average adjusters."

"without prejudice" and that the party making the payment reserves the right to contest the liability in general average and to dispute the adjustment.[67] When the adjustment is issued, credit will be granted for payments on account.

Where a vessel encounters difficulties on the voyage and puts in to a port of refuge, the shipowner may decide to forward some or all of the cargo to its ultimate destination using other means. The cargo owner may wish to do the same. Where cargo is forwarded, in the absence of an agreement to the contrary, there is a "separation" of the interests of ship and cargo. The result is that any general average expenses incurred *after* this separation are not recoverable from the forwarded cargo, since it is no longer a part of the "adventure" and cannot be regarded as having received a benefit from these expenses. To prevent this, the average adjuster may require that cargo interests execute a "non-separation agreement", confirming that the transshipment or forwarding of cargo to its original destination does not affect rights and liabilities in general average. The purpose is to ensure that cargo forwarded to its destination continues to contribute in general average, and preserves the shipowner's right to an allowance for the wages and maintenance of the crew at a port of refuge after the forwarding of the cargo. It has been held in Canada that the shipowner has no right to demand a non-separation agreement, provided the cargo owner pays the full freight at an intermediate port and gives a guarantee for payment of general average expenses incurred up to that point.[68] A major change brought about by the *YAR 1994* is the incorporation of a non-separation agreement, possibly reversing the effect of *Ellerman Lines v. Gibbs, Nathaniel (Canada) Ltd.*, in cases to which these rules apply. Contracts of affreightment subject to the *YAR 1994* will therefore incorporate this non-separation agreement.[69]

---

[67]   See, for example, *Ultramar Canada Inc. v. Mutual Marine Office Inc. (The "Pointe Levy")* (1994), 82 F.T.R. 1 (T.D.) where this practice was acknowledged.

[68]   (1983), 4 D.L.R. (4th) 645 (F.C.T.D.), aff'd. (1986), 26 D.L.R. (4th) 161 (F.C.A.). See S. J. Harrington, "General Average - York-Antwerp Rules 1974", *J.M.L.C.* 20:1, p. 80. See also P. J. Cullen, "General Average - The Future of Non-Separation Agreements" (A comment on *Ellerman Lines Ltd. v. Gibbs, Nathaniel (Canada) Ltd.* in *L.M.C.L.Q.* 160.

[69]   Rule G provides, in part:

> When a ship is at any port or place in circumstances which would give rise to an allowance in general average under the provisions of Rules X and XI, and the cargo or part thereof is forwarded to destination by other means, rights and liabilities in general average shall, subject to cargo interests being notified if practicable, remain as nearly as possible the same as they would have been in the absence of such forwarding as if the adventure had continued in the original ship for so long as justifiable under the contract of affreightment and the applicable law.
>
> The proportion attaching to cargo of the allowances made in general average by reason of applying the third paragraph of this Rule shall not exceed the cost which would have been borne by the owners of cargo if the cargo had been forwarded at their expense.

PART IV

MARINE INSURANCE PRACTICE

Chapter 23

The Marine Insurance Broker

23.1 INTRODUCTION

The broker — an intermediary who procures insurance on behalf of the insured — is a vital participant in the marine insurance business. While the agent of the insured,[1] the broker must enjoy the trust and confidence of the insurer and must conduct himself or herself with the utmost good faith and integrity in dealing with the insurer. This applies when the insurance is placed, and also when an insurance claim is presented. There may be circumstances where the broker will be considered to act as the agent for the insurer, for example, where the insurer "holds out" the broker as its agent,[2] but these are exceptions to the rule.

Most commercial hull and cargo insurance in Canada is effected through specialist marine insurance brokers who are familiar with the coverage available in the domestic and international marine insurance markets. Private pleasure craft and yacht insurance is often handled by general insurance brokers, placing the business with companies specializing in such risks.

A marine insurance broker performs several functions on behalf of its client. It analyzes the client's business and provides advice on the coverages available to protect the client's assets and income and to insure against potential liabilities. It approaches insurers to negotiate coverage and premiums. Sometimes, when a subscription policy is necessary, the broker formulates a proposal containing premium, conditions and deductibles and then attempts to find a leading insurer to take a percentage of the risk at or close to the proposed terms. The broker then approaches other insurers to follow the "leader" until there is a 100 per cent placement.

The price that the client is willing to pay, the breadth of the insuring conditions and the financial strength of the insurers will be significant issues for the broker. Finding the right insurance is often a matter of price — part of the

---

[1]   This principle has been repeatedly recognized in Canada: see *Queen Charlotte Lodge Ltd. v. Hiway Refrigeration Ltd. & Royal Insurance of Canada*, unreported (17 October 1997), B.C. Supreme Court, citing *Arnould's Law of Marine Insurance and Average*, 16th ed., Vol. 1 (London: Stevens & Sons); *Adams-Eden Furniture Ltd. v. Kansa General Insurance Inc.* (1996), 141 D.L.R. (4th) 288, [1997] 2 W.W.R. 65 (Man. C.A.), aff'g. (1995), 103 Man. R. (2d) 284, leave to appeal refused (1997) 123 Man. R. (2d) 79*n* (S.C.C.); and *Dickie v. Merchants Marine Insurance Co.* (1883), 16 N.S.R. 244 (C.A.).

[2]   See *Fallas v. Continental Insurance Co.*, [1973] 6 W.W.R. 379 (B.C.S.C.).

broker's skill lies in tailoring the coverage the client requires to the price the client is prepared to pay. It is common for negotiations with underwriters and clients to be protracted.[3] If, after the insurance has been placed, an insured claim arises, the broker will be informed by the insured and will, in turn, inform the underwriters. Underwriters often give comments to the broker concerning the appointment of an approved surveyor to investigate the claim. The broker is the conduit of information between underwriters and the insured, and has a duty to keep both parties fully and accurately informed. The broker will provide assistance to the client in the preparation, quantification and presentation of the claim to the insurer.

The Canadian *Marine Insurance Act* (*"C.M.I.A."*) does not deal with the responsibilities of brokers, although it recognizes the role of the broker in effecting the marine insurance policy, confers obligations of disclosure and good faith on the broker when procuring the insurance[4] and imposes rights and obligations on the broker in relation to premiums.[5] The law surrounding the broker's duties and liabilities is based on common law rather than statute. As there has been a proliferation of legal decisions in Canada relating to the obligations and liabilities of non-marine insurance brokers, we will examine some of the most important of these cases. In most respects, the law in this area applies to both marine and non-marine brokers.

The *C.M.I.A.* is not concerned with the licensing or regulation of either marine insurers or marine insurance brokers. This is left to the laws of the jurisdictions in which they are engaged in business.

23.2   THE BROKER'S OBLIGATIONS

There are some features of marine insurance that expose brokers to particular risks. It is a specialized field, and those practising in the area are expected to have an appropriate level of skill and competence. As well, brokers are often directly involved in the preparation of the policy — particularly complex policies on broker's "manuscript" wordings. If the wording is imprecise or

---

[3]   In *Kalkinis (litigation guardian of) v. Allstate Insurance Co. of Canada* (1996), 28 O.R. (3d) 237 (Gen. Div.), rev'd. (1998), 41 O.R. (3d) 528, 117 O.A.C. 193, leave to appeal ref'd. (2000), 255 N.R. 199*n* (S.C.C.), the court pointed out that a private agent has a duty to "provide appropriate advice about the form of coverage that best suits the needs" of the customer, referring to *Fletcher v. Manitoba Public Insurance Co.*, [1990] 3 S.C.R. 191, 74 D.L.R. (4th) 636, rev'g. (1989), 68 O.R. (2d) 193, 58 D.L.R. (4th) 23 (C.A.), rev'g. (1987), 60 O.R. (2d) 629, 26 C.C.L.I. 236 (H.C.J.). The court stated at (1996), 28 O.R. (3d) 237 at 245-46: "Policyholders require guidance and advice from their insurance agents as to what coverage is sensible for their circumstances and bearing in mind the affordability of the cost of such coverage." It was held that Allstate's agent was negligent in failing to provide advice on a reasonable level of coverage in light of recent awards. It should have also provided advice about the risks of cancelling $1,000,000 coverage in favour of $500,000 coverage.

[4]   S.C. 1993, c. 22, subss. 21(2) and 22(8).

[5]   Sections 48, 49, and 50.

ambiguous, the broker may be responsible.[6] Where an insurer denies coverage, it has become commonplace for the insured to sue the broker as well as the insurer.[7] Indeed, where the insurer's position is that the policy does not cover the particular loss, or that coverage was available but on different terms or at a greater premium, the insured may be well-advised to join the broker as a defendant in the suit.[8]

In the 1993 case of *Dueck (c.o.b. Peter P. Dueck & Son) v. Manitoba Mennonite Mutual Insurance Co.*,[9] which involved non-marine insurance, the Manitoba Court of Appeal gave a useful summary of the duties of an insurance broker. It was held that:

(a) the duty of the broker is to use a reasonable degree of skill and care to obtain the policy the client wants;

(b) if the broker is unable to obtain the desired policy, he or she must advise the client;

(c) the broker has a duty to provide information about the coverage available;

(d) the broker has a duty to provide information about the coverage the client requires to meet his or her needs;

(e) where the insured is unsophisticated, the broker has a duty to explain the coverage available as well as the gaps in the coverage provided; and

(f) in the context of this case, the broker should have explained the difference between an all perils policy and a specific perils policy.[10]

---

[6] On the other hand, if the insurer accepts imprecise wording prepared by the broker, it is arguably bound by the wording, however deficient it may have been: *1013799 Ontario Ltd. v. Kent Line International Ltd.* (2000), 21 C.C.L.I. (3d) 312, [2000] O.T.C. 635 (S.C.J.).

[7] See, for example: *Stevenson v. Continental Insurance Co. & Breen Agencies Ltd.*, [1973] 6 W.W.R. 316, [1973] I.L.R. ¶1-553 (B.C. Dist. Ct.); *C.C.R. Fishing Ltd. v. British Reserve Insurance Co.*, [1990] 1 S.C.R. 814, 69 D.L.R. (4th) 112, rev'g. (1998), 55 D.L.R. (4th) 429, 38 C.C.L.I. 134 (B.C.C.A.), rev'g. (1986), 21 C.C.L.I. 297 (B.C.S.C.); *Toron Construction Ltd. v. Continental Insurance Co.* (1982), 34 A.R. 456 (Alta Q.B.); *Catherwood Towing Ltd. v. Commercial Union Assurance Co.* (1996), 78 B.C.A.C. 257, 35 C.C.L.I. (2d) 124 (B.C.C.A.), var'g. (1995), 30 C.C.L.I. (2d) 135; and *DeGroot v. J.T. O'Bryan & Co.* (1979), 15 B.C.L.R. 271, [1979] I.L.R. ¶1-1152 (C.A.), rev'g. [1977] I.L.R. ¶1-863 (B.C.S.C.).

[8] See *Crate Marine Sales Ltd. v. Graham Neale Insurance Brokers Ltd.*, [1990] I.L.R. ¶1-2610 (Ont. S.C.J.), where the trial judge suggested that alternative claims for relief against the broker and the insurer might be the safest course of action. In other cases, where it is clear that the insurance procured by the broker does not cover the loss, the insured may proceed only against the broker. This was the course ultimately adopted in *1013799 Ontario Ltd. v. Kent Line International Ltd.* (2000), 21 C.C.L.I. (3d) 312, [2000] O.T.C. 635 (S.C.J.).

[9] [1993] 4 W.W.R. 531, 13 C.C.L.I. (2d) 155 (Man. C.A.), aff'g. (1992), 80 Man. R. (2d) 173, 11 C.C.L.I. (2d) 87 (Q.B.).

[10] See also *Evans v. State Farm Fire & Casualty Co.* (1993), 15 O.R. (3d) 86, 19 C.C.L.I. (2d) 76 (H.C.), where the issue was whether the agent was in breach of its duty as a result of its failure to cover the replacement cost of the property. It was held that the broker: (a) failed to ask questions of the client concerning the value of the property; (b) failed to obtain information relevant to the question of replacement value; (c) made use of a software program which was out of date and inadequate; (d) failed to convey information; (e) failed to provide counsel and advice as to the

The modern Canadian statement of the law concerning insurance brokers is found in the case of *Fine's Flowers Ltd. v. General Accident Assurance Co.,*[11] which has been followed in numerous subsequent cases. The Ontario Court of Appeal found that the plaintiff insured, who operated a greenhouse business, had asked the insurance agent to obtain "full coverage" for his business. The policy procured by the agent did not cover the loss that ultimately occurred — freezing of plants as a result of the failure of a water pump. The Court of Appeal, agreeing with the trial judge, found the insurance agent liable. In giving the judgment of the majority of the Court of Appeal, Justice Wilson stated:

> The main ground of appeal from the judgment of the learned trial Judge is that he put far too broad and sweeping a duty on insurance agents. They are not insurers. It is not part of their duty to know everything about their clients' businesses so as to be in a position to anticipate every conceivable form of loss to which they might be subject. The agent's duty, counsel submits, is to 'exercise a reasonable degree of skill and care to obtain policies in the terms bargained for and to service those policies as circumstances might require'.

> I take no issue with counsel's statement of the scope of the insurance agent's duty except to add that the agent also has a duty to advise his principal if he is unable to obtain the policies bargained for so that his principal may take such further steps to protect himself as he deems desirable. The operative words, however, in counsel's definition of the scope of the agent's duty, are 'policies in the terms bargained for'.

> In many instances, an insurance agent will be asked to obtain a specific type of coverage and his duty in those circumstances will be to use a reasonable degree of skill and care in doing so or, if he is unable to do so, 'to inform the principal promptly in order to prevent him from suffering loss through relying upon the successful completion of the transaction by the agent': Ivamy, *General Principles of Insurance Law*, 2nd ed. (1970), at p. 464.

> But there are other cases, and in my view this is one of them, in which the client gives no such specific instructions but rather relies upon his agent to see that he is protected and, if the agent agrees to do business with him on those terms, then he

---

risk assessment; and (f) failed to tailor the policy to the specific needs of the client. See, as well, *Breen v. Donald T. Ritchie Insurance Agencies Ltd.* (1983), 2 C.C.L.I. 182 (Ont. H.C.J.).

[11]   (1977), 17 O.R. (2d) 529, 81 D.L.R. (3d) 139 (C.A.), aff'g. (1974), 5 O.R. (2d) 137, 49 D.L.R. (3d) 641 (H.C.J.). In the same year as *Fine's Flowers Ltd. v. General Accident Assurance Co.*, the standard of care owed by an insurance broker to its customer was stated in a New Brunswick case, *Centre Sportif de Caraquet Ltée. v. Edmond E. Lundry Assurance Ltd.* (1977), 16 N.B.R. (2d) 489 at 494 (Q.B.), in which the court quoted *Halsbury's Laws of England*, 3rd ed., to the following effect: "All agents, whether paid or unpaid, skilled or unskilled, are under a legal obligation to exercise due care and skill in performance of the duties which they have undertaken, a greater degree of care being required from a paid than from an unpaid, and from a skilled than from an unskilled, agent. The question in all such cases is whether the act or omission complained of is inconsistent with that reasonable degree of care and skill which persons of ordinary prudence and ability might be expected to show in the situation and profession of the agent."

cannot afterwards, when an uninsured loss arises, shrug off the responsibility he has assumed. If this requires him to inform himself about his client's business in order to assess the foreseeable risks and insure his client against them, then this he must do. It goes without saying that an agent who does not have the requisite skills to understand the nature of his client's business and assess the risks that should be insured against should not be offering this kind of service. As Mr. Justice Haines said in *Lahey v. Hartford Fire Ins. Co.*, [1968] 1 O.R. 727 at p. 729, 67 D.L.R. (2) 506 at p. 508; varied [1969] 2 O.R. 883, 7 D.L.R. (3d) 315:

> The solution lies in the intelligent insurance agent who inspects the risks when he insures them, knows what his insurer is providing, discovers the areas that may give rise to dispute and either arranges for the coverage or makes certain the purchaser is aware of the exclusion.

> I do not think this is too high a standard to impose on an agent who knows that his client is relying upon him to see that he is protected against all foreseeable, insurable risks.[12]

Applying this test, the court found the agent liable.

In *Fletcher v. Manitoba Public Insurance Co.*,[13] a decision of the Supreme Court of Canada, Justice Wilson (who by this time had been elevated to the Supreme Court) referred to her decision in the *Fine's Flowers* case as a correct statement of the law and added:

> In my view, it is entirely appropriate to hold private insurance agents and brokers to a stringent duty to provide both information and advice to their customers. They are, after all, licensed professionals who specialize in helping clients with risk assessment and in tailoring insurance policies to fit the particular needs of their customers. Their service is highly personalized, concentrating on the specific circumstances of each client. Subtle differences in the forms of coverage available are frequently difficult for the average person to understand. Agents and brokers are trained to understand these differences and to provide individualized insurance advice. It is both reasonable and appropriate to impose upon them a duty not only to convey information but also to provide counsel and advice.[14]

In *Truman v. Sparling Real Estate Ltd.*,[15] a broker was held liable for 25 per cent of the damages suffered by a boat owner whose uninsured vessel sank in a storm. The boat owner had asked the broker to place insurance, but launched his boat some days later without knowing whether or not insurance had been placed. The court held that the broker had failed to display reasonable diligence in obtaining coverage:

---

[12] (1977), 81 D.L.R. (3d) 139 at 148-49.
[13] [1990] 3 S.C.R. 191.
[14] *Ibid.*, at 217.
[15] [1977] I.L.R. ¶1-893 at 694 (B.C.S.C.).

The defendant owed a duty, consequently, to the plaintiff to exercise reasonable care, skill and diligence. The defendant did not owe a duty to obtain coverage but rather to use its best endeavours in a reasonable way to achieve that end.[16]

The court held that the plaintiff was justified in assuming that the broker would attend to his business promptly and that the broker had failed to carry out his promise to obtain coverage even though he knew that the plaintiff was relying on him. The plaintiff was substantially to blame for his own loss and was held contributorily negligent to the extent of 75 per cent of his damages.

In *1013799 Ontario Ltd. v. Kent Line International Ltd.*,[17] an insured sued its freight forwarder, which had procured cargo insurance, and the insurance broker, alleging negligence. The complaint was that the insured's cargo was insured under the Institute Frozen Foods Clauses (under which there was no coverage), whereas, according to the evidence, there were extensions to these clauses available in the insurance market, which would have covered the loss. The judge found that this broad coverage:

> ...was not drawn to the attention of Multi-Foods [the plaintiff]. In my view, on the basis of *Fine's Flowers* and *Fletcher*, it was part of the defendants' duty to make the extension provisions known to Multi-Foods, thus giving it the opportunity to apply for coverage that would have provided protection against the events that happened. ...[The broker] failed in his duty to his customer in not bringing the extension clauses to its attention.[18]

Significantly, the court held that it was not up to the plaintiff to show that the protection of the extension clauses would have been given to it if requested:

> It is more appropriate that the defendants, having failed to bring the extension clauses to Multi-Foods' attention, should have the burden of showing that even if they had done so and even if Multi-Foods had applied for the clauses to be part of its coverage the clauses would not have become part of the insurance contract. No evidence was adduced by the defendants to show — or even to suggest — that the clauses, if requested, would not have been written into the policy.[19]

The judge therefore found that the defendants had breached their duty to the plaintiff in failing to explore and explain the additional coverage available.

In the marine insurance context, the performance of the broker's duty to the client requires not only an understanding of the scope and limitations of the various coverages available in the marine insurance market, but also an appreciation of the intricacies of the client's business. The broker must be familiar with the client's marine activities and assets, and must appreciate the exposures or risks which those assets face. Most marine operations do not remain static and new acquisitions or operations may require adjustments to the client's insurance program. The legal requirements expressed in *Fine's Flowers* and *Fletcher* —

---

16   *Ibid.*, at 695.
17   (2000), 21 C.C.L.I. (3d) 312, [2000] O.T.C. 635 (Ont. S.C.J.).
18   (2000) 21 C.C.L.I. (3d) 312 at 318.
19   *Ibid.*, at 318.

that the broker must procure insurance against the "foreseeable exposures" or explain why such insurance is not available, and must explain to the client any exclusions or limitations on coverage — put a heavy responsibility on the broker. In the following sections, we will examine some particular aspects of that responsibility.

23.3 PARTICULAR OBLIGATIONS

23.3.1 To Understand the Client's Needs

The broker has a duty to learn about and understand the client's requirements.[20] A broker cannot properly advise the client concerning its insurance needs without a full understanding of the client's business and assets. The more sophisticated the client's business, the greater the obligation on the broker to investigate.

23.3.2 To Explain Coverage Available

The choice of coverage is ultimately the client's and cost is always a consideration. Generally, the more comprehensive the coverage sought, the more difficult it is to obtain and the more expensive it will be. In marine insurance, possibly more so than any other type of insurance, the rates and to some extent the insuring conditions, are set by the market — that is, the interplay of the many insurers competing for business. When markets are described as being "soft", there is generally a substantial amount of insurance capacity due to many insurers competing for a relatively fixed amount of business. In these types of markets, lower premiums may be offered for what insurers consider to be desirable business. As well, insurers may be prepared to give broader insuring conditions than they would be prepared to do in more normal market conditions. A soft market generally comes to an end when a number of insurers, having sustained adverse financial results, either withdraw from the market or insist on higher premiums.

Although insurance pricing, and to a limited extent, insuring conditions, vary with market cycles, there are certain risks which more knowledgeable underwriters will only insure on restricted conditions. For instance, goods stowed on deck which would normally be stowed under deck will generally be assigned restricted insuring conditions, such as "free of particular average" ("F.P.A.") plus jettison and washing overboard or the Institute Cargo Clauses 1/1/82 (B) or

---

[20] See *Fine's Flowers Ltd. v. General Accident Assurance Co.* (1977), 17 O.R. (2d) 529, 81 D.L.R. (3d) 139 (C.A.), aff'g. (1974), 5 O.R. (2d) 137, 49 D.L.R. (3d) 641 (H.C.J.). See also: *Elite Marine Co. v. Southlands Insurance Inc.*, [1994] B.C.J. No. 3188 (B.C. Prov. Ct.) (QL). The insurance on a pleasure craft contained a warranty that it was to be used only for private pleasure use. The insured had told the broker that he used the boat from time to time in his business. The broker was found liable for failing to advise the client concerning the limitation in the policy to recreational uses.

(C) (reproduced in Appendices C and D). A shipment of used goods will generally only be granted F.P.A. conditions, unless they are warranted reconditioned and in like-new condition. If they comply with this warranty, they might be considered for broader "all risks" conditions, for example the Institute Cargo Clauses 1/1/82 (A) (reproduced in Appendix B).

The marine insurance broker has a duty to know these alternatives and to explain to its client the insurance options as well as the costs and risks associated with them.[21] If a loss occurs that is not covered by the policy issued, but which might have been covered by a more expensive but nonetheless available insurance, there is an onus on the broker to prove that the option of such coverage was explained to the client and that the client chose not to take it, presumably as a result of cost considerations.[22] The prudent broker will confirm such advice in writing.

Some non-marine cases suggest that the broker has an obligation to find the type of insurance coverage which the insured's business requires or to explain why it was unable to do so.[23] For example, in *Rivard v. Mutual Life Insurance Co. of Canada*,[24] the plaintiff was the beneficiary of a life insurance policy on his business partner. The policy was void for misrepresentation of the insured's smoking history. The court stated:

> In summary, an insurance agent does have a duty to his client to either provide the insurance requested or advise the client that such coverage is not available. It is reasonable for the client to rely upon the insurance agent to provide this service. Insurance agents hold themselves out as possessing the expertise to arrange insurance coverage and to advise clients on insurance matters.[25]

The agent was found negligent in the performance of this duty.

In an Alberta case, *Jessett v. Conacher*, the court accepted the following statement:[26]

---

[21] See *1013799 Ontario Ltd. v. Kent Line International Ltd.* (2000), 21 C.C.L.I. (3d) 312, [2000] O.T.C. 635 (Ont. S.C.J.).

[22] *Ibid.*

[23] See *G.K.N. Keller Canada Ltd. v. Hartford Fire Insurance Co.* (1983), 1 C.C.L.I. 34, 27 C.C.L.T. 61 (Ont. H.C.J.), rev'd. in part (1984), 4 C.C.L.I. xxxvii, 28 C.C.L.T. xxxv (Ont. C.A.).

[24] (1992), 9 O.R. (3d) 545 (Gen. Div.).

[25] (1992), 9 O.R. (3d) 545 at 556 (Gen. Div.).

[26] [1981] I.L.R. ¶1-1429 at 476 (Alta. Q.B.), citing *Peter Unruh Construction Ltd. v. Kelly-Lucy & Cameron Adjusters Ltd.* (1976), 4 W.W.R. 419 at 426. The judge in *Jessett v. Conacher* also quoted with approval from two other Alberta cases imposing a heavy burden on the broker at [1981] I.L.R. ¶1-429 at 476. In the first of those cases, *Hornburg v. Toole, Peet & Co. Ltd.*, [1981] I.L.R. ¶4997 at 5001, *per* Power J., the court stated: "I do not think this is too high a standard to impose upon an agent who knows that his client is relying upon him to see that he is protected against all foreseeable insurance risks." In the second case, *Neil's Tractor & Equipment Ltd. v. Butler, Maveety & Maryland Casualty Co.* (1977), 75 D.L.R. (3d) 151, 2 Alta. L.R. (2d) 187 (Alta. S.C.) the trial judge had stated: "An insurance agent owes a duty of care to an insured who relies upon that agent to provide proper and full insurance coverage for the insured's entire operation."

Insurance brokers are agents who make it their business to provide contracts of insurance for those who employ them. Having undertaken to obtain insurance an insurance broker must exercise proper care and skill in carrying out the assured's instructions and he cannot excuse himself from accepting a policy that gives insufficient coverage by saying that the assured ought to have examined it.

23.3.3   To Explain Coverage to the Client

Marine insurance is a complex and technical area. There may be limitations or exceptions to the coverage, warranties or conditions to be observed by the insured that may not be readily understood, even by experienced insureds. The broker must explain all these aspects of coverage to the client and, once again, this advice should be given in writing.[27]

In *New Forty Four Mines Ltd. v. St. Paul Fire & Marine Insurance Co.*,[28] the trial judge had found a broker liable for failing to bring a "watchman's warranty" to the attention of the insured. There was a fire at the mine when there was no watchman in place and the insurer was able to avoid liability. The Court of Appeal, reversing the trial judgment, held that the insurance binder was brief and the warranty was plainly visible on the binder. The principal shareholder of the insured and the president of the insured were both lawyers, and presumably were sophisticated enough to read and understand the policies.[29]

---

[27] See *Desgagnes v. Antonin Belleau Inc.*, [1970] I.L.R. ¶1-348 (Que. C.A.), leave to appeal ref'd. [1970] S.C.R. vii, in which the broker was found liable for failing to advise the client that it was insured against actual total loss but not against *constructive* total loss. In *Fine's Flowers*, Mr. Justice Estey, then of the Ontario Court of Appeal, found that the broker was liable in negligence for failing to advise his client of the limitations on coverage. Had the plaintiff known of these limitations, he would have been able to procure other insurance. See also: *Tradelink Distribution Ltd. (Canada) v. Rand & Fowler Insurance Ltd.* (2001), 33 C.C.L.I. (3d) 299 (B.C.S.C.), where the Canadian broker failed to read the cover note provided by the London broker and failed to inform the insured of significant restrictions on coverage. The broker was liable for failing to inform the client of these restrictions; *Percy v. West Bay Boat Builders & Shipyards Ltd.* (1996), 36 C.C.L.I. (2d) 284 (B.C.S.C.), aff'd. (1997), 49 C.C.L.I. (2d) 1, 98 B.C.A.C. 256 (B.C.C.A.): broker held liable for failing to understand and appreciate the client's business, assets and risks to which the client was exposed and to point out gaps in the client's new policy that would have been covered under its former policy; *Elite Marine Co. v. Southlands Insurance Inc.*, [1994] B.C.J. No. 3188 (B.C. Prov. Ct.) (QL), where the broker failed to explain to the client that a warranty as to private pleasure use restricted the operation of the vessel.

[28] [1984] 9 C.C.L.I. 91, [1985] I.L.R. ¶1-1872 (Alta. Q.B.), rev'd. [1987] 5 W.W.R. 673, 28 C.C.L.I. 81 (Alta. C.A.), leave to appeal ref'd. (1987), 86 N.R. 238n (S.C.C.).

[29] See also *Waldman's Fish Inc. v. Anderson Insurance Ltd.* (1979), 25 N.B.R. (2d) 482, [1979] I.L.R. ¶1-1145 (C.A.), rev'g. (1978), 20 N.B.R. (2d) 600 (Q.B.), leave to appeal refused (1979), 29 N.R. 359n, 30 N.B.R. (2d) 626n (S.C.C.), in which it was held that an agent was negligent in failing to notify the insured of changes in the terms of the insurance which had been made by the insurer; and *Niagara Frontier Caterers Ltd. v. Continental Insurance Co. of Canada* (1990), 74 O.R. (2d) 191, 5 C.C.L.I. (2d) 54 (H.C.J.), where there was negligence on the part of a broker in explaining the consequences of a co-insurance requirement in the policy of insurance.

In *G.K.N. Keller Canada Ltd. v. Hartford Fire Insurance Co.*,[30] it was held that the broker was negligent. Although aware of the insured's needs, the broker failed to provide the insurance coverage the insured required and failed to inform the client that the coverage he needed was not provided by the policy of insurance.

23.3.4   To Investigate the Solvency of Insurers

In *Norlympia Seafoods Ltd. v. Dale & Co.*, it was held that a broker has a duty to make reasonable investigations of the solvency and security of the insurers with whom the risk has been placed.[31] In *Norlympia*, the broker was held liable for placing the risk with inferior companies who became insolvent. It had misrepresented to the plaintiff that the risk had been placed with "highly secure" insurers. The Court reviewed the obligations of the broker and stated:

> As brokers for the plaintiff, the defendant was under a contractual obligation to obtain and service the insurance request in a reasonably competent manner. It was also an implied term of that contract for professional services that the broker would not misrepresent material facts to the assured.[32]

The Court stated that the broker had a duty to know the basic principles of insurance law and should have advised the insured that there was no insurance in place so that it could take steps to obtain other insurance. The broker had a duty to advise the insured of all facts relevant to the decisions it might be required to make and to advise it of all the available options in terms of coverage.

Larger brokers maintain security committees to monitor the financial health of the insurers with which they deal. International brokerage firms with operations in several countries have representatives in principal cities to monitor local insurers. These representatives exchange information so that an up-to-date record of worldwide insurers can be maintained. There are also several financial reporting services providing information on the financial viability of insurers.[33]

In Canada, insurers are subject to audit by the federal Department of Financial Institutions if they are federally-licensed or by the provincial authorities if they are provincially-licensed. In fulfilling their obligations to investigate the insurer's solvency, brokers would be unwise to rely on the fact that a particular insurer is licensed by a government agency. Whenever it appears that an insurer on an existing policy is in danger of becoming insolvent, a prudent broker

---

[30]   (1983), 1 C.C.L.I. 34, 27 C.C.L.T. 61 (Ont. H.C.J.), var'd. (1984), 4 C.C.L.I. xxxvii, 28 C.C.L.T. xxxv.

[31]   [1983] I.L.R. ¶1-1688 (B.C.S.C.), aff'd. [1988] B.C.J. No. 107 (B.C.C.A.). See also *Chidley v. Thompson, Osen & Sherban Canada Ltd.* (1987), 28 C.C.L.I. 267 (B.C.S.C.) where the broker was found liable for assuring his client that the insurer was secure, in the face of evidence to the contrary.

[32]   [1983] I.L.R. ¶1-1688 at 6491.

[33]   The most well known financial service is probably A.M. Bests, an agency which provides an opinion on the ability of any particular insurer to pay claims. Standard & Poor's and Moody's are two other rating firms which can be consulted by a broker.

should advise its client and should attempt to replace the insurance with a financially sound insurer. This could cost the insured an additional premium if the original insurer refuses a mutual cancellation with a refund of a portion of the premium. Additionally, in some cases, the broker may, with the insured's permission, place insurance with an unapproved insurer. This may occur because of difficulty completing the placement at the price required by the insured. In this situation, it is wise for the broker to obtain the insured's written consent to the use of an unapproved insurer.

23.3.5 Duty With Respect to Expiry and Renewal

The broker may have a duty to advise the client that the policy has expired or is about to expire.[34] This will depend on the facts of the particular case; the nature of the relationship between the broker and the insured; the custom and practice of the business; and all the surrounding circumstances.[35]

23.3.6 Liability for Negligent Misrepresentation

Brokers are frequently asked by third parties, such as financial institutions and others doing business with the insured, to provide confirmation that a particular property or liability is insured. If the broker provides misinformation or incomplete information, it may find itself liable if the third party suffers loss as a result. For example, in *Random Ford Mercury Sales Ltd. v. Noseworthy*,[36] the plaintiff, an unpaid seller of a boat, was only prepared to release it to the buyer on confirmation that his interest was insured. The insurance agent gave that assurance when, in fact, the boat was not insured. The seller released the boat, which later burned and sank. The agent was subsequently held liable for negligent misrepresentation.

23.4 CLAIMS

The marine insurance broker's duties do not end with the procuring of the policy. When a loss or casualty occurs, the insured usually notifies its broker with the expectation that the broker will communicate with insurers to ensure

---

[34] See *Grove Service Ltd. v. Lentart Agencies Ltd.* (1979), 10 C.C.L.T. 101 (B.C.S.C.): the broker was negligent in failing to advise the client that its policy had expired and that it had been unable to find new coverage. The client was found to have been 50 per cent contributorily negligent. See also *Lewis v. C.M. & M. Insurance Services Ltd.* (1983), 51 N.B.R. (2d) 433, 4 C.C.L.I. 1 (N.B.Q.B.), a non-marine case, in which the broker was partly to blame for failing to notify the client that the policy was about to expire. The client was held contributorily negligent for failing to take reasonable measures for its own protection.

[35] See *Roy v. Atlantic Underwriters Ltd.* (1984), 9 C.C.L.I. 77 (N.B.Q.B.), rev'd. (1986), 17 C.C.L.I. 266, 67 N.B.R. (2d) 16 (N.B.C.A.), where the Court of Appeal held that in the absence of a contract or an undertaking to renew, there was no obligation on the broker to renew the contract.

[36] (1992), 95 D.L.R. (4th) 168, 98 Nfld. & P.E.I.R. 221 (Nfld. T.D.).

that the insured's rights under the policy are protected. The broker has a duty to inform the insured of any particular requirements of the insurance policy, such as the need to appoint a surveyor and the need to take reasonable measures to mitigate the loss. In Canada and the United States, large brokers handling hull fleets generally have accredited average adjusters on staff to deal with the most complicated claims. These professionals will ensure that the insurers are properly notified of the claim and that adjustments are presented in a timely fashion in accordance with policy terms and the rules and practices pertaining to adjustments. Similarly, in the case of cargo claims, many of the larger brokers have experienced claims staff who can assist the insured in the preparation of the claim and its submission in accordance with the applicable principles and practices.

23.5 DUTY OF THE INSURED

What duty does the insured have to take reasonable measures for its own protection? If the loss is not covered by the insurance which the broker pro-cured, does the insured bear some responsibility for not taking the time to read and understand its own insurance coverage?

There have been a number of Canadian cases in which courts have found the insured partly to blame, and therefore contributorily negligent, in failing to take reasonable steps for his or her own protection.[37] For example, in *Eedy v. Stephens*,[38] the client had been warned that it would be difficult to obtain insurance and before the insurance could be placed, the boat was destroyed by fire. The broker was not liable for failing to put insurance in place. In *Curry Construction (1973) Ltd. v. Reed Stenhouse Ltd.*,[39] the insured claimed that he was unaware of an exclusion in the policy, which he had not read. It was held that the broker did not have a duty to read the policy to the client clause-by-clause — it was sufficient that the broker warned the client to read the policy and to pay particular attention to the exclusions. Whether this approach would apply in all cases is doubtful. The more complex the policy, the more significant the exclusions; the less sophisticated the client, the greater the broker's duty to ensure that the client fully appreciates the important terms of the policy.

The knowledge and sophistication of the insured will affect the court's judg-ment as to whether or not the insured failed to take reasonable measures for his or her own protection and therefore whether he or she was contributorily negligent. In *Olanick v. R. Cholkan & Co. Ltd.*,[40] the plaintiff was a real estate lawyer who had failed to read the policy. The defendant had obtained the only

---

[37] See *Grove Service Ltd. v. Lentart Agencies Ltd.* (1979), 10 C.C.L.T. 101 (B.C.S.C.); *Lewis v. C.M. & M. Insurance Services Ltd.* (1983), 51 N.B.R. (2d) 433, 4 C.C.L.I. 1 (Q.B.), where the insured was also found to blame; and *Truman v. Sparling Real Estate Ltd.*, [1977] I.L.R. ¶1-893 at 694 (B.C.S.C.).

[38] [1976] I.L.R. ¶1-735 (B.C.S.C.).

[39] (1988), 35 C.C.L.I. 275 (N.W.T. S.C.), aff'd. (1990), 40 C.C.L.I. xxxvii (N.W.T.C.A.).

[40] [1980] I.L.R. ¶1-1282 (Ont. H.C.J.).

kind of policy that was practically available and the court found he was not negligent.[41] Similarly, in *Marler v. Schmucki*,[42] the plaintiff was an Ontario lawyer, who understood the significance of a "laid up and out of commission" warranty in the policy, and the consequences of a breach of that warranty. The plaintiff breached the warranty by operating his boat without the consent of the insurer and his claim against the broker and the insurer was dismissed.

23.6 ESTABLISHING A CLAIM AGAINST THE BROKER

What must the insured prove in order to establish a claim against the insurance broker? In *Crate Marine Sales Ltd. v. Graham Neale Insurance Brokers Ltd.*,[43] the judge quoted with approval from Madam Justice McLachlin, in the *Norlympia v. Dale* case:

> To succeed in their claim [against the broker] with respect to the hull and machinery coverage, the plaintiffs must establish: (1) that they suffered a loss on account of hull and machinery; (2) that there was no hull and machinery insurance in effect at the time on [sic] of the grounding; (3) that the absence of hull and machinery insurance at the time of the grounding was caused by Dale & Company's acts or omissions; and (4) that such acts or omissions constitute breach of contract or actionable negligence at law.[44]

The judge held that the plaintiffs had not pleaded the second and third items and suggested that there was possibly some reluctance to plead that there was no insurance coverage. On this point, he stated:

> The approach that may cover the complete claim is to sue the insurer and the broker in the alternative, that is, that in the event that it is found that the policies are not properly in effect, then to claim against the broker for not properly procuring that which it is alleged they undertook to procure on the advice received from the plaintiff.[45]

In many cases, the issue will be more complicated and not simply a matter of alleging that the broker did not obtain insurance. The insured will have to plead that the insurance procured by the broker did not cover the loss, that there was other insurance available on the market which would have covered the loss and that the broker either failed to explain the limitations of the insurance or failed to bring the availability of the broader coverage to the insured's attention.

The duty of care owed by the broker to its client may depend on the broker's degree of sophistication and the extent to which he or she holds out a degree of expertise in the field of marine insurance. A broker specializing in marine

---

[41] See also *Weston v. Pilot Insurance Co.* (1994), 22 C.C.L.I. (2d) 114, [1994] I.L.R. 1-3030 (Ont. Ct. Gen. Div.); *Marler v. Schmucki*, [1996] O.J. No. 3865 (Ont. Gen. Div.).

[42] [1996] O.J. No. 3865 (Ont. Gen. Div.).

[43] [1990] I.L.R. ¶1-2610 (Ont. S.C.J.)

[44] *Ibid.*, at 10,180, citing *Norlympia Seafoods Ltd. v. Dale & Co.*, [1983] I.L.R. ¶1-1688 (B.C.S.C.).

[45] [1990] I.L.R. ¶1-2610 at 10,181.

insurance will probably be expected to display more skill and expertise in such matters than a general insurance broker and will be held to a higher standard of care.

The broker may be in a difficult position where the insurer defends the claim on the basis that the loss is simply not covered by the terms of the policy. The broker's position becomes worse where the insurer contends that another form of coverage was available, but that it was not requested by the broker. The broker's first line of defence may be to argue that the claim is in fact covered by the policy and that the insurer should pay it. However, the broker may be liable if the court disagrees and finds that although the coverage might have been available on other terms, the broker simply did not advise the client of the availability of those terms.

Where the broker is sued for negligence it is entitled to raise any defences under the policy that are or would have been available to the insurers.[46] The broker may also plead that it procured the ordinary form of policy and that there is no superior form of policy available, even though the policy in question does not cover the loss.[47]

23.7   THE BROKER'S REMUNERATION

Traditionally, brokers have been paid a percentage commission of the insurance premium. This means that if the insurer raises the premium, the broker's earnings will increase proportionately. If, on the other hand, the premium is reduced, there will be a corresponding reduction in the broker's earnings. In the case of fleet insurances, clients often prefer to compensate their brokers by means of a negotiated fee. This practice applies principally to the larger insurance exposures where the premium could reach hundreds of thousands or even millions of dollars.

It is common for the broker to advance the premium on behalf of its client and the broker has the right to sue the client for the premium so advanced.[48] The broker has a "lien" on the insurance policy to protect its right to recover the premium it pays on behalf of the insured.[49] The broker's lien enables it to hold

---

[46]   See *Buck v. Knowlton* (1891), 31 N.B.R. 417, aff'd. (1892), 21 S.C.R. 371.

[47]   See *Silverthorne v. Gillespie, Moffat* (1852), 9 U.C.Q.B. 414; *Olanick v. R. Cholkan & Co.*, [1980] I.L.R. ¶1-1282 (Ont. H.C.J.).

[48]   See *Tomenson Saunders Whitehead Ltd. v. Smith* (1984), 12 C.C.L.I. 89, [1985] I.L.R. ¶1-1890 (B.C. Co. Ct.).

[49]   Canadian *Marine Insurance Act* ("*C.M.I.A.*"), S.C. 1993, c. 22, subs. 49(1):
      49(1) Unless otherwise agreed, where a broker effects a marine policy on behalf of the insured,
      (a) the broker is directly responsible to the insurer for the premium;
      (b) the broker has, as against the insured, a lien on the policy for the amount of the premium and the broker's charges in effecting the policy; and
      (c) the insurer is directly responsible to the insured for any amount that may be payable in respect of losses or a returnable premium.

the policy until reimbursed by its client for the premium. On a practical level, this may not be of much assistance unless there is a claim under the policy, in which case, technically, the original policy is presented to the insurer as part of the claim process. The broker would be entitled to present the claim on behalf of its client and obtain compensation for its charges out of the settlement of the claim. In *Marler v. Schmucki*,[50] the insured complained that the policy had not been delivered to him in a timely manner, with the result that he did not have a full appreciation of the language of a warranty contained in the policy. The court held that any delay was attributable to the fact that the insured had failed to pay the premium and the broker had exercised its right to a lien on the policy.

It has been held that the broker has an action *in rem* against the insured vessel to recover its premium. The broker has the right to sue the vessel (the *res*) to recover the premium it paid on behalf of the vessel. The reasoning is that because the *insurer* had the right to bring an action *in rem*, the broker, having paid the insurer for the premium, was "entitled to the insurer's right to bring an action *in rem* for the premiums".[51]

On the other hand, payment by the insured to the broker is customarily treated as payment to the insurer. In *Green Forest Lumber Ltd. v. General Security Insurance Co.*,[52] Mr. Justice Addy of the Federal Court of Canada stated:[53]

> Due to long established practice among insurers and insurance brokers, payment by the assured to its broker discharges the duty of the assured in order to complete its contract with the insurer. The broker becomes the debtor of the insurer for payment.

The subject of the premium and the rights and obligations of brokers in respect of premium is discussed in detail in Chapter 16.

---

(2) Unless otherwise agreed, where a broker effects a marine policy on behalf of a person who employs the broker as a principal, the broker has a lien on the policy in respect of any balance on any insurance account that may be due to the broker from that person unless, when the debt was incurred, the broker had reason to believe that the person was only an agent.

C.M.I.A., s. 50:

50. Where a broker effects a marine policy on behalf of an insured, an acknowledgment in the policy of the receipt of the premium is, in the absence of fraud, conclusive as between the insurer and the insured, but not as between the insurer and the broker.

[50]   [1996] O.J. No. 3865 (Ont. Gen. Div.) (QL).

[51]   *Fairway Life & Marine Insurance v. "Susan Darlene" (The)*, [1987] 2 F.C. 547, 21 C.C.L.I. 83 (T.D.). The decision appears to be based, not on the combined effect of subss. 22(2)(*r*) and 43(2) of the *Federal Court Act*, R.S.C. 1985, c. F-7 which provide for an action *in rem* in a claim in connection with a contract of marine insurance, but rather on the fact that, under civil law there was a lien for premiums.

[52]   [1980] 1 S.C.R. 176, 34 N.R. 303, aff'g. [1978] 2 F.C. 773, 34 N.R. 308 (C.A.), aff'g. [1977] 2 F.C. 351, 34 N.R. 308 (T.D.).

[53]   [1977] 2 F.C. 351 at 358.

23.8   JURISDICTION OF THE COURTS OVER BROKERS

Can a marine insurance broker be sued in the Federal Court of Canada, which has jurisdiction in relation to matters falling within the category of "navigation and shipping"? There is no question that marine insurance is a matter falling within the jurisdiction of the Federal Court of Canada, but it was held in *Intermunicipal Realty & Development Corp. v. Gore Mutual Insurance Co.*[54] that the Federal Court of Canada did not have jurisdiction in an action for damages against a marine insurance broker based on negligence and agency principles. These principles were said not to be part of maritime law and therefore not within the Federal Court's jurisdiction. The *Intermunicipal Realty* case was decided at what might be described as the "low-water mark" of the case law with respect to the jurisdiction of the Federal Court of Canada in admiralty matters. Since that time, there have been a number of decisions expanding the scope of the court's jurisdiction.[55] As the marine insurance broker is an integral part of the process of procuring marine insurance, one would hope that in future cases the court would consider either distinguishing or overruling *Intermunicipal Realty.*[56] On a practical level, the insured may have no choice but to sue both the insurer and the broker but it would be inadvisable and impractical to sue the insurer in one court and the broker in another court.

---

[54]   *Intermunicipal Realty Corp. v. Gore Mutual Insurance Co.*, [1981] 1 F.C. 151, 112 D.L.R. (3d) 432 (T.D.).

[55]   See *ITO - International Terminal Operators Ltd. v. Miida Electronics Inc.*, [1986] 1 S.C.R. 752, 28 D.L.R. (4th) 641, aff'g. [1982] 1 F.C. 406, 124 D.L.R. (3d) 33 (C.A.), aff'g. [1979] 2 F.C. 283, 96 D.L.R. (3d) 518 (T.D.); *Whitbread v. Walley*, [1990] 3 S.C.R. 1273, [1991] 2 W.W.R. 195, aff'g. (1988), 51 D.L.R. (4th) 509, [1988] 5 W.W.R. 313 (B.C.C.A.), rev'g. (1987), 45 D.L.R. (4th) 729, 19 B.C.L.R. (2d) 120 (S.C.); *Porto Seguro Companhia de Seguros Gerais v. Belcan S.A.*, [1997] 3 S.C.R. 1278, 153 D.L.R. (4th) 577, rev'g. [1996] 2 F.C. 751, 195 N.R. 241 (C.A.), aff'g. (1994), 82 F.T.R. 127 (T.D.); *Bow Valley Husky (Bermuda) Ltd. v. St. John Shipbuilding Ltd.*, [1997] 3 S.C.R. 1210, 153 D.L.R. (4th) 385, aff'g. (1995), 126 D.L.R. (4th) 1, 130 Nfld. & P.E.I.R. 92 (Nfld. C.A.), rev'g. (1994), 118 Nfld. & P.E.I.R. 271, 120 Nfld. & P.E.I.R. 228 (Nfld. S.C.T.D.); *Monk Corporation v. Island Fertilizers Ltd.*, [1991] 1 S.C.R. 779, 80 D.L.R. (4th) 58, rev'g. (1989), 97 N.R. 384 (F.C.A.), aff'g. in part (1988), 19 F.T.R. 220 (T.D.); and *Ordon Estate v. Grail*, [1998] 3 S.C.R. 437, 166 D.L.R. (4th) 193, aff'g. (1996), 30 O.R. (3d) 643, 140 D.L.R. (4th) 52 (C.A.), leave to appeal allowed (1997) 225 N.R. 238n (S.C.C.).

[56]   See Chapter 25, *Practice and Procedural Issues*, for a further discussion of this issue.

Chapter 24

The Marine Surveyor

24.1 INTRODUCTION

Marine insurance policies often stipulate that prompt notice must be given to the insurer in the event of a potential claim or that a particular survey firm must be notified in the event of an occurrence giving rise to a claim under the policy. In practice, where the insured is represented by a broker, the insured will notify the broker who will, in turn, consult with the insurer concerning the appointment of a surveyor to investigate the claim on the insurer's behalf. This Chapter will examine the functions and responsibilities of the marine surveyor.

24.2 THE SURVEYOR'S ROLE

The insurer should have the loss investigated at an early stage, when the evidence is still fresh and while it is still possible to take appropriate measures to reduce the amount of the potential loss and to preserve rights against third parties. While these obligations rest squarely on the shoulders of the insured, at least until the claim has been paid, it is undoubtedly in the insurer's interest to assist the insured in order to reduce the amount of the claim and to protect the insurer's rights of subrogation. The marine surveyor is frequently appointed to fulfil several roles, one of which is to provide expert advice and assistance to the insured.

In Canada, as in the United States and the United Kingdom, marine surveyors are independent private contractors. They are not affiliated with insurance companies and should not be confused with insurance adjusters employed in non-marine claims. The relationship between a surveyor and the client, generally the underwriter, is purely a matter of private contract.

Canadian survey firms range in size from branch offices of large international surveying organizations to single-surveyor companies. There is no formal training system for marine surveyors in Canada, nor are surveyors required to be licensed under federal or provincial law. Most surveyors have previous experience in shipping matters, often as ship captains, chief engineers, ship's officers, marine engineers, naval architects or shipyard managers. In Canada, most surveyors specialize in one or more of cargo damages, hull and machinery damages, third party (protection and indemnity) claims, salvage cases or risk assessment surveys. Some surveyors, with particular expertise in yacht and pleasure craft surveys, restrict themselves to the survey of this class of vessel. The Canadian Association of Marine Surveyors, a purely voluntary organization, concerns itself with the education and training of marine surveyors. The National Association of Marine Surveyors of the United States, which has an Eastern Canadian chapter, has as its stated purpose the development and improvement of the competence and professional ethics of marine surveyors. The Society of Accredited Marine Surveyors in the United States has similar purposes.

While it has been frequently said that the surveyor is the "eyes and ears" of the underwriter, the surveyor is not, however, the underwriter's spokesperson. Although usually appointed by the underwriter, the surveyor does not normally have the authority to comment on coverage issues or to adjust the claim. The surveyor who does so without specific instructions oversteps his or her authority and runs the risk of committing the underwriter to a liability. If the underwriter "holds out" the surveyor as its agent, or if the surveyor leads the insured to reasonably believe that the surveyor has the underwriter's authority to give binding commitments on coverage or the claim, the underwriter may find itself bound by the surveyor's representations. For this reason, in spite of the persistence of an insured who may wish to obtain confirmation of its coverage, the surveyor should refer all queries on such issues to the broker or to the insurer itself.

Nor should the surveyor take over the insured's fundamental responsibility to deal with its own property and to manage its own insurance claim. We have seen in Chapter 11, *Duties of the Insured: Sue and Labour*, that the insured has an obligation to take reasonable measures to mitigate damages and to act — as the saying goes — "as a prudent uninsured". It is appropriate for the surveyor to offer advice and recommendations to the insured on the mitigation of damages, but the surveyor should not, unless specifically instructed by the underwriter, direct the insured to a specific location for repairs, authorize salvage of property, or sell property that is a constructive total loss. In one Canadian case, where the surveyor appointed by the underwriter had directed the arrangements for the repair of the vessel after an alleged breach of warranty, the surveyor's actions were held to be a waiver of the breach of warranty by the insurer.[1]

The surveyor's role, when acting on behalf of an underwriter, is to attend to provide the client with a professional and independent opinion concerning the "cause, nature and extent of the damage", together with recommendations concerning repairs; comments on the reasonableness of the cost of repairs or reconditioning; and on the reasonableness of actions that are being taken or that could be taken by a prudent owner to minimize a loss. Whether the claim is large or small, the surveyor plays a major part in the assessment of the claim by the insurer who will seldom pay a claim unless the surveyor has commented that it is "fair and reasonable".

The surveyor's greatest assets are marine experience, independence, common sense, and integrity. While the surveyor is usually appointed by the underwriter, he or she must report "on behalf of whom it may concern" and without prejudice to underwriters' liability. This means that the surveyor must report solely on the facts and must give an independent professional opinion without reference to

---

[1]   *Daneau v. Laurent Gendron Ltée.*, [1964] 1 Ll. L.R. 220 (Exch. Ct.).

which party will ultimately bear the loss, be it the insurer, the insured or some other third party.[2]

The fees of the surveyor are usually paid by the insured, but if there is a proper claim under the policy, survey fees are recoverable as part of the adjustment.[3] In some cases, where underwriters require a survey as a condition to acceptance of the risk, they will require that the costs of any survey be paid by the insured.

24.3 TYPES OF SURVEYS

The activities carried out by marine surveyors acting on behalf of underwriters are limited only by the risks insured by underwriters. The following are the most common functions of marine surveyors, and are carried out on behalf of underwriters or other party requiring an independent assessment.

24.3.1 Hull and Machinery Surveys[4]

Hull and machinery policies frequently specify the surveying firm to be notified in the event of an accident affecting the vessel. The surveyor will attend the vessel to report on the cause, nature and extent of the damage. The investigation of the cause of the incident is an important part of the surveyor's responsibility since the policy will invariably be on a "named perils" basis and the surveyor's opinion will be important in determining whether the loss was caused by one of the perils named in the policy.

In addition to determining the cause of the incident, the surveyor will carry out a detailed inspection of the nature and extent of the damage. Sometimes it may be necessary to employ other professionals to assist in the process, such as divers to inspect the bottom of a vessel, machinery specialists to evaluate damage to equipment or engines (if the firm has no marine engineers on staff) or metallurgists to determine the cause of failure. In a serious case, drydocking may be required in order to fully determine the extent of the damage and to carry out repairs. In conjunction with the insured, the surveyor should be capable of preparing a repair specification and setting out the work and materials necessary to effect repairs. The Surveyor may also assist the insured in obtaining bids for that work.

---

[2] See *Continental Insurance Co. v. Almassa International Inc.*, unreported (24 March 2003), Toronto (Ont. Sup. Ct. of Justice), in which the court discounted the surveyor's opinion because some of the language of his report had been provided by the insurer's representatives.

[3] See *James Richardson & Sons Ltd. v. Standard Marine Insurance Co.*, [1936] S.C.R. 573, [1936] 3 D.L.R. 513.

[4] In November 1992, the Association of Marine Underwriters of British Columbia issued a set of guidelines entitled "General Guidelines and Principles for Use by Hull Surveyors when Acting in the Capacity of Underwriters' Surveyor in the Instance of a Loss." This document lists some of the information that underwriters expect to be included in a survey report, and also cautions surveyors about becoming involved in discussions of coverage or in committing the insured or underwriters to the payment of particular costs.

The appointment of a surveyor does not relieve the insured of its responsibility to act prudently to mitigate the amount of the claim against the underwriter. It is the duty of the insured to obtain estimates for the repair of the damage, to select the most appropriate contractor to carry out the repairs and to give instructions to the repairer concerning the work to be done. While the surveyor will invariably consult with the insured throughout this operation, and may offer advice and commentary, the responsibility to carry out these activities rests with the insured, not with the surveyor. Some hull and machinery policies give the underwriters the right to override the insured's choice of repair firm, in which case the insurer's preference must be determined before a commitment is made.

The surveyor will typically review the repair accounts submitted by contractors to determine whether they are fair and reasonable and attributable to the casualty in question. The surveyor's opinion on the accounts will be set out in the survey report. This is done by the surveyor on a "without prejudice" basis and is subject to proper adjustment under the terms of the policy. If repairs have been done to the vessel by the owner as part of "owner's work", the necessary costs will be identified and commented upon by the surveyor. At the conclusion of the investigation, the surveyor will usually submit a report to the broker, who will use the report in the preparation of the claim to underwriters.

24.3.2 Salvage Surveys

In the case of major damage, such as a grounding, fire or flooding of the ship, the marine surveyor will attend at the scene on the insurer's behalf to assist and advise in the salvage operations until the vessel is taken to a place of safety or returned to its pre-accident condition. This salvage work is one of the most specialized of the surveyor's functions and requires considerable skill and experience. After the salvage of the vessel has been completed, the surveyor's role may return to the more usual function of determining the cause, nature and extent of the damage and the associated costs.

24.3.3 P. & I. Surveys

As noted elsewhere in this book, most larger vessels, particularly commercial vessels, carry third party liability insurance which is frequently but not exclusively provided by protection and indemnity ("P. & I.") Clubs on a mutual basis.[5] Third party claims can encompass many situations, but the most common occurrences a surveyor may encounter are collisions, groundings, dock or fixed structure damages, wreck removals, cargo claims and any other incident having the potential for a claim to be made against the insurer. Unlike hull and machinery underwriters, P. & I. Clubs have marine surveyors on staff, but they generally engage independent surveyors around the world in the case of all but the most serious incidents.

---

[5]   See Chapter 20, *Protection and Indemnity Insurance.*

24.3.4 Risk Management/Towage Surveys

The towage of a vessel, particularly a vessel with no means of propulsion, presents particular risks. Underwriters frequently insist on a pre-towage survey to inspect and approve the suitability of the towed vessel; the towing vessel (typically one or more tugs); the towing arrangements; the nature and quality of the tow line and connections; and the emergency equipment. The surveyor will usually inspect all of these items and may initially issue recommendations for the preparation of the tow and the towing vessel. These recommendations may include limitations on the operation, such as a maximum speed at which the tug is permitted to proceed; requiring the operation to be confined to a specified route; and limiting the weather conditions or forecasts under which the tug is permitted to leave the port of departure or other intermediate ports.[6]

24.3.5 Condition Surveys

While surveyors are sometimes called upon to perform valuations of ships for buyers, lenders and insurers, this work is usually left to the expertise of ship brokers and valuators whose job it is to establish the market value of a vessel at a given time. Most commonly, the surveyor carries out a "condition survey" (also called a "condition and detail survey" or "condition and valuation survey"[7]). This refers to an inspection of the ship for the purpose of determining its overall condition and state of repair. For example, a buyer may want an expert inspection of the ship before entering into an agreement of purchase and sale, or financial institutions and other lenders may require a condition and valuation survey to ensure that the vessel provides adequate security for the loan. Occasionally, underwriters will request a condition survey prior to coming on risk, relying on the surveyor to identify any deficiencies that may need to be rectified before the insurance is bound or any circumstances which might prompt the underwriter to give restricted cover.[8]

24.3.6 On/Off Hire Surveys

Where the ship is about to go under charter for a period of time, the owner and the charterer may agree that an "on hire" survey will be carried out to determine

---

[6] See, for example, *Riverside Landmark Corp. v. Northumberland General Insurance Co.* (1984), 8 C.C.L.I. 118 (Ont. S.C.J.).

[7] In *Armac Diving Services Ltd. v. Meadows Marine Surveys Ltd.*, [1983] B.C.J. No. 479 (B.C.S.C.) (QL), the plaintiff sued a surveyor for alleged deficiencies in the survey. The court distinguished between three different types of condition surveys, the least complex being a condition and detail survey for insurance purposes, the next being a valuation survey for a lending institution and the most comprehensive being a purchaser's survey.

[8] For an example of underwriters imposing limitations on coverage as a result of a surveyor's recommendations concerning a vessel's need for repair, see: *Marler v. Schmucki*, [1996] O.J. No. 3865 (Ont. Gen. Div.) (QL), for another example of a condition survey, see *Silva v. British Columbia* (1992), 67 B.C.L.R. (2d) 75 (C.A.) where the insurer denied liability because the recommendations of the surveyor had not been complied with.

the condition of the ship and to note any damages. At the end of the charter period there will be an "off hire" survey to establish whether the ship has suffered any damage since the commencement of the charter, for which the charterer will be held liable.

24.3.7 Cargo Surveys

Cargo insurance policies frequently stipulate that in the event of damage to a shipment, the holder of the certificate of insurance must notify the insurer's designated agent at the destination to inspect the goods. The agent (sometimes a survey firm itself) will arrange for the appointment of a cargo surveyor to investigate the loss. Like a hull and machinery surveyor, the cargo surveyor's responsibility is to ascertain the "cause, nature and extent" of the loss. This will entail an inspection of the damaged goods and of any packing or shipping container to determine how the goods were damaged. A frequent cause of damage to containerized shipments is the mishandling of the container itself. If the container can be located, the surveyor will inspect it for holes, scrapes or other evidence of abuse. If damage by seawater is suspected, the surveyor will frequently test a sample of the goods to determine whether they have been in contact with salt water. Further testing for other types of contamination may also be required. In exceptional cases, the surveyor, after discussing the matter with the underwriter and the insured, may retain the services of other experts such as chemists, biologists, or metallurgists, to assist in determining the cause of the damage.

The surveyor will also investigate and report on the nature of the damage and its extent in both physical and financial terms. Deficiencies in the packing of the goods which may have caused or contributed to the loss will be noted by the surveyor. The surveyor will examine the insured's expenses in relation to the claim as well as the insured's assessment of the amount of the claim, and will comment on whether the costs claimed by the insured are considered fair and reasonable and attributable to the cause alleged.

In the course of carrying out his or her functions, the surveyor will locate all relevant documentation, including commercial invoices, customs documents, shipping contracts such as bills of lading and waybills, and other documents and records generated during the transportation process.

Where the goods have been damaged and are unusable by the receiver, but nevertheless have some salvage value, the surveyor will, if requested by the insured, assist in arrangements for a salvage sale. He or she will contact known salvage sources for bids on the goods and will arrange a sale to the highest bidder on behalf of the insured. Where there is a possibility that the goods can be reconditioned and restored, the surveyor will assist the insured in finding ways to do so, at a reasonable cost. Sometimes, the most cost-effective way of dealing with damaged goods is to reach an agreement with the receiver to retain them, subject to a discount or "depreciation" factor, which the surveyor will recommend and which the insurer will consider (and generally accept) after the surveyor submits a report.[9]

In the context of cargo claims, it is understandable that an insured would consider the surveyor to be the insurer's representative — after all, the surveyor is stipulated in the insurance policy and is usually better known to the insurer than the insured. The commercial reality is that experienced cargo surveyors are relatively few in number in Canada's maritime centres and they are usually well-known and respected by the insurance companies who appoint them. Neverthe-less, the duty to "sue and labour" after a loss remains the insured's duty, not the insurer's, and the appointment of a surveyor does not relieve the insured of this obligation. The insured is not bound to follow the surveyor's advice, and, thus, disputes occasionally arise concerning the most appropriate and cost-effective method of mitigating the damages. The surveyor's approval of the insured's claim will generally be accepted by the insurer, but where the insured departs from the surveyor's advice, he or she will have to justify the reason or reasons to the underwriters.

The surveyor must avoid creating the impression that he or she is the under-writer's agent and must avoid taking over responsibility for decision-making in the mitigation of cargo claims.

One of the usual acts of the surveyor in a marine cargo claim is to assist the insured in making sure that recovery rights against third parties are protected. Appropriate notice will be given to carriers and other parties potentially responsible for the loss.

24.3.8 Draft Surveys

A surveyor may be hired as an independent expert, before and after the loading of a particular cargo or fuel, to carry out a draft survey for the purpose of calculating the amount of cargo or fuel loaded on the vessel.

24.3.9 Loading Surveys

In the case of special cargos, such as heavy machinery or large cumbersome goods, the shipper or underwriter may retain a surveyor to make recommenda-tions concerning the preparation of the goods for transit and their stowage and securing on-board the vessel. As shipments of heavy machinery or large vehicles, such as railcars or tractors, frequently require special lifting gear, stowage and lashing, it is common to engage a professional (generally someone with seafaring experience as an officer) to make recommendations concerning stowage.

---

[9] See Section 24.7, "Depreciation", for a discussion of some of the problems that may arise where a claim is settled on a depreciation basis.

24.3.10 Out-turn Surveys

Where a party has a particular concern about the potential condition of goods at the time of discharge from the ocean vessel (for example, where some loss or damage to the goods has occurred during transport or where there is a risk of damage during discharge), the interested parties may appoint surveyors to inspect the goods before, during and after discharge to determine when, how and to what extent damages have occurred.

24.3.11 General Average Surveys

Where general average is declared, the several interested parties will generally appoint surveyors to represent their individual interests, but the general average adjuster will likely appoint a surveyor to investigate the circumstance of the loss, oversee the general average operation and to identify charges and expenses of a general average nature.[10] This surveyor's responsibilities are described in one text as follows:

1) To advise all parties on the steps necessary to ensure the common safety of ship and cargo.

2) To monitor the steps actually taken by the parties to ensure that proper regard is taken of the general interest.

3) To review general average expenditure incurred and advise the adjuster as to whether the costs are fair and reasonable.

4) To identify and quantify any general average sacrifice of ship and cargo.

5) To ensure that the general average damage is minimised wherever possible, *i.e.*, by reconditioning or sale of damaged cargo. Except in cases of extreme urgency or where communications are difficult any significant action with regard to cargo (*i.e.*, arranging for its sale at a port of refuge) must be taken in consultation with the concerned in cargo. [*i.e.*, the cargo owners and their underwriters][11]

It is part of the general average surveyor's duty to inspect the damage to vessel and cargo and to separate out and quantify general average damage as against particular average damage.

24.3.12 Yacht Surveys

While similar to hull and machinery surveys, the surveying of yachts and pleasure craft is generally carried out by surveyors specializing in such vessels, rather than by commercial hull surveyors. However, their roles and responsibilities are very similar.

---

[10] See Chapter 22, *General Average*.

[11] G. Hughes & R. Cornah, *A Guide to General Average* (London: Richards Hogg Limited, 1994) at p. 23.

24.3.13 Miscellaneous Surveys

The surveyor may also be called upon to carry out a variety of other types of surveys, such as surveys to determine the angle of impact or speed in the case of collision, charterer's legal liability surveys (where there may be damage to a ship while under charter), fuel shortage investigations, lay-up and reactivation surveys, loss of earnings (or hire) surveys, mooring approvals, stevedore's liability surveys and ship builder's legal liability surveys.

24.4 JOINT SURVEYS

When a marine accident occurs, whether involving damage to cargo during a voyage, a collision between ships, or another kind of shipping incident, it is common for the underwriters of the interested parties to appoint surveyors to investigate the occurrence and the damage. Very often, the surveyors will carry out a "joint survey", inspecting the damaged property together, and attempting to reach agreement on the nature and extent of the damage. Often, a list of the damages will be made up, to be signed or otherwise agreed upon by the surveyors present. Areas of dispute will be noted. In the case of damage that is capable of being repaired, the surveyors may jointly agree upon a repair specification. In the case of a cargo claim, the surveyors may attempt to reach agreement on a suitable percentage of depreciation, permitting the consignee to retain the cargo subject to an appropriate allowance. These surveys are conducted on a "without prejudice" basis, that is, without the admission of liability by the responsible parties. While the damages agreed upon by the surveyors are not absolutely binding on the underwriters they represent, the insurers usually accept the surveyors' agreement, thus simplifying the settlement of the insurance claim and future subrogation proceedings against the responsible party.

24.5 CLASS SURVEYS

Most commercial vessels are required by the terms of their insurance policies to be registered with a recognized "classification society" — an international body charged with the responsibility of ensuring that the ship is constructed and maintained in accordance with the legal requirements of the flag state and with international conventions. These organizations retain their own surveyors who inspect the ship and its machinery during its construction and on a periodic basis through the life of the ship, to ensure that its condition meets the requirement of the classification society. In such case, the ship is said to be "in class". If deficiencies are noted, the shipowner is advised and is generally given a reasonable period of time within which to correct the problem, failing which "class" may be withdrawn.

24.6 SURVEY REPORTS

After the surveyor's work has been completed, a report is generally prepared for submission to the underwriter, frequently with photographs, test reports and relevant documents attached. In some parts of the country, particularly for smaller claims and in cases where the broker lacks a qualified adjuster to prepare an adjustment of the claim, the survey report and appended documents will serve as the claim under the insurance policy. The insurer may well settle and pay the claim based on that report.

It is occasionally contended that the surveyor's report is a "privileged" document and therefore immune from production in legal proceedings. The Canadian cases have generally held that survey reports commissioned in the ordinary course of the insurer's business are not privileged. The onus is on the party claiming privilege to establish that the dominant purpose behind the preparation of the report was litigation which was in actual contemplation.[12]

24.7 DEPRECIATION

As noted above, where cargo suffers partial damage, the insured and the surveyor may agree on a "depreciation" percentage to be applied against the insured value of the cargo in order to settle the claim. The adjustment of loss on a depreciated basis may create difficulties when it comes time for underwriters to pursue subrogation against the carrier or another party responsible for the loss. The amount recoverable against that party must be the *actual loss* suffered by the insured and not the amount of depreciation agreed between the insurer and insured. Where the goods have subsequently been sold by the insured, or used in the insured's manufacturing process, the actual loss, if any, may be difficult to prove. For example, in *Redpath Industries Ltd. v. "Cisco" (The)*,[13] a cargo of sugar had been damaged by seawater. The insurer and the insured agreed upon a depreciation figure and the insured then used the sugar, on a gradual basis over time, to mix with other product. In an action against the ocean carrier, it was held that the depreciation figure was not the true measure of

---

[12] There have been numerous cases on this issue, of which the following are examples: *Snyder v. Hall Corp. of Canada*, [1974] F.C.J. No. 110 (T.D.) (QL); *Santa Ursula Navigation S.A. v. St. Lawrence Seaway Authority* (1981), 25 C.P.C. 78 (F.C.T.D.); *W.K. Construction Ltd. v. Maritime Insurance Co.*, [1985] B.C.J. No. 2095 (B.C.C.A.) (QL); *Sauder Industries Ltd. v. A/S J. Ludwig Mowinckels Rederi* (1986), 3 F.T.R. 190 (T.D.): onus on the party claiming privilege to show that the dominant purpose for ordering the report was litigation or a reasonable prospect thereof; *T.O. Forest Products Inc. v. Fednav Ltd.* (1993), 72 F.T.R. 39 (T.D.); *Standard Machine Ltd. v. Royal Insurance. Co. of Canada*, [1997] 3 W.W.R. 364, 150 Sask. R. 161 (Q.B.): reports ordered produced because the dominant purpose was not litigation but rather the investigation of the claim; *Jordan v. Towns Marine Electronics Ltd.* (1996), 113 F.T.R. 226 (T.D.): reports not prepared for the purpose of legal advice or defending action and were therefore to be produced; *Pusan Pipe America Inc. v. Pan Ocean Shipping Co.* (1996), 119 F.T.R. 25 (T.D.): claim of privilege upheld because reports prepared in contemplation of litigation; *Marubeni Corp. v. Gearbulk Ltd.* (1986), 4 F.T.R. 265 (T.D.); *Commercial Union Assurance Company PLC v. M.T. Fishing Co. Ltd.* (1999), 162 F.T.R. 74 (F.C.T.D.), aff'd. (1999), 244 N.R. 372 (F.C.A.): where the reports were held to be privileged because the dominant purpose of their preparation was litigation.

[13] [1994] 2 F.C. 279, 110 D.L.R. (4th) 583 (C.A.), leave to appeal ref'd. (1994), 179 N.R. 319*n* (S.C.C.); see, however, *Canastrand Industries Ltd. v. "Lara S" (The)*, [1993] 2 F.C. 553, 16 C.C.L.T. (2d) 1 (T.D.), aff'd. (1994), 176 N.R. 31 (F.C.T.D.), confirming that the usual measure of damages is the arrived sound market value less the arrived damaged market value.

damages. Accordingly, in cases where there is potential recovery against a third party, it may be desirable to attempt to obtain the agreement of the carrier's surveyor to the proposed depreciation with the understanding that it is the most economical course of action and that it will be binding on all parties in the event of subrogation.

24.8 THE LIABILITY OF A MARINE SURVEYOR

Like all professionals, the marine surveyor is held to a standard of care commensurate with that of a reasonably competent individual engaged in the same vocation. The surveyor can be found liable in negligence if he or she fails to meet that standard and if its customer suffers damage as a result.[14] In *Armac Diving Services Ltd. v. Meadows Marine Surveys Ltd.*,[15] the British Columbia Supreme Court found that it was an implied term of the contract with a survey company that it would supply a suitably skilled individual to conduct the survey. It is noted in Chapter 23, *The Marine Insurance Broker*, that it has become commonplace for the insured to sue both the insurer and the broker where an insurance claim is declined. In some cases, where there is a dispute about the surveyor's work or conclusions, the surveyor may find itself targeted as well.

---

[14] See B. Beck, "Liability of Marine Surveyors for Loss of Surveyed Vessels: When Someone other than the Captain Goes Down with the Ship" (1989) Notre Dame L. Rev., 64:246; and *Marc Rich & Co. v. Bishop Rock Marine Co. Ltd.*, [1995] 2 Ll. L.R. 299 (H.L.).

[15] [1983] B.C.J. No. 479 (B.C.S.C.) (QL).

Chapter 25

Practice and Procedural Issues

25.1 INTRODUCTION

This Chapter will consider some practical and procedural issues that can arise in marine insurance, particularly in the legal context.

25.2 CLAIMS PRACTICE

There are no provisions in the Canadian *Marine Insurance Act* (*"C.M.I.A."*)[1] that deal with claims procedures. While in earlier times the advancement of a claim under a marine insurance policy was somewhat formalistic, modern marine insurance claims practice is less so.[2] In a British Columbia case, *Knight Towing Ltd. v. Guardian Insurance Co. of Canada*, the court noted that:[3]

> Unlike general insurance, neither marine insurance policies nor the *Insurance (Marine) Act* provide for the filing of proofs of loss by the insured with the insurer. Instead, adjustments are prepared, usually by the average adjuster, and submitted to the underwriters for payment.

In recent years, the use of average adjusters to prepare routine adjustments has become less common. The preparation and adjustment of the claim is usually the responsibility of the insured's broker, who prepares the claim and submits it to the underwriter for consideration and payment. In a typical cargo claim, the insured or the surveyor will provide proof of insurance, such as the certificate of insurance; a copy of the bill of lading or contract of carriage; the commercial invoice and customs forms; a survey report or other confirmation of the damage; transportation documents such as interchange records and receipts; and copies of any communications with carriers or third parties. Claims under hull and machinery policies will require different documentation, but a survey report together with repair invoices and proof of ownership of the vessel are generally required.

---

[1] Canadian *Marine Insurance Act* (*"C.M.I.A."*), S.C. 1993, c. 22.

[2] In an early New Brunswick case, *Watson v. Summers* (1842), 4 N.B.R. 62 (C.A.), also reported at (1843), 4 N.B.R. 101(C.A.), the court rejected the claim on the procedural ground that the plaintiff had failed to prove that there had been a proof of loss and adjustment and proof of the insured's interest.

[3] (1989), 37 C.C.L.I. 222, [1989] I.L.R. ¶1-2456 at 9501 (B.C.S.C.).

Where the policy sets forth a claims procedure, it must be followed.[4] Some policies contain express provisions with respect to the giving of notice to underwriters or their agents, the appointment of a surveyor and the submission of claims. The policy should be carefully reviewed to ensure compliance with its requirements.

25.3　JURISDICTION OF THE COURTS IN MARINE INSURANCE MATTERS

Canada has a dual court system consisting of the Federal Court of Canada, which has jurisdiction over matters that are "federal" or national in nature, and a provincial court system in each province and territory. Section 22(1) of the *Federal Court Act*[5] gives the Federal Court of Canada concurrent jurisdiction with the provincial courts "in all cases in which a claim for relief is made or a remedy is sought under or by virtue of Canadian maritime law or any other law of Canada relating to any matter coming within the class of subject of navigation and shipping, except to the extent that jurisdiction has been otherwise specially assigned". Subsection 22(2)(*r*) provides that the Federal Court has concurrent jurisdiction in claims for general average as well as claims "arising out of or in connection with a contract of marine insurance". This means that a marine insurance dispute may be litigated in either the Federal Court of Canada[6] or in a provincial court — usually the superior court of the province in which the contract was made.[7]

After the enactment of the *Federal Court Act* in 1971, there was a succession of cases, spanning almost 30 years, dealing with the scope of the Federal Court's jurisdiction in maritime law matters.[8] Some of these cases resulted in narrow interpretations of the court's jurisdiction, with unfortunate results. However, the

---

[4]　See *McFaul v. Montreal Inland Insurance Co.* (1845), 2 U.C.Q.B. 59.

[5]　R.S.C. 1985, c. F-7.

[6]　It has been authoritatively held that the Federal Court has jurisdiction in an action under a contract of marine insurance: *Zavarovalna Skupnost Triglav (Insurance Community Triglav Ltd.) v. Terrasses Jewellers Inc.*, [1983] 1 S.C.R. 283, [1983] I.L.R. ¶1-1627. It has also been held that the federal court has jurisdiction in an action *in rem* by an insurance broker for premiums it paid to the insurer for insurance on a ship: *Fairway Life & Marine Insurance Ltd. v. "Susan Darlene" (The)*, [1987] 2 F.C. 547, 5 F.T.R. 212. There is also jurisdiction over an action by a marine insurer for premiums due from its insured: *Insurance Co. of North America v. Barbalic Steel Sales Corp.*, [1978] F.C.J. No. 816 (QL).

[7]　In *Gould v. Cornhill Insurance Co.* (1983), 1 D.L.R. (4th) 183, 2 C.C.L.I. 148 (Nfld. C.A.), leave to appeal to S.C.C. refused (1983), 1 D.L.R. (4th) 183*n*, 44 Nfld. & P.E.I.R. 270*n* (S.C.C.), it was held that the Newfoundland District Court had jurisdiction in relation to a contract of marine insurance, which was a matter over which the common law courts had historically exercised jurisdiction. In *Amo Containers Ltd. v. Drake Insurance Co.* (1984), 8 C.C.L.I. 97, 51 Nfld. & P.E.I.R. 55 (Nfld. S.C.), it was held that the Newfoundland Supreme Court had jurisdiction to hear a claim under a marine insurance policy. It was also held that in the absence of a provincial marine insurance act in Newfoundland, it was appropriate to look to the English *M.I.A. 1906*, 6 Edw. VII, c. 41, as a codification of the common law.

[8]　For a review of the evolution of the jurisdiction of the Federal Court of Canada, see A. Stone, "Canada's Admiralty Court in the Twentieth Century", (2000) 47:3 McGill L.J. at p. 511.

Supreme Court of Canada's landmark decision in *Zavarovalna Skupnost Triglav (Insurance Community Triglav Ltd.) v. Terrasses Jewellers Inc.*[9] (*"Terrasses Jewellers"*) clearly confirmed the essentially maritime and federal nature of marine insurance. That case established that a suit on a marine insurance contract could be brought in the Federal Court of Canada. Nevertheless, even after *Terrasses Jewellers*, there remained doubts created by earlier decisions regarding the Federal Court's jurisdiction over parties or transactions that could be regarded as incidental to marine insurance. In a case decided before *Terrasses Jewellers* reached the Supreme Court, *McAllister Towing & Salvage Ltd. v. General Security Insurance Co.*,[10] the Federal Court of Canada struck out a third party notice by the insurer against its insured. The insurer had given an undertaking to a salvor. Later, the salvor sued the insurer and the insurer sought to join the insured as a third party. It was held by the majority of the Federal Court of Appeal that the claim did not arise out of a contract of marine insurance. The dissenting judge, Mr. Justice Lalande, would have held that the claim in question was one "in connection with" a contract of marine insurance and therefore within the court's jurisdiction.

In *Transport Insurance Co. v. "Ondine" (The)*,[11] it was held that subsection 22(2)(*r*) of the *Federal Court Act* did not bring within the court's jurisdiction an action against an insurer for breach of a warranty of authority to settle a claim. The court held that the cause of action was not founded in the contract of marine insurance, but rather was based on the course of dealings between the defendant and the plaintiff's insurer.

Similarly, in *Intermunicipal Realty & Development Corp. v. Gore Mutual Insurance Co.*,[12] (*"Intermunicipal Realty"*) it was held that the Federal Court of Canada did not have jurisdiction in an action for damages against a marine insurance broker. The suit was based on common law concepts of agency and misrepresentation which the court held were not part of "maritime law" and therefore not federal in nature. In applying this law to a marine insurance broker, the court would not be administering "the law of Canada", but rather provincial common law.

In light of the decisions of the Supreme Court of Canada in *Terrasses Jewellers* and *Ordon Estate v. Grail*,[13] and other cases confirming an expanded jurisdiction of the Federal Court in maritime matters,[14] it is quite possible that

---

[9]　[1983] 1 S.C.R. 283, [1983] I.L.R. ¶1-1627.

[10]　[1982] 2 F.C. 34, 41 N.R. 239 (C.A.), aff'g. [1981] 1 F.C. 758 (T.D.).

[11]　(1982), 138 D.L.R. (3d) 745 (Fed. C.A.), leave to appeal to S.C.C. refused (1982), 138 D.L.R. (3d) 745*n*, 44 N.R. 630*n* (S.C.C.).

[12]　[1978] 2 F.C. 691, 108 D.L.R. (3d) 494 (T.D.).

[13]　[1998] 3 S.C.R. 437, 166 D.L.R. (4th) 193, aff'g. (1996), 30 O.R. (3d) 643, 140 D.L.R. (4th) 52 (C.A.), leave to appeal allowed (1997) 225 N.R. 238*n* (S.C.C.).

[14]　See *ITO - International Terminal Operators Ltd. v. Miida Electronics Inc.*, [1986] 1 S.C.R. 752, 28 D.L.R. (4th) 641, aff'g. [1982] 1 F.C. 406, 124 D.L.R. (3d) 33 (C.A.), aff'g. [1979] 2 F.C. 283, 96 D.L.R. (3d) 518 (T.D.); *Whitbread v. Walley*, [1990] 3 S.C.R. 1273, [1991] 2 W.W.R. 195, aff'g. (1988), 51 D.L.R. (4th) 509, [1988] 5 W.W.R. 313 (B.C.C.A.), rev'g. (1987), 45 D.L.R. (4th) 729, 19 B.C.L.R. (2d) 120 (S.C.) to the effect that federal jurisdiction in relation to navigation and shipping includes inland waters and waterways; *Porto Seguro Companhia de*

the decisions in *McAllister*, *"Ondine"* and *Intermunicipal Realty* would be reconsidered in future cases. In *H. Smith Packing Corp. v. Gainvir Transport Ltd.*,[15] the Federal Court of Canada held that it had jurisdiction to hear a claim for negligent misrepresentation against a shipping agent for misrepresenting the extent of the insurance coverage. The plaintiff's counsel submitted that the *Intermunicipal Realty* case would have been decided differently in light of the decision of the Supreme Court of Canada in *ITO - International Terminal Operators Ltd. v. Miida Electronics Inc.*[16] which had broadened the scope of the Federal Court's jurisdiction. Mr. Justice Martin stated:

> I consider the conditions under which cargo is to be carried aboard a vessel, and the extent of insurance carried by the owner and manager of that vessel on its cargo are maritime and admiralty matters within the wider context suggested by McIntyre, J [in *I.T.O.*]. In my view negligent misrepresentations made with respect to those matters do not cause them to lose their maritime and admiralty character-istics. I conclude that this court has jurisdiction to hear such claims. ...[17]

A similar argument could be made with respect to the claim against the broker in *Intermunicipal Realty* and it has been suggested that the case may no longer be good law.[18] It is certainly arguable that the activities of insurance brokers have been an integral part of marine insurance for several centuries and are inextrica-bly linked with the business.

In actions against insurers on a policy where coverage is denied, it has be-come common for the plaintiff insured to add the broker as a defendant.[19] The usual allegation is that if the insurer's defence is successful, and there is no coverage, then the broker was negligent in failing to properly advise and represent its client. Suing both parties in the same action prevents the possibility of inconsistent verdicts. If the *Intermunicipal Realty* decision stands, it means that the prudent plaintiff should sue both broker and insurer in the provincial superior court, rather than run the risk of having part of the case thrown out of the Federal Court on jurisdictional grounds, or of having different results in different courts.

    Seguros Gerais v. Belcan S.A., [1997] 3 S.C.R. 1278, 153 D.L.R. (4th) 577, rev'g. [1996] 2 F.C. 751, 195 N.R. 241 (C.A.), aff'g. (1994), 82 F.T.R. 127 (T.D.); *Bow Valley Husky (Bermuda) Ltd. v. St. John Shipbuilding Ltd.*, [1997] 3 S.C.R. 1210, 153 D.L.R. (4th) 385, aff'g. (1995), 126 D.L.R. (4th) 1, 130 Nfld. & P.E.I.R. 92 (Nfld. C.A.), rev'g (1994), 118 Nfld. & P.E.I.R. 271, 120 Nfld. & P.E.I.R. 228 (Nfld. S.C.T.D.); *Monk Corp. v. Island Fertilizers Ltd.*, [1991] 1 S.C.R. 779, 80 D.L.R. (4th) 58, rev'g. (1989), 97 N.R. 384 (F.C.A.), aff'g. in part (1988), 19 F.T.R. 220 (T.D.).

[15] (1988) 30 C.C.L.I. 256, 20 F.T.R. 54, aff'd. (1989), 99 N.R. 54, 61 D.L.R. (4th) 489. See also *Ingle v. Her Majesty the Queen In Right of Canada*, [1984] 2 F.C. 57, [1984] I.L.R. ¶1-1764 (T.D.).

[16] [1986] 1 S.C.R. 752, 28 D.L.R. (4th) 641, aff'g. [1982] 1 F.C. 406, 124 D.L.R. (3d) 33 (C.A.), aff'g. [1979] 2 F.C. 283, 96 D.L.R. (3d) 518 (T.D.).

[17] *H. Smith Packing Corp. v. Gainvir Transport Ltd.* (1988), 20 F.T.R. 54 at 57, aff'd. (1989), 61 D.L.R. (4th) 489.

[18] *Royal & Sun Alliance Insurance Co. v. Sinclair* (2001), 220 F.T.R. 28, 33 C.C.L.I. (3d) 228 (F.C. Prothonotary).

[19] See Chapter 23, *The Marine Insurance Broker*.

25.4 JURISDICTION AND ARBITRATION CLAUSES

A jurisdiction clause is an agreement between the parties to a contract concerning the place for the resolution of their disputes. A simple jurisdiction clause might state: "All disputes arising under this policy of insurance shall be heard by the Federal Court of Canada at Vancouver." The policy form currently in use at Lloyd's, the MAR 91 form (which replaced the earlier form which, in turn, had replaced the S.G. Form), contains a jurisdiction clause: "This insurance shall be subject to the exclusive jurisdiction of the English courts, except as may be expressly provided herein to the contrary." Although many of the Institute clauses (which are meant to be attached to this form) are in common use in Canada, the form itself is not. In the case of a policy issued in the U.K. and covering a Canadian risk, it would be preferable to delete the English jurisdiction clause.

A foreign jurisdiction clause does not necessarily deprive the Canadian court of the power to deal with the case, and must be specifically invoked by the party relying on it, usually the defendant. In general, Canadian courts will give effect to such clauses where one party commences an action in violation of the clause and the other party objects.[20] If the plaintiff commences an action in Canada in defiance of a foreign jurisdiction clause, and the defendant does not object and defends the proceedings, the court will usually hold that the defendant has "attorned" to the court's jurisdiction and has "waived" any right to object based on the jurisdiction clause.

The jurisdiction clause must be a part of the contract between the parties in order to be enforceable. In *Ronald A. Chisholm Ltd. v. Agro & Diverses Souscriptions Internationales — A.D.S.I. – S.A.*,[21] it was held that a jurisdiction clause in the underlying cargo insurance policy was not binding on the purchaser of goods who had received an assignment of the insurance certificate containing no reference to the clause. The court stated that if the insurer considered the provision to be important, it should have included it in the certificate. As this had not been done, it was not binding on the assignee of the certificate who was not a party to the underlying policy.

While a particular case may be within their jurisdiction, Canadian courts will nevertheless ask whether Canada is the appropriate forum or *forum conveniens* for the determination of the dispute. In *Maxwell-Humm v. Mauran*,[22] the Federal Court of Canada referred to *Amchem Products Inc. v. British Columbia (Workers' Compensation Board)* in which it was held that:

---

[20] See, for example, *Jian Sheng Co. v. Great Tempo S.A.*, [1998] 3 F.C. 418, 225 N.R. 140 (C.A.), leave to appeal ref'd. (1998), 236 N.R. 388n (S.C.C.), rev'g. (1997), 132 F.T.R. 166, rev'g. (1997) 129 F.T.R. 55, with respect to a jurisdiction clause; *M/V Seapearl v. Seven Seas Dry Cargo Shipping Corp.*, [1983] 2 F.C. 161 (C.A.) with respect to arbitration clause.

[21] (1991), 6 C.C.L.I. (2d) 132 (Gen. Div.), aff'g. (1991), 2 C.P.C. (3d) 120 at 121 (Ontario Master).

[22] (1998) 50 C.C.L.I. (2d) 219 at 222, 141 F.T.R. 222 at 225, quoting [1993] 1 S.C.R. 897, 102 D.L.R. (4th) 96 at 104, aff'g. (1990), 75 D.L.R. (4th) 1, [1991] 1 W.W.R. 243 (B.C.C.A.), aff'g. (1989), 65 D.L.R. (4th) 567, [1990] 2 W.W.R. 601 (B.C.S.C.).

The choice of the most appropriate forum, in the application of the 'forum non conveniens' doctrine, 'is to be made on the basis of factors designed to ensure, if possible, that the action is tried in the jurisdiction that has the closest connection with the action and the parties and not to secure a juridical advantage to one of the litigants at the expense of others in a jurisdiction that is otherwise inappropriate.'

The court said that the onus is on the defendant to establish that there is a more convenient forum.[23]

Parties to a contract may decide to have their disputes referred to a panel of arbitrators, rather than to the courts. For example, a marine insurance contract might provide:

> Any dispute under this contract of marine insurance shall be submitted to binding arbitration at Toronto, Ontario, before a panel of three arbitrators, to be appointed in accordance with the Rules of the Association of Maritime Arbitrators of Canada.

Parties may select arbitration for a variety of reasons, including a perceived speed of adjudication, reduced costs and, perhaps most significantly, the prospect of submitting the claim to knowledgeable specialists.[24] While Canadian courts were at one time sceptical of arbitration clauses, viewing them as an infringement on the courts' authority, they have become increasingly supportive of arbitration and such clauses are almost invariably enforced.[25]

25.5　CHOICE OF LAW — ENGLISH LAW AND PRACTICE CLAUSE

Many of the standard Institute of London Underwriters clauses, including the Institute Cargo Clauses (1/1/82), provide "This policy is subject to English law and practice".[26] This means that in the interpretation or construction of the policy, or the settlement of claims under the policy, English marine insurance

---

[23] See also *Insurance Co. of North America v. Barbalic Steel Sales Corp.*, [1978] F.C.J. No. 816, where the court refused to give effect to an alleged foreign jurisdiction clause in a marine insurance contract without receiving evidence concerning the factors which would govern the exercise of the court's discretion in determining whether to grant a stay of the Canadian proceedings. These considerations, elaborated in the English case of *Eleftheria* (*The*), [1969] 2 All E.R. 641, [1969] 1 Ll. L. Rep. 237 (P.D.) include: the location of the evidence on factual questions; whether foreign law is applicable; the degree of connection between the parties and one jurisdiction or another; whether the defendant genuinely desires trial in the foreign jurisdiction or is simply seeking procedural advantage; and whether the plaintiff would be prejudiced in suing in the foreign court by being deprived of security, being unable to enforce the judgment, being faced with a time-bar, or subjected to racial, political or other prejudice to a fair trial.

[24] For an example of the arbitration process, see *Anchor Marine Insurance Co. v. Corbett* (1882), 9 S.C.R. 73.

[25] See, however, *Ocean Fisheries Ltd. v. Pacific Coast Fishermen's Mutual Marine Insurance Co.*, [1998] 1 F.C. 586, [1998] I.L.R. ¶1-3492 (C.A.), aff'g. (1997), 128 F.T.R. 232, rev'g. (1997), 125 F.T.R. 20, where the Federal Court of Appeal held that an arbitration clause in the by-laws of a mutual insurance association did not require a claim under the policy of insurance to go to arbitration.

[26] Institute Cargo Clauses (A), (B) and (C) can be found at Appendices B, C and D.

law and the practice of English insurers, brokers or adjusters is to be applied. As Canadian law and practice are similar in most respect to English law and practice, this particular clause is not usually of great significance. It should be noted, however, that this clause is not a "jurisdiction clause". It is not an agreement as to where the dispute will be heard or litigated, but simply an agreement as to what law will be applied to the resolution of the dispute, wherever it may be heard.

In Canada, as in most common law countries, where one party asserts that foreign law applies, that foreign law must be proven as a fact, usually through the testimony of an expert witness on foreign law. In the absence of such proof, the court will assume that the foreign law is the same as Canadian law.

Although not absolutely necessary, it may be prudent for Canadian insurers to provide in their policies that the policy is to be governed by the *C.M.I.A.* and by Canadian law and practice. The Canadian Hulls (Pacific) Clauses (Sept. 1/91) stipulate "This insurance is subject to Canadian law and usage as to liability for and settlement of any and all claims."[27] Brokers' manuscript policies will frequently contain a similar provision. It may also be prudent to specify that disputes are to be subject to the jurisdiction of the Federal Court of Canada or a provincial superior court.

25.6 SERVICE OF SUIT CLAUSES

Marine insurance policies sometimes contain a "service of suit" clause, permitting the insured to serve legal process on a particular representative of this insurer. This is often done in the case of foreign insurers doing business in Canada or the United States, who permit the insured to serve legal proceedings on some named individual in the country where the risk is located, rather than in the insurer's home jurisdiction.[28]

In *Maxwell-Humm v. Mauran*,[29] the underwriters sued in Canada, where the insured was domiciled, to recover money which had been paid out to the insured under the policy. The insured argued that a United States "service of suit" clause required the action to be brought in the United States. The court held that the clause dealt simply with service of process on underwriters and not with jurisdiction — it did not require suit to be brought by the underwriters in the United States.

---

[27] See Appendix E, clause 25 at lines 369-70.

[28] It was, at one time, common that policies, particularly those issued in the United Kingdom, named a designated Canadian representative, often a lawyer, to accept service of suit on the underwriters' behalf. In other cases, the broker will receive instructions from underwriters, sometimes simply the leading underwriter, to appoint counsel for the acceptance of service and defence of the action on the underwriters' behalf. For a discussion of some of the difficulties that can arise in such cases, see *Mischke v. Tomenson Saunders Whitehead Ltd.*, unreported (17 December 1982), British Columbia Supreme Court.

[29] (1998), 50 C.C.L.I. (2d) 219 (F.C.T.D.).

25.7   PUNITIVE DAMAGES

The usual measure of damages in an action on an insurance policy is the amount that should have been paid by the insurer had the claim been properly adjusted. The insured is entitled to be put in the position it would have been in, had the contract been performed in accordance with its terms.[30] In several Canadian marine insurance cases, however, plaintiffs have sought to use the duty of good faith as a springboard for an award of punitive damages against the insurer who declined a claim. For example, in *Central Native Fishermen's Co-op. v. Commonwealth Insurance Co.*,[31] the plaintiff, having overcome the insurer's nondisclosure defence, claimed an award of punitive damages on the basis of the House of Lords' decision in *Rookes v. Barnard.*[32] It was argued that the insurer had breached its duty of good faith by failing to pay a valid claim. Justice Fawcus of the British Columbia Supreme Court rejected this contention, holding that the insurer was entitled to resist this claim and that, in his view, "its conduct in so doing cannot and should not be disapproved of by this Court by the awarding of such damages".[33]

In *Riverside Landmark Corp. v. Northumberland General Insurance Co.*,[34] there was a claim for punitive damages based on the allegation that the insurer had made a decision to reject the claim even before a formal claim was submitted. After referring to earlier Ontario decisions where punitive damages had been awarded in employment cases,[35] the trial judge distinguished the defendants' behaviour in those cases as involving "conduct several orders of magnitude removed from anything that can be said of the defendant in this action"[36] and refused to award punitive damages. Quoting from a previous decision, he stated:

> The goal of punitive or exemplary damages, on the other hand, is to punish and deter. They are meant to furnish retribution against a defendant, to prevent him from repeating his conduct and to dissuade others from following his example. Although an award for punitive damages is granted to the plaintiff, its chief aim is not compensatory but prophylactic and retributive. It is administered to teach the wrongdoer that tort does not pay. There is no need to show any actual loss by a plaintiff. It is akin to a civil fine.[37]

---

[30]   See *Suchy v. Zurich Insurance Co.* (1993), 16 C.C.L.I. (2d) 10 (B.C.S.C.), also reported at (1994), 25 C.C.L.I. (2d) 177 (B.C.S.C.).

[31]   [1979] I.L.R. ¶1-1091 (B.C.S.C.).

[32]   [1964] A.C. 1129.

[33]   [1979] I.L.R. ¶1-1091 at 167.

[34]   (1984), 8 C.C.L.I. 118 (Ont. S.C.J.).

[35]   *Brown v. Waterloo Regional Board of Commrs. of Police* (1982), 37 O.R. (2d) 277, var'd. (1983), 43 O.R. (2d) 113 (C.A.); *Pilato v. Hamilton Place Convention Centre Inc.* (1984), 45 O.R. (2d) 652, 7 D.L.R. (4th) 342 (H.C.J.).

[36]   (1984), 8 C.C.L.I. 118 at 146 (S.C.J.).

[37]   (1984), 8 C.C.L.I. 118 at 146, citing *Brown v. Waterloo Regional Board of Commissioners of Police* (1982), 37 O.R. (2d) 277 at 289, 136 D.L.R. (3d) 49 (H.C.J.), var'd. (1983), 43 O.R. (2d) 113, 150 D.L.R. (3d) 729 (C.A.). See also *Pilato v. Hamilton Place Convention Centre Inc.*

The Supreme Court of Canada in *Whiten v. Pilot Insurance Co.*[38] confirmed that punitive damages could be awarded in appropriate cases and upheld a jury's punitive damages award of $1 million. The action was brought on a home-owner's insurance policy for the loss of the plaintiffs' home by fire. At trial, the insurer's defence based on arson was wholly discredited and the court found that the insurer had denied the claim in the hope of pressuring the plaintiffs to make an unfair settlement. In upholding the jury's award (and overruling the Court of Appeal, which had reduced the award to $100,000), the Supreme Court stated that punitive damages are awarded not to compensate the plaintiff, but for reasons of "retribution, deterrence and denunciation". Before punitive damages can be awarded, there must be an "actionable wrong", separate and distinct from the insurer's breach of contract in failing to pay the claim. In the *Whiten* case, the actionable wrong was the insurer's breach of its independent duty to deal with its insured in good faith. The court noted that punitive damages should be the exception rather than the rule and that such damages should only be awarded where there has been "high-handed, malicious, arbitrary or highly reprehensible conduct that departs to a marked degree from ordinary standards of decent behaviour".[39]

No doubt claimants in marine insurance cases will use the insurer's duty of good faith — a cornerstone of marine insurance — to support an independent duty of fair dealing, the breach of which may result in an award of punitive damages. The *Whiten* case confirms the court's jurisdiction to award such damages in cases where the insurer's conduct is so far beyond the norm as to offend the court's sense of fairness and decency.

25.8 PRE-JUDGMENT INTEREST

Pre-judgment interest — interest on the plaintiff's damages from the date the claim arose or notice of the claim was given — is awarded as an integral part of the plaintiff's damages in Canadian maritime cases.[40] In *MacMillan Bloedel Ltd.*

(1984), 45 O.R. (2d) 652, 3 C.C.E.L. 241, 84 C.L.L.C. 14,039, 7 D.L.R. (4th) 342 (Ont. H.C.J.) See *Continental Insurance Co. v. Almassa International Inc.*, unreported (24 March 2003), Toronto (Ont. Sup. Ct. of Justice), a marine insurance case, where the court held that although there was some conduct of the insurer that breached the duty of good faith, it was not so outrageous that punitive damages were required to act as a deterrent.

[38] (2002), 209 D.L.R. (4th) 257, 35 C.C.L.I. (3d) 1 (S.C.C.), rev'g. (1999), 42 O.R. (3d) 641, 170 D.L.R. (4th) 280 (C.A.), rev'g. (1996), 27 O.R. (3d) 479 (Gen. Div.).

[39] (2002), 209 D.L.R. (4th) 257 at 295 (S.C.C.). See also *Labelle v. Guardian Insurance Co. of Canada* (1989), 38 C.C.L.I. 274, [1989] I.L.R. ¶1-2465 (Ont. S.C.): punitive damages awarded where evidence of malice, including a wanton and reckless disregard for the rights of another; *Kogan v. Chubb Insurance Co. of Canada* (2001), 27 C.C.L.I. (3d) 16, [2001] I.L.R. ¶I-3987 7054 (Ont. S.C.J.): punitive damages of $100,000 were awarded for breach of the insurer's duty of good faith to the insured and engaging in "reprehensible, callous and high-handed" conduct. The purpose in awarding punitive damages was to deter the insurer from exploiting the vulnerability of the insured.

[40] *Canadian General Electric Co. v. Pickford & Black Ltd.*, [1972] S.C.R. 52, 20 D.L.R. (3d) 432, rev'g. [1970] Ex. C.R. 552; *Bell Telephone Co. of Canada v. "Mar-Tirenno" (The)*, [1974] 1 F.C. 294, 52 D.L.R. (3d) 702 (T.D.), aff'd. [1976] 1 F.C. 539, 71 D.L.R. (3d) 608n (C.A.).

v. Youell,[41] the British Columbia Court of Appeal held that this principle applied in marine insurance cases and that the provincial superior court had inherent jurisdiction to award interest in such cases. In *Cleveland v. Sunderland Marine Mutual Insurance Co.*,[42] the rules of a protection and indemnity ("P. &. I.") association stated that interest would not be paid on claims against the association. The court held that this provision did not oust the inherent jurisdiction of the court to award interest and proceeded to do so.

Legislation governing actions in the Federal Court of Canada[43] and in the provincial courts[44] provides for the award of pre-judgment and post-judgment interest. The rate of interest to be applied, although sometimes fixed by statute, is generally a matter within the discretion of the court. The court can award compound interest in appropriate cases.[45]

In practice, interest is seldom paid on a claim, provided that the claim is settled by the insurer within a reasonable time, unless legal proceedings have been commenced. Where there has been an unreasonable delay after the insurer has had an opportunity to examine and assess the claim, it is arguable that interest should be paid since the insurer has had the benefit of money which really belonged to the insured.

25.9 COSTS

Legal costs are not payable as part of a typical marine insurance claim unless the insured has incurred legal expenses as part of its duty to "sue and labour" — for example, by retaining counsel in order to protect rights against third parties. If a lawsuit has been commenced against the insurer for recovery of a claim which has been denied, however, different rules apply. In Canada, a successful litigant is entitled to be awarded costs of the action. While these are generally awarded on a "party and party" or "partial indemnity" scale and do not provide a full indemnity for the litigant's costs, they usually amount to between 50 and 70 per cent of the party's legal fees and disbursements.

A trial judge has a discretion in appropriate cases, to award an enhanced scale of costs, known as "solicitor and client" or "substantial indemnity" costs. In *Riverside Landmark Corp. v. Northumberland General Insurance Co.*, the

---

[41] (1993), 23 C.C.L.I. (2d) 18 (B.C.C.A.). The case contains an excellent exposition by Justice Southin of the considerations with respect to the award of interest.

[42] (1987), 45 D.L.R. (4th) 340, 81 N.S.R. (2d) 1 (S.C.).

[43] *Federal Court Act*, R.S.C. 1985, c. F-7, s. 36.

[44] See, for example, Ontario *Courts of Justice Act*, R.S.O. 1990, c. C.43, s. 127.

[45] See also the earlier case of *Pacific Coast Coal Freighters Ltd. v. Westchester Insurance Co. of New York*, [1926] 4 D.L.R. 963, [1926] 3 W.W.R. 356 (B.C.S.C.), aff'd. [1927] 2 D.L.R. 590, [1927] 1 W.W.R. 878 (B.C.C.A.) in which it was held that where an insured succeeds under a marine insurance policy, the court may allow interest. There was also a good discussion of the subject of interest in *Piedmontese Breeding Co-operative Ltd v. Madill* (1983), 40 Sask. R. 152 (Q.B.), rev'd. in part (1984), 40 Sask. R. 151 (C.A.), add'l. reasons at [1985] 5 W.W.R. 289, 40 Sask. R. 144 (C.A.). See also *Central Native Fishermen's Co-op. v. Commonwealth Insurance Co.*, [1979] I.L.R. ¶1-1091 (B.C.S.C.) as another example of a case in which pre-judgment interest was awarded.

successful plaintiff in an action against a marine insurer asked for an award of costs on a solicitor and client basis. The trial judge identified the different considerations applicable but declined to award costs at the higher level:

> The conflicting considerations which a trial Judge must have in mind in making his disposition, exercising his discretion to determine the scale of costs, seem to me to be these: on the one hand, it is tempting to say that the contract was a contract of insurance, that in its claim on that contract the plaintiff's case has succeeded and, therefore, it should be made economically whole as to the loss insured. This can only be accomplished by an award of costs on a solicitor-and-client basis.

> Viewing the matter from the opposite perspective of the defendant, it must surely be said that a defendant entertaining doubts as to its legal liability which are entertained in good faith and which cannot be said to be wanting in substance, is entitled to put the plaintiff's rights to the testing involved in an action, and that in so doing such a defendant should hazard nothing more upon losing than that which is inflicted upon any other unsuccessful defendant.

> There is, I am sure, no perfect or certain answer to the manner in which the discretion is to be exercised. I am much influenced, however, by the fact that this has been a long trial in which real issues have been raised, real and difficult issues, the reality and difficulty of which are reflected in the detailed arguments of counsel and in the not inconsiderable length of time it has taken me to deal with them.

> Doing the best I can with the question, my conclusion is that the ordinary order as to costs as between party and party is the proper order.[46]

In *Cleveland v. Sunderland Marine Mutual Insurance Co.*,[47] a P. & I. policy provided that the insurer was not obliged to pay "law costs" unless the directors of the association had consented to the commencement of the action. The trial judge described this provision as "outrageous" and held that it did not oust the jurisdiction of the court to award costs.

The rules of procedure in the Federal Court of Canada[48] and in most provinces[49] provide that where one of the parties has made an "offer to settle" prior to trial which has not been accepted, and the party making the offer ultimately does as well as or better than the offer, that party is entitled to recover costs on an enhanced scale.[50]

---

46 (1984), 8 C.C.L.I. 118 at 147-48.

47 (1987), 45 D.L.R. (4th) 340, 81 N.S.R. (2d) 1 (S.C.).

48 *Federal Court Rules, 1998*, S.O.R. 98/106, Rules 419-422.

49 See, for example, Ontario *Rules of Civil Procedure*, R.R.O. 1990, Reg. 194, Rule 49.10.

50 See *Cleveland v. Sunderland Mutual Marine Insurance Co.* (1987), 45 D.L.R. (4th) 340, 81 N.S.R. (2d) 1 (S.C.) and *Fiske v. Hartford Insurance Co. of Canada*, [1994] I.L.R. ¶1-3009 (Ont. Gen. Div.), aff'd (July 17, 1995), Doc. C.A. C176-22 (Ont. C.A.).

25.10   TIME FOR SUIT: LIMITATION AND NOTICE PERIODS

The *C.M.I.A.* does not stipulate time limits for notice of a claim under a marine insurance policy or for the commencement of legal proceedings in the event the claim is denied by the insurer. Nor is there a Canadian federal statute containing general limitation periods, although subsection 39(1) of the *Federal Court Act* provides that in actions in the Federal Court, the limitation period of the province in which the cause of action arose will apply. Presumably, this refers to the general provincial limitations statute as opposed to specific statutes such as insurance legislation, although the intent is by no means clear. Subsection 39(2) stipulates that in causes of action arising otherwise than within the province, the limitation period is six years. It remains a troublesome practical question as to whether or not the limitations contained in provincial insurance legislation apply to claims under marine policies and whether the result will be any different if suit is brought in the Federal Court of Canada or in the provincial superior court.

In *Knight Towing Ltd. v. Guardian Insurance Co. of Canada*,[51] the British Columbia Supreme Court held that in the absence of any limitation period in the British Columbia *Insurance (Marine) Act*,[52] the one-year limitation in the British Columbia general insurance statute, the *Insurance Act*,[53] which was expressed to apply to marine policies except where specifically excluded, would apply to a claim under a marine insurance policy. The Court held, however, that there had not been an unequivocal denial of coverage by the insurer so as to trigger the commencement of the limitation period.[54] However, the validity of *Knight Towing* is in question in light of the combined effect of the decisions of the Supreme Court of Canada in *Zavarovalna Skupnost Triglav (Insurance Community Triglav Ltd.) v. Terrasses Jewellers Inc.*[55] and *Ordon Estate v. Grail.*[56]

The *Terrasses Jewellers* case, which is discussed in more detail in Chapter 1 and in Section 25.3 above, established that marine insurance is a matter falling within exclusive federal jurisdiction. *Ordon Estate v. Grail* confirmed the uniformity and national scope of Canadian maritime law. As a result of these decisions, it is arguable that the time for suit under a marine insurance policy is not regulated by the insurance legislation of the province in which the insurance contract was made or in which suit was brought on the policy. It is also arguable that the rights of the parties to the contract do not vary depending upon the court in which the plaintiff chooses to sue. If the time limitations in the provincial insurance legislation do not apply, however, what limitation period is applicable? The general provincial limitations statutes, applicable to contractual claims, are not uniform and in the absence of a federal limitations statute, there is no clear legislative guidance on the point. Until the issue is addressed by the courts

---

[51]   (1989), 37 C.C.L.I. 222, [1989] I.L.R. ¶1-2456 (B.C.S.C.).

[52]   R.S.B.C. 1996, c. 230.

[53]   R.S.B.C. 1996, c. 226.

[54]   See *Dachner Investments Ltd. v. Laurentian Pacific Insurance Co.* (1988), 32 C.C.L.I. 261, 22 B.C.L.R. (2d) 254 (B.C.S.C.), rev'd. (1989), 59 D.L.R. (4th) 123, 36 B.C.L.R. (2d) 98 (C.A.).

[55]   [1983] 1 S.C.R. 283, [1983] I.L.R. ¶1-1627.

[56]   [1998] 3 S.C.R. 437, 166 D.L.R. (4th) 193, aff'g. (1996), 30 O.R. (3d) 643, 140 D.L.R. (4th) 52 (C.A.).

or Parliament, the only practical advice is that great care should be exercised. In appropriate cases, an agreement may be reached with the insurer as to the time within which litigation may be commenced.

Of course, some policies contain specific limitation periods. For example, the marine insurance policy may contain a provision requiring that a proof of claim be filed or that a suit be brought within a specific time. Such provisions are valid and have been upheld by Canadian courts.[57] In *Robertson v. Lovett*,[58] the Nova Scotia Supreme Court gave effect to a clause in a marine insurance policy requiring any action to be brought within 12 months after the claim for loss was presented. In *Allen v. Merchants Marine Insurance Co. of Canada*,[59] the Supreme Court of Canada held that the insurer was entitled to rely on a clause in the policy that all claims under the policy would be void unless prosecuted within one year from the date of the loss.

The language of the notice or limitation clause will dictate the circumstances which start the time running. It may be the date of the loss or the denial of the claim by the insurer. In the latter case, the insurer's denial must be clear and unequivocal. In *Dachner Investment v. Laurentian Pacific Insurance Co.*,[60] Justice Taggart of the British Columbia Court of Appeal stated:

> In my opinion, when an insurer seeks to rely on the running of a period of limitation whose commencement is fixed by the conduct of the insurer in denying coverage under a policy of insurance, the denial of coverage must be clear and unequivocal.[61]

In that case, the insurer had agreed to cooperate with the insured's surveyor, thus leading the insured to believe that the claim was still under consideration and that time was not running. The court found that the insurer's denial of liability was equivocal and the insured was not to be prejudiced as a result. The court also held that where the insurer unequivocally denies liability, there is no need to file a proof of loss, and the limitation period runs from the date of the denial.[62]

The Institute Cargo Clauses (1/1/82) contain no specific provisions with respect to notice of claim or time for suit. Marine open cargo policies occasionally contain provisions with respect to time for suit, but it is arguable that in order to be binding upon an assignee of an insurance certificate, such a provision must be included on the certificate, so that the assignee would be taken to have

---

[57] See *Robertson v. Pugh* (1887), 20 N.S.R. 15 (C.A.), aff'd. (1888), 15 S.C.R. 706; *O'Leary v. Pelican Insurance Co.* (1889), 29 N.B.R. 510 (C.A.); and see *Provincial Insurance Co. v. Aetna Insurance Co.* (1858), 16 U.C.Q.B. 135 with respect to the time for suit under a reinsurance agreement.
[58] (1874), 9 N.S.R. 424 (S.C.).
[59] (1887), M.L.R. 3 Q.B. 293, 16 R.L.O.S. 232 (Que. C.A.), aff'd. (1888), 15 S.C.R. 488.
[60] (1989), 59 D.L.R. (4th) 123, 37 C.C.L.I. 212 (B.C.C.A.), rev'g. (1988), 32 C.C.L.I. 261, 22 B.C.L.R. (2d) 254.
[61] (1989), 59 D.L.R. (4th) 123 at 130.
[62] See also *Browning v. Provincial Insurance Co.* (1873), L.R. 5 P.C. 263.

notice of the requirement.[63] There is a final provision, or "Note" at the end of the Institute Cargo Clauses:

> NOTE: - It is necessary for the Assured when they become aware of an event which is 'held covered' under this insurance to give prompt notice to the Underwriters and the right to such cover is dependent upon compliance with this obligation.

The use of the technical term "held covered" suggests that this is not a requirement pertaining to all claims, but rather refers to a variety of circumstances in which there is a change of the "adventure" covered by the insurance. Underwriters nonetheless agree that the assured will continue to be insured, either subject to the original premium and terms, or on terms and premium to be agreed.[64]

The Institute Time Clauses Hulls (1/11/95) stipulate that notice of claim must be given within 12 months from the date on which the insured, owners or managers become aware of the loss or damage, failing which the underwriters are discharged from liability for the claim. There is not, however, an express limitation of time for suit. The C.B.M.U. Great Lakes Hull Clauses (Sept. 1, 1971)[65] require the insured to give "prompt notice" to underwriters "in the event of any accident or occurrence which could give rise to a claim under this Policy". The clause requires that, where practical, underwriters are to be advised prior to survey so that they can appoint their own surveyor. They are entitled to stipulate where the vessel is to proceed for repair and may veto any repair firm proposed. The clause continues: "In the event of failure to comply with the conditions of this clause 15 per cent shall be deducted from the amount of the ascertained claim." This, coupled with the lack of any other sanction for breach of the notice requirements, supports the conclusion that the failure to give prompt notice to underwriters does not invalidate or otherwise jeopardize a claim. The Canadian Hulls (Pacific) Clauses (1/9/91) contain a substantially similar provision.

To conclude, most marine insurance claims are submitted and settled promptly. If a dispute develops, the policy should be scrutinized to determine whether it contains a notice requirement or limitation period. The insured will commonly rely on the broker to give advice in this regard, and if the broker is dealing with the claim, to ensure that appropriate notice is given to the insurer. In view of the absence of clear federal limitations legislation, and the uncertainty concerning the application of provincial insurance and general limitations legislation, it may be safest to assume that the shortest limitation period is applicable or to obtain the insurer's written waiver of any limitation defence.

---

[63] See *Ronald A. Chisholm Ltd. v. Agro & Diverses Souscriptions Internationales — A.D.S.I – S.A.* (1991), 6 C.C.L.I. (2d) 132 (Gen. Div.), aff'g. (1991), 2 C.P.C. (3d) 120 at 121 (Ontario Master).

[64] For example, where there is a termination of the contract of carriage at a place other than the destination named in the policy or certificate, the insured may extend the insurance by giving prompt notice to the insurer and paying an additional premium if required.

[65] Appendix G.

25.11 JUDICIAL RELIEF FROM FORFEITURE

Suppose the insured fails to give notice as required by the provisions of the policy in the event of a loss. Does the court have the authority or discretion to waive this provision or extend the time for giving notice? The purpose of a notice provision is to enable the insurer to investigate the claim, to offer advice or assistance to the insured in responding to the claim or mitigating the damages, and to post reserves. Although there is no provision of the *C.M.I.A.* dealing with this issue, if the court is satisfied that the insurer did not suffer prejudice as a result of the late reporting, it would generally be equitable to extend the relevant period. This is routinely done in non-marine insurance claims.[66] However, where prejudice is established, the insurer may be entitled to decline the claim on the basis of late notice.

In *Demitri v. General Accident Indemnity Co.*,[67] the British Columbia Supreme Court declined to give relief from forfeiture under a marine insurance policy on a pleasure craft. The plaintiff had been awarded damages against the defendant's insured as a result of a pleasure boat accident. Unable to collect the judgment from the insured, the plaintiff brought a direct action against the liability insurer under the British Columbia general insurance statute. The insurer argued, successfully, that it had not been given notice of the claim until some 14 months after the incident and that it had been prejudiced. The court held that the insured's failure to give timely notice was a bar to the claim and the third party making a claim against the insurer stood in no better position than the insured.[68]

Different considerations apply to the expiry of a contractual limitation period for the commencement of suit. Insurers are reasonably entitled to close their books on policy years if a claim has not been presented within the limitation period.

---

[66] *Canadian Equipment Sales & Service Co. Ltd. v. Continental Insurance Co.* (1975), 9 O.R. (2d) 7 (C.A.); *Minto Construction Ltd. v. Gerling Global General Insurance Co.* (1978), 19 O.R. (2d) 617 (C.A.); *McNish & McNish v. American Home Assurance Co.* (1989), 68 O.R. (2d) 365 (H.C.J.).

[67] (1996) 41 C.C.L.I. (2d) 49 (B.C.S.C.).

[68] *Ibid.*

Appendix A

Marine Insurance Act

S.C. 1993, c. 22
[Unofficial Chapter No. M-0.6]

An Act respecting marine insurance

Her Majesty, by and with the advice and consent of the Senate and House of Commons of Canada, enacts as follows:

SHORT TITLE

1. **Short title** — This Act may be cited as the Marine Insurance Act.
S.C. 1993, c. 22, s. 1.

INTERPRETATION AND APPLICATION

2. **Definitions** — (1) In this Act,
"action"
"action" includes a counterclaim and a set-off;
"contract"
"contract" means a contract of marine insurance as described in subsection 6(1);
"freight"
"freight" includes the profit derivable by a shipowner from the use of the shipowner's ship to carry the shipowner's goods or movables and freight payable by a third party, but does not include passenger fares;
"goods"
"goods" means goods in the nature of merchandise, but does not include personal effects or provisions or stores for use on board a ship;
"insurable property"
"insurable property" means any ship, goods or movables;
"marine adventure"
"marine adventure" means any situation where insurable property is exposed to maritime perils, and includes any situation where

    (a) the earning or acquisition of any freight, commission, profit or other pecuniary benefit, or the security for any advance, loan or disbursement, is endangered by the exposure of insurable property to maritime perils, and

(b) any liability to a third party may be incurred by the owner of, or other person interested in or responsible for, insurable property, by reason of maritime perils;

"marine policy"

"marine policy" means the instrument evidencing a contract;

"maritime perils"

"maritime perils" means the perils consequent on or incidental to navigation, including perils of the seas, fire, war perils, acts of pirates or thieves, captures, seizures, restraints, detainments of princes and peoples, jettisons, barratry and all other perils of a like kind and, in respect of a marine policy, any peril designated by the policy;

"movable"

"movable" means any movable tangible property, other than a ship or goods, and includes money, valuable securities and other documents;

"ship"

"ship" includes the hull, machinery, materials and outfit and the stores and provisions for the officers and crew and also includes fuel, oils and engine stores, if they are owned by the insured, and, in the case of a ship engaged in a special trade, the ordinary fittings required for the trade.

(2) **Other terms** — The following terms have the meanings assigned by the provisions indicated beside them:

(a) actual total loss, subsection 56(1);

(b) constructive total loss, section 57;

(c) general average act, subsection 65(2);

(d) general average contribution, subsection 65(3);

(e) general average expenditure, subsection 65(2);

(f) general average loss, subsection 65(1);

(g) general average sacrifice, subsection 65(2);

(h) particular average loss, subsection 63(1);

(i) particular charges, subsection 63(2);

(j) salvage charges, subsection 64(1);

(k) time policy, subsection 29(3);

(l) unvalued policy, subsection 30(3);

(m) valued policy, subsection 30(2); and

(n) voyage policy, subsection 29(2).

S.C. 1993, c. 22, s. 2.

3. Construction of marine policies — Subject to this Act and unless a contrary intention appears, the words and terms set out in the schedule have, when used in a marine policy, the meanings assigned by the schedule.

S.C. 1993, c. 22, s. 3.

4. Rules of Canadian maritime law — The rules of Canadian maritime law continue to apply in respect of contracts, except in so far as the rules are inconsistent with this Act.

S.C. 1993, c. 22, s. 4.

5. Application — This Act applies in respect of contracts concluded on or after the coming into force of this Act.

S.C. 1993, c. 22, s. 5.

CONTRACT OF MARINE INSURANCE

6.(1) **Contract of marine insurance** — A contract of marine insurance is a contract whereby the insurer undertakes to indemnify the insured, in the manner and to the extent agreed in the contract, against

    (a) losses that are incidental to a marine adventure or an adventure analogous to a marine adventure, including losses arising from a land or air peril incidental to such an adventure if they are provided for in the contract or by usage of the trade; or

    (b) losses that are incidental to the building, repair or launch of a ship.

(2) **Coverage** — Subject to this Act, any lawful marine adventure may be the subject of a contract.

S.C. 1993, c. 22, s. 6.

INSURABLE INTEREST

7.(1) **Insurable interest required** — In order to recover under a contract for a loss, the insured must have an insurable interest in the subject-matter insured at the time of the loss, but need not have such an interest when the contract is concluded.

(2) **"Lost or not lost" insurance** — Notwithstanding subsection (1), where the subject-matter is insured "lost or not lost", the insured may recover in respect of an insurable interest in the subject-matter acquired after a loss unless, at the time the contract was concluded, the insured was aware of the loss and the insurer was not.

(3) **Where no interest** — An insured who has no insurable interest in the subject-matter insured at the time of a loss cannot acquire an insurable interest by any act or election after becoming aware of the loss.

S.C. 1993, c. 22, s. 7.

8.(1) **Insurable interest — general principle** — Subject to this Act, a person who has an interest in a marine adventure has an insurable interest.

(2) **Interest in marine adventure** — A person has an interest in a marine adventure if the person has a legal or equitable relation to the adventure, or to any insurable property at risk in the adventure, and may benefit from the safety or due arrival of insurable property, may be prejudiced by its loss, damage or detention or may incur liability in respect of it.

S.C. 1993, c. 22, s. 8.

9.(1) **Defeasible or contingent interests** — A defeasible interest and a contingent interest are insurable interests.

(2) **Buyer of goods** — A buyer of goods who has insured them has an insurable interest even though the buyer might have elected to reject the goods or to treat them as at the seller's risk for any reason, including a delay in delivering them.

S.C. 1993, c. 22, s. 9.

10. Partial interest — A partial interest of any nature is an insurable interest.

S.C. 1993, c. 22, s. 10.

11. Master and crew's wages — The master and any member of the crew of a ship have insurable interests in their own wages.

S.C. 1993, c. 22, s. 11.

12. Advance freight — A person who advances freight has an insurable interest, in so far as the freight is not repayable in case of loss.

S.C. 1993, c. 22, s. 12.

13. Charges of insurance — An insured has an insurable interest in the charges for any insurance that the insured has effected.

S.C. 1993, c. 22, s. 13.

14. Reinsurance — The insurer under a contract has an insurable interest in the risk insured and may reinsure in respect of it, but, unless the marine policy provides otherwise, the original insured has no right or interest in the reinsurance.

S.C. 1993, c. 22, s. 14.

15. Bottomry — A lender of money on the security of a ship or a ship's cargo has an insurable interest in respect of the loan.

S.C. 1993, c. 22, s. 15.

16.(1) **Quantum of mortgagor's interest** — A mortgagor of insurable property has an insurable interest in its full value, and the mortgagee has an insurable interest in any sum due or to become due under the mortgage.

(2) **Interest of mortgagee, consignee or other person** — A mortgagee, consignee or other person who has an insurable interest in the subject-matter insured may insure on the person's own behalf, on behalf and for the benefit of any other interested person or both on the person's own behalf and on behalf and for the benefit of any other interested person.

(3) **Quantum of owner's interest** — The owner of insurable property has an insurable interest in its full value, even where a third person has agreed, or is liable, to indemnify the owner in case of loss.

S.C. 1993, c. 22, s. 16.

17.(1) **Assignment of interest** — An insured who assigns or otherwise parts with an insurable interest in the subject-matter insured does not thereby transfer the rights of the insured under the contract, unless there is an express or implied agreement to that effect.

(2) **Exception** — Subsection (1) does not apply in respect of a transmission of interest by operation of law.

S.C. 1993, c. 22, s. 17.

18.(1) **Gaming or wagering contracts void** — Every contract by way of gaming or wagering is void.

(2) **Presumption** — A contract is deemed to be a contract by way of gaming or wagering if

    (a) the insured has no insurable interest within the meaning of this Act and the contract is concluded with no expectation of acquiring such an interest; or

    (b) the marine policy is made "interest or no interest", "without further proof of interest than the policy itself" or "without benefit of salvage to the insurer" or is subject to any other like term.

(3) **Exception** — Paragraph (2)(b) does not apply in respect of a marine policy that is made "without benefit of salvage to the insurer" or is subject to any other like term, if there is no possibility of salvage.

S.C. 1993, c. 22, s. 18.

INSURABLE VALUE

19.(1) **Calculation of insurable value** — Subject to any express provision of, or any value specified in, the marine policy, the insurable value of the subject-matter insured is

    (a) in the case of insurance on a ship, the aggregate of the value of the ship at the commencement of the risk and the charges of insurance;

    (b) in the case of insurance on freight, whether paid in advance or not, the aggregate of the gross amount of the freight at the risk of the insured and the charges of insurance;

    (c) in the case of insurance on goods, the aggregate of the prime cost of the goods, the expenses of and incidental to shipping and the charges of insurance on those goods and expenses; and

    (d) in the case of insurance on any other subject-matter, the aggregate of the amount at the risk of the insured when the policy attaches and the charges of insurance.

(2) **Value of ship** — For the purposes of paragraph (1)(a), the value of a ship includes money advanced for officers' and crew's wages and other disbursements incurred to make the ship fit for the marine adventure contemplated by the marine policy.

S.C. 1993, c. 22, s. 19.

DISCLOSURE AND REPRESENTATIONS

20. Utmost good faith — A contract is based on the utmost good faith and, if the utmost good faith is not observed by either party, the contract may be avoided by the other party.

S.C. 1993, c. 22, s. 20.

21.(1) **Disclosure by insured** — Subject to this section, an insured must disclose to the insurer, before the contract is concluded, every material circumstance that is known to the insured.

(2) **Disclosure by agent of insured** — Subject to this section, an agent who effects insurance for an insured must disclose to the insurer, before the contract is concluded,

- (a) every material circumstance that is known to the agent; and
- (b) every material circumstance that the insured must disclose, unless the insured learned of it too late to communicate it to the agent.

(3) **Material circumstance** — A circumstance is material if it would influence the judgment of a prudent insurer in fixing the premium or determining whether to take the risk.

(4) **Question of fact** — Whether any circumstance that is not disclosed is material or not is a question of fact.

(5) **Circumstances not disclosed** — In the absence of any inquiry, the following circumstances need not be disclosed:

- (a) any circumstance that diminishes the risk;
- (b) any circumstance that is known to the insurer;
- (c) any circumstance as to which information is waived by the insurer; and
- (d) any circumstance the disclosure of which is superfluous by reason of any express warranty or implied warranty.

(6) **Presumptions** — For the purposes of this section,

- (a) an insured is deemed to know every circumstance that, in the ordinary course of business, ought to be known by the insured;
- (b) an agent is deemed to know every circumstance that, in the ordinary course of business, ought to be known by, or to have been communicated to, the agent; and
- (c) an insurer is presumed to know circumstances of common notoriety and every circumstance that, in the ordinary course of an insurer's business, ought to be known by an insurer.

(7) **Effect of non-disclosure** — If an insured or an agent of an insured fails to make a disclosure as required by this section, the insurer may avoid the contract.

(8) **Definition of "circumstance"** — In this section, "circumstance" includes any communication made to, or information received by, the insured.

S.C. 1993, c. 22, s. 21.

22.(1) **Representations by insured or agent** — Every material representation made by the insured or the insured's agent to the insurer during the negotiations for the contract and before the contract is concluded must be true.

(2) **Material representation** — A representation is material if it would influence the judgment of a prudent insurer in fixing the premium or determining whether to take the risk.

(3) **Question of fact** — Whether any representation is material or not is a question of fact.

(4) **Types of representations** — A representation may be as to a matter of fact or as to a matter of expectation or belief.

(5) **Fact** — A representation as to a matter of fact is deemed to be true if the difference between what is represented and what is actually correct would not be considered material by a prudent insurer.

(6) **Expectation or belief** — A representation as to a matter of expectation or belief is deemed to be true if it is made in good faith.

(7) **Withdrawal or correction** — A representation may be withdrawn or corrected before a contract is concluded.

(8) **Effect of false representations** — If any material representation made by the insured or the insured's agent to the insurer during the negotiations for the contract is not true and is not withdrawn or corrected before the contract is concluded, the insurer may avoid the contract.

S.C. 1993, c. 22, s. 22.

CONCLUSION AND RATIFICATION OF CONTRACTS

23. When contract is deemed to be concluded — A contract is deemed to be concluded when the proposal of the insured is accepted by the insurer, whether the marine policy is then issued or not, and for the purpose of establishing when the proposal is accepted, the slip or covering note or other customary memorandum of the contract may be referred to.

S.C. 1993, c. 22, s. 23.

24. Ratification — A contract effected in good faith by a person on behalf of another person may be ratified by that other person even after the other person becomes aware of a loss.

S.C. 1993, c. 22, s. 24.

THE MARINE POLICY

25.(1) **Marine policy required** — A contract is inadmissible in evidence, unless it is evidenced by a marine policy in accordance with this Act.

(2) **Issue of marine policy** — A marine policy may be executed and issued when the contract is concluded or afterwards.

S.C. 1993, c. 22, s. 25.

26. Contents of marine policy — A marine policy must specify

   (a) the name of the insured or of a person who effects the insurance on behalf of the insured;

   (b) the subject-matter insured;

   (c) the perils insured against;

   (d) the voyage or period, or both, covered by the insurance;

   (e) the sum insured; and

   (f) the name of the insurer.

S.C. 1993, c. 22, s. 26.

27.(1) **Signature of insurer** — A marine policy must be signed by or on behalf of the insurer.

(2) **Exception** — Notwithstanding subsection (1), where the insurer is a corporation, the corporate seal is sufficient.

(3) **Subscription by two or more insurers** — Where a marine policy is subscribed by or on behalf of two or more insurers, each subscription, unless the contrary is expressed, constitutes a distinct contract with the insured.

S.C. 1993, c. 22, s. 27.

28.(1) **Specification of subject-matter** — A marine policy must specify the subject-matter insured with reasonable certainty, but need not specify the nature and extent of the interest of the insured in that subject-matter.

(2) **Specification in general terms** — A marine policy that specifies the subject-matter insured in general terms shall be construed to apply to the interest intended by the insured to be covered.

(3) **Usage** — Any usage regulating the specification of the subject-matter insured shall be taken into consideration in applying this section.

S.C. 1993, c. 22, s. 28.

29.(1) **Voyage and time policies** — A marine policy may be a voyage policy or a time policy.

(2) **Voyage policy** — A marine policy is a voyage policy if the contract insures the subject-matter "at and from", or "from", one place to another place or other places.

(3) **Time policy** — A marine policy is a time policy if the contract insures the subject-matter for a definite period.

(4) **Combined policies** — A marine policy may include a contract insuring the subject-matter as described in subsections (2) and (3).

S.C. 1993, c. 22, s. 29.

30.(1) **Valued and unvalued policies** — A marine policy may be a valued policy or an unvalued policy.

(2) **Valued policy** — A marine policy is a valued policy if it specifies the agreed value of the subject-matter insured.

(3) **Unvalued policy** — A marine policy is an unvalued policy if it does not specify the value of the subject-matter insured and, subject to the limit of the sum insured, leaves the value to be determined in accordance with section 19.

(4) **Value specified** — Subject to this Act and in the absence of fraud, the value specified by a valued policy is, as between the insurer and the insured, conclusive of the insurable value of the subject-matter intended to be insured, regardless of whether any loss is a total loss or a partial loss.

(5) **Idem** — Unless a valued policy otherwise provides, the value specified by the policy is not conclusive for the purpose of determining whether there has been a constructive total loss.

S.C. 1993, c. 22, s. 30.

31.(1) **Floating policy** — A marine policy may be a floating policy, that is to say, a policy that describes the insurance in general terms and leaves the name of the ship and other particulars to be defined by subsequent declarations, either by endorsement on the policy or in any other customary manner.

(2) **Declarations** — Unless a floating policy otherwise provides, declarations must be made in the order of dispatch or shipment and must, in the case of goods, include all consignments within the terms of the policy and honestly state the value of the goods.

(3) **Rectification** — An omission in a declaration or an erroneous declaration may be rectified even after loss or arrival if the omission or declaration was made in good faith.

(4) **Idem** — Unless a floating policy otherwise provides, where a declaration of value is not made until after notice of loss or arrival, the policy shall be treated as an unvalued policy with respect to the subject-matter of that declaration.

S.C. 1993, c. 22, s. 31.

WARRANTIES

32.(1) **Definition of "warranty"** — In this section and sections 33 to 39, "warranty" means a promissory warranty by which the insured

    (a) undertakes that some particular thing will or will not be done or that some condition will be fulfilled; or

    (b) affirms or negates the existence of particular facts.

(2) **Types of warranty** — A warranty may be an express warranty or an implied warranty.

S.C. 1993, c. 22, s. 32.

33.(1) **Express warranties** — An express warranty may be in any form of words from which the intention to warrant may be inferred.

(2) **Inclusion in policy** — An express warranty must be included in, or written on, the marine policy or be contained in a document incorporated by reference into the policy.

(3) **Exclusion of implied warranty** — An express warranty does not exclude an implied warranty, unless they are inconsistent.

S.C. 1993, c. 22, s. 33.

34. Warranty of legality — There is an implied warranty in every marine policy that the marine adventure insured is lawful and, in so far as the insured has control, will be carried out in a lawful manner.
S.C. 1993, c. 22, s. 34.

35. No implied warranty of nationality — There is no implied warranty in any marine policy as to the nationality of a ship or that the nationality of a ship will not be changed during the risk.
S.C. 1993, c. 22, s. 35.

36.(1) **Warranty of neutrality** — Where in any marine policy insurable property is expressly warranted to be neutral, there is an implied condition in the policy

(a) that the property will have a neutral character at the commencement of the risk and that, in so far as the insured has control, that character will be preserved during the risk; and

(b) where the property is a ship, that, in so far as the insured has control, the papers necessary to establish the neutrality of the ship will be carried on the ship and will not be falsified or suppressed and no simulated papers will be used.

(2) **Breach of condition** — If any loss occurs through a breach of the implied condition referred to in paragraph (1)(b), the insurer may avoid the contract.
S.C. 1993, c. 22, s. 36.

37.(1) **Warranty of seaworthiness of ship in voyage policy** — There is an implied warranty in every voyage policy that, at the commencement of the voyage, the ship will be seaworthy for the purpose of the particular marine adventure insured.

(2) **Warranty of fitness against perils of the port** — Where a voyage policy attaches while the ship is in port, there is an implied warranty in the policy that the ship will, at the commencement of the risk, be reasonably fit to encounter the ordinary perils of the port.

(3) **Warranty of fitness for each stage of voyage** — Where a voyage policy relates to a voyage performed in different stages during which the ship requires different or further preparation or equipment, there is an implied warranty in the policy that, at the commencement of each stage, the ship is seaworthy for the purposes of that stage.

(4) **No implied warranty of seaworthiness in time policy** — There is no implied warranty in any time policy that the ship will be seaworthy at any stage of the marine adventure, but where, with the privity of the insured, the ship is sent to sea in an unseaworthy state, the insurer is not liable for any loss attributable to unseaworthiness.

(5) **When ship deemed seaworthy** — A ship is deemed to be seaworthy if it is reasonably fit in all respects to encounter the ordinary perils of the seas of the marine adventure insured.
S.C. 1993, c. 22, s. 37.

38.(1) **No implied warranty that goods are seaworthy** — There is no implied warranty in any marine policy on insurable property, other than a ship, that the insurable property is seaworthy.

(2) **Voyage policy on goods** — There is an implied warranty in every voyage policy on insurable property, other than a ship, that, at the commencement of the voyage, the ship is seaworthy and reasonably fit to carry the insurable property to the destination contemplated by the policy.

S.C. 1993, c. 22, s. 38.

39.(1) **Compliance with warranty** — Subject to this section, a warranty must be exactly complied with, whether or not it is material to the risk.

(2) **Effect of breach of warranty** — Subject to any express provision in the marine policy or any waiver by the insurer, where a warranty is not exactly complied with, the breach of the warranty discharges the insurer from liability for any loss occurring on or after the date of the breach, but does not affect any liability incurred by the insurer before that date.

(3) **Breach of warranty of good safety** — A warranty that the subject-matter insured is "well" or "in good safety" on a particular day is not breached if the subject-matter is safe at any time during that day.

(4) **When breach of warranty excused** — A breach of a warranty is excused if, because of a change of circumstances, the warranty ceases to be applicable to the circumstances contemplated by the contract or if compliance with the warranty is rendered unlawful by any subsequent law.

(5) **Limit on defence to breach of warranty** — It is no defence to a breach of a warranty that the breach was remedied and the warranty complied with before any loss was incurred.

S.C. 1993, c. 22, s. 39.

THE VOYAGE

40.(1) **Implied condition as to commencement** — Where the subject-matter is insured by a voyage policy, the ship need not, when the contract is concluded, be at the place at and from, or from, which the subject-matter is insured, but there is an implied condition in the policy that the marine adventure will commence within a reasonable time and, if it is not so commenced, the insurer may avoid the contract.

(2) **Exception** — The implied condition may be negated by establishing that the delay was caused by circumstances known to the insurer before the contract was concluded or that the insurer waived the condition.

S.C. 1993, c. 22, s. 40.

41.(1) **Change of port of departure** — Where the place of departure is specified by a marine policy and the ship sails from a different place, the risk does not attach.

(2) **Change of destination** — Where the destination is specified by a marine policy and the ship sails for a different destination, the risk does not attach.

S.C. 1993, c. 22, s. 41.

42.(1) **Change of voyage** — Unless a marine policy otherwise provides, a change of voyage discharges the insurer from liability for any loss occurring on or after the time when the intention to change is manifested, whether or not the ship has in fact left the course of voyage contemplated by the policy when the loss occurs.

(2) **Idem** — There is a change of voyage where, after the commencement of the risk, the destination of the ship is voluntarily changed from that contemplated by the marine policy.

S.C. 1993, c. 22, s. 42.

43.(1) **Deviation from voyage** — A deviation without lawful excuse from the voyage contemplated by a marine policy discharges the insurer from liability for any loss occurring on or after the time when the deviation occurs, regardless of the intention to deviate and whether or not the ship returns to its course of voyage before the loss occurs.

(2) **Idem** — There is a deviation from the voyage contemplated by a marine policy where

> (a) the course of the voyage is specified by the policy and is departed from; or
> (b) the course of the voyage is not specified by the policy but the usual and customary course is departed from.

(3) **Idem** — Where a marine policy specifies the ports of discharge, the ship may proceed to any or all of them, but if, in the absence of any usage or sufficient cause, the ship does not proceed to them, or such of them as it goes to, in the order specified, there is a deviation from the voyage contemplated by the policy.

(4) **Idem** — Where a marine policy specifies that the ports of discharge are within a given area and does not otherwise name them, the ship may proceed to any or all of them, but if, in the absence of any usage or sufficient cause, the ship does not proceed to them, or such of them as it goes to, in their geographical order, there is a deviation from the voyage contemplated by the policy.

S.C. 1993, c. 22, s. 43.

44. Delay in voyage — The marine adventure insured by a voyage policy must be carried out with reasonable dispatch and a delay, without lawful excuse, in carrying it out discharges the insurer from liability for any loss occurring on or after the time when the delay becomes unreasonable.

S.C. 1993, c. 22, s. 44.

45.(1) **Excuses for deviation or delay** — A deviation or delay referred to in section 43 or 44 is excused if it is

> (a) authorized by any special term in the marine policy;
> (b) caused by circumstances beyond the control of the master and the master's employer;
> (c) reasonably necessary in order to comply with an express warranty or an implied warranty;

(d) reasonably necessary for the safety of the ship or subject-matter insured;

(e) for the purpose of saving human life or aiding a ship in distress where human life may be in danger;

(f) reasonably necessary for the purpose of obtaining medical aid for any person on board the ship; or

(g) caused by the barratrous conduct of the master or crew, if barratry is one of the perils insured against.

(2) **Resumption** — When the excuse for a deviation or delay ceases, the voyage must be resumed with reasonable dispatch.

S.C. 1993, c. 22, s. 45.

46. Transhipment — Where the voyage contemplated by a marine policy is interrupted, by a peril insured against, at an intermediate port or place in such circumstances as, apart from the contract of affreightment, justify the master in landing and reshipping, or transhipping, the goods or movables and sending them to their destination, the insurer continues to be liable for a loss occurring on or after the landing or transhipment.

S.C. 1993, c. 22, s. 46.

THE PREMIUM

47.(1) **Premium to be arranged** — A reasonable premium is payable if insurance is effected at a premium to be arranged and no arrangement is made.

(2) **Additional premium** — A reasonable additional premium is payable if insurance is effected on the terms that an additional premium is to be arranged on the happening of a given event and that event happens but no arrangement is made.

S.C. 1993, c. 22, s. 47.

48. Payment of premium — Unless otherwise agreed, the duty of the insured or the insured's agent to pay the premium and the duty of the insurer to issue the marine policy to the insured or the insured's agent are concurrent conditions, and the insurer is not required to issue the policy until the premium is paid or tendered.

S.C. 1993, c. 22, s. 48.

49.(1) **Policy effected through broker** — Unless otherwise agreed, where a broker effects a marine policy on behalf of the insured,

(a) the broker is directly responsible to the insurer for the premium;

(b) the broker has, as against the insured, a lien on the policy for the amount of the premium and the broker's charges in effecting the policy; and

(c) the insurer is directly responsible to the insured for any amount that may be payable in respect of losses or a returnable premium.

(2) **Idem** — Unless otherwise agreed, where a broker effects a marine policy on behalf of a person who employs the broker as a principal, the broker has a

lien on the policy in respect of any balance on any insurance account that may be due to the broker from that person, unless, when the debt was incurred, the broker had reason to believe that the person was only an agent.

S.C. 1993, c. 22, s. 49.

50. Acknowledgement of receipt of premium — Where a broker effects a marine policy on behalf of an insured, an acknowledgement in the policy of the receipt of the premium is, in the absence of fraud, conclusive as between the insurer and the insured, but not as between the insurer and the broker.

S.C. 1993, c. 22, s. 50.

ASSIGNMENT OF MARINE POLICY

51.(1) **Marine policy assignable** — A marine policy is assignable either before or after a loss, unless it expressly prohibits assignment.

(2) **Manner of assignment** — A marine policy may be assigned by endorsement on the policy or in any other customary manner.

(3) **Effect of assignment** — Where a marine policy is assigned so as to transfer the beneficial interest in the policy, the assignee of the policy is entitled to sue on it in the assignee's name and, in any such action, the defendant is entitled to raise any defence arising out of the contract that the defendant would have been entitled to raise if the action had been brought in the name of the person by or on behalf of whom the policy was effected.

S.C. 1993, c. 22, s. 51.

52.(1) **Loss of interest** — Where an insured transfers or loses an interest in the subject-matter insured and does not, before or at the time of so doing, expressly or impliedly agree to assign the marine policy, no subsequent assignment of the marine policy is operative.

(2) **Exception** — Subsection (1) does not apply in respect of an assignment of a marine policy after a loss.

S.C. 1993, c. 22, s. 52.

LOSS AND ABANDONMENT

53.(1) **Losses covered** — Subject to this Act and unless a marine policy otherwise provides, an insurer is liable only for a loss that is proximately caused by a peril insured against, including a loss that would not have occurred but for the misconduct or negligence of the master or crew.

(2) **Losses specifically excluded** — Without limiting the generality of subsection (1), an insurer is not liable for any loss attributable to the wilful misconduct of the insured nor, unless the marine policy otherwise provides, for

(a) in the case of insurance on a ship or goods, any loss proximately caused by delay, including a delay caused by a peril insured against;

(b) ordinary wear and tear, ordinary leakage or breakage or inherent vice or nature of the subject-matter insured;

(c) any loss proximately caused by vermin; or

(d) any loss or damage to machinery not proximately caused by maritime perils.

S.C. 1993, c. 22, s. 53.

54. Total and partial losses — A loss may be a total loss or a partial loss.

S.C. 1993, c. 22, s. 54.

55.(1) **Types of total loss** — A total loss may be an actual total loss or a constructive total loss.

(2) **Losses covered** — Unless a marine policy otherwise provides, insurance against total loss includes both actual total loss and constructive total loss.

S.C. 1993, c. 22, s. 55.

56.(1) **Actual total loss** — A loss is an actual total loss if the subject-matter insured is destroyed or is so damaged as to cease to be a thing of the kind insured or if the insured is irretrievably deprived of the subject-matter.

(2) **Idem** — Where a ship engaged in a marine adventure is missing and no news of the ship is received within a reasonable period, an actual total loss may be presumed.

S.C. 1993, c. 22, s. 56.

57.(1) **Constructive total loss** — Unless a marine policy otherwise provides, a loss is a constructive total loss if the subject-matter insured is reasonably abandoned because the actual total loss of the subject-matter appears unavoidable or the preservation of the subject-matter from actual total loss would entail costs exceeding its value when the costs are incurred.

(2) **Idem** — Without limiting the generality of subsection (1), a loss is a constructive total loss if

(a) in the case of a ship or goods, the insured is deprived of possession of the ship or goods by reason of a peril insured against and either the insured is unlikely to recover the ship or goods or the cost of recovery would exceed the value of the ship or goods when recovered;

(b) in the case of a ship, the ship is so damaged by a peril insured against that the cost of repairing it would exceed the value of the ship when repaired; or

(c) in the case of goods, the goods are so damaged that the cost of repairing and forwarding them to their destination would exceed the value of the goods on arrival.

(3) **Cost of repair of ship** — For the purposes of paragraph (2)(b), in estimating the cost of repairing a ship, no deduction may be made in respect of general average contributions to the repairs payable by other interested persons, but account is to be taken of the cost of future salvage operations and of any future general average contributions to which the ship would be liable if repaired.

S.C. 1993, c. 22, s. 57.

58.(1) **Treatment** — An insured may treat a constructive total loss as a partial loss or may abandon the subject-matter insured to the insurer and treat the constructive total loss as an actual total loss.

(2) **Notice of abandonment** — Subject to this section and section 59, an insured who elects to abandon the subject-matter insured to the insurer must give a notice of abandonment to the insurer with reasonable diligence after the insured receives reliable information of the loss.

(3) **Time for inquiry** — An insured who receives doubtful information of a loss is entitled to a reasonable time to make inquiries before giving a notice of abandonment.

(4) **Manner of giving notice** — An insured may give a notice of abandonment orally or in writing, or partly orally and partly in writing, and in any terms that indicate the insured's intention to abandon unconditionally the insured interest in the subject-matter to the insurer.

(5) **Failure to give notice** — If an insured fails to give a notice of abandonment as required by this section, the constructive total loss may be treated only as a partial loss.

S.C. 1993, c. 22, s. 58.

59.(1) **Notice not required** — An insured is not required to give a notice of abandonment to the insurer if

    (a)   the loss is an actual total loss;

    (b)   notice is waived by the insurer; or

    (c)   at the time the insured receives information of the loss, there is no possibility of benefit to the insurer if notice were given to the insurer.

(2) **Idem** — An insurer who has reinsured a risk is not required to give a notice of abandonment to the reinsurer.

S.C. 1993, c. 22, s. 59.

60.(1) **Refusal of abandonment** — If an insured gives a notice of abandonment as required by section 58, the rights of the insured are not prejudiced by a refusal of the insurer to accept the abandonment.

(2) **Acceptance of abandonment** — An acceptance of an abandonment may be either express or implied from the conduct of the insurer, but the mere silence of an insurer after a notice of abandonment is given does not constitute an acceptance.

(3) **Effect of acceptance on insured** — On acceptance of an abandonment, the abandonment is irrevocable.

(4) **Effect of acceptance on insurer** — On acceptance of an abandonment, the insurer

    (a)   conclusively admits liability for the loss and the sufficiency of the notice of abandonment; and

    (b)   is entitled to acquire the interest of the insured in whatever remains of the subject-matter insured, including all proprietary rights incidental thereto.

(5) **Abandonment of ship** — On acceptance of the abandonment of a ship, the insurer is entitled to

  (a) any freight being earned at the time of, or earned subsequent to, the casualty causing the loss, less the costs incurred in earning it after the casualty; and

  (b) if the ship is carrying the shipowner's goods, reasonable remuneration for the carriage of the goods subsequent to the casualty.

S.C. 1993, c. 22, s. 60.

61.(1) **Partial loss** — A partial loss is any loss that is not a total loss.

(2) **Idem** — Where insured goods reach their destination in specie but cannot be identified by reason of obliteration of marks or otherwise, the loss, if any, is a partial loss.

(3) **Recovery for partial loss** — Unless a marine policy otherwise provides, an insured who brings an action for a total loss but establishes only a partial loss may recover for a partial loss.

S.C. 1993, c. 22, s. 61.

62. Types of partial losses — A partial loss may be a particular average loss, a general average loss, salvage charges or particular charges.

S.C. 1993, c. 22, s. 62.

63.(1) **Particular average loss** — A particular average loss is a loss of the subject-matter insured that is caused by a peril insured against and is not a general average loss, but does not include particular charges.

(2) **Particular charges** — Particular charges are expenses incurred by or on behalf of an insured for the purpose of preserving the subject-matter insured from a peril insured against, but do not include a general average loss or salvage charges.

S.C. 1993, c. 22, s. 63.

64.(1) **Salvage charges** — Salvage charges are charges recoverable under maritime law by a salvor independently of any contract, but do not include expenses incurred for services in the nature of salvage rendered by the insured or the insured's agent, or any person hired by the insured or the insured's agent, for the purpose of averting a loss by a peril insured against.

(2) **Recovery of salvage charges** — Subject to any express provision in the marine policy, salvage charges incurred for the purpose of averting a loss by a peril insured against may be recovered from the insurer as a loss by such a peril.

(3) **Recovery of other expenses** — The expenses referred to in subsection (1) that are not salvage charges may, when properly incurred, be recovered from the insurer as particular charges or as a general average loss, according to the circumstances under which they were incurred.

S.C. 1993, c. 22, s. 64.

65.(1) **General average loss** — A general average loss is a loss caused by or directly consequential on a general average act, and includes a general average sacrifice and a general average expenditure.

(2) **General average act, sacrifice and expenditure** — A general average act is any extraordinary sacrifice or expenditure, known as a general average sacrifice and a general average expenditure, respectively, that is voluntarily and reasonably incurred in time of peril for the purpose of preserving the property from peril in a common adventure.

(3) **General average contribution** — Subject to the conditions imposed by maritime law, a person who incurs a general average loss is entitled to receive from the other interested persons a rateable contribution, known as a general average contribution, in respect of the loss.

(4) **Recovery of general average expenditure and general average sacrifice** — Subject to any express provision in the marine policy,

(a) an insured who incurs a general average expenditure may recover from the insurer in respect of the proportion of the loss falling on the insured; and

(b) an insured who incurs a general average sacrifice may recover from the insurer in respect of the whole loss, without having enforced the insured's right to contribution from other persons.

(5) **Recovery of general average contribution** — Subject to any express provision in the marine policy, an insured who has paid, or is liable to pay, a general average contribution in respect of the subject-matter insured may recover the contribution from the insurer.

(6) **Condition** — Subject to any express provision in the marine policy, an insurer is not liable for a general average loss or a general average contribution, unless the loss was incurred for the purpose of averting, or in connection with the avoidance of, a peril insured against.

(7) **Where single ownership** — Where any ship, freight and goods, or any two of them, are owned by the same insured, the liability of the insurer for a general average loss or a general average contribution shall be determined as if they were owned by different persons.

S.C. 1993, c. 22, s. 65.

MEASURE OF INDEMNITY

66. Measure of indemnity — The measure of indemnity in respect of a loss under a marine policy is the amount that the insured can recover in respect of the loss under the policy, such amount not exceeding

(a) in the case of an unvalued policy, the insurable value of the subject-matter insured; or

(b) in the case of a valued policy, the value of the subject-matter insured specified by the policy.

S.C. 1993, c. 22, s. 66.

67. Total loss — Subject to this Act and any express provision in the policy, the measure of indemnity in respect of a total loss of the subject-matter insured is

(a) in the case of an unvalued policy, the insurable value of the subject-matter; and

(b) in the case of a valued policy, the value of the subject-matter specified by the policy.

S.C. 1993, c. 22, s. 67.

68. Partial loss of ship — Subject to any express provision in the marine policy, the measure of indemnity in respect of a partial loss of a ship is

(a) where the ship is repaired, the reasonable cost of the repairs less the customary deductions, but not exceeding the sum insured in respect of any one casualty;

(b) where the ship is partially repaired, the aggregate of the reasonable cost of the repairs, as determined under paragraph (a), and the reasonable depreciation, if any, arising from the unrepaired damage, the aggregate not exceeding the cost, as determined under paragraph (a), of repairing the whole damage; and

(c) where the ship is not repaired and is not sold in a damaged state during the risk, the reasonable depreciation arising from the unrepaired damage, but not exceeding the cost, as determined under paragraph (a), of repairing the damage.

S.C. 1993, c. 22, s. 68.

69. Partial loss of freight — Subject to any express provision in the policy, the measure of indemnity in respect of a partial loss of freight is that proportion of the insurable value of the freight, in the case of an unvalued policy, or the value of the freight specified by the policy, in the case of a valued policy, that the part of the freight lost by the insured bears to the whole freight at the risk of the insured under the policy.

S.C. 1993, c. 22, s. 69.

70.(1) **Partial loss of goods or movables** — Subject to any express provision in the policy, the measure of indemnity in respect of a partial loss of goods or movables is

(a) where part of the goods or movables insured by an unvalued policy is totally lost, the insurable value of the part lost, ascertained as in the case of a total loss;

(b) where part of the goods or movables insured by a valued policy is totally lost, that proportion of the value of the goods or movables specified by the policy that the insurable value of the part lost bears to the insurable value of all the goods or movables, ascertained as in the case of an unvalued policy; and

(c) where the whole or any part of the goods or movables is delivered damaged at its destination, that proportion of the insurable value of all the goods or movables, in the case of an unvalued policy, or the value of all the goods or movables specified by the policy, in the case of a valued policy, that the difference between the gross value of all the goods or movables in a sound condition at that destination and their gross value in their damaged condition at that destination bears to the gross value of all the goods or movables in a sound condition at that destination.

(2) **Definition of "gross value"** — For the purposes of paragraph (1)(c), "gross value"

    (a) in the case of goods or movables customarily sold in bond, means the bonded price of the goods or movables; and

    (b) in the case of any other goods or movables, means the wholesale price, or if there is no wholesale price, the estimated value, of the goods or movables, together with any freight, landing charges and duty paid in respect of them.

(3) **Gross proceeds** — For the purposes of paragraph (1)(c), where the goods or movables are sold at their destination and all charges on the sale are paid by the sellers, their gross value in their damaged condition at that destination is the actual price obtained for them, which price is known as the gross proceeds.

S.C. 1993, c. 22, s. 70.

71.(1) **Apportionment of specified value** — In determining the measure of indemnity under a valued policy that specifies a single value for different types of goods,

    (a) the value must be apportioned to those types in proportion to their respective insurable values, as determined under this Act; and

    (b) the value of any part of any type of the goods is that proportion of the value of all the goods of that type that the insurable value of that part bears to the insurable value of all the goods of that type, as determined under this Act.

(2) **Idem** — Where the insurable value of goods cannot be determined for the purposes of subsection (1) because the prime cost of a type of goods is not ascertainable, the value specified by the valued policy may be apportioned to the different types of goods in proportion to their respective net arrived sound values.

S.C. 1993, c. 22, s. 71.

72.(1) **General average contribution** — Subject to any express provision in the marine policy, the measure of indemnity in respect of a general average contribution that an insured has paid or is liable to pay is

    (a) where the subject-matter of the contribution is fully insured for its contributory value, the full amount of the contribution; and

    (b) where the subject-matter of the contribution is not fully insured for its contributory value or only part of it is insured, that proportion of the full amount of the contribution that the insured value of the subject-matter bears to its contributory value.

(2) **Idem** — In order to determine the measure of indemnity under paragraph (1)(b) in a case where a particular average loss that is to be deducted from the contributory value has been incurred and is payable by the insurer, the amount of the loss must be deducted from the insured value of the subject-matter.

(3) **Salvage charges** — Where salvage charges are recoverable under a marine policy, the measure of indemnity in respect of the charges is to be determined in accordance with the principles set out in subsections (1) and (2).
S.C. 1993, c. 22, s. 72.

73. Third party liability — Subject to any express provision in the policy, the measure of indemnity in respect of any liability to a third party that is expressly insured against by a marine policy is the amount paid or payable by the insured to the third party in respect of the liability.
S.C. 1993, c. 22, s. 73.

74. Other losses — The measure of indemnity in respect of a loss not provided for in any of sections 67 to 73 is to be determined, as much as possible, in accordance with those sections.
S.C. 1993, c. 22, s. 74.

75. Proportional liability — Where a loss is recoverable under a marine policy, the insurer, or each insurer if there is more than one, is liable for that proportion of the measure of indemnity in respect of the loss that the amount subscribed by the insurer is of
    (a)   in the case of an unvalued policy, the insurable value of the subject-matter; and
    (b)   in the case of a valued policy, the value of the subject-matter specified by the policy.
S.C. 1993, c. 22, s. 75.

76. Construction — Nothing in sections 66 to 75 shall be construed as affecting the provisions of this Act relating to double insurance or prohibiting an insurer from disproving an interest in whole or in part or from establishing that, at the time of a loss, the whole or any part of the subject-matter insured was not at risk under the marine policy.
S.C. 1993, c. 22, s. 76.

77.(1) **Particular average warranties** — Where the subject-matter insured under a marine policy is warranted free from particular average, the insured cannot recover for a loss of part of the subject-matter, other than a loss incurred by a general average sacrifice, unless the contract evidenced by the policy is apportionable, in which case the insured may recover for a total loss of any apportionable part.

(2) **Idem** — Where the subject-matter insured under a marine policy is warranted free from particular average, either wholly or under a specified percentage, the insurer is nevertheless liable for salvage charges and, if the policy contains a sue and labour clause, for particular charges and other expenses properly incurred under the clause for the purpose of averting a loss by a peril insured against.

(3) **Addition of general to particular average loss** — Unless the policy otherwise provides, where the subject-matter insured under a marine policy is warranted free from particular average under a specified percentage, a general

average loss cannot be added to a particular average loss in order to attain that percentage.

(4) **Calculation of percentage** — Where the subject-matter insured under a marine policy is warranted free from particular average under a specified percentage, for the purpose of determining whether that percentage has been attained, only the actual loss incurred in respect of the subject-matter may be considered, and no particular charges or expenses incurred in establishing the loss may be included.

S.C. 1993, c. 22, s. 77.

78.(1) **Recovery of successive losses** — Subject to this Act and unless the marine policy otherwise provides, an insurer is liable for successive losses, even if the total amount of the losses exceeds the sum insured.

(2) **Exception** — Where, under a marine policy, a partial loss that has not been repaired or otherwise made good is followed by a total loss, the insurer is liable only for the total loss.

(3) **Liability under sue and labour clause** — Nothing in subsections (1) and (2) shall be construed as affecting the liability of an insurer under a sue and labour clause.

S.C. 1993, c. 22, s. 78.

79.(1) **Sue and labour clause** — Where a marine policy contains a sue and labour clause, the engagement thereby entered into is supplementary to the contract and the insured may recover from the insurer any expenses properly incurred under the clause, even if the insurer has paid for a total loss of the subject-matter insured or the subject-matter insured is warranted free from particular average, either wholly or under a specified percentage.

(2) **Idem** — General average losses, general average contributions, salvage charges, and expenses incurred for the purpose of averting or diminishing a loss by a peril not insured against are not recoverable under a sue and labour clause.

S.C. 1993, c. 22, s. 79.

80. Duty to avert or diminish loss — It is the duty of an insured and an insured's agent to take such measures as are reasonable for the purpose of averting or diminishing a loss under the marine policy.

S.C. 1993, c. 22, s. 80.

RIGHTS OF INSURER ON PAYMENT

81.(1) **Subrogation where total loss** — On payment by an insurer for a total loss of the whole of the subject-matter insured or, if the subject-matter insured is goods, for any apportionable part of the subject-matter insured, the insurer becomes entitled to assume the interest of the insured in the whole or part of the subject-matter and is subrogated to all the rights and remedies of the insured in respect of that whole or part from the time of the casualty causing the loss.

(2) **Subrogation where partial loss** — On payment by an insurer for a partial loss of the subject-matter insured, the insurer acquires no title to the subject-

matter but is subrogated to all the rights and remedies of the insured in respect of the subject-matter from the time of the casualty causing the loss to the extent that the insured is indemnified, in accordance with this Act, by the payment for the loss.
S.C. 1993, c. 22, s. 81.

RETURN OF PREMIUM

82.(1) **Recovery or retention** — A premium or part of a premium that is returnable to the insured may, if paid, be recovered by the insured from the insurer and may, if not paid, be retained by the insured or the insured's agent.

(2) **When premium returnable** — A premium or part of a premium is returnable to the insured in any of the circumstances described in sections 83 to 85.
S.C. 1993, c. 22, s. 82.

83. Return on happening of specified event — Where a marine policy contains a provision for the return of the premium or part of the premium on the happening of a specified event, the premium or part is returnable to the insured on the happening of that event.
S.C. 1993, c. 22, s. 83.

84.(1) **Return on total failure of consideration** — Where the consideration for a premium totally fails and there is no fraud or illegality on the part of the insured or the insured's agent, the premium is returnable to the insured on the failure.

(2) **Idem** — Where any apportionable part of the consideration for a premium totally fails and there is no fraud or illegality on the part of the insured or the insured's agent, a proportionate part of the premium is returnable to the insured on the failure.
S.C. 1993, c. 22, s. 84.

85.(1) **Particular circumstances** — Without limiting the generality of section 84, a premium or part of a premium is returnable or not returnable to the insured in the particular circumstances described in subsections (2) to (11).

(2) **Void or avoided marine policy** — Where a marine policy is void, or is avoided by the insurer as of the commencement of the risk, and there is no fraud or illegality on the part of the insured or the insured's agent, the premium is returnable.

(3) **Exception** — Where the risk is not apportionable and has once attached, subsection (2) does not apply and the premium is not returnable.

(4) **Subject-matter never imperilled** — Where the subject-matter insured or part of the subject-matter insured has never been exposed to any peril insured against, the premium or a proportionate part of the premium, as the case may be, is returnable.

(5) **Exception** — Where the subject-matter is insured "lost or not lost" and has arrived at its destination safely before the contract is concluded, subsection

(4) does not apply and the premium is not returnable unless, at the time the contract is concluded, the insurer knows of the safe arrival.

(6) **No insurable interest** — Where an insured has no insurable interest throughout the period of the risk, the premium is returnable.

(7) **Exception** — Subsection (6) does not apply in respect of a contract by way of gaming or wagering and the premium is not returnable.

(8) **Over-insurance under one policy** — Where an insured is over-insured under an unvalued policy, a proportionate part of the premium is returnable.

(9) **Defeasible interest** — Where an insured has a defeasible interest in the subject-matter insured that is terminated during the period of the risk, the premium is not returnable.

(10) **Over-insurance under several policies** — Subject to subsections (2) to (9), where an insured is over-insured by double insurance, a proportionate part of the premiums is returnable.

(11) **Exceptions** — Subsection (10) does not apply

    (a) where the double insurance is knowingly effected by the insured, in which case none of the premiums is returnable; and

    (b) where the policies are effected at different times and either the earlier policy has at any time borne the entire risk or a claim has been paid on the earlier policy in respect of the full sum insured by it, in which case the premium for the earlier policy is not returnable and the premium for the later policy is returnable.

S.C. 1993, c. 22, s. 85.

DOUBLE INSURANCE

86.(1) **Double insurance where over-insured** — An insured is over-insured by double insurance if two or more marine policies are effected by or on behalf of the insured on the same marine adventure and interest or part thereof and the sums insured exceed the indemnity allowed by this Act.

(2) **Where over-insurance** — An insured who is over-insured by double insurance

    (a) may claim payment from the insurers in any order, unless the marine policy under which the claim is made provides otherwise, but may not receive more than the indemnity allowed by this Act;

    (b) if claiming under a valued policy, shall give credit, as against the value specified in the policy, for any sum received by the insured under any other policy without regard to the actual value of the subject-matter insured;

    (c) if claiming under an unvalued policy, shall give credit, as against the full insurable value, for any sum received by the insured under any other policy; and

    (d) is deemed to hold any sum received in excess of the indemnity allowed by this Act in trust for the insurers, according to their right of contribution among themselves.

S.C. 1993, c. 22, s. 86.

87.(1) **Right of contribution** — Where an insured is over-insured by double insurance, each insurer is liable, as between the insurer and the other insurers, to contribute rateably to the payment of a loss in proportion to the amount for which the insurer is liable under the insurer's contract.

(2) **Remedies for overcontribution** — An insurer who contributes more to the payment of a loss than required by subsection (1) is entitled to bring an action against the other insurers for contribution and to such other remedies as a surety is entitled to for paying more than the surety's proportion of a debt.

S.C. 1993, c. 22, s. 87.

UNDER-INSURANCE

88. Under-insurance — Where an insured is insured for a sum that is less than the insurable value of the subject-matter insured, in the case of an unvalued policy, or less than the value of the subject-matter insured specified by the policy, in the case of a valued policy, the insured is deemed to be self-insured in respect of the uninsured difference.

S.C. 1993, c. 22, s. 88.

MUTUAL INSURANCE

89.(1) **Mutual insurance** — Mutual insurance is insurance whereby two or more persons mutually agree to insure one another against marine losses.

(2) **Application of Act** — Subject to subsections (3) and (4), this Act applies in respect of mutual insurance.

(3) **Premium** — The provisions of this Act relating to premiums do not apply in respect of mutual insurance, but a guarantee, or such other arrangement as may be agreed on, may be substituted for the premium for mutual insurance.

(4) **Amendment by mutual insurance association** — The provisions of this Act may, in the case of mutual insurance effected by an association, be modified by a marine policy issued by the association, or by the rules and regulations of the association, to the extent that the provisions may be modified by agreement of the parties to the insurance.

S.C. 1993, c. 22, s. 89.

GENERAL

90. Exclusion or variation of rights, duties or liabilities — Any right, duty or liability that arises under a contract by implication of law, or that is established by this Act and may be lawfully modified by the parties to a contract, may be negated or varied by express agreement or by usage of the trade if the usage binds both parties to the contract.

S.C. 1993, c. 22, s. 90.

91. Question of fact — Any question as to what constitutes a reasonable time, a reasonable premium or reasonable diligence for the purposes of this Act is a question of fact.

S.C. 1993, c. 22, s. 91.

SCHEDULE

(Section 3)

CONSTRUCTION OF MARINE POLICIES

1.(1) **Definitions** — In a marine policy,

"barratry"

"barratry" includes every wrongful act wilfully committed by the master or crew of the insured ship to the prejudice of the owner or charterer of the ship;

"goods"

"goods" means goods in the nature of merchandise, but does not include personal effects or provisions, stores for use on board a ship or, in the absence of any usage to the contrary, deck cargo or live animals;

"pirates"

"pirates" includes passengers on the insured ship who mutiny and persons who attack the ship from land;

"thieves"

"thieves" does not include persons who commit a clandestine theft or passengers, officers or members of the crew of the insured ship who commit a theft.

(2) **Other definitions** — In a marine policy, the words "freight" and "ship" have the meaning assigned by subsection 2(1) of this Act.

2. References — In a marine policy, a reference

    (a) to "all other perils" means perils similar to the perils specifically mentioned in the policy;

    (b) to "arrests, &c., of kings, princes, and people" includes political or executive acts, but does not include riot or ordinary judicial process;

    (c) to "average unless general" means a partial loss of the subject-matter insured, other than a general average loss, but does not include particular charges; and

    (d) to "perils of the seas" means fortuitous accidents or casualties of the seas, but does not include ordinary action of the wind and waves.

3. "Lost or not lost" — Where the subject-matter of a marine policy is insured "lost or not lost" and a loss occurs before the contract is concluded, the risk attaches unless, at the time the contract was concluded, the insured was aware of the loss and the insurer was not.

4. "From" — Where the subject-matter of a marine policy is insured "from" a particular place, the risk does not attach until the voyage covered by the policy is commenced.

5.(1) **"At and from"** — **ship** — Where a marine policy insures a ship "at and from" a particular place and the ship is at that place in good safety when the contract is concluded, the risk attaches when the contract is concluded.

(2) **Idem** — Where a marine policy insures a ship "at and from" a particular place and the ship is not at that place when the contract is concluded, the risk attaches when the ship arrives there in good safety, and, unless the policy otherwise provides, it is immaterial that the ship is insured by another marine policy for a specified time after the arrival.

6.(1) **"At and from"** — **chartered freight** — Where a marine policy insures chartered freight "at and from" a particular place and the ship is at that place in good safety when the contract is concluded, the risk attaches when the contract is concluded.

(2) **Idem** — Where a marine policy insures chartered freight "at and from" a particular place and the ship is not at that place when the contract is concluded, the risk attaches when the ship arrives there in good safety.

(3) **"At and from"** — **other freight** — Where a marine policy insures freight, other than chartered freight, "at and from" a particular place and the freight is payable without special conditions, the risk attaches proportionately as the goods are shipped, except that if the goods are ready for shipping and belong to the shipowner or are to be shipped under a contract with the shipowner, the risk attaches when the ship is ready to receive the goods.

7. "From the loading thereof" — Where a marine policy insures goods or movables "from the loading thereof", the risk does not attach until they are on board the ship.

8. "Safely landed" — Where the risk on any goods or movables continues until they are "safely landed", the risk ceases if they are not landed in the customary manner within a reasonable time after the arrival of the ship at the port of discharge.

9. "At any port or place whatsoever" — In the absence of any licence or usage, the liberty to touch and stay "at any port or place whatsoever" does not authorize a change in the course of the ship's voyage from the port of departure to the port of destination.

10. "Stranded" — Where a marine policy excepts a loss unless a ship is "stranded", the insurer is liable for any excepted loss, whether or not the loss is attributable to the stranding, if the risk has attached before the stranding and, in the case of a marine policy on goods, the damaged goods are on board the ship.

S.C. 1993, c. 22, Sch.

Appendix B

INSTITUTE CARGO CLAUSES (A)

RISKS COVERED

1. This insurance covers all risks of loss of or damage to the subject-matter insured except as provided in Clauses 4, 5, 6 and 7 below.

Risks Clause

2. This insurance covers general average and salvage charges, adjusted or determined according to the contract of affreightment and/or the governing law and practice, incurred to avoid or in connection with the avoidance of loss from any cause except those excluded in Clauses 4, 5, 6 and 7 or elsewhere in this insurance.

General Average Clause

3. This insurance is extended to indemnify the Assured against such proportion of liability under the contract of affreightment "Both to Blame Collision" Clause as is in respect of a loss recoverable hereunder. In the event of any claim by shipowners under the said Clause the Assured agree to notify the Underwriters who shall have the right, at their own cost and expense, to defend the Assured against such claim.

"Both to Blame Collision" Clause

EXCLUSIONS

4. In no case shall this insurance cover

General Exclusions Clause

4.1 loss damage or expense attributable to wilful misconduct of the Assured

4.2 ordinary leakage, ordinary loss in weight or volume, or ordinary wear and tear of the subject-matter insured

4.3 loss damage or expense caused by insufficiency or unsuitability of packing or preparation of the subject-matter insured (for the purpose of this Clause 4.3 "packing" shall be deemed to include stowage in a container or liftvan but only when such stowage is carried out prior to attachment of this insurance or by the Assured or their servants)

4.4 loss damage or expense caused by inherent vice or nature of the subject-matter insured

4.5 loss damage or expense proximately caused by delay, even though the delay be caused by a risk insured against (except expenses payable under Clause 2 above)

4.6 loss damage or expense arising from insolvency or financial default of the owners managers charterers or operators of the vessel

4.7 loss damage or expense arising from the use of any weapon of war employing atomic or nuclear fission and/or fusion or other like reaction or radioactive force or matter.

5.

5.1 In no case shall this insurance cover loss damage or expense arising from
unseaworthiness of vessel or craft,
unfitness of vessel craft conveyance container or liftvan for the safe carriage of the subject-matter insured,
where the Assured or their servants are privy to such unseaworthiness or unfitness, at the time the subject-matter insured is loaded therein.

Unseaworthiness and Unfitness Exclusion Clause

5.2 The Underwriters waive any breach of the implied warranties of seaworthiness of the ship and fitness of the ship to carry the subject-matter insured to destination, unless the Assured or their servants are privy to such unseaworthiness or unfitness.

6. In no case shall this insurance cover loss damage or expense caused by

War Exclusion Clause

6.1 war civil war revolution rebellion insurrection, or civil strife arising therefrom, or any hostile act by or against a belligerent power

6.2 capture seizure arrest restraint or detainment (piracy excepted), and the consequences thereof or any attempt thereat

6.3 derelict mines torpedoes bombs or other derelict weapons of war.

7. In no case shall this insurance cover loss damage or expense

Strikes Exclusion Clause

7.1 caused by strikers, locked-out workmen, or persons taking part in labour disturbances, riots or civil commotions

7.2 resulting from strikes, lock-outs, labour disturbances, riots or civil commotions

7.3 caused by any terrorist or any person acting from a political motive.

DURATION

8. This insurance attaches from the time the goods leave the warehouse or place of storage at the place named herein for the commencement of the transit, continues during the ordinary course of transit and terminates either

    8.1.1 on delivery to the Consignees' or other final warehouse or place of storage at the destination named herein,

    8.1.2 on delivery to any other warehouse or place of storage, whether prior to or at the destination named herein, which the Assured elect to use either

        8.1.2.1 for storage other than in the ordinary course of transit or

        8.1.2.2 for allocation or distribution,

        or

    8.1.3 on the expiry of 60 days after completion of discharge overside of the goods hereby insured from the oversea vessel at the final port of discharge,

    whichever shall first occur.

8.2 If, after discharge overside from the oversea vessel at the final port of discharge, but prior to termination of this insurance, the goods are to be forwarded to a destination other than that to which they are insured hereunder, this insurance, whilst remaining subject to termination as provided for above, shall not extend beyond the commencement of transit to such other destination.

8.3 This insurance shall remain in force (subject to termination as provided for above and to the provisions of Clause 9 below) during delay beyond the control of the Assured, any deviation, forced discharge, reshipment or transshipment and during any variation of the adventure arising from the exercise of a liberty granted to shipowners or charterers under the contract of affreightment.

Transit Clause

9. If owing to circumstances beyond the control of the Assured either the contract of carriage is terminated at a port or place other than the destination named therein or the transit is otherwise terminated before delivery of the goods as provided for in Clause 8 above, then this insurance shall also terminate *unless prompt notice is given to the Underwriters and continuation of cover is requested when the insurance shall remain in force, subject to an additional premium if required by the Underwriters, either*

9.1 until the goods are sold and delivered at such port or place, or, unless otherwise specially agreed, until the expiry of 60 days after arrival of the goods hereby insured at such port or place, whichever shall first occur,

or

9.2 if the goods are forwarded within the said period of 60 days (or any agreed extension thereof) to the destination named herein or to any other destination, until terminated in accordance with the provisions of Clause 8 above.

Termination of Contract of Carriage Clause

10. Where, after attachment of this insurance, the destination is changed by the Assured, *held covered at a premium and on conditions to be arranged subject to prompt notice being given to the Underwriters*

Change of Voyage Clause

Continued . . .

CLAIMS

11. 11.1 In order to recover under this insurance the Assured must have an insurable interest in the subject-matter insured at the time of the loss.

11.2 Subject to 11.1 above, the Assured shall be entitled to recover for insured loss occurring during the period covered by this insurance, notwithstanding that the loss occurred before the contract of insurance was concluded, unless the Assured were aware of the loss and the Underwriters were not.

Insurable Interest Clause

12. Where, as a result of the operation of a risk covered by this insurance the insured transit is terminated at a port or place other than that to which the subject-matter is covered under this insurance, the Underwriters will reimburse the Assured for any extra charges properly and reasonably incurred in unloading storing and forwarding the subject-matter to the destination to which it is insured hereunder.

This Clause 12, which does not apply to general average or salvage charges, shall be subject to the exclusions contained in Clauses 4, 5, 6 and 7 above, and shall not include charges arising from the fault negligence insolvency or financial default of the Assured or their servants.

Forwarding Charges Clause

13. No claim for Constructive Total Loss shall be recoverable hereunder unless the subject-matter insured is reasonably abandoned either on account of its actual total loss appearing to be unavoidable or because the cost of recovering, reconditioning and forwarding the subject-matter to the destination to which it is insured would exceed its value on arrival.

Constructive Total Loss Clause

14. 14.1 If any Increased Value insurance is effected by the Assured on the cargo insured herein the agreed value of the cargo shall be deemed to be increased to the total amount insured under this insurance and all Increased Value insurances covering the loss, and liability under this insurance shall be in such proportion as the sum insured herein bears to such total amount insured.

In the event of claim the Assured shall provide the Underwriters with evidence of the amounts insured under all other insurances.

14.2 **Where this insurance is on Increased Value the following clause shall apply:**
The agreed value of the cargo shall be deemed to be equal to the total amount insured under the primary insurance and all Increased Value insurances covering the loss and effected on the cargo by the Assured, and liability under this insurance shall be in such proportion as the sum insured herein bears to such total amount insured.

In the event of claim the Assured shall provide the Underwriters with evidence of the amounts insured under all other insurances.

Increased Value Clause

BENEFIT OF INSURANCE

15. This insurance shall not inure to the benefit of the carrier or other bailee.

Not to Inure Clause

MINIMISING LOSSES

16. It is the duty of the Assured and their servants and agents in respect of loss recoverable hereunder

16.1 to take such measures as may be reasonable for the purpose of averting or minimizing such loss, and

16.2 to ensure that all rights against carriers, bailees or other third parties are properly preserved and exercised

and the Underwriters will, in addition to any loss recoverable hereunder, reimburse the Assured for any charges properly and reasonably incurred in pursuance of these duties.

Duty of Assured Clause

17. Measures taken by the Assured or the Underwriters with the object of saving, protecting or recovering the subject-matter insured shall not be considered as a waiver or acceptance of abandonment or otherwise prejudice the rights of either party.

Waiver Clause

AVOIDANCE OF DELAY

18.   It is a condition of this insurance that the Assured shall act with reasonable despatch in all circumstances within their control.

Reasonable Despatch Clause

LAW AND PRACTICE

19.   This insurance is subject to English law and practice.

English Law and Practice Clause

NOTE.– It is necessary for the Assured when they become aware of an event which is "held covered" under this insurance to give prompt notice to the Underwriters and the right to such cover is dependent upon compliance with this obligation.

Reprinted with the permission of Witherby & Co.

Appendix C

INSTITUTE CARGO CLAUSES (B)

RISKS COVERED

1. This insurance covers, except as provided in Clauses 4, 5, 6 and 7 below,

   1.1   loss of or damage to the subject-matter insured reasonably attributable to

      1.1.1   fire or explosion

      1.1.2   vessel or craft being stranded grounded sunk or capsized

      1.1.3   overturning or derailment of land conveyance

      1.1.4   collision or contact of vessel craft or conveyance with any external object other than water

      1.1.5   discharge of cargo at a port of distress,

   1.2   loss of or damage to the subject-matter insured caused by

      1.2.1   general average sacrifice

      1.2.2   jettison or washing overboard

      1.2.3   entry of sea lake or river water into vessel craft hold conveyance container liftvan or place of storage,

   1.3   total loss of any package lost overboard or dropped whilst loading on to, or unloading from, vessel or craft.

Risks Clause

2. This insurance covers general average and salvage charges, adjusted or determined according to the contract of affreightment and/or the governing law and practice, incurred to avoid or in connection with the avoidance of loss from any cause except those excluded in Clauses 4, 5, 6 and 7 or elsewhere in this insurance.

General Average Clause

3. This insurance is extended to indemnify the Assured against such proportion of liability under the contract of affreightment "Both to Blame Collision" Clause as is in respect of a loss recoverable hereunder. In the event of any claim by shipowners under the said Clause the Assured agree to notify the Underwriters who shall have the right, at their own cost and expense, to defend the Assured against such claim.

"Both to Blame Collision" Clause

EXCLUSIONS

4. In no case shall this insurance cover

   4.1   loss damage or expense attributable to wilful misconduct of the Assured

   4.2   ordinary leakage, ordinary loss in weight or volume, or ordinary wear and tear of the subject-matter insured

   4.3   loss damage or expense caused by insufficiency or unsuitability of packing or preparation of the subject-matter insured (for the purpose of this Clause 4.3 "packing" shall be deemed to include stowage in a container or liftvan but only when such stowage is carried out prior to attachment of this insurance or by the Assured or their servants)

   4.4   loss damage or expense caused by inherent vice or nature of the subject-matter insured

   4.5   loss damage or expense proximately caused by delay, even though the delay be caused by a risk insured against (except expenses payable under Clause 2 above)

   4.6   loss damage or expense arising from insolvency or financial default of the owners managers charterers or operators of the vessel

   4.7   deliberate damage to or deliberate destruction of the subject-matter insured or any part thereof by the wrongful act of any person or persons

   4.8   loss damage or expense arising from the use of any weapon of war employing atomic or nuclear fission and/or fusion or other like reaction or radioactive force or matter.

General Exclusions Clause

5. 5.1 In no case shall this insurance cover loss damage or expense arising from
           unseaworthiness of vessel or craft,
           unfitness of vessel craft conveyance container or liftvan for the safe carriage of the subject-matter insured,
    where the Assured or their servants are privy to such unseaworthiness or unfitness, at the time the subject-matter insured is loaded therein.

5.2 The Underwriters waive any breach of the implied warranties of seaworthiness of the ship and fitness of the ship to carry the subject-matter insured to destination, unless the Assured or their servants are privy to such unseaworthiness or unfitness.

6. In no case shall this insurance cover loss damage or expense caused by
   6.1 war civil war revolution rebellion insurrection, or civil strife arising therefrom, or any hostile act by or against a belligerent power
   6.2 capture seizure arrest restraint or detainment (piracy excepted), and the consequences thereof or any attempt thereat
   6.3 derelict mines torpedoes bombs or other derelict weapons of war.

7. In no case shall this insurance cover loss damage or expense
   7.1 caused by strikers, locked-out workmen, or persons taking part in labour disturbances, riots or civil commotions
   7.2 resulting from strikes, lock-outs, labour disturbances, riots or civil commotions
   7.3 caused by any terrorist or any person acting from a political motive.

DURATION
8. 8.1 This insurance attaches from the time the goods leave the warehouse or place of storage at the place named herein for the commencement of the transit, continues during the ordinary course of transit and terminates either
       8.1.1 on delivery to the Consignees' or other final warehouse or place of storage at the destination named herein,
       8.1.2 on delivery to any other warehouse or place of storage, whether prior to or at the destination named herein, which the Assured elect to use either
          8.1.2.1 for storage other than in the ordinary course of transit or
          8.1.2.2 for allocation or distribution,
                  or
       8.1.3 on the expiry of 60 days after completion of discharge overside of the goods hereby insured from the oversea vessel at the final port of discharge,
              whichever shall first occur.

8.2 If, after discharge overside from the oversea vessel at the final port of discharge, but prior to termination of this insurance, the goods are to be forwarded to a destination other than that to which they are insured hereunder, this insurance, whilst remaining subject to termination as provided for above, shall not extend beyond the commencement of transit to such other destination.

8.3 This insurance shall remain in force (subject to termination as provided for above and to the provisions of Clause 9 below) during delay beyond the control of the Assured, any deviation, forced discharge, reshipment or transshipment and during any variation of the adventure arising from the exercise of a liberty granted to shipowners or charterers under the contract of affreightment.

Unseaworthiness and Unfitness Exclusion Clause

War Exclusion Clause

Strikes Exclusion Clause

Transit Clause

continued...

Appendix D

INSTITUTE CARGO CLAUSES (C)

RISKS COVERED

1. This insurance covers, except as provided in Clauses 4, 5, 6 and 7 below,   Risks Clause

  1.1 loss of or damage to the subject-matter insured reasonably attributable to

    1.1.1 fire or explosion

    1.1.2 vessel or craft being stranded grounded sunk or capsized

    1.1.3 overturning or derailment of land conveyance

    1.1.4 collision or contact of vessel craft or conveyance with any external object other than water

    1.1.5 discharge of cargo at a port of distress,

  1.2 loss of or damage to the subject-matter insured caused by

    1.2.1 general average sacrifice

    1.2.2 jettison.

2. This insurance covers general average and salvage charges, adjusted or determined according to the contract of affreightment and/or the governing law and practice, incurred to avoid or in connection with the avoidance of loss from any cause except those excluded in Clauses 4, 5, 6 and 7 or elsewhere in this insurance.   General Average Clause

3. This insurance is extended to indemnify the Assured against such proportion of liability under the contract of affreightment "Both to Blame Collision" Clause as is in respect of a loss recoverable hereunder. In the event of any claim by shipowners under the said Clause the Assured agree to notify the Underwriters who shall have the right, at their own cost and expense, to defend the Assured against such claim.   "Both to Blame Collision" Clause

EXCLUSIONS

4. In no case shall this insurance cover   General Exclusions Clause

  4.1 loss damage or expense attributable to wilful misconduct of the Assured

  4.2 ordinary leakage, ordinary loss in weight or volume, or ordinary wear and tear of the subject-matter insured

  4.3 loss damage or expense caused by insufficiency or unsuitability of packing or preparation of the subject-matter insured (for the purpose of this Clause 4.3 "packing" shall be deemed to include stowage in a container or liftvan but only when such stowage is carried out prior to attachment of this insurance or by the Assured or their servants)

  4.4 loss damage or expense caused by inherent vice or nature of the subject-matter insured

  4.5 loss damage or expense proximately caused by delay, even though the delay be caused by a risk insured against (except expenses payable under Clause 2 above)

  4.6 loss damage or expense arising from insolvency or financial default of the owners managers charterers or operators of the vessel

  4.7 deliberate damage to or deliberate destruction of the subject-matter insured or any part thereof by the wrongful act of any person or persons

  4.8 loss damage or expense arising from the use of any weapon of war employing atomic or nuclear fission and/or fusion or other like reaction or radioactive force or matter.

5.

5.1 In no case shall this insurance cover loss damage or expense arising from
unseaworthiness of vessel or craft,
unfitness of vessel craft conveyance container or liftvan for the safe carriage of the subject-matter insured,
where the Assured or their servants are privy to such unseaworthiness or unfitness, at the time the subject-matter insured is loaded therein.

5.2 The Underwriters waive any breach of the implied warranties of seaworthiness of the ship and fitness of the ship to carry the subject-matter insured to destination, unless the Assured or their servants are privy to such unseaworthiness or unfitness.

Unseaworthiness and Unfitness Exclusion Clause

6. In no case shall this insurance cover loss damage or expense caused by

6.1 war civil war revolution rebellion insurrection, or civil strife arising therefrom, or any hostile act by or against a belligerent power

6.2 capture seizure arrest restraint or detainment (piracy excepted), and the consequences thereof or any attempt thereat

6.3 derelict mines torpedoes bombs or other derelict weapons of war.

War Exclusion Clause

7. In no case shall this insurance cover loss damage or expense

7.1 caused by strikers, locked-out workmen, or persons taking part in labour disturbances, riots or civil commotions

7.2 resulting from strikes, lock-outs, labour disturbances, riots or civil commotions

7.3 caused by any terrorist or any person acting from a political motive.

Strikes Exclusion Clause

DURATION

8.

8.1 This insurance attaches from the time the goods leave the warehouse or place of storage at the place named herein for the commencement of the transit, continues during the ordinary course of transit and terminates either

8.1.1 on delivery to the Consignees' or other final warehouse or place of storage at the destination named herein,

8.1.2 on delivery to any other warehouse or place of storage, whether prior to or at the destination named herein, which the Assured elect to use either

8.1.2.1 for storage other than in the ordinary course of transit or

8.1.2.2 for allocation or distribution,
or

8.1.3 on the expiry of 60 days after completion of discharge overside of the goods hereby insured from the oversea vessel at the final port of discharge,
whichever shall first occur.

8.2 If, after discharge overside from the oversea vessel at the final port of discharge, but prior to termination of this insurance, the goods are to be forwarded to a destination other than that to which they are insured hereunder, this insurance, whilst remaining subject to termination as provided for above, shall not extend beyond the commencement of transit to such other destination.

8.3 This insurance shall remain in force (subject to termination as provided for above and to the provisions of Clause 9 below) during delay beyond the control of the Assured, any deviation, forced discharge, reshipment or transshipment and during any variation of the adventure arising from the exercise of a liberty granted to shipowners or charterers under the contract of affreightment.

Transit Clause

continued...

9. If owing to circumstances beyond the control of the Assured either the contract of carriage is terminated at a port or place other than the destination named therein or the transit is otherwise terminated before delivery of the goods as provided for in Clause 8 above, then this insurance shall also terminate *unless prompt notice is given to the Underwriters and continuation of cover is requested when the insurance shall remain in force, subject to an additional premium if required by the Underwriters, either*

   9.1 until the goods are sold and delivered at such port or place, or, unless otherwise specially agreed, until the expiry of 60 days after arrival of the goods hereby insured at such port or place, whichever shall first occur,

      or

   9.2 if the goods are forwarded within the said period of 60 days (or any agreed extension thereof) to the destination named herein or to any other destination, until terminated in accordance with the provisions of Clause 8 above.

                                Termination of Contract of Carriage Clause

10. Where, after attachment of this insurance, the destination is changed by the Assured, *held covered at a premium and on conditions to be arranged subject to prompt notice being given to the Underwriters.*

        Change of Voyage Clause

CLAIMS

11. 11.1 In order to recover under this insurance the Assured must have an insurable interest in the subject-matter insured at the time of the loss.

     11.2 Subject to 11.1 above, the Assured shall be entitled to recover for insured loss occurring during the period covered by this insurance, notwithstanding that the loss occurred before the contract of insurance was concluded, unless the Assured were aware of the loss and the Underwriters were not.

        Insurable Interest Clause

12. Where, as a result of the operation of a risk covered by this insurance the insured transit is terminated at a port or place other than that to which the subject-matter is covered under this insurance, the Underwriters will reimburse the Assured for any extra charges properly and reasonably incurred in unloading storing and forwarding the subject-matter to the destination to which it is insured hereunder.

This Clause 12, which does not apply to general average or salvage charges, shall be subject to the exclusions contained in Clauses 4, 5, 6 and 7 above, and shall not include charges arising from the fault negligence insolvency or financial default of the Assured or their servants.

        Forwarding Charges Clause

13. No claim for Constructive Total Loss shall be recoverable hereunder unless the subject-matter insured is reasonably abandoned either on account of its actual total loss appearing to be unavoidable or because the cost of recovering, reconditioning and forwarding the subject-matter to the destination to which it is insured would exceed its value on arrival.

        Constructive Total Loss Clause

14. 14.1 If any Increased Value insurance is effected by the Assured on the cargo insured herein the agreed value of the cargo shall be deemed to be increased to the total amount insured under this insurance and all Increased Value insurances covering the loss, and liability under this insurance shall be in such proportion as the sum insured herein bears to such total amount insured.

In the event of claim the Assured shall provide the Underwriters with evidence of the amounts insured under all other insurances.

     14.2 **Where this insurance is on Increased Value the following clause shall apply:**
        The agreed value of the cargo shall be deemed to be equal to the total amount insured under the primary insurance and all Increased Value insurances covering the loss and effected on the cargo by the Assured, and liability under this insurance shall be in such proportion as the sum insured herein bears to such total amount insured.

In the event of claim the Assured shall provide the Underwriters with evidence of the amounts insured under all other insurances.

        Increased Value Clause

BENEFIT OF INSURANCE

15. This insurance shall not inure to the benefit of the carrier or other bailee.

Not to
Inure Clause

MINIMISING LOSSES

16. It is the duty of the Assured and their servants and agents in respect of loss recoverable hereunder

  16.1   to take such measures as may be reasonable for the purpose of averting or minimizing such loss,
        and

  16.2   to ensure that all rights against carriers, bailees or other third parties are properly preserved and exercised
        and the Underwriters will, in addition to any loss recoverable hereunder, reimburse the Assured for any charges properly and reasonably
        incurred in pursuance of these duties.

Duty of
Assured
Clause

17. Measures taken by the Assured or the Underwriters with the object of saving, protecting or recovering the subject-matter insured shall not be
considered as a waiver or acceptance of abandonment or otherwise prejudice the rights of either party.

Waiver
Clause

AVOIDANCE OF DELAY

18. It is a condition of this insurance that the Assured shall act with reasonable despatch in all circumstances within their control.

Reasonable
Despatch
Clause

LAW AND PRACTICE

19. This insurance is subject to English law and practice.

English Law
and
Practice
Clause

*NOTE.– It is necessary for the Assured when they become aware of an event which is "held covered" under this insurance to give prompt notice to the
Underwriters and the right to such cover is dependent upon compliance with this obligation.*

Reprinted with the permission of Witherby & Co.

INSTITUTE CARGO CLAUSES (C)   page 2

Appendix E

CANADIAN HULLS (PACIFIC) CLAUSES

1. Touching the Adventures and Perils which we, the Underwriters, are contented to bear and take upon us, they are of the Seas, Men-of-War, Fire, Enemies, Pirates, Rovers, Thieves, Jettisons, Letters of Mart and Counter-Mart, Surprisals, Takings at Sea, Arrests, Restraints and Detainments of all Kings, Princes and Peoples, of what nation, condition or quality soever, Barratry of the Master and Mariners and of all other like Perils, Losses and Misfortunes that have or shall come to the Hurt, Detriment or Damage of the subject matter insured (hereafter the "Vessel") or any part thereof; excepting, however, such of the foregoing Perils as may be excluded by provisions elsewhere in these clauses or by endorsement.

2. It is the duty of the Assured, their servants, agents or assigns, in case of loss or misfortune to take such measures as may be reasonable for the purpose of averting or minimizing a loss which would be recoverable under this insurance. For the purpose of this insurance, such measures shall be designated as Sue and Labour.

The reasonable charges therefor will be reimbursed by Underwriters in accordance with their rateable proportion as provided for herein.

It is expressly agreed that no acts of Underwriters or the Assured in recovering, saving or preserving the Vessel shall be considered as successive ports shall be treated as being due to one accident. In the case of such heavy weather extending over a period not wholly covered by this insurance, the deductible to be applied to the claim recoverable hereunder shall be the proportion of the above deductible that the number of days of such heavy weather falling within the period of this insurance bears to the number of days of heavy weather during the single sea passage.

Unless the Assured and Underwriters shall have agreed in writing prior to commencement of suit to participate jointly in recoveries and concomitant legal costs, then net recoveries (excluding interest comprised therein) made against any claim subject to the above deductible, or any other deductions by reason of the difference between the insured and sound values, shall first be credited to the Underwriters up to the amount of the claim paid by them and then to the Assured.

Interest comprised in recoveries shall be apportioned between the Assured and the Underwriters, taking into account the sums paid by Underwriters and the dates when such payments were made.

8. Unless this insurance otherwise provides, claims for partial loss recoverable hereunder shall not be subject to depreciation.

23 either a waiver or acceptance or abandonment or otherwise prejudice
24 the rights of either party.
25   When expenses are incurred pursuant to this clause, the liability
26 under this insurance shall not exceed the proportion of such expenses
27 that the amount insured hereunder bears to the value of the Vessel as
28 stated herein, or to the sound value of the Vessel at the time of the
29 occurrence giving rise to the expenditure if the sound value exceeds
30 that value. Where the Underwriters have admitted a claim for total
31 loss and subject matter insured by this insurance is saved, the foregoing
32 provisions shall not apply unless the expenses of suing and labouring
33 exceed the value of such property saved and then shall apply only to the
34 amount of the expenses which is in excess of such value.
35   When a claim for total loss of the Vessel is admitted under this
36 insurance and expenses have been reasonably incurred in salving or
37 attempting to salve the Vessel and other property and there are no
38 proceeds, or the expenses exceed the proceeds, then this insurance
39 shall bear its pro rata share of such proportion of the expenses, or of
40 the expenses in excess of the proceeds, as the case may be, as may
41 reasonably be regarded as having been incurred in respect of the Vessel;
42 but if the Vessel be insured for less than its sound value at the time of
43 the occurrence giving rise to the expenditure, the amount recoverable
44 under this clause shall be reduced in proportion to the under-
45 insurance.
46   The sum recoverable under this clause shall be in addition to the loss
47 otherwise recoverable under this insurance but shall in no
48 circumstances exceed the amount insured under this insurance in
49 respect of the Vessel.

50 3. This insurance includes loss of or damage to the Vessel directly
51 caused by:-
52   (a) Accidents in loading, discharging or shifting cargo or fuel
53   Explosions on shipboard or elsewhere
54   Breakdown of or accident to nuclear installations or reactors
55   on shipboard or elsewhere
56   Bursting of boilers, breakage of shafts or any latent defect in
57   the machinery or hull
58   Negligence of Master, Charterers other than an Assured,

116 9. From the cost of cleaning and painting the bottom of the Vessel
117 (exclusive of dry dock charges) recoverable hereunder there shall be
118 deducted one-twelfth for every month since the Vessel was last painted,
119 but no allowance shall be made for cleaning and painting on account
120 of exposure to air unless the Vessel has been more than twenty four
121 hours out of the water.
122   Notwithstanding the foregoing, no claim in respect of bottom
123 painting shall be recoverable hereunder unless evidence is provided to
show date of the last bottom painting prior to the loss.

124 10. General Average, Salvage and Special Charges payable as provided
125 in the contract of affreightment, or failing such provision, or there be
126 no contract of affreightment, payable in accordance with the York-
127 Antwerp Rules. Provided always that when an adjustment according to
128 the laws and usages of the port of destination is properly demanded by
129 the owners of the cargo General Average shall be paid in accordance
130 with same.
131   When the Vessel sails in ballast, not under charter, the provisions
132 of the York-Antwerp Rules, 1974 (excluding Rules XX and XXI) shall
133 be applicable, and the voyage for this purpose shall be deemed to
134 continue from the port or place of departure until the arrival of the
135 Vessel at the first port or place thereafter other than a port or place of
136 refuge or a port or place of call for bunkering only. If at any such
137 intermediate port or place there is an abandonment of the adventure
138 originally contemplated, the voyage shall thereupon be deemed to be
139 terminated.
140   When the contributory value of the Vessel is greater than the
141 valuation herein, the liability of these Underwriters for General Average
142 contribution (except in respect to amount made good to the Vessel) or
143 Salvage shall not exceed that proportion of the total contribution due
144 from the Vessel that the amount insured hereunder bears to the
145 contributory value. If because of damage for which these Underwriters
146 are liable as partial loss, the value of the Vessel has been reduced for the
147 purpose of contribution, the net amount of the partial loss under this
148 insurance shall be deducted from the amount insured hereunder and
149 these Underwriters shall be liable only for the proportion which such
150 net amount bears to the contributory value.

Officers, Crew or Pilots

Negligence of repairers provided such repairers are not Assured(s) hereunder, but this exclusion shall not apply to loss or damage resulting from the operation by the Assured of a commercial repair division or facility

(b) Contact with aircraft or similar objects, or objects falling therefrom

Contact with any land conveyance, dock or harbour equipment or installation

Earthquake, volcanic eruption or lightning

Provided such loss or damage has not resulted from want of due diligence by the Assured, Owners or Managers.

Masters, Officers, Crew or Pilots not to be considered as part Owners within the meaning of this clause should they hold shares in the Vessel.

4. This insurance excludes claims due to or resulting from ice and/or freezing howsoever caused on inland waters above ocean tidal influence.

5. The Vessel is covered subject to the provisions of this insurance at all times and has leave to sail or navigate with or without pilots, to go on trial trips and to assist and tow vessels or craft in distress, but it is warranted that the Vessel shall not otherwise tow or be towed, except as is customary or to the first safe port or place when in need of assistance.

6. The Vessel is covered in case of any breach of warranty as to cargo, employment, towage, salvage services or date of sailing, provided notice be given to the Underwriters immediately after receipt of advices and any amended terms of cover and any additional premium required by them be agreed.

7. The sum of $ shall be deducted from the total of all claims arising out of one accident or occurrence (including claims under the Running Down Clause). Nevertheless, the expense of sighting the bottom after stranding, if reasonably incurred specially for that purpose, shall be paid in full even if no damage be found.

11. In ascertaining whether the Vessel is a constructive total loss, the insured value shall be taken as the repaired value and nothing in respect of the damaged or break-up value of the Vessel or wreck shall be taken into account.

No claim for constructive total loss based upon the cost of recovery and/or repair of the Vessel shall be recoverable hereunder unless such cost would exceed the insured value. In making this determination, only the cost relating to a single accident or sequence of damages arising from the same accident shall be taken into account.

12. In the event of total or constructive total loss, no claim to be made by the Underwriters for freight whether notice of abandonment has been given or not.

13. In no case shall Underwriters be liable for unrepaired damage in addition to a subsequent total loss sustained from any cause during the term covered by this insurance or extension thereof.

14. It is further agreed that if the Vessel shall come into collision with any other vessel and the Assured shall in consequence thereof become liable to pay to any other person or persons any sum or sums in respect of such collision for:

(i) loss of or damage to any other vessel or property on any other vessel,

(ii) delay to or loss of use of any such other vessel or property thereon, or

(iii) general average of, salvage under contract of any such other vessel or property thereon,

the Underwriters will pay the Assured such proportion of such sum or sums as their respective subscriptions hereto bear to the insured value of the Vessel provided always that their liability in respect of any one such collision shall not exceed their proportionate part of the insured value of the Vessel, and in cases in which, with the prior consent in writing of the Underwriters, the liability of the Vessel has been contested or proceedings have been taken to limit the liability, they will also pay a like proportion of the costs which the Assured shall thereby

92 This paragraph shall not apply to Sue and Labour, Salvage Expenses,
93 General Average nor to a claim for Total or Constructive Total Loss.
94   Claims for damage by heavy weather (which includes contact with floating ice) occurring during a single sea passage between two

185 incur. But when both vessels are to blame then, unless the liability of
186 the Owners of one or both of such vessels becomes limited by law,
187 claims under this clause shall be settled on the principle of cross-liabilities as if the Owners of each vessel had been compelled to pay to

188 the Owners of the other such vessels such proportion of the latter's
189 damages as may have been properly allowed in ascertaining the balance
190 or sum payable by or to the Assured in consequence of such collision.
191   Provided always that this clause shall in no case extend to any sum
192 which the Assured may become liable to pay for or in respect of:-
193 (a) removal or disposal of obstructions, wrecks, cargoes or any
194   other thing whatsoever,
195 (b) any real or personal property or thing whatsoever except
196   other vessels or property on other vessels,
197 (c) pollution or contamination of any real or personal property or
198   thing whatsoever (except other vessels with which the insured
199   Vessel is in collision or property on such other vessels),
200 (d) the cargo or other property on or the engagements of the
201   insured Vessel,
202 (e) loss of life, personal injury or illness.

203   15. Should the Vessel come into collision with or receive salvage
204 services from another vessel belonging wholly or in part to the same
205 Owners or under the same management, the Assured shall have the
206 same rights under this insurance as they would have were the other
207 vessel entirely the property of Owners not interested in the Vessel; but
208 in such cases the liability for the collision or the amount payable for the
209 services rendered shall be referred to a sole arbitrator to be agreed
210 upon between the Underwriters and the Assured.

211   16. This insurance covers loss of or damage to the Vessel directly
212 caused by any governmental authority acting under the powers vested
213 in them to prevent or mitigate a pollution hazard, or threat thereof,
214 resulting directly from the damage to the Vessel for which the
215 Underwriters are liable under this insurance, provided such act of
216

279 respect of a full period of thirty days as the number of days attaching
280 thereto bear to thirty.
281   22. Additional insurances as follows are permitted:
282 (a) DISBURSEMENTS, MANAGERS' COMMISSIONS,
283   PROFITS OR EXCESS OR INCREASED VALUE OF HULL
284   AND MACHINERY AND/OR SIMILAR INTERESTS
285   HOWEVER DESCRIBED, AND FREIGHT (INCLUDING
286   CHARTERED FREIGHT OR ANTICIPATED FREIGHT)
287   INSURED FOR TIME. A sum not exceeding in the
288   aggregate 25 percent of the insured value of the vessel.
289 (b) FREIGHT OR HIRE, UNDER CONTRACTS FOR VOYAGE.
290   A sum not exceeding the gross freight or hire for the
291   current cargo passage and next succeeding cargo passage
292   (such insurance to include, if required, a preliminary and
293   an intermediate ballast passage) plus the charges of
294   insurance. In the case of a voyage charter where payment is
295   made on a time basis, the sum permitted for insurance shall
296   be calculated on the estimated duration of the voyage
297   subject to the limitation of two cargo passages as laid down
298   herein. Any sum insured under this Section shall be reduced
299   as the freight or hire is earned by the gross amount so
300   earned.
301
302 (c) ANTICIPATED FREIGHT IF THE VESSEL SAILS IN
303   BALLAST AND NOT UNDER CHARTER. A sum not
304   exceeding the anticipated gross freight on next cargo
305   passage, such sum to be reasonably estimated on the basis of
306   the current rate of freight at time of insurance, plus the
307   charges of insurance. Provided, however, that no insurance
308   shall be permitted under this Section if any insurance is

governmental authority has not resulted from want of due diligence by the Assured, the Owners or Managers of the Vessel or any of them to prevent or mitigate such hazard or threat, Masters, Officers, Crew or Pilots not to be considered Owners within the meaning of this clause should they hold shares in the Vessel.

17. This insurance also covers loss of or damage to the Vessel caused by strikers, locked out workmen or persons taking part in labour disturbances, riots or civil commotions; also destruction of or damage to the Vessel caused by persons acting maliciously.

18. In the event of accident whereby loss or damage may result in a claim under this insurance, notice shall be given in writing to the Underwriters, where practicable, prior to survey, so that they may appoint their own surveyor if they so desire. The Underwriters shall be entitled to decide the port to which the Vessel shall proceed for docking or repairing (the actual additional expense of the voyage arising from compliance with Underwriters' requirements being refunded to the Assured). The majority of Underwriters (in amount) shall also have a right of veto in connection with the place of repair or repairing firm proposed and may take, or may require to be taken, tenders for the repair of such damage.

In the event of failure to comply with the conditions of this clause pertaining to the repair of the Vessel, 15 percent shall be deducted from the amount of the ascertained claim.

19. If the Vessel is sold or transferred voluntarily or otherwise to new management or chartered on a bare boat basis then, unless the Underwriters agree in writing to continue this insurance, this insurance shall become cancelled from the time of sale or transfer, unless the Vessel has cargo on board and has already sailed from her loading port or is at sea in ballast, in either of which cases such cancellation shall, if required, be suspended until arrival at final port of discharge, if with cargo, or at port of destination if in ballast. A pro rata daily return of net premium shall be made.

For the purposes of this clause, arrest shall not be considered a

effected under Section (b).

(d) TIME CHARTER HIRE OR CHARTER HIRE FOR SERIES OF VOYAGES. A sum not exceeding 50% of the gross hire which is to be earned under the charter in a period not exceeding 18 months. Any sum insured under this Section shall be reduced as the hire is earned under the charter by 50% of the gross amount so earned but where the charter is for a period exceeding 18 months the sum insured need not be reduced while it does not exceed 50% of the gross hire still to be earned under the charter. An insurance under this Section may begin on the signing of the charter.

(e) PREMIUMS. A sum not exceeding the actual premiums of all interests insured for a period not exceeding 12 months (excluding premiums insured under the foregoing Sections but including if required the premium or estimated calls on any Protection and Indemnity or War etc. Risk insurance) reducing pro rata monthly.

(f) RETURNS OF PREMIUM. A sum not exceeding the actual returns which are allowable under any insurance but which would not be recoverable thereunder in the event of a total loss of the Vessel, whether by insured perils or otherwise.

(g) INSURANCE IRRESPECTIVE OF AMOUNT AGAINST:-
(i) Risks excluded by Clause 24 herein; and
(ii) General Average and Salvage Disbursements.

It is a condition precedent to the recovery of any claims hereunder that no insurance on any interests enumerated in the foregoing Sections (a) to (f), inclusive, in excess of the amounts permitted herein and no insurance whatever subject to P.P.I., F.I.A. or other like term, on any interests whatever excepting those enumerated in Section (a), is or shall be effected to operate during the currency of this insurance by or for account of the Assured, Owners, Managers or Mortgagees. Provided always that a breach of this condition precedent shall not afford Underwriters any defense to a claim by a Mortgagee who has accepted this insurance without knowledge of such breach.

23. Should the Vessel at the expiration of this insurance be at sea, or

250   transfer to new management.

251   This clause shall prevail notwithstanding any provision whether written, typed or printed in this insurance inconsistent therewith.

252

253   20. If payment of premium is not made by the Assured within thirty
254 (30) days after attachment of this insurance or, in the event
255 Underwriters shall have agreed to accept deferred payments, if any
256 payment of any premium is not made on the day agreed, this insurance
257 may be cancelled at any time thereafter by Underwriters giving to the
258 Assured named herein, and to third party payee or payees (if any)
259 named in this insurance, five (5) days' notice of such cancellation.
260   Such notice may be given by Underwriters or on their behalf by
261 an authorized Agent or by the Agent or Broker effecting this insurance.
262   Such cancellation shall be without prejudice to the premiums
263 earned and due for the period the insurance was in force.
264   In the event of total loss sustained from any cause occurring prior to cancellation, full annual premium shall be deemed earned.

265   21. Underwriters will return _____ percent (net) for every thirty
266 days of unexpired time if it be mutually agreed to cancel this insurance,
267 but there shall be no cancellation or return of premium in event the
268 Vessel is lost from any cause.
269   At expiration, Underwriters will return _____ percent (net)
270 for every thirty consecutive days the Vessel was laid-up in port out of
271 commission with no cargo on board and not under repair for
272 Underwriters' account.
273   In the event of the Vessel being laid-up in port for a period of
274 thirty consecutive days, a part only of which attaches to this insurance,
275 it is hereby agreed that the laying up period in which either the
276 commencing or ending date of this insurance falls shall be deemed to
277 run from the first day on which the Vessel is laid-up and that on this
278 basis Underwriters shall pay such proportion of the return due in

344 in distress, or at a port of refuge or of call, she shall, provided previous
345 notice be given to the Underwriters, be held covered at a pro rata
346 monthly premium, to her port of destination.

347   24. THIS CLAUSE SHALL BE PARAMOUNT AND SHALL
348 OVERRIDE ANYTHING CONTAINED IN THIS INSURANCE
349 INCONSISTENT THEREWITH.
350   (a) In no case shall this insurance cover loss, damage, liability or
351   expense directly caused by
352   (i) war, civil war, revolution, rebellion, insurrection, or
353   civil strife arising therefrom, or any hostile act by or
354   against a belligerent power
355   (ii) capture, seizure, arrest, restraint or detainment
356   (barratry and piracy excepted) and the consequences
357   thereof or any attempt thereat
358   (iii) derelict mines, torpedoes, bombs or other derelict
359   weapons of war.
360   (b) In no case shall this insurance cover loss, damage, liability or
361   expense arising from
362   (i) the detonation of an explosive
363   (ii) any weapon of war
364   and caused by any terrorist or any person acting from a
365   political motive.
366   (c) In no case shall this insurance cover loss, damage, liability or
367   expense arising from any weapon of war employing atomic
368   or nuclear fission and/or fusion or other like reaction or
369   radioactive force or matter.

369   25. This insurance is subject to Canadian law and usage as to liability
370 for and settlement of any and all claims.

(Association of Marine Underwriters of British Columbia)
5000-9-91

Reprinted with the permission of the Marine Insurance Association of British Columbia.

Appendix F

Canadian (Pacific) Special Fishing Vessel Endorsement

To be attached to Canadian Hulls (Pacific) Clauses — 1991

1. In the event any equipment or apparatus not owned by the Assured but for which the Assured has assumed responsibility is installed on the Vessel, such equipment or apparatus shall be considered part of the insured value of the hull and machinery of the Vessel, unless more specifically insured elsewhere or unless specifically added by endorsement to this insurance. In the event of loss of or damage to such equipment or apparatus if insured hereunder. Underwriters shall not be liable for an amount greater than the Assured's legal responsibility to the owners or lessors of such equipment or apparatus, subject to the conditions of this insurance.

2. The following shall not be considered as part of the hull and machinery of the Vessel:

(a) Bait;
(b) Nets, traps and/or other overside gear used in conjunction therewith:
(c) Aircraft;
(d) Power boats, dories, or skiffs (other than craft used solely for life saving purposes) valued in excess of $5,000, unless specifically agreed and scheduled hereon.

3. Warranted that a survey by a surveyor approved by these Underwriters on the suitability of the Vessel for the herring trade be conducted prior to the Vessel being so employed.

Further, it is warranted that any recommendations of the surveyor be completed by the Assured prior to the employment of the Vessel in the herring trade and/or complied with during the time that the Vessel is so employed.

ASSOCIATION OF MARINE UNDERWRITERS
OF BRITISH COLUMBIA

Appendix G

CANADIAN BOARD OF MARINE UNDERWRITERS
GREAT LAKES HULL CLAUSES
September 1, 1971

To be attached to and form a part of Policy No.

The terms and conditions of the following clauses are to be regarded as substituted for those of the policy form to which they are attached, the latter being hereby waived, except provisions required by law to be inserted in the Policy. All captions are inserted only for purposes of reference and shall not be used to interpret the clauses to which they apply.

ASSURED

1 This Policy insures .... *as attached* ....

2 .... hereinafter referred to as the Assured.

3

4 If claim is made under this Policy by anyone other than the Owner of the Vessel, such person shall not be entitled to recover

5 to a greater extent than would the Owner, had claim been made by the Owner as an Assured named in this Policy.

6 Underwriters waive any right of subrogation against affiliated, subsidiary or interrelated companies of the Assured, provided

7 that such waiver shall not apply in the event of a collision between the Vessel and any vessel owned, demise chartered or other-

8 wise controlled by any of the aforesaid companies, or with respect to any loss, damage or expense against which such companies

9 are insured.

LOSS PAYEE

10 Loss, if any, (excepting claims required to be paid to others under the Collision Liability clause), payable to .... *as attached* ....

11 .... or order.

12

VESSEL

13 The Subject Matter of this insurance is the Vessel called the .... *as attached* ....

14 or by whatsoever name or names the said Vessel is or shall be called, which for purposes of this insurance shall consist of and be

15 limited to her hull, launches, lifeboats, rafts, furniture, bunkers, stores, supplies, tackle, fittings, equipment, apparatus, machinery,

16 boilers, refrigerating machinery, insulation, motor generators and other electrical machinery.

17 In the event any such equipment or apparatus not owned by the Assured is installed for use on board the Vessel and the

18 Assured has assumed responsibility therefor, it shall also be considered part of the Subject Matter and the aggregate value thereof

19 shall be included in the Agreed Value.

20 Notwithstanding the foregoing, cargo containers, barges and lighters shall not be considered a part of the Subject Matter

21 of this insurance.

DURATION OF RISK

22   From the.................... day of........................ 19........, ... *as attached*..............C.S.T.

23   to the.................... day of........................ 19........, ... *as attached*..............C.S.T.

24   In the event of payment by the Underwriters for Total Loss of the Vessel this Policy shall thereupon automatically terminate.

AGREED VALUE

25   The Vessel, for so much as concerns the Assured, by agreement between the Assured and the Underwriters in this Policy, is

26   and shall be valued at .... *as attached*.................... Dollars.

27   **EASTERN LIMIT OF NAVIGATION (line 76)**

     AMOUNT INSURED HEREUNDER

28   .... *as attached*.................... Dollars.

DEDUCTIBLE

29   Notwithstanding anything in this Policy to the contrary, there shall be deducted from the aggregate of all claims (including

30   claims under the Collision Liability clause) arising out of each separate accident, the sum of $ *as attached* ...., unless the accident

31   results in a Total Loss or Constructive Total Loss of the Vessel in which case this clause shall not apply. A recovery from other

32   interests, however, shall not operate to exclude claims under this Policy provided the aggregate of such claims arising out of one

33   separate accident if unreduced by such recovery exceeds that sum. For the purpose of this clause each accident shall be treated

34   separately, but it is agreed that (a) a sequence of damages arising from the same accident shall be treated as due to that accident

35   and (b) all heavy weather damage which occurs during a single sea passage between two successive ports shall be treated as

36   though due to one accident. Also there shall be no deductible average applied to claims arising under the Sue and Labor Clause,

37   nor claims for salvage expenses, or general average.

38   PROVIDED, however, that claims arising from damage by ice, (excepting claim for Total or Constructive Total Loss), shall be

39   subject to a deductible of $50,000. or 10% of the insured value of the entire Vessel as stated herein, whichever is less, in respect of

40   each accident as defined herein, but in no case less than the deductible stated in line 30 above. Also there shall be no deductible

41   average applied to claims arising under the Sue and Labor Clause, nor claims for salvage expenses, or general average.

42   In the event of a claim for loss of or damage to any boiler, shaft, machinery or associated equipment, arising from any of the

43   causes enumerated in the ADDITIONAL PERILS (INCHMAREE) clause, lines 106 to 115 hereunder, attributable in part or in whole

44   to negligence of Master Officers or Crew and recoverable under this insurance only by reason of the said Clause, then the Assured

45   shall, in addition to the deductible, also bear in respect of each accident or occurrence an amount equal to 10% of the balance

46   of such claim, but not to exceed a further $50,000. This clause shall not apply to a claim for total or constructive total loss of the

47   Vessel.

PREMIUM

48

49 The Underwriters to be paid in consideration of this insurance.................................*as attached*.................................

50 ....Dollars being at the rate of .*as attached* ....per cent. ... *as attached* .... payable in cash, and in case the said premium shall not be paid to these

51 Underwriters **within** sixty days after the date of attachment of navigating insurance in force under this Policy, or before November

52 first next succeeding the date of attachment if there be less than sixty days between the date of attachment and such November

53 first, this Policy shall automatically terminate upon such sixtieth day, at noon, or upon November first at noon, as the case may be.

54 Such proportional part of the premium, however, as shall have been earned up to the time of such termination shall thereupon

55 remain and become immediately due and payable.

56 Additional premiums, if any, shall be due at commencement of the risk for which such additional premiums have been

57 assessed .

58 Full premium (Port Risk, Navigating for the entire Season of Navigation and any additional premium due) shall be considered

59 earned in the event the Vessel becomes a Total Loss during the term of this Policy.

60 UNDERWRITER'S SURVEYOR

RETURNS OF PREMIUM

61 Port Risk and/or Navigating premium returnable as follows:

62 Pro rata daily net in the event of termination under the Change of Ownership clause;

63 Pro rata monthly net for each uncommenced month if it be mutually agreed to cancel this Policy;

64 Pro rata daily net of the Navigating rate for each period of 15 consecutive days between March 31st–December 15th,

65 Midnight C.S.T. that the Vessel may be laid up in port not under repair and for which Navigating premium has been paid;

66 provided always that:

67   (a) a Total Loss of the Vessel has not occurred during the currency of this Policy;

68   (b) in no case shall a return for lay-up be allowed when the Vessel is lying in exposed or unprotected waters or in any

69   location not approved by the Underwriters;

70   (c) in no case shall a return be allowed when the Vessel is used for lightering purposes.

71 If, for account of the Assured, the Vessel is laid up for a period of 15 consecutive days, a part only of which attaches under

72 this Policy, the Underwriters shall pay such proportion of the return due in respect of a full period of 15 days as the number of

73 days attaching hereto bears to 15. Should the lay up period exceed 15 consecutive days, the Assured shall have the option to elect

    the period of 15 consecutive days for which a return is recoverable.

TRADING WARRANTY AND SEASON OF NAVIGATION

75 Warranted that the vessel shall be confined to the waters, bays, harbors, rivers, canals and other tributaries of the Great Lakes,
76 not east of the point specified in line 27 above and shall engage in navigation only between March 31st, Midnight and December
77 15th, Midnight, C.S.T. (referred to in this Policy as the Season of Navigation).
78 Navigation prior to March 31st, Midnight, C.S.T. and subsequent to December 15th, Midnight, C.S.T. is held covered provided
79 (a) prompt notice is given to the Underwriters (b) any amended terms of cover and any additional premium required by the Under
80 writers are agreed to by the Assured and (c) prior approval of each sailing is obtained from Underwriter's Surveyor.
81 The Vessel may discharge inward cargo, take in outward cargo, retain cargo on board, and move in port during the period she is
82 in Winter lay-up. For purposes of this provision such of the following places as are designated by a single numeral shall be deemed
83 one port: (1) Duluth -- Superior (2) Detroit -- Dearborn -- River Rouge -- Ecorse -- Wyandotte -- Windsor (3) Kingston --
84 Portsmouth.
85 Permission is hereby granted for the Vessel to carry grain without shifting boards on the Great Lakes. This privilege also
86 applies to navigation on the St. Lawrence River as far as permitted hereunder, but not East of 65° West Longitude.

WINTER MOORINGS

87 Warranted that the Vessel be properly moored in a safe place and under conditions satisfactory to the Underwriter's Surveyor
88 during the period the Vessel is in Winter lay-up.

ADVENTURE

89 Beginning the adventure upon the Vessel, as above, and so shall continue and endure, subject to the terms and conditions of
90 this Policy, as employment may offer, in port or at sea, in docks and graving docks, and on ways, gridirons and pontoons, at all
91 times, in all places, and on all occasions, services and trades; with leave to sail or navigate with or without pilots, to go on trial
92 trips and to assist and tow vessels or craft in distress, but the Vessel may not be towed, except as is customary or when in need of
93 assistance, nor shall the Vessel render assistance or undertake towage or salvage services under contract previously arranged by
94 the Assured, the Owners, the Managers or the Charterers of the Vessel.
95 The Vessel is held covered in case of any breach of conditions as to towage or salvage activities, provided (a) notice is given to
96 the Underwriters immediately following receipt of knowledge thereof by the Assured, and (b) any amended terms of cover and any
97 additional premium required by the Underwriters are agreed to by the Assured.

PERILS

98 Touching the Adventures and Perils which the Underwriters are contented to bear and take upon themselves, they are of the
99 Seas, Men-of-War, Fire, Lightning, Earthquake, Enemies, Pirates, Rovers, Assailing Thieves, Jettisons, Letters of Mart and Counter-
100 Mart, Surprisals, Takings at Sea, Arrests, Restraints and Detainments of all Kings, Princes and Peoples, of what nation, condition
101 or quality soever, Barratry of the Master and Mariners and of all other like Perils, Losses and Misfortunes that have or shall come
102 to the Hurt, Detriment or Damage of the Vessel, or any part thereof, excepting, however, such of the foregoing perils as may be
103 excluded by provisions elsewhere in the Policy or by endorsement thereon.

ADDITIONAL PERILS (INCHMAREE)

104 Subject to the conditions of this Policy, this insurance also covers loss of or damage to the Vessel directly caused by the
following:

105 Accidents in loading, discharging or handling cargo, or in bunkering;
106 Accidents in going on or off, or while on drydocks, graving docks, ways, gridirons or pontoons;
107 Explosions on shipboard or elsewhere;
108 Breakdown of motor generators or other electrical machinery and electrical connections thereto, bursting of boilers,
109 breakage of shafts, or any latent defect in the machinery or hull, (excluding the cost and expense of replacing or repairing
110 the defective part);
111 Breakdown of or accidents to nuclear installations or reactors not on board the insured Vessel;
112 Contact with aircraft, rockets or similar missiles, or with any land conveyance;
113 Negligence of Charterers and/or Repairers, provided such Charterers and/or Repairers are not an Assured hereunder;
114 Negligence of Master, Officers, Crew or Pilots;
115 provided such loss or damage has not resulted from want of due diligence by the Assured, the Owners or Managers of the Vessel,
116 or any of them. Masters, Officers, Crew or Pilots are not to be considered Owners within the meaning of this clause should they
117 hold shares in the Vessel.
118

CLAIMS (GENERAL PROVISIONS)

119 In the event of any accident or occurrence which could give rise to a claim under this Policy, prompt notice thereof shall be
120 given to the Underwriters, and:
121 (a) where practicable, the Underwriters shall be advised prior to survey, so that they may appoint their own surveyor, if they
122 so desire;
123 (b))the Underwriters shall be entitled to decide where the Vessel shall proceed for docking and/or repair (allowance to be
124 made to the Assured for the actual additional expense of the voyage arising from compliance with the Underwriters'
125 requirement);
126 (c) the Underwriters shall have the right of veto in connection with any repair firm proposed;
127 (d) the Underwriters may take tenders or may require tenders to be taken for the repair of the Vessel, in which event, upon
128 acceptance of a tender with the approval of the Underwriters, an allowance shall be made at the rate of 30 per cent. per
129 annum on the amount insured, for each day or pro rata for part of a day, for time lost between the issuance of invitations
130 to tender and the acceptance of a tender, to the extent that such time is lost solely as the result of tenders having been
131 taken and provided the tender is accepted without delay after receipt of the Underwriters' approval.
132 Due credit shall be given against the allowances in (b) and (d) above for any amount recovered:
133 (1) in respect of fuel, stores, and wages and maintenance of the Master, Officers and Crew members allowed in General or
134 Particular Average;

in respect of damages for detention and/or loss of profit and/or running expenses;

      ... covered by the allowances or any part thereof.

138   No claim shall be allowed in Particular Average for wages and maintenance of the Master, Officers and Crew, except when the
139 Crew are employed in lieu of shore or other labour with the view to minimizing expense or when incurred solely for the necessary
140 removal of the vessel from one port to another for average repairs or for trial trips to test average repairs, in which cases wages and maintenance
140 will be allowed only while the vessel is under way.

141   General and Particular Average shall be payable without deduction, new for old.
142   Claims hereunder to be adjusted in accordance with the Rules of Practice for the Great Lakes of the Association of Average
143 Adjusters of Canada so far as they may be applicable.

144   The expense of sighting the bottom after stranding shall be paid, if reasonably incurred especially for that purpose, even if
145 no damage be found.
146   If repairs have not been executed within 15 months from the date of the accident, Underwriters are not to be liable for any
147 increased cost of repairs which may be incurred by reason of such repairs being executed after 15 months from the date of the
148 accident.

149   No claim shall in any case be allowed in respect of scraping or painting the Vessel's bottom.
150   In the event of failure to comply with the conditions of this clause 15 per cent. shall be deducted from the amount of the
151 ascertained claim.

152   In the event of loss or damage to equipment or apparatus as covered hereunder not owned by the Assured but installed for use on
153 board the Vessel and for which the Assured has assumed responsibility, claim shall not exceed (1) the amount the Underwriters
154 would pay if the Assured were owner of such equipment or apparatus, or (2) the contractual responsibility assumed by the Assured
155 to the owners or lessors thereof, whichever shall be less.

156   It is understood and agreed that the fees of the Assured, his Superintendent, and the Assured's Officers, Manager and/or other
157 servants are not collectible under this Policy, except that in the event of loss or damage, where the Assured chooses not to employ
158 an Owner's surveyor and uses his own Marine Superintendent, a reasonable fee will be allowed.

GENERAL AVERAGE AND SALVAGE

159   General Average and Salvage shall be payable as provided in the contract of affreightment, or failing such provision or there
160 be no contract of affreightment payable in accordance with the Rules of Practice for the Great Lakes of the Association of Average Adjusters of
161 Canada. Provided always that when an adjustment according to the laws and usages of the port of destination is
162 properly demanded by the owners of the cargo, General Average shall be paid accordingly.

163   In the event of salvage, towage or other assistance being rendered to the Vessel by any vessel belonging in part or in whole to
164 the same Owners or Charterers, the value of such services (without regard to the common ownership or control of the vessels) shall
165 be ascertained by arbitration in the manner provided for under the Collision Liability clause in this Policy, and the amount so
166 awarded so far as applicable to the interest hereby insured shall constitute a charge under this Policy.

167   When the contributory value of the Vessel is greater than the Agreed Value herein, the liability of the Underwriters for General
168 Average contribution (except in respect to amounts made good to the Vessel), or Salvage, shall not exceed that proportion of the
169 total contribution due from the Vessel which the amount insured hereunder bears to the contributory value; and if, because of
170 damage for which the Underwriters are liable as Particular Average, the value of the Vessel has been reduced for the purpose of contribution, the
171 amount of such Particular Average damage recoverable under this Policy shall first be deducted from the amount

172 insured hereunder, and the Underwriters shall then be liable only for the proportion which such net amount bears to the
173 contributory value.

TOTAL LOSS

174 There shall be no recovery for a constructive Total Loss hereunder unless the expense of recovering and repairing the Vessel
175 shall exceed the Agreed Value. In making this determination, only expenses incurred by reason of a single accident or a sequence
176 of damages arising from the same accident shall be taken into account.
177 In ascertaining whether the Vessel is a constructive Total Loss the Agreed Value shall be taken as the repaired value and
178 nothing in respect of the damaged or break-up value of the Vessel or wreck shall be taken into account.
179 In the event of Total Loss (actual or constructive), no claim to be made by the Underwriters for freight, whether notice of
180 abandonment has been given or not.
181 In no case shall the Underwriters be liable for unrepaired damage in addition to a subsequent Total Loss sustained during the
182 period covered by this Policy.

SUE AND LABOR

183 And in case of any Loss or Misfortune, it shall be lawful and necessary for the Assured, their Factors, Servants and Assigns, to
184 sue, labor and travel for, in, and about the defense, safeguard and recovery of the Vessel, or any part thereof, without prejudice
185 this insurance, to the charges whereof the Underwriters will contribute their proportion as provided below. And it is expressly
186 declared and agreed that no acts of the Underwriters or Assured in recovering, saving or preserving the Vessel shall be considered
187 as a waiver or acceptance of abandonment.
188 In the event of expenditure under the Sue and Labor clause, the Underwriters shall pay the proportion of such expenses that
189 the amount insured hereunder bears to the Agreed Value, or that the amount insured hereunder, less loss and/or damage payable
190 under this Policy, bears to the actual value of the salved property; whichever proportion shall be less.
191 If claim for Total Loss is admitted under this Policy and sue and labor expenses have been reasonably incurred in excess of
192 any proceeds realized or value recovered, the amount payable under this Policy will be the proportion of such excess that the
193 amount insured hereunder (without deduction for loss or damage) bears to the Agreed Value or to the sound value of the Vessel at
194 the time of the accident, whichever value was greater. The foregoing shall also apply to expenses reasonably incurred in salving or attempting to
195 salve the Vessel and other property to the extent that such expenses shall be regarded as having been incurred in
196 respect of the Vessel.

COLLISION LIABILITY

And it is further agreed that:

(a) if the Vessel shall come into collision with any other ship or vessel, and the Assured or the Surety in consequence of the Vessel being at fault shall become liable to pay and shall pay by way of damages to any other person or persons any sum or sums in respect of such collision, the Underwriters will pay the Assured or the Surety, whichever shall have paid, such proportion of such sum or sums so paid as their respective subscriptions hereto bear to the Agreed Value, provided always that their liability in respect to any one such collision shall not exceed their proportionate part of the Agreed Value;

(b) in cases where, with the consent in writing of a majority (in amount) of Hull Underwriters, the liability of the Vessel has been contested, or proceedings have been taken to limit liability, the Underwriters will also pay a like proportion of the costs which the Assured shall thereby incur or be compelled to pay.

When both vessels are to blame, then, unless the liability of the owners or charterers of one or both such vessels becomes limited by law, claims under the Collision Liability clause shall be settled on the principle of Cross-Liabilities as if the owners or charterers of each vessel had been compelled to pay to the owners or charterers of the other vessel such one-half or other proportion of the latter's damages as may have been properly allowed in ascertaining the balance or sum payable by or to the Assured in consequence of such collision.

The principles involved in this clause shall apply to the case where both vessels are the property, in part or in whole, of the same owners or charterers, all questions of responsibility and amount of liability as between the two vessels being left to the decision of a single Arbitrator, if the parties can agree upon a single Arbitrator, or failing such agreement, to the decision of Arbitrators, one to be appointed by the Assured and one to be appointed by the majority (in amount) of Hull Underwriters interested; the two Arbitrators chosen to choose a third Arbitrator before entering upon the reference, and the decision of such single Arbitrator, or of any two of such three Arbitrators, appointed as above, to be final and binding.

Provided always that this clause or any other provision of this policy shall in no case extend to any sum which the Assured or the Surety may become liable to pay or shall pay in consequence of, or with respect to:

(a) removal or disposal of obstructions, wrecks, cargoes, or any other thing whatsoever under statutory powers or otherwise pursuant to law;

(b) injury to real or personal property of every description;

(c) the discharge, spillage, emission or leakage of oil, petroleum products, chemicals or other substances of any kind or description whatsoever;

(d) cargo or other property on or the engagements of the Vessel;

(e) loss of life, personal injury or illness.

Provided further that exclusions (b) and (c) above shall not apply to injury to other vessels or property thereon except to the extent that such injury arises out of any action taken to avoid, minimize or remove any discharge, spillage, emission or leakage described in (c).

CHANGE OF OWNERSHIP

229 In the event of any change, voluntary or otherwise, in the ownership or flag of the Vessel, or if the Vessel be placed under new
230 management, or be chartered on a bareboat basis or requisitioned on that basis, or if the Classification Society of the Vessel or her
231 class therein be changed, cancelled or withdrawn, then, unless the Underwriters agree thereto in writing, this Policy shall
232 automatically terminate at the time of such change of ownership, flag, management, charter, requisition or classification; provided, however, that:
233   (a) if the Vessel has cargo on board and has already sailed from her loading port, or is at sea in ballast, such automatic
234   termination shall, if required, be deferred until arrival at final port of discharge if with cargo, or at port of destination if in
235   ballast;
236   (b) in the event of an involuntary temporary transfer by requisition or otherwise, without the prior execution of a written
237   agreement by the Assured, such automatic termination shall occur fifteen days after such transfer.
238 This insurance shall not inure to the benefit of any transferee or charterer of the Vessel and, if a loss payable hereunder should occur
239 between the time of change or transfer and any deferred automatic termination, the Underwriters shall be subrogated
240 to all of the rights of the Assured against the transferee or charterer in respect of all or part of such loss as is recoverable from the transferee or
241 charterer, and in the proportion which the amount insured hereunder bears to the Agreed Value.
242 The term "new management" as used above refers only to the transfer of the management of the Vessel from one firm or
243 corporation to another, and it shall not apply to any internal changes within the offices of the Assured.

ADDITIONAL INSURANCES

244 It is a condition of this Policy that no additional insurance against the risk of Total Loss of the Vessel shall be effected to
245 operate during the currency of this Policy by or for account of the Assured, Owners, Managers, Operators or Mortgagees except
246 on the interests and up to the amounts enumerated in the following Sections (a) to (g), inclusive, and no such insurance shall be
247 subject to P.P.I., F.I.A. or other like term on any interests whatever excepting those enumerated in Section (a): provided always and
248 notwithstanding the limitation on recovery in the Assured clause a breach of this condition shall not afford the Underwriters any
249 defense to a claim by a Mortgagee who has accepted this Policy without knowledge of such breach:
250   (a) DISBURSEMENTS, MANAGERS' COMMISSIONS, PROFITS OR EXCESS OR INCREASED VALUE OF HULL AND
251   MACHINERY AND/OR SIMILAR INTERESTS HOWEVER DESCRIBED, AND FREIGHT (INCLUDING CHARTERED FREIGHT
252   OR ANTICIPATED FREIGHT) INSURED FOR TIME. An amount not exceeding in the aggregate 25% of the Agreed Value.
253   (b) FREIGHT OR HIRE, UNDER CONTRACTS FOR VOYAGE. An amount not exceeding the gross freight or hire for the current
254   cargo passage and next succeeding cargo passage (such insurance to include, if required, a preliminary and an inter-
255   mediate ballast passage) plus the charges of insurance. In the case of a voyage charter where payment is made on a time
256   basis, the amount shall be calculated on the estimated duration of the voyage, subject to the limitation of two cargo
257   passages as laid down herein. Any amount permitted under this Section shall be reduced, as the freight or hire is earned
258   by the gross amount so earned. Any freight or hire to be earned under the form of Charters described in (d) below shall
259   not be permitted under this Section (b) if any part thereof is insured as permitted under said Section (d).

(c) ANTICIPATED FREIGHT IF THE VESSEL SAILS IN BALLAST AND NOT UNDER CHARTER. An amount not exceeding the ..... anticipated gross freight on next cargo passage, such amount to be reasonaby estimated on the basis of the current rate of freight at time of insurance, plus the charges of insurance. Provided, however, that no insurance shall be permitted by this Section if any insurance is effected as permitted under Section (b).

(d) TIME CHARTER HIRE OR CHARTER HIRE FOR SERIES OF VOYAGES. An amount not exceeding 50% of the gross hire which is to be earned under the charter in a period not exceeding 18 months. Any amount permitted under this Section shall be reduced as the hire is earned under the charter by 50% of the gross amount so earned but, where the charter is for a period exceeding 18 months, the amount insured need not be reduced while it does not exceed 50% of the gross hire still to be earned under the charter. An insurance permitted by this Section may begin on the signing of the charter.

(e) PREMIUMS. An amount not exceeding the actual premiums of all interests insured for a period not exceeding 12 months (excluding premiums insured as permitted under the foregoing Sections but including, if required, the estimated calls or premium on any Protection and Indemnity or War Risks and Strikes Insurance) reducing pro rata monthly.

(f) RETURNS OF PREMIUM. An amount not exceeding the actual returns which are recoverable subject to "and arrival" or equivalent provision under any policy of insurance.

(g) INSURANCE IRRESPECTIVE OF AMOUNT AGAINST: -- Risks excluded by the War, Strikes and Related Exclusions clause; risks enumerated in the American Institute War Risks and Strikes Clauses; and General Average and Salvage Disbursements.

WAR STRIKES AND RELATED EXCLUSIONS

The following conditions shall be paramount and shall supersede end nullify any contrary provisions of the Policy.

This Policy does not cover any loss, damage or expense caused by, resulting from, or incurred as a consequence of:

(a) Capture, seizure, arrest, restraint or detainment, or any attempt thereat; or

(b) Any taking of the Vessel, by requisition or otherwise, whether in time of peace or war and whether lawful or otherwise; or

(c) Any mine, bomb or torpedo not carried as cargo on board the Vessel; or

(d) Any weapon of war employing atomic or nuclear fission and/or fusion or other like reaction or radioactive force or matter; or

(e) Civil war, revolution, rebellion, insurrection, or civil strife arising therefrom, or piracy; or

(f) Strikes, lockouts, political or labor disturbances, civil commotions, riots, martial law, military or usurped power, malicious acts or vandalism; or

(g) Hostilities or warlike operations (whether there be a declaration of war or not) but this subparagraph (g) not to exclude collision or contact with aircraft, rockets or similar missiles, or with any fixed or floating object, or stranding, heavy weather, fire or explosion unless caused directly by a hostile act by or against a belligerent power which act is independent of the nature of the voyage or service which the Vessel concerned or, in the case of a collision, any other vessel involved therein, is performing. As used herein, "power" includes any authority maintaining naval, military or air forces in association with a power.

If war risks or other risks excluded by this clause are hereafter insured by endorsement on this Policy, such endorsement shall supersede the above conditions only to the extent that the terms of such endorsement are inconsistent therewith and only while such endorsement remains in force.

Appendix H

CANADIAN (Pacific) TOTAL LOSS AND EXCESS LIABILITIES CLAUSES

December 31, 1991

1. Touching the Adventures and Perils which we, the Underwriters, are contented to bear and take upon us, they are of the Seas, Men-of-War, Fire, Enemies, Pirates, Rovers, Thieves, Jettisons, Letters of Mart and Counter-Mart, Surprisals, Takings at Sea, Arrests, Restraints and Detainments of all Kings, Princes and Peoples, of what nation, condition or quality soever, Barratry of the Master and Mariners and of all other like Perils, Losses and Misfortunes that have or shall come to the Hurt, Detriment or Damage of the subject matter insured (hereafter the "Vessel") or any part thereof; excepting, however, such of the foregoing Perils as may be excluded by provisions elsewhere in these clauses or by endorsement.

2. It is the duty of the Assured, their servants, agents or assigns, in case of loss or misfortune to take such measures as may be reasonable for the purpose of averting or minimising a loss which would be recoverable under this insurance. For the purpose of this insurance, such measures shall be designated as Sue and Labour.

   The reasonable charges therefor will be reimbursed by Underwriters in accordance with their rateable proportion as provided for herein.

   It is expressly agreed that no acts of Underwriters or the Assured in recovering, saving or preserving the Vessel shall be considered as either a waiver or acceptance of abandonment or otherwise prejudice the rights of either party.

3. THIS INSURANCE COVERS ONLY ACTUAL OR CONSTRUCTIVE TOTAL LOSS OF THE VESSEL:
   (a) Caused by the perils enumerated in clause 1 hereof.
   (b) Directly caused by:
      (i) Accidents in loading, discharging or shifting cargo or fuel
          Explosions on shipboard or elsewhere
          Breakdown of or accident to nuclear installations or reactors on shipboard or elsewhere
          Bursting of boilers, breakage of shafts or any latent defect in the

and machinery by reason of the difference between the insured value of the Vessel as stated therein and the value of the Vessel adopted for the purpose of ascertaining the amount recoverable under the insurances on hull and machinery, the liability under this insurance being for such proportion of the amount not recoverable as the amount insured hereunder bears to the said difference or to the total sum insured against excess liabilities if it exceeds such difference.

(c) Collision Liability not recoverable in full under the Running Down and Sister Ship Clauses in the insurances on hull and machinery by reason of such liability exceeding the insured value of the Vessel as stated therein, in which case the amount recoverable under this insurance shall be such proportion of the difference so arising as the amount insured hereunder bears to the total sum insured against excess liabilities.

Underwriters' liability under clauses 3 and 4(a), (b) and (c), separately, in respect of any one claim, shall not exceed the amount insured hereunder.

5. This insurance excludes claims due to or resulting from ice and/or freezing howsoever caused on inland waters above ocean tidal influence.

6. The Vessel is covered subject to the provisions of this insurance at all times and has leave to sail or navigate with or without pilots, to go on trial trips and to assist and tow vessels or craft in distress, but it is warranted that the Vessel shall not otherwise tow or be towed, except as is customary or to the first safe port or place when in need of assistance.

7. The Vessel is covered in case of any breach of warranty as to cargo, employment, towage, salvage services or date of sailing, provided notice be given to the Underwriters immediately after receipt of advices and any amended terms of cover and any additional premium required by them be agreed.

8. Should the Vessel at the expiration of this insurance be at sea, or in distress, or at

machinery or hull

Negligence of Master, Charterers other than an Assured, Officers, Crew or Pilots

Negligence of repairers provided such repairers are not Assured(s) hereunder, but this exclusion shall not apply to loss or damage resulting from the operation by the Assured of a commercial repair division or facility

(ii) Contact with aircraft or similar objects, or objects falling therefrom

Contact with any land conveyance, dock or harbour equipment or installation

Earthquake, volcanic eruption or lightning

Provided such loss or damage has not resulted from want of due diligence by the Assured, Owners or Managers.

(c) Masters, Officers, Crew or Pilots not to be considered as part Owners within the meaning of this Clause 3(b) should they hold shares in the Vessel.

Directly caused by any governmental authority acting under the powers vested in them to prevent or mitigate a pollution hazard, or threat thereof, resulting directly from the damage to the Vessel for which the Underwriters are liable under this insurance, provided such act of governmental authority has not resulted from want of due diligence by the Assured, the Owners or Managers of the Vessel or any of them to prevent or mitigate such hazard or threat. Masters, Officers, Crew or Pilots not to be considered Owners within the meaning of this Clause 3(c) should they hold shares in the Vessel.

(d) Caused by strikers, locked-out workmen or persons taking part in labour disturbances, riots or civil commotions; also destruction of or damage to the Vessel caused by persons acting maliciously.

In ascertaining whether the Vessel is a constructive total loss the insured value in the insurances on hull and machinery shall be taken as the repaired value and nothing in respect of the damaged or break-up value of the Vessel or wreck shall be taken into account.

No claim for constructive total loss based upon the cost of recovery and/or repair of the Vessel shall be recoverable hereunder unless such cost would exceed the insured value in the insurances on hull and machinery. In making this determination, only the costs relating to a single accident or sequence of damages arising from the same accident shall be taken into account.

Should the Vessel be a constructive total loss but the claim on the insurances on hull and machinery be settled as a claim for partial loss, no payment shall be due under this clause.

a port of refuge or of call, she shall, provided previous notice be given to the Underwriters, be held covered at a pro rata monthly premium, to her port of destination.

9. If the Vessel is sold or transferred voluntarily or otherwise to new management or chartered on a bare boat basis then, unless the Underwriters agree in writing to continue this insurance, this insurance shall become cancelled from the time of sale or transfer, unless the Vessel has cargo on board and has already sailed from her loading port or is at sea in ballast, in either of which cases such cancellation shall, if required, be suspended until arrival at final port of discharge, if with cargo, or at port of destination if in ballast. A pro rata daily return of net premium shall be made.

For the purposes of this clause, arrest shall not be considered a transfer to new management.

This clause shall prevail notwithstanding any provision whether written, typed or printed in this insurance inconsistent therewith.

10. If payment of premium is not made by the Assured within thirty (30) days after attachment of this insurance or, in the event Underwriters shall have agreed to accept deferred payments, if any payment of any premium is not made on the day agreed, this insurance may be cancelled at any time thereafter by Underwriters giving to the Assured named herein, and to third party payee or payees (if any) named in this insurance five (5) days' notice of such cancellation.

Such notice may be given by Underwriters or on their behalf by an authorized Agent or by the Agent or Broker effecting this insurance.

Such cancellation shall be without prejudice to the premiums earned and due for the period the insurance was in force.

In the event of total loss sustained from any cause occurring prior to cancellation full annual premium shall be deemed earned.

11. Underwriters will return _____ percent (net) for every thirty days of unexpired time if it be mutually agreed to cancel this insurance, but there shall be no cancellation or return of premium if the Vessel is lost from any cause.

At expiration, Underwriters will return _____ percent (net) for every thirty consecutive days the Vessel was laid up in port out of commission with no cargo on board and not under repair for Underwriters account.

In the event of the Vessel being laid up in port for a period of thirty consecutive days, a part only of which attaches to this insurance, it is hereby agreed that the laying up period in which either the commencing or ending date of this insurance falls shall be deemed to run from the first day on which the Vessel is laid up and that on this basis Underwriters shall pay such proportion of the return due in respect of a full period of thirty days as the number of days attaching thereto bear to thirty.

67 Provided that the Valuation Clause, lines 55/58 above, or a clause having a
68 similar effect, is contained in the insurances on hull and machinery, the settlement of a
69 claim for constructive total loss thereunder shall be accepted as proof of the constructive
70 total loss of the Vessel and in the event of a claim for total loss or constructive total loss
71 being settled on the insurances on hull and machinery as a compromised total loss the
72 amount payable hereunder shall be the same percentage of the sum insured as is paid on
73 the said insurances.
74 4. This insurance also covers:
75 (a) General Average, Salvage and Salvage Charges not recoverable in full
76 under the insurances on hull and machinery by reason of the difference
77 between the insured value of the Vessel as stated therein (or any reduced
78 value arising from the deduction therefrom in process of adjustment of
79 any claim which law or practice or the terms of the insurances covering hull
80 and machinery may have required) and the value of the Vessel adopted for
81 the purpose of contribution to general average, salvage or salvage charges,
82 the liability under this insurance being for such proportion of the amount not
83 recoverable as the amount insured hereunder bears to the said difference or
84 to the total sum insured against excess liabilities if it exceeds such difference.
85 (b) Sue and Labour Charges not recoverable in full under the insurances on hull

150 12. THIS CLAUSE SHALL BE PARAMOUNT AND SHALL OVERRIDE
151 ANYTHING CONTAINED IN THIS INSURANCE INCONSISTENT THEREWITH:
152 (a) In no case shall this insurance cover loss, damage, liability or expense
153 directly caused by
154 (i) war, civil war, revolution, rebellion, insurrection, or civil strife arising
155 therefrom, or any hostile act by or against a belligerent power
156 (ii) capture, seizure, arrest, restraint or detainment (barratry and piracy
157 excepted) and the consequences thereof or any attempt thereat
158 (iii) derelict mines, torpedoes, bombs or other derelict weapons of war.
159 (b) In no case shall this insurance cover loss, damage, liability or expense
160 arising from
161 (i) the detonation of an explosive
162 (ii) any weapon of war
163 and caused by any terrorist or any person acting from a political motive.
164 (c) In no case shall this insurance cover loss damage liability or expense
165 arising from any weapon of war employing atomic or nuclear fission and/or
166 fusion or other like reaction or radioactive force or matter.
167 13. This Insurance is subject to Canadian law and usage as to liability for and
settlement of any and all claims.

Reprinted with the permission of the Marine Insurance Association of British Columbia.

Appendix I

BRITISH COLUMBIA BUILDERS' RISKS CLAUSES (1989)

GENERAL SECTION

1/1/89

1.   This policy contains warranties and general conditions none of which are to be interpreted as suspensive conditions, The Underwriters have agreed to accept the risk of insuring the Vessel on the condition precedent that the Assured will comply strictly and literally with these warranties and conditions. If the Assured breaches any of these warranties or conditions, the Underwriters at their option will not pay any claim arising thereafter, regardless of whether or not such breach is causative or in any way connected to such claim.

2.   ASSURED

This policy insures _____

_____

(Herein referred to as the "Assured") for account of themselves and/or any owner or owners of the Vessel as their interest may appear at the time of the happening of a loss

3.   SUBJECT MATTER

The subject matter of this insurance (hereinafter referred to as the Vessel) is the Hull, Engines, Boilers, Machinery, Appurtenances, etc. (including plans, patterns, moulds, etc.) Boats and other Furniture and Fixtures and all material belonging to and/or allocated to _____

under construction at _____

This policy does not cover any materials, furniture and equipment for the Vessel furnished by the owner, the cost of which is not included in the construction contract price, but permission is granted to effect additional

In the event of such delivery not being effected by _____

this policy may be extended at _____ monthly additional premium provided notice of the extension be given to Underwriters prior to _____

In no case shall this insurance extend beyond delivery of the vessel.

10.   SUBROGATION

It is agreed that upon payment of any loss, damage, or expense the Underwriters are to be subrogated to all the rights of the Assured to the extent of such payment, and the Assured will cooperate fully in all subrogated proceedings brought by Underwriters.

Unless the Assured and Underwriters shall have otherwise agreed in writing, the Assured and Underwriters shall participate jointly in recoveries, with net recoveries (excluding interest comprised therein) made against any claim **pro rated** between the respective interests of the Assured and Underwriters.

Interest comprised in net recoveries shall be apportioned between the Assured and the Underwriters, taking into account the sums paid by Underwriters and the dates when such payments were made.

11.   ASSIGNMENT

It is agreed that no assignment of any interest in this policy or in any moneys which may be or become payable thereunder is to be binding on or recognized by the Underwriters unless a dated notice of such assignment or interest signed by the Assured and (in the case of subsequent assignment) by the assignor be endorsed on this policy and the policy with such endorsement being produced before payment of any claim or return of premium thereunder, but nothing in

insurance covering the value of such interests.

4. PREMIUM

Underwriters to be paid in consideration of this insurance _____ Dollars being at the rate of _____ per cent.

5. CHANGE OF INTEREST

It is agreed that any changes of interest in the vessel hereby insured shall not affect the validity of this policy.

6. AMOUNT INSURED

In the event of loss prior to completion of the vessel, Underwriters liability hereunder shall not exceed the actual value, if any, of the Vessel at the commencement of the risk plus the cost of work and materials subsequently incorporated into the vessel to the time of such loss, less such deductible as is stated within the policy, but in no event to exceed the completed contract price of _____ Dollars.

In the event of loss, the Underwriters shall not be liable for a greater proportion thereof than the amount of this insurance bears to the completed contract price.

7. OTHER INSURANCE

In the event there is other valid insurance covering the same loss, this insurance shall not pay more than its proportion of the total of all insurance.

8. DEDUCTIBLE

The sum of $_____ shall be deducted from the total of all claims arising out of one accident or occurrence. This paragraph shall not apply to a claim for total or constructive total loss of the Vessel.

9. DURATION OF RISK

Commencing _____

and ending _____

or until delivery at _____

if delivered at an earlier date.

this clause is to have effect as an agreement by the Underwriters to a sale or transfer to new management.

12. CANCELLATION

If payment of premium is not made by the Assured within thirty (30) days after attachment of the insurance, or, in the event the Underwriters shall have agreed to accept deferred payments, if any payment of any premium is not made on the day agreed, this policy may be cancelled at any time thereafter by the Underwriters giving to the Assured named herein, and to third party payee or payees (if any) named in the policy, five (5) days' notice of such cancellation. Such notice may be given by the Underwriters or on their behalf by an authorized Agent or by the Agent or Broker effecting this insurance. Such cancellation shall be without prejudice to the premiums earned and due for the period the policy was in force. In event of Total or Constructive Total Loss occurring prior to cancellation, full annual premium shall be deemed earned.

13. BRITISH COLUMBIA LAW

Warranted to be subject to British Columbia Law and Usage as to Liability for and settlement of any and all claims.

14. NOTICE

The Assured must give the Underwriters immediate notice upon becoming aware of the happening of any event which may lead to a claim under this policy.

15. SUIT TIME LIMITATION

It is a condition of this Policy that no suit, action or proceeding for the recovery of any claim under this Policy shall be sustainable in any court of law or equity unless the same be commenced within twelve months next after the time a cause of action for the loss accrues. Provided, however, that if by the laws of the province within which this policy is issued such limitation is invalid, then any such claim shall be void unless such action, suit or proceeding be commenced within the shortest limit of time permitted, by the laws of such province, to be fixed therein.

HULL SECTION

16. HULL RISKS

This insurance covers all risks of physical loss or damage to the Vessel, from any external cause, while under construction and/or fitting out, and/or trial trips, including materials on the premises of the Assured, and while in transit (within 100 miles of the construction site) to and from the Vessel wherever she may be.

17. SEA TRIALS

Warranted all trials shall be carried out within a radius of 100 miles of the construction site.

18. FAILURE TO LAUNCH

In the case of failure to launch, Underwriters shall bear, up to the amount insured hereunder, their proportion of all necessary expenses incurred in completing the launch.

19. NEW FOR OLD

General and Particular Average shall be payable without deduction, new for old.

20. TOTAL LOSS

There shall be no recovery for a Constructive Total Loss under this Policy unless the expense of recovering and restoring the Vessel to the stage of her construction at time of loss would exceed her value at such stage of construction (which value shall be taken to be the cost of labour actually expended by the Builder in the construction of the Vessel and material actually incorporated therein at the time of loss, including accrued overhead and profit on such labour and material, not exceeding the Agreed Value). In making this determination expenses incurred prior to tender of abandonment shall not be considered if such are to be claimed separately under the Sue and Labour clause.

In ascertaining whether the Vessel is a constructive total loss, the completed contract price shall be taken as the repaired value and nothing in respect of the damaged or breakup value of the Vessel or wreck shall be taken into account. No claim for constructive total loss based upon the cost of recovery and/or repair of the Vessel shall be recoverable hereunder unless such cost would exceed the completed contract price.

21. UNREPAIRED DAMAGE

In no case shall the Underwriters be liable for unrepaired damage in addition to a subsequent Total Loss sustained during the period covered by this Policy, or any extension thereof.

22. SUE AND LABOUR

In case of any Loss or Misfortune, it shall be lawful and necessary for the Assured, their Factors, Servants and Assigns, to sue, labour and travel for, in and about the defense, safeguarding and recovery of the Vessel, or any part thereof, without prejudice to this insurance, to the charges whereof Underwriters will contribute their proportion as provided below. It is expressly declared and agreed that no acts of Underwriters or Assured in recovering, saving or preserving the Vessel shall be considered as a waiver or acceptance of abandonment.

In the event of expenses being incurred pursuant to the Sue and Labour Clause, the liability under this policy shall not exceed the proportion of such expenses that the amount insured hereunder bears to the value of the Vessel as stated herein, or to the sound value of the Vessel at the time of the occurrence giving rise to the expenditure if the sound value exceeds that value. Where Underwriters have admitted a claim for total loss and property insured by this policy is saved, the foregoing provisions shall not apply unless the expenses of suing and labouring exceed the value of such property saved and then shall apply only to the amount of the expenses which is in excess of such value.

Where a claim for total loss of the Vessel is admitted under this policy and expenses have been reasonably incurred in salving or attempting to salve the Vessel and other property and there are no proceeds, or the expenses exceed the proceeds, then this policy shall bear its **pro rata** share of such proportion of the expenses, or of the expenses in excess of the proceeds, as the case may be, as may reasonably be regarded as having been incurred in respect of the Vessel; but if the Vessel be insured for less than its sound value at the time of the occurrence giving rise to the expenditure, the amount recoverable under this clause shall be reduced in proportion to the under-insurance.

23. GENERAL AVERAGE AND SALVAGE

General Average and Salvage to be adjusted according to the law and practice obtaining at the place where the adventure ends, as if the contract of affreightment contained no special terms upon the subject; but where the contract of affreightment so provides the adjustment shall be according to York-Antwerp Rules.

When the Vessel sails in ballast, not under charter, the provisions of the York-Antwerp Rules, 1974 (excluding Rules XX and XXI) shall be applicable, and the voyage for this purpose shall be deemed to continue from the port or place of departure until the arrival of the Vessel at the first

When the contributory value of the Vessel is greater than the valuation herein, the liability of these Underwriters for General Average contribution

LIABILITY SECTION

24. COLLISION LIABILITY

If the Vessel hereby insured shall come into collision with any other vessel and the Assured shall in consequence thereof become liable to pay and shall pay by way of damages to any other person or persons any sum or sums in respect of such collision for

(i)   loss of or damage to any other vessel or property on any other vessel;

(ii) delay to or loss of use of any such other vessel or property thereon, or;

(iii) general average of, salvage of, or salvage under contract of, any such other vessel or property thereon;

the Underwriters will pay the Assured such proportion of such sum or sums so paid as their respective subscriptions hereto bear to the completed value of the Vessel hereby insured, provided always that their liability in respect of any one such collision shall not exceed their proportionate part of the completed value of the Vessel hereby insured, and in cases in which, with the prior consent in writing of the Underwriters, the liability of the Vessel has been contested or proceedings have been taken to limit the liability, they will also pay a like proportion of the costs which the Assured shall thereby incur or be compelled to pay; but when both vessels are to blame, then

(except in respect to amount made good to the Vessel) or Salvage shall not exceed that proportion of the total contribution due from the Vessel that port or place thereafter other than a port or place of refuge or a port or place of call for bunkering only. If at any such intermediate port or place there is an abandonment of the adventure originally contemplated the voyage shall thereupon be deemed to be terminated.

the amount insured hereunder bears to the contributory value; and if because of damage for which these Underwriters are liable as Particular Average the value of the Vessel has been reduced for the purpose of contribution, the amount of the Particular Average loss under this policy shall be deducted from the amount insured hereunder and these Underwriters shall be liable only for the proportion which such net amount bears to the contributory value.

chosen shall choose a third arbitrator before entering upon the reference, and the decision of the sole arbitrator or of any two of such three arbitrators appointed as above, shall be final and binding. The arbitration shall be conducted pursuant to the **Commercial Arbitration Act** of British Columbia.

25. PROTECTION AND INDEMNITY

It is further agreed that if the Assured by reason of its interest in the Vessel or the Surety for the Assured in consequence of its undertaking shall become liable to pay and shall pay any sum or sums in respect of any responsibility, claim, demand, damages, and/or expenses arising from or occasioned by any of the following matters or things during the currency of this policy, that is to say:

(a) Loss of or damage to any other ship or goods, merchandise, freight, or other things or interests whatsoever, on board such other ship, caused proximately or otherwise by the Vessel insured insofar as the same is not covered by the collision liability clause set out above;

(b) Loss or damage to any goods, merchandise, freight, or other things or interest whatsoever, other than as aforesaid (not being builders' gear or material or cargo on the insured Vessel), whether on board the insured

Vessel or not, which may arise from any cause whatsoever;

(c) Loss of or damage to any harbour, dock (graving or otherwise), slipway, way, gridiron, pontoon, pier, quay, jetty, stage, buoy, telegraphic cable or other fixed or movable thing whatsoever, or to any goods or property in or on the same, howsoever caused:

(d) Loss of life, personal injury, illness or life salvage;

(e) Any attempted or actual raising, removal, or destruction of the wreck of the insured ship or the cargo thereof, or any neglect or failure to raise, remove, or destroy the same.

(f) Any sum or sums for which the Assured may become Liable or incur from causes not hereinbefore specified, but which would be covered by the Canadian (Pacific) Protection and Indemnity Clauses, unamended.

The Underwriters will pay the Assured such proportions of such sum or sums so paid, or which may be required to indemnify the Assured for such loss, as their respective subscriptions bear to the completed contract price of the ship hereby insured, provided always that the amount recoverable hereunder in respect of any one accident or series of accidents shall not exceed their proportionate part of the completed value of the vessel hereby insured, and where the liability of the Assured has been contested with the consent in writing of a majority (in amount) of the Underwriters on the vessel hereby insured, the Underwriters will also pay a like proportion of the costs which the Assured shall thereby incur or be compelled to pay.

26. CO-OPERATION BY ASSURED

The Assured will co-operate fully with Underwriters in the defense of all claims arising from alleged liability of the Assured, and the Assured will not admit liability or incur any expense for which the Underwriters may be liable, without the written approval of the Underwriters.

unless the liability of the Owners of one or both of such vessels becomes limited by law, claims under this clause shall be settled on the principle of cross liabilities as if the Owners of each vessel had been compelled to pay to the Owners of the other of such vessels such one-half or other proportion of the latter's damages as may have been properly allowed in ascertaining the balance or sum payable by or to the Assured in consequence of such collision.

Provided always that this clause shall in no case extend or be deemed to extend to any sum which the Assured may become liable to pay or shall pay for or in respect of:

(a) removal or disposal, under statutory powers or otherwise, of obstructions, wrecks, cargoes or any other thing whatsoever;

(b) any real or personal property or thing whatsoever except other vessels or property on other vessels;

(c) pollution or contamination of any real or personal property or thing whatsoever (except other vessels with which the insured Vessel is in collision or property on such other vessels);

(d) the cargo or the property on or the engagements of the insured Vessel;

(e) loss of life, personal injury or illness.

Should the Vessel hereby insured come into collision with or receive salvage services from another vessel belonging wholly or in part to the same Owners or under the same management, the Assured shall have the same rights under this Policy as they would have were the other vessel entirely the property of Owners not interested in the Vessel hereby insured; but in such cases the liability for the collision or the amount payable for the services rendered shall be referred to arbitration at Vancouver, British Columbia, before a sole arbitrator to be agreed upon between the majority (in amount) of the Underwriters and the Assured, or if they cannot agree on an arbitrator, then each shall appoint an arbitrator, and the two arbitrators so

EXCLUSIONS

The following exclusions shall be paramount and shall supercede and nullify any contrary provisions in the policy. This insurance shall not cover any losses arising directly or indirectly from the causes described below:

(a) Notwithstanding anything to the contrary contained in these clauses, warranted free of capture, seizure, arrest, restraint or detainment, and the consequences thereof or of any attempt thereat; also from the consequences of hostilities or warlike operations, whether there be a declaration of war or not; but this warranty shall not exclude collision, contact with any fixed or floating object (other than a mine or torpedo), stranding, heavy weather or fire unless caused directly (and independently of the nature of the voyage or service which the Vessel concerned or in the case of a collision, any other vessel involved therein, is performing) by a hostile act by or against a belligerent power; and for the purpose of this warranty "power" includes any authority maintaining naval, military or air forces in association with a power.

(b) Warranted free from the consequences of civil war, revolution, rebellion, insurrection, or civil strife arising therefrom, piracy, strikes, lockouts, political or labour disturbances, civil commotions, military or unsurped power.

(c) Warranted free from loss, damage, liability or expense arising from any weapon of war employing ionizing radiation, atomic or nuclear fission and/or fusion or other like reaction or radioactive force or matter.

(d) Warranted free from loss, damage, liability or expense arising from:-

    (1) the detonation of an explosive;

    (2) any weapon of war;

    and caused by any person acting from a political motive.

(e) Warranted free from liability to any employee of the Assured or in the case of death, to his beneficiaries or others, under any Workers Compensation Acts or similar legislation, order or regulations, where the Assured is required to insure under such compensation provisions.

(f) Warranted free of any consequential damages or claims for loss through delay however caused, including, but not limited to loss of earnings or use of the Vessel.

(g) Warranted free from any claims arising from defects in materials, defects in design, failure to comply with specifications, or deliberate, dishonest, fraudulent or criminal acts of the builders.

(h) Nothing in this policy shall be construed to insure against or cover any loss, damage or expense in connection with docks, shipways, tools or any other property of the shipyard not intended to be incorporated in the vessel, excepting staging, scaffolding and similar temporary construction the value of which is included in the contract price of the vessel and excepting any loss, damage or expense for which Underwriters may be liable under the Protection and Indemnity clauses; provided, nevertheless, that in case of failure to launch, Underwriters shall bear their proportion of all subsequent expenses incurred in completing launch.

(i) Nothing in this policy shall be construed to insure against punitive damages, or fines or penalties imposed by any level of government, nor for any liability, assumed by the Assured under any contract or agreement unless specifically endorsed hereon.

(j) Warranted free from any claims arising from earthquakes, volcanoes, or tidal waves.

Reprinted with the permission of the Marine Insurance Association of British Columbia.

Appendix J

B.C. YACHT FORM (FULL COVER) 1964

In consideration of the premium hereinafter mentioned, these Assurers do hereby insure

Upon the _____ Built _____

from Noon _____ to Noon _____ Pacific Standard Time

This insurance is limited to those coverages named in the schedule below which are indicated by a premium set opposite thereto

COVERAGES	AMOUNT OF INSURANCE	AGREED VALUATION AS PER VALUATION CLAUSE IN SEC. A PAGE 2	RATE	PREMIUM
1 (a) Hull Insurance, as per section A			%	$
1 (b) As per Endorsement attached			%	$
2 Land transportation as included under Section A of these clauses within _____ miles of vessel's home port			%	$

	LOSS OF LIFE AND BODILY INJURY		PROPERTY DAMAGE	
	LIMIT, ANY ONE PERSON	LIMIT, ANY ONE ACCIDENT	LIMIT, ANY ONE ACCIDENT	
3 (a) Protection and Indemnity Insurance as per Section B of these clauses	$	$	$	s
3 (b) Medical Payments Insurance, as per Section C of these clauses	$	LIMIT, ANY ONE ACCIDENT $		$
			TOTAL PREMIUM	$

WARRANTED that the said vessel shall be laid up and out of commission from _____ at noon P.S.T., until _____ at noon P.S.T.

RETURN PREMIUMS FOR LAYUP

Return premium will be paid at the rate of _____ % net for each period of 15 consecutive days during which the vessel, while at the risk of these Assurers, shall be laid up and out of commission during the navigating period, and arrival.

RETURN PREMIUMS FOR CANCELLATION

If this policy be cancelled, return premiums will be paid as follows:

(1) With respect to Coverage 1 (a) above, for each 15 consecutive days of unexpired time, of the navigating period, at the rate of _____ % net; of the layup period at the rate of _____ % net.

(2) With respect to Land Transportation Insurance, Coverage 2 above, no return of premium.

(3) With respect to Coverage 3 above:

Should this policy be cancelled in accordance with its terms by the Assured or by this Assurer after the premium has been paid return premium payable under this section shall be computed as follows:

Where this policy provides for six (6) months navigation or less, these Assurers shall return under this section of the policy 6% net of the annual premium for every fifteen (15) consecutive days of the unexpired time of the navigating period and 1% net of the annual premium for every fifteen (15) consecutive days of the unexpired time of the layup period. Minimum premium to be retained $10.00.

Where this policy provides for more than six (6) months navigation, these Assurers shall return 3% net of the annual premium for every fifteen (15) consecutive days of the unexpired time. Minimum premium to be retained $10.00.

SPECIAL CONDITIONS

GENERAL CONDITIONS

PRIVATE PLEASURE WARRANTY

Warranted to be used solely for private pleasure purposes and not to be chartered unless approval and permission is endorsed hereon.

TRANSFER OF INTEREST

Warranted this insurance shall be void in case this policy or the interest insured thereby shall be sold or transferred without the previous consent in writing of these Assurers.

PRIVILEGES

To cover in port and at sea, at all times, in all places on shore or afloat, and on all occasions not conflicting with warranties and clauses contained herein and with leave to sail with or without pilots, to be towed by vessels, and to assist vessels in all situations.

CONTINUATION CLAUSE

If the vessel insured hereunder is at sea at the expiration of this policy this insurance may be continued until the vessel has been anchored or moored at her port of destination for twenty-four (24) hours in good safety, provided notice be given to these Assurers and additional premium paid as required.

NOTICE OF PAYMENT OF LOSS

In the event of any accident, loss, damage or injury for which claim may be made under this policy, the Assured must give immediate notice thereof to these Assurers or their authorized agent, as soon as such loss or accident becomes known to the Assured.

In case of loss covered by this policy, such loss to be paid within thirty (30) days after proof of loss and proof of interest in the said vessel, all indebtedness between the Assured and these Assurers being first deducted.

NOTICE OF CANCELLATION

This policy may be cancelled at any time at the Assured's request, or by these Assurers giving ten (10) days written notice of such cancellation, calculated from the time of receipt of the letter of cancellation at the Post Office, at the point of mailing.

TIME FOR SUIT

It is a condition of this policy that no suit, action or proceeding for the recovery of any claim under this policy shall be sustainable in any court of law or equity unless the same be commenced within twelve months next after the time a cause of action for the loss accrues. Provided, however, that if by the laws of the province within which this policy is issued such limitation is invalid, then any such claim shall be void unless such action, suit or proceeding be commenced within the shortest limit of time permitted, by the laws of such province, to be fixed therein.

NEGLIGENCE AND PRIVITY

Personal negligence or fault of the Assured in the navigation of the vessel or privity or knowledge in respect thereto (excepting loss, damage or liability wilfully or intentionally caused by the Assured) shall not relieve these Assurers of liability under this policy.

LEGAL REPRESENTATION AND COOPERATION CLAUSE

The Assured shall not assume any obligation or admit any liability for which the Assurers may be liable, without the written approval of the Assurers. In case the liability of the Assured shall be contested with the written approval of the Assurers first obtained, the Assurers will pay the cost and expense of such defense, in which event the Assurers shall have the option of naming the attorneys who shall represent the Assured in the said defense, and, if such option is exercised, shall have the exclusive direction and control thereof.

OMNIBUS CLAUSE

The Assured shall, whenever required, attend hearings and trials and shall assist in effecting settlements, securing and giving evidence, obtaining the attendance of witnesses, and in the conduct of suits and limitation proceedings.

It is understood and agreed that the word Assured whenever used in the Collision Clause, Section A of these clauses, and in the Protection and Indemnity Insurance, Section B of these clauses, includes in addition to the named Assured any person, firm, corporation or other legal entity who may be operating the insured vessel with the prior permission of the named Assured, but does not include a paid master or a paid member of the crew of the insured vessel or a person, firm, corporation or other legal entity, or any agent or employee thereof, operating a shipyard, boat repair yard, marina, yacht club, sales agency, boat service station, or similar organization. Notwithstanding anything contained herein the insurance provided by this clause does not cover liability of such additional Assureds to the Assured and/or Assureds named in this policy. The insurance provided by this clause is conditional upon compliance by an Assured with all the terms, conditions and warranties applicable to the named Assured. Nothing contained in this clause shall be construed to increase the limits of the Assurers' liability as stated in the policy.

PROPORTION OF LOSSES COVERED

Where the amount of insurance as set forth in Coverage 1(a) is less than the Agreed Valuation stated therein, these Assurers shall be liable only for such proportion of any loss recoverable under this policy as the said amount of insurance bears to the said Agreed Valuation.

STRIKES AND RIOTS

Warranted free of loss or damage caused by strikers, locked out workmen or persons taking part in labor disturbances, riots or civil commotions.

F.C. AND S. CLAUSE

Unless physically deleted by these Assurers, the following warranty shall be paramount and shall supersede and nullify any contrary provision of these clauses:

Warranted free of capture, seizure, arrest, restraint or detainment, and the consequences thereof or of any attempt thereat; also from the consequences of hostilities or warlike operation, whether there be a declaration of war or not; but this warranty shall not exclude collision, contact with any fixed or floating object (other than a mine or torpedo), stranding heavy weather or fire unless caused directly (and independently of the nature of the voyage or service which the vessel concerned or, in the case of a collision, any other vessel involved therein, is performing) by a hostile act by or against a belligerent power; and for the purpose of this warranty "power" includes any authority maintaining naval, military or air forces in association with a power.

Further warranted free from the consequences of civil war, revolution, rebellion, insurrection, or civil strife arising therefrom, or piracy.

ENGLISH LAW AND USAGE

Warranted to be subject to English Law and Usage as to liability for and settlement of any and all claims.

SECTION A — HULL AND MACHINERY INSURANCE

COVERAGES

The insurance provided by this Section shall cover, subject to the exclusions, stipulations, conditions and warranties contained herein, afloat and ashore, against ALL RISKS of direct physical loss or damage including physical loss or damage directly caused by the following:

Explosions, bursting of boilers, breakage of shafts, or any latent defect in the Hull or Machinery (excluding the cost of repairing or replacing the defective part):

Negligence of Master, Mariners, Engineers or Pilots; providing such loss or damage has not resulted from want of due diligence by the Assured, or any of them, or by the Manager.

COLLISION CLAUSE

It is further agreed that if the vessel hereby insured shall come into collision while water borne, with any other vessel or craft, and the Assured shall, in consequence thereof, become legally liable to pay and shall pay by way of damages to any other person or persons any sum or sums in respect of such collision, the Assurers will pay the Assured such sum or sums so paid not exceeding in respect of any one such collision the total limit of liability specified in Coverage No. 1, "Agreed Valuation". And in cases where the liability of the Assured has been contested, with the consent, in writing, of the Assurers, the Assurers will also bear a like proportion of the costs and expenses that may be incurred in contesting the liability resulting from said collision.

PROVIDED always that the foregoing clause shall in no case extend to any sum which the Assured may become liable to pay, or shall pay for removal of obstructions under statutory powers, or for loss of life or personal injury.

PROPERTY COVERED

Upon the vessel including her sails, tackle, apparel, machinery, dinghies, tenders, outboard motors, furniture and such other equipment as is generally required aboard for the operation and maintenance of the vessel.

HULL VALUATION

The vessel, including all the property insured under this Section, for so much as concerns the Assured by agreement between the Assured and these Assurers, is and shall be valued at the amount stated in "Agreed Valuation" on Page 1, but no recovery for a Total or Constructive Total Loss shall be had hereunder unless all said property is lost absolutely or unless the expenses of recovering and repairing the vessel shall exceed such amount.

DEDUCTIBLE

The sum of $ shall be deducted from each and every claim under this policy except for total and/or Constructive Total Loss.

Notwithstanding the foregoing, where the vessel is being loaded to or from, or conveyed in or on, any land conveyance a deductible of 5% of the insured value or a maximum of $250 whichever shall be the less, shall apply to each and every claim. For purposes of this clause, a marine railway, dockside crane or elevator are not to be regarded as land conveyances.

DEPRECIATION

Losses payable without deduction for depreciation, except in respect to sails, protective covers and running rigging. No deductions to be made for depreciation in the event of Total or Constructive Total Loss of the vessel due to perils insured against.

EQUIPMENT SEPARATED AND ON SHORE

It is also agreed that should any part of the furniture, tackle, boats, or other property of the said vessel be separated and laid up on shore during the period of this policy then this shall cover the same to an amount not exceeding % of the sum stated under the heading "Amount of Insurance" in Coverage 1 on Page 1. The amount attaching on the said vessel shall be decreased by the amount so covered.

SUE AND LABOUR

In case of any loss or misfortune, it shall be lawful and necessary for the Assured, their factors, servants and assigns, to sue, labour and travel for, in and about the defense, safeguard and recovery of the said property or any part thereof, without prejudice to this insurance, to the charges whereof these Assurers will contribute their proportion, not exceeding the "Agreed Valuation" as specified in Coverage 1 on Page 1. And it is especially declared and agreed that no acts of these Assurers or the Assured in recovering, saving or preserving the property insured shall be considered as a waiver or acceptance of abandonment.

UNREPAIRED DAMAGE

In no case shall these Assurers be liable for unrepaired damage in addition to a subsequent total loss sustained during the period covered by this policy.

FIBERGLASS AND PATCH CLAUSE

If the hull of the insured vessel is made in whole or in part of Plywood, Plastic, Fiberglass or other material of similar nature, it is understood and agreed that in the event of damage caused by a peril insured against, these Assurers shall only be liable for repairs made by applying suitable patches to the damaged hull area, in accordance with good repair practice.

It is also agreed that these Assurers will not be liable for the cost or expense of painting or impregnating colour beyond the immediate damaged area or areas. These principles shall also govern in determining whether or not the insured vessel is a Constructive Total Loss.

Also to pay General Average and Salvage Charges, where properly and reasonably incurred, not exceeding however, the amount in Coverage 1 on Page 1, of this policy under "Agreed Valuation".

Warranted that the Assured shall not insure excess or increased value of Hull and Machinery or other total loss Policy Proof of Interest or Full Interest Admitted insurances, without the written consent of these Assurers.

EXCLUSIONS

GENERAL AVERAGE AND SALVAGE CHARGES

OTHER INSURANCE

THIS POLICY DOES NOT COVER:

Loss, damage or expense, caused directly or indirectly by wear and tear, gradual deterioration (including Marine life), marring, denting, scratching, electrolysis, corrosion, rust, dampness of atmosphere, ice or in consequence of ice freezing other than collision with floating ice, extremes of temperature, weathering or wilful misconduct of the Assured;

Loss or damage to electrical apparatus, including wiring, caused by electricity other than lightning, unless fire ensues and then only for loss or damage by such ensuing fire;

Wrongful conversion or infidelity of persons to whom the insured property may be entrusted;

Loss or damage to spars and/or sails while racing unless added hereon by endorsement at an additional premium to be agreed upon;

SECTION B — PROTECTION AND INDEMNITY INSURANCE

PROPERTY DAMAGE

The Assurers further agree that if the Assured shall by reason of his interest in the insured vessel become liable to pay, and shall pay, any sum or sums in respect of any responsibility, claim, demand, damages, expenses or other loss arising from or occasioned by any of the following matters or things during the currency of this policy in respect to the vessel hereby insured, that is to say:

(1) Loss or damage to any other ship or boat or goods, merchandise, freight or other things or interests whatsoever, on board such other ship or boat, caused proximately or otherwise by the vessel insured, including collision liability, in so far as the same is not covered in amount by the Collision Clause in Section A of this policy but in no event shall these Assurers be liable for the amount of any deductible applied to a claim under said Collision Clause;

Loss of or damage to any goods, merchandise, freight or other things or interest whatsoever other than as aforesaid, whether on board said vessel or not, which may arise from any cause whatever;

Loss or damage to any harbor, dock (graving or otherwise), slipway, way, gridiron, pontoon, pier, quay, jetty, stage, buoy, telegraph cable or other fixed or movable thing whatsoever or to any goods or property in or on the same, howsoever caused;

Any attempted or actual raising, removal or destruction of the wreck of the insured vessel or property thereon, or any neglect or failure to raise, remove or destroy the same;

the Assurers will pay the Assured such sum or sums so paid or which may be required to indemnify the Assured for such loss;

PROVIDED always that the amount recoverable hereunder in respect to any one accident or series of accidents arising out of the same event shall not exceed the sum stated under Coverage 3(a), "Property Damage Limit Any One Accident".

PERSONAL INJURY

(2) Loss of life or bodily injury and payments made on account of life salvage; the Assurers will pay the Assured such sum or sums so paid or which may be required to indemnify the Assured for such loss;

PROVIDED always that the liability of these Assurers, in respect to any one person, is limited to the sum stated under Coverage 3(a), "Loss of Life and Bodily Injury Limit Any One Person"; and, subject to the same limit for each person, up to the sum therein stated under Coverage 3(a), "Loss of Life & Bodily Injury Limit Any One Accident", it being understood that this limit applies to any one accident or series of accidents arising out of the same event.

COSTS

(3) And in case the liability of the Assured shall be contested in any suit or action, these Assurers will also pay their proportion of such ensuing costs as the Assured may incur with the consent in writing of these Assurers.

No liability shall exist under this Protection and Indemnity Insurance unless as a condition precedent thereto, all the stipulations, conditions and warranties of this policy have been fully complied with, and until the fact and amount of the Assured's obligation to pay shall have been finally determined either by judgment against the Assured after actual trial or by written agreement between the Assured, the claimant and the Assurers, and the Assured has paid the amount of liability so determined.

ASSUMPTION OF LIABILITY

This Protection and Indemnity Insurance does not cover any liability assumed by the Assured under contract or otherwise if such liability is greater than or different from liability imposed upon the Assured by law in the absence of such contract.

OTHER INSURANCE

If the Assured has other insurance (except under this Policy) against a liability covered by this Protection and Indemnity Insurance, the Assurers shall not be liable under this Protection and Indemnity Insurance for a greater proportion of such loss than the applicable limit of liability stated in this policy bears to the total applicable limit of liability of all valid and collectible insurance against such loss.

SECTION C — MEDICAL PAYMENTS INSURANCE

The Assurers agree to pay to or for each person, except as hereinafter excluded, who sustains bodily injury caused by accident while in or upon, boarding or alighting from the vessel insured hereunder, the reasonable expense of necessary medical, surgical, ambulance, hospital and professional nursing services, and, in event of death resulting from such injury, the reasonable funeral expense, all incurred within one (1) year from the date of accident.

LIMIT OF LIABILITY

Notwithstanding the foregoing these Assurers shall not be liable hereunder for any expense or combined expenses incurred by one person in excess of the sum stated as "Limit of Liability, Any One Person" in Coverage 3(b); and subject to that limit for any one person, the Assurers shall not be liable for any sum in excess of that stated as "Limit, Any One Accident" in the Coverage 3(b) incurred by more than one person as a result of any one accident or series of accidents arising out of the same event.

EXCLUSIONS

The coverage afforded by this Section C shall not apply:

(a) to liability assumed by the Assured under any contract or agreement;

(b) to bodily injury to or death of:

   (1) any person to or for whom benefits are payable under any Workmen's Laws because of such injury or death, or

   (2) any employee of the Assured while engaged in the employment, other than domestic, of the Assured, or while engaged in the operation, maintenance, or the repair of the within insured vessel, or

   (3) the Assured or registered owner of the within insured vessel.

MEDICAL AND OTHER REPORTS EXAMINATION

The injured person or someone on his behalf shall, as soon as practicable furnish reasonably obtainable information, pertaining to the accident and injury, and execute authorization to enable the Assurers to obtain medical reports and copies of records.

The injured person shall submit to physical examination by physicians selected by the Assurers when and as often as the Assurers may reasonably require.

PROOF AND PAYMENT OF CLAIM

As soon as practicable after completion of the services or after the rendering of services which in cost equal or exceed the limit of liability for medical payments or after the expiration of one year from the date of the accident, whichever is the first, the injured person or someone on his behalf shall give to the Assurers written proof of claim under oath, stating the name and address of each person or organization which has rendered services, the nature and extent and the dates of rendition of such services, the itemized charges thereof and the amounts paid thereon. Upon the Assurers' request, the injured person or someone on his behalf shall cause to be given to the Assurers by each such person and organization written proof of claim under oath, stating the nature and extent and dates of rendition of such services, the itemized charges and the payments received thereon.

The Assurers shall have the right to make payments at any time to the injured person or to any such person or organization on account of the services rendered, and a payment so made shall reduce to the extent thereof the amount payable hereunder to or for such injured person on account of such injury. Payment hereunder shall not constitute admission of liability of the Assured or, except hereunder, of the Assurers.

Reprinted with the permission of the Marine Insurance Association of British Columbia.

Appendix K

Subrogation Receipt

Name of Insurer: [the "Insurance Company"]

Policy No.:

Certificate No.:

Cargo: [Description of Cargo]

Bill of Lading: [Number] [Date] [Place of Issue]

Vessel: [Name of Vessel]

The undersigned acknowledges receipt of the sum of $[amount of payment] ([amount] dollars) in full and final settlement of its claim for loss or damage to the cargo described above and in consideration of the payment of the said sum:

1. We hereby guarantee that we are entitled to receive the said sum and to enforce the terms of the contract contained in the bill of lading or other document described above.

2. We acknowledge and agree that the Insurance Company is subrogated to all our rights of recovery from the party or parties liable for our loss or damage.

3. We agree to assist the Insurance Company to effect such recovery and in connection therewith agree to provide it with all documents, correspondence and records (including electronic records) pertaining to our loss or damage and to make any such affidavits or declarations and to give such oral evidence as we can properly make or give and generally render such assistance as may from time to time be reasonably required, subject to reimbursement of any reasonable expenses incurred in connection therewith.

4. We authorize the Insurance Company to file suit against any such party or parties in our name, with authority to begin, prosecute, compromise or withdraw, in our name, but at the sole expense of the Insurance

Company, any and all legal proceedings which they may consider necessary to give effect to this agreement.

5. We agree to execute in our name any documents (including any release) which may be necessary to carry out the purpose of this agreement.

6. We acknowledge and agree that any monies collected from any such party or parties, whether received in the first instance by us or by the Insurance Company, shall be the property of the Insurance Company.

The payment referred to herein is accepted on the understanding and agreement that it shall not enure to the benefit of any carrier under the provisions of any contract of carriage or otherwise.

[Name of insured]

Date:_____

Signed by: _____

Name:

Title:

I have authority to bind the corporation.

Appendix L

Loan Receipt

Name of Insurer:

Policy No.:

Certificate No.:

Cargo: [Description of Cargo]

Bill of Lading: [Number] [Date] [Place of Issue]

Vessel: [Name of Vessel]

Received from [name of insurer], the sum of $[amount of payment] ([amount] dollars), as a loan and not as payment of any claim, repayable only out of any net recovery the undersigned may make from any carrier, vessel, bailee or others upon or by reason of any claim for the loss of or damage to the above-described cargo, from any insurance effected by the undersigned or by any carrier, bailee or others on said property, and as security for such payment we hereby pledge to the said [name of insurer] all such claims and any recovery thereon.

This payment is made and accepted with the express agreement that the payee will refund to the said insurance company the amount named herein should the property described herein be recovered and delivered in good order and condition to the consignees or to the consignors, and the undersigned so agrees. Should the said property be recovered in other than good order and condition, the undersigned will refund to the said insurance company the difference between the amount named herein and the amount of the loss or damage adjusted in accordance with the policy of insurance.

In further consideration of the said loan, we further agree that we are the persons entitled to enforce the terms of the contracts of transportation set forth in the bills of lading covering the said property; and we hereby appoint the agents and officers of the said insurance company and their successors, sever-ally, our agents and attorneys in fact, with irrevocable power to collect any such claim and to begin, prosecute, compromise or withdraw, in our name, but at the expense of the said insurance company, any and all legal proceedings which they may deem necessary to enforce such claim or claims, and to execute in our name any documents which may be necessary to carry into effect the purposes of this agreement. We further agree to assist the said insurance company and its agents in the prosecution of any such claim, subject to reimbursement of any reasonable expenses incurred in connection therewith.

[Name of insured]

Date:_____

Signed by: _____

Name:

Title:

I have authority to bind the corpo-ration.

Appendix M

Letter of Undertaking

Name of Protection and Indemnity Association
(or correspondent or law firm providing letter on behalf of association)

To: Claimant or Claimant's Solicitor

Dear Sirs/Mesdames:

Re.: [Name of Vessel(s)/Description of Incident/Date of Incident]

In consideration of your refraining from arresting [or releasing from arrest] or detaining or interfering in any other way with the use or trading of the above Vessel or any other vessel or property or asset in the same or associated ownership or management, we [name of Protection and Indemnity Association] hereby agree:

1. To submit to the jurisdiction of the Federal Court of Canada and to appoint counsel [or identify name of authorized legal counsel] to accept service of legal proceedings issued against the Vessel and its owners in the Federal Court of Canada for recovery of your claim and to appear in said proceedings on behalf of the Vessel and its owners;

2. On demand, or at our option, whether or not the Vessel has been lost or sold, to cause to be filed in the said proceedings a bailbond in the usual form by an approved corporate surety in the total amount of Cdn$[amount of security] ([amount] Canadian dollars), as security for the said claim, inclusive of principal, interest and costs;

3. If the said owners shall not pay and satisfy in full what may be adjudged against them or against the Vessel by final judgment or settlement, to satisfy such judgment or settlement in full up to the said amount of Cdn$[amount of security] ([amount] Canadian dollars), inclusive of principal, interest and costs.

This undertaking shall remain in full force and effect during any appeal and the same shall apply to any compromise or settlement among the parties of the subject matter of the said proceedings or to any admission of liability therein or to any amount of damages, interest and costs agreed by the undersigned to be paid in the said proceedings or assessed after admission of liability or compromise, so that if the undersigned does not pay such amounts it shall be liable for them in the same manner as if they had been adjudged by the court but not in excess of the said maximum amount and provided always that such compromise, settlement or admission has our prior approval.

This undertaking is given without prejudice to any and all defences and limitations which may be available to the Vessel and to its owners and under reserve of the right of the said owners to file a counterclaim or institute limitation proceedings.

This undertaking or any substitution therefore shall lapse unless a Statement of Claim for the claim referred to herein is issued and served within two years from the date of the said claim, in which case it shall remain in full force and effect until a bailbond has been filed or any final judgment or settlement against the Vessel and her owners has been satisfied.

This undertaking shall be governed by Canadian law and any dispute arising hereunder shall be subject to the jurisdiction of the Federal Court of Canada.

Dated at [City], [Province], the [day] day of [month], [year].

Yours truly,

[Name of Protection and Indemnity Association]

per: _____

[Where signed by law firm or correspondent add name of firm and:
As agents only.

We warrant that we have authority to issue this letter of undertaking.]

Appendix N

Canadian (Pacific) Protection and Indemnity Clauses

The Assurer(s) hereby undertakes to make good to the Assured or the Assured's executors, administrators and/or successors all such Liabilities and/or Expenses as the Assured or the Assured's executors, administrators and/or successors shall have become liable to pay and shall have in fact paid on account of the liabilities, risks, events and/or happenings arising out of ownership, use or operation of the vessel(s) hereby insured (hereinafter referred to as "The Vessel"), as follows:

1. LIABILITY FOR LOSS OF LIFE, BODILY INJURY

Liability for loss of life of, or bodily injury to, or illness of any person, excluding however, unless otherwise agreed by endorsement hereon, liability to any employee of the Assured or in the case of death, to his beneficiaries or others, under any Compensation Acts or similar legislation, order or regulations, where the Assured is required to insure under such compensation provisions.

Protection hereunder for loss of life or injury arising in connection with the handling of cargo shall commence from the time of receipt by the Assured of the cargo on dock or wharf or on craft alongside the vessel for loading thereon, and shall continue until delivery thereof from dock or wharf of discharge or until discharge from the vessel on to another vessel or craft.

2. HOSPITAL, MEDICAL OR OTHER EXPENSES

(a) Liability for hospital, medical or other expenses necessarily and reasonably incurred in respect of loss of life of or bodily injury to, or illness of any member of the crew of the vessel or any other person. Protection hereunder shall also include burial expenses not exceeding $500.00 when necessarily and reasonably incurred by the Assured for the burial of any seaman of the vessel and such burial expenses shall not be subject to any deductible provision in the policy.

This insurance EXCLUDES any claim recoverable under any Provincial or other applicable Hospital or Medical Insurance Plan where the claimant is required to be insured under such a plan.

(b) **Port Charges and Owner's Expenses**
Port Charges incurred solely for the purpose of landing an injured or sick person shall be allowed as well as the net loss of the Assured in respect of bunkers, insurance, stores and provisions solely caused by the landing of such person.

3. REPATRIATION EXPENSES

Liability for repatriation expenses of any members of the crew of the vessel necessarily and reasonably incurred in case of wreck or abandonment of the vessel or under statutory obligation, excepting such liability and expenses as arise out of or ensue from the termination of any agreement in accordance with the terms thereof, or by mutual consent, or by the sale of the vessel, or by any other act of the Assured. Wages shall only be included in such expenses where payable under statutory obligations during unemployment due to wreck or loss of the vessel.

4. LIABILITY FOR DAMAGE TO OTHER VESSELS

(a) **By Collision**

(i) Loss of or damage to any other vessel or craft or to the freight thereof or property thereon, caused by collision with the vessel to the extent that the same would not be recoverable if the vessel were at all times fully insured under hull and machinery and, where applicable, excess liabilities policies on terms at least equivalent to those of the current Canadian Hulls (Pacific) Clauses and current Canadian (Pacific) Total Loss and Excess Liabilities Clauses.

(ii) Where there would be a valid claim hereunder but for the fact that the damaged property belongs to the same Assured, the Assurer(s) shall be liable in the same way and shall have the same rights as if the damaged property belonged to different owners.

(iii) When both vessels are to blame, then unless the liability of the Owners of one or both of such vessels becomes limited by law, claims under this clause shall be settled on the principle of cross liabilities as if the Owner of each vessel had been compelled to pay to the Owner of the other vessel one half or other proportion of the latter's damages as may have been properly allowed in ascertaining the balance or sum payable by or to the Assured in consequence of such collision.

Notwithstanding the foregoing, if any one or more of the various liabilities arising from such collision has been compromised, settled or adjusted without the written consent of the Assurer(s), the Assurer(s) shall be relieved of liability for any and all claims under this clause.

(b) **Other Than By Collision**

    (i) Loss of or damage to any other vessel or craft or to the freight thereof or property thereon not caused by collision with the vessel provided such liability does not arise solely by reasons of a contract made by the Assured.

    (ii) Where there would be a valid claim hereunder but for the fact that the damaged property belongs to the Assured, the Assurer(s) shall be liable in the same way and shall have the same rights as if the damaged property belongs to different owners.

5. LIABILITY FOR DAMAGE TO FIXED OR MOVABLE OBJECTS

    (i) Loss of or damage to any fixed or movable object or property thereon, except another vessel or craft or property on board another vessel or craft.

    (ii) Where there would be a valid claim hereunder but for the fact that the damaged property belongs to the Assured, the Assurer(s) shall be liable in the same way and shall have the same rights as if the damaged property belongs to different owners.

6. LIABILITY FOR POLLUTION

Loss, damage, cost, liability or expense that the Assured, as owner of the vessel(s), shall have become liable to pay and shall pay in consequence of the accidental, actual or potential discharge, spillage or leakage of oil, fuel, cargo, petroleum products, chemicals or other substances of any kind or description; provided, however, that this policy shall not insure any liability resulting directly or indirectly or arising out of or having relation to:

    (a) Any loss, damage, cost, liability or expense paid or incurred in consequence of any such actual or potential discharge, spillage or leakage unless proximately caused by fault on the part of the Assured.

    (b) Punitive or exemplary damages.

7. REMOVAL OF WRECK

Liability for costs or expenses of, or incidental to the removal of the wreck of the vessel, when such removal is compulsory by law, PROVIDED, HOWEVER, that the value of all stores and materials saved as well as the value of the wreck itself, shall first be deducted from such costs or expenses and only the balance thereof, if any, shall be recoverable from the Assurers, ALWAYS PROVIDED THAT the Assurers are not liable for such costs, or expenses as would be covered by insurance under the current Canadian Hulls (Pacific) Clauses, and where applicable, current Canadian (Pacific) Total Loss and Excess Liabilities Clauses.

8. FINES IMPOSED BY GOVERNMENT OR CUSTOMS AUTHORITIES

Liability for fines and penalties, including expenses necessarily and reasonably incurred in avoiding or mitigating same, for the violation of any laws of Canada or of any Province thereof, or of any foreign country including fines imposed by Government or Customs Authorities in respect of short or over-delivery of cargo, smuggling, breach of Immigration Regulations or in respect of other neglect or default of captains or crew for which the vessel or Assured may he held responsible, PROVIDED, HOWEVER, that the Assurer(s) shall not be liable to indemnify the Assured against any such fines or penalties resulting directly or indirectly from the failure, neglect or default of the Assured or his managing officers or managing agents to exercise the highest degree of diligence to prevent a violation of any such laws.

With respect to claims for pollution, this policy shall not indemnify the Assured against any fine or penalty arising out of the actual or potential discharge, spillage or leakage of oil, fuel, cargo, petroleum products, chemicals or other substances of any kind or description.

9. EXTRAORDINARY EXPENSES IN CASES OF QUARANTINE, ETC.

Extraordinary expenses incurred in cases of outbreak of plague or other contagious disease, for disinfection of the vessel or persons on board, or for quarantine but not including the ordinary expenses of loading or discharge, nor the wages and/or provisions of crew or passengers. Where the vessel is chartered or not being under contract, is ordered to proceed to a port where it is or ought to be known that she will be subjected to quarantine, the Assured shall receive no benefit from the Assurer(s) under this clause.

10. MUTINY OR OTHER MISCONDUCT

Expenses incurred in resisting any unfounded claim by the master or crew or other persons employed on the vessel, or in prosecuting such persons in case of mutiny or other misconduct.

11. COSTS

(a) **Legal Costs**
Where the Assured is successful in defending a claim or suit, the Legal Costs incurred with the Assurer(s) or their agent's approval shall be payable by Assurers without application of any deductible. Where however, payment has to be made to dispose of a claim and the amount so paid by the Assured, including Legal Costs, exceeds the amount of the deductible stipulated in this policy, the Assurer(s) shall be liable only for the amount in excess of such deductible.

(b) **Costs and Charges**

Other costs, charges and expenses, reasonably incurred and paid by the Assured in defence against any liabilities herein insured against in respect of the vessel shall be subject to the agreed deductibles applicable, and subject further to the conditions and limitations herein provided.

GENERAL CONDITIONS AND/OR LIMITATIONS

PROMPT NOTICE OF CLAIM — WARRANTED that in the event of any occurrence which may result in loss, damage and/or expense for which the Assurer(s) is/are or may become liable, the Assured will give prompt notice thereof and forward to the Assurer(s) as soon as practicable after receipt thereof, all communications, processes, pleadings and other legal papers or documents relating to such occurrences.

SETTLEMENT OF CLAIM — The Assured shall not make any admission of liability, either before or after any occurrence which may result in a claim for which the Assurer(s) may be liable without the Assurer(s) prior written consent.

The Assured shall not interfere in any negotiations of the Assurer(s) for settlement of any legal proceedings in respect of any occurrences for which the Assurer(s) are liable under this policy, PROVIDED, HOWEVER, that in respect of any occurrence likely to give rise to a claim under this insurance, the Assured is obligated to and shall take steps to protect its (and/or the Assurer(s)) interests as would reasonably be taken in the absence of this or similar insurance. If the Assured shall fail or refuse to settle any claim as authorized by the Assurer(s), the liability of the Assurer(s) to the Assured shall be limited to the amount for which settlement could have been made.

ASSURED TO ASSIST WITH EVIDENCE IN DEFENCE, ETC. — Whenever required by the Assurer(s), the Assured shall aid in securing information and evidence and in obtaining witnesses and shall cooperate with the Assurer(s) in the defence of any claim or suit or appeal from any judgment, in respect of any occurrence as hereinbefore provided.

SUBROGATION — The Assurer(s) shall be subrogated to all the rights which the Assured may have against any other person or entity in respect of any payment made under this insurance, to the extent of such payment, and the Assured shall, upon the request of the Assurer(s), execute all documents necessary to secure to the Assurer(s) such rights. The Assurer(s) shall be entitled to take credit for any profit accruing to the Assured by reason of any negligence or wrongful act of the Assured's servants or agents, up to the measure of their loss, or to recover for their own **account** from third parties any damage that may be provable by reason of such negligence or wrongful act.

COVER ELSEWHERE — Where the Assured is, irrespective of this insurance covered or protected against any loss or claim which would otherwise have been paid by the Assurer(s) under this insurance, there shall be no contribution by the Assurer(s) on the basis of double insurance or otherwise.

EXCLUSIONS AND WARRANTIES

Notwithstanding anything to the contrary contained in this policy, no liability attaches to the Assurer(s);

(i) For any loss, damage, or expense which would be payable if the vessel were fully insured under the Hull & Machinery and Excess Liability policies on terms at least equivalent to those of the current Canadian Hulls (Pacific) Clauses and, where applicable, current Canadian (Pacific) Total Loss and Excess Liabilities Clauses.

(ii) For any loss, damage or expense sustained by reason of capture, seizure, arrest, restraint or detainment, and the consequences thereof or of any attempt thereof; also from the consequences of hostilities or warlike operations, whether there be a declaration of war or not; but this shall not exclude collision, contact with any fixed or floating object (other than a mine or torpedo), stranding, heavy weather or fire unless caused directly (and independently of the nature of the voyage or service which the vessel or, in the case of a collision, any other vessel involved therein, is performing) by a hostile act by or against a belligerent power; and for the purpose of this exclusion, "power" includes any authority maintaining naval, military or air forces in association with a power.

Warranted free from the consequences of civil war, revolution, rebellion, insurrection, or civil strife arising therefrom, or piracy.

Warranted free from loss, damage, liability or expense arising from any weapon of war employing atomic or nuclear fission and/or fusion or other like reaction or radioactive force or matter.

Warranted free from loss, damage, liability or expense arising from:

(a) The detonation of an explosive

(b) Any weapon of war

and caused by any person acting from a political motive.

ASSIGNMENTS — This insurance shall be void in case the vessel or any part thereof, shall be sold, transferred or mortgaged, or if there be any change of management or charter of the vessel, or if this policy be assigned or pledged, without the previous consent in writing of the Assurer(s).

TITLES OF PARAGRAPH — The titles of paragraphs of this Policy including endorsement and supplementary contracts, if any, now or hereafter attached to this Policy are included solely for the convenience of reference and should not be deemed in any way to limit, alter or affect the provisions to which they relate.

ACTIONS AGAINST THE ASSURER — No Action shall lie against the Assurer(s) for the recovery of any loss sustained by the Assured unless such action is brought against the Assurer(s) within one year of the final judgment or decree is entered in the litigation against the Assured or, in case the claim against the Assurer(s) accrues without the entry of such final judgment or decree, unless such action is brought within one year of the date of the payment of such claim.

CONTINUATION CLAUSE — Should the vessel at the expiration of this insurance be at sea, or in distress, or at a port of refuge or of call, she shall, provided previous written notice be given to the Assurer(s), be held covered to her port of destination and until completion of discharge upon payment of a *pro rata* monthly premium each 30 days (or part thereof) during which this insurance is held covered.

CANCELLATION CLAUSE — A *pro rata* net premium for every 30 consecutive days of unexpired time shall be returned if it be mutually agreed to cancel this policy, but there shall be no cancellation or return of premium in event vessel is lost from any cause whatsoever.

It is understood and agreed that in the event of non-payment of premiums by the Assured to the Agent or to the Assurer(s), the Agent or the Assurer(s) may cancel this insurance by giving to the Assured five days notice in writing by registered letter.

If the vessel named herein should be sold or requisitioned and this policy be cancelled and surrendered, a *pro rata* net premium for each 30 consecutive days of the unexpired term of this insurance shall be returned.

EACH VESSEL SEPARATELY INSURED CLAUSE — As a matter of convenience, one policy is issued covering the vessels scheduled herein, but as a matter of construction, the limit of liability applicable to each vessel is to be deemed a separate interest, separately insured, in all respects as if a separate policy for the limit of liability set against each vessel were issued, and the policy is to be read and applied accordingly. The limit of liability on one vessel is not applicable to any other.

(iii) For any loss, damage, or expense arising from the cancellation or breach of any charter, had debts, fraud of agents, insolvency, loss of freight, hire or demurrage, or as a result of the breach of any undertaking to load any cargo, or in respect of the vessel engaging in any unlawful trade or performing any unlawful act, with the knowledge of the Assured.

(iv) For any loss, damage, expense or claim arising out of or having relation to the towage by the vessel (not being a tug) of any other vessel or craft, whether under agreement or not, unless such towage was to assist such other vessel or craft in distress to a port or place of safety, PROVIDED, HOWEVER, that this clause shall not apply to claims under this policy for loss of life or bodily injury to passengers and/or members of the crew of the vessel arising as a result of towing.

(v)   When the insured vessel is a tug, this insurance shall remain in force during the towage of any other vessel, craft or log raft, but shall in no way extend to cover loss, damage or expense to (or caused by) her tow or the property thereon, whether liability arises under contract or otherwise.

(vi)   For any claim involving loss of life or bodily injury resulting from or in relation to the handling of cargo where such claim arises from a contract of indemnity between the Assured and a third party.

(vii)   For any claim in respect of cargo carried on board the vessel.

(viii)   Oil pollution resulting from or during services provided under a contract of salvage.

(ix)   The U.S. *Water Quality Improvement Act* and/or any similar acts enacted by any State or duly constituted legal authority, or any statutory amendment or modification thereof.

It is expressly understood and agreed if and when the Assured under this policy has any interest other than as a shipowner in the vessel, in no event shall the Assurer(s) be liable hereunder to any greater extent than if such Assured where the owner and were entitled to all the rights of limitation to which a shipowner is entitled.

Unless otherwise agreed by endorsement to this insurance, liability hereunder shall in no event exceed that which would be imposed on the Assured by law in the absence of contract.

Index